# Kylix Developer's Guide

Charles Calvert
Marjorie Calvert
John Kaster
Bob Swart

201 West 103rd St., Indianapolis, Indiana, 46290 USA

# Kylix Developer's Guide

## Copyright © 2002 by Sams Publishing

All rights reserved. No part of this book shall be reproduced, stored in a retrieval system, or transmitted by any means, electronic, mechanical, photocopying, recording, or otherwise, without written permission from the publisher. No patent liability is assumed with respect to the use of the information contained herein. Although every precaution has been taken in the preparation of this book, the publisher and authors assume no responsibility for errors or omissions. Nor is any liability assumed for damages resulting from the use of the information contained herein.

International Standard Book Number: 0-672-32060-6

Library of Congress Catalog Card Number: 00-107408

Printed in the United States of America

First Printing: October 2001

04  03  02  01        4  3  2  1

## Trademarks

All terms mentioned in this book that are known to be trademarks or service marks have been appropriately capitalized. Sams Publishing cannot attest to the accuracy of this information. Use of a term in this book should not be regarded as affecting the validity of any trademark or service mark.

## Warning and Disclaimer

Every effort has been made to make this book as complete and as accurate as possible, but no warranty or fitness is implied. The information provided is on an "as is" basis. The authors and the publisher shall have neither liability nor responsibility to any person or entity with respect to any loss or damages arising from the information contained in this book.

**EXECUTIVE EDITOR**
Michael Stephens

**ACQUISITIONS EDITOR**
Carol Ackerman

**DEVELOPMENT EDITOR**
Tiffany Taylor

**MANAGING EDITOR**
Matt Purcell

**PROJECT EDITOR**
Andy Beaster

**COPY EDITOR**
Kate Givens

**INDEXER**
Diane Brenner

**PROOFREADER**
Debra Neel

**TECHNICAL EDITORS**
Bob Swart
Paul Qualls

**TEAM COORDINATOR**
Pamalee Nelsen

**INTERIOR DESIGNER**
Anne Jones

**COVER DESIGNER**
Aren Howell

# Overview

# Contents

# Foreword

## The Creation of Kylix

*by David Intersimone*

*"David I"* davidi@borland.com
Vice President, Developer Relations
Borland® Software Corporation

One of the joys of working at Borland is the opportunity to watch creation in progress. I love taking a little time out from my daily grind to go down to where the Delphi team sits. It's great fun to visit with Chuck, Danny, Allen, Eddie, and other team members to see what they are cooking up this week.

The creation of Kylix was, of course, a very special event. I was privileged to watch its development from the very first days of its planning all the way through completion. It was, at times, a tough road. Nevertheless, it was a wondrous joy to watch the product emerge step by step by step over the months.

It was thrilling to get the first successful builds of Kylix. Now at last I could boot up Linux, start a high-powered development environment, and begin creating powerful applications with a few clicks of the mouse. Tasks in Linux that had once seemed formidable soon were easily within reach.

I have always been a big fan of Delphi. Having it transported to Linux intact was a very exciting event for me personally, and one that I think will end up, in the long run, having a huge impact on the future of not only Linux development, but also the entire Linux operating system.

## Learning the Ropes with the *Kylix Developer's Guide*

Throughout the development of Kylix, I shared the joy in watching its creation with my two friends and co-workers, John Kaster and Charlie Calvert. We spent many hours together hovered over Linux machines testing new code, trying experiments, and sharing in the excitement of a new product. Both John and Charlie worked with Kylix from the very beginning, and indeed, they sat in on some of the earliest meetings involving the planning. The other authors, especially Bob Swart, were also working with the product from the moment it was released to field test. Bob worked closely with both the development team itself, and with those of us who work elsewhere in Borland.

Development in Kylix is relatively easy compared to the trials encountered under other Linux development systems. If you know how to use Kylix, then database, Web, and even system development can be made relatively simple. Nevertheless, the product has a rich feature set, and mastering it can take time.

Having Charlie, John, Bob, and the other authors to guide you through the product is the next best thing to being able to sit down with Danny, Allen, Eddie, or even Chuck himself. This book examines all the major features, and many of the smaller features, of both the product itself, and the Delphi language. It contains a treasure trove of Kylix programming jewels, replete with a shimmering panoply of information that you can use again and again in your Linux project development.

I look forward to the upcoming months and years, when both Kylix and this book will help programmers create solutions and tools that will prove useful to businesses, users, and the whole Linux movement. Kylix is a great product, and having this book in your hands will help you take part in the exciting world of Linux development.

*by Chuck Jazdzewski*

Chief Architect of Kylix™ and Delphi™
Office of Chief Scientist
Borland® Software Corporation

As the chief architect of Kylix, I have had a chance to oversee this product from the moment of its conception until its release to the general public. It's very exciting for me to now see books on our compiler hitting the shelves. In particular, *Kylix Developer's Guide* provides developers with all the knowledge they need to begin creating powerful Linux applications. Whether you come from a Windows or a Linux background, and whether or not you have experience with similar tools, this book will provide you with all the information you need to create tools that users will love.

Linux has proved to be one of the fastest growing and most exciting areas in computer development. Its success as a server platform is already fully established. What is needed now are technologies that will help the Linux community develop powerful, attractive, fast, and easy to use applications. That's the role Kylix is designed to fill.

When we put our Linux compiler and IDE together, we aimed from the beginning to create a practical, easy to use tool that would allow developers to create applications users will enjoy. Although still providing deep access to the low-level functionality available in Linux, Kylix gives users easy to use components from which they can create the kind of cutting edge applications that users have come to expect. Developers, on the other hand, will love the sophisticated debugging and program analysis tools that are built into the IDE.

Our goal in developing Kylix was to bring all the key features of Delphi to the Linux platform. In particular, that meant focusing on database- and Web-based applications. Databases form the backbone on which many corporate applications are based, and we did everything we could to ensure that there is no easier way for Linux developers to build data-centric applications than Kylix itself. With just a few clicks of the mouse, you can put together simple database applications that give users access to data from both open source and proprietary database servers. With a little more work, you can construct powerful applications that access dozens, or even hundreds, of tables residing on multiple heterogeneous servers.

Creating Kylix was an exciting, but often difficult, task for the Borland development team. Throughout our effort, we continuously sought out and found ways to encapsulate the most complex parts of Linux development inside easy to use components. The result is a set of more than one hundred extensible controls that you can use to assemble the highest possible quality applications.

# Developer Expertise

I can't think of anyone better prepared to write a book about Kylix than Charlie Calvert, John Kaster, Bob Swart, and the other authors of this book. Charlie and John in particular were involved with Kylix before it even became an official project at Borland. They participated in the planning of the product as part of the Kylix core team. They helped decide what would be in the initial product release. I frequently saw them in the offices of various R&D engineers throughout the development of Kylix, making sure they understood the nuances of the engineering decisions that were made for Kylix.

Along with David Intersimone, they hosted the Kylix Kick Start on March 20, 2000, which was the first time we talked to anyone who was not a Borland employee about Kylix. The Kick Start was a technology briefing for hundreds of technology partners and authors. Charlie and John put together the agenda for this meeting and worked directly with Kylix R&D to determine the most useful information to provide the attendees. In the months following this initial Kick Start, Charlie, John, and David went on the road, hosting Kylix Kick Starts in more than 50 cities worldwide.

Charlie and John frequently communicated with R&D to ensure that they completely understood the technological decisions we made. They know and understand the issues developers face. Charlie and John provided the original information on which all external Kylix publications are based, including any other Kylix book you may buy. They have continued to provide and refine information on Kylix.

All the authors of this book explain not only how Kylix works, but why it works the way it does. This book is the culmination of more than two years of intimate involvement with both Kylix the product and the project.

I hope you enjoy the *Kylix Developer's Guide*, and I hope you enjoy your development experiences with Kylix. We have lots of great things planned for future releases of the product, and Charlie, John, Bob, and the other authors provide you an excellent foundation for developing any kind of application with Kylix.

# About the Authors

**Charlie Calvert** is a programmer and writer who lives and works with his wife Margie and his two cats in Santa Cruz, California. He is the author of *Delphi 4 Unleashed*, C++*Builder 3 Unleashed, Delphi 2 Unleashed, Teach Yourself Windows 95 Programming in 21 Days, Delphi Unleashed, Teach Yourself Windows Programming, Turbo Pascal Programming 101*, and a contributing author of *CBuilder 4 Unleashed*. He worked with his wife Margie to create an interactive Java tutorial, and he has been published in many different technical magazines. Charlie has spoken on technical subjects such as Delphi, C++, and Java at major industry conferences, and in many smaller conferences from Europe to Australia to the Far East. Originally trained as an English major, Charlie worked as a journalist and college English teacher before turning to the world of computers. He has a BA in both Journalism and Computer Science from Evergreen State College in Olympia, Washington.

His interests include bicycling, hiking, playing folk guitar, listening to jazz, and writing poetry and fiction. A considerable portion of his free time is dedicated to spiritual pursuits within the Episcopal Church and various Buddhist and Hindu meditation traditions.

Online, he can be found at `http://www.elvenware.com`.

**Margie Calvert** has been working with computers for the past six years. Her focus is on graphics and the Internet. She has collaborated with Charlie Calvert on several books, helping with editing and graphics. Margie also has an MBA in business, an MA in English, and a background in nursing.

**John Kaster** is a Senior Developer Relations Manager for Borland, and architect for the Borland Community Web site. Previously, he was a product manager, responsible for distributed computing and database connectivity for Delphi and C++ Builder. John is the author of the CodeCentral repository and other custom applications for the community Web site, all built with Borland technology. Before coming to Borland, he produced several award-winning software development tools. He is co-author of *Delphi Database Development, Programming in Clipper 5*, and numerous articles for various computing magazines. He has been speaking at conferences and providing training around the world for more than 15 years. John loves to share his discoveries about software development and discuss design philosophy with other developers.

**Bob Swart** (www.drbob42.com) is a UK Borland User Group (UK-BUG) and UK Borland Connections member and an independent technical author, trainer, and consultant using Delphi, Kylix and C++Builder based in Helmond, The Netherlands. Bob writes regular columns for *The Delphi Magazine, Delphi Developer, UK-BUG Developer's Magazine*, as well as the DevX, TechRepublic and the Borland Community Web sites. *Kylix Developer's Guide* is the second book where Bob Swart's name appears on the cover (the first one was *C++Builder 5 Developer's Guide*), but he has also participated and written chapters for *The Revolutionary Guide to Delphi 2, Delphi 4 Unleashed, C++Builder 4 Unleashed* and the upcoming *Delphi 6 Developer's Guide* (SAMS).

Bob is a frequent speaker at Borland and Delphi/Kylix related seminars all over the world, and writes his own training material for Dr.Bob's Delphi Clinics (in The Netherlands and the UK).

In his spare time, Bob likes to watch video tapes of Star Trek Voyager and Deep Space Nine with his 7-year old son Erik Mark Pascal and 5-year old daughter Natasha Louise Delphine.

# About the Contributing Authors

**Paul J. Freitas**, Ph.D., has more than 10 years experience in object-oriented programming. After earning his bachelor's degrees at Santa Clara University in 1991, he worked for several years as a software developer using rapid application development tools. Seeking greater challenges, he entered graduate school, where he developed C++ software for use in his computational physics research. He completed his doctoral studies in 2000; now he puts his programming, teaching, and writing skills to work as a technical writer at Borland Software Corporation. He lives in Santa Cruz, California with his cat Sassy, whom he tends to annoy with his drum studies.

**Bruno Sonnino** is a Delphi Client/Server Developer certified by Borland Brazil and has worked with Delphi since its first version, in 1995, developing medical and commercial applications. He was a speaker at Borland Conference 2001, in Long Beach, California, and writes a monthly column in the Delphi Informant magazine, "At Your Fingertips," and articles for Brazilian magazines.

He has written the books *Kylix—Delphi for Linux, Developing Applications with Delphi 6*, and *365 Delphi Tips*, published in Brazil by Pearson Education Brazil.

# Dedication

*I would like to dedicate this book to all those who lost their lives in the World Trade Center and Pentagon attacks of Sept 11, 2001. My hope is that their sacrifice will, through some miracle, lead us to a safer, saner, and more peaceful world—a world filled with understanding rather than hatred and suspicion.*

*–Charlie Calvert*

*This book is dedicated to my daughter Sydney Leilani Kaster, who decided to arrive in the world eight weeks early, so I couldn't finish the "book project" before my life-long one started. I also want to thank my wife, Patricia White-Kaster, for her extreme patience with the time I spent on this book. I earnestly hope this book in some small way helps lead to a more educated and tolerant world where tragedies like the bombings of the World Trade Center and the Pentagon, and the crash in Pennsylvania will no longer occur. My heart goes out to those who were killed or injured, and their family and friends. I could easily have been one of those passengers—something I will strive to always remember.*

*–John Kaster*

*To Yvonne, Erik, and Natasha*

*–Bob Swart*

# Acknowledgments

I want to thank the following people: my fellow authors for their hard work, the people at Borland for their support, and everyone at Sams for their hard work and support.

I also want to thank the members of the Open Source community for the many resources they have made available, and for their ability to put a spirit of excitement, common decency, and even altruism back into the art of computer software development.

In particular my thanks go to John Kaster for the many days and nights he put into this project, and all the help he gave me preparing this book. Carol Ackerman also went well beyond the call of duty in her efforts. She was a continual source of support, and offered me an inspiring example of human decency and consideration.

Most of all, my thanks goes to my wife Margie, who not only worked hard on this book, but also supported me through the various ups and downs that always seem to accompany the production of a book.

*–Charlie Calvert*

I would like to thank TeamB members Jeff Overcash and Rob Schieck, who provided indispensable help, material, and suggestions for the database chapters he wrote. I would also like to thank the Kylix R&D team for their patience in answering questions, no matter how many times I pestered them.

*–John Kaster*

# Tell Us What You Think!

As the reader of this book, *you* are our most important critic and commentator. We value your opinion and want to know what we're doing right, what we could do better, what areas you'd like to see us publish in, and any other words of wisdom you're willing to pass our way.

As an Executive Editor for Sams, I welcome your comments. You can fax, e-mail, or write me directly to let me know what you did or didn't like about this book—as well as what we can do to make our books stronger.

*Please note that I cannot help you with technical problems related to the topic of this book, and that due to the high volume of mail I receive, I might not be able to reply to every message.*

When you write, please be sure to include this book's title and author as well as your name and phone or fax number. I will carefully review your comments and share them with the author and editors who worked on the book.

Fax:        317-581-4770

E-mail:     feedback@samspublishing.com

Mail:       Michael Stephens, Executive Editor
            Sams Publishing
            201 West 103rd Street
            Indianapolis, IN 46290 USA

# Introduction

## Book Overview

This book will teach you how to use Kylix. In these pages you'll learn how to produce quality applications appropriate for open source development, the corporate marketplace, the consumer marketplace, or private use.

## The Intended Audience for this Book

This book is designed for experienced object-oriented programmers at the intermediate level or above. Programmers who have experience with C++, Java, or Object Pascal will all be in a good position to understand this text.

You need to know

- How to program
- Structured programming
- Object-oriented programming

You don't need to know

- It is not important that you have experience with any particular computer language, though knowledge of Object Pascal will be helpful. A complete explanation of Object Pascal is, however, included in the text.
- It is not important that you have experience with any particular operating system, though a basic understanding of Linux will be helpful.

## What's in the Text

The text of this book places a big emphasis on providing information for experienced programmers. It is not expected that the reader have a knowledge of Kylix's sister product, Delphi for Windows. However, there will be numerous passages that directly address readers who have that background.

Newcomers to Object Pascal who have never seen Delphi will find many things to interest them in this text. In particular, it lightly covers the basics of the language, in a fashion that will be useful to experienced programmers. This is not an attempt to teach beginners how to program, but rather the goal is to give Java, C++, Python, Perl and VB programmers the information they need to quickly get up to speed on Kylix.

After covering the basic syntax of the language, the text explains how visual programming works in Kylix. A certain emphasis will also be placed on assuring newcomers to the language that Kylix does not rely on black boxes or sleight of hand. In particular, you will see that the visual tools are designed to help you write code quickly, without concealing the inner workings of the language. This is a programmer's tool, and you can do everything in code if you so desire.

The book begins with an explanation of Object Pascal designed for experienced programmers. It is not a tutorial on how to program, but rather an overview of Object Pascal designed to be read by experienced C++, Java, Perl, Python, or VB users. In particular, developers with a C++ or Java background will find many useful tips to help them get up to speed quickly.

Visual programming in Kylix is dependent on an object-oriented library called CLX. The text explains the CLX architecture and how it is structured. The study of this library consumes the major portion of the second section of the book.

With this foundation material out of the way, the next step is to plunge into Linux systems programming. You will learn how to push the GUI and high-end tools aside and interface directly with the low-level functionality of the Linux operating system. These chapters should convince skeptical readers that Object Pascal gives you full access to all the major services of the operating system. Other readers with more Delphi experience might be getting their first in-depth look at the internal workings of the Linux operating system, and so the text will also include enough detail to help them grasp the fundamentals of a complicated new subject.

The fourth section of the book, written primarily by John Kaster, deals with databases. Databases are one of Kylix's great strengths. As a result, you can expect this section to be full of important information. It will contain in-depth explorations of the Kylix database architecture and the act of constructing Delphi database applications. It will also contain explications of how to use the tools Delphi provides to connect to and manipulate data. The text covers SQL databases such as InterBase and MySQL.

Web development is the theme of the fifth and last section of the book. The text works primarily with the Apache server, since it is the dominant tool for Web development on the Linux platform. The text shows how to create CGI applications, how to expand the applications to encompass more complex data models, and how to use JavaScript and DOM to enhance applications.

I'm Charlie Calvert, and I'll write the sections of the book on Object Pascal and CLX. As you know, the database tools will be described by John Kaster. Bob Swart will be the primary author handling the Web development chapters. The sections on the native Linux APIs were written by Paul Freitas. You can read more about us at the beginning of this book.

As writers, we strive to:

- Explain technology in a relatively clear and easy to read manner.
- Provide plenty of working code available in numerous sample programs.
- Organize material so it is easy to find important passages.

Most of the code will be released as open source, and can be downloaded as a zip file or via CVS from `http://sourceforge.net/projects/elvenware`. For updates on the code found in the book, check the sourceforge site, and also `www.elvenware.com`.

Rather than talk about it further, it will probably be best if we begin our exploration right away. The first step will be to define Kylix itself.

## What Is Kylix?

Kylix is a tool for creating cross-platform applications. It is made by Borland, a highly respected tools development company.

The application source code Kylix produces is cross-platform. The product is not based on an emulation layer, but instead allows you to recompile your source to create high performance native applications for both Linux and Windows.

Kylix is based on the award winning product Delphi for Windows. Like Delphi, Kylix uses the Object Pascal language and a visual programming metaphor to allow programmers to develop high performance applications easily.

It is the opinion of the authors of this book that Delphi is an excellent tool for building Windows applications. The product has won many prestigious awards, and it is highly respected by some of the best programmers in the industry. The act of creating Kylix by porting Delphi to Linux is a major event in the programming world, and will hopefully become an important milestone in the history of Linux.

Like Delphi, Kylix allows you to create the interface for an application by dropping components down on a form. For instance, Figure I.1 shows a Kylix application that consists of several buttons and edit controls. Creating applications of this type is simple in Kylix. An experienced Kylix programmer could easily build such an application in less than 30 seconds.

Kylix has many features that help you arrange, align, resize, and reformat the components you drop on your form. Visual design is easy in Kylix, and there are repositories and other mechanisms available that make it easy for you to reuse or share your creations in multiple projects.

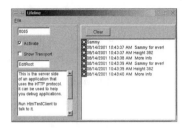

**FIGURE I.1**

*A simple Kylix form with components on it.*

Included in Kylix are sophisticated debuggers that help you explore your code at runtime. Browsers are available to help you examine your code in depth at design time. Kylix will optionally help you write code, popping up windows showing the parameters for a particular call, or alphabetized lists of legal calls you can make at any one place in your code. Figure I.2 shows Kylix popping up a window showing the methods available on a particular object. Though I personally find tools of this kind invaluable, it is nice to know that they can be turned on and off to suit your needs or preferences.

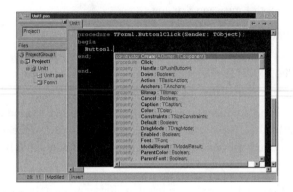

**FIGURE I.2**

*Kylix pops up a list showing all the legal methods you can call on an instance of a button component.*

There are many other excellent features of the Kylix programming environment. You will find tools for creating shared objects, wizards to help you build forms, dialog boxes for helping you create components, and a Tools API that can help you program the Kylix development environment itself. There is not enough room here to explain all these things in depth, but most of them will be covered in the first two sections of this text.

## Object Pascal

Delphi and Kylix both use the Object Pascal programming language. Object Pascal is a wonderful language. It fully supports basic OOP features such as polymorphism, inheritance, and encapsulation. It has support for most of the features of sophisticated modern programming languages, such as pointers and interfaces.

The programming language that most closely mirrors the features of Object Pascal is Java. The biggest difference between Java and Object Pascal is that the latter is a compiled language with performance characteristics similar to C++. Just as Java was based on C, so is Object Pascal based on Niklas Wirth's original Pascal programming language. However, Object Pascal, like Java, has many powerful modern programming features that make it architecturally much more sophisticated than the language on which it is based.

Hopefully, you now have some very general sense of the feature set found in Kylix. Throughout this brief overview, I've stressed that one of the primary goals of the Kylix project was to bring Delphi to Linux. The aim was to give Linux programmers a chance to work with a state of the art development environment similar in quality to Delphi. It is, however, important to stress that Kylix is not identical to Delphi. Instead, it is based on Delphi. In the next section you will learn something about the Kylix architecture and its relationship to Delphi.

# The Kylix Architecture

Delphi for Windows is based on an objected-oriented library called the VCL. The creators of Kylix could have set 100% compatibility with the Delphi VCL as their goal. However, they did not end up taking that position. Delphi is a Windows product based on the Windows API. The Windows API is not natively available on Linux, though it is available on that platform through an API called WINE. The Kylix team, decided, however, not to use WINE. Instead, they decided to create a compiler that generated applications that were truly native to Linux.

To port Delphi to Linux, the developers had a number of choices. In the end, they chose to write an OOP layer called CLX that allowed Delphi apps to run on Linux with a minimum set of modifications.

# What Is This Thing Named CLX?

CLX is an OOP library whose visual controls are based on Qt, a native Linux library that forms the basis for the KDE, which is the most popular Linux desktop. (In this case, the word "desktop" refers to the GUI interface of the Linux operating system. KDE plays much the same role in Linux that the Start bar and core utilities such as Notepad, Wordpad, Calc, and the Control Panel do in Windows. Qt is the C++ OOP library that was used to build the KDE.)

Later chapters include an in-depth description of Qt, KDE, and the entire Linux GUI architecture. In particular, see Chapter 1, "Visual Development," and Chapter 7, "CLX Architecture and Visual Development."

CLX allows developers to create applications that integrate seamlessly with Linux. In particular, it allows you to produce truly native Linux applications with no reliance on Windows code or any sort of emulation layer. It does, however, force existing Delphi developers to rewrite their code—at least, in part. Furthermore, it forces customers to use a Qt DLL when they take their Kylix applications back to Windows. (Remember, the apps must run on both Windows and Linux, so you are in a bind no matter which way you go. This is a Catch-22 factor. However the Qt DLL required on Windows is only about a megabyte in size, which is not a significant factor in an OS such as Windows that routinely uses more than 80MB of RAM and swap space just to load its basic tools.)

It is important to stress that although CLX and the VCL are very much alike, they are not identical. They are enough alike, however, that Delphi apps can run on Linux with a minimum set of modifications.

The decision that the team made when deciding how to port Delphi to Linux brought numerous consequences. Perhaps the largest was that Delphi programmers had to abandon their familiar object-oriented library, named the Visual Component Library (VCL). In its place, a new library was born: CLX.

It is possible to place too much significance on that fact that Qt was developed by a different group of developers than those who created the Linux Kernel. Qt, however, is no more a layer on top of Linux than the buttons or list boxes found on Windows are part of a layer that sits on top of the Windows OS. Both Linux and Windows have a core OS with buttons and list boxes sitting on top of it. Windows has the controls as part of the OS; Linux delivers them separately. They both have the same architecture, but Linux gives you the option to choose which widget set you want to use. (Of course, the Linux world does not have the luxury of needing to refine and plan for only one set of widget tools!)

Whatever compromises the Kylix team made in other areas, it did a conscientious job of finding a good way to allow programmers to write native GUI applications that perform well on Linux. There is no denying that Qt is a real native Linux widget set. Furthermore, the team chose an architecture that closely mirrored the Linux way of thinking about applications. Within reasonable limitations, the team did everything that it could to help you produce high-performance Linux applications. The only caveat is that these applications contain as many features of the Delphi architecture as could be preserved without fundamentally violating the architectural vision of native Linux programs.

# Compatibility Between Delphi for Windows and Kylix for Linux

You can perform two kinds of programming tasks in Delphi and Kylix:

1. Application programming tasks
2. Component writing tasks

The Delphi team tried to maintain a high degree of compatibility between Delphi and Kylix when it comes to application development tasks. However, the Kylix team decided that it would be impossible to maintain this same charmed relationship when it came to writing components.

In short, if you know how to build an application in Delphi with the visual tools, it should not be hard to learn how to do the same thing in Kylix. If you know how to write components in Delphi, however, those skills will not transfer as readily. The same can be said of porting apps from Windows to Linux: Applications should come over fairly easily, but custom components could be quite difficult to port. In many cases, you will be able to take a form designed for Delphi for Windows and port it to Kylix with only a small amount of fuss, if you have a certain degree of patience and a good knowledge of both Kylix and Delphi. (Giving you a good understanding of Kylix is the task of this book.)

## Porting Applications

The Kylix team's stated goal was to make it possible to move a large application from Delphi to Kylix in one to two months. Except in the most trivial cases, you should not expect a port from the VCL to CLX to be a simple recompile. As we've tried to make clear, significant differences exist between the two models.

A one- or two-month port of a large application from Windows to Linux might sound like a fairly substantial effort. However, large applications can take six months to a year to write—perhaps even longer. If you can move that app to Linux in one month, you are saving between one-sixth and one-twelfth the time involved in a full rewrite.

---

### NOTE

Don't become confused: We're talking about porting VCL apps from Windows to Kylix. If you have a Kylix app that you developed on Linux, you can port it to Windows with a simple recompile—at least, in theory. Your success will be based on your ability to avoid using Linux APIs in your program. If you write directly to the Linux APIs, your app will not port easily to Windows. However, if all your code is CLX-based, it should port to Windows with a simple recompile.

One of the most severe problems you're likely to encounter when porting VCL apps to Kylix is a dependency on third-party controls. It will be important for Borland to get the third parties to move over their controls.

## Porting Components

Component writers likely will not find their tasks as easy to perform as the tasks of application developers. Applications are based on CLX, and CLX looks a lot like the VCL. Components, on the other hand, are often based on the Windows API, and the Linux API looks nothing like the Windows API. Even components based on the VCL will be hard to port. The problem will be that components usually rely on the very lowest, most complex parts of the VCL. It is this part of the object-oriented library that changed most radically when ported to Linux.

Borland's goal was to make sure that CLX meshed well with Qt and decided not to try to make CLX fit in with the Windows architecture. In particular, it did not try to set up a close relationship between Qt messages and Windows messages. If your Windows code sticks to Borland's known events, such as OnKeyDown and OnMouseDown, then it will be easy to port to Linux. On the other hand, if you use the Windows messages WM_KEYDOWN and WM_LBUTTONDOWN, you will have trouble.

The more Delphi programmers rely on the Windows API, the harder time they will have porting components. Porting non-visual components should be simpler than porting visual components, if you don't rely on the Windows API too heavily.

With Kylix, Borland introduces a new architecture named dbExpress for accessing databases. Designed to work with SQL servers, dbExpress performs much better than the old SQL links tools that were part of the BDE. (dbExpress provides no tools for Paradox, Access or dBase tables. Instead, Borland is focusing on SQL databases.)

Just as CLX is as much like the VCL as possible, so is dbExpress as much like the BDE as possible. Moving from the BDE to dbExpress is a challenge, but many of the tools will seem very familiar to Delphi developers.

Borland has great hopes for this architecture. In fact, the company would like to make this the database access API that is standard under Linux.

## Types of Kylix Programs

Linux is used most frequently as a server. As a result, many of the tools used in Linux run from the command line. Kylix is primarily aimed at people who want to build GUI applications with widgets on them; However, it's a flexible tool and will be of use to people who just want to build utilities or servers that run from the command line.

Kylix comes with a wizard that automatically generates a default, nearly empty, command-line, or console, program. (You will read about this utility in Chapter 1.) You have complete access to the core OS-level functions that such command-line programs will typically need to call. For instance, experienced Linux programmers will be glad to know that Kylix offers full and ready access to nearly everything in Libc. (For those who don't know Linux well, Libc is a shared object containing all the core functions in the C library.) But Kylix doesn't stop at merely letting you build command-line and widget-based tools. You can also use Kylix to build applications that use only the X Window Library but contain no widgets. Such an application would run in a GUI environment but would not need to include Qt. In short, it would have no controls, only text or bitmaps. Programs of this type are usually very small and very fast, but they still contain some of the features of typical GUI applications. However, Kylix does nothing to help you build this kind of program; constructing it is just as difficult as building the program in C. (Windows programmers can think of it as being similar in difficulty to building a typical Windows API program from scratch. In fact, there are many direct parallels between the two types of programs—for example, the Windows call `CreateWindow` becomes `XCreateSimpleWindow` or `XCreateWindow`. We discuss this topic in depth in Chapter 6, "Understanding the Linux Environment.")

## Further Questions: GTK and Kernel Development

In the first version of Kylix, Borland has done nothing to make it easy for you to use the GTK. You can use it, if you want, but doing so requires considerable effort.

The Linux kernel is not a part of Kylix development. The kernel is intimately wed to the GNU C++ compiler; it is built with the GNU compiler, and it depends on certain bugs in that compiler. As a result, there is no practical way to program the Linux kernel with Kylix—that is still a task for programmers armed with GCC.

However, most of the low-level functionality for Linux development is not in the kernel itself, but instead is in Libc. Libc contains routines for opening and closing files, creating and deleting files and directories, changing directories, working with threads, setting the time, working with dates, scheduling tasks, and so on.

## Kylix and Databases

Delphi is most famous as a database development tool. As mentioned earlier, Delphi depends on a database access layer named the BDE; however, the Kylix team decided not to port the BDE to Linux.

Because of the shift away from local databases and toward SQL databases, the Kylix team decided that the new dbExpress database engine would target SQL databases. Currently, you cannot use dbExpress to access Paradox, dBase, or Access tables; instead, dbExpress targets InterBase, MySQL, and other SQL databases.

dbExpress is designed to be small, fast, and modular. This contrasts with the BDE, which has many tools but is large and somewhat awkward; dbExpress does not have has many features, but it does its primary job very well. In particular, you can expect to see a 100% increase in performance for many tasks when moving from the BDE to dbExpress. Your guide to the dbExpress will be John Kaster; his description of dbExpress tells you all you need to know about this powerful new database development tool.

## Kylix and Web Development

The Delphi Web development tools are powerful and easy to use. However, they have never quite reached the state of sophistication found in the Delphi GUI and database development tools. New features in Delphi 6 should help to rectify the situation, but it is not clear at this time whether all the new Web development features in Delphi 6 will make it into Kylix. (In fact, many of the features found in Delphi 5 might not appear in the first version of Kylix.)

The Delphi WebBroker architecture provides the capability to easily create CGI- or DLL-based applications. These tools can be used to construct simple Web pages, to respond to events that occur on the Web, and to display database tables in an HTML form. The Delphi WebBroker appears fully formed in Kylix. The best news regarding Web development in Kylix is that your WebBroker code will recompile virtually unchanged in Delphi. In fact, most WebBroker code developed in Delphi 5 or earlier versions should recompile in Kylix.

Kylix Web development is designed primarily to work with the Apache Server. You will be able to easily create both standard CGI programs and Apache Shared Modules. (For those of you from the Windows world, Apache Shared Modules are much like ISAPI.) The Web architecture is not based on Qt, so the presence of Qt is not a prerequisite for its use.

At this time, Linux offers few GUI tools that can help you quickly develop powerful Web applications. As a result, the Kylix WebBroker architecture should be a welcome tool in the hands of experienced programmers. Over time, Borland plans to port the more advanced Delphi Web development tools to Kylix.

Bob Swart will be your primary guide through the WebBroker architecture. You can find his description of this subject in Chapters 17–19.

## Summary

In this introduction, you have been introduced to both Kylix and the subject matter of this book. Kylix has some great strengths, as well as some parts where technical challenges forced the developers to make hard choices and difficult compromises. Certainly we wouldn't have written this book if we did not believe that Kylix stands a good chance of stepping into the shoes of its excellent forbearer: Delphi for Windows.

Thank you for buying our book. Now sit down someplace comfortable, fire up your computer, put on your thinking cap, and prepare to have some fun exploring a powerful new technology.

# Understanding Delphi and Linux

## PART

# I

## IN THIS PART

# Visual Development

*By Charlie Calvert*

## IN THIS CHAPTER

This chapter gives you an introduction to the Kylix visual development tools. The text introduces the Kylix IDE, the form designer, and a few simple tricks for doing visual development.

By the end of the chapter, you will know something about the kind of programs Kylix produces, and you will see how easy it is to create them using the tools found in the IDE.

This is also the place to tell experienced Delphi programmers about the adjustments they need to make when switching their Object Pascal development from Windows to Kylix. The Kylix IDE is a port of the Delphi 5 IDE to Linux. As a result, it is very similar—but not identical—to the IDE used by Delphi 5 programmers. Throughout the text, I'll highlight the differences between the two environments and give the readers with Windows backgrounds some tips on how to begin to feel comfortable in the Linux world.

## The Kylix IDE

The Kylix IDE is customizable. You can rearrange, add to, delete from, and generally reconfigure the toolbars so that they suit your style of development.

The IDE's most obvious feature is that it enables you to drag and drop visual objects such as edit controls and list boxes onto a form. You can then modify and rearrange these controls, creating a powerful interface for your application.

The editor itself supports several different key mappings, and you can change its colors, its font size, and the fonts themselves. Many other features of the editor are configurable, including the tab settings, the width of the borders, insert mode, syntax highlighting, and other features too numerous to mention.

When you are working in the editor, you can get instant context-sensitive help on the methods you are using. That help can come from the help system itself or from a tool named Code Insight, which can show you the parameters for the method you are calling or for the methods available on a particular object. Code Insight works not only on the code from the official CLX API, but it also automatically works on the code that you write, as you write it.

Even the menu system in Kylix is extensible. You can add new menu items to the IDE that enable you to call other applications. For instance, as you will see in this chapter, you can easily configure the IDE to pop up the current source file that you are working on in emacs or some other editor.

This chapter explores all these features of the IDE. Later portions of this book expand on the information that you see here and cover some of the more complex subjects in depth. For instance, I can give you an overview of dragging components onto forms in this chapter, but a full understanding of components and their relationship to the IDE is complex subject. As a result, I will devote most of Part II, "CLX," to teaching you how to build your own components.

I've been using the Delphi IDEs since before the Earth's crust began cooling, and I've been pounding on the Kylix IDE since well before it was even remotely usable. As a result, I know a number of tips for taking advantage of its features. I will share as many of them as possible with you in this text.

## A Plan of Attack

By now, you might be getting a sense of the size and complexity of the Kylix IDE. This is a big and very powerful tool. Even people who have been using Delphi for years might not know all its in and outs.

Fortunately, many of the features of the IDE should be relatively familiar to experienced computer users. The IDE follows many of the same conventions and metaphors found in StarOffice, Microsoft Office, Visual Basic, Visual C++, KDeveloper, and other widely used tools. Furthermore, even the advanced and lesser-known features are usually relatively intuitive and easy to understand.

I will try to cover all the highlights so that you know the major features. I will also take time to point out key or very useful features that might not be obvious to newcomers.

I'll begin by looking at the toolbars, showing you how to rearrange and configure them. I'll then focus on the basics of visual development, highlighting techniques for using components and designing interfaces. Then I'll zero in on the editor and show you how to configure it, how it can help you browse your code, how it can help you find the methods and parameters that you need, and how it can generally make the act of writing code a relatively pleasant and intuitive process. With all the major topics out of the way, I'll come back and hit some of the smaller features that add power to the IDE. These include wizards, frames, calls to third-party utilities, and the help system.

Although not all the features of the IDE are obvious to a newcomer, none are particularly difficult to understand. As a result, this chapter should not be particularly demanding, and I will make an effort to keep the tone relatively light-hearted. Throughout, I'll keep an eye out for tips useful to Java, VB, and Visual C++ programmers who might be interested in trying a new technology. And, of course, I'll give as many hints as possible to emacs or vi users who might be venturing into relatively new and, perhaps from their perspective, somewhat suspect territory. Hopefully all the newcomers will come to feel at home with this powerful and friendly tool.

This chapter has a close kinship with Chapter 5, "The Editor and Debugger." Together they present an overview of the entire Kylix IDE. Along with the other chapters in Part I, "Understanding Delphi and Linux," they give you an overview of the Object Pascal way of life.

## The IDE from 20,000 Feet

To help get you oriented, Figure 1.1 names the IDE's major features. These include the Menu, the Object Inspector, the Component Palette, the Editor, the Form Designer, and the Toolbars.

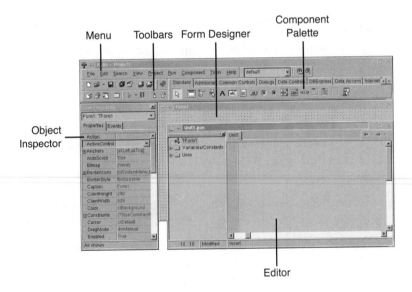

**FIGURE 1.1**
*The major features of the IDE.*

Throughout the rest of this book, I will tackle each of these major features and explain them in depth. However, sometimes I will reference some feature in a relatively offhand way before I have time to fully explain its purpose. In such cases, you can refer to Figure 1.1 to understand which feature of the IDE I am discussing. Then just be patient, and you will soon encounter a more in-depth explanation of that feature.

# The Menus

We have to start somewhere, and the menus are perhaps as good a place as any to get our feet wet. The intended readers for this book are entirely capable of exploring the menus for themselves. However, there are some things I can say that might be of use to at least a few readers.

You can use the menus to perform a wide range of tasks, including opening and closing files, manipulating the debugger, and customizing the environment. As a general rule, all the features of the IDE, by default, are accessible through the menus.

## Menu Shortcuts

The menus provide a very fast interface to the Kylix environment because they can be manipulated through a configurable set of key strokes. They also provide a handy reference for the hotkeys that enable you to easily perform routine tasks such as saving files or projects, as well as compiling and debugging your application.

If you open the Edit menu, you will see the window shown in Figures 1.2 and 1.3. Take a second to compare the two figures. At first, they might seem identical. However, if you look closely, you will see that the keyboard shortcuts associated with each menu item are different in each screenshot. Why is this?

**FIGURE 1.2**

*The Edit menu as it appears with the default key mappings.*

To understand what is happening, open the Tools menu, choose Editor Options, and then choose the Key Mappings menu item. Change the Key Mapping Module from Default to Brief and finally to Epsilon. As you make each selection, click OK and then open the Edit menu. As you can see, the shortcuts on each menu item change, depending on the type of key mapping you have chosen.

**FIGURE 1.3**

*The Edit menu as it appears with the brief key mappings.*

---

**NOTE**

You can create your own key mappings and supply your own key shortcuts. I will show how to do that in Chapter 8.

---

**LINUX NOTE**

If you are an emacs or vi user who is new to IDEs, I encourage you to take the tlme to become familiar with the menu system. The default key mapping enables you to open any menu by pressing the Alt key plus the first letter of the menu. For instance, Alt+F opens the File menu. Now you can select an item in the menu by pressing the underlined letter in the menu, such as S for save, or C for close.

---

**VC NOTE**

If you are a Microsoft C++ programmer, consider choosing the Visual C++ key mapping emulation so that you can use your familiar shortcuts when in the IDE. Select the Tools menu and choose Editor Options, Key Mappings, and then Visual Studio Emulation.

## Right-Click Pop-up Menus

Another key feature of the Kylix menu system is the right-click pop-up menus. In fact, right-clicking to bring up pop-up menus is a bit of a religion at Borland because the company was a pioneer in this field. In general, whenever you are in the Kylix IDE and you feel a little unsure about what to do next, try right-clicking on whatever is nearest to you, and you might find your answer. There are different and often quite complex pop-up menus for all the major windows in the IDE. For instance, the Form Designer, the Object Inspector, the Editor, the Component Palette, and the toolbars all have their own menus. Remember to right-click!

## Adding New Tools to the Menu

Here's another useful feature of the menu system. Go to the Tools menu and choose Configure Tools. Click Add. In the Title field, type **emacs**. (If emacs is not installed on your system, choose another utility that you want to use, such as vi, kwrite, or joe.) In the Program field, type **/usr/bin/emacs** or whatever the path is to your utility. In the Working Dir field, type in the name of your home directory, such as **/home/ccalvert**. Click Macros, and scroll through the list and choose $EDNAME. This macro gives you the fully qualified path to the topmost file in the editor. Click OK on the Tools Property dialog box and then click the Close button in the Tool Options dialog box. Figure 1.4 shows how the dialog box should appear when correctly configured to load emacs on a standard Red Hat install.

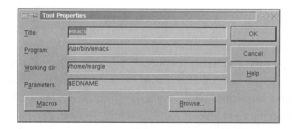

**FIGURE 1.4**
*Tool Properties dialog box.*

Open the Tools menu: You should now see emacs listed as an item in your menu. If it is not there, or if it is not enabled, then go back to the Tools menu and repeat the steps outlined in the previous paragraph.

To test your new menu item, you need a file to edit. To ensure that you have a valid file, open an existing Kylix project. (For instance, go to the Kylix/demos directory and open the BasicEd project. Choose View, Units from the menu and select BasicEd1.) When you see the code from a saved file in the Kylix editor, choose Tools, emacs. emacs should open, and you should see your Pascal source in the classic GNU editor. The new versions of emacs should even automatically provide syntax highlighting for your code. If you make edits in emacs and save your changes, they will be preserved when you return to the Kylix IDE.

That's all I'm going to say about the Kylix menu system for now. I will focus on menus again when talking about key topics, such as the debugger or the editor. In those passages, I will focus on the parts of the menu that are germane to that particular topic being discussed.

## The Toolbars

By default, the toolbars appear directly beneath and to the right of the main menu. By clicking the toolbars with the mouse, you can accomplish many of the same tasks that you can perform via the menus and a keyboard. The toolbars are also easier to customize than the menu. Whether you use the toolbars or the menus to perform certain tasks is totally up to you.

If you right-click the menu bar or the speed bar, a pop-up window will appear. You can hide many of the toolbars by simply deselecting them in this window. Conversely, you will notice that there is a small handle on the far left of each toolbar. (The handle actually looks more like two miniature speed bumps than a handle.) You can grab the toolbar by this handle. To do this, left-click, hold down the button, and drag. You can use this handle to move the location of the toolbar or to completely remove the toolbar from its home. After you pull the toolbar off the main window of the IDE, it will float on top of the other windows and will not disappear behind them.

It is also possible for you to add elements to the toolbars. Start by right-clicking a toolbar. Choose the Customize option at the bottom of the pop-up window. The Customize dialog box appears. It will be open to the Toolbars page, which lists the toolbars that you can select or hide. Move to the Commands page by clicking on it; this page is divided into two parts, with categories on the left and commands on the right. If you click a category, such as Debug, various commands appear on the right side of the dialog box. You can click any of the icons and drag them to the toolbar. For instance, you can click the Breakpoints icon from the Debug category and drag it to the toolbar. The icon will then appear on the toolbar. See Figures 1.5 and 1.6 for an illustration of this process.

You can also drag items off the toolbars. For instance, I rarely use the Step Into, Step Over, and Pause buttons on the Debug toolbar. As a result, I often remove them from the toolbars and replace them with the Cut, Copy, and Paste icons from the Edit category. I also like to put the Compile and Build icons from the project category on the Desktops toolbar found to the right of the menu. My point is not that you should necessarily perform this same operation, but that you should be aware that similar courses of action are open to you.

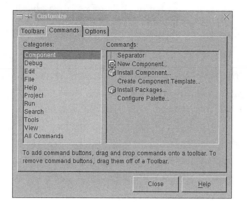
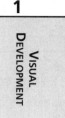

**FIGURE 1.5**
*The Commands page in the Customize dialog box.*

**FIGURE 1.6**
*Two pictures of the same toolbar—first as it appears by default, and second as it appears with some new icons added to it.*

# Visual Development

Now that some of the preliminaries are out of the way, it's time to explore the subject of visual programming. This subject, of course, is very much at the heart of Kylix programming. Visual programming technologies are the single biggest benefit that Kylix brings to programmers, and they are the ones that can save you the most time. (Probably the second most important feature is the debugger, which will be covered in Chapter 5.) Before getting down to the details, let me add just a few words of introduction. Visual programming is still a new idea, and, like all new ideas, it meets resistance from people who are reluctant to change. I would like to take a moment to debunk a few common objections to this technology.

1. **Objection One:** *Visual Programming feels like cheating. In my gut, I sense that there is something wrong with making a complex job this simple.* The real goal for programmers is to find the best way to do a job. We all know that, if given enough time, most healthy people can walk all the way from San Francisco to New York. However, in most cases—particularly when business is involved—airplanes are a cheaper, safer, and more expedient means of crossing the continent. In the same way, visual programming provides an economical and efficient means of creating the interface to most applications. No doubt,

everyone can create the same interface in the Kylix editor by writing code, but it is easier, simpler, and usually safer to build it with the visual tools.

2. **Objection Two:** *I've heard that visual components are big and unwieldy and that they can't be linked directly into my executable.* For some visual tools, this is a valid objection—but not for Kylix. Via inheritance, components contain a very small amount of extra Object Pascal code that allow them to be manipulated visually at design time. This code is not bulky. Other types of visual components might be bulky, but Kylix components are not outsized. Furthermore, you can directly link components into your application—or not, depending on your needs. The part of the code that makes a component a component is all written directly in Object Pascal. Therefore, it can be linked directly into your program in exactly the same manner as you would link in any other object. (Parts of some components are not written in Object Pascal but are instead part of the C/C++–based Qt library. That subject is covered in the second part of this book, on CLX.) To be fair, I should say that the entire CLX library is fairly large, just as MFC, Qt, the GTK, and other OOP-based libraries are fairly large. But on a component-by-component basis, the amount of code needed to create a visual control is not large at all.

3. **Objection Three:** *Anybody can do visual programming. I'm a real programmer, and I want to do work commensurate with my skills. (Besides, where's my job security if programming becomes nothing more than dragging things around with a mouse?)* If you truly are a good programmer, it would be a waste of your time to do the kind of tedious, repetitive programming that is generally the heart and soul of most interface-development chores. Visual development tools let you get the boring stuff out of the way quickly so that you can concentrate on the more interesting and challenging tasks. Secondly, visual programming actually creates programming jobs in the field of generating interface components. It takes programmers with great coding skills to build good components, and there is plenty of opportunity for good programmers to find work in this area. Finally, the heart and soul of good interface programming is ultimately an aesthetic chore—and partly a test of finding ways to make things easy for the end user. It is rare to find a expert at hacking algorithms who is also gifted in interface design. Visual programming tools such as Kylix enable you to hand off the aesthetic tasks to people with the appropriate gifts, while handing off the heavyweight intellectual tasks to hard-core coders.

4. **Objection Four:** *The applications created by visual programming are larger and more complex than what I would produce if I wrote the code all by hand.* This is probably the best of the classic objections to visual programming. However, I believe that this complaint applies not to visual programming per se, but to the OOP libraries that underlie visual programming. Nonvisual programming environments, such as Microsoft's Visual C++ programming environment, also use large OOP-based libraries. (Don't let the name

throw you: Visual C++ is not a visual programming tool.) VC programmers depend on MFC, just as GNOME programmers depend on the GTK and KDE programmers depend on Qt. All these libraries add bulk to your code. Furthermore, the libraries are intimidatingly intricate. Nevertheless, they have become popular because they create standards and make complex chores relatively manageable. Furthermore, just as VC programmers can write code that does not use MFC, Kylix programmers can write code that does not use CLX. In Chapter 6, "Understanding the Linux Environment," for instance, you will learn how to write directly to the XLIB API when creating X programs. These programs do not use CLX at all. Throughout the book, you will see small command-line applications that also do not use CLX. By today's standards, these programs are quite small, weighing in at less than 25KB. You can develop these or any other Kylix applications using nothing more than emacs; the Kylix command-line compiler, dcc; and gdb.

5. **Objection Five:** *I don't like visual programming because I worry that it involves black boxes. I want access to the complete code for my project.* There need be no black boxes in Kylix programming. The product ships with the complete source to CLX. The visual tools provide a quick way for you to write additional code. However, you can usually view all the code that is being produced while you work in the Kylix Form Designer. (The exception occurs when you buy components from a third party that does not also give you the source.) The code produced during visual programming appears in one of two places: directly in the source file for your application or in the xfm file that is stored in the same directory as your source file. To learn more about xfm files, see the section "Editing an xfm File," later in this chapter.

Over the years, I've watched OOP go from an infrequently used technology to one that is a predominate force in the programming world. Visual programming does not yet have the prestige that OOP has, but I expect that over time it will match or perhaps even surpass the importance of OOP in the minds of most programmers.

## The Component Palette

It's time now to get down to cases. I'll start by discussing the Component Palette, and then I'll go on to discuss the Form Designer itself, which is usually used in conjunction with the Object Inspector. Figure 1.7 contains a picture of the Component Palette, and you can see the Form Designer in Figure 1.8. A closely related tool, the Object Inspector, is shown in Figure 1.9.

**FIGURE 1.7**

*The Component Palette opened to the Standard page.*

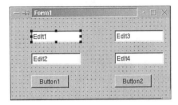

**FIGURE 1.8**

*The Form Designer with several components on it.*

**FIGURE 1.9**

*The Object Inspector, as it appears when you are looking at an edit control.*

The Component Palette appears under the menu bar on the right. Arranged on these tabbed pages are the components that come with the product. You can fairly easily create new components and add them to this palette. The topic of creating components will be extensively explored in Part II.

On the pages of the Component Palette, you will find many useful components. Included are components that enable you to create database applications and Web-based applications. Also present, of course, are many standard elements of form design, such as edit controls and labels.

The order in which the pages appear on the Component Palette is entirely configurable. Right-click the Component Palette and choose Properties. As shown in Figure 1.10, a dialog box appears titled Palette Properties. On the left of the dialog box is a list of pages, and on the right is a list of the components found on any one page. By clicking items on the left, you change the list of components found on the right.

You can left-click on the text in the Pages box and drag it into a new position. For instance, you can scroll to the bottom of the list, find the last item listed there, and then drag it up to the top of the list. When you close the dialog box, you will see that the last has become the first, and the first has become, well, not the last, but the second.

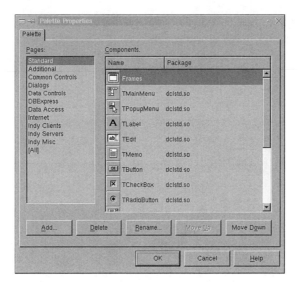

**FIGURE 1.10**

*The Palette Properties dialog box enables you to change the layout of the Component Palette.*

Further explorations of the Palette Properties dialog box reveal options to rearrange the components themselves, to delete items, and to hide items. A second way to reach this dialog box is through the Component menu, under the listing Configure Palette. Additional options for configuring the palette are available if you simply right-click the Component Palette itself. (Remember, when you are using the IDE, try right-clicking on just about everything.)

## Thinking About Packages

The components on the Component Palette are stored in multiple libraries known as *packages*. On disk, each library is simply a special kind of shared object—what Windows programmers would call a DLL. To create a component, you write an object that descends from one of a particular set of Object Pascal classes, and then you compile your component into one of these libraries. If you make the right moves, the IDE knows how to search through the libraries and display an iconic representation of your object on the Component Palette.

---

**NOTE**

As you will learn in Part II, there is an entirely different way to change the Component Palette. This second technique uses some relatively advanced technologies involving libraries.

If you choose Component, Install Packages from the menu, you can see a list of these libraries, as shown in Figure 1.11. (You can also reach this dialog box by choosing Project, Options, Packages.) If you click the Components button from the dialog box, you can see which components are found in a particular package. As you can see, most of the packages that ship with Kylix are stored in the kylix/bin directory.

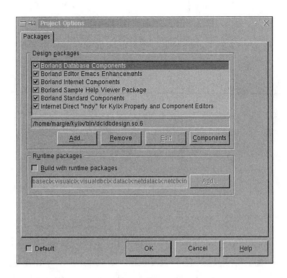

**FIGURE 1.11**
*A list of currently used packages, shown in the Project Options dialog box.*

A check box found in the Design Packages list box enables you to display or hide the components from any one particular package. The Remove button in the Project Options dialog box enables you to completely remove a package so that it is no longer loaded by Kylix. If you choose not to load certain big packages—most notably the database packages—the entire Kylix IDE will load much more quickly. This can also be a means of creating a less cluttered and more comprehensible Component Palette.

At the bottom of the Project Options dialog box is the option to use runtime packages in the currently open project. This option lets you decide whether you want the components from a particular package to be linked into your executable. If you choose not to link them into your binary executable, you can simply access them from the library in which they are stored. Programs built with runtime packages are much smaller than programs that link all their objects directly into the executable. However, you must distribute the runtime packages with your product if you chose to use them and want others to be able to access your application.

But I already am starting to focus on matters that will be better discussed in Part II. I merely wanted to give you a glimpse here and provide a discreet peek at the Kylix component architecture. You just need to know enough to begin to see how things work; then, in later chapters, we can delicately draw back the curtain all the way, revealing Kylix's most treasured assets.

## Using the Kylix Form Designer

The Form Designer enables you to design the interface for your project. It consists primarily of a single window on which you can arrange various items from the Component Palette. The components that you add to your project may be visual or nonvisual. Regardless, when you drop a component onto the Form Designer, Kylix automatically instantiates an instance of the component. You can manipulate this component at design time. At runtime, your project will display the interface that you created in the Form Designer.

## Arranging Components

The Component Palette contains standard components displayed on tabbed pages. To add a component to the Form Designer, click the component that you want in the Component Palette, and then click the Form Designer. For instance, you might click a button component and then drop it on the Form Designer, creating a form like the one shown in Figure 1.12.

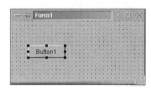

**FIGURE 1.12**
*A comely button resting demurely on the Kylix Form Designer.*

After a component has been added to the Form Designer, you can move it by clicking it and dragging it to a new spot. You can also resize the component by using the tabs at its edges, known as handles, to stretch or shrink its size. Or, if you prefer, you can select the Object Inspector, find the Width and Height properties of the component, and change their values, as shown in Figure 1.13.

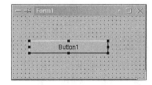

**FIGURE 1.13**
*Setting the Width property of the button to 160, causes it to stretch out luxuriously across the form.*

Note that you can also go up to the Caption property and change the text that appears on the button. Notice that many other properties are associated with this component. You can select any property and press F1 to bring up help on it, as shown in Figure 1.14.

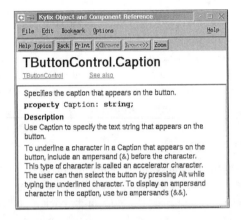

**FIGURE 1.14**

*The context-sensitive help found for the Caption property of a TButton object.*

Left-click the button that you placed on your form. Now hold down the Ctrl key and press the arrow keys on your keyboard. You will find that the button moves up or down, left or right, one pixel at a time. Take your finger off the Ctrl key, and hold down the Shift key instead. Now lean on one of the arrow keys; you will find that you can increase or decrease the width or height of the component one pixel at a time. These are small touches, but they can prove to be invaluable when you are creating a form.

If you right-click a component on the Form Designer, a pop-up menu gives you options for aligning components, such as Align, Size, Scale and Align to Grid. These options are extremely helpful. For instance, if you have four edit controls and want them all to be the same size, you can press the Shift key and then click each control in turn to select them all. Then right-click one of the edit controls, select Size, and choose the appropriate selection, such as Grow To Largest.

## The Object Inspector

The Object Inspector is one of Kylix's most powerful tools. With it, you can modify the properties of a component or generate events associated with the component. If the Object Inspector is not visible in the IDE, select View, Object Inspector to display it.

If you click a component in the Form Designer, its name will appear in the Object Inspector. You can also choose which component you want to work with by selecting it from the drop-down list in the Object Inspector.

The Properties page of the Object Inspector reveals properties of the component that you can modify. Each property has two parts. On the left of the Object Inspector, you see the name of the property. To the right, you see a blank field, which is known as a property editor. Sometimes property editors are simply input text fields. Sometimes they are lists of options, such as the True, False fields. Sometimes they are more complex entities. To see a complex property editor, drop a TEdit control from the Standard page. Double-click the small … icon that appears in the property editor for the TEdit control's font property. The Font dialog box, shown in Figure 1.15, appears. Use this dialog box to select the font that you want to appear in your edit control.

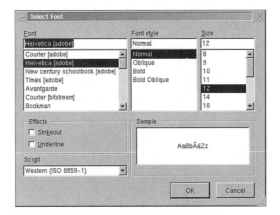

**FIGURE 1.15**

*The Font dialog box.*

In general, when you click the property editor to the right of a property, you are selecting an option for the property. For instance, a TPanel component has an `align` property. To see how it works, first select the TPanel component on the Standard page and drop it on a form. Then, click the property editor to its right; a drop-down list appears, and you can choose the alignment of the control.

## Tweaking the Object Inspector

The Object Inspector is configurable. To display items by category or by name, right-click the Object Inspector and choose either Arrange, By Category or Arrange, By Name. The two different views are shown in Figures 1.16 and 1.17.

You can also filter the events in the Object Inspector. Drop a button on a form, and then focus the Object Inspector. Make sure that the button is selected on the form and is visible in the Object Inspector. Right-click the Object Inspector and choose View, None. All the items in the Inspector will disappear. Right-click again and choose View, Action. A subset of the properties for the TButton object will become visible.

**FIGURE 1.16**

*The Object Inspector with values arranged by name.*

**FIGURE 1.17**

*The Object Inspector with values arranged by category.*

## Editing an xfm File

When you drop a button on a form, code is generated behind the scenes. Some of that code is in the editor itself. Other code appears in the xfm file that accompanies your form.

The xfm file is referenced in the source to your form-based units, just below the keyword implementation:

```
{$R *.xfm}
```

This statement tells the compiler that part of the definition for the form in this unit is found in the xfm file. All units that contain a direct TForm descendant contain this statement, and source files that do not contain forms would normally have no reason to contain this statement.

**DELPHI NOTE**

Delphi programmers should note that the letters xfm are lowercase. When you translate Delphi programs to Kylix, you need to switch from {$R *.DFM} to {$R *.xfm}. In fact, you will find that Kylix will sometimes accept unchanged Delphi dfm files with their dfm extension intact. However, you will still probably need to change the reference to them from uppercase DFM to lowercase dfm.

One other change will be needed in all these forms. The Pixels Per Inch property in Delphi is usually set to 96. In Kylix, it generally is best when set to 75. If you open a Delphi form in Kylix and the controls and text appear too small and cramped, try changing the Pixels Per Inch property from 96 to 75.

At no time do you need to edit the code in an xfm file; doing so is strictly optional. Normally, you would control its contents by making changes in the Form Designer or in the Object Inspector. However, you can edit this code, and sometimes it is useful to do so.

xfm files can be either binary or text-based, depending on what you select in Tools, Environment, Preferences, Form Designer, New Forms As Text menu. (You can achieve the same effect on a local rather than global basis by right-clicking a form and choosing Text xfm.) To see the source for a form, you can either open a text xfm file in an editor or right-click on a form at design time and choose the View As Text menu option.

**NOTE**

There is also a command-line utility named `convert` that will convert a text-based form to a binary form, and vice versa. To run the program, just type a command similar to the following at the command line:

```
convert MyForm.xfm
```

Make sure that you have your path set up correctly before issuing the convert command: Utilities named `convert` ship with some Linux distributions.

The code in an xfm file is very much real code. You can edit it by hand, if you want, and you can even paste it into the IDE. To see how this works, start a new project and then drop a button onto the project's form. Right-click the form and choose View As Text. In the code for the form, you will find the following code:

```
object Button1: TButton
  Left = 264
  Top = 24
```

```
      Width = 75
      Height = 25
      Caption = 'Button1'
      TabOrder = 0
   end
```

Change the Caption property so that instead of "Button1," it reads, "If there is any religion that would cope with modern scientific needs, it would be Buddhism. —Albert Einstein." Right-click and choose View As Form from the menu. Now resize the button and view the results of your handiwork. You might want to experiment further by changing the Width, Height, and other properties while viewing the form as text.

Now go into a text editor. You can use the Kylix editor, if you want, or choose an editor such as KWrite or KEdit that will share a clipboard with Kylix. In your text editor, write the following:

```
   object Button2: TButton
      Left = 20
      Top = 10
      Width = 75
      Height = 25
      Caption = 'Wisdom is oft times nearer when we stoop, than when we soar. --
➥William
      Wordsworth'
      TabOrder = 0
   end
```

Use your editor to make a block copy of this entire piece of text. Now go back to Kylix and start a new application, viewing the form in normal mode, not in text mode. With the form focused, choose Edit, Paste from the menu. The button that you designed in the editor should appear in the upper-left corner of the form. You can now resize the button with the mouse so that all the text appears.

The technique of pasting in controls to the Form Designer from an editor can be quite useful. I have found it particularly helpful when repairing a damaged form or when straightening out a form that has lapsed into chaos. This can also be a very useful technique when you are porting Delphi applications to Kylix.

**DELPHI NOTE**

The xfm file format, both binary and text, is identical to the dfm file format used in Delphi Windows development. You can use dfm files in a Kylix application, as long as all the components, properties, and events used in the dfm file exist in both the VCL and the CLX. The xfm extension for Kylix files exists simply so that you can have a quick way of checking to see that the components in the file are CLX components rather than VCL components. As a general rule, you will find that you can use your dfm files unchanged in Kylix programs, as long as the form that they describe is relatively simple. If the form is complex, you are likely to have trouble. Even in the worst cases, an edited dfm file can help you get started creating a Kylix form.

---

**JAVA NOTE**

Java programmers who use JBuilder will be familiar with most of the visual programming technologies found in Kylix. However, there is no xfm file in JBuilder. Instead, all the results of your actions with the mouse are stored in your source file, usually in your jbInit method. Whether you like the Kylix method or the JBuilder method of visual programming better is a matter of taste—or perhaps a matter that must be settled on a case-by-case basis. Personally, when I first starting using the JBuilder technology, I thought that it was better than my beloved Delphi technology. However, as I began to develop larger and more complex Java programs, I grew weary of scrolling through jbInit methods that consisted of screenful after screenful of information produced by the visual design tools. (Certainly it was better to use the visual tools to produce the code than to write the code by hand, and certainly the code was at least as good as—and, in fact, usually identical to—what I would have written by hand. Nevertheless, there was a lot of it, and it was in the way.) In the end, I'd probably call it a draw. Java has the admirable trait of keeping all your source code in one file and one language. Delphi/Kylix has the benefit of isolating all that generally unsightly code in an xfm file. Furthermore, the format found in that xfm file is easy to understand. It represents a particularly apt way of storing the kind of information created by people who are doing visual programming.

## Constraints and Anchors

Java programmers use a technology known as layout managers to control the size of components at runtime. These layout managers can help define the way a form behaves when it comes up in an unexpected resolution or when the user begins to resize it. Kylix has nothing as complex as layout managers to offer, but it does have properties named Constraints and Anchors that can prove to be surprisingly powerful in similar situations.

Place a button at the bottom-right corner of a form. Now grab the bottom-right corner of the form and begin to shrink it, as shown in Figure 1.18.

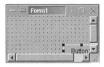

**Figure 1.18**

*As the user resizes a form, a component can become partially or completely hidden.*

As you can see, a component can easily become either partly or completely hidden at design time or runtime. If this is a problem in your application, one simple solution is to use the Anchor property.

Notice that the Anchor property in the Object Inspector has a small plus beside it. Click this plus sign to open all the fields of the Anchor property. Select the button and set the akLeft and akTop fields of the property to False, and set the akRight and akBottom fields of the property to True. Now resize the form again and you will see that the button will maintain its place at the bottom-right corner of the form as you resize it.

If you want, you can add additional buttons to the form. For instance, you might drop down four buttons, one for each corner of the form. Use the Anchor property to anchor each button in place. Now try resizing the form. If you've done the task right, the buttons won't become hidden as you resize the form. (While performing this action, you might discover that a double-click on a Boolean field reverses its setting, changing a False value to True or a True value to False.) See the ButtonAnchor program on disk for an example of how the program should work if you have set the Boolean options correctly.

> **Note**
>
> Absolute newcomers to Object Pascal may be interested to note that the True and False variables begin with a capital letter and use lowercase letters for other values. This contrasts with C, which uses all caps for the variables, and Java, which uses all lowercase letters. Furthermore, True and False are values built into the compiler, so they are never declared in any of the Pascal source files. Of course, Pascal is not a case-sensitive language; it does not care whether you write False, false, fALSE, or faLsE. The convention, however, is to start all variable names and most type names with a capital letter. The exception to the rule is enumerated types, the elements of which usually begin with small letters:
>
> ```
> TNavigateBtn = (nbFirst, nbPrior, nbNext, nbLast, nbInsert, nbDelete,
>     nbEdit, nbPost, nbCancel, nbRefresh)
> ```
>
> If you put two words in a single variable, they should each be capitalized, as in MyVariable. Reserved words, which the editor always prints in bold, should be in

lowercase letters, with the exception of the String type, which is usually capitalized. (This exception for the capitalization of the word String provides a rather homey touch to an otherwise rather rigidly structured language.) All other reserved words, such as begin, end, if, implementation, and interface, are written by convention in lowercase letters.

By now you should have four buttons visible, each one anchored to a different corner of the form. If all is well, you can resize the form and each button will stay in its place, like well–brought-up children. Your impulse is to see what happens if you make the form as small as possible. The answer, of course, is that chaos ensues. To forbid your users from making the form too small, you can set the Constraints property of the form itself to appropriate values.

Click once on the gray background of the form to select it. Notice that the Object Inspector now lists the properties for the currently selected object, which in this case is the form. Double-click the Constraints property for the form in the Object Inspector. It opens, enabling you to enter in values of 200 and 250 for the MinWidth and MinHeight properties of the form, respectively. When you try to resize your form, you will find that it now stops short of allowing your users to make a mess.

> **NOTE**
>
> The conventions in Pascal are usually to be as literal as possible. Hence, the use of abbreviations in variable names is not as common as in other languages. In general, Pascal programmers will approve variable names such MinWidth and MinHeight, but would turn a jaded eye on mWidth, or mHght, as variable names. I tend to carry this literalness to an extreme, and might even name a variable MinimumWidth or MinimumHeight. The compiler, of course, will not use these literal strings in your code compiled with debug options turned off, so you are not changing the size of your final executable by electing to use larger variable names.

## Tab Order

In some applications, tab order can be important. If you want to rearrange the tab order of your components, right-click a component and then choose Tab Order from the pop-up menu. In the Edit Tab Order dialog box, select the name of a component. By clicking the up or down arrow, you can change the component's place in the tab order for your application.

# The Object Inspector and Events

It is now time to discuss events. This is a significantly more complex subject than any broached so far in this chapter. It represents the transition between the discussion of the visual tools and a discussion of the editor itself. The discussion of events involves writing code, and writing code is an act performed in the editor.

The next few pages of text involve some complex discussion of the intersection between the Object Inspector, the editor, and the syntactical rules of the Object Pascal language itself. Even the compiler will be dragged into the discussion at one point. When this explication is complete, however, the road will be clear to cover a few last points about the editor and Code Insite, and then finally a chance to look at some Object Pascal programs.

The Events page of the Object Inspector displays the events associated with the component. If you click the property editor for an event, Kylix generates code in the Source Code Editor, and the Source Code Editor will immediately be brought to the fore so that you can add additional logic.

To see how events work, first choose File, New to start a new project. Now drop a TButton control from the Standard page on the main form for the project. Select the button with the mouse. Open the Object Inspector to the Events page. Double-click the property editor for the OnClick event. The editor is brought to the front, and the following lines of code are inserted into your program:

```
procedure TForm1.Button1Click(Sender: TObject);
begin

end;
```

You also could have created this code by double-clicking the button itself. This second technique works because the OnClick event is the default event for the TButton control. The default event usually is activated automatically when you double-click a control.

Edit the code button click method so that it appears as follows:

```
procedure TForm1.Button1Click(Sender: TObject);
begin
  ShowMessage('This very place is the Lotus Land; this body, the buddha')
end;
```

Now run the program that you have created, and press the button. A dialog box appears, showing the text that you passed to the ShowMessage method.

# The Source for a Kylix Unit

If you followed the text in the previous section exactly and created the default event for a form, a FormCreate event was inserted into your program:

```
procedure TForm1.FormCreate(Sender: TObject);
begin

end;
```

After you run the program, if you go back and look at the source for your project, you will find that the header for your FormCreate event has disappeared. Where did it go?

Methods generated by the IDE that have no code in them are automatically deleted when you either save your source or run the program. More particularly, this rule holds true for all event handlers that are created in a standard fashion, regardless of whether they are generated by the IDE.

And what, you might ask, is the "standard fashion" for an event handler? To answer this question correctly, it will help to see the complete source for the unit we have created, in Listing 1.1.

**LISTING 1.1**   The Source for a Simple Unit with Two Event Handlers

```
unit Unit1;

interface

uses
  Windows, Messages, SysUtils,
  Classes, Graphics, Controls,
  Forms, Dialogs, StdCtrls,
  ExtCtrls;

const
  Diamond = 'All composed things are like a dream, ' +
    'a phantom, a drop of dew, a flash of lightening';

type
  TForm1 = class(TForm)
    Button1: TButton;
    procedure Button1Click(Sender: TObject);
    procedure FormCreate(Sender: TObject);
  private
    { Private declarations }
```

**LISTING 1.1**  Continued

```
public
  { Public declarations }
end;

var
  Form1: TForm1;

implementation

{$R *.DFM}

procedure TForm1.Button1Click(Sender: TObject);
begin
  ShowMessage(Diamond);
end;

procedure TForm1.FormCreate(Sender: TObject);
begin

end;

end.
```

The next few sections describe the various elements of this source file in detail. In particular, I will focus on the distinction between the interface and the implementation.

## The Interface of a Kylix Unit

Listing 1.1 shows the declaration for a typical Kylix form. The code is divided into three sections. The first section is the name of the unit, which in this case looks like this:

```
unit Unit1;
```

The second section begins with the word interface and ends just before the word implementation:

```
interface
```

```
uses
  Windows, Messages, SysUtils,
  Classes, Graphics, Controls,
  Forms, Dialogs, StdCtrls,
  ExtCtrls;
```

```
const
  Diamond = 'All composed things are like a dream, ' +
    'a phantom, a drop of dew, a flash of lightening';

type
  TForm1 = class(TForm)
    Button1: TButton;
    procedure Button1Click(Sender: TObject);
    procedure FormCreate(Sender: TObject);
  private
    { Private declarations } public
    { Public declarations }
  end;

var
  Form1: TForm1;
```

Needless to say, this section of the code is called the interface of your program. Beneath the interface is the implementation. The implementation reaches from the beginning of the word `implementation` to the bottom of the source, which is always marked with the keyword `end`, followed by a period.

The interface contains declarations for your unit but has no actual code. It is like the header file for a C or C++ program, except that it is integrated into the same source as your implementation. Hence, Pascal takes the middle road between Java and C/C++. Unlike C/C++, all your code for one module is kept in one source file. Unlike Java, there is a clean separation in Pascal between the declaration for an object and its implementation.

The interface contains four sections:

1. **The uses clause**—Here you find a list of other units upon which this unit depends. This is the equivalent of the `#include` statements in C++ and the import statements in Java. Although it is never explicitly listed, all Pascal units use the `System` unit. Borland ships the complete source for the `System` unit.

2. **The const section**—Here you can declare constants. If you declare a constant without declaring its type, you cannot change that constant in your program. If you declare a constant along with its type, you can change the constant in your program. This latter technique is really a way of predeclaring an object outside an implementation block. Here is a declaration for a constant that includes a type declaration:

   ```
   MyNumber: Integer = 2;
   ```

   If you tried to change the constant that I have declared as `Diamond` in your `Button1Click` method, the compiler generates an error. This is not an error to change the value of `MyNumber`.

3. **The type section**—Here you declare the types that you want to use in your program. In this particular case, the unit declares a type named TForm1 that descends from the TForm object. The TForm object is part of CLX. A TForm object knows how to instantiate an instance of a form. TForm1 is your variation on this particular object. In particular, TForm1 takes a basic TForm object and adds in a button control and two methods. I will discuss those two methods in more depth later in this section.

4. **The var section**—Here you can declare any global variables that you want to add to your program. These variables will have global scope throughout your entire program. As all experienced programmers know, a global variable is considered to be a bad thing. As a result, you generally should not add anything to the var section for the implementation of a unit unless you are absolutely sure that you know what you are doing.

Each of the sections that appear in the interface can also appear in the implementation. In fact, all the sections except the uses clause can appear even inside a single method. You should choose the location for your declarations depending on the scope that you want to give your variable. If you want it to be global, put it in the implementation. If you want it to be available throughout a whole unit, but not throughout a whole program, put it at the top of your implementation section. If you want the type, constant, or variable to be visible only to a single method, place it inside that method, as shown here:

```
procedure Foo;
const
  S = 'My String constant';
type
  TMyArray = array[0..5] of Integer;
var
  MyArray: TMyArray;
  i: Integer;
begin
  ShowMessage(S);
  for i := 0 to 5 do
    MyArray[i] := i;
  ... // Code omitted here
end;
```

## The Implementation of a Kylix Unit

In the type section where you declared the TForm object, you find the following line of code:

```
procedure Button1Click(Sender: TObject);
```

This is the declaration for the Button1Click method. As you might recall, the Button1Click method is called every time the user clicks on Button1. Here is the implementation for the Button1Click method:

```
procedure TForm1.Button1Click(Sender: TObject);
begin
  ShowMessage(Diamond);
end;
```

If you put your cursor on the Button1Click method, hold down the Shift and Ctrl keys, and press the up arrow key, you will be taken to the declaration for this method. If you now press the down arrow key, you will be taken back to the implementation for the method. In short, the IDE is fully conscious of the relationship between these two code blocks, even before you compile your code. I discuss this matter in more depth in Chapter 5, in the section "The Code Explorer."

If you know how to program, then you surely understand the relationship between the declaration and the implementation for this method. However, what might not be clear is the relationship between the TButton object and this method. In other words, how does the TButton object know to call this method when it is clicked?

Java programmers already know one method for creating a relationship between an object and its event handlers. Windows API programmers know another method. However, Object Pascal takes a third route, which is fortunately quite simple and easy to understand.

All TButton objects descend from an object named TControl that has a field in it of type TNotifyEvent:

```
type
  TNotifyEvent = procedure(Sender: TObject) of object;

  TControl = class(TComponent)
  private
    FParent: TWinControl;
    FWindowProc: TWndMethod;
    ... // Code omitted here
    FOnEndDrag: TEndDragEvent;
    FOnClick: TNotifyEvent;
    ... // Code omitted here
  protected
    property OnClick: TNotifyEvent read FOnClick write FOnClick stored
    IsOnClickStored;
  end;
```

The OnClick property of TButton is set to nil by default. The value nil evaluates to 0; it is equivalent to what C++ programmers call NULL, and it is very similar to what Java programmers call null. If OnClick is set equal to nil, then a user can click on a button all day, and nothing will happen. However, if the OnClick property of a TButton is assigned to a method such as Button1Click, the Button1Click method will be called.

When you double-click a button in the Form Designer, or when you double-click the property editor for the OnClick event in the Object Inspector, you are assigning the OnClick property of a TButton object to a particular method.

Please note that you cannot assign just any method to an OnClick property. Instead, the method must be of type TNotifyEvent:

```
TNotifyEvent = procedure(Sender: TObject) of object;
```

TNotifyEvent is a declaration for a method with the following signature:

```
procedure TForm1.Button1Click(Sender: TObject);
```

If you omit the phrase "of object" from the end of the TNotifyEvent declaration, you would be declaring a pointer to a procedure rather than a method. A procedure, of course, is not part of an object. For instance, this declaration is a pointer to a procedure, not to a method:

```
TMyNotifyEvent = procedure(Sender: TObject);
```

Here is an implementation of procedure of this type:

```
procedure Button1Click(Sender: TObject);
```

The difference here is that a routine of type TNotifyEvent is part of an object, while a routine of type TMyNotifyEvent is not part of an object.

A function is a routine that returns a value, and a procedure is a routine that returns nothing.

In C/C++ and Java programs, a method that returns nothing is declared to return void:

```
void Button1Click(TObject Sender);
```

## C++ NOTE

Here is what the declaration for TNotifyEvent would look like in C++:

```
typedef void __fastcall (__closure *TNotifyEvent)(System::TObject*
Sender);
```

## JAVA NOTE

You cannot declare a pointer to a method in Java because Java does not support the pointer type. This is one of the reasons that Java has a different event mechanism from Object Pascal. The great virtue of the Java event system is that the OnClick event for Java (known in the vernacular as actionPerformed) can point to more than one method at a time. In Object Pascal, a single instance of TButton can have only one OnClick event handler at a time. On the other hand, the great advantage of the Pascal system is that it is much easier to understand than the Java system and it does not involve the creation of any intermediate objects, such as EventListeners.

## Mystery Theater: Where Did the FormCreate Method Go?

As you perhaps recall, this discussion began when we noted that the FormCreate method had disappeared:

```
procedure TForm1.FormCreate(Sender: TObject);
begin

end;
```

As you now know, this method has a declaration in the interface section and an implementation in the implementation section of your code. If you wanted to remove the method manually, you would have to delete code in two places. In a normal text editor, this does not a represent a problem because you probably would not have inserted the code unless you meant to insert it. However, in a visual programming environment such as Kylix, it is easy to do a little double-clicking here and there, and before you know it, your unit is filled up with event handlers that you don't necessarily want. To make this little annoyance go away, Kylix implements a rule that says that any event handlers that contain no code at the time you run or save your program will be completely deleted. This does not apply to all methods—only to event handlers.

If Kylix deletes an event handler that you did not want deleted, it usually is a very simple thing to re-create it. You just go back to the Object Inspector, find the relevant property on the Events page, and delete the code.

Conversely, if you have an event handler that suddenly begins to look like dead code, you can simply delete all the code that you added to the method and press Save—voilá, the method disappears.

If you don't want to implement a method immediately but you also don't want the method to disappear, you can just add a comment to it:

```
procedure TForm1.FormCreate(Sender: TObject);
begin
  // foobar
end;
```

Just putting in the initial two slashes with no text is enough to tell the Kylix IDE to keep the method around.

# Pascal Source Files

You place Pascal source code in three types of files:

- The main program file, or, as it is sometimes referred to, the Delphi project file
- A unit
- An include file

## Delphi Project Files

The main source file for your project contains the main program block. This block starts with the reserved word begin and ends with the reserved word end. Here's a very simple Pascal program:

```
program SimpleProgram;
begin
  WriteLn('Simple Program');
end.
```

This program consists of nothing more than a program header and a main program block. As you can see, the program block starts with the word begin and terminates with the word end. The final end has a period after it because it marks the end of the program. This is the only place inside this file where an end can have a period.

If a project consists of single file, the main block for that program is the entry point for that program. As such, it is equivalent to the main or WinMain function in a C++ program.

The main file for a program can have one of two extensions. In most Delphi programs, the main file should have a .dpr extension (which stands for "Delphi Project"), as in SimpleProgram.dpr. It is also legal to have a .pas extension for the main file in your program. However, I would not use this extension in most cases because the IDE won't provide quite the same set of services for a .pas file as a .dpr file.

## Units

*Units* are the names of Pascal files that belong to a project. The main file, or project file, typically has multiple units that it owns.

Units have .pas as an extension. Therefore, in the typical Delphi application, the main file has an extension of .dpr and the other files have an extension of .pas.

Units are broken up into two sections. The top section is known as the *interface*, and the main body of the file is referred to as the *implementation*. Both the interface and the implementation appear in one file. However, C or C++ programmers can think of the interface as corresponding to what they think of as a header.

Listings 1.2 and 1.3 show an example of a very simple program consisting of a project file and a simple unit.

**LISTING 1.2**   The Main File for the SimpleUnit Project

```
program SimpleUnit;

uses
  MyUnit;

begin
  DoSomething;
end.
```

**LISTING 1.3**   The Unit That Belongs to the SimpleUnit Program

```
unit MyUnit;

interface

procedure DoSomething;

implementation

procedure DoSomething;
begin
  WriteLn('I am the poet of the body and I am the poet of the soul -Whitman');
end;

end.
```

Units were originally designed to allow programmers to break up their code into logical segments. For instance, you could put all the code in your program that deals with file input/output in one unit. A second unit could hold your database code, among other things.

In Delphi, units have a second purpose. Each form in your program must go in its own unit, if you want to edit that form with the Visual Form Designer. You can put multiple forms in one unit, but if you do so, the Visual Form Designer will not work properly.

In Listing 1.3, you can see that the interface for a unit can contain declarations. The implementation, on the other hand, contains executable code in a unit. The unit in Listing 1.3 is very simple. In most programs, a unit will contain many different elements, such as constant, type, class, and function definitions.

## Pascal Program Entry Points

The main block of a Pascal program is not always the entry point. Listing 1.4 shows a rewrite of the unit shown in Listing 1.3.

**LISTING 1.4**   Rewritten Unit That Belongs to the SimpleUnit Program

```
unit MyUnit;

interface

procedure DoSomething;

implementation

var
  MyString: string;

procedure DoSomething;
begin
  WriteLn(MyString);
end;

initialization

  MyString:= 'I say to you, if anyone keeps my word, he will never see death';
finalization
  MyString = '';
end.
```

This versiona Pascal program is not always the entry point. of MyUnit contains an initialization and finalization clause. The code in the initialization section is called when the unit is first loaded into memory. This occurs even before the main program block of the main file is executed. As soon as the program is loaded into memory, the code jumps to the first file listed in the main file's uses block. If there is an initialization section in that unit, the code in that initialization section will be executed.

If there are many units in a project, all their initialization sections will be executed before the code ever gets to the main program block in the main file! To put it mildly, this is very different from what happens in a C/C++ program.

Object Pascal has initialization blocks, to give developers an opportunity to initialize any variables listed in a particular unit. The finalization section is included to give developers a chance to clean up the code that might have executed in a particular unit.

## Uses Clauses and Circular Unit References

At the top of Listing 1.2, you can see a syntactical element known as a uses clause. In the optional uses clause for a file, you can list all the units upon which that file depends. In this case, the main file of program SimpleUnit depends on MyUnit.

In the previous section, I described what happens when a program is executed. It is interesting to note that something very similar happens when files are parsed at compile time. The first uses clause in the program's main file is parsed by the compiler. In the example we've been discussing, the compiler first opens SimpleUnit.dpr and discovers that MyUnit is used in its uses clause. It then begins parsing MyUnit. When it is done, it comes back to the main file, finds the next unit in its uses clause, and begins parsing it. If any unit in the uses clause of the main program contains a uses clause that references other units, those other units will be parsed before the unit listed in the uses clause of the main program.

Units can contain their own uses clauses. The first uses clause for a unit is listed directly under the reserved word interface. The second uses clause for a unit is listed under the reserved word implementation:

```
unit Foo;

interface

uses
  unit1, unit2;

implementation

uses
  unit2, unit3;

end.
```

If unit1 lists unit2 in its topmost uses clause, then unit2 may not list unit1 in its topmost uses clause. If you attempt to do this, you will get a *circular unit reference* error. To fix the error, move the reference to unit1 in unit2 down to the uses clause in the implementation section. Conversely, move the reference to unit2 in unit1 down to the `implementation` section.

Most of the time, this will resolve the problem. In a few cases, this solution will not work. To understand why this solution might not work, you need to know that unit1 cannot see any elements in unit2 until it has listed unit2 in its uses clause. Thus, if you need to reference something declared in the interface of unit2 in the interface of unit1, you must reference unit2 in the first uses clause of unit1. If you also need to reference something in the interface of unit1 in unit2's interface, you will be out of luck. Consider the examples shown in Listings 1.5 and 1.6.

**LISTING 1.5** Unit Declaring a Type Named TMyArray and Listing a Unit Named unit2 in Its uses Clause

```
unit unit1;

interface

uses
  unit2;

type
  TMyArray = array[1..0] of Unit2Type;

var
  Unit2Type: TUnit2Type;

implementation

end.
```

**LISTING 1.6** The Unit Used by unit1, Using the TMyArray Type from unit1 and with a Type Named Unit2Type That Is Used by unit1

```
unit unit2;

interface

uses
  unit1;

type
  TUnit2Type: Integer;
```

**LISTING 1.6**   Continued

```
var
  TFooArray: TMyArray;

implementation

end.
```

These examples have a deeply rooted problem that necessitates careful thought to resolve. Both units reference one another in their topmost uses clause. This is not allowed because it causes a circular unit reference. You cannot resolve the problem through the standard technique of moving one of the references in the uses clause from the interface section to implementation. In this case, this standard solution will not work because both files reference elements declared in the interface section of the other file. In particular, unit2 references the type declaration TMyArray, while unit1 references the type declaration Unit2Type.

When you encounter a problem of this kind, the solution is to either start combining the two files or create a third file. In some cases, it is easiest to simply merge the two files into one file. In other cases it is easiest to move some elements of unit1 into unit2, or vice versa. In yet a third case, the best solution is to create a third unit and move certain declarations from the first two units into that third unit. Which solution to the problem is best is a matter of opinion and probably also depends on the particulars of each example.

> **NOTE**
>
> The circular unit reference problem does not plague C/C++ programmers. As a result, in this one case, the C/C++ language has an advantage over the Object Pascal language. It's worth pointing out, however, that problems like this usually arise only when programs are poorly organized. For instance, the structures of the units shown in Listings 1.5 and 1.6 are obviously haphazard and nonsensical. If you structure your programs correctly, problems like this should not arise very often. To put the matter differently, if you get the error, it is sometimes the compiler's way of telling you that you should rethink the structure of your program because it has a design flaw. Having said all this, I will concede that, in some very rare instances, it makes sense to create units that have circular unit references; in those cases, this error can be quite annoying. Nevertheless, if you do get the error, you must implement one of the solutions outlined in the previous paragraph.

Here's one final point to keep in mind while considering the structure of units: As a rule, it does not matter what order you declare the sections in your interface. Usually the const section comes first, then the type section, and then the var section. However, you can reverse the order if you want. Furthermore, you can have multiple instances of each section in the interface. For instance, a const section can be followed by a type section, which is followed by a second const section.

## Compilation Time in Kylix

Some readers might be surprised to learn that Kylix often knows what code you have even if the code has not yet been compiled. It turns out that the IDE is continually compiling the code that you create, on the fly, as you type it in. None of the code gets written to disk as a binary image, but it is kept in memory and is used to detect certain things about the state of your code. For instance, the IDE knows whether you are working on an event handler or some other method that you wrote yourself. This information is used by the IDE in the events page of the Object Inspector, and it is used to automatically delete empty event handlers when you save your code. It also is used in the Code Insight features discussed in Chapter 5.

This leads us to one last point on this subject. As you have no doubt noticed, Kylix applications compile in very little time. Small projects appear to compile immediately, and large projects compile in only a few seconds. There are two reasons for this:

1. Object Pascal is a fairly straightforward language. Enormously ambiguous syntactical elements such as operator overloading and multiple inheritance have been kept out of the language. As a result, the code that you write is fairly easy not only for end users to understand but also for the compiler to parse. This leads to very fast compile times.

2. The link cycle is expedited because Object Pascal uses its own binary format, which is often little more than a simple copy of existing memory structures to disk. In particular, the compiler parses your code and stores the information that it gleans from this process in memory. When it comes time to write the binary code, it does little more than dump these in memory structures to disk. The format for the .o and .obj files produced by C++ programs is very complex and has little to do with the image that the compiler has stored in memory after compiling the code. The Object Pascal equivalent of .o or .obj file is a .dcu file. From the compiler's point of view, these files are quite simple to write and to reload back into memory. In short, the compiler thinks of them as easy to parse.

As a rule, the speed of a compiled Kylix application run outside the IDE, with debug information stripped from it, should be comparable to the speed of a C or C++ application. At the time I write, the final figures are not in on this for Kylix, but, historically, Borland's Object Pascal–compiled code has been either as fast as C/C++ compiled code or only a few percentage points slower. Unlike Java or Visual Basic code, compiled Object Pascal code is almost never three or four times slower than C/C++ code.

# Working with Containers

Another common task performed in the Form Designer has to do with allocating space by working with panels or page controls. For instance, you might want to create an application with a list box along its left side. When the user clicks in the list box, additional information can be shown in two areas to the right of the list box, as shown in Figure 1.19. Furthermore, you might want the user to be able to resize the various sections of the window.

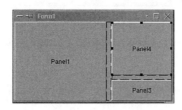

**FIGURE 1.19**
*A complex form with multiple areas on it—a splitter control enables you to resize each area.*

To create this form, follow these steps:

1. Drop down a panel on a form. Set its Align property to **alLeft**.

2. Turn to the Additional page, and drop down a TSplitter to the right of the panel. Set its Width property to **10** so that it is easy for the user to grab hold of it at runtime.

3. Drop down a second panel on the blank right side of the form, and set its Align property to **alClient**.

4. Drop down a third panel on top of the second panel, and set its Align property to **alBottom**.

5. Drop down a second splitter on the second panel. Set its Align property to **alBottom** and its Height property to **10**.

6. Drop down a fourth panel on top of the second panel and above the second splitter. Set its Align property to **alClient**.

Run the program, and use the splitters to resize the window, as shown in Figure 1.20. Note that this arrangement gives you three fully resizable areas that can act, if desired, as nested forms inside a larger form.

You can use this basic layout for various kinds of applications, such as the one found in the PanelDesign program in the Chap01 directory for the code that came with this book. The program is shown in Figure 1.21. The program itself is discussed in the next section, "The PanelDesign Program."

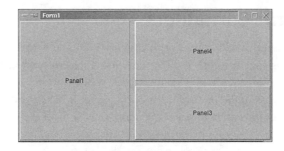

**FIGURE 1.20**
*You can use splitters to create resizable panels that you can use in your programs.*

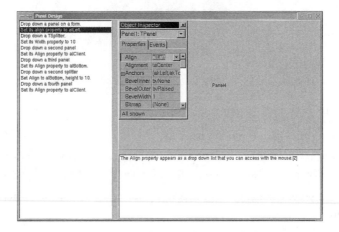

**FIGURE 1.21**
*A program based on resizable panels that itself is a tutorial on creating programs with resizable panels.*

## The PanelDesign Program

The PanelDesign program brings together many of the ideas discussed so far in this chapter. It is found in Listings 1.7 through 1.9.

**LISTING 1.7**   Code for the PanelDesign Program

```
unit Main;

interface

uses
  SysUtils, Types, Classes,
  QGraphics, QControls, QForms,
  QDialogs, QExtCtrls, QStdCtrls;
```

**LISTING 1.7**   Continued

```
type
  TForm1 = class(TForm)
    Panel1: TPanel;
    Splitter1: TSplitter;
    Panel2: TPanel;
    Panel3: TPanel;
    Splitter2: TSplitter;
    Panel4: TPanel;
    ListBox1: TListBox;
    Image1: TImage;
    Memo1: TMemo;
    procedure FormShow(Sender: TObject);
    procedure ListBox1Click(Sender: TObject);
  private
    FList: TStringList;
    function GetSelNum: String;
    procedure ParseListRes(var TempList: TStringList; StartNum: Integer);
    { Private declarations }
  public
    { Public declarations }
  end;

var
  Form1: TForm1;

implementation

uses
  LCodeBox;

{$R *.xfm}

procedure TForm1.FormShow(Sender: TObject);
var
  TempList: TStringList;
begin
  ListBox1.Items.LoadFromFile('instructions.txt');
  FList := TStringList.Create;
  TempList := TStringList.Create;
  TempList.LoadFromFile('descriptions.txt');
  ParseListRes(TempList);
  FList.SaveToFile('Foo.txt');
  TempList.Free;
end;
```

**LISTING 1.7** Continued

```
function TForm1.GetSelNum(): String;
var
  ListNum: Integer;

begin
  ListNum := ListBox1.ItemIndex + 1;
  Result := Int2StrPad0(ListNum, 2);
end;

procedure TForm1.ListBox1Click(Sender: TObject);
var
  PicName: string;
begin
  PicName := GetStartDir() + 'step' + getSelNum + '.bmp';
  if FileExists(PicName) then
    Image1.Picture.LoadFromFile(PicName);
  if ListBox1.ItemIndex < FList.Count then
    Memo1.Text := FList.Strings[ListBox1.ItemIndex];
end;

procedure TForm1.ParseListRes(var TempList: TStringList);
var
  i: Integer;
  S, WholeLine: string;
  NewPar: Boolean;
begin
  WholeLine := '';

  for i := 0 to 2 do        // I check TempList.Strings[i + 1] so
    TempList.Append('');    // these lines must be here!

  NewPar := False;
  for i := 0 to TempList.Count - 1 do begin
    S := TempList.Strings[i];
    S := StripEndChars(S, #32);
    if (S <> '') then
      S := S + #32;
    if (i = 0) or (NewPar and (S <> '')) then begin
      WholeLine := S;
      if TempList.Strings[i + 1] <> '' then begin
        NewPar := False;
      end else begin
        NewPar := True;
        FList.Add(WholeLine);
```

**Listing 1.7** Continued

```
      WholeLine := '';
    end;
  end else if S = '' then
    // Do nothing
  else if (i < (TempList.Count - 1)) and (TempList.Strings[i + 1] = '') then
  begin
    NewPar := True;
    WholeLine := WholeLine + S;
    FList.Add(WholeLine);
    WholeLine := '';
  end else begin
    S := StripBlanks(S);
    S := S + #32;
    WholeLine := WholeLine + S
  end;
  end;
end;

end.
```

**Listing 1.8** The Instructions.txt File, Which Describes in Rough Outline the Steps for Building a Multipanel Kylix Application

```
Drop down a panel on a form.
Set its align property to alLeft.
Drop down a TSplitter.
Set its Width property to 10
Drop down a second panel
Set its Align property to alClient.
Drop down a third panel
Set its Align property to alBottom.
Drop down a second splitter
Set Align to alBottom, height to 10.
Drop down a fourth panel
Set its Align property to alClient.
```

**Listing 1.9** The directions.txt File, Which Gives Commentary on Each of the Steps Required to Build a Multipanel Kylix Application

```
The panel is on the standards page.[1]

The Align property appears as a drop-down list
that you can access with the mouse.[2]
```

**LISTING 1.9** Continued

The TSplitter component is on the Additional
page of the Component palette.[3]

The two most important properties of TSplitter
are its Align property and its Width (or Height)
property. In this case, the default Align
property of alLeft is just what we want, so we
need to set only the Width property.[4]

When you drop down the second panel, make
sure it rests on the blank part of the form,
which appears to the right. Where you drop
a component is very important. If you dropped
it on top of Panel1, then it would be tricky
to move it off the panel.

When you set a component's Align property to
alClient, it fills up all the available
space on its parent. In this case, the parent
is the form.

Again, be sure to drop this panel on the right
side of the form.

By setting the Align property alBottom, the new
panel will fill in the bottom of its parent, which
in this case is not the form, but a panel.

Don't worry about how the Splitter aligns itself
when you first drop it down. Just get it on top
of the control that you want to be its parent.

By setting the Align property of the Splitter,
and by adjusting its height, you can move it
right into the place you desire for it.

Again, be sure you put it right on top of the
empty space in Panel2. Don't let any part of
it touch Panel1 or Panel3 when you drop
the control.

Set the Align property of the Panel to move
it into position. Don't bother trying to move
the panel into place by hand.

The interface for the PanelDesign program has a list box on the left for storing single lines of text. On the bottom right, it has a TMemo control, which holds multiple lines of text. At the top, it has a TImage control, which enables a developer to easily display a picture to the user.

The list box contains the instructions.txt file, which enumerates the steps necessary to create a multipanel Kylix program. The image control shows pictures of what the user does in each step. The Memo control provides a commentary on each step and provides details that might be of use to someone new to Kylix.

The program allows the user to click on the single lines of text in the list box. As each click occurs, you see an accompanying picture in the image control and an accompanying description in the Memo control.

Now that you understand what the program is about, let's find out how it is put together. Hopefully, you will see that Kylix makes it easy for you to create this relatively sophisticated type of program. I will not explain how the interface of the program is put together at design time because the program itself is a tutorial on that very subject. Instead, I will show you the code needed to make the program behave properly at runtime.

## Initializing the Form of the PanelDesign Program

The OnShow event for a component is called just before the control is displayed to the user. By the time this event is called, all the background pieces that hold together your application have been initialized. Another event, OnCreate, is called before OnShow. OnCreate is a good place to put code that does not affect the interface of your program. If you want to set the form up before it is shown to the user, however, it is usually best to do this in OnShow, not in OnCreate.

Here is the OnShow event for the main form in the PanelDesign program:

```
procedure TForm1.FormShow(Sender: TObject);
var
  TempList: TStringList;
begin
  ListBox1.Items.LoadFromFile('instructions.txt');
  FList := TStringList.Create;
  TempList := TStringList.Create;
  TempList.LoadFromFile('descriptions.txt');
  ParseListRes(TempList);
  FList.SaveToFile('Foo.txt');
  TempList.Free;
end;
```

Notice that it takes one line of code to load the contents of the instructions.txt file into the list box on the left side of the main form. The Items property of the list box is of type TStrings. The TStrings object is designed to hold a list of strings. If you place a string in the Items property of a TListBox, that string will be displayed to the user in the list box.

The TStringList object is a descendant of TStrings. TStringList is meant for general use as a container of strings. It has all the same properties as the TStrings object, but it is not attached to a control such as a list box. Instead, it stands on it own.

## C/C++ NOTE

The TStringList object has a sister object named TList. TList is designed to hold any object, while the TStringList object is designed to hold strings. Together, these two objects play a similar role in Object Pascal programs that key classes in the STL play in C++ programs.

## JAVA NOTE

The Object Pascal classes TStringList and TList play much the same role in Object Pascal programs as an array of String or the ArrayList object might play in a Java program.

Here is how you create an instance of a TStringList object:

```
FList := TStringList.Create;
```

This is code that first creates a TStringList object, then loads the descriptions.txt file into it, and finally passes the list object off to another routine:

```
TempList := TStringList.Create;
TempList.LoadFromFile('descriptions.txt');
ParseListRes(TempList);
```

The ParseListRes function breaks up the contents in the descriptions.txt file so that each paragraph is regarded as a single string. The algorithm starts at the top of the file, reads in the first line, strips off any whitespace at the beginning or end of the line, and saves the result in a variable named WholeLine. It then loops around, finds the next line in the file, strips off its end bits, and appends it to WholeLine. It continues in this manner until it comes to a blank line of text. This it regards as the mark between one paragraph and the next. When it has a full paragraph, it appends the text it has found to the TStringList object:

```
FList.Add(WholeLine);
```

The algorithm continues on its merry way through the entire file, adding one paragraph after another to the TStringList. When it is done, it exits the loop and returns control back to the FormShow method.

## Handling User Input in the PanelDesign Program

The ListBox object has an event named OnClick, which is called each time the user clicks on the list box. Here is the implementation of that event in this program, along with a helper method named GetSelNum:

```
function TForm1.GetSelNum(): String;
var
  ListNum: Integer;
begin
  ListNum := ListBox1.ItemIndex + 1;
  Result := Int2StrPad0(ListNum, 2);
end;

procedure TForm1.ListBox1Click(Sender: TObject);
var
  PicName: string;
begin
  PicName := GetStartDir() + 'step' + GetSelNum + '.bmp';
  if FileExists(PicName) then
    Image1.Picture.LoadFromFile(PicName);
  if ListBox1.ItemIndex < FList.Count then
    Memo1.Text := FList.Strings[ListBox1.ItemIndex];
end;
```

The Sender parameter that is passed to ListBox1Click is a copy of the object that created the event. In this case, it will always be the list box itself. To access the object, I would take advantage of the principles of polymorphism and write code that looks like this:

```
procedure TForm1.ListBox1Click(Sender: TObject);
var
  MyListBox: TListBox;
begin
  if Sender is TListbox then begin
    MyListBox := TListBox(Sender);
    MyListBox.Items.Add('Sam');
  end;
end;
```

All this is well and good, but it is of only academic interest in the PanelDesign program. There is no real need for me to use the Sender object, so I just ignore it.

My first concern in the ListBox1Click method is to discover the name of the picture that will accompany the selection made by the user. To create this name, I call the GetSelNum method. GetSelNum uses the TListBox.ItemIndex property to discover the item in the list box that the user clicked:

```
ListNum := ListBox1.ItemIndex + 1;
```

I then call a method named `Int2StrPad0`, which ensures that the result returned from the function has two characters in it, not just one. For instance, if the user clicked on the first item in the list, we want to return 01, not just 1:

```
Result := Int2StrPad0(ListNum, 2);
```

## Functions and the Built-in Result Variable

`Int2StrPad0` is found in a unit named LCodeBox.pas. `LCodeBox` does not ship with Kylix. Instead, it comes with this book and is also available on my Web site, www.elvenware.com.

```
function Int2StrPad0(N: LongInt; Len: Integer): string;
begin
  FmtStr(Result, '%d', [N]);
  while Length(Result) < Len do
    Result := '0' + Result;
end;
```

The `Result` variable is predeclared in all Kylix functions. It will always be the type of the return value of your current function. In this case, `Result` is a string.

---

**C/C++,
JavaNote**

In C/C++ and Java, you designate the return value of a function by using the `return` statement:

```
int result;
result = 2 + 2;
return result;
```

The big difference between the Object Pascal technology and the Java and C way of doing things is twofold. First, there is the matter of whether you or the compiler declares the return variable. Second, in Pascal the `return` statement is implied, while in C and Java it is explicit. In my opinion, both technologies are intuitive and easy to use.

---

`Int2StrPad0` calls the Object Pascal `FmtStr` procedure. This function is similar to the C/C++ function `sprintf`. It takes a string in its first two parameters and an array of values in its third parameter:

```
procedure FmtStr(
    var StrResult: string;        // The return value of the procedure
    const Format: string;         // A string with embedded format characters
    const Args: array of const);  // Values to embed in the format string
```

The format string can contain the same types of format characters that are used in the `sprintf` function. The values that you can pass include %d (integer), %u (decimal), %e (scientific), %f (fixed), %g (general), %m (money), %n (number), %p (pointer), %s (string), and %x (hex). For details, look up Format String in the online help.

The `Args` parameter contains an array of arguments. For instance, consider this code fragment:

```
procedure TForm1.Button1Click(Sender: TObject);
var
  S, Temp: string;
begin
  S := 'Sammy';
  Temp := 'Variable S has value %s, the address $%p, and is %d chars long.';
  FmtStr(S, Temp, [S, @S, Length(S)]);
  Edit1.Text := S;
end;
```

Here you can see that three values are passed in the `Args` parameter. The first value is a string, the second is the address of the string, and the third is the length of the string. After the procedure is called, `StrResult` is set as follows: The variable S has the value `Sammy`, the address `$0012F5E0`, and it is 5 characters long.

## C/C++ NOTE

In C/C++, you take the address of a variable with the & symbol. In Pascal, you use the @ symbol. In C/C++ you designate a hex value with 0x, as in 0xFFFF; in Pascal, you use the $, as in $FFFF. The technology and behavior of the symbols in each language is identical, but the actual symbols are different.

In Object Pascal, there is a second way to translate an integer to a string:

```
var
  S: string;
  i: Integer;
begin
  i := 2;
  S := IntToStr(i);
end;
```

The extremely intuitive `IntToStr` function is one that I will use repeatedly throughout this book. It is accompanied by the `StrToInt` function, which works like this:

```
var
  S: string;
  i: Integer;
begin
  S := '2';
  i := StrToInt(S);
end;
```

If either function fails, it will raise an exception. These two functions are extremely intuitive and beautifully designed. Like all well-designed technologies, they are so simple and obvious that one can only wonder why people ever tried to perform this task in a different manner.

The `Int2StrPad0` function ends with the following simple `while` loop:

```
while Length(Result) < Len do
  Result := '0' + Result;
```

This code fragment says that the string `'0'` should be inserted at the start of the `Result` string until `Result` is as long as the value designated in the `Len` parameter passed to the function. For instance, if `Result` is 2 and `Len` is 3, then the first time through the loop `Result` would become 02, and the second time through it would become 002. At that point, the exit requirements for the loop would be satisfied, and it would return.

---

**NOTE**

I will not explain how Object Pascal `while` loops work in this book. Experienced programmers can find out all they need to know about `while` loops simply by typing the word **while** in the Kylix editor, placing the cursor on the word, and pressing the F1 key. The online help will pop up, giving you all the information you need to construct a `while` statement in Object Pascal. Essentially, a `while` statement is a `while` statement, regardless of whether you write it in C, Object Pascal, Java, or BASIC.

---

## Loading an Image from Disk

At this stage, you should be able to understand the first two lines of the `ListBox1Click` method:

```
PicName := GetStartDir() + 'step' + GetSelNum + '.bmp';
if FileExists(PicName) then
  Image1.Picture.LoadFromFile(PicName);
```

The `String PicName` is set equal to the word `'step'`, plus the padded string translation of the index of the currently selected item in the list box, plus the extension `'.bmp'`. For instance, if the user clicked the third item in the list box, the value of `PicName` would be `step03.bmp`.

The `GetStartDir` function from the `LCodeBox` unit looks like this:

```
function GetStartDir: string;
begin
  Result := ExtractFilePath(ParamStr(0));
  Result := IncludeTrailingPathDelimiter(Result)
end;
```

All the functions that `GetStartDir` calls are Pascal built-ins. `ParamStr(0)` returns the fully qualified name of the currently running program. `ExtractFilePath` returns the path part of a fully qualified filename. For instance, if `ParamStr(0)` is set to `/home/ccalvert/src/srcpas/PanelDesign/PanelDesign`, then `ExtractFilePath` strips off the name of the executable and returns `/home/ccalvert/src/srcpas/PanelDesign/`. `IncludeTrailingPathDelimiter` makes sure that you return `/home/ccalvert/src/srcpas/PanelDesign/` and not either `/home/ccalvert/src/srcpas/PanelDesign` or `/home/ccalvert/src/srcpas/PanelDesign\`. If you used the function in a Windows program, it would make sure that a backslash rather than a forward slash was appended to the path string.

| C/C++, |
| :--- |
| **JAVANOTE** |

Both C and Java use the first value of the `Args` parameter passed to the entry point function main to accomplish the same task as `ParamStr(0)` does in Pascal.

After composing the correct path to find the name of the bitmap file, the code calls the built-in `FileExists` function to make sure that the file step03.bmp is actually in the directory where the executable is running. Assuming that it is present, it then calls `Image1.Picture.LoadFromFile(PicName);` to actually load the file into memory and display it to the user.

## Displaying Multiple Lines of Text

As you recall, code presented earlier in this chapter showed how to parse the instructions.txt file and place it in the `TStringList` object called `FList`. The following line of code takes the contents of one of the items in the `TStringList` and displays it in a `Memo` control:

```
if ListBox1.ItemIndex < FList.Count then
  Memo1.Text := FList.Strings[ListBox1.ItemIndex];
```

Memo controls automatically handle word wrap and will automatically insert scrollbars, if they are needed. The Strings property of a TStringList takes the index of the string in the list that you want to display and returns the associated string. For instance, if the string list contains the strings "Father", "Son", and "Holy Ghost", then FList.Strings[0] would return "Father" and FList.Strings[2] would return "Holy Ghost".

The Count property of the TStringList object tells how many items there are in a list. Be careful when using this variable: It is 1-based, while the Strings property of TStringList is 0-based. For instance, if there is one element in the TStringList, then Count would equal 1, but you would access that element with the code MyStringList.Strings[0].

The one part of the PanelDesign program that I have not explored is the underlying CLX code. There are no black boxes in Kylix. If you want to see how the TStringList object is implemented, just open Kylix, place your cursor under the word *TStringList* in the editor, right-click, and select FindDeclaration. You will be taken to the declaration for the object. Then you can press Ctrl+Shift+DownArrow to move to the implementation. But now I am getting ahead of myself by talking about code navigation. Learning how to navigate in the editor is really a whole subject in itself, so I will cover it in Chapter 5.

I've finally reached the end of this discussion on the PanelDesign program. Hopefully hearing about it has helped you gain some insight into how to construct a simple Kylix program.

## Summary

This chapter introduced you to visual programming in Kylix. You learned about the menu system, the toolbars, the Component Palette, the Object Inspector, and the Form Designer.

In the next three chapters, you will learn some necessary facts about the Object Pascal language. Then in Chapter 5, you will learn more about the Kylix IDE. The advanced exploration of the Kylix IDE found in Chapter 5 contains discussions of the advanced tools that you can use to explore your code in depth. By the time you have finished reading these chapters, you should have a good sense of what the Kylix IDE and the Object Pascal language can do for you.

# Looping and Branching, Operators, and Recursion

*By Charlie Calvert*

## IN THIS CHAPTER

This chapter introduces you to the basic statements available in the Object Pascal language. In particular, this chapter is designed to be a short, concise reference to looping and branching in Object Pascal. I will also briefly talk about the Pascal operators and give a brief discussion of recursion.

The goal of the chapter is to give experienced programmers examples of Pascal syntax. The ideal reader for this chapter is someone who knows all about basic programming statements and just wants to how it is done in Object Pascal. "Just show me how it is done, and then let's get on with it," is the guiding phrase for this chapter. However, I do take the time to express the ideas in this chapter in plain English.

It's possible to express things more concisely and tersely in symbolic language, but I believe that the point of a book is to express ideas in written English.

This chapter holds nothing for you here if you already know the basics of the Pascal language. On the other hand, if you don't know what `for` statements or `if` statements are, you will find this material too advanced. For that kind of information, you need a more basic primer on computer programming.

A more rigorous definition of the Pascal language appears in the Style Guide found on this book's accompanying CD-ROM. The main purpose of the Style Guide is to show the preferred way to capitalize and indent Object Pascal code. In the process, however, it presents a fairly rigorous definition of much of the Object Pascal syntax.

# Defining Our Terms: Statements and Expressions

I'll use the terms *statement* and *expression* a number of times in this chapter. As far as I know, there are no settled, cross-language definitions for these terms. The following sections define what I mean by the terms when I use them in this chapter or in later parts of the book.

## Expressions

An *expression* yields a result. For instance, in the following statement, the code `1 + 2` is an expression:

```
X := 1 + 2;
```

Note that `1 + 2` can be placed on the right side of an assignment operator. Anything that you can legally place on the right side of an assignment operator can generally be thought of as an expression.

In the following statement, the value e is an expression:

```
X := e;
```

Here, e is an expression because it yields a result—namely, the value of e.

Here is one last example of an expression:

```
Edit1.Text := IntToStr(y) + ' ' + Format('%d%e', [TotalValue, LostValue]);
```

In this case, everything to the right of the := operator is an expression. This expression also contains some subexpressions. For instance, the call to IntToStr(y) is also an expression because it yields a result.

## Statements

*Statements* are code fragments that usually end with a semicolon or period. Sometimes people define statements as chunks of code that the compiler can process as a single unit without reference to anything other than type declarations. Many of the statements written in programs are looping or branching statements. For instance, if clauses, while loops, and for loops are all statements.

Here is a typical statement:

```
for i := 0 to 10 do
  x := 3 + i;
```

This code fragment is a statement because it ends with a semicolon. If you add type declarations, it makes sense to think of compiling this code by itself. On the other hand, it would not make sense to try to compile the code 0 to 10 by itself. That is why the code 0 to 10 is not considered to be a statement. Furthermore, the for loop shown here is not an expression because it does not yield a result: You can't use it on the right side of an assignment statement.

*Compound statements* are statements that consist of two or more substatements:

```
for i := 0 to 10 do begin
  x := x + 3;
  y := y + 2;
end;
```

This for loop contains three statements:

```
Statement 1:  x := x + 3;
Statement 2:  y := y + 2;
Statement 3:  for i := 0 to 10 do begin
              end;
```

2

LOOPING AND
BRANCHING

Some of the most common kinds of Object Pascal statements appear between `begin..end` pairs. For instance, most procedures consist of a compound statement delineated by a `begin..end` pair:

```
procedure TForm1.Button1Click(Sender: TObject);
var
  x, y: Integer;
begin
  y := 3;
  x := y + 2;
end;
```

This is a Pascal procedure—or, more correctly, a Pascal *method*. It is passed a single parameter, which in this example is ignored. The compound statement in this method looks like this:

```
begin
  y := 3;
  x := y + 2;
end;
```

The following complete Object Pascal program consists primarily of a single compound statement delineated by a `begin..end` pair:

```
program Project2;

{$APPTYPE CONSOLE}

begin
  WriteLn('The fourth noble truth is the noble eightfold path.');
end.
```

In this case, the compound statement ends not with a semicolon, but with a period.

---

> **NOTE**
>
> Project2 is a console application. *Console applications* are programs that have no GUI front end. Instead, they output text to a shell window. To create a console application in Kylix, enter the code shown in Project2, or choose File, New, Console Application from the Kylix menu. The main file in a Kylix console application should end with .dpr, not with .pas.
>
> When you start a new console application, the default name is Project1.dpr. Even if you save the project, you are prompted to supply a name. By default, the .dpr extension is used. You need to perform extra work (take additional steps) *not* to save it with a .dpr extension.

You have seen that Pascal statements end with a semicolon or a period, and they can be thought of as standing on their own without reference to the other code in your program. Most Pascal statements are either assignments, a branching or looping statement, or the compound statement that appears between `begin..end` pairs in a method, function, or procedure.

# if Statements

if statements in Pascal consist of the word `if`, followed by a Boolean expression, the word then, and a statement—for example:

```
procedure TForm1.DHLawrenceClick(Sender: TObject);
var
  i: Integer;
begin
  i := 3;
  if i < 3 then
    ShowMessage('Slowly the moon is rising out of the ruddy haze.');
end;
```

if statements come in a second form, known as an `if..else` statement:

```
procedure TForm1.DHLawrenceClick(Sender: TObject);
var
  i: Integer;
begin
  i := 3;
  if i < 3 then
    ShowMessage('Slowly the moon is rising out of the ruddy haze.')
  else
    ShowMessage('Divesting herself of her golden shift,');
end;
```

The key point to absorb when looking at this statement is the absence of the semicolon before the else clause. In my opinion, this is something that Pascal gets right that most other languages get wrong. The statement ends not before the else statement, but after it.

The confusing part is that the rule about omitting a semicolon before an else statement does not apply if there are compound statements between the else clauses:

```
procedure TForm1.DHLawrenceClick(Sender: TObject);
const
  CR = #10;
var
  i: Integer;
  S: String;
begin
```

```
  i := 2;
  if i < 3 then begin
    S := 'Slowly the moon is rising out of the ruddy haze.' + CR +
    'Divesting herself of her golden shift, and so' + CR +
    'Emerging white and exquisite';
    ShowMessage(S)
  end else
    ShowMessage('A tiny moon as small and white as a single jasmine flower.');
end;
```

Here you can see that I have left off the semicolon before the word end. However, it would also be acceptable to include it:

```
procedure TForm1.DHLawrenceClick(Sender: TObject);
const
  CR = #10;
var
  i: Integer;
  S: String;
begin
  i := 2;
  if i < 3 then
  begin
    S := 'Slowly the moon is rising out of the ruddy haze.' + CR +
    'Divesting herself of her golden shift, and so' + CR +
    'Emerging white and exquisite';
    ShowMessage(S);
  end else
    ShowMessage('A tiny moon as small and white as a single jasmine flower.');
end;
```

Note also that in this second example, I have dropped the opening begin statement down on its own line. Furthermore, I have lined it up with the closing end statement. This is the preferred way to indent your code in a Pascal program. However, I usually use the first method because it buys me an extra line of screen real estate.

The expression in a Pascal if statement can be quite complex, but I will show you one of moderate complexity because it is of the type most commonly formed:

```
procedure TForm1.DHLawrenceClick(Sender: TObject);
const
  CR = #10;
var
  i, j: Integer;
  S: String;
begin
  i := 2;
  j := 3;
```

```
  if ((i < 3) and (j > 3)) then
  begin
    S := 'Take off your cloak and your hat.' + CR +
    'And your shoes, and draw up at my hearth' + CR +
    'Where never woman sat.';
    ShowMessage(S);
  end else begin
    S := 'I have made the fire up bright;' + CR +
    'Let us leave the rest in the dark' + CR +
    'And sit by the firelight.';
    ShowMessage(S);
  end;
end;
```

The key point here is that it is best to use parentheses to set off the various sections of the expression part of an if statement.

## Case Statements

Pascal case statements work the same way that switch statements do in C or Java:

```
procedure TForm1.DHLawrenceClick(Sender: TObject);
var
```

```
  Value: Integer;
begin
  Value := 3;
  case Value of
    0: ShowMessage('In the window full of sunlight');
    1: ShowMessage('Concentrates her golden shadow');
    2: ShowMessage('Fold on fold, until it glows as');
    3: ShowMessage('Mellow as the glory roses.');
  else
    ShowMessage('The sluicing of their rain-disheveled petals.');
  end;
end;
```

Here is the same code rendered in C++ Builder:

```
void __fastcall TForm1::DHLawrenceClick(TObject *Sender)
{
  int Value = 3;

  switch (Value)
  {
    case 0: ShowMessage("In the window full of sunlight"); break;
    case 1: ShowMessage("Concentrates her golden shadow"); break;
    case 2: ShowMessage("Fold on fold, until it glows as"); break;
    case 3: ShowMessage("Mellow as the glory roses."); break;
  default:
    ShowMessage("The sluicing of their rain-disheveled petals.");
  }
}
```

Six of one, half dozen of the other—both syntaxes achieve the same end.

Ironically, in this "case," the Pascal syntax is somewhat more concise because there is no need for the repetitive case or break keywords that clutter up the usually terse C++ syntax.

If you want multiple lines in a particular part of the Pascal case statement, use a begin..end pair:

```
procedure TForm1.LongFellowClick(Sender: TObject);
const
  CR: Char = #10;
var
  Value: Integer;
  S: String;
begin
  Value := 1;
  case Value of
    0: begin
```

```
      S := 'The day is done, and the darkness' + CR +
      'Falls from the wings of Night,';
    end;

  1: begin
      S := 'As a feather is wafted downward' + CR +
      'From an eagle in his flight';
    end;
  else
    ShowMessage('The Day is done.');
  end;
  ShowMessage(S);
end;
```

2

> **NOTE**
>
> In this example, I explicitly designate the type when I declare the constant CR: CR: Char = #10. In particular, the variable is declared to be a Char. According to the traditional rules of Pascal syntax, a constant declared in this way can be changed at runtime. A constant declared as in the previous declarations for the identifier cannot be changed at runtime:
>
> ```
> CR: Char = #10; // Can be changed
> CR = #10;       // Can't be changed
> ```
>
> However, in the first shipping version of Kylix and in Delphi 6, neither type of constant can be changed at runtime. The issue is the assignable type constant option, which you can reach by using Project, Options, Compiler from the Kylix menu. In Delphi 5, this option was checked by default. From here on, it will be unchecked by default.

## for Loops

for loops in Pascal look quite different than in C/C++ or Java:

```
procedure TForm1.LongFellowClick(Sender: TObject);
const
  CR = #10;
  MyArray: array[1..8] of String = (
    'I see the lights of the village'#10,
    'Gleam through the rain and the mist'#10,
    'And a feeling of sadness comes o''er me'#10,
    'That my soul cannot resist.'#10,
```

```
    'Come read to me some poem,'#10,
    'Some simple and heartfelt lay'#10,
    'That shall soothe this restless feeling,'#10,
    'And banish the thoughts of day.'#10);
var

  S: String;
  i: Integer;
begin
  S := '';

  for i := 1 to 8 do
    S := S + MyArray[i];

  ShowMessage(S);
end;
```

Here you see a `for` statement that iterates over the values 1 to 8. During each iteration, a different member of an array is accessed: `S := S + MyArray[i]`.

This is the classic structure for a Pascal `for` loop. In particular, such loops follow this pattern:

`for VariableToIncreate := AnInitialValue to AFinalValue do statement`.

Using the keyword `downto`, you can perform the same act in reverse:

```
procedure TForm1.NapoleonClick(Sender: TObject);
const
  CR = #10;
  A: array[1..7] of String = (' able ', ' was ', ' I ',
    ' ere ', ' I ', ' saw ', ' elba ');
var
  S: String;
  i: Integer;
begin
  S := '';

  for i := 7 downto 1 do
    S := S + A[i];

  ShowMessage(S);
end;
```

The first example gives us the stanza from Longfellow, as we would expect to see it. The second example counts backward from 7 "down to" 1 and gives us a bit of doggerel in reverse, as shown in Figure 2.1.

**FIGURE 2.1**

*No matter how he reads it, Napoleon cannot escape his fate.*

Although not as fruitful a pursuit as Lawrence or Longfellow, palindromes are amusing, so let's till that soil a while longer. You might have noticed a flaw in my earlier work with the Napoleonic palindrome. In particular, the word *able* was not rendered backward. A for loop is still the right tool to fix the problem:

```
procedure TForm1.NapoleonClick(Sender: TmObject);
var
  S, Temp: String;
  Len, i, j: Integer;
begin
  S := 'able was I ere I saw elba';
  Len := StrLen(PChar(S));
  SetLength(Temp, Len);
  j := Len;
  for i := 1 to Len do begin
    Temp[i] := S[j];
    Dec(j);    //decrement the value of j by 1
  end;
  ShowMessage(Temp);
end;
```

The results of this function are shown in Figure 2.2.

**FIGURE 2.2**

*The NapoleonClick method renders a string in reverse, which in this case means that it appears to be unchanged.*

As this example illustrates, you can include a begin..end part in a for statement, if you want.

> **NOTE**
>
> I use StrLen to return the length of the string in NapoleonClick rather than the function Length. Length works fine in most circumstances, but in some object Pascal compilers Length returns the amount of space allocated for a string, while StrLen returns the actual length of the string.

> **NOTE**
>
> The Dec and Inc functions decrement or increment a value by a prescribed value. By default, this value is 1. However, you can also write Dec(j, 3), which decrements the value of j by 3. Needless to say, you can decrement or increment the value by whatever integer value you want to use: Inc(j, 5). The Dec and Inc functions are highly optimized and play the same general role in Pascal that the ++ or -- operators play in C++ or Java.

The NapoleonClick method is really a technology for reversing a string. Such technology cries out to be generalized:

```
function ReverseStr(S: string): string;
var
  Len: Integer;
  Temp: String;
  i,j: Integer;
begin
  Len := StrLen(PChar(S)); // Length returns allocation, not length
  SetLength(Temp, Len);
  j := Len;
  for i := 1 to Len do begin
    Temp[i] := S[j];
    dec(j);
  end;
  ReverseStr := Temp;
end;
```

The ReverseString function, shown here, is stored in the LCodeBox.pas program found on the CD that accompanies this book. It is kept in a directory named lunits, which stands for "Linux units." I will use the LCodeBox unit frequently throughout the course of this book. Other generally useful routines are found in LCodeBox and in the other source files found in the lunits directory.

# While Statements

while statements in Pascal are much like while statements in Java or C++. In general, while statements follow this pattern:

```
while SomeBooleanExpressionIsTrue do SomeStatement
```

Consider this example:

```
while x < 3 do
  Inc(x);
```

Here is a more practical example of how to use the syntax:

```
function StripFrontChars(S: string; Ch: Char): string;
begin
  while (Length(S) > 0) and (S[1] = Ch) do
    Delete(S,1,1);

  StripFrontChars := S;
end;
```

This code will remove all instances of the character Char that appear at the front of a string. For instance, the following call would remove the x's from the front of the string S:

```
S := 'xxxxxxTo me what is and what seems are often one and the same.';
MyString := StripFrontChars(S, 'x');
```

> **NOTE**
>
> The StripFrontChars function indexes not to element 0 in a string, but instead to element 1. As you will learn in the next chapter, element 0 in a Pascal AnsiString is something we shouldn't touch.

The GetFirstWord function from the LCodeBox unit illustrates a somewhat more complex use of a while loop. This function returns the first word from a string.

Rather than raising an exception, I could have set the length of the new string to the length of the string that is passed:

```
function GetFirstWord(const S: string): string;
var
    i: Integer;
    S1: String;
begin
  i := 1;
  if S = '' then Exit;
```

```
  SetLength(S1, Length(S)); // Large buffer, changed later
  while (S[i] <> ' ') and (i < Length(S)) do begin
     S1[i] := S[i];
     Inc(i);
  end;
  Dec(i);
  SetLength(S1, i);
  GetFirstWord := S1;
end;
```

This while loop has two parts, tied together by the Boolean operator and:

```
(S[i] <> ' ') and (i < Length(S))
```

By default, if the first part of this Boolean expression evaluates to false, then the second part will never be tested. If, for some odd reason, you want to ensure that both parts are tested, you can select Project, Options from the Kylix menu, turn to the Compiler page, and make sure that the Complete Boolean Evaluation option is checked, as shown in Figure 2.3.

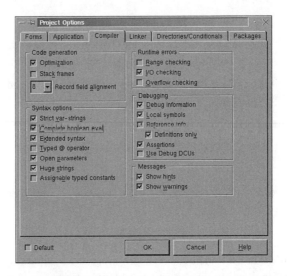

**FIGURE 2.3**

*Turning on Complete Boolean Evaluations in the Compiler page of the Project Options dialog box.*

Note that I pass in the string S as a const. This means that the string is passed by reference rather than by value. That is, you receive a pointer to the string rather than a copy of the string. However, this particular string is declared as a const, which means that you do not intend to change its value. Nevertheless, passing a string as a pointer is much more efficient than passing it by value. In particular, it is easier for the compiler to pass a pointer to the string than it is to make a copy of the string and then pass that copy. Despite the fact that a pointer is being passed, the const directive does not force you to treat the variable as a pointer. You can still treat it as a normal type. Only in the background, behind the scenes, is the value treated as a pointer.

---

### NOTE

Here is a second version of the GetFirstWord function:

```
function GetFirstWord(const S: string): string;
var
    i: Integer;
    S1: String;
begin
  i := 1;
  if Length(S) > 1024 then
    raise ECodeBoxException.Create('String too long');
  SetLength(S1, 1024); // Large buffer, changed later
  while (S[i] <> ' ') and (i < Length(S)) do begin
    S1[i] := S[i];
    Inc(i);
  end;
  Dec(i);
  SetLength(S1, i);
  GetFirstWord := S1;
end;
```

This function raises an exception if the string that the user passes is longer than 1,024 characters. The ECodeBoxException type is made explicitly for the LCodeBox unit:

```
type
   InfoProc = procedure (Info: String) of Object;
   ECodeBoxException = class(Exception);
```

The nice thing about this syntax is that it enables you to easily and quickly create an exception type that not only helps you handle errors, but that also defines the type and location of the error. In particular, all errors of this type occur in the LCodeBox unit. When the compiler reports the error, it states the name of the exception raised. Because this exception is named ECodeBoxException, it is easy to trace it back to the LCodeBox unit.

---

## repeat Statements

repeat statements are like do..while statements in C/C++ or Java. You use while statements for loops that will execute 0 to $N$ times, but you use repeat statements for loops that will repeat 1 to *N* times. In other words, if you know that the loop should occur at least once, use a repeat statement; otherwise, use a while or for loop.

The following method is from the ShowAllWords example found on the CD that accompanies this book:

```
procedure TForm1.Button1Click(Sender: TObject);
var
  S, Temp: string;
begin
  S := Memo1.Lines.GetText;
  repeat
    Temp := RemoveFirstWord(S);
    Temp := CleanString(Temp);
    S := CleanString(S);
    if Temp <> '' then
      ListBox1.Items.Add(Temp);
  until S = '';
end;
```

The program from which this method is taken is shown in Figure 2.4. This is the only method in the program.

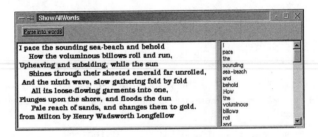

**FIGURE 2.4**

*The ShowAllWords program breaks a poem into its individual constituent parts.*

The point of this exercise is to show how the repeat..until statement works. In particular, this loop will continue until all the words found in the string from the Memo control have been deleted. At that time, S will be equal to the empty string, and the loop will exit:

```
repeat
  ... // Code omitted here
until S = '';
```

Needless to say, the method is not designed to handle a situation in which there is no text in Memo1. If you expect that to ever be the case, you should use a while loop rather than a repeat until loop. Nevertheless, the RemoveFirst and CleanString methods can handle empty strings, so the method would not fail even in the worst-case scenario.

The ShowAllWords program presents the user with a partial stanza from a poem by Longfellow. The words of the poem are split out and shown one by one in a list box. The RemoveFirstWord and CleanString functions are found in the LCodeBox unit:

```
function RemoveFirstWord(var S: String): String;
var
  i, Size: Integer;
  S1: String;
begin
  i := Pos(#32, S);
  if i = 0 then begin
    RemoveFirstWord := S;
    S := '';
    Exit;
  end;
  SetLength(S1, i);
  Move(S[1], S1[1], i);
  SetLength(S1, i-1);
  Size := (Length(S) - i);
  Move(S[i + 1], S[1], Size);
  SetLength(S, Size);
  RemoveFirstWord := S1;
end;

function CleanString(const S: string): string;
var
  Temp: String;
begin
  Temp := '';
  if Length(S) <> 0 then begin
    Temp := StripFrontChars(S, #32);
    Temp := StripEndChars(Temp, #32);
    Temp := StripFrontChars(Temp, #13);
    Temp := StripFrontChars(Temp, #10);
    Temp := StripEndChars(Temp, #10);
    Temp := StripEndChars(Temp, #13);
  end;
  CleanString := Temp;
end;
```

Both are very similar to routines that you have already seen in this chapter. Notice that CleanString takes its parameter as a const, while RemoveFirstWord takes a var parameter. var parameters are passed by reference, and any changes that you make to a var parameter will be maintained after the function returns.

## Last Words on Looping and Branching

You have now seen the Pascal `if` statements, `while` statements, and `repeat..until` statements. These are the core building blocks out of which most programs are made. These constructs are innately simple and easy to understand, so I have tried to cover them as quickly as possible, while still taking enough time to explore their key features.

# A Few Words About Operators

The Pascal operators are laid out very nicely in the online help. To learn about them, simply search using the word Operators. In particular, the tables that you find in the online help tell you most of what you need to know about operators. Therefore, I limit this section of the text to a few short comments on the areas where Pascal operators can cause confusion.

## The Assignment Operator

Use `:=`, not `=`, to take the result of an expression:

```
x := i + j;
```

To read this out loud, you would say: "x colon equals i + j," or "x gets i + j." Most developers, including myself, use the first manner of speaking, but I believe I have heard some of the key architects of Kylix use the latter wording.

If you want to use an equals sign in a Boolean expression, use `=`, and not `= =`, as in this example:

```
if x = y then
  DoSomething;
```

## The Division Operators

Use the `div` operator if you want the result of an expression to yield an integer. Use the `/` operator if you want the result to yield a floating-point number:

```
procedure TForm1.FloatButtonClick(Sender: TObject);
var
  i, j: Integer;
  x: Double;
begin
  i := 3;
  j := 2;
  x := i / j;  // Yields a floating point number
  Edit1.Text := Format('%f', [x]);
end;
```

```pascal
procedure TForm1.IntegerButtonClick(Sender: TObject);
var
  i, j, x: Integer;

begin
  i := 3;
  j := 2;
  x := i div j;  // Yields an Integer
  Edit1.Text := IntToStr(x);
end;
```

The first example shown here yields 1.5 as the result, and the second yields 1. div always rounds numbers down toward 0. As a result, even though 9 / 10 yields 0.90, the result of 9 div 10 is 0. The fractional part of the result of division based on the div operator is always rounded down to the next whole number. If you want more control over the rounding of fractions, use the / operator and convert the result to an integer value using the built-in Object Pascal functions Round, Int or Trunc:

```pascal
var
  i, j, k: Integer;
  y, z: Double;
begin
  y := j / i;
  k := Round(y); // Rounds to the nearest whole number.
  k := Trunc(y); // Like the div operator, trunc rounds y toward zero.
  z := Int(y);   // Rounds like the div operator, but yields a float.
end;
```

When using the Round function, if the value of y were halfway between the two nearest whole numbers, then Round would yield the nearest even number. Rounding to the nearest even number is also called "bankers rounding" because the banks use this technique as well.

## Boolean and Logical Operators

Rather than &&, !, and ||, the Boolean operators in Pascal are and, or, not, and xor. The fact that Pascal uses words rather than symbols for these operators does not affect the performance of your code. The and operator works the same way and has the same performance characteristics in Pascal as the && operator does in C or C++.

The logical operators in Pascal are and, or, not, xor, shl, and shr. Again, the shift left operator, shl, works exactly the same way in Pascal as the << operator does in C++ or Java. There is no performance penalty incurred for using the letters shl rather than the symbol <<.

The famous trick of shifting a value to the left to multiply by two works just as effectively and just as quickly in Pascal as it does in C/C++:

```
procedure TForm1.QuickMultiplyClick(Sender: TObject);
var
  i, j: Integer;
begin
  i := 1;
  for j := 0 to 29 do begin
    i := i shl 1;
    ListBox1.Items.Add(IntToStr(i));
  end;
end;
```

This function yields the values 2, 4, 8, 16, 32, 64, and so on. You can view the output of this function in Figure 2.5. The program shown in Figure 2.5 is named Operators and it is found on the CD that accompanies this book. Many of the other examples from this section on operators are also found in that program.

**FIGURE 2.5**

*The output of the Operators program.*

## Relational Operators

As mentioned earlier, the test for equality is performed not with the = = operator, but with the = operator:

```
if x = y then
  ShowMessage('X equals Y');
```

The expression x = = y has no meaning in Pascal.

To test for inequality, don't use !=; instead, use <>:

```
if x <> y then
  ShowMessage('Not equal');
```

To read this statement out loud, say, "If x does not equal y, then show message, open parenthesis, single quote, not equal, close single quote, close parenthesis, semicolon."

Pascal includes the less than or equal to and greater than or equal to operators: <=, >=.

## Getting the Address of a Variable

Rather than use the & symbol, Pascal developers take the address of a variable by using the @ symbol:

```
procedure TForm1.Button1Click(Sender: TObject);
var
  P: Pointer;
begin
  P := @Form1;
  Edit1.Text := Format('The address of Form1 is $%p', [P]);
end;
```

Here I am using the @ symbol to place the address of the Form1 variable in the pointer variable P. I could have placed @Form1 directly in the call to Format, but it's easier to understand the significance of the @ operator this way. Here is how to do the same thing in C++ Builder:

```
void __fastcall TForm1::Button1Click(TObject *Sender)
{
  char C[1024];
  void *P = &Form1;
  sprintf(C, "The address of Form1 is 0x%p", P);
  Edit1->Text = C;
}
```

In both the C++ and Pascal examples, I use the %p format specifier to tell Format or sprintf that I want to convert the pointer variable P into a string representation of the address of the pointer in question. The $ symbol in Pascal designates a hexadecimal value, just as the 0x symbol in C/C++ designates a hexadecimal value. Hence, the number 10 in hex is written $A.

## Operators In Strings and In Pointer Arithmetic

There are certain noteworthy ways to use Pascal operators that I did not mention, primarily because I consider them relatively obvious to most users:

- **Concatenating strings**—The most important operator used with Pascal strings is the plus operator (+). You can use it to concatenate two strings:

  ```
  S := 'This is part one ' + 'and this is part two.'
  ```

  After the assignment, S would contain the string 'This is part one and this is part two.'

- **Relational operators**—You can also use the relational operators such as =, <>, and >= to test the relationship between strings. For instance, the expression if `String1` > `String2` asks whether `String1` is larger than `String2`. To state the matter somewhat differently, it asks whether `String1` would be listed after `String2` in a dictionary.

- **Quotes**—Pascal uses single quotes rather than double quotes for listing strings:

  ```
  S := 'This is a string.'
  ```

  If you need to embed a single quote in a string, just use the normal practice of using the quote twice:

  ```
  'This is a ''string'' with the word string in single quotes embedded in
  it.'
  ```

  The word *string* is surrounded by two single quotes, not a double quote. See Figure 2.6 as an aid to help you understand this issue. If you want a string that consists solely of one single quote, you would write `''''`, which is four single quotes in a row. This would yield a string that looks like this: `'`.

- **Pointer Arithmetic**—You can use operators to perform pointer arithmetic. That subject is complex enough that it gets its own section in Chapter 5, "The Editor and Debugger."

In addition, a number of operators can be used with sets. I do not, however, cover sets in the main text of this book. Instead, see Appendix A, included on the CD that accompanies this book.

**FIGURE 2.6**
*Here is a string with embedded single quotes inside it.*

## Final Words on Operators

As you have seen, Pascal has a very rich set of operators. In most languages, operators are operators, and everyone who knows how to use any other computer language can figure out how they work in Pascal. For instance, `x := 2 + 2;` is a statement that makes sense to all programmers, so there's not much need to explain the particulars of how it works in Pascal. However, there are a few tricky or confusing bits of operator usage in every language, and I have tried to cover those cases here. For examples of the more obvious ways to use Pascal operators, simply look up "Operator" in the online help.

# Recursion

Recursion is a technology commonly found in nature. Many plants, most obviously ferns and palms, grow through an iterative process very similar to recursion in a computer program.

Two classic examples of recursion in programming are the calculation of factorials and the calculation of Fibonacci numbers. I'll have to confess that I have never had a real-world reason for needing to know the factorial of a number or for having to know any number in the Fibonacci series. And, with any luck, I never will! However, I have had reason to use recursion in my programs, and calculating these numbers provides an excellent way to demonstrate recursion in any generally useful programming language.

## Factorials

Given a number *n*, the factorial of it is expressed as this:

```
n * (n - 1) * (n - 2) * ... * 1
```

or, somewhat more rigorously, as this:

```
N! = N * (N - 1)!, for N > 0 with 0! = 1
```

Here, you can read N! as the factorial of N. If all that seems like so much gibberish to you, then a simpler way to think of the matter is simply to consider the factorial of 3 being equal to 3×2×1, or 6. The factorial of 5 is 5×4×3×2×1, or 120. And so on.

You can use recursion to calculate factorials in Object Pascal much as you would in any other language:

```
function Factorial(Value : Integer): Integer;
begin
  if Value <= 0 then
    Result := 1
  else
    Result := Value * Factorial(Value - 1);
end; { Factorial }
```

This function must be passed a positive number. If you pass 0 or a negative number, the function simply returns 1. If you pass any other positive number, the function calls itself recursively. For instance, calling the function 11 times with the values 0, 1, 2, 3, and so on, you get:

```
Factorial of 0 is 1
Factorial of 1 is 1
Factorial of 2 is 2
Factorial of 3 is 6
```

```
Factorial of 4 is 24
Factorial of 5 is 120
Factorial of 6 is 720
Factorial of 7 is 5040
Factorial of 8 is 40320
Factorial of 9 is 362880
Factorial of 10 is 3628800
```

If you call the function with a value of 3, the first time it is called, `Value` is set equal to 3. The second time, it is set to 2; the third time, it is set to 1, and the last time, it is set to 0. Thus, you multiply 3×2×1×1, which equals 6.

Listing 2.1 shows a console program that lets you play with the algorithm for calculating factorials. In this instance of the function, I add a few lines of code to ensure that the function never tries to calculate the value for a negative number.

---

**NOTE**

As mentioned earlier, console applications run at the command prompt rather than on top of the X Window Library. You can create a console application in Kylix by choosing File, New, Console Application from the Kylix menu. You can also simply open a text editor and type in the code shown here. However, if you want to use the code in the Kylix IDE, it is best to save the file with an extension of .dpr rather than an extension of .pas. You can compile the program at the command prompt with the dcc utility that ships with Kylix, or you can compile it inside Kylix in the usual manner.

---

**LISTING 2.1**   A Program That Calculates Factorials and Fibonacci Numbers

```pascal
program Recursion;

{$APPTYPE CONSOLE}

function Factorial(Value : Integer): Integer;
begin
  if Value < 0 then begin
    WriteLn('Number must be positive');
    Result := -1;
    Exit;
  end;

  if Value = 0 then
    Result := 1
```

**LISTING 2.1**   Continued

```
  else
    Result := Value * Factorial(Value - 1);
end; { Factorial }

function Fibonacci(Value: Integer): Integer;
begin
  if (Vaue = 0) or (Value = 1) then
    Result := Value
  else
    Result := Fibonacci(Value - 1) + Fibonacci(Value - 2);
end; { Fibonacci }

var
  Temp, OldTemp, i : Integer;
begin
  Temp := Factorial(5);
  WriteLn('Factorial: ', Temp);

  for i := 0 to 10 do begin
    Temp := Factorial(i);
    WriteLn('Factorial of ', i, ' is ', Temp);
  end;

  WriteLn;
  WriteLn('Fibonacci values');
  WriteLn('----------------');
  Temp := Fibonacci(10);
  WriteLn('Fibonacci: ', Temp);

  Temp := 0;
  OldTemp := Temp;
  for i := 0 to 25 do begin
    Temp := Fibonacci(i);
  if Temp <> OldTemp then
    WriteLn('Fibonacci ', i, ' is ', Temp);
  OldTemp := Temp;
end;

end.
```

# Fibonacci Series

Calculating the Fibonacci series is a lot like calculating factorials. You start the series with the numbers 1 and 1, and you calculate each successive number in the series by adding the two previous numbers together:

1, 1, 2, 3, 5, 8, 13, 21, 34, 55, 89, 144, 233 ...

As expressed in Pascal, here is how to calculate these numbers:

```
function Fibonacci(Value: Integer): Integer;
begin
  if (Value = 0) or (Value = 1) then
    Result := Value
  else
    Result := Fibonacci(Value - 1) + Fibonacci(Value - 2);
end; { Fibonacci }
```

As you can see, this algorithm calls for a form of double recursion, where the function recursively calls itself twice. Technically, when I dig down and see how this function really works, the end result is deep contemplation of a piece of code that makes my head hurt. However, if I don't think about it too carefully and I just look at what the function does from a superficial level, then my head doesn't hurt so much.

When recursion makes my head hurt, I do one of three things:

1. I search through my books or the Web and try to find someone whose head does not hurt when they think recursively, and I use their solutions to the problem. If that fails, I search for someone who does not mind having his head hurt and who is generous enough to share the fruits of his suffering with the rest of us.

2. I try to think of ways to solve the same problem without using recursion.

3. I bite the bullet and prepare to endure the challenge as best I can.

Listing 2.2 shows an alternative way to calculate Fibonacci numbers, which offers two benefits over the first method shown:

1. It calculates the results in a much shorter period of time.

2. Instead of making my head hurt, it makes me feel as though my head has had a pleasant workout.

In particular, this second version of the program does not use recursion. Instead, it uses a simple for loop.

**LISTING 2.2**  The ezFibonacci Program, Which Offers an Exponential Improvement in Performance over the Recursive Solution for Calculating the Numbers in the Fibonacci Series

```
program ezFibonacci;

{$APPTYPE CONSOLE}

const
  MAX = 25;

type
  TFibArray = array[0..MAX] of Integer;

function Fibonacci: TFibArray;
var
  i: Integer;
begin
  Result[0] := 1;
  Result[1] := 1;
  for i := 2 to MAX do
    Result[i] := Result[i -1] + Result[i - 2];
end;

var
  FibArray: TFibArray;
  i: Integer;
begin
  FibArray := Fibonacci;
  for i := 0 to MAX do
    Write(FibArray[i], ' ');
end.
```

When creating this program, I deliberately kept the number of values in the series that it calculates to a minimum. This is done as a courtesy to people who are running the code on slower machines. However, if you are working on a 600MHZ or higher machine, you can crank up the values quite high and still get very fast results. The same cannot be said of the recursive solution to this problem.

The ezFibonacci program also shows an example of returning a complex type from a function. Notice that I request that the Fibonacci function itself return an array of Integers. In many languages, code like that would not compile. However, Object Pascal handles the problem easily and takes care of all the necessary allocation of memory for you automatically.

## Drawing Recursion

One of the people I turn to whenever I'm in danger of encountering an algorithm that might
make my head hurt is Robert Sedgewick. His book, *Algorithms in C++*, includes an interesting
recursive program that draws the pattern shown in Figure 2.7. My translation of his algorithm
into Object Pascal is shown in Listing 2.3.

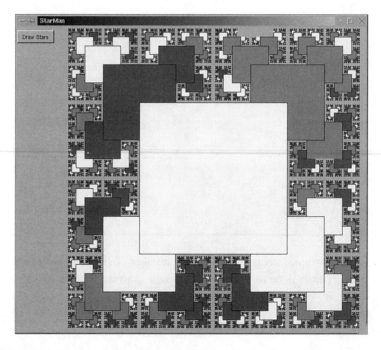

**FIGURE 2.7**

*The stars program shows recursion in action.*

**LISTING 2.3**  A Recursive Program for Drawing Patterns

```
program stars;

uses
  SysUtils, Classes, QForms,
  QControls, QStdCtrls, QGraphics,
  Qt;

type
  TForm1 = class(TForm)
  public
    constructor Create(AOwner: TComponent); override;
    procedure DoPaint(Sender : TObject);
    procedure DrawStars(x, y, r : Integer);
  end;

var
  Form1: TForm1;

constructor TForm1.Create(AOwner : TComponent);
begin
  inherited Create(AOwner);
  OnPaint := DoPaint;
  SetBounds(10, 10, 800, 600);
end;
i
procedure TForm1.DrawStars(x, y, r : Integer);
const
  Colors: array [0..3] of TColor = (clBlue, clYellow, clRed, clGreen);
begin
  if r > 0 then begin
    DrawStars(x - r, y + r, r div 2);
    DrawStars(x + r, y + r, r div 2);
    DrawStars(x - r, y - r, r div 2);
    DrawStars(x + r, y - r, r div 2);
    Canvas.Brush.Color := Colors[Random(3)];
    Canvas.Rectangle(x - r, y - r, x + r, y + r);
  end;
end;

procedure TForm1.DoPaint(Sender : TObject);
begin
  DrawStars(400, 300, 150);
end; { TForm1 }
```

**2**

**LISTING 2.3**   Continued

```
begin
  Application.CreateForm(TForm1, Form1);
  Application.Run;
end.
```

The stars program is a full GUI-based program that pops up a main form. It uses the OnPaint method to call the function that does the actual drawing. OnPaint events are designed to be called whenever the program's main form needs to be redrawn. Thus, iyou can guarantee that the program will always be painted correctly, even if it is temporarily covered by another program.

## Summary

This chapter introduced you to basic Pascal syntax for looping, branching, using operators, and performing recursion. I have tried to keep the examples short and to the point without ever being cryptic.

In the next two chapters, you will get a deeper look at the Object Pascal language. First, you will learn about the basic types in the language. Then, you will move on to increasingly complex subjects, and you'll end with an overview of objects and interfaces.

# Basic Pascal Syntax

*By Charlie Calvert*

## IN THIS CHAPTER

This chapter is dedicated to some of the more advanced features of the most commonly used Pascal types. Subjects covered include integers, strings, floating-point types, arrays, records, and pointers.

I'm writing for experienced programmers, and the text is not meant to be a primer on Object Pascal for newcomers. I assume that the reader already understands simple types such as integers, floating-point types, and even complex types such as arrays, records, and pointers. I will highlight the unexpected or advanced features of these types as they are implemented in Object Pascal.

Some readers might have last used Pascal many years ago and might no longer have a sure feeling of the language. Many programmers have had experience with ANSI Pascal but not with Object Pascal. Object Pascal is to ANSI Pascal as C++ is to C. If you're expecting the Object Pascal universe to resemble the relatively bland world of ANSI Pascal, then you may be in for some surprises.

The material in this chapter will be necessary for an understanding of the material in Chapter 5, "The Editor and Debugger." In short, I can't discuss the finer points of writing and debugging code in the Object Pascal editor without first covering a few crucial syntactical issues.

DELPHI NOTE

Experienced Object Pascal programmers will want to at least skim this chapter because there might be some issues such as variant records or dynamic arrays that you want to bone up on. Advanced topics are spread throughout the chapter. For instance, one section that even experienced Delphi users should read is "The TBcd type and Floating-Point Accuracy," which covers the new routines for handling the TBcd type.

## The Content of This Chapter

Pascal is a strongly typed language. The compiler cares a great deal about your type declarations, and the things you can do with variables are severely restricted by your type choices. In the old days, this was considered a bad thing because it was felt to be restricting. Over the years, however, the general consensus on this topic has changed. All modern languages, such as C++ and Java, have followed in Pascal's footsteps by placing a strong emphasis on typing.

Pascal was invented back in 1968 and was first implemented in 1970. Any language that old is going to have some quirks in it. However, overall, I consider Pascal to be a very good language. If you come to this book with a different prejudice, I ask that you put those ideas aside while you read this chapter. You might be surprised at the power of this language. In particular, C++ programmers probably will be surprised to find that the language is so flexible, and Java programmers will be surprised to find that it has so many modern features.

Most major Pascal types will be covered in one fashion or another. However, there are two major topics that I will just touch on:

- **Objects**—The Object Pascal syntax for declaring and building objects will be explored in Chapter 4, "Objects and Interfaces," and also throughout nearly all the chapters in Part II, "CLX." However, this chapter covers allocating and deallocating memory for objects. You will find this material in this chapter's coverage of pointers. In particular, you should see the sections "Working with Pointers to Objects" and "Pointers, Constructors, and Destructors." Included are a brief overview of the Pascal constructor and destructor syntax and a few words on writing virtual methods.

- **Interfaces**—Interfaces enable you to define the structure for a class without creating an implementation for it. I will cover this important topic in Part II.

# Integer Types and Floating-Point Types

I assume that readers of this book can quickly come to terms with basic Pascal types. I will say a few words on the basics of the subject and then go on to cover some issues that might trip up experienced programmers new to this language or experienced programmers who need a refresher course on Pascal syntax. This approach will not be helpful for a newcomer to programming, but it should be enough information to get experts up to speed on Object Pascal in short order.

I'll start by talking briefly about integers and floating-point types. After getting that basic material out of the way, I'll discuss strings, pointers, and typecasting.

Here are two very basic definitions:

- Integers are whole numbers, such as –1, 0, 1, 2, and 5,000,000.
- Floating-point numbers are sometimes known as decimal numbers, such as 7.0, 3.2, –5.004, and 32,000.0000000034.

## Ordinal Types

A whole series of types in Pascal are based on whole numbers. These include the Byte, Integer, Char, and Boolean types. All of these types are ordinal types.

Understanding the definition of the ordinal types is helpful for programmers who want to set sail on the good ship Pascal. All but the first and last members of ordinal types have a predecessor and a successor. For instance, an ordinal number such as 1 is followed by 2 and preceded by 0. The same cannot be said of a floating-point type. What is the predecessor to

1.0002? Is it 1.0001? Maybe. But perhaps it is 1.00019—or maybe 1.000199. How about 1.000199999999? Ultimately, there is no clearly defined predecessor to a floating-point number, so it is not an ordinal value.

Whole numbers are ordinal numbers. Simple types such as `Char` and `Boolean` are also ordinal numbers. For instance, the letter B is succeeded by the letter C and preceded by the letter A. It makes sense to talk about the successor and predecessor of a `Char`. The same is true of `Boolean` values. `False`, which is equivalent to 0, is succeeded by `True`, which is usually equivalent to 1. `False` is the predecessor of `True`, and `True` is the successor to `False`.

**NOTE**

When I use the word *integer* in a generic sense, I am talking about the numeric ordinal types such as `Byte`, `LongInt`, `Integer`, or `Cardinal`. When I talk specifically about `Integers`, with a capital I, then I mean the Pascal type named `Integer`. C and Java programmers make a similar distinction between the floating-point types and the type named `float`.

Two integer types exist in Pascal: generic and fundamental. The generic types, called `Integer` and `Cardinal`, will transform themselves to fit the compiler you are currently using. If you use `Integers` on a 16-bit platform, they will be 16 bits in size. Use them on a 32-bit platform with a 32-bit compiler, and they will be 32 bits in size. Use them on a 64-bit platform with a 64-bit compiler, and they will be 64 bits in size.

`Integers` are always signed values, which means that they use 1 bit to signal whether they are positive or negative and then use the remaining bits to record a number.

**NOTE**

Some readers might not be clear on the difference between signed and unsigned types. Consider the `Byte` and `ShortInt` types, both of which contain 8 bits. A `Byte` is unsigned, and a `ShortInt` is signed. The largest unsigned 8-bit number is 255, while its smallest value is 0. The largest signed 8-bit number is 127, while its smallest value is −128. The issue is simply that you can have 256 possible numbers that can be held in 8 bits. These 256 numbers can range from either −128 to 127, or from 0 to 255. The difference between signed and unsigned types is whether one of the bits is used to designate the plus and minus sign. Unsigned numbers have no plus and minus sign and, therefore, are always positive. Signed numbers range over both positive and negative values.

> **NOTE**
>
> At this time, there is only a 32-bit compiler in Kylix. On the Windows platform, at the time of this writing, there is a 16-bit and a 32-bit Delphi compiler.

In contrast to generic types, fundamental types are always a set size, regardless of what platform you use. For instance, a Byte is an 8-bit, unsigned number, regardless of the platform. The same rule applies to LongInts, which are always 32-bit signed numbers, regardless of the platform.

The generic types are shown in Table 3.1, and the fundamental types appear in Table 3.2.

**TABLE 3.1**  The Generic Types Are Ordinal Values with a Range That Changes Depending on the Number of Bits in the Native Type Word for Your Platform

| Type | Range | Format |
|------|-------|--------|
| Integer | –2147483648 to 2147483647 | Signed 32-bit |
| Cardinal | 0 to 4294967295 | Unsigned 32-bit |

**TABLE 3.2**  The Fundamental Type Stays the Same, Regardless of Platform

| Type | Range | Format |
|------|-------|--------|
| ShortInt | –128 to 127 | Signed 8-bit |
| SmallInt | –32768 to 32767 | Signed 16-bit |
| LongInt | –2147483648 to 2147483647 | Signed 32-bit |
| Int64 | $-2^{63}$ to $2^{63-1}$ | Signed 64-bit |
| Byte | 0 to 255 | Unsigned 8-bit |
| Word | 0 to 65535 | Unsigned 16-bit |
| LongWord | 0 to 4294967295 | Unsigned 32-bit |

Most knowledgeable programmers try to use the generic types whenever possible. They help you port your code to new platforms, and they make your code backward compatible with old platforms. Furthermore, the generic Integer type should always be the fastest numeric type on any platform because it fits exactly the size of a word on that particular processor. Thus, the Integer type will usually be the best choice for producing fast code, even though it is larger than the ShortInt or SmallInt types. On 32-bit platforms, LongInts and Integers are equally fast, but when we move to 64-bit computers, LongInts will no longer be the native type, while Integers will continue in the anointed position. In short, Integers will have 64 bits on a 64-bit platform, 16 bits on a 16-bit platform, and 32 bits on a 32-bit platform.

If you have code that assumes that a particular variable has a certain number of bits in it or will always contain only a certain range of numbers, you should use fundamental types to make sure that your code does not break if you move to another platform. Obviously, most of the code that you write will not be dependant on the number of bits in a variable, but if your code does depend on such a thing, choose your types carefully. For instance, if you are writing a routine that needs to handle numbers larger than 32,767, don't use Integers if you think that the code will ever be run on a 16-bit platform. If you do choose Integers, they will not be large enough to hold the values that you want to use. If you choose LongInts, the type will be large enough, even if ported to a 16-bit platform. (Of course, the odds that you will port your code back to a 16-bit platform are low.)

## Pascal Routines for Using Ordinal Numbers

The Integer types, by definition, are ordinal numbers. Ordinal numbers can be manipulated with the following routines: Ord, Pred, Succ, High, and Low. If applied to a Char, the Ord function returns its numeric value. For instance, the Ord of $A$ is 65, and the Ord of a space is 32. In the following example, Num will be set to 66:

```
var
  MyChar: Char;
  Num: Integer;
begin
  MyChar := 'B';
  Num := Ord(MyChar);
end;
```

The Pred routine returns the predecessor of a number. For instance, the Pred of 1 is 0. The Succ of 1 is 2.

High and Low give you the highest and lowest numbers that you can use with a type. Examples of how to use High and Low are shown in the SimpleTypes program, found on your CD and in Listing 3.1.

**LISTING 3.1**   The SimpleTypes Program

```
unit Main;

interface

uses
  SysUtils, Types, Classes,
```

**LISTING 3.1**   Continued

```pascal
  QGraphics, QControls, QForms,
  QDialogs, QStdCtrls, QExtCtrls;

type
  TForm1 = class(TForm)
    ListBox1: TListBox;
    RadioGroup1: TRadioGroup;
    procedure RadioGroup1Click(Sender: TObject);
  private
    procedure DoLongInt;
    procedure DoInteger;
    procedure DoCardinal;
    procedure DoLongWord;
    procedure DoWord;
    procedure DoShortInt;
    procedure DoSmallInt;
    { Private declarations }
  public
    { Public declarations }
  end;

var
  Form1: TForm1;

implementation

{$R *.xfm}

type
  TMethodType = (mtInteger, mtCardinal, mtLongInt,
    mtLongWord, mtWord, mtShortInt, mtSmallInt);

procedure TForm1.DoInteger;
var
  Value: Integer;
begin
  ListBox1.Items.Add('Integer high value: ' + IntToStr(High(Value)));
  ListBox1.Items.Add('Integer low value: ' + IntToStr(Low(Value)));
  ListBox1.Items.Add('Size of Integer: ' + IntToStr(SizeOf(Value)) + ' bytes or
➥' + IntToStr(8 * SizeOf(Value)) + ' bits.');
end;

procedure TForm1.DoLongInt;
var
```

**LISTING 3.1**   Continued

```
  Value: LongInt;
begin
  ListBox1.Items.Add('LongInt high value: ' + IntToStr(High(Value)));
  ListBox1.Items.Add('LongInt low value: ' + IntToStr(Low(Value)));
  ListBox1.Items.Add('Size of LongInt: ' + IntToStr(SizeOf(Value)) + ' bytes or
➥' + IntToStr(8 * SizeOf(Value)) + ' bits.');
end;

procedure TForm1.RadioGroup1Click(Sender: TObject);
begin
  case TMethodType(RadioGroup1.ItemIndex) of
    mtInteger: DoInteger;
    mtCardinal: DoCardinal;
    mtLongInt: DoLongInt;
    mtLongWord: DoLongWord;
    mtWord: DoWord;
    mtShortInt: DoShortInt;
    mtSmallInt: DoSmallInt;
  end;
end;

procedure TForm1.DoCardinal;
var
  Value: Cardinal;
begin
  ListBox1.Items.Add('Cardinal high value: ' + IntToStr(High(Value)));
  ListBox1.Items.Add('Cardinal low value: ' + IntToStr(Low(Value)));
  ListBox1.Items.Add('Size of Cardinal: ' + IntToStr(SizeOf(Value)) + ' bytes
➥or ' + IntToStr(8 * SizeOf(Value)) + ' bits.');
end;

procedure TForm1.DoLongWord;
var
  Value: LongWord;
begin
  ListBox1.Items.Add('LongWord high value: ' + IntToStr(High(Value)));
  ListBox1.Items.Add('LongWord low value: ' + IntToStr(Low(Value)));
  ListBox1.Items.Add('Size of LongWord: ' + IntToStr(SizeOf(Value)) + ' bytes
➥or ' + IntToStr(8 * SizeOf(Value)) + ' bits.');
end;

procedure TForm1.DoWord;
var
  Value: Word;
```

**LISTING 3.1**   Continued

```
begin
  ListBox1.Items.Add('Word high value: ' + IntToStr(High(Value)));
  ListBox1.Items.Add('Word low value: ' + IntToStr(Low(Value)));
  ListBox1.Items.Add('Size of Word: ' + IntToStr(SizeOf(Value)) + ' bytes or '
➥+ IntToStr(8 * SizeOf(Value)) + ' bits.');
end;

procedure TForm1.DoShortInt;
var
  Value: ShortInt;
begin
  ListBox1.Items.Add('ShortInt high value: ' + IntToStr(High(Value)));
  ListBox1.Items.Add('ShortInt low value: ' + IntToStr(Low(Value)));
  ListBox1.Items.Add('Size of ShortInt: ' + IntToStr(SizeOf(Value)) + ' bytes
➥or ' + IntToStr(8 * SizeOf(Value)) + ' bits.');
end;

procedure TForm1.DoSmallInt;
var
  Value: SmallInt;
begin
  ListBox1.Items.Add('SmallInt high value: ' + IntToStr(High(Value)));
  ListBox1.Items.Add('SmallInt low value: ' + IntToStr(Low(Value)));
  ListBox1.Items.Add('Size of SmallInt: ' + IntToStr(SizeOf(Value)) + ' bytes
➥or ' + IntToStr(8 * SizeOf(Value)) + ' bits.');
end;

end.
```

This program rather laboriously calls High and Low for all the integer types. Notice that it also uses the SizeOf function, which returns the size in bytes of any variable or type. The point of this program is to show you that you can discover this information at runtime.

You can learn even more about a type using Run Time Type Information (RTTI). An introduction to RTTI appears in the upcoming section "Floating-Point Types."

# Enumerated Types

All major languages have enumerated types. This is an ordinal type. In fact, enumerated types are really nothing more than a few numbers starting from 0 and rarely ranging much higher than 10. The interesting thing about these numbers is that you can give them names.

Consider this example:

```
procedure TForm1.Button1Click(Sender: TObject);
type
  TComputerLanguage = (clC, clCpp, clJava, clPascal, clVB);
var
  ComputerLanguage: TComputerLanguage;
begin
  ComputerLanguage := clPascal
end;
```

Here the values clC, clCpp, clJava, clPascal, and clVB are just fancy ways to write 0, 1, 2, 3, and 4. In short, enumerated types are just a way to associate numbers with names. However, if you want to associate numbers with names, you are always in danger of forgetting which number belongs to which name. For instance, you might want to reference Java and accidentally write 3, when what you meant to write was 2. To avoid confusion, the enumerated type enables you to associate a name with a number. Furthermore, you can enforce that relationship through Pascal's strong type checking. For instance, you can't assign even a valid identifier named clTunaFish to the variable ComputerLanguage unless it is part of the TComputerLanguage type.

> **NOTE**
>
> The letters cl prefacing each name are a Pascal convention. The convention says that you put the letters of the name of the type before the name. So, Computer *Language* becomes cl.

You can use the Ord routine to convert an enumerated value to a number:

```
i := Ord(clPascal);
```

In this case, i is set equal to 3. In fact, you can go from the number to the name, but that is a complex operation involving routines found in the TypInfo unit. The TypInfo unit will be discussed in Chapter 4, and in the next section "Floating-Point Types."

Here is an example by Bob Swart that shows a simple way to write out the name of a type:

```
program BobEnum;
{$APPTYPE CONSOLE}
type
  TEnum = (zero, one, two, three);
var
  E: TEnum;
```

```
begin
  E := TEnum(2); // E := two;
  if E = two then WriteLn('Two!');
  ReadLn
end.
```

## Floating-Point Types

Pascal has lots of floating point-types for helping you work with decimal numbers, or fractions of whole numbers. Table 3.3 lists the fundamental types you can choose from.

**TABLE 3.3**  The Fundamental Floating-Point Types—the Generic Type, Known as a `Real`, Is Currently Equivalent to a `Double`

| Type | Range |
|------|-------|
| Real48 | $2.9 \times 10^{-39}$ to $1.7 \times 10^{38}$ 11–12 6 |
| Single | $1.5 \times 10^{-45}$ to $3.4 \times 10^{38}$ 7–8 4 |
| Double | $5.0 \times 10^{-324}$ to $1.7 \times 10^{308}$ 15–16 8 |
| Extended | $3.6 \times 10^{-4951}$ to $1.1 \times 10^{4932}$ 19–20 10 |
| Comp | $-2^{63+1}$ to $2^{\wedge}63 - 1$ 19–20 8 |
| Currency | $-922337203685477.5808$ to $922337203685477.5807$ 19–20 8 |

The most commonly used type is the `Double`. However, there is a generic floating point type known as a `Real`. It is currently the same as a `Double`, much as an `Integer` is currently the same as a `LongInt`. If you declare your floating-point values to be `Reals`, they can be automatically converted to any new optimal floating-point type that might come along.

The `Comp` type is the floating-point type that is used the least frequently. In fact, it isn't really meant to represent floating-point numbers. In the bad old days of 16-bit computing, this used to be the best way to work with very large whole numbers. Now it has no function other than to support old code. If you need to work with really large `Integer` types, then you should now use the `Int64` type.

> **NOTE**
>
> Back in the aforementioned bad old days, Pascal used to have a set of routines for working with a type of unique floating-point type known as a `Real`. (This is not the same thing as the current `Real` type, but it's a strange 48-bit beast that was custom-

made by optimization-obsessed Borland programmers. Back in this time, the `Real` type and its associated code were considered to be very fast. However, those days are now little more than a memory. Modern operating systems and modern processors now have built-in routines that are superior to the once–ground-breaking code that supported the 48-bit `Real` type.

The current `Real` is the same as a `Double`. However, a type known as a `Real48` is compatible with the old `Real` type used long ago, when Windows was a failed project that provided fodder for jokes and everyone believed that Apple might end up ruling the computer desktop. If you are an old Pascal programmer who has some code dependant on the implementation of the old Pascal `Real` type, then use `Real48`.

Remember that `Real` types, which are synonymous with the `Double` type, are now back in fashion. I'm having trouble adopting to this new state of affairs because I'm used to thinking of `Reals` as being out-of-date. So, you will find a lot of `Doubles` in my code, but I am trying to make the move to using `Reals` instead. I never use `Real48s` because I have no code dependant on them.

## The `TBcd` and Floating-Point Accuracy

We now broach the treacherous topic of floating-point accuracy. This is a sea in which no ship is safe, and only caution can protect us from the reefs.

All experienced programmers know that floating-point types such as `Doubles` and `Singles` lose precision nearly every time they are part of a calculation. This loss of precision is usually not a problem in a standard math or graphics program, but it can be a serious issue in financial calculations. As a result, you should consider using the `Currency` type to avoid rounding errors. However, this is not a perfect solution.

The best way to avoid problems with rounding errors is to use the `TBcd` type, found in the `FMTBcd` unit. *BCD* stands for "binary coded decimal," and it is a widely used technology to avoid rounding errors when working with floating-point numbers. Borland did not invent the BCD technology any more than it invented the idea of the floating-point type. It's just a technology that it employs in this product.

Here is what the `TBcd` type looks like:

```
PBcd = ^TBcd;
TBcd  = packed record
  Precision: Byte;                        { 1..64 }
  SignSpecialPlaces: Byte;                { Sign:1, Special:1, Places:6 }
  Fraction: packed array [0..31] of Byte; { BCD Nibbles, 00..99 per Byte,
high Nibble 1st }
  end;
```

Each of the numbers in your floating-point type is stored in a *nibble*, which is 4 bits in size. You can specify the number of digits in your number in the `Precision` field, and you can specify the number of places after the decimal in the `SignSpecialPlaces` field. In practice, you rarely end up working so directly with this type. Instead, you can use a series of routines to make working with the `TBcd` type a more palatable exercise.

Kylix provides a large number of routines in the `FMTBcd` unit for manipulating BCD values. A large sampling of these routines is found in Listing 3.2. You should find the time to open the unit itself and examine it as well.

> **NOTE**
>
> In the Kylix editor, if you put your cursor over any unit in your uses clause and then press Ctrl+Enter, the source for that unit should open in your editor.

**LISTING 3.2**    Routines in `FMTBcd` That You Can Use to Help You Work with the BCD Type

```
procedure VarFMTBcdCreate(var ADest: Variant; const ABcd: TBcd); overload;
function VarFMTBcdCreate: Variant; overload;
function VarFMTBcdCreate(const AValue: string;
  Precision, Scale: Word): Variant; overload;
function VarFMTBcdCreate(const AValue: Double;
  Precision: Word = 18; Scale: Word = 4): Variant; overload;
function VarFMTBcdCreate(const ABcd: TBcd): Variant; overload;
function VarIsFMTBcd(const AValue: Variant): Boolean; overload;
function VarFMTBcd: TVarType;


// convert String/Double/Integer to BCD struct
function StrToBcd(const AValue: string): TBcd;
function TryStrToBcd(const AValue: string; var Bcd: TBcd): Boolean;
function DoubleToBcd(const AValue: Double): TBcd; overload;
procedure DoubleToBcd(const AValue: Double; var bcd: TBcd); overload;
function IntegerToBcd(const AValue: Integer): TBcd;
function VarToBcd(const AValue: Variant): TBcd;


function CurrToBCD(const Curr: Currency; var BCD: TBcd; Precision: Integer =
32;
  Decimals: Integer = 4): Boolean;


// Convert Bcd struct to string/Double/Integer
function BcdToStr(const Bcd: TBcd): string; overload;
function BcdToDouble(const Bcd: TBcd): Double;
```

**3**

**LISTING 3.2**  Continued

```
function BcdToInteger(const Bcd: TBcd; Truncate: Boolean = False): Integer;
function BCDToCurr(const BCD: TBcd; var Curr: Currency): Boolean;

// Formatting Bcd as string
function BcdToStrF(const Bcd: TBcd; Format: TFloatFormat;
  const Precision, Digits: Integer): string;
function FormatBcd(const Format: string; Bcd: TBcd): string;
function BcdCompare(const bcd1, bcd2: TBcd): Integer;
```

Most of these routines are encapsulations of technologies for converting back and forth from TBcd values to most major types. For instance, BcdToStr converts a TBcd value to a string, and StrToBcd performs the opposite task. However, there are more routines than the ones I show you here. Perhaps the best way to get up to speed is to simply look at the BCDVariant program, found in Listing 3.3.

**LISTING 3.3**  The BCDVariant Program Gives You a Number of Examples on How to Use the BCD Type

```
unit Main;

interface

uses
  SysUtils, Types, Classes,
  QGraphics, QControls, QForms,
  QDialogs, QStdCtrls;

type
  TForm1 = class(TForm)
    Button1: TButton;
    Button2: TButton;
    Button3: TButton;
    ListBox1: TListBox;
    procedure Button1Click(Sender: TObject);
    procedure Button2Click(Sender: TObject);
    procedure Button3Click(Sender: TObject);
    procedure SimpleMathButtonClick(Sender: TObject);
  private
    { Private declarations }
  public
    { Public declarations }
  end;
```

**LISTING 3.3**    Continued

```pascal
var
  Form1: TForm1;

implementation

uses
  FMTBcd;

{$R *.xfm}

procedure TForm1.Button1Click(Sender: TObject);
var
  B: TBcd;
  V: Variant;
begin
  V := VarFMTBcdCreate(36383.530534346, 32, 9);
  ListBox1.Items.Add(BCDToStr(VarToBCD(V)));
end;

procedure TForm1.Button2Click(Sender: TObject);
var
  B: TBcd;
  D: Double;
  V: Variant;
  S: String;
begin
  D := 32.346;
  V := VarFMTBcdCreate(D, 18, 3);
  B := VarToBcd(V);
  S := BcdToStr(B);
  ListBox1.Items.Add(S);
end;

procedure TForm1.Button3Click(Sender: TObject);
var
  C: Currency;
  D: Double;
  B: TBcd;
  V: Variant;
  S: String;
begin
  C := 33334.43;
  CurrToBCD(C, B, 32, 4);
  D := BcdToDouble(B);
```

**LISTING 3.3**    Continued

```
  S := Format('%m', [D]);
  ListBox1.Items.Add(S);
end;

procedure TForm1.SimpleMathButtonClick(Sender: TObject);
var
  V1, V2, V3: Variant;
  B1, B2, B3: TBcd;
  S1, S2: String;
begin
  V1 := VarFMTBcdCreate(3.5011, 32, 12);
  V2 := VarFMTBcdCreate(3.5020, 32, 12);
  V3 := V1 + V2;
  ListBox1.Items.Add(BcdToStr(VarToBcd(V3)));
  V3 := V1 * V2;
  ListBox1.Items.Add(BcdToStr(VarToBcd(V3)));
  V3 := V1 / V2;
  ListBox1.Items.Add(BcdToStr(VarToBcd(V3)));
  V3 := V1 - V2;
  ListBox1.Items.Add(BcdToStr(VarToBcd(V3)));
  B1 := VarToBcd(V1);
  B2 := VarToBcd(V2);
  S1 := BcdToStr(B1);
  S2 := BcdToStr(B2);
  BcdAdd(B1, B2, B3);
  ListBox1.Items.Add(S1 + ' + ' + S2 + '=' + BcdToStr(B3));
  BcdMultiply(B1, B2, B3);
  ListBox1.Items.Add(S1 + ' * ' + S2 + '=' + BcdToStr(B3));
  BcdDivide(B1, B2, B3);
  ListBox1.Items.Add(S1 + ' / ' + S2 + '='  + BcdToStr(B3));
  BcdSubtract(B1, B2, B3);
  ListBox1.Items.Add(S1 + ' - ' + S2 + '='  + BcdToStr(B3));
end;

end.
```

The most important code found here is seen in the lines at the beginning of the
`SimpleMathButtonClick` method:

```
  V1 := VarFMTBcdCreate(3.5011, 32, 12);
  V2 := VarFMTBcdCreate(3.5020, 32, 12);
  V3 := V1 + V2;
  ListBox1.Items.Add(BcdToStr(VarToBcd(V3)));
  V3 := V1 * V2;
  ListBox1.Items.Add(BcdToStr(VarToBcd(V3)));
```

This code uses `VarFMTBcdCreate` to create two BCD numbers as `Variants`. Pass the number that you want to encapsulate in a BCD type in the first parameter. In the second parameter, pass the number of digits used to capture your number. For instance, in the first case shown previously, I could safely pass 5 because there are only five digits in 3.5011. Passing 32 is probably overkill. The last parameter is the number of those digits that appear after the decimal point. Again, 12 is more than ample for the job because there are only four numbers after the decimal point. (Obviously, these later two values are simply being used to fill in the `Precision` and `SignSpecialPlaces` fields of the `TBcd` type.)

The big question here is not how to call `VarFMTBcdCreate`, but why I am calling it. After all, this function returns not a `TBcd` value, but a `Variant`. I create `Variants` because you can directly add, multiply, divide, and subtract `TBcd` values when they are inside `Variants`:

```
V3 := V1 + V2;
```

Go back again to the declaration for `TBcd`. Clearly, there is no simple way to add or multiply values of type `TBcd`. However, if we convert them to `Variants`, the chore of performing basic math with `TBcd` values is marvelously simplified!

> **NOTE**
>
> For now, you need know little more than that `Variants` are like variables declared in a BASIC program, or like variables in Perl or Python. They are very loosely typed—or, at least, *appear* to be loosely typed. You can assign an `Integer`, `Real`, `Byte`, `String` or `Object`, to a `Variant`. In fact, you can assign almost anything to a `Variant`.
>
> Kylix will allow you to implement particular kinds of `Variants`, and then give them interesting characteristics. For instance, you can create a kind of `Variant` that handles BCD values, and then you can teach this kind of `Variant` to do all sorts of interesting things In particular, you can teach it to handle addition, multiplication, and division. Clearly, this is the closest thing that Pascal has to the wonders of C++ operator overloading. If you are a Delphi programmer, you might find my definition of `Variants` at odds with what you learned about `Variants` in the Windows world. That is because `Variants` in Linux (and also in Delphi 6) do wondrous things that they did not do in the old Delphi 5 days.

Later in the `MathButtonClick` method, you see that there is a way to add, subtract, multiply, and divide `TBcd` variables without converting them to `Variants`:

```
BcdAdd(B1, B2, B3);
ListBox1.Items.Add(S1 + ' ' + ' ' + S2 + '=' + BcdToStr(B3));
BcdMultiply(B1, B2, B3);
```

```
ListBox1.Items.Add(S1 + ' * ' + S2 + '=' + BcdToStr(B3));
BcdDivide(B1, B2, B3);
ListBox1.Items.Add(S1 + ' / ' + S2 + '='  + BcdToStr(B3));
BcdSubtract(B1, B2, B3);
ListBox1.Items.Add(S1 + ' - ' + S2 + '='  + BcdToStr(B3));
```

This code shows you the `BcdAdd`, `BcdMultiply`, `BcdDivide`, and `BcdSubtract` routines, all of which do precisely what their names imply. However, most programmers would probably prefer the `Variant` code shown earlier because it is provides a more intuitive syntax.

Again, the point of the `TBcd` type is to ensure that you have no loss of precision when working with floating-point numbers. It goes without saying that there is overhead associated with the `TBcd` type and that, if possible, you should stick with `Doubles` or `Reals` if speed is an issue for you.

I should perhaps make clear that floating-point types are not inordinately inaccurate. The problems that you encounter with them occur when you do the kind of rounding necessary when working with money. If you don't have to round the values that you are working with to two decimal places, the standard floating-point types will probably meet your needs in all but the most rigorous of circumstances. More specifically, `Doubles` will generally be accurate to at least seven or eight decimal places, which in most cases is all the accuracy you will need. But if you keep rounding those values back to two decimal places, as you do when working with money, then the process of rounding the numbers will lead to errors of at least one penny.

## Pascal Strings

I've included this section on strings because this feature of the language has a number of very confusing aspects. Under normal circumstances, Pascal strings are very easy to use. However, there happen to be a number of different kinds of Pascal strings, and that proliferation of types really cries out for a clear explanation.

Object Pascal has four different kinds of strings: `ShortStrings`, `AnsiStrings`, `PChars`, and `WideStrings`. All Object Pascal strings except `WideStrings` are, at heart, little more than an array of `Char`. A `WideString` is an array of `WideChars`. A `Char` is 8 bits in size, while a `WideChar` is 16 bits—going on 32 bits—in size. I will explain more about `WideStrings` and `WideChars` at the end of this section on strings.

The following code fragment gives you examples of the types of things you can do with a `Char` or a `String`. The code explicitly uses `AnsiStrings`, but most of it would work the same regardless of whether the variables S and S2 were declared as `ShortStrings`, `PChars`, or `AnsiStrings`. Of course, I will explain the differences among these three types later in this section. Here is the example:

```
var
  a, b: Char;
  S, S2: String;
begin
  S := 'Sam';      // Valid: Set a string equal to a string literal
  S := '1';        // Valid: Set a string equal to character
  S := '';         // Valid: Set a string equal to an empty string literal
  a := '1';        // Valid: Set a Char equal to a character literal
  b := a;          // Valid: Set a Char equal to Char
  a := 'Sam';      // Invalid: You can't set a Char equal to a string
  a := #65;        // Valid: Set a Char equal to a character literal
  a := Char(10);   // Valid: Set a Char equal to an integer converted to a char
  a := S[1];       // Valid: Set a Char equal to the first Char in a string
  S2 := 'Sam'#10;  // Valid: Set a string equal to a string with Char appended
  S := S + S2;     // Valid: Concatenate two strings
  if (S = S2) then
    ShowMessage('S and S2 contain equivalent strings');
  if (S > S2) then
    ShowMessage('S would appear in a dictionary after S2');
end;
```

The Pascal language originated in Europe, so strings follow the traditional European syntax and are set off with single rather than double quotes. The code shown here declares two Chars and two Strings. The first statement after the begin correctly sets the String equal to a string literal that contains three letters. You can also set a String equal to a string literal that contains a single character or no characters. You can set a Char equal to a single character such as a, b, A, or B. You cannot set a Char equal to a string such as Sam. You can, however, set a Char equal to the first character in a String, as in a := S[1]. You can also set a String equal to the 65th character in a character set by writing this syntax: a := #65. In the standard ANSI character set, the 65th character is a capital A, so this is equivalent to setting a Char equal to the letter A: a := 'A';. The expression Char(10) is equivalent to the expression #10. Both expressions reference the 10th ANSI character, which is usually the linefeed character. It is also legal to append or insert characters into a string using the following syntax: S := 'Sam'#10;. This adds a linefeed to the end of the string. Notice that the character is appended outside the closing quote.

---

**C/C++, JAVA NOTE**

In Java or C++ you would write "Sam\n" rather than 'Sam'#10. The two statements are equivalent.

Studying the examples in this section should give you some sense of how to use strings in your programs. Notice that in one of the examples, you can use the + operator to concatenate two strings. You can also use the < and > operators to test whether a String is larger than another String, and you can use the = operator to test whether two Strings point to identical sets of characters.

---

### JAVA NOTE

The = operator in Pascal does the same thing as the String::equals method does in Java. You are not testing to see whether the strings point at the same memory; you are testing to see whether they point at strings that contain the same sets of characters.

---

## ShortStrings

The ShortString is the oldest kind of Pascal string, and it is rarely in use today. A ShortString is essentially a glorified array of Char with a maximum length of 256 characters. The first byte, the *length byte*, designates the length of the string. ShortStrings are not null-terminated; their length is determined only by the length byte. Remember that the length byte takes up 1 of the 256 bytes in the string, so the longest possible ShortString contains 255 characters. The limitation on the length of a ShortString exists because the first byte is 8 bits in size, and you can fit only 256 possible values in 8 bits.

---

### NOTE

ShortStrings are used mostly for backward compatibility with old Pascal code. However, you might use a ShortString if you need to be sure that a block of memory has a prescribed size. For instance, you know that ShortStrings are usually 256 bytes long, so if you want to create an array of 4 Strings and you want to be sure that it occupies exactly 1,024 bytes of memory, regardless of the length of each string (and assuming that each string is 255 characters in length or less), you might decide to use ShortStrings rather than AnsiStrings. ShortStrings can also be useful in variant records, as described in the later section of this chapter titled "Variant Records."

---

Here is the syntax for using a ShortString:

```
var
  S: ShortString;
```

```
begin
  S := 'Hello';
end;
```

This string is represented in memory as such: [#5][H][e][l][l][o]. The first byte of the string, which the user never sees, represents the length of the string. The remaining bytes contain the string itself.

You can also declare a ShortString like this:

```
var
  S: String[10];
```

This string contains only 10 characters rather than 255. More commonly, you might declare a type of string that is a custom length and then reuse that type throughout your program:

```
type
  String5 = String[5];
  String15 = String[15]
var
  S5: String5;
  S15: String15;
```

The compiler appears not to object to you assigning strings larger than 5 or 16 characters to the types declared previously. However, the string that you create will display only the appropriate number of characters. The others will be ignored.

Again, I want to stress that ShortStrings are not in common use today. In Java parlance, one might even say that they are *deprecated*, although I doubt that they will ever cease to be a part of the language.

## AnsiStrings

AnsiStrings are also known as *long strings*. On 32-bit platforms, the maximum length for an AnsiString is 2GB. This type is the native Object Pascal string and the kind that you will use in most programs.

If you declare a variable as a String, it is assumed to be an AnsiString. In other words, if you do not specify that a string is an AnsiString, a ShortString, or a custom string such as String[10], you can assume that it is an AnsiString. The one exception to this rule occurs if you explicitly turn off the $H directive, where H can be thought of as standing for "huge" strings. In such cases, all strings are assumed to be ShortStrings unless explicitly declared otherwise. If you place the {$H-} directive at the top of a module, that entire module will use ShortStrings by default. If you deselect Project, Options, Compiler, Huge Strings from the menu, your entire program will use ShortStrings by default.

> **NOTE**
>
> When using the default key mappings, you can press Ctrl+O+O (that's the letter O) to get a list of all the compiler directives for the current module.

When a CLX method needs to be passed a string, it almost always expects to be passed an AnsiString. The AnsiString is the native type expected by CLX controls. Despite the simplicity of this statement, there are some twists and turns to it. As a result, I will discuss this in more depth both in this section and in the section "PChars."

An AnsiString is a pointer type, although you should rarely, if ever, need to explicitly allocate memory for it. The compiler notes the times when you make an assignment to a string, and it calls routines at that time for allocating the memory for the string. (Many of these routines are in System.pas, and you can step right into them with the compiler on some versions of Kylix.)

> **NOTE**
>
> You will find that many of the routines in the System unit use Assembly language. In general, they follow one of two different formats:
>
> ```
> procedure Foo;
> asm
>   mov oax, 1
> end;
>
> procedure FooBar;
> var
>   X: Integer;
> begin
>   X := 7;
>   asm
>     mov eax, X;
>   end;
> end;
> ```
>
> Procedure Foo uses asm where a normal Pascal procedure would use begin. In this type of procedure, all the code is written in Assembler until the closing end statement. The second example embeds an asm statement in a begin..end block. Both syntaxes are valid. When using the debugger, after starting your program, choose View, Debug Windows, CPU to step through your code. I will talk more about debugging in Chapter 5. However, I am not going to say anything more about Assembler in this book. Use System.pas as a reference if you are interested in this technology.

The only time that you might need to allocate memory for an AnsiString is if you are going to pass it to a routine that does not know about AnsiStrings—that is, when you are passing it a routine written in some language other than Pascal or when you are passing it to some exceptionally peculiar Pascal routine. In such a case, you would normally want to pass a PChar rather than an AnsiString. But it is possible to pass an AnsiString to such a routine; you allocate memory for it first and then pass it. (Use the SetLength routine to allocate memory for an AnsiString, as described at the very end of this section.)

Routines that take PChars are generally routines that are written in some other language, such as C or C++. If you pass an AnsiString into such a routine and you expect it to pass the string back with a new value in it (passing by reference), you probably need to allocate memory for the string before passing it. If you are passing an AnsiString into an Object Pascal routine, you can assume that the compiler will know how to allocate memory for it. In your day-to-day practice as an Object Pascal programmer, you should never need to think about allocating memory for an AnsiString. The cases when you need to do it are very rare and are not the type that beginning or intermediate-level programmers are ever likely to encounter.

AnsiStrings are null-terminated. This means that the end of the string is marked with #0, the first character in the ANSI character set. This is the same way that you mark the end of a string in C/C++. AnsiStrings are different than C/C++ strings, however, because they are usually prefaced with two 32-bit characters; one character holds the length of the string, and the other holds the reference count for a string. The only time that an AnsiString is not prefaced by these values is when the string variable references a 0-length string. As a programmer, you will almost certainly never have an occasion to explicitly reference either of these values.

It is a simple matter to understand the 32-bit value that holds the length of the string. It is similar to the length byte in a ShortString, except that it is 32 bits in size rather than 8 bits, so it can reference a very large string. What is the point, though, of the 32-bit value used for reference counting?

Reference counting is a means of saving memory and decreasing the time necessary to make string assignments. If two strings contain the same values, it is thriftiest to have them both point at the same memory. If possible, Object Pascal will do this by default. (You can override this behavior, as explained later in this section in the note on the UniqueString procedure.) When reference counting, the compiler simply points a second string at the memory allocated for a first string and then ups the reference count of the strings. Consider the following code fragment:

```
var
  Sam: String;
  Fred: String;
begin
```

```
  Sam := 'Look at all beings with the eyes of compassion. -- Lotus Sutra';
  Fred := Sam; // Reference count incremented, no memory allocated for chars.
  Fred := 'Learn to ' + Fred; // Strings not equal, memory must be allocated.
end;
```

When you set `Sam` equal to the quote from the Lotus Sutra, the compiler allocates sufficient memory for the variable `Sam`. When you set `Fred` equal to `Sam`, no new memory for character values is allocated. Instead, the reference count for the string is incremented and `Fred` is pointed at the same string as `Sam`. This kind of assignment is very fast and also saves memory. In short, you avoid both the extra memory consumed by allocating memory for the characters in the string and also the extra time required to copy the memory from one location in memory to another.

So far, so good. But what happens if you change one of the values that either variable addresses? That is what happens in the third line of the code fragment. When you change the value of `Fred` in the last line of the method, new memory is allocated for `Fred` and the reference count for the string is decremented by 1. At this point, `Fred` and `Sam` point at two entirely separate strings.

> **NOTE**
>
> You can use the `UniqueString` procedure to force a string to have a reference count of 1, even if it would normally have a higher count.

I want to stress that all these complicated machinations mean that you normally don't have to think about string memory allocation at all. You can just use a string type in a manner similar to the way you would use an `Integer` type. The compiler handles the allocation, and you don't have to think about it. However, it helps to know the inner workings of the `AnsiString` type, both so that you know what happens in unusual cases and so that you can design your code to be as efficient as possible.

Strings are generally allocated for you automatically. However, you can use the `SetLength` procedure to set or reset the length of a string:

```
var
  S: string;
begin
  SetLength(S, 10);
  SetLength(S, 12);
end;
```

Many routines built into the Object Pascal language can help you work with strings. In particular, see the FmtStr and Format functions. You might also want to browse the entire SysUtils unit and become familiar with the many useful routines found there. Also see the LCodeBox unit that ships with this book.

## PChars

A PChar is a standard null-terminated string and is structurally exactly like a C string. In fact, this type was created primarily to provide compatibility with C class libraries. In particular, it was created for compatibility with the Windows API, which is written in C. It has proven to be a generally useful type, and it will come in handy when you are calling functions from the Linux C libraries such as Libc.

---

**NOTE**

To call most of the routines in the Libc library, just add Libc to your uses clause and go to work. This process is described in more depth in Chapter 6, "Understanding the Linux Environment."

---

The native Object Pascal string type is known as a String—or, more properly, as a long string or AnsiString. However, in most cases you are free to use either the native String type or the PChar type. Both types of strings are null-terminated. The difference between them is that a Pascal string has data placed in front of the String that determines the string's length and its reference count.

In most cases in a Kylix program, you should use the AnsiString type. A Kylix control such as a TEdit would never expect you to pass it a PChar. However, it is usually legal, but unorthodox, to pass it a PChar. This is confusing enough that an example might be helpful. Consider the following block of code:

```
procedure TForm1.Button1Click(Sender: TObject);
var
  Sam: PChar;
begin
  Sam := 'Fred';
  Edit1.Text := Sam;
end;
```

This code will compile and run without error. In short, it is legal to assign a PChar to a property that is declared to be of type AnsiString. (Actually the Text property is declared to be of type TCaption, but TCaption is declared to be of type String.)

> **NOTE**
>
> CLX is built on top of the C++ library called Qt. As a result, many of the controls in CLX ultimately end up working with native C strings, or a C String object. However, none of that is any concern to us as Pascal programmers. CLX is expecting AnsiStrings and, when you work with CLX controls, you should use the native String type.

You can assign a PChar to a string directly. However, if you assign a String to a PChar, you need to typecast it:

```
var
  S: string;
  P: PChar;
begin
  P := PChar(S);
```

As you recall, an AnsiString is simply a PChar with some data in front of it. This data appears at a negative offset from the pointer to the AnsiString. As a result, typecasting the AnsiString as a PChar is really just a confirmation that *from the pointer to the AnsiString and onward*, an AnsiString is nothing more than a PChar. You will use this typecasting technique quite often if you need to pass AnsiStrings to routines written in C that are expecting a regular C string rather than an AnsiString.

Once the decision was made to make PChars part of Object Pascal there needed to be a set of routines to help you work with such strings. These routines are based closely on the functions you would use for manipulating strings in a C/C++ program. For instance, these routines have names such as StrLen, StrCat, StrPos, and StrScan. Again, you should look in the SysUtils unit for more information on these routines. You will find that there are dozens of such routines and that they are quite flexible and powerful.

## WideStrings

WideStrings are very much like AnsiStrings, except that they point at wide characters of 16 bits rather than normal Chars of 8 bits. These large characters, known as WideChars, are a means of manipulating Unicode characters. Unicode in particular, and WideChars, in general, provide a means for working with large character sets that will not fit in the 256 bits of a Char. For instance, the kanji character sets from Asia have thousands of characters in them. You can't capture them using standard AnsiStrings; instead, you must use WideStrings.

> **NOTE**
>
> In Windows, the native wide character type (WCHAR) is 16 bits in size. In Linux, wide characters are 32 bits in size. The Kylix team decided to reuse the 16 bit WideChar in place for Windows rather than to rewrite the routines explicitly for the 32-bit Linux WideChar. As a result, your programs work with 16-bit WideChars, even though Linux defaults to 32-bit WideChars. Unless we are invaded from Alpha Centauri, where very large character sets are in common use, you should find that 16-bit WideChars are large enough for all practical purposes.

Starting with Kylix and Delphi 6, WideStrings are reference counted just as AnsiStrings are reference counted. In fact, you use a WideString exactly as you would use an AnsiString:

```
procedure TForm1.Button1Click(Sender: TObject);
var
  S: WideString;
begin
  S := 'Sam';
  Edit1.Text := S;
end;
```

This example shows that you can convert an AnsiString to a WideString and also convert a WideString to an AnsiString through the simple use of the assignment operator. In Kylix and Delphi 6, code based on WideStrings is actually quite efficient. If you have good reason to use WideStrings, go ahead and use them. The compiler handles them quite easily.

This is the end of the section on Strings. Next up are typecasts, a technology used very widely in Kylix programs. After that, we will look at the array and record types, and then we'll take a quick tour of Object Pascal pointers.

## Typecasts

Typecasts can be used to coerce a type declared one way to be treated as some other type that descends from it. For instance, in the following code a typecast is used to enable an object declared as type TPersistent to be treated as a TStringList:

```
procedure TForm1.Button2Click(Sender: TObject);
var
  F: TPersistent;
  L: TStringList;
begin
  L := TStringList(F);
end;
```

You perform a typecast by stating the name of the type that you want to declare and then placing the object that you want to typecast in parenthesis. The compiler is smart enough to know that this is a typecast, not a function call. The user can often make the same deduction simply by seeing that TStringList begins with the telltale T, which stands for "type." That particular initial consonant gives away the fact that TStringList is a type, not a function.

## The as and is Operators and the Sender Parameter

Typecasts are an essential part of working with a language that supports polymorphism. In many Kylix programs, the IDE generates event handlers that are passed objects declared to be one type but that are actually descendants of the type passed. The classic example of this is the Sender parameter, seen in many event handlers:

```
procedure TForm1.Button1Click(Sender: TObject);
begin

end;
```

The Button1Click method in a typical Delphi application is called when the user clicks on Button1. In that case, the Sender parameter really contains a TButton object. Flexibility is gained, however, if you declare the parameter as a TObject. The declaration enables you to pass any Pascal object to this method, not just a TButton.

> **NOTE**
>
> All Object Pascal classes must descend from TObject or one of its descendants. Even if you declare an object to have no ancestor, the Pascal compiler automatically descends the class from TObject. You simply can't declare an Object Pascal class that does not descend from TObject or one of its descendants. As a result of this rule, it is legal to pass any object in the Sender parameter of the Button1Click method. This extraordinary flexibility is possible because all these objects, by definition, descend from TObject.

Let's look at a practical example of how declaring the Button1Click method to take a TObject might be useful in a real program. Imagine that a message handler that you want to respond to clicks on not only a TButton, but also a TBitButton and TSpeedButton. The previous declaration could work with any of those types because they are all descendants of TObject. More particularly, the magic of polymorphism grants TButton, TBitButton, or TSpeedButton the capability to masquerade as a lowly TObject.

> **NOTE**
>
> Never forget the hierarchical nature of polymorphism: The king can masquerade as a pawn, but a pawn cannot pretend to be a king. A `TButton` can go disguised as a `TObject`, but a `TObject` cannot put on airs and pretend to be a `TButton`.

Here is how you can get at the object passed in the `Sender` parameter:

```
procedure TForm1.Button1Click(Sender: TObject);
var
  Button: TButton;
begin
  Button := TButton(Sender);
end;
```

As you can see, you need do nothing more than perform a simple typecast, and the `Sender` object is uncloaked and its true nature as an instance of `TButton` is revealed. In this case, the typecast again plays the role of the truth-teller, stripping off the object's disguise.

But doesn't trouble lurk amid the players of this game of cat and mouse? What would happen if the truth-teller were wrong? If you typecast a `Sender` object as a `TButton`, but it was really a `TBitButton`, `TSpeedButton`, `TPanel`, or something else passed unexpectedly, your typecast would be allowed at compile time, but an exception would be raised at runtime. Here is what you can do in such cases:

```
procedure TForm1.Button1Click(Sender: TObject);
var
  Button: TButton;
begin
  if Sender is TButton then
    Button := TButton(Sender);
end;
```

This code uses the `is` operator to test whether `Sender` is of type `TButton`. If it is, the `if` statement evaluates to `true` and the call succeeds. If it is not, the second line attempting the typecast is never called.

There is another way to perform a typecast that is perhaps a bit more modern than the way I have shown you so far:

```
procedure TForm1.Button1Click(Sender: TObject);
var
  Button: TButton;
begin
  Button := Sender as TButton;
end;
```

This code yields that same result as writing `Button := TButton(Sender)`. The difference is that the code will raise an exception if `Sender` is not of type `TButton`. The as operator is a prophylactic ensuring that the typecast will not be made if it is not valid. I also find the code easy to read because it cannot be mistaken as a method call, per the discussion earlier in this section. On the other hand, the code might take longer to execute than the other kind of typecast because it is adding the overhead of type checking. (An actual ruling on the performance of the two forms of typecasts will have to be left to someone else because I am not an expert in this kind of performance issue. But certainly the additional type checking must add at least some overhead to your program.)

The as operator is most typically used in statements that look like this:

```
procedure TForm1.Button2Click(Sender: TObject);
var
  F: TPersistent;
  L: TStringList;
begin
  (F as TStringList).Add('Sam');
end;
```

Here you can see the way parentheses have been added to give precedence to the as operator and ensure that the compiler can make proper sense of your statement.

Hopefully you now understand the basics of how typecasts work in an Object Pascal program. If you still feel that you could use more enlightenment on this issue, just be patient—the subject will come up numerous times throughout the course of this book.

## Arrays

Pascal is a very clean and easy-to-read language. If you can write code at all, you should be able to understand the basics of the Pascal syntax. The Pascal array syntax is no exception to this rule. Artfully constructed and robustly engineered, Pascal arrays are a powerful feature of the language.

Here is how to declare an array of `Integers` in Pascal:

```
procedure TForm1.Button1Click(Sender: TObject);
var
  MyArray: array [0..10] of Integer;
  MyNum: Integer;
begin
  MyArray[0] := 1;
  MyNum := MyArray[0];
end;
```

In this code, you find an array of 11 `Integer`s. The first member of the array is at offset 0, and the last is at offset 10. The syntax for capturing this construction is simplicity itself. It is hard to imagine how the concept of an array could be expressed more elegantly or more clearly.

Pascal arrays are very flexible. Note that you can declare not only the top of the range of values in an array, but also the bottom:

```
procedure TForm1.Button1Click(Sender: TObject);
var
  MyArray: array [12..24] of Integer;
  MyNum: Integer;
begin
  MyArray[12] := 1;
  MyNum := MyArray[12];
end;
```

In this example, the first element of the array is at offset 12, and the last is at 24. You can discover at runtime the range of values in an array:

```
procedure TForm1.Button1Click(Sender: TObject);
var
  MyArray: array [12..24] of Integer;
  HighValue, LowValue: Integer;
begin
  HighValue := High(MyArray);
  LowValue := Low(MyArray);
  Label1.Caption := 'High Value: ' + IntToStr(HighValue);
  Label2.Caption := 'Low Value: ' + IntToStr(LowValue);
end;
```

The `High` function returns the upper limit of an array, which, in this case, is 24. `Low` returns the low range, which, in this case, is 12.

## Array Constants

When I pick up a new language, I always seem to struggle to find an example of how to declare array constants. This next sample shows two array constants, one with `Integer`s and the other with `String`s:

```
procedure TForm1.Button1Click(Sender: TObject);
type
  TMyStringArray = array[0..2] of String;
const
  MyIntArray: array[0..3] of Integer = (1, 2, 3, 4);
  MyStringArray: TMyStringArray = ('One', 'Two', 'Three');
```

```
begin
  ListBox1.Items.Add(IntToStr(MyIntArray[0])); // prints 1
  ListBox1.Items.Add(MyStringArray[0]); // prints 'one'
end;
```

In this example, I declare the type of the Integer array in the const statement and the type of the String array in a type section. I do this simply to show that, depending on your needs or preferences, you can use either syntax.

## Dynamic Arrays and Arrays of Objects

Unlike C/C++, Pascal has no trouble handling arrays of objects. The following syntax discovers all the buttons on a form, places them in an array, and gives you access to their properties and methods:

```
procedure TForm1.Button3Click(Sender: TObject);
var
  ButtonArray: array of TButton;
  i, j, Num: Integer;
begin
  Num := 0;
  for i := 0 to ComponentCount - 1 do
    if Components[i] is TButton then
      Inc(Num);

  SetLength(ButtonArray, Num);

  j := 0;
  for i := 0 to ComponentCount - 1 do
    if Components[i] is TButton then begin
      ButtonArray[j] := TButton(Components[i]);
      Inc(j);
    end;

  for i := 0 to High(ButtonArray) do
    ListBox1.Items.Add(ButtonArray[i].Caption);
end;
```

The Button3Click method shows the Pascal language doing all sorts of glorious thing to delight and amuse us. The code discovers all the TButton objects on a form, declares an array just large enough to hold these buttons, and then places the buttons in the array. Finally, the captions of each button are placed in a list box, as shown in Figure 3.1.

ButtonArray is declared to be an array of TButton, with no declared bottom or top range. Instead, the range of the array will be discovered at runtime.

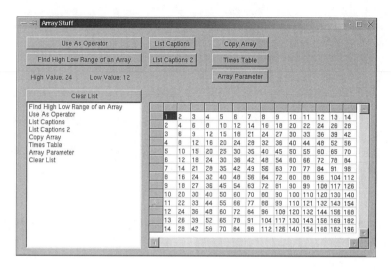

**FIGURE 3.1**

*A list box is put to use holding the captions of each button placed on this form.*

To find out how many elements we need in the array, the code makes use of information maintained by the main form of this application. In particular, all forms maintain a list of the components that have been dropped on them.

The program uses the `Form1.ComponentCount` property to determine how many components are on the form:

```
for i := 0 to ComponentCount - 1 do
```

Then each element of the array of components maintained by the main form is iterated over and is checked to see if it is a button:

```
if Components[i] is TButton then
```

Perhaps some clarity could be gained if these methods were written thus:

```
procedure TForm1.Button3Click(Sender: TObject);
var
  ButtonArray: array of TButton;
  i, j, Num: Integer;
begin
  Num := 0;
  for i := 0 to Self.ComponentCount - 1 do
    if Self.Components[i] is TButton then
      Inc(Num);
```

In this rewrite of the first lines of the `Button3Click` method, I make explicit the fact that `ComponentCount` and the `Components` array both belong to `Form1`.

---

**C/C++, JAVA**
**NOTE**

Object Pascal uses the term `Self` where Java or C++ would use `this`. Depending on your frame of mind, this personification of objects could be appealing or distracting. Despite the different flavors associated with the two terms, their meaning is ultimately identical.

---

When you know the number of buttons that were dropped on the form, you can set the size of the array of buttons:

```
SetLength(ButtonArray, Num);
```

The `SetLength` method does exactly what you would expect: It allocates memory in the array for the number of buttons that you have dropped on the form.

---

**NOTE**

You will perhaps recall that `SetLength` can also be used to set the length as an `AnsiString`. Because a string is really just an array of `Char`, this is not quite the coincidence that it might appear at first. Other functions that you can use on both types include `Copy` and `Length`.

---

The next chunk of code simply iterates over the components again, adding the buttons into the array as each is discovered:

```
for i := 0 to ComponentCount - 1 do
  if Components[i] is TButton then begin
    ButtonArray[j] := TButton(Components[i]);
    Inc(J);
  end;
```

Finally, the code displays the names of the buttons in a list box:

```
for i := 0 to High(ButtonArray) do
  ListBox1.Items.Add(ButtonArray[i].Caption);
```

Note that the syntax for accessing the members of the array of buttons is utterly clean and intuitive:

```
ButtonArray[i].Caption
```

It turns out that the `SetLength` procedure can be used not only to allocate memory for a `String`, but also to reallocate it. The following rewrite of the `Button3Click` method shows how to put this to use:

```pascal
procedure TForm1.Button3Click(Sender: TObject);
var
  ButtonArray: array of TButton;
  i, Num: Integer;
begin
  Num := 0;
  for i := 0 to Self.ComponentCount - 1 do
    if Self.Components[i] is TButton then begin
      Inc(Num);
      SetLength(ButtonArray, Num);
      ButtonArray[Num - 1] := TButton(Components[i]);
    end;

  for i := 0 to High(ButtonArray) do
    ListBox1.Items.Add(ButtonArray[i].Caption);
end;
```

Here the method is shortened and cleaned up a bit by continually reallocating the memory for the `ButtonArray` with the `SetLength` method.

> **NOTE**
>
> You might expect that repeatedly reallocating memory has some overhead associated with it, so it is possible that this second solution is not necessarily any faster than the first technique. People who are interested in such matters can explore the matter further on their own. Unless you are using these methods in a large, frequently called loop, don't worry about using one method or the other—they both execute in essentially zero time.

If you want to shorten the length of a dynamic array, use the `Copy` function:

```pascal
procedure TForm1.Button5Click(Sender: TObject);
const
  BigLen = 24;
  SmallLen = 12;
```

3

BASIC PASCAL
SYNTAX

```
var
  MyArray: array of Double;
  i: Integer;
begin
  SetLength(MyArray, BigLen);
  for i := 0 to High(MyArray) do
    MyArray[i] := Sqr(i);

  MyArray := Copy(MyArray, 0, SmallLen);

  for i := 0 to High(MyArray) do
    ListBox1.Items.Add(Format('Value of array = %f', [MyArray[i]]));
end;
```

This code first sets the length of MyArray to 24. Next it assigns values to each member of the array. The array is then shortened to length 12. Finally, the program displays the elements of the array to show that the shortening did not destroy the values that it held. Note that you can use High, Low and Length on dynamic arrays, just as you can on normal arrays and on strings.

Pascal arrays can contain multiple dimensions. Here is an example of how multi-dimensional arrays works:

```
procedure TForm1.Button6Click(Sender: TObject);
const
  XSize = 5;
  YSize = 5;
var
  MyTwoDim: array[0..XSize, 0..YSize] of Integer;
  i, j: Integer;
begin
  for i := 0 to YSize do
    for j := 0 to XSize do
      MyTwoDim[j, i] := j * i;

  for i := 0 to YSize do
    for j := 0 to XSize do
      StringGrid1.Cells[j, i] := IntToStr(MyTwoDim[j, i]);
end;
```

The code declares a two-dimensional array of Integer. Both dimensions contain five elements. The code then fills out the array with the first five elements of the multiplication table. A TStringGrid allows the program to display the content of the array, as shown in Figure 3.2. The key to the TStringGrid object is the Cells property, which represents the array of cells in the grid. The syntax for using the Cells property is the same as for using a two-dimensional array of String.

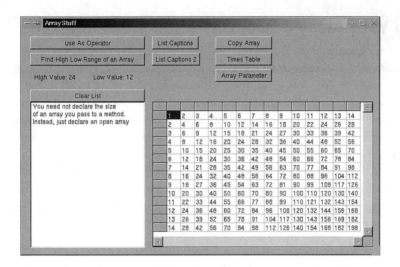

**FIGURE 3.2**

*The* TStringGrid *object from the Additional page in the Component Palette can help you display your data in a clean and logical fashion.*

You may declare an array in the normal fashion and then pass it to a method as a parameter. In such cases, you need not specify the size of the parameter in the function that you pass to it:

```pascal
procedure TForm1.ShowArray(MyArray: array of String);
var
  i: Integer;
begin
  for i := 0 to High(MyArray) do
    ListBox1.Items.Add(MyArray[i]);
end;

procedure TForm1.Button7Click(Sender: TObject);
var
  MyArray: array [0..2] of String;
begin
  MyArray[0] := 'You need not declare the size';
  MyArray[1] := 'of an array you pass to a method.';
  MyArray[2] := 'Instead, just declare an open array';
  ShowArray(MyArray);
end;
```

Here you can see that I do not explicitly state the size of the array to be passed to the ShowArray method. Instead, I declare it as an open array of String and then use the High method to determine its actual dimensions.

## Debug Your Arrays: Turn on Range Checking

When developing applications that use arrays, it is best to select Project, Options, Compiler and turn on Range Checking. Range Checking is off, by default. This is a technique used by the compiler to check that you are not trying to write past the end of an array. For instance, if you allocate an array of 10 bytes in size and try to write to the nonexistent 11th byte of the array, the Range Checking mechanism would catch the error and raise an exception. Without range checking, sometimes writing past the end of an array will raise an exception; at other times, it will corrupt the memory of a program in some subtle and seemingly undetectable manner. This can lead to debugging sessions that last for hours or even days. If you turn on Range Checking, however, the error will appear immediately, and it will be clearly flagged. After debugging your code that uses arrays, you should turn off Range Checking because it slows down your code.

In this section on arrays, I discussed the basic facts about arrays in a few short paragraphs and then covered the more complex subject of dynamic arrays and open arrays. This look at arrays ended with a brief meditation on the importance of range checking.

# Records

*Records* are a technique for binding together multiple data types into a single structure. Examples of using records can be found in the RecordWorks program found in the Chap03 directory of your accompanying CD.

Consider the following method:

```
procedure TForm1.Button1Click(Sender: TObject);
var
  FirstName: String;
  LastName: String;
  Address: String;
  City: String;
  State: String;
  Zip: String;
begin
  FirstName := 'Blaise';
  LastName := 'Pascal';
  Address := '1623 Geometry Lane';
  City := 'Clemont';
  State := 'CA';
  Zip := '81662'
end;
```

The `String` declarations in the `var` section are all part of an address. Here is how you can bind these identifiers into one record:

```pascal
procedure TForm1.Button2Click(Sender: TObject);
type
  TAddress = record
    FirstName: String;
    LastName: String;
    Address: String;
    City: String;
    State: String;
    Zip: String;
  end;
var
  Address: TAddress;
begin
  Address.FirstName := 'Blaise';
  Address.LastName := 'Pascal';
  Address.Address := '1623 Geometry Lane';
  Address.City := 'Clemont';
  Address.State := 'CA';
  Address.Zip := '81662'
end;
```

In this second example, a record declaration has been added to the type section of the Button2Click method. A variable of type TAddress has been declared in the var section. Dot notation is used in the body of the Button2Click method to enable you to reference each field of the record: Address.FirstName. People often will read out loud such a declaration as "Address dot FirstName," hence the term *dot notation*.

## C/C++ NOTE

A record in Object Pascal is the same thing as a struct in C/C++. However, in C/C++, the line between a struct and an object is blurred, while in Object Pascal they are two distinctly different types. Pascal records do not support the concept of a method, although you can have a pointer to a method or function as a member of a record. However, that pointer references a routine outside the record itself. A method, on the other hand, is a member of an object.

## Records and with Statements

You can create a with statement to avoid the necessity of using dot notation to reference the fields of your record. Consider the following code fragment:

```pascal
procedure TForm1.Button3Click(Sender: TObject);
type
```

```
TPerson = Record
  Age: Integer;
  Name: String;
end;
var
Person: TPerson;
begin
  with Person do begin
    Age := 100046;
    Name := 'ET';
  end;
end;
```

The line with Person do begin is a with statement that tells the compiler that the identifiers Age and Name belong to the TPerson record. In effect, with statements offer a kind of short-hand to make it easier to use records or objects.

**NOTE**

with statements are a double-edged sword. If used properly, they can help you write cleaner code that's easier to understand. If used improperly, they can help you write code that not even you can understand. Frankly, I tend to avoid the syntax because it can be so confusing. In particular, the with syntax can break the connection between a record or object and the fields of that record or object.

For instance, you have to use a bit of reasoning to realize that Age belongs to the TPerson record and is not, for instance, simply a globally scoped variable of type Integer. In this case, the true state of affairs is clear enough, but in longer, more complex programs, it can be hard to see what has happened. A good rule of thumb might be to use with statements if they help you write clean code and then to avoid them if you are simply trying to save time by cutting down on the number of key-strokes you type.

## Variant Records

A variant record in Pascal enables you to assign different field types to the same area of memory in a record. In other words, one particular location in a record could be either of type A or of type B. This can be useful in either/or cases, where a record can have either one field or the other field, but not both. For instance, consider an office in which you track employees either by their name or by an ID, but never by both at the same time. Here is a way to capture that idea in a variant `record`:

```
procedure TForm1.VariantButtonClick(Sender: TObject);
type
  TMyVariantRecord = record
    OfficeID: Integer;
    case PersonalID: Integer of
      0: (Name: ShortString);
      1: (NumericID: Integer);
  end;
var
  TomRecord, JaneRecord: TMyVariantRecord;
begin
  TomRecord.Name := 'Sammy';
  JaneRecord.NumericID := 42;
end;
```

The first field in this record, `OfficeID`, is just a normal field of the record. I've placed it there just so you can see that a variant record can contain not only a variant part, but also as many normal fields as you want.

The second part of the record, beginning with the word `case`, is the variant part. In this particular record, the `PersonalID` can be either a `String` or an `Integer`, but not both. To show how this works, I declare two records of type `TMyVariantRecord` and then use the `Name` part of one variant record and the `NumericID` of the other record instance.

`Name` and `NumericID` share the same block of memory in a `TVariantRecord`—or, more precisely, they both start at the same offset in the record. Needless to say, a `String` takes up more memory than an `Integer`. In any one instance of the record at any one point in time, you can have either the `String` or the `Integer`, but not both. Assigning a value to one or the other field, will, at least in principle, overwrite the memory in the other field.

The compiler will always allocate enough memory to hold the largest possible record that you can declare. For instance, in this case, it will always allocate 4 bytes for the field `OfficeID` and then 256 bytes for the `String`, giving you a total of 260 bytes for the record. This is the case even if you use only the `OfficeID` and `NumericID` fields, which take up only 8 bytes of memory.

For me, the most confusing part of variant records is the line that contains the word `case`. This syntax exists to give you a means of telling whether the record uses the `NumericID` or the `Name` field. Listing 3.4 shows a second example that focuses on how to use the `case` part of a variant record.

**3**

BASIC PASCAL SYNTAX

**LISTING 3.4**  The case Part of a Variant Record Used in the ShowRecordType Method

```
unit Main;

interface

uses
  Windows, Messages, SysUtils,
  Classes, Graphics, Controls,
  Forms, Dialogs, StdCtrls;

type
  TMyVariantRecord = record
    OfficeID: Integer;
    case PersonalID: Integer of
      0: (Name: ShortString);
      1: (NumericID: Integer);
  end;

  TForm1 = class(TForm)
    Button1: TButton;
    procedure Button1Click(Sender: TObject);
  private
    procedure ShowRecordType(R: TMyVariantRecord);
    { Private declarations }
  public
    { Public declarations }
  end;

var
  Form1: TForm1;

implementation

{$R *.DFM}

procedure TForm1.ShowRecordType(R: TMyVariantRecord);
begin
  case R.PersonalID of
    0: ShowMessage('Uses Name field: ' + R.Name);
    1: ShowMessage('Uses NumericID: ' + IntToStr(R.NumericID));
  end;
end;

procedure TForm1.Button1Click(Sender: TObject);
var
```

**LISTING 3.4**    Continued

```
  Sam, Sue: TMyVariantRecord;
begin
  Sam.OfficeID := 1;
  Sue.PersonalID := 0;
  Sue.Name := 'Sue';
  ShowRecordType(Sue);
  Sam.OfficeID := 2;
  Sam.PersonalID := 1;
  Sam.NumericID := 1;
  ShowRecordType(Sam);
end;

end.
```

In this example, the two records are passed into the ShowRecordType method. One record has the PersonalID set to 0; the other has it set to 1. ShowRecordType uses this information to sort out whether any one particular record uses the Name field or the RecordID field:

```
case R.PersonalID of
  0: ShowMessage('Uses Name field: ' + R.Name);
  1: ShowMessage('Uses NumericID: ' + IntToStr(R.NumericID));
end;
```

As you can see, if PersonalID is set to 0, the Name field is valid; if it is set to 1, the NumericID field is valid.

> **NOTE**
>
> A case statement plays the same role in Object Pascal that switch statements play in C/C++ and Java. Other than the obvious syntactical similarities, there is no significant connection between the case part of a variant record and case statements. In and of themselves, case statements have nothing to do with variant records. It is simply coincidence that, in this example, case statements are the best way to sort out the two different types of records that can be passed to the ShowRecordType procedure. The following code, however, would also get the job done:
>
> ```
> procedure TForm1.ShowRecordType2(R: TMyVariantRecord);
> begin
>   if R.PersonalID = 0 then
>     ShowMessage('Uses Name field: ' + R.Name)
>   else
>     ShowMessage('Uses NumericID: ' + IntToStr(R.NumericID));
> end;
> ```

Here is one last variant record that shows how far you can press this paradigm:

```
procedure TForm1.HonkerButtonClick(Sender: TObject);
type
  TAnimalType = (atCat, atDog, atPerson);
  TFurType = (ftWiry, ftSoft);
  TMoodType = (mtAggressive, mtCloying, mtGoodNatured);
  TAnimalRecord = record
    Name: String;
    Age: Integer;
    case AnimalType: TAnimalType of
      atCat: (Talk: ShortString;
              Fight: ShortString;
              Food: ShortString);
      atDog: (Fur: TFurType;
              Description: ShortString;
              Mood: TMoodType);
      atPerson:(Rank: ShortString;
              SerialNumber: ShortString);
  end;

var
  Cat, Dog, Person: TAnimalRecord;
begin
  Cat.Name := 'Valentine';
  Cat.Age := 14;
  Cat.Talk := 'Meow';
  Cat.Fight := 'Scratch';
  Cat.Food := 'Cheese';
  Dog.Name := 'Rover';
  Dog.Age := 2;
  Dog.AnimalType := atDog;
  Dog.Fur := ftWiry;
  Dog.Description := 'Barks';
  Dog.Mood := mtGoodNatured;
end;
```

In this example, I declare an enumerated type named TAnimalType. I use this type in the case part of the variant record, which enables me to use descriptive names rather than numbers for each case:

```
TAnimalType = (atCat, atDog, atPerson);
TAnimalRecord = record
  case AnimalType: TAnimalType of
    atCat:
    atDog:
    atPerson:
end;
```

The other important bit of code in this example is the fact that you can place multiple fields in each element of the case part:

```
atDog: (Fur: TFurType;
        Description: ShortString;
        Mood: TMoodType);
```

Here you can see that the atDog part of the variant records has three separate fields: Fur, Description, and Mood.

---

**NOTE**

I use ShortStrings in these examples because you cannot use the system-allocated variables of type AnsiStrings, WideStrings, dynamic arrays, or Interfaces in a variant record. However, you can use pointers to these forbidden types.

---

Variant records don't play a large role in Object Pascal programming. However, they are used from time to time in some fairly crucial places, and they fit nicely into our search for the more advanced parts of the language that might not be obvious at first glance to a newcomer. In fact, I've seen many experienced Pascal programmers get tripped up by this syntactically complex entity.

## Pointers

Pascal pointers are just like C or C++ pointers: They are the key to what makes the language so powerful, but they can also cause you considerable pain.

I'll start by showing you what the untamed pointer type looks like in Object Pascal. Most people won't want to use pointers this way, but I think it helps to start by seeing the low-level usage. Then I'll show you the somewhat more civilized way pointers most often appear in Kylix programs. This is the undomesticated version:

```
procedure TForm1.Button1Click(Sender: TObject);
var
  P: Pointer;
  S, Temp: String;
begin
  S := 'Sam';                 // Set S = 'Sam'
  GetMem(P, 10);              // Allocate 10 bytes
  FillChar(P^, 10, 0);        // Zero out all 10 bytes
  Move(S[1], P^, Length(S));  // Move 'Sam' into P^
  SetLength(Temp, 4);         // Make Temp four bytes long
  Move(P^, Temp[1], 1);       // Move S from P to temp
```

```
Inc(PChar(P));            // Make P point to am
Move(P^, Temp[2], 1);     // Move a from P to temp
Inc(PChar(P));            // Make P point to m
Move(P^, Temp[3], 1);     // Move m from P to temp
Temp[4] := #0;            // Set the null terminator for temp
Dec(PChar(P), 2);         // Make P point at Sam
FreeMem(P, 10);           // Free memory allocated for Sam
Edit1.Text := Temp;
end;
```

This code is from a program named Pointers, which is in the Chap03 directory on your accompanying CD. The Button1Click method shown here does nothing practical other than show how to use pointer syntax in Object Pascal. In particular, the code creates a pointer of 10 bytes of memory. It zeroes out the bytes that the pointer addresses. Then it copies a string into the bytes address by the pointer. Finally, it accesses the contents of pointer, 1 byte at a time.

The Pascal pointer type is, logically enough, referred to as a pointer. Use the ^ operator operator>to address the memory associated with a pointer. The ^ operator performs more or less the same function in Pascal as the -> operator does in C and C++.

I have commented this code so heavily that you can probably best follow it by simply reading the code itself. Notice, in particular, the following calls:

- The GetMem procedure allocates memory for a pointer. Pass the pointer in the first parameter and the number of bytes that you want to allocate in the second parameter. You will receive a copy of a fully initialized pointer to the amount of memory that you requested.

- FillChar can be used to spray a single-character value into multiple contiguous bytes in a very efficient manner. Commonly, it is used to zero out the bytes in a contiguous chunk of memory. In this case, I tell FillChar to fill the 10 bytes pointed to by P with the value 0. This is the first character in the character set, not the number 0. The first parameter of the function specifies the memory that you want to fill, the second specifies the number of bytes of that memory that you want to address, and the third parameter is the character that you want to spray into those bytes. Needless to say, the routine is designed to be very fast.

- The Move procedure moves *n* number of bytes from one place in memory to another place. In this case, I move the 3 bytes addressed by the String variable into the bytes address by the pointer. The first parameter of the Move procedure is the source memory, the second is the destination memory, and the third is the number of bytes to be moved.

- Notice that I use the Inc and Dec procedures to iterate over particular bytes in the memory addressed by the pointer. This technique is known as pointer arithmetic, and it should be familiar to all C or C++ programmers. You will get a more detailed look at pointer arithmetic in Chapter 5, in the sections on the debugger. After the call to Move, the pointer points at the letters S, a, and m. The last 7 bytes addressed by the pointer are still zeroed out. If I call Inc(P) one time, then the first byte addressed by the pointer is no longer S, but a. In C or C++, you would achieve the same effect by writing P++.

- The FreeMem procedure deallocates the memory assigned to the pointer P. Notice that I use Dec to unwind the memory addressed by the variable P back to the place initially allocated by the call to get GetMem. Failure to do this can yield undefined results.

The best way to understand these lines of code is to watch them very carefully in the debugger. Unfortunately, I have not yet talked to you about using the debugger. Furthermore, the parts of the debugger that you can use to really get a look at this code are relatively advanced features. As a result, I'm going to have to ask you to put this code aside for a time. Then, in Chapter 5, in the section "Using the Debugger," I will show you how to get a good look at what happens under the hood when this code is executed.

## Working with Pointers to Objects

The type of pointer that I showed you in the last section is really an advanced technique, not one that you are likely to employ in many sections of your code. Pointers to objects, however, are ubiquitous in Object Pascal, and you must understand them if you want to work with Kylix.

> **NOTE**
>
> In this section and the next, I talk a good deal about how objects work in Kylix. I assume that all readers of this book already understand objects as well as polymorphism, inheritance, encapsulation, virtual methods, and related topics. My goal in this text is not to explain OOP in and of itself, but instead to introduce or reintroduce Pascal objects to experienced programmers from other languages such as C++, VB, and Java.

Like Strings, pointers have a rather checkered history in Object Pascal. For many years, a Pascal pointer was a Pascal pointer, and as long as you understood how memory is addressed by a computer, they were fairly simple to use. In recent years, however, the waters have been muddied to make some changes that make programming easier for certain types of developers.

For many years, the basic rule for pointers was that if you wanted to address the memory they referenced, you used pointer syntax. For instance, you wrote MyPointer^.SomeBlockOfMemory. Spoken out loud, this is usually rendered as, "MyPointer points to SomeBlockOfMemory." This

**3**

BASIC PASCAL
SYNTAX

syntax is easy for intermediate and advanced-level programmers to use. However, inexperienced programmers can find it disconcerting. To solve their feelings, the Pascal team decided to drop the ^ operator. The result is simple dot notation: `MyPointer.SomeBlockOfMemory`. When working with Pascal objects, you can now leave off the ^.

Note, in particular, that all CLX objects should be addressed using dot notation. No one writes `TEdit^.Text`; they all write `TEdit.Text`.

You and I know, however, that this dropping of the pointer syntax is a simple affectation. It is a euphemism. Underneath this thin veneer, the untamed beast sharpens its claws on the bark of exotic tropical trees, its lidded eyes never still, its body crouching as it waits for you to make a false move. At this point it will—well, I'm not allowed to talk about that kind of thing in a book intended for general audiences. But if you have ever used a Microsoft product or attended a Bill Gate's demo, or if you have had a glimpse of the dreaded blue screen of death, then I'm sure you know something of what can happen.

> **NOTE**
>
> When they dropped the pointer syntax for objects, the Delphi and Kylix engineers also decided to place a T rather than a P before the declarations for these objects. For instance, it is proper to write `TEdit` or `TButton`, but not `PEdit` or `PButton`. Normally, you would put a P rather than a T before a pointer type. However, the game is properly afoot, and to play along you should use a T rather than a P.

The biggest issue when you use pointers is to make sure that the pointer is allocated properly and, even more importantly, that it is disposed of properly. In Kylix, these chores are largely taken out of the users' hands by two mechanisms:

1. In design mode, when you drop a component onto a form or onto another component, memory for that component is allocated automatically.

2. When a form closes, it automatically disposes of the memory associated with all the components that it owns. In fact, when any component that owns another component is destroyed, that component frees the memory for all the components that it owns. (In the section "Arrays", you saw the `Component` array that belongs to a form. We used that array for our purposes, but its primary purpose is to allow the form to track the components that it owns and to dispose of them properly when the time comes.)

Now you can begin to understand what the designers of Pascal have done:

- They've made Pascal allocate memory for you automatically most of the time when you're working in the Form Designer.

- When the time comes, Pascal will automatically dispose of the components.
- They've unburdened developers of the need to use the ^ syntax.

If you put these three pieces together, you can see that Delphi goes a long way toward entirely relieving you of the duty to think about pointers or to even know that pointers are being used.

All of that is well and good—except for one crucial fact: Object Pascal uses pointers everywhere! Every component that you drop on a form is a pointer to an object. In fact, it is not possible to create a static instance of an object in Pascal. All Pascal components must be created as pointers to components. Indeed, all Pascal objects must be instantiated as pointers!

Listing 3.5 shows how to explicitly create an instance of an object. This is information that you must understand for those times when you create objects on your own rather than by dropping them onto the Component Palette:

**LISTING 3.5**   A Short Console Application Found on Disk as ObjectAllocate1.dpr

```
program ObjectAllocateOne;

{$APPTYPE CONSOLE}

uses SysUtils;

type
  TMyObject = class(TObject)
    procedure SayYourName;
  end;

{ MyObject }

procedure TMyObject.SayYourName;
begin
  WriteLn(ClassName);
end;

var
  MyObject: TMyObject;
begin
  MyObject := TMyObject.Create;
  MyObject.SayYourName;
  MyObject.Free;
end.
```

This program is a console application. You can create console applications by choosing File, New, Console Application from the menu system. Console applications are not run as part of X. Instead, they are run from the shell prompt and usually output only raw text.

---

### Note

It is traditional to end console applications with the ReadLn statement while you are debugging them in the IDE. This ensures that the window that the program creates stays open until you press the Enter key. If you start Kylix from the shell prompt, there is no reason to use this mechanism. Instead, the text from your program will be seen at the shell prompt from which you started Kylix. (In fact, it might be the case in the first version of Kylix that this latter mechanism is the only way to see the output from your console applications.) Remember that when you start Kylix from the shell prompt, you should use the command startkylix.

---

The ObjectAllocateOne program declares a simple Object Pascal class named TMyObject. With rare exceptions, all Object Pascal classes should begin with T, which stands for "type." To declare the class, you write TMyObject = class(TObject), where TObject is the name of the parent class.

To create an instance of TMyObject, you write the following code:

```
var
  MyObject: TMyObject;
begin
  MyObject := TMyObject.Create;
  ... // Code omitted here
```

This code allocates memory for an object. Java and C++ programmers would achieve the same ends by writing MyObject = new TMyObject(). VB programmers would write Dim MyObject as TMyObject. But parallels with VB and Java are inappropriate because Pascal treats pointers the same way C++ does. If you allocate memory for an object, you must free that memory or risk crippling your program!

Here is how to free memory for a Pascal object:

```
MyObject.Free;
```

This code destroys the memory associated with TMyObject. After you have made this call, you can no longer safely reference MyObject.

## Pointers, Constructors, and Destructors

When you call Free on an object, the compiler also calls the destructor for your object, if there is one. The ObjectAllocateTwo program, shown in Listing 3.6, demonstrates how this works.

**LISTING 3.6** The ObjectAllocateTwo Program, Featuring a Constructor That Allocates Memory and a Destructor That Destroys That Same Memory

```pascal
program ObjectAllocateTwo;
{$APPTYPE CONSOLE}
uses
  SysUtils;

type
  TMyObject = class(TObject)
  private
    FMyPointer: Pointer;
  protected
    constructor Create; virtual;
    destructor Destroy; override;
  public
    procedure SayYourName;
  end;

{ MyObject }

constructor TMyObject.Create;
begin
  inherited Create;
  GetMem(FMyPointer, 10);
end;

destructor TMyObject.Destroy;
begin
  FreeMem(FMyPointer, 10);
  inherited;
end;

procedure TMyObject.SayYourName;
begin
  WriteLn(ClassName);
end;

var
  MyObject: TMyObject;
```

**LISTING 3.6**  Continued

```
begin
  MyObject := TMyObject.Create;
  MyObject.SayYourName;
  FreeAndNil(MyObject);
end.
```

Many programs contain pointers that need to be allocated and deallocated. When allocating memory for an object that will belong to another object, you should do one of two things:

- Declare the pointer or object as a method-scoped variable, and then allocate and deallocate the memory for that object inside one single method. This is the way the variable P is treated in the Button1Click method from the earlier section of this chapter titled "Pointers." In that method, P belongs to the Button1Click method, and the Button1Click method therefore takes on the chore of both allocating and deallocating memory for that object.

- The second method is shown in the AllocateObjectTwo program. In that program, the variable FMyPointer is declared as a field of TMyObject. (The name of all fields of Pascal objects should begin with F, which stands for "field.") The memory for FMyPointer is allocated in the object's constructor and deallocated in the object's destructor. If you do things in this way, you are unlikely to forget to either allocate or deallocate memory for your object. In particular, all you need do is see what pointers or objects are declared as fields of your object and then make sure that they are allocated in the constructor and deallocated in the destructor. If you have declared five fields for your object but only four of those fields are cleaned up in your destructor, you likely have a problem.

There is nothing in Object Pascal to keep you from allocating and deallocating memory for your objects and pointers wherever you please. These rules are merely guidelines. In some cases, it will not be possible to follow these guidelines, but you should heed them if you can.

## `virtual` Methods and the `override` Directive

In the AllocateObjectTwo program, the directive virtual is placed after the constructor for TmyObject, and the directive override follows the destructor. The first time you declare a method that you want to be virtual, use the directive virtual. If you are overriding an already existing virtual method, use the directive override.

All Pascal objects are guaranteed to have a destructor named Destroy and a method named Free. The purpose of the Free method is to call the destructor. More particularly, the Free method ensures that the object is not already set to nil; if it is not, the method calls Destroy.

Pascal objects inherit the `Free` and `Destroy` methods from `TObject`. When it comes time for a component to deallocate the memory for all the components that it owns, it simply calls `TObject.Free` on all the objects in its `Components` array. Through the miracle of polymorphism, this single call ensures that the destructors for each object are called. The end result is that all the memory for these objects is destroyed. This mechanism will not work, however, unless you override the `Destroy` method in your programs whenever you need to deallocate the memory associated with any of the fields of your object.

There is no need to override `Destroy` in the AllocateObjectOne program because the instance of `TMyObject` in that program does not have any fields for which it allocates memory. This is not the case in the AllocateObjectTwo program, so it is necessary to create a destructor for that object. Note further that in the AllocateObjectTwo program, `TMyObject` is not owned by a component. As a result, you must specifically call its destructor, as shown in that program. If `TMyObject` were owned by a component, you would not need to explicitly call `Free` on that object because its owner would perform the task for you.

> **NOTE**
>
> Newcomers to Object Pascal likely will have further questions at this point about the difference between objects and components. In general, a component is simply an object that you can place on the Component Palette. Saying as much, however, raises as many questions as it answers. Part II is dedicated to components, and there you will learn about them in depth.

I've tried to cover most of the major subjects about pointers that I think can cause confusion. If you want to hear more about pointers to objects, don't worry—the subject will come up again in Part II, when the focus of the text becomes CLX.

# What You Won't Find in Object Pascal

I want to close with a few words on what you won't find in Object Pascal:

- There is no support for multiple inheritance. However, you can descend from multiple interfaces, just as you can in Java.

- There is no support for operator overloading. This feature was deemed inappropriate for the language by its developers. They felt that it would make the syntax of the language too complex and possibly could lead to much longer compile times, similar to those found in C++. However, you will find that a clever use of variants will enable you to do something very similar to operating overloading.

- No garbage collection takes place. This is a feature that the team has often contemplated adding to the language. However, you can use numerous tricks to help you clean up memory automatically in Pascal; many of these were discussed in the section on pointers found earlier in this chapter.

## Summary

In this chapter, you learned about Object Pascal types. This information is essential if you want to use Object Pascal successfully.

The chapter began with a look at the simple types, such as integers, strings, and the floating-point types. Stepping into wilder terrain, you had a look at typecasting, arrays, and records. The last few pages of the text took you into the untamed jungle for a look at pointers and memory allocation for objects.

Hopefully this chapter has given you some sense of the power and subtlety of Object Pascal. The language is a subtle tool with many modern features. It gives you the speed and flexibility of C or C++, many of the modern programming features of Java, and the ease of use that you might expect from Perl or Python.

In the next chapter, you will learn more about working with objects and interfaces in an Object Pascal program. From there you will go on to learn more about the IDE and the editor. Finally, at the end of Part I, "Understanding Delphi and Linux," you will see how to use Object Pascal to access the core features of the X Window library.

# Objects and Interfaces

*by Charlie Calvert*

## IN THIS CHAPTER

You will need to know a few basic facts about the Kylix object model to understand much of the material found in the rest of this book. This chapter presents that information in a condensed form.

The information presented here is intended for experienced programmers who already thoroughly understand object-oriented programming. If you are unclear about what an object is, what polymorphism is, or how inheritance works, then you need to turn to a different book for further enlightenment.

> **NOTE**
>
> One subject that will not be covered in this chapter is working with constructors and destructors. Material on that subject can be found in Chapter 3, "Basic Pascal Syntax," in the section "Pointers, Constructors, and Destructors."
>
> A second subject related to objects that will not be covered in this chapter is properties. You can read about properties in Chapter 10, "Advanced Component Design," in the section "Properties." Properties are part of the Pascal object model. However, many of the interesting things that you can do with properties are related to components and the Object Inspector. As a result, it is hard to give a complete summation of what you can do with properties if you do not first understand components. Hence, my discussion of properties is in the section on component design rather than this section of the text.

## The Kylix Object Model

There's no mbetter way to get started than to simply plunge right into the heart of the matter. Here is how you declare an object in Pascal:

```
type
  TMyObject = class(TObject)
    // Particulars of the class declaration appear here
  end;
```

In this case, TMyObject is the name of the class being declared. The object name is followed by an equals sign and the reserved word class. Next you insert a parenthesis and the name of the object from which your class is descending. If you do not include this last part, the class is assumed to descend from TObject. All classes in Pascal, except for TObject, have an ancestor. It is impossible for Object Pascal programmers to declare classes that have no ancestor.

The end of a class is marked by the reserved word end, followed by a semicolon. The body of your declaration appears in the lines between the word TMyObject and the final word end.

## Where to Declare an Object

The declaration for a class appears in a type section. You can declare as many objects as you want in any one type section, and you can have as many type sections as you want in your code.

Most class declarations that you make will appear in a Pascal unit. However, a type section containing a class declaration can appear at the top of a DPR file. In a unit, it can appear anywhere in the interface after the uses clause. In the implementation, it can appear anywhere except inside the declaration of a function, procedure or method, or inside the finalization or initialization clauses.

In Listings 4.1 and 4.2, you will see some examples of the correct and incorrect locations to declare classes. Listing 4.1 shows the correct way to proceed. Listing 4.2 shows all the kind of mistakes that you can easily make if you don't yet feel comfortable with the language.

**LISTING 4.1** Two Correctly Declared Classes—TMyObject Is In the Interface After the Uses Clause, and TMyObject2 Is In the Implementation

```
unit Unit2;

interface

uses
  SysUtils;

type
  TMyObject = class(TObject)
    procedure Foo;
  end;

implementation

type
  TMyObject2 = class(TObject)
    procedure Foo;
  end;

procedure TMyObject.Foo;
begin
end;
```

**LISTING 4.1**   Continued

```
procedure TMyObject2.Foo;
begin
end;

end.
```

---

JAVA AND C++
NOTE

When studying the declaration in Listing 4.1, please note that the implementations of TMyObject.Foo and TMyObject2.Foo both appear in the implementation section of the unit. In Java, the declaration for an object and its implementation are united in one long listing of code. In C++, you generally declare objects in a header file and implement them in a CPP file. Neither of these models corresponds to the syntax found in Object Pascal. In Kylix, the declaration for an object can be in either the interface or the implementation of a file, and the implementation of the object's methods must be in the implementation section of the unit. As a rule, you must always declare and implement an object in the same unit. A descendant of an object can appear in a second unit, but any one object is almost always declared and implemented in a single file.

---

**LISTING 4.2**   Three Incorrectly Declared Classes—TMyObject Is Incorrectly Declared Before the Uses Clause, TMyObject2 Is Incorrectly Declared Inside the Scope of a Method, and TMyObject3 Is Incorrectly Declared in the Initialization Clause

```
unit Unit2;

interface

type
  TMyObject = class(TObject)
    procedure Foo;
  end;

uses
  SysUtils;


implementation
```

**LISTING 4.2** Continued

```
procedure TMyObject.Foo;
type
  TMyObject2 = class(TObject)
    // Particulars of the class declaration appear here
  end;
begin
end;

initialization
type
  TMyObject3 = class(TObject)
    // Particulars of the class declaration appear here
  end;

end.
```

## Scoping in Object Pascal Classes

The methods or variables in a class can have private, protected, public, or published scope:

```
TEdit1 = class(TEdit)
private
  { Private declarations }
protected
  { Protected declarations }
public
  { Public declarations }
published
  { Published declarations }
end;
```

`private` methods or variables can be seen only by classes or methods declared inside the scope of this one unit. Any class in the unit can access these variables. Not just the `TEdit1` class can access the variables in its `private` section; any other class in the same unit can also access those variables. There is no way to hide a method or variable from other classes declared in its unit. Any class outside the unit cannot directly access the variables. Instead, you/ must use properties or `getter` and `setter` methods to access the variables. In Object Pascal, it is traditional for programmers to use properties rather than `getter` or `setter` methods to provide access to private data.

`protected` methods or variables can be seen only by objects in the current unit or by descendants of this object. A descendant of `TEdit1` that exists in an entirely different unit can access the protected variables and methods of TEdit1, as long as the second unit lists the first unit in its uses clause.

public methods or variables can be accessed from virtually any location in your program. If you are in Unit1, you can access public methods and variables declared in any object found in Unit1. If you are in a second unit, you can access public variables and methods of an object as long as the second unit lists the first unit in its uses clause.

published variables and methods have the same scope as public methods or variables. However, they have additional runtime information (RTTI). In particular, the RTTI in the published section of a class is used by the IDE when it displays properties in the Object Inspector. All properties shown in the Object Inspector were declared, by definition, in the published section of a class. It usually makes no sense to use published sections in classes that are not also components.

## Scoping Issues with Classes That Reference One Another

When declaring several classes in one unit, you often want to access one class in the declaration of a second class. Consider the following code:

```
type
  TLineCollection = class
    FLine: TLine;
  end;

  TLine = class
    FLineCollection: TLineCollection;
  end;
```

In these declarations, TLine references TLineCollection, and TLineCollection references TLine. Given the normal rules of scoping in Object Pascal, it would not be possible for TLineCollection to include its reference to the TLine object:

```
    FLine: TLine;
```

The problem here is simply that the declaration for TLineCollection comes before the declaration for TLine. The compiler reads the code from the top to the bottom. As a result, the compiler knows nothing about TLine at the time it reaches the declaration for TLineCollection. That lack of knowledge will cause the compiler to issue an error, stating that you are trying to use a variable about which it knows nothing.

The solution to this problem is simple—to write a single line predeclaring the TLine class:

```
type
  TLine = class;
```

```
TLineCollection = class
  FLine: TLine;
end;

TLine = class
  FLineCollection: TLineCollection;
end;
```

The forward declaration for `TLine` looks a bit forlorn sitting there all by itself. Nonetheless, the compiler recognizes this brave outpost of the `TLine` object and takes it as sufficient evidence to accept the reference to `TLine` in `TLineCollection`.

---

I occasionally catch myself using the words *class* and *object* interchangeably. Technically, a *class* is the code, particularly the declaration, for an object. An *object*, on the other hand, is an instantiated instance of a class. You see classes when you are writing code, and you create objects at runtime. A source file contains class declarations; a compiled program creates and manipulates objects at runtime.

In theory, the line between a class and an object is clear and fairly easy to understand. In practice, however, the line between classes and objects becomes a bit blurred in the speech and minds of all but the most compulsive programmers. In the few instances when the distinction between the two entities really matters, I will try to make that fact abundantly clear. The rest of the time, I will try to avoid what I sometimes regard as an overly pedantic reliance on the subtle differences between two such easily confused terms.

A similar syntactical situation arises over the proper name to call the object from which another object descends. I often talk in terms of *parent objects* and *child objects*. In the examples that I have been showing here, `TMyObject` is the parent of `TMyObject2`, and `TMyObject2` is the child of `TMyObject`. I rarely, if ever, push the metaphor so far that I start speaking of grandchildren and grandparents. Instead, I often use the terms *ancestor* and *descendant* to refer to the same relationship if it extends over several "generations." For the most part, though, I use the terms *parent* and *ancestor* as synonyms, and *child* and *descendant* as synonyms.

---

**4**

## Declaring a Method

You declare an Object Pascal method by writing the word `procedure` or `function`, followed by the name of the class, followed by a period, followed by the method's name, and finally followed by any parameters or return values:

```
type
  TMyObject = class(TObject)
```

```
    procedure Foo;
    function Goober(InValue: Integer): String;
  end;

procedure TMyObject.Foo;
begin
end;

function TMyObject.Goober(InValue: Integer): String;
begin
end;
```

When declaring the method inside the class declaration, you do not include the name of the class:

```
type
  TMyObject = class(TObject)
    procedure TMyObject.Foo;  // Wrong. No class names in method declarations.
  end;
```

The code shown here produces an error, not a warning, from the compiler.

## The Object Pascal Inheritance Model: `virtual` and `override`

Virtual and dynamic methods make polymorphism possible. In this section, I show you the syntax for those technologies as they manifest themselves in an Object Pascal program. Again, none of the syntax shown in this section will make sense to you unless you first understand polymorphism and inheritance. I assume, however, that readers of this text already understand those terms and have experience using them in some other language, such as C++ or Java.

If you want to allow users of your object to override any of its methods, you must declare one or more of the methods as `virtual`:

```
TMyObject = class(TObject)
  procedure Foo; virtual;   // TMyObject.Foo is virtual
end;
```

To override a `virtual` method, use the `override` directive:

```
TMyObject2 = class(TMyObject)
  procedure Foo; override;   // TMyObject2.Foo overrides TMyObject.Foo;
end;
```

If you want to declare a new method with the same name that is not `virtual`, you can do so using regular Object Pascal method syntax:

```
TMyObject3 = class(TMyObject)
  procedure Foo; // Does not override the virtual method TMyObject.Foo.
end;
```

The declaration of Foo in TMyObject3 will cause the compiler to generate a warning stating that you have "hidden" the virtual method TMyObject.Foo with your own copy of Foo. Here is the warning: "Method Foo hides virtual method of base type TMyObject." If you want to suppress the warning, use the reintroduce directive:

```
TMyObject3 = class(TMyObject)
  procedure Foo; reintroduce;
end;
```

As a rule, however, you do not want to reintroduce a method name that hides a virtual method. In most cases, it's just not good programming practice.

> **NOTE**
>
> The compiler will also raise its voice in irritation if you place an overridden instance of a virtual method in the protected or private section when the method that you are overriding was originally declared in the public section. The solution to the problem is obvious: Move your new method back to the public section.

## Using dynamic Rather Than virtual in a Declaration

The words dynamic and virtual have essentially the same semantics in Object Pascal. They are all but synonyms of one another. The differences between them have to do only with the way they perform at runtime. They mean the same thing, but the technology behind the two syntaxes gives your program its own unique performance characteristics.

If you want to save memory, you can use the word dynamic instead of the word virtual:

```
TMyObject = class(TObject)
  procedure Bar(i: Integer); dynamic;
end;
```

To override the method, use the same syntax that you would use to override a virtual method:

```
TMyObject2 = class(TMyObject)
  procedure Foo; override;  // TMyObject2.Foo overrides TMyObject.Foo;
end;
```

A dynamic method takes up less memory than a virtual method, but it takes longer to execute. A virtual method takes up more memory than a dynamic method, but it executes more quickly.

> **NOTE**
>
> `virtual` methods are included in the Virtual Method Table (VMT) for the original instance and all descendant instances of an object. As such, they are easy to access, but they take up a significant amount of memory. (You can think of a VMT as a record or array in memory containing a list of all the `virtual` methods declared for an object and its ancestors.) A `virtual` method does not take up memory in the VMT of the original object and in the VMT of each descendant of that object. A `dynamic` method, on the other hand, is stored in a single table that is looked up each time it is called. It takes longer to look up a `dynamic` method than to call a `virtual` method. However, it appears only once and thus takes up less space. If you are uncertain which technique to use, the Kylix team recommends that you use `virtual` methods.

An example program, ObjectModel.dpr, is included in the Chapter04 directory on the CD that accompanies this book. It gives examples of all the syntax shown in this section of the chapter. Listing 4.3 shows the ObjectUnit.pas file from the ObjectModel program.

**LISTING 4.3**  The `ObjectUnit` Shows How to Use the `dynamic`, `virtual`, `reintroduce`, `abstract`, `inherited`, and `overload` Directives

```
unit ObjectUnit;

interface

uses
  SysUtils;

type
  TMyObject = class(TObject)
    procedure Foo; virtual;
    procedure Bar(i: Integer); dynamic;
    procedure Goober; overload;
    procedure Goober(s: String; i: integer = 2); overload;
  end;

procedure UseAllObjects;

implementation

uses
  QDialogs;

type
  TMyObject2 = class(TMyObject)
```

**LISTING 4.3**    Continued

```
    procedure Foo; override;
    procedure Bar(i: Integer); override;
  end;

  TMyObject3 = class(TMyObject)
    procedure Foo; reintroduce;
  end;

  TMyObject4 = class(TMyObject)
    procedure BeEsoteric; virtual; abstract;
  end;

{------------------------------------------------------------}
{-- TMyObject -----------------------------------------------}
{------------------------------------------------------------}

procedure TMyObject.Bar(i: Integer);
begin
  ShowMessage(IntToStr(i));
end;

procedure TMyObject.Foo;
begin
  Goober;
  Goober('Sam');
  Goober('Sam', 2);
end;

procedure TMyObject.Goober;
begin

end;

procedure TMyObject.Goober(s: String; i: integer);
begin

end;

{------------------------------------------------------------}
{-- TMyObject2 ----------------------------------------------}
{------------------------------------------------------------}

procedure TMyObject2.Bar(i: Integer);
begin
```

**LISTING 4.3**   Continued

```
  inherited Bar(i);

end;

procedure TMyObject2.Foo;
begin
  inherited;
end;

{-----------------------------------------------------------}
{-- TMyObject3 ---------------------------------------------}
{-----------------------------------------------------------}

procedure TMyObject3.Foo;
begin

end;

procedure UseAllObjects;
var
  MyObject: TMyObject;
  MyObject2: TMyObject2;
  MyObject3: TMyObject3;
  MyObject4: TMyObject4;
begin
  MyObject := TMyObject.Create;
  MyObject.Foo;
  MyObject.Free;

  MyObject2 := TMyObject2.Create;
  MyObject2.Bar(3);
  MyObject2.Free;

  MyObject3 := TMyObject3.Create;
  MyObject3.Foo;
  MyObject3.Free;

  // Attempting to create an instance of abstract object
  // TMyObject4 will create a warning at compile time.
  MyObject4 := TMyObject4.Create;
  // It is legal to call BeEsoteric. However,
  // it will raise exception. In fact, it might crash Kylix 1.0.
  // As a result, I will comment out the method here.
  // MyObject4.BeEsoteric;
```

**LISTING 4.3**   Continued

```
  MyObject4.Free;
end;

end.
```

Take a moment to study this code. Note the examples of the syntax explored over the last few pages of the text. The purpose of the program is simply to provide a concise reference for these key features of the Object Pascal syntax. The program doesn't really do anything useful other than provide a single, short piece of code that shows you how to use all these key features of the Pascal language. Use it as a reference when you have questions about how to implement a technique in Object Pascal that you are already familiar with from some other language, such as Java or C++.

Parts of the program will be unfamiliar. The next few sections of this chapter describe those unfamiliar sections.

## Calling the Ancestor of an Overridden Method: `inherited`

When looking at Listing 4.3, pay special attention to the Bar and Foo methods. They show how to use the `inherited` keyword:

```
procedure TMyObject2.Bar(i: Integer);
begin
  inherited Bar(i);

end;

procedure TMyObject2.Foo;
begin
  inherited;
end;
```

If you are inside TMyObject2.Foo and you want to be sure that TMyObject.Foo gets called, you must place the keyword inherited in your code. If you don't place it there, then TMyObject.Foo will not get called.

So what happens if you have to call an ancestor method that takes parameters? How do you pass them on? Fortunately, that job is taken care of for you automatically by the inherited keyword. When you use the inherited keyword, all the parameters passed to a method automatically are passed on to the ancestor method when it is called. To help you understand this, let me show you an example. The Bar method shows one rather explicit way to extend the syntax of the inherited keyword to pass parameters to an ancestor method. In particular, you

**4**

OBJECTS AND
INTERFACES

enter the name of the ancestor method that you want to call and then pass the parameters in the usual manner. Note, however, that it is not necessary to use this technique if you do not want explicit control of how and where parameters are passed. For instance, the following two methods are semantically identical:

```
procedure TMyObject2.Bar(i: Integer);
begin
  inherited Bar(i);

end;

procedure TMyObject2.Bar(i: Integer);
begin
  inherited;

end;
```

In particular, both methods pass the variable i on to the inherited method Bar. The first method does so explicitly; the second does the same thing implicitly.

---

**C++ AND JavaNote**

Object Pascal constructors and destructors use the exact same model for inheritance that regular methods use. In Java and C++, inherited constructors and destructors are called first and are called automatically. This is not the case in Object Pascal. Instead, the constructor for the current object is called first, and no inherited constructors are called unless you explicitly call them by using the inherited keyword. In Java and C++, constructors and destructors are given the same name as a class. In Pascal, you can give a constructor any name that you want. The fact that it is a constructor is designated by the use of the keyword constructor, not by the fact that the constructor has the same name as the class. Destructors in Object Pascal can have any name you want, but by convention they are almost always named Destroy, and they use the override directive.

---

## The abstract Directive

It is time now to delve into a rather esoteric aspect of the Object Pascal inheritance model. This technology is not needed on a day-to-day basis, but it is a very powerful technique in the appropriate circumstances.

If you declare a method of an object to be abstract, then you do not need to implement that method. Instead, it is assumed that descendant objects will create the implementation. In short, this is a technique for declaring the specification for a class. It is not a technique for creating classes that you actually want to instantiate. As a result, it occupies a middle ground between an Object Pascal interface and an Object Pascal class.

All `abstract` methods must be declared `virtual` or `dynamic`. It is legal to create an instance of an object with `abstract` methods. However, doing so generates warnings at compile time. If you call one of these `abstract` methods at runtime, you will raise an exception. (In fact, in the first version of Kylix, calling an `abstract` method could produce undefined results.)

Here is how to declare an `abstract` method:

```
TMyObject4 = class(TMyObject)
  procedure BeEsoteric; virtual; abstract;
end;
```

As you can see, the `BeEsoteric` method looks very much like the code for a `virtual` method. The difference is simply that the directive `abstract` has been appended to the end of the declaration. There is no implementation for a method that is declared with the `abstract` directive. It is meant simply as a reminder to descendant objects that they must implement that particular method if they want to live up to the specification outlined by the `abstract` methods in their parent's declaration. Any one object can have any number and any combination of `abstract` and non-`abstract` methods.

It might help in this case to reference an example. The native Object Pascal class `TStream` has `abstract` methods in it. It is declared in Classes.pas; if you have access to the source for that class, you might want to look it up.

Because `TStream` has at least one `abstract` method in it, you would never directly create an instance of this class. If you create descendants of this class, you should fill in the methods of the `TStream` class that are declared as abstract. For instance, the Object Pascal team created `TFileStream` and `TMemoryStream`. Both objects override and implement the abstract `TStream.Write` method. In particular, `TFileStream.Write` implements a technique for writing to files, and `TMemoryStream.Write` implements a technique for writing to memory.

The key point to grasp here is that `abstract` methods, combined with the basic principles of inheritance and polymorphism, provide a powerful mechanism for defining a single technology for working with a whole set of classes. When you know how `TStream` works, you can easily use any of its descendants. If you understand `TFileStream`, then you automatically understand most of what you need to know about `TMemoryStream`. Both classes follow the specification laid out in the `TStream` object. Furthermore, through the magic of polymorphism, you can call one instance of the `TStream` object that will act like a memory stream, and you can call a second instance that will act like a file stream.

**4**

**OBJECTS AND INTERFACES**

## The `overload` Directive

You can overload methods in Object Pascal. An overloaded method has the same name as some other method in your object, but it has a different list of parameters:

```
type
  TMyObject = class(TMyObject)
    procedure Foo; virtual;
    procedure Goober; overload;
    procedure Goober(s: string; i: integer = 2); overload;
  end;
```

Two methods in TMyObject have the name Goober. Neither is either virtual or dynamic. Instead, these are overloaded methods, distinguished by their parameter list. The second instance of Goober has one parameter of type string and a second of type integer. The second parameter has a default value of 2.

Consider the following method:

```
procedure TMyObject.Foo;
begin
  Goober;
  Goober('Sam');
  Goober('Sam', 3);
end;
```

In this method, Goober calls TMyObject.Goober. The second example, Goober('Sam'), calls this:

```
TMyObject.Goober(s: string; i: integer = 2)
```

In particular, it allows the default value of 2 to be passed in the second parameter. Goober('Sam', 3) calls this:

```
TMyObject.Goober(s: string; i: integer = 2)
```

Needless to say, it ignores the default value of 2 for the i parameter and instead passes the value 3 in the second parameter of the method.

> **Note**
>
> You can overload functions and procedures exactly the same way that you overload methods.

JAVA AND
C++NOTE

Both Java and C++ support method overloading and default parameters. Semantically, there are few differences in the way overloading works in Java, C++, and Object Pascal. From a syntactic perspective, however, you must remember to include the overload directive when working with overloaded methods in an Object Pascal program.

## Instantiating and Freeing Instances of Classes

Consider the following procedure:

```pascal
procedure UseAllObjects;
var
  MyObject: TMyObject;
  MyObject2: TMyObject2;
  MyObject3: TMyObject3;
  MyObject4: TMyObject4;
begin
  MyObject := TMyObject.Create;
  MyObject.Foo;
  MyObject.Free;

  MyObject2 := TMyObject2.Create;
  MyObject2.Bar(3);
  MyObject2.Free;

  MyObject3 := TMyObject3.Create;
  MyObject3.Foo;
  MyObject3.Free;

  // Attempting to create an instance of abstract object
  // TMyObject4 will create a warning at compile time.
  MyObject4 := TMyObject4.Create;
  MyObject4.BeEsoteric;
  MyObject4.Free;
end;
```

Here you see code for instantiating instances of all the classes that have been discussed in this section of the text. Notice that I first create the class, then call one of its methods, and finally, free the memory associated with the class.

**4**

The call to instantiate an instance of `TMyObject4` generates a warning at compile time because it contains a method that is declared `abstract`. If you actually call the `abstract` method, as shown here, an exception should be raised.

That is all I'm going to say about the object model used in Kylix programs. Further points could be made about this subject, but I believe that most of them are matters for language lawyers. In this text, I have done my best to lay out the matters of practical concern for most programmers who want to use OOP in a day-to-day programming context.

## Class Methods

Class methods are a special kind of method used very rarely in Pascal programs. However, some objects, such as `TObject` itself, include a large number of class methods that are called frequently by CLX itself.

---

**C++ AND JAVA NOTE**

In C++ and Java, a class method is called a static method.

---

The important thing about a class method is that you can call it without first creating an instance of the object to which it belongs. To do so, you just use the class name and the name of the method that you want to call: `TObject.ClassName`.

In Object Pascal, you can declare a class method as follows:

```
TMyObject = class(TObject)
  class procedure DoIt; // This is a class method.
end;
```

The implementation of this method might look like this:

```
class procedure TMyObject.DoIt;
begin
  ShowMessage('Foobar');
end;
```

You can then call the method without first instantiating an instance of the method.

```
procedure TForm1.Button1Click(Sender: TObject);
begin
  TMyObject.DoIt;
end;
```

Notice that there was no need to call `TMyObject.Create`. Instead, you can call the class method `DoIt` directly off the class name. When making the call, you include the initial `T` at the beginning of the name. Further discussion of this topic occurs in Chapter 7, "CLX Architecture and Visual Development," in the section "Signals and Slots."

That is all I'm going to say about the object model used in Kylix programs. Further points could be made about this subject, but I believe that most of them are matters for language lawyers. In this text, I have done my best to lay out the matters of practical concern for most programmers who want to use OOP in a day-to-day programming context.

# Interfaces

Interfaces provide a means for creating standards. They provide a means for defining the best means of accessing a body of code. They also provide a means for abstracting the means of accessing a set of objects.

An object implements a set of declarations. An interface is just the declaration itself. It is a promise to the user that a certain set of methods will or should be implemented somewhere.

Suppose that you want to build a set of objects for creating games that can use DirectX, OpenGL, the Windows GDI, or Xlib. In this situation, you need to create four complete sets of objects. One set will let you implement the game in DirectX, and the others will let you use OpenGL, the Windows GDI, Xlib. Of course, the user of your objects would hope that each set of objects would work the same way. For instance, the method for drawing a bitmap to the screen should look the same whether the underlying technology is OpenGL or DirectX. Interfaces can help you be sure that your technology actually does present a uniform face to the user.

In particular, you could declare an interface for drawing things to the screen. The interface would say nothing about the implementation of your object. In practice, one implementation would draw things to the screen using DirectX, and another would draw things to the screen using OpenGL. The user of your objects, however, would never need to think about the implementation; instead, he could focus on the interface. Furthermore, the developers of the various sets of objects would have a blueprint to follow, outlined in the interface.

Kylix programmers can think of an interface as nothing more than a set of virtual abstract public methods for manipulating an object. If you stripped away the protected and private sections from a standard CLX object and then declared all the remaining methods as virtual abstract, you would have something very much like an interface.

The big difference between the public section of a CLX object and an interface is that the interface has no implementation. Its methods are abstract. An interface simply defines a set of public methods for accessing an object, but it says nothing about the actual implementation of that object. In this sense, an interface is a great deal like a virtual abstract public interface to a standard Pascal object.

**4**

**OBJECTS AND INTERFACES**

In the last few paragraphs, I've given you a number of fairly concrete ways to think about interfaces. However, interfaces are very flexible. An interface can simply be a means of providing a layer of abstraction around an object. If you want to talk about a specific set of behaviors that an object is capable of, but you don't want to talk about its actual implementation, then you might use an interface. For instance, this can be helpful if you have built a set of routines in C++ and you want programmers from other languages to use it. In such a case, you might create a set of interfaces that define what the objects do and then let developers in other languages figure out how to access the interfaces. This is what Microsoft did with the COM interfaces to DirectX.

I've tried to be as clear as possible, but newcomers to interfaces probably still might be unclear about this subject. If you are finding the subject hard to grasp, I assure you that this subject is not really that difficult to understand. After a time, you will almost certainly have an "ah-ha" moment, an epiphany, and you will suddenly see that the subject is not really that complicated. For now, perhaps the best way to fully get your arms around this subject matter is just to jump right in and see some code. Object Pascal makes interfaces very easy to implement, so I'll show you how things work before I explain any more about why they work that way—or even why they exist at all.

## The Interface Type

Here is what an interface looks like:

```
type
  IMyInterface = interface
    procedure MyProcedure;
  end;
```

This simple interface has one method, MyProcedure. To declare the interface, I first stated the name of the interface and then wrote an equals sign and the interface keyword. Finally, I declared a simple method and wrote the keyword end to wrap things up.

If I wanted to, I could have stated in parentheses the name of an interface from which this interface will descend:

```
IMyObject = interface(IInterface)
  Procedure MyProcedure;
end;
```

For now, you don't have to understand anything about IInterface other than it is another interface. An interface cannot descend from a class; it must descend either from nothing or from another interface.

Now, it so happens that the two declarations I have shown you here are actually identical, just as the following two class declarations are identical:

```
TMyObject = class
end;

TMyObject = class(TObject)
end;
```

These two declarations are identical because all Kylix classes descend, by default, from a class named TObject. Therefore, even if you don't say that TMyObject descends from another class, it still descends from TObject.

Just as all Kylix classes must descend either directly or indirectly from TObject, all Kylix interfaces must descend either directly or indirectly from IInterface. (However, I will not explain IInterface to you yet.)

Immediately below the declaration for IInterface in System.pas, you will find this statement:

```
IUnknown = IInterface;
```

For all intents and purposes, you can consider all interfaces to descend from either IUnknown or IInterface. In Delphi 5 and earlier, all interfaces descended from IUnknown, and there was no IInterface. However, IUnknown is a word rooted in Microsoft's COM technology. In an attempt to distance Object Pascal interfaces from the Windows world, the team decided to call the base object IInterface rather than IUnknown. To provide compatibility with old Delphi 5 code, they set IUnknown equal to IInterface.

> **NOTE**
>
> For those who are curious, IInterface is declared exactly as IUnknown was declared in Delphi 5. Furthermore, IDispatch is still declared almost immediately after IUnknown.

**4**

OBJECTS AND INTERFACES

## An Interface Is Not a Class!

Interfaces look a lot like classes, but they are not classes. For instance, interfaces have no data. There are no fields and no instance data in an interface. The following declaration is entirely illegal:

```
IMyObject = interface
  FMyData: Integer;  // This is illegal!
  Procedure MyProcedure;
end;
```

This declaration is no good because you cannot declare any data inside an interface. That's completely against the rules.

Furthermore, all members of interfaces are public, by default. In fact, you can't add any scoping directives to an interface. For instance, the following declaration is illegal:

```
IMyObject = interface(IUnknown)
private  // This scoping directive is illegal!
  procedure MyProcedure;
end;
```

This declaration is no good because you can't use scoping directives such as private, public, protected, or published in an interface declaration. All methods are declared public by default, and that's all there is to it.

## You Can't Directly Implement an Interface

You never implement an interface by itself. Instead, you make it part of a class. Using interfaces is a way to create a specification for an object, not a way to declare an object. For instance, the following unit will not compile:

```
unit Unit2;

interface
type
  IMyObject = interface(IUnknown)
    procedure MyProcedure;
  end;

implementation

procedure IMyObject.MyProcedure;
begin
  ShowMessage('Hi from MyObject');
end;

end.
```

The problem here is that I am attempting to declare an implementation of the IMyObject.MyProcedure method. You can't directly implement any of the methods of an interface. Instead, you must use a class to implement an interface. This all sounds like a mouthful when spoken out loud, but you will find that, in practice, it is quite simple.

## Using a Class to Implement an Interface

In this section, I'll show you a very simple program named SimpleInterface, which shows how to declare an interface, implement it, and then call it. The program is found on the CD that comes with this book, and the code for the program is shown in Listings 4.4 and 4.5.

**LISTING 4.4**   A Simple Unit That Declares an Interface and Implements It

```
//////////////////////////////////////
// Purpose: Declare and implement a simple interface
// Project: SimpleInterface.dpr
// Copyright  1998..2001 by Charlie Calvert
//
unit SimpleObject;

interface

type
  IMyInterface = interface
    function GetName: string;
  end;

  TMyClass = class(TInterfacedObject, IMyInterface)
    function GetName: string;
    constructor Create;
    destructor Destroy; override;
  end;

implementation

uses
  QDialogs;

constructor TMyClass.Create;
begin
  inherited Create;
  ShowMessage('Constructor called');
end;

destructor TMyClass.Destroy;
begin
  ShowMessage('Destroy');
  inherited Destroy;
end;

function TMyClass.GetName: string;
begin
  Result := Self.ClassName;
end;

end.
```

**LISTING 4.5**  The Main Form for a Kylix Application That Uses an Interface and Its Implementation

```
/////////////////////////////////////
// Purpose: Use an interface declared in SimpleObject.pas
// Project: SimpleInterface
// Copyright  1998..2001 by Charlie Calvert
//
unit Main;

interface

uses
  SysUtils, Classes, QGraphics,
  QControls, QForms, QDialogs,
  QStdCtrls;

type
  TForm1 = class(TForm)
    UseInterface2Btn: TButton;
    UseObjectBtn: TButton;
    UseInterface1Btn: TButton;
    procedure UseInterface2BtnClick(Sender: TObject);
    procedure UseObjectBtnClick(Sender: TObject);
    procedure UseInterface1BtnClick(Sender: TObject);
  end;

var
  Form1: TForm1;

implementation

uses
  SimpleObject;

{$R *.xfm}

{-----------------------------------------------------------------
  Just call the method of an object
------------------------------------------------------------------}
procedure TForm1.UseObjectBtnClick(Sender: TObject);
var
  MyClass: TMyClass;
begin
  MyClass := TMyClass.Create;
  ShowMessage(MyClass.GetName);
```

**LISTING 4.5**   Continued

```
  MyClass.Free;
end;

{- - - - - - - - - - - - - - - - - - - - - - - - - - - - - - - - - - - - - - - - - - - - - - - - - - - - - - -
  Retrieve an interface, and call one of its methods
- - - - - - - - - - - - - - - - - - - - - - - - - - - - - - - - - - - - - - - - - - - - - - - - - - - - -}
procedure TForm1.UseInterface1BtnClick(Sender: TObject);
var
  MyInterface: IMyInterface;
  MyClass: TMyClass;
begin
  MyClass := TMyClass.Create;
  MyInterface := MyClass;
  ShowMessage(MyInterface.GetName);
//  MyInterface := nil;
  MyClass := nil;
  ShowMessage('Foo');
end;

{- - - - - - - - - - - - - - - - - - - - - - - - - - - - - - - - - - - - - - - - - - - - - - - - - - - - - - -
  Retrieve an interface, and call one of its methods
- - - - - - - - - - - - - - - - - - - - - - - - - - - - - - - - - - - - - - - - - - - - - - - - - - - - -}
procedure TForm1.UseInterface2BtnClick(Sender: TObject);
var
  MyInterface: IMyInterface;
begin
  MyInterface := TMyClass.Create;
  ShowMessage(MyInterface.GetName);
end;

end.
```

4

When you run this program, you see a form with three buttons on it, as shown in Figure 4.1. If you click the buttons on the form, various methods of the interface or the object that implements it are called.

**FIGURE 4.1**

*The form to the* SimpleInterface *program.*

The following is the declaration for the interface used in this program and for the class used to implement the interface:

```
IMyInterface = interface
  function GetName: string;
end;

TMyClass = class(TInterfacedObject, IMyInterface)
  function GetName: string;
end;
```

The simple interface shown here declares a single method called GetName. This method is implemented in TMyClass as follows:

```
function TMyClass.GetName: string;
begin
  Result := 'MyInterface';
end;
```

As you can see, nothing is unusual about the implementation for this method. It could not possibly be simpler. It's just a normal implementation of a very simple method. So what ties TMyClass.GetName to IMyInterface.GetName? What is the relationship between these two syntactical entities?

To understand what is happening here, you need to take a careful look at the declaration for TMyClass:

```
TMyClass = class(TInterfacedObject, IMyInterface)
```

This line of code says that TMyClass descends from another class named TInterfacedObject, and it implements an interface named IMyInterface.

> **NOTE**
>
> You need to understand that TMyClass does not support true multiple inheritance. True multiple inheritance occurs when one class descends from at least two other classes. TMyClass descends from one class and one interface. This difference is actually more than a semantic quibble because an interface is fundamentally different from a class in that it cannot implement any methods.
>
> The end result is that you cannot have two implementations of the same method of an interface in the same inheritance tree. I will discuss this topic more fully when I examine the program MultipleInterface later in this chapter.

`TMyClass` descends from one standard Kylix class named `TInterfacedObject` and one interface named `IMyInterface`. It declares a single method named `GetName` that implements the `GetName` method declared in `IMyInterface`. The thing that ties `TMyClass.GetName` to `IMyInterface.GetName` is the simple fact that the two methods have the same name. (There is slightly more to this story, but again I will ask you to wait for a full explanation until you see the `MultipleInheritance` program.)

You are probably wondering about `TInterfacedObject` and where it comes from. `TInterfacedObject` is a special class that does certain things to make it possible for the class from which it descends to automatically and easily implement an interface. In particular, `TInterfacedObject` implements the methods of `IInterface`, just as `TMyClass` implements the single method of `IMyInterface`.

If you wanted, you could implement the methods of `Interface` in `TMyClass`. In other words, you could write something like the following:

```
TMyClass = class(TObject, IMyInterface);
```

In this case, though, `TMyClass` would have to implement not only `GetName`, but also the methods declared in `IInterface`.

If you want, you can think about this situation in a slightly different way. If you want to create a form to use in your own program, then you descend from `TForm`:

```
TForm1 = class(TForm)
```

In the same way, if you want to implement an interface, just descend from `TInterfacedObject` or for some other object that itself descends from `TInterfacedObject`:

```
TMyClass = class(TInterfacedObject, IMyInterface)
```

## Calling the Methods of an Interface

The main form for the `SimpleInterface` program contains three buttons. The first button enables you to call the sole method of `TMyClass`. The second two buttons show you two different ways to call a method of `IMyInterface`. In the next few paragraphs, I will explain all these methods.

This method does nothing more than create an instance of `TMyClass` and call its method:

```
procedure TForm1.UseObjectBtnClick(Sender: TObject);
var
  MyClass: TMyClass;
begin
  MyClass := TMyClass.Create;
  ShowMessage(MyClass.GetName);
  MyClass.Free;
end;
```

This example is as simple a piece of code as you can write in Kylix. I just want to give you a base point to start from so that you can see what is different when you start working with an interface:

```
procedure TForm1.UseInterface1BtnClick(Sender: TObject);
var
  MyInterface: IMyInterface;
  MyClass: TMyClass;
begin
  MyClass := TMyClass.Create;
  MyInterface := MyClass;
  ShowMessage(MyInterface.GetName);
end;
```

In this example, you first create an instance of TMyClass:

```
MyClass := TMyClass.Create;
```

Then you retrieve the interface from that class:

```
MyInterface := MyClass;
```

This line of code is very important. It enables you to create a reference to an interface through a simple assignment statement.

> **NOTE**
>
> People who understand the Windows-based Microsoft COM technology might have some pretty pressing questions by this time, so I will take a moment to answer one of them. In particular, those who understand COM are probably wondering whether the rules of COM apply over here in the land of Linux. For better or worse, the answer to that question is yes. In particular, the following call is legal and will succeed:
>
> ```
> MyInterface.QueryInterface(IUnknown, Unknown);
> ```

After you have retrieved an instance of IMyInterface from an object, then you can call the method of IMyInterface:

```
ShowMessage(MyInterface.GetName);
```

As you know, this is really the same thing as calling TMyClass.GetName. In fact, you are literally calling TMyClass.GetName. In other words, UseObjectClick and UseInterface1BtnClick end up doing pretty much the same thing. The only difference is that one uses an interface and the other doesn't.

The following is the second method that retrieves the interface from `TMyClass` and calls the `IMyInterface.GetName` method:

```
procedure TForm1.UseInterface2BtnClick(Sender: TObject);
var
  MyInterface: IMyInterface;
begin
  MyInterface := TMyClass.Create;
  ShowMessage(MyInterface.GetName);
end;
```

## Destroying Interfaces

The watchful readers of this book will have noticed that I do nothing to destroy the interfaces that I create. As it happens, this is the correct thing to do. An interface does not need to be destroyed because Kylix will do so automatically.

To understand what is happening here, the first thing you want to do is see for yourself that what I am saying is really true. To understand what is happening, you need only focus on the destructor shown in the SimpleObject.pas file:

```
destructor TMyClass.Destroy;
begin
  ShowMessage('Destroy');
  inherited Destroy;
end;
```

Because I call `ShowMessage` in the destructor of this object, you have a simple way to tell whether the object is being freed.

If you call the first method on the main form, the destructor gets called for an obvious reason:

```
procedure TForm1.UseObjectBtnClick(Sender: TObject);
var
  MyClass: TMyClass;
begin
  MyClass := TMyClass.Create;
  ShowMessage(MyClass.GetName);
  MyClass.Free;
end;
```

Here I explicitly call `MyClass.Free`, so it's obvious that the destructor is going to be called. Now take a look at the second example:

```
procedure TForm1.UseInterface1BtnClick(Sender: TObject);
var
  MyInterface: IMyInterface;
```

**4**

OBJECTS AND
INTERFACES

```
  MyClass: TMyClass;
begin
  MyClass := TMyClass.Create;
  MyInterface := MyClass;
  ShowMessage(MyInterface.GetName);
end;
```

If you run this example, you will see that the destructor gets called in this case, too. But why? Why should the destructor be called in this second case when there obviously is no explicit call to free or destroy?

Well, the answer is simply that, behind the scenes, Kylix is keeping track of this object and frees it the moment it goes out of scope. These objects work exactly the same way that local objects work in C++; or the way variants, WideChars, and strings work in Kylix: As soon as they go out of scope, they are automatically destroyed.

All this is fine, but what if you want to explicitly destroy an object? Intelligent readers not already in the know are likely to make one of two guesses regarding how an interface should be destroyed:

- Programmers with a strong Object Pascal background would assume that you can call the Free method on these objects.
- Programmers with a COM background would assume that you can call Release on these objects.

Both are intelligent, reasonable guesses. However, neither approach will end up generating an access violation. The correct way to destroy these objects is to set them equal to nil:

```
MyInterface := nil;
```

If you make this call, the method Release is automatically called, as is the destructor for TMyClass. I find this behavior to be extremely surprising, so I need to make explicit note of it and keep it in mind at all times.

To test this behavior, try conducting a few experiments. For instance, try the following method:

```
procedure TForm1.UseInterface1BtnClick(Sender: TObject);
var
  MyInterface: IMyInterface;
  MyClass: TMyClass;
begin
  MyClass := TMyClass.Create;
  MyInterface := MyClass;
  ShowMessage(MyInterface.GetName);
  MyInterface := nil;
  ShowMessage('Foo');
end;
```

Or, try things this way:

```
procedure TForm1.UseInterface1BtnClick(Sender: TObject);
var
  MyInterface: IMyInterface;
  MyClass: TMyClass;
begin
  MyClass := TMyClass.Create;
  MyInterface := MyClass;
  ShowMessage(MyInterface.GetName);
  MyClass := nil;
  ShowMessage('Foo');
end;
```

Again, you might find the results of this little experiment surprising. For instance, in the first case, the program pops up the name of the object, then says that the destructor is being called, and then shows the message 'Foo'. In the second case, however, the object name is popped up, then the message Foo is displayed, and then the destructor for the object is called. In other words, you can free TMyClass by setting MyInterface equal to nil, but you cannot free TMyClass by setting MyClass equal to nil. In the first case, you are causing things to happen behind the scenes; in the second case, you are merely setting a pointer variable equal to nil.

An important point to grasp here is that an interface has no separate life apart from the object that implements it. The interface is just an abstraction; it's just an idea. The only thing that gets created is TMyClass. IMyInterface is just an abstraction of some subset of functionality of TMyClass and TInterfacedObject.

## Multiple Interfaces on One Object

The SimpleInterface program works with an object that implements only one interface. However, you can implement as many interfaces as you want on a single object. Listings 4.6 and 4.7 show how this works.

LISTING 4.6   A Program That Shows How to Handle a Class That Supports Multiple Interfaces

```
////////////////////////////////////
// Purpose: Use an interface declared in SimpleObject.pas
// Project: SimpleInterface
// Copyright  1998..2001 by Charlie Calvert
//
unit Main;

interface
```

4

OBJECTS AND
INTERFACES

**LISTING 4.6**   Continued

```
uses
  SysUtils, Classes, QGraphics,
  QControls, QForms, QDialogs,
  QStdCtrls;

type
  TForm1 = class(TForm)
    SimpleInterfaceBtn: TButton;
    ComplexInterface1Btn: TButton;
    MultipleClassBtn: TButton;
    procedure SimpleInterfaceBtnClick(Sender: TObject);
    procedure ComplexInterface1BtnClick(Sender: TObject);
    procedure MultipleClassBtnClick(Sender: TObject);
  end;

var
  Form1: TForm1;

implementation

uses
  ComplexObject;

{$R *.xfm}

{-------------------------------------------------------------------
  Retrieve an interface, and call one of its methods. This is the
  simple example meant to set off the complex example shown in
  ComplexInterface1BtnClick.
-------------------------------------------------------------------}
procedure TForm1.SimpleInterfaceBtnClick(Sender: TObject);
var
  MyInterface: IMyInterface;
begin
  MyInterface := TMyClass.Create;
  ShowMessage(MyInterface.GetName);
end;

{-------------------------------------------------------------------
  Create an instance of the Complex class and calls its
  GetName method. This shows that we are not working
  with true multiple inheritance. When you create
  TMyComplexClass, you get the Complex version of the
  GetName method, and the original version is
```

**LISTING 4.6**   Continued

```
  obliterated. Look at ComplexObject.pas to see what
  is happening. This is why you don't have to worry about
  multiple inheritance tripping you up in Delphi.
-----------------------------------------------------------------------------}
procedure TForm1.ComplexInterface1BtnClick(Sender: TObject);
var
  MyInterface: IMyInterface;
begin
  MyInterface := TMyComplexClass.Create;
  ShowMessage(MyInterface.GetName);
end;


{-----------------------------------------------------------------------------
  This routine shows how to work with method-resolution
  clauses.
-----------------------------------------------------------------------------}
procedure TForm1.MultipleClassBtnClick(Sender: TObject);
var
  MultipleInterface: TMyMultipleInterface;
begin
  MultipleInterface := TMyMultipleInterface.Create;
  ShowMessage(MultipleInterface.GetName + #13 +
    MultipleInterface.MyOtherInterfaceGetName);
end;

end.
```

**LISTING 4.7**   A Single Object That Implements Two Interfaces

```
////////////////////////////////////////
// Purpose: Declare and implement a simple interface
// Project: SimpleInterface.dpr
// Copyright  1998..2001 by Charlie Calvert
//
unit ComplexObject;

interface

type
  IMyInterface = interface
    function GetName: string;
  end;
```

**LISTING 4.7**   Continued

```pascal
  TMyClass = class(TInterfacedObject, IMyInterface)
    function GetName: string;
  end;


{------------------------------------------------------------------------
  IMyInterface appears twice in this class's hierarchy, but
  only TMyComplexClass.GetName will be called. There are not
  two implementations of GetName in the hierarchy of this class,
  thus it is not true multiple inheritance.
-------------------------------------------------------------------------}
  TMyComplexClass = class(TMyClass, IMyInterface)
    function GetName: string;
  end;


  IMyOtherInterface = interface
    function GetName: string;
  end;


{------------------------------------------------------------------------
  Show how to use a method resolution clause
-------------------------------------------------------------------------}
  TMyMultipleInterface = class(TInterfacedObject,
    IMyInterface, IMyOtherInterface)
    function IMyOtherInterface.GetName = MyOtherInterfaceGetName;
    function GetName: string;
    function MyOtherInterfaceGetName: string;
  end;


implementation


function TMyClass.GetName: string;
begin
  Result := Self.ClassName + '.MyInterface';
end;


{ TMyComplexClass }


function TMyComplexClass.GetName: string;
begin
  Result := Self.ClassName + '.GetName';
end;


{ TMyMultipleInterface }
```

**LISTING 4.7**   Continued

```
function TMyMultipleInterface.GetName: string;
begin
  Result := 'IMyInterface';
end;

function TMyMultipleInterface.MyOtherInterfaceGetName: string;
begin
  Result := 'IMyOtherInterface';
end;

end.
```

This program has a very simple interface with three buttons on it. Clicking any of the buttons on the form allows the user to exercise the interface supplied in the ComplexObject.pas unit. Needless to say, this program also has no real-world application beyond teaching someone how interfaces work.

TMyComplexClass gets its name because it has two instances of IMyInterface in its inheritance tree:

```
IMyInterface = interface
  function GetName: string;
end;

TMyClass = class(TInterfacedObject, IMyInterface)
  function GetName: string;
end;

TMyComplexClass = class(TMyClass, IMyInterface)
  function GetName: string;
end;
```

In particular, notice that TMyClass implements IMyInterface, as does TMyComplexClass. Because TMyComplexClass inherits from TMyClass, this makes it appear that TMyComplexClass has two implementations of GetName in it. Although it's not an exact duplicate of the truly troublesome situations, this is nonetheless the kind of situation that can lead to sleepless nights over the debugger in standard C++ multiple inheritance programming.

But in this program, TMyComplexClass knows nothing about TMyClass's implementation of the GetName method. When Kylix finds two implementations of the same class in a hierarchy, only the most recent one is kept, and any inherited instances are discarded. This keeps things very clean and simple. You always know which instance of a particular method will execute.

**4**

You should also note that the Kylix form of inheritance is kept simple because you can inherit from multiple interfaces, but from only one class. This means that you can't have two implementations of a single interface coming at you from two different directions. Any implementations of an interface can come up as a single line of inheritance; if there is more than one implementation of an interface in that line of inheritance, then it is only the most recent one that is active.

## Method Resolution Clauses

The `TMyMultipleInterface` implements two interfaces, and both of these interfaces have methods with the same name:

```
IMyInterface = interface
  function GetName: string;
end;

IMyOtherInterface = interface
  function GetName: string;
end;

TMyMultipleInterface = class(TInterfacedObject,
  IMyInterface, IMyOtherInterface)
  function IMyOtherInterface.GetName = MyOtherInterfaceGetName;
  function GetName: string;
  function MyOtherInterfaceGetName: string;
end;
```

This particular case might look a lot like the programming problem discussed in the last section, but it is fundamentally different. In this case, there are not two implementations of the `GetName` method. Instead, you have a problem because there are two interfaces that have declared a method with the same name.

To handle this problem, you can declare a method-resolution clause that assigns the implementation of a particular interface method declaration to a method of your current class that sports a slightly different name:

```
function IMyOtherInterface.GetName = MyOtherInterfaceGetName;
```

Here the `IMyOtherInterface.GetName` method will be implemented by a method called `MyOtherInterfaceGetName`. If you look at the declaration for `TMyMultipleInterface`, you will see that the `IMyInterface.GetName` method is handled by `TMyMultipleInterface.GetName`.

Overall, this is a pretty simple matter to digest. There is nothing complicated about method-resolution clauses other than simply remembering that they exist. You might not get hit by the problem shown here right away, but sooner or later you will stumble across it. If you can just remember this solution, you will have no trouble navigating these potentially treacherous shores.

> **NOTE**
>
> I have a terrible time remembering the exact syntax for method-resolution clauses, but I have managed to keep the name of the technology tucked away in my brain. Fortunately, this is a case in which the online help can come to your rescue. Just plug the phrase *method resolution clause* into the Index page of the online help, and you will be taken to an example of the syntax.

## The Declaration of `IInterface`

Here is the declaration of `IInterface`:

```
IInterface = interface
  ['{00000000-0000-0000-C000-000000000046}']
  function QueryInterface(const IID: TGUID; out Obj): HResult; stdcall;
  function _AddRef: Integer; stdcall;
  function _Release: Integer; stdcall;
end;
```

The method `_AddRef` is called automatically by the Kylix compiler each time you create an instance of this interface. When you let go of an instance of this interface, Kylix automatically calls `_Release` for you. In Linux, you never need to explicitly call these methods. To see how this works, take a look at the program shown in Listing 4.8.

**LISTING 4.8** A second version of the SimpleObject File That Implements `_AddRef` and `_Release`

```
///////////////////////////////////////
// Purpose: Declare and implement a simple interface
// Project: AddRefRelease.dpr
// Copyright  1998..2001 by Charlie Calvert
//
unit SimpleObject;

(* Here is the declaration for IInterface:

  IInterface = interface
    ['{00000000-0000-0000-C000-000000000046}']
    function QueryInterface(const IID: TGUID; out Obj): HResult; stdcall;
```

**LISTING 4.8** Continued

```pascal
    function _AddRef: Integer; stdcall;
    function _Release: Integer; stdcall;
  end; *)

interface

type
  IMyInterface = interface(IInterface)
    function GetName: string;
  end;

  TMyClass = class(TObject, IMyInterface)
  private
    FRefCount: Integer;
  public
    function GetName: string;
    constructor Create;
    destructor Destroy; override;
    function QueryInterface(const IID: TGUID; out Obj): HResult; stdcall;
    function _AddRef: Integer; stdcall;
    function _Release: Integer; stdcall;
  end;

implementation

uses
  QDialogs;

constructor TMyClass.Create;
begin
  inherited Create;
  ShowMessage('Constructor called');
end;

destructor TMyClass.Destroy;
begin
  ShowMessage('Destroy');
  inherited Destroy;
end;

function TMyClass.GetName: string;
begin
  Result := Self.ClassName;
end;
```

**LISTING 4.8**   Continued

```
function TMyClass._AddRef: Integer;
begin
  ShowMessage('AddRef');
  Inc(FRefCount);
  Result := FRefCount;
end;

function TMyClass.QueryInterface(const IID: TGUID; out Obj): HResult;
begin
  ShowMessage('QueryInterface');
  if GetInterface(IID, Obj) then
    Result := 0
  else
    Result := E_NOINTERFACE;
end;

function TMyClass._Release: Integer;
begin
  ShowMessage('Release');
  Dec(FRefCount);
  if FRefCount <= 0 then
    Free;
end;

end.
```

The implementation for _AddRef shown here simply increments a variable named FRefCount. In the _Release method, FRefCount is decremented. If FRefCount ever reaches 0, the object is freed.

I have placed this unit in the directory AddRefReleaseInterface. The other files in that unit are identical to the files in the SimpleInterface program. Consider for a moment the UseInterface1BtnClick method:

```
procedure TForm1.UseInterface1BtnClick(Sender: TObject);
var
  MyInterface: IMyInterface;
  MyClass: TMyClass;
begin
  MyClass := TMyClass.Create;
  MyInterface := MyClass;
  ShowMessage(MyInterface.GetName);
  // Switch which line you comment out, and run the program
  //  MyInterface := nil;
```

**4**

**OBJECTS AND
INTERFACES**

```
  MyClass := nil;
  ShowMessage('Foo');
end;
```

The moment the line that says MyInterface := MyClass is called, _AddRef is called. The moment the line that says MyInterface := nil is called, _Release is called. In the sample shown here, MyInterface := nil is commented out. As a result, _Release will be called after ShowMessage but before the end; statement.

Again, you don't have to do anything to make these calls happen. Kylix does it all for you. Most people will probably want to experiment some with the AddRefReleaseInterface program. A little hands-on work can help you get a good feeling for what is happening here.

As a rule, in Kylix, QueryInterface never comes into play. The underlying version of QueryInterface implemented in TInterfacedObject will work as QueryInterface is supposed to work in COM programming, but there is no real need for it in most Kylix programs. Instead, the compiler will do some hand waving in the background and return to you pointers to the relevant offsets in the object's VMT. This is much faster than calling QueryInterface. In other words, Kylix has optimized code in it that will return just that portion of an object that contains the methods used by a particular interface. As result, there is no need to call QueryInterface.

Here is another way to think about what QueryInterface does:

```
function TMyClass.QueryInterface(const IID: TGUID; out Obj): HResult;
begin
  Obj := self;
  Result := 0;
end;
```

This code returns a copy of the current object to anyone who wants access to an interface supported by this object. This is an oversimplification of what happens in QueryInterface, but it sums up the purpose of the method.

The one subject not addressed yet in this section is the GUID that is associated with an interface:

```
IInterface = interface
  ['{00000000-0000-0000-C000-000000000046}']
```

The GUID part of an interface is optional. In Linux, there is very little need to use it. Its sole purpose is to uniquely identify an interface. The GUID is just a very large number. Each interface that is created in this world should have its own unique GUID. In fact, there are ways of creating numbers guaranteed to be unique. However, that subject generally is not important to Kylix programmers who want to use interfaces. As a result, I will not cover it in this text, although I do discuss the subject in depth in my book, *Delphi 4 Unleashed* by Sams Publishing.

You do not need to have a separate declaration for a GUID if you do find a reason to use it. Simply referencing the interface itself is equivalent to referencing the GUID. For instance, the following code will compile:

```
var
  Guid: TGuid;
begin
  Guid := IDispatch;
```

Everything said in this section on IInterface can be summed up by simply recommending that you always use TInterfacedObject and let it implement IInterface for you. If you want to have a frame or a form support an interface, you do not need to worry about implementing the methods of IInterface. TForm and TFrame do not descend from TInterfacedObject, but they do implement the methods of IInterface.

## The Theory Behind Interfaces

You learned earlier that interfaces provide a simple way to create standards or specifications. If you define an interface, then you or others can implement it according to a predefined and easily understood standard. The TStrings and TStream classes play roles similar to this in CLX: They are abstract classes that are used primarily as a way to define the behavior to be exhibited by a whole series of other classes such as TFileStream and TStringList.

Suppose that you want to create a specification for creating objects that deliver a specific set of functionality. For instance, you might want to define a set of objects that enable people to create certain geometrical shapes. Your goal is to allow multiple vendors to create their own shapes but to define a common API that all vendors would use. That way, you could write one set of code for displaying shapes but create different results by plugging in different vendors' objects. For instance, you might write code for manipulating a spherical shape, but when you use Vendor A's implementation of the sphere shape, you would get a sphere with polka dots; if you used Vendor B's implementation, you would get a sphere with a hippie tie-dye pattern on it. Or, perhaps one vendor's sphere would have fewer facets than another vendor's sphere, making it more purely round.

To give your objects this kind of plug-and-play functionality, each vendor would have to conform to a predefined specification for defining geometric shapes. To start defining that specification, you might create a simple interface that defines points in space:

```
IPoint = Interface(IUnknown)
  procedure SetPoints(X, Y: Integer);
  procedure Draw;
end;
```

This declaration says nothing about the actual implementation of class `IPoint`. It just represents a specification for the class. A particular vendor might choose to implement it as follows:

```
TPoint = class(TInterfacedObject, IPoint)
private
  XPos: Integer;
  YPos: Integer;
public
  procedure SetPoints(X, Y: Integer);
  procedure Draw; virtual;
end;
```

But this implementation is really beside the point. What matters here is that a specification has been laid out, and all the vendors who want to participate must follow that specification. They can develop their own implementations to suit their own needs; it's the specification that can't change. This is not a fascistic call for conformism—rather, it gives people the freedom to choose from an array of vendors who support the interface. Or, if they prefer, they can implement the interface as they choose.

## Reasons for Using Interfaces

Interfaces might provide a better way to define a set of objects than the technologies provided by traditional OOP. This fact was not at all clear to me when I first started using interfaces, but the more I have played with this technology, the more I have come to see how valuable it can be.

To understand what I am driving at, it might be helpful to see a concrete example. Suppose that you want to create a set of objects that will be used to communicate with a piece of hardware that will control some fanciful object such as an automated kite. The object that you create might look something like this:

```
TKite = class(TObject)
  Procedure Launch;
  Procedure Land;
  Procedure LetOutString;
  Procedure ReelInString;
  Procedure Swoop(Direction: TDirection);
  Procedure UntangleString;
  Procedure FreeStringFromTelephoneWire;
end;
```

The company that you are working for might create a whole line of automated kites, and the implementation for each of these methods would differ depending on the kind of kite you create. Interfaces provide a simple mechanism for defining the way each of these kite objects should look, without saying anything about their implementation.

For instance, you could recast the class shown previously as an interface:

```
IKite = interface(Interface)
  Procedure Land;
  Procedure LetOutString;
  Procedure ReelInString;
  Procedure Swoop(Direction: TDirection);
  Procedure UntangleString;
  Procedure FreeStringFromTelephoneWire;
end;
```

This simple declaration is more powerful than it might seem. It serves as a specification for the kite object. You can give these few lines to several teams of programmers and tell them to create objects that implement this interface. When they are finished, you will have a series of entirely compatible objects guaranteed to behave in a similar manner. In other words, an interface can be a simple means of documenting and designing shallow hierarchies of objects. At the same time, these interfaces provide a built-in means of enforcing a clearly defined and especially lucid design standard.

To help emphasize this point, let me show you what some of these implementations might look like. For instance, the kite teams might end up implementing the following classes:

```
TBatKite = class(TInterfacedObject, IKite);
  Procedure Land;
  Procedure LetOutString;
  // Code omitted here to avoid repetition
end;

TChineseKite = class(TInterfacedObject, IKite)
  Procedure Land;
  Procedure LetOutString;
  // Other methods of IKite interface defined here...
end;
```

These two objects will behave in the same way. After you have taught someone to work with one of these kites, he will know how to work with all of them because they support the same interface. The adoption of interfaces by the kite team can make a lot of programming and design issues quite simple. (Now, if only we could figure out a way to get the bugs out of that darn FreeStringFromTelephoneWire method.)

Of course, as shown here, this technology does not provide much in the way of reuse. In some cases, you might just forgo the reuse of code and say that the benefits of interfaces are sufficient for the particular situation at hand. Or, if you want, you can create an intermediate class that implements some of the functionality of the interface and leaves it up to each individual class to implement the rest.

**4**

OBJECTS AND
INTERFACES

You must understand, however, that some people like the fact that interfaces don't tend to promote deep hierarchies. Consider what happens when you are in hierarchy several levels deep and you want to implement a particular virtual method. To be reminded of the complications that can ensue, consider the following hierarchy:

```
TKite = class;
TChineseKite = class(Kite);
TEagleKite = class(TChineseKite);
TTwoStringedEagleKite = class(TEagleKite);
```

Suppose that a virtual method named Launch is implemented in each of these objects. If you are creating or maintaining the TTwoStringedEagleKite class, you might have to decide whether you want to call the ancestor class's version of Launch from your implementation of the Launch method. Well, perhaps you should. On the other hand, maybe you should skip the implementation of Launch in TEagleKite and go directly to the one in TChineseKite. Hmm. Maybe. The truth is, when you get right down to it, knowing for sure what the best course of action is might be a bit hard. You will have to study quite a bit of source code and maybe do some guesswork or experimentation before you can make a decision.

The difficult decisions outlined in the preceding paragraph do not exhaust the list of ambiguous situations that OOP commonly creates. For instance, imagine that you are a programmer called in to maintain an existing implementation of the code, and you see that TTwoStringedEagleKite.Launch calls TEagleKite.Launch, but you missed the fact that TEagleKite.Launch skips calling TChineseKite.Launch and instead calls TKite.Launch. What are the potential ramifications of that particular oversight? Well, again, it's a bit hard to say without doing a considerable amount of guesswork and experimentation.

The more you ponder the difficulties inherent in the scenarios described in the previous paragraphs, the better it sounds to implement simple interface/object pairs that go only one level deep. Sure, you can't reuse the code as easily as you can reuse traditional OOP code, but the code that you do write will be easy to understand and easy to maintain. If you are working in C++, you will also know that you don't have to worry about true multiple inheritance throwing even more monkey wrenches into the works.

My point here is not that interfaces and shallow inheritance are necessarily better than traditional OOP—only that the issue is more open to debate than it might seem at first glance. Keeping code as simple and clean as possible is a very worthwhile goal, one that might be worth pursuing even at the cost of losing certain fun-to-use features. Certainly, it's hard to argue with the fact that you can teach most programmers how to take advantage of interfaces in just a few days, whereas it usually takes years for a programmer to fully grasp all the nuances of traditional OOP programming.

Before closing this section, let me just remind you that interfaces can be used as a way of defining a standard for very deep hierarchies. That's not a misuse of interfaces, nor is it uncommon practice. I'm merely pointing out that sometimes you might find it useful to use a very shallow hierarchy. Interfaces could provide an enticing alternative to standard OOP-based programming practices.

## Maintaining or Updating an Interface

It might be helpful to make one more important point about interfaces and the way they are used in most programming environments. As a rule, you should never attempt to update or improve an interface. After you have created it and released it to the public, that is the final draft and it should never be changed.

If you want to make changes to an interface, you should create a new version of the interface and release it under a new name:

```
IKite2 = class(TObject)
  Procedure Launch;
  Procedure Land;
  Procedure LetOutString(NumInches: Integer);
  Procedure ReelInString(NumInches: Integer);
  Procedure Swoop(Direction: TDirection);
  Procedure UntangleString;
  Procedure FreeStringFromTelephoneWire;
  Function GetWindStatus: TDirection;
end;
```

This new interface is identical to the original IKite interface, except that it supports a new function named GetWindStatus. Furthermore, the LetOutString and ReelInString methods now take parameters.

If a developer wants to access the new features in IKite2, he can use that interface. But your object should also still support the IKite interface so that you do not break old code. In other words, you should consider creating one object server that supports at least two interfaces, one named IKite and the other named IKite2.

Programming is difficult because of the complexity inherent in many of the real-world problems that need to be solved. Maybe it's best not to try to solve these complex problems with complex tools. Sometimes the best tools are the simplest tools that provide good flexibility and performance. When used correctly, interfaces encourage the creation of simple programs with good performance characteristics.

**4**

OBJECTS AND
INTERFACES

# Variants

As promised in Chapter 3, in the section on BCD development, I will now go on to describe variants and how they work.

Variants can be assigned to a wide range of variable types. Some people jokingly refer to variants as a typeless type, because they can be used to represent a string, an integer, an object, or several other types.

The following is a simple procedure that illustrates the flexible nature of variants:

```
procedure TForm1.Button2Click(Sender: TObject);
var
  V:Variant;
begin
  V := 1;
  V := 'Sam';
end;
```

As you can see, you are allowed to assign both a string and an integer to the same variant variable.

The following procedure, however, is not legal:

```
procedure TForm1.Button1Click(Sender: TObject);
var
  V: Variant;
begin
  V := 1;
  Caption := 'Sam' + V;
end;
```

The attempt to assign `Edit1.Text` to a variant concatenated with a string will be flagged as a type mismatch by the compiler because a variant takes on some of the attributes of an integer after being assigned to that type.

Underneath the surface, variant types are represented by a 16-byte structure found in System.pas. At the time of this writing, that structure looks like this:

```
TVarType = Word;
PVarData = ^TVarData;
TVarData = packed record
  VType: TVarType;
  case Integer of
    0: (Reserved1: Word;
         case Integer of
           0: (Reserved2, Reserved3: Word;
```

```
          case Integer of
            varSmallInt: (VSmallInt: SmallInt);
            varInteger:  (VInteger: Integer);
            varSingle:   (VSingle: Single);
            varDouble:   (VDouble: Double);
            varCurrency: (VCurrency: Currency);
            varDate:     (VDate: TDateTime);
            varOleStr:   (VOleStr: PWideChar);
            varDispatch: (VDispatch: Pointer);
            varError:    (VError: LongWord);
            varBoolean:  (VBoolean: WordBool);
            varUnknown:  (VUnknown: Pointer);
            varShortInt: (VShortInt: ShortInt);
            varByte:     (VByte: Byte);
            varWord:     (VWord: Word);
            varLongWord: (VLongWord: LongWord);
            varInt64:    (VInt64: Int64);
            varString:   (VString: Pointer);
            varAny:      (VAny: Pointer);
            varArray:    (VArray: PVarArray);
            varByRef:    (VPointer: Pointer);
          );
      1: (VLongs: array[0..2] of LongInt);
    );
  2: (VWords: array [0..6] of Word);
  3: (VBytes: array [0..13] of Byte);
end;
```

Notice that this is a variant record—that is, the various types represented in the case statement are overlaid in memory. (Variant records have nothing to do with the Variant type. The occurrence of the two names in the same context is just a coincidence.) The structure ends up being 16 bytes in size because the VType field is 2 bytes, the three reserved fields total 6 bytes, and the largest of the types in the variant section is the double, which is 8 bytes in size. (2 + 6 + 8 = 16.) Again, the case statement in the declaration is not a list of separate fields, but a list of different ways to interpret the 8 bytes of data contained in the second half of the space allocated for the record.

The following are the declarations for the values used with variants:

```
varEmpty     = $0000; { vt_empty     }
varNull      = $0001; { vt_null      }
varSmallint  = $0002; { vt_i2        }
varInteger   = $0003; { vt_i4        }
varSingle    = $0004; { vt_r4        }
varDouble    = $0005; { vt_r8        }
```

**4**

**OBJECTS AND INTERFACES**

```
     varCurrency = $0006; { vt_cy          }
     varDate     = $0007; { vt_date        }
     varOleStr   = $0008; { vt_bstr        }
     varDispatch = $0009; { vt_dispatch    }
     varError    = $000A; { vt_error       }
     varBoolean  = $000B; { vt_bool        }
     varVariant  = $000C; { vt_variant     }
     varUnknown  = $000D; { vt_unknown     }
//varDecimal    = $000E; { vt_decimal $0e } {UNSUPPORTED}
                         { undefined  $0f } {UNSUPPORTED}
     varShortInt = $0010; { vt_i1      $10 }
     varByte     = $0011; { vt_ui1         }
     varWord     = $0012; { vt_ui2     $12 }
     varLongWord = $0013; { vt_ui4     $13 }
     varInt64    = $0014; { vt_i8      $14 }
//varWord64     = $0015; { vt_ui8     $15 } {UNSUPPORTED}

     varStrArg   = $0048; { vt_clsid    }
     varString   = $0100; { Pascal string; not OLE compatible }
     varAny      = $0101; { Corba any }
     varTypeMask = $0FFF;
     varArray    = $2000;
     varByRef    = $4000;
```

> **NOTE**
>
> When you study these declarations, it's important to understand that Kylix defines a certain set of behaviors to be associated with variants, but it might not guarantee that the implementation will remain the same from version to version. In other words, you can almost surely count on the fact that assigning both a string and an integer to the same variant will always be safe. However, you might not necessarily be sure that variants will always be represented by the same constants and record shown previously. To check whether these implementations have been blessed as being permanent, refer to your Kylix documentation.
>
> Please note that this structure might change over time in different versions of the product.

It should be clear from the preceding code examples that knowing what type is represented by a variant at a particular moment can be important. To check the variant's type, you can use the VarType function, as shown here:

```
var
  Atype: Integer;
  V: Variant;
```

```
begin
  Atype := VarType(V);
  ...
end;
```

In this example, the Integer variable AType will be set to one of the constants shown previously. In particular, it will probably be assigned to varEmpty because, in the preceding example, this variable has not yet been assigned to another type.

If you want to get a closer look at a variant, you can typecast it to learn more about it, as shown in the following example:

```
procedure TForm1.Button1Click(Sender: TObject);
var
  V: Variant;
  VarData: TVarData;
begin
  V := 1;
  VarData := TVarData(V);
  Atype := VarData.vType;
end;
```

In this particular case, AType will be set to the same value that would be returned from a call to VarType.

To understand more about how all this works, see Listing 4.9, in which you can find the code for the VarDatas program. This code sets a single variant to a series of different values and then examines the variant to discover the current value of its VType field.

**LISTING 4.9**   The VarDatas Program Lets You Examine Variant Types

```
unit Main;

{  Program demonstrates some traits of Variants. }

interface

uses
  SysUtils, Classes, QGraphics,
  QControls, QForms, QDialogs,
  QStdCtrls;

type
  TForm1 = class(TForm)
    bVariantPlay: TButton;
    ListBox1: TListBox;
```

**LISTING 4.9** Continued

```
    procedure bVariantPlayClick(Sender: TObject);
  public
    procedure ShowVariant(V: Variant);
  end;

var
  Form1: TForm1;

implementation

uses
  Variants;

{$R *.xfm}

function GetVariantType(V: Variant): string;
var
  VarData: TVarData;
  S: string;
begin
  VarData := TVarData(V);
  case VarData.VType of
    varEmpty: S := 'varEmpty';
    varNull:  S := 'varNull';
    varSmallint: S := 'varSmallInt';
    varInteger: S := 'varInteger';
    varSingle: S := 'varSingle';
    varDouble: S:= 'varDouble';
    varCurrency: S := 'varCurrency';
    varDate: S := 'varDate';
    varOleStr: S := 'varOleStr';
    varDispatch: S := 'varDispatch';
    varError: S := 'varError';
    varBoolean: S := 'varBoolean';
    varVariant: S := 'varVariant';
    varUnknown: S := 'varUnknown';
    varString: S := 'varString';
    varTypeMask: S := 'varTypeMask';
    varByRef: S := 'varByRef';
    varByte: S := 'varByte';
    varArray: S := 'varArray';
  end;
  Result := S;
end;
```

**LISTING 4.9**   Continued

```
procedure TForm1.ShowVariant(V: Variant);
var
  S, Temp: string;
begin
  if VarIsNull(V) then begin
    Temp := 'Null';
    S := Format('Value: %-15s  Type: Null', [Temp]);
  end else begin
    Temp := V;
    S := Format('Value: %-15s  Type: %s', [Temp, GetVariantType(V)]);
  end;
  ListBox1.Items.Add(S);
end;

procedure TForm1.bVariantPlayClick(Sender: TObject);
var
  V: Variant;
begin
  ShowVariant(V);
  V := Null;
  ShowVariant(V);
  V := 1;
  ShowVariant(V);
  V := 'Sam';
  ShowVariant(V);
  V := 1.25;
  ShowVariant(V);
end;

end.
```

**4**

A typical run of this program is shown in Figure 4.2.

The data shown in the list box in Figure 4.2 represents the value and internal representation of a single variant that is assigned a series of different types. It's important to understand that Variant can't simultaneously represent all types; instead, at any one moment it can take on the characteristics of only one particular type.

The code that assigns different types to a variant is easy to understand:

```
procedure TForm1.Button1Click(Sender: TObject);
var
  V: Variant;
  S: TObject;
begin
```

```
    ShowVariant(V);
    V := Null;
    ShowVariant(V);
    V := 1;
    ShowVariant(V);
    V := 'Sam';
    ShowVariant(V);
    V := 1.25;
    ShowVariant(V);
end;
```

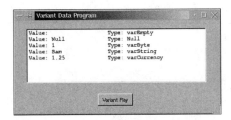

**FIGURE 4.2**

*The VarDatas program uses the* TVarData *structure to examine how variants are put together.*

The code that reports on the current type of a variant is somewhat more complex, but it's still relatively straightforward:

```
function GetVariantType(V: Variant): string;
var
  VarData: TVarData;
  S: string;
begin
  VarData := TVarData(V);
  case VarData.VType of
    varEmpty: S := 'varEmpty';
    varNull:  S := 'varNull';
    varSmallint: S := 'varSmallInt';
    varInteger: S := 'varInteger';
    varSingle: S := 'varSingle';
    varDouble: S:= 'varDouble';
    varCurrency: S := 'varCurrency';
    varDate: S := 'varDate';
    varOleStr: S := 'varOleStr';
    varDispatch: S := 'varDispatch';
    varError: S := 'varError';
    varBoolean: S := 'varBoolean';
```

```
    varVariant: S := 'varVariant';
    varUnknown: S := 'varUnknown';
    varString: S := 'varString';
    varTypeMask: S := 'varTypeMask';
    varByRef: S := 'varByRef';
  end;
  Result := S;
end;
```

This code first converts a variant into a variable of type `TVarData`. In doing so, it is merely surfacing the true underlying type of the variant. However, a variable of type `TVarData` will not act the same as a variable of type `Variant`. This is because the compiler provides special services for variants that it would not provide for a simple record type such as `TVarData`.

It's important to note that there are at least two ways to write the first lines of code in this function. For instance, I could have written this:

```
function GetVariantType(V: Variant): string;
var
  I: Integer;
  S: string;
begin
  i := VarType(V);
  case i of
    varEmpty: S := 'varEmpty';
    varNull:  S := 'varNull';
    ...
  end;
end;
```

This code works the same as the code shown in the actual program found on the CD that accompanies this book.

However you decide to implement the function, the key point is that variants can take on the appearance of a certain type. The chameleon-like behavior of `Variant` is sparked by the type of variable to which it is assigned. If you want, you can think of a variant as being a chameleon that hides itself from view by assuming the coloration of the variable to which it is assigned. A variant is never of type `Variant`; it's always either empty, `NULL`, or the type of the variable to which it is assigned. In the same way, a chameleon has no color of its own but is always changing to adapt its color to the environment around it. Either that or it is unborn, dead, nonexistent, or has no color at all!

The following routines can all be used with variants. To learn more about these routines, look in the online help.

**4**

**OBJECTS AND INTERFACES**

```
function VarType(const V: Variant): TVarType;
function VarAsType(const V: Variant; AVarType: TVarType): Variant;
function VarIsType(const V: Variant; AVarType: TVarType): Boolean; overload;
function VarIsType(const V: Variant;
  const AVarTypes: array of TVarType): Boolean; overload;
function VarIsByRef(const V: Variant): Boolean;
function VarIsEmpty(const V: Variant): Boolean;
procedure VarCheckEmpty(const V: Variant);
function VarIsNull(const V: Variant): Boolean;
function VarIsClear(const V: Variant): Boolean;
function VarIsCustom(const V: Variant): Boolean;
function VarIsOrdinal(const V: Variant): Boolean;
function VarIsFloat(const V: Variant): Boolean;
function VarIsNumeric(const V: Variant): Boolean;
function VarIsStr(const V: Variant): Boolean;
function VarToStr(const V: Variant): string;
function VarToStrDef(const V: Variant; const ADefault: string): string;
function VarToWideStr(const V: Variant): WideString;
function VarToWideStrDef(const V: Variant; const ADefault: WideString):
WideString;
function VarToDateTime(const V: Variant): TDateTime;
function VarFromDateTime(const DateTime: TDateTime): Variant;
function VarInRange(const AValue, AMin, AMax: Variant): Boolean;
function VarEnsureRange(const AValue, AMin, AMax: Variant): Variant;
function VarIsEmptyParam(const V: Variant): Boolean;
function VarSupports(const V: Variant; const IID: TGUID; out Intf): Boolean;
{ Variant copy support }
procedure VarCopyNoInd(var Dest: Variant; const Source: Variant);
```

Here are some routines to use with Variant arrays, which, unfortunately, I do not have room to discuss in this book:

```
function VarArrayCreate(const Bounds: array of Integer;
  AVarType: TVarType): Variant;
function VarArrayOf(const Values: array of Variant): Variant;
function VarArrayDimCount(const A: Variant): Integer;
function VarArrayLowBound(const A: Variant; Dim: Integer): Integer;
function VarArrayHighBound(const A: Variant; Dim: Integer): Integer;
function VarArrayLock(const A: Variant): Pointer;
procedure VarArrayUnlock(const A: Variant);
function VarArrayRef(const A: Variant): Variant;
function VarIsArray(const A: Variant): Boolean;
function VarTypeIsValidArrayType(const AVarType: TVarType): Boolean;
function VarTypeIsValidElementType(const AVarType: TVarType): Boolean;
```

Before closing this section, I want to make it clear that variants are not meant to be used broadly in your program whenever you need to work with a variable. I have no doubt that many people will, in fact, program that way, but I want to emphasize that the developers didn't really want variants to be used that way, mainly because they have some overhead associated with them that can slow down the compiler. (Some tricks performed by variants, such as string manipulation, happen to be very highly optimized. However, you should never consider a variant to be as fast or efficient as a standard Object Pascal type such as an `Integer`, `Cardinal`, or `string`.)

Variants are almost certainly best used in database applications. In particular, variants were brought into the language because they played a role in Windows-based OLE automation. These unusual types also prove useful in database applications. As a rule, so much overhead is involved in referencing any value from a database that a little additional variant manipulation code will not make a significant difference.

# RTTI and Floating-Point Types

I now want to talk briefly about Run Time Type Information, or RTTI. The integer types have many easy-to-use routines for finding out about the range and size of a type. I will now show you a tricky way to get that same kind of information about floating-point numbers. I should emphasize, however, that this technology is extremely generic and can be applied to nearly any Pascal type.

The best way to get started is to take a look at the BasicType program, found in Listing 4.10. This program shows how to use the poorly documented `TypInfo` unit to get information about types.

---

**NOTE**

The word *TypInfo* is pronounced "Tip-Info," as in giving a waiter a tip, or giving someone a tip about the stock market. This unit has never been very well documented, partly because the Pascal team hopes one day to provide a more intuitive interface to this same functionality. At that time portions of the `TypInfo` unit could be made obsolete. As a rule, if you can find information about a routine in the online help, then it is a part of the language and you can count on its continuance, unless the help specifically states otherwise. If a routine is not in the online help, then all bets are off.

**LISTING 4.10**  The BasicType Program Shows Some of the Simplest Tricks You Can Perform Using the `TypInfo` Unit

```
unit Main;

interface

uses
  SysUtils,Classes, QGraphics,
  QControls, QForms, QDialogs,
  QStdCtrls, TypInfo, QComCtrls;

type
  TForm1 = class(TForm)
    Button1: TButton;
    ListView1: TListView;
    procedure Button1Click(Sender: TObject);
  private
    procedure GetInfo(Info: PTypeInfo);
    { Private declarations }
  public
    { Public declarations }
  end;

var
  Form1: TForm1;

implementation

{$R *.xfm}

procedure TForm1.GetInfo(Info: PTypeInfo);
var
  TypeData: PTypeData;
  ListItem: TListItem;
begin
  TypeData := GetTypeData(Info);
  ListItem := ListView1.Items.Add;
  ListItem.Caption := Info^.Name;
  ListItem.SubItems.Add(IntToStr(TypeData^.MinValue));
  ListItem.SubItems.Add(IntToStr(TypeData^.MaxValue));
end;

procedure TForm1.Button1Click(Sender: TObject);
begin
  GetInfo(TypeInfo(Boolean));
  GetInfo(TypeInfo(Byte));
```

**LISTING 4.10**  Continued

```
  GetInfo(TypeInfo(ShortInt));
  GetInfo(TypeInfo(Char));
  GetInfo(TypeInfo(SmallInt));
  GetInfo(TypeInfo(Word));
  GetInfo(TypeInfo(Integer));
  GetInfo(TypeInfo(Cardinal));
  GetInfo(TypeInfo(LongInt));
  GetInfo(TypeInfo(LongWord));
  GetInfo(TypeInfo(Int64));
  GetInfo(TypeInfo(Double));
  GetInfo(TypeInfo(Single));
  GetInfo(TypeInfo(Real));
  GetInfo(TypeInfo(Extended));
  GetInfo(TypeInfo(Comp));
  GetInfo(TypeInfo(Currency));
end;

end.
```

The BasicType program gives you type information on the Pascal integer and floating-point types. To do this, it uses the TypInfo unit, which contains routines for mining the type information that the compiler carries for all Pascal types.

Using the TypInfo unit, you can do many wonderful things, such as print the names of all the values of a particular enumerated type. You can also find out whether a variable is a floating-point type, an ordinal type, an object, or something else.

There is no room to explore the TypInfo unit in depth in this chapter. However, I believe that there is value in at least propping open the door leading to this subject. That way you will at least know that the TypInfo unit exists, and you will perhaps begin to see some of the wondrous things it can do for you.

Perhaps the most fundamental type in the TypInfo unit is TTypeInfo:

```
  TTypeKind = (tkUnknown, tkInteger, tkChar, tkEnumeration, tkFloat,
    tkString, tkSet, tkClass, tkMethod, tkWChar, tkLString, tkWString,
    tkVariant, tkArray, tkRecord, tkInterface, tkInt64, tkDynArray);

  TTypeInfo = record
    Kind: TTypeKind;
    Name: ShortString;
    {TypeData: TTypeData}
  end;
```

When applied to a variable, this record will tell you the name of variable's type. For instance, consider this code fragment:

```
var
  T: PTypeInfo;
begin
  T := TypeInfo(Currency);
  ListBox1.Items.Add(T.Name);
```

This code adds the word *Currency* to a list box. The value of Kind will be tkFloat.

The PTypeData type provides more information than the TTypeInfo type:

```
PTypeData = ^TTypeData;
TTypeData = packed record
  case TTypeKind of
    tkUnknown, tkLString, tkWString, tkVariant: ();
    tkInteger, tkChar, tkEnumeration, tkSet, tkWChar: (
      OrdType: TOrdType;
      case TTypeKind of
        tkInteger, tkChar, tkEnumeration, tkWChar: (
          MinValue: Longint;
          MaxValue: Longint;
          case TTypeKind of
            tkInteger, tkChar, tkWChar: ();
            tkEnumeration: (
              BaseType: PPTypeInfo;
              NameList: ShortStringBase));
        tkSet: (
          CompType: PPTypeInfo));
    tkFloat: (
      FloatType: TFloatType);
    tkString: (
      MaxLength: Byte);
    tkClass: (
      ClassType: TClass;
      ParentInfo: PPTypeInfo;
      PropCount: SmallInt;
      UnitName: ShortStringBase;
     {PropData: TPropData});
    tkMethod: (
      MethodKind: TMethodKind;
      ParamCount: Byte;
      ParamList: array[0..1023] of Char
     {ParamList: array[1..ParamCount] of
        record
          Flags: TParamFlags;
```

```
      ParamName: ShortString;
      TypeName: ShortString;
    end;
  ResultType: ShortString});
tkInterface: (
  IntfParent : PPTypeInfo; { ancestor }
  IntfFlags : TIntfFlagsBase;
  Guid : TGUID;
  IntfUnit : ShortStringBase;
 {PropData: TPropData});
tkInt64: (
  MinInt64Value, MaxInt64Value: Int64);
end;
```

Let's take a look at one more very short program that shows how to get an enumerated type to give the name of its currently selected element. The example is found on the accompanying CD as the TypeInfoGet.dpr, from the Chapter04 directory. You can see the program in Listing 4.11.

**LISTING 4.11**    The TypeInfoGet Program Shows How to Get an Enumerated Type to Speak Its Name

```
unit Main;

////////////////////////////////////////
// Purpose: Work with TypInfo and Enumerated types
// Program: TypeInfoGet
// Copyright  2001 by Charlie Calvert
//

interface

uses
  SysUtils, Classes, QGraphics,
  QControls, QForms, QDialogs,
  QStdCtrls, TypInfo;

type
  TStuff = (tsNancy, tsPaul, tsLucy, tsMary, tsSam, tsSarah);

  TForm1 = class(TForm)
    Button1: TButton;
    ListBox1: TListBox;
    procedure Button1Click(Sender: TObject);
  private
```

**4**

**LISTING 4.11**    Continued

```
  FStuff: TStuff;
public
  property Stuff: TStuff read FStuff write FStuff;
end;

var
  Form1: TForm1;

implementation

{$R *.xfm}

procedure TForm1.Button1Click(Sender: TObject);
const
  Alpha = ['A'..'Z', 'a'..'z', '_', ' '];
  AlphaNumeric = Alpha + ['0'..'9'];

var
  T: PTypeInfo;
  D: PTypeData;
  i, Index, WordLen: Integer;
  P: ShortString;
begin
  ListBox1.Items.Add('Tell me the name of the types we''re using.');
  T := TypeInfo(Currency);
  ListBox1.Items.Add(T.Name);
  T := TypeInfo(TStuff);
  ListBox1.Items.Add(T.Name);
  ListBox1.Items.Add('Show enumerated values by brute force');
  Stuff := tsNancy;
  ListBox1.Items.Add(GetEnumName(TypeInfo(TStuff), Ord(Stuff)));
  Stuff := tsSam;
  ListBox1.Items.Add(GetEnumName(TypeInfo(TStuff), Ord(Stuff)));
  Stuff := tsMary;
  ListBox1.Items.Add(GetEnumName(TypeInfo(TStuff), Ord(Stuff)));


  ListBox1.Items.Add('Show all enumerated values the easy way');
  D := GetTypeData(T);
  for i := 0 to D.MaxValue do
    ListBox1.Items.Add(GetEnumName(TypeInfo(TStuff), i));

  ListBox1.Items.Add('Show all enumerated values the hard way');
  Index := 0;
  for i := 0 to D.MaxValue do begin
```

**LISTING 4.11** Continued

```
    WordLen := Ord(D.NameList[Index]) + 1;
    Move(D.NameList[Index], P, WordLen);
      ListBox1.Items.Add(P);
    Inc(Index, WordLen);
  end;
end;

end.
```

The output from this program is shown in Figure 4.3. Note that the program prints the name of the currency type and prints the element associated with an instance of the TStuff type. In particular, the program prints the words Currency and tsSam.

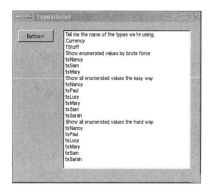

**FIGURE 4.3**

*The output from the TypeInfoGet program.*

This program uses the TypeInfo function to get the Currency and TStuff types to say their names. This is only marginally useful. More valuable is the second statement, which gets the name of the current value of the enumerated variable Stuff. The GetEnumName function, from the TypInfo unit, takes a pointer to a TTypeInfo records in its first parameter, and the ordinal value of an enumerated type in its second parameter.

**4**

OBJECTS AND
INTERFACES

| NOTE |

The fifth line of this program does not explicitly set the value of the property Stuff. This is not necessary because all objects automatically zero out their fields at the moment the object is created. As a result, Stuff is set to 0, which, in this case, is

> equivalent to tsSam. Note, however, that this rule does not apply to local variables in a method or procedure.
>
> Furthermore, you could not get type information on TStuff if it were not a property of an object. The fact that TStuff is a property makes the variable worthy of containing type information.

Here is an easy way to enumerate over all the types in an enumeration:

```
D := GetTypeData(T);
for i := 0 to D.MaxValue do
  ListBox1.Items.Add(GetEnumName(TypeInfo(TStuff), i));
```

The key point here is that the TTypeData.MaxValue field tells you how many different types are in the enumeration. When you have that value, it is easy to use GetEnumName to iterate over the relevant values.

The last bit of code in the Button1Click method digs a little deeper into the TTypeData record structure:

```
ListBox1.Items.Add('Show all enumerated values the hard way');
Index := 0;
for i := 0 to D.MaxValue do begin
  WordLen := Ord(D.NameList[Index]) + 1;
  Move(D.NameList[Index], P, WordLen);
    ListBox1.Items.Add(P);
  Inc(Index, WordLen);
end;
```

The variable D.NameList is an array containing the names of all the members of the enumerated type. Each name is preceded by a value designating the length of the value. For instance, #5 would proceed tsSam, and #6 would proceed tsMark. I use this information to find each of the type names hidden in the NameList and to print them to the ListBox. This works because the compiler treats each chunk of the array that you discover as a ShortString.

# Frames

This section discusses one of the more important features in CLX programming. If you really understand what frames are about, you can use this very easy-to-understand device to significantly improve the maintainability of your code.

Frames provide a form of visual encapsulation for your program. When you first learn about OOP, there is a tendency to see inheritance and polymorphism as its flashiest and most important features. But years of experience has taught me that no part of standard OOP is more important than the simple capability to partition code into neatly organized compartments via encapsulation.

Frames bring encapsulation to the visual portions of the code that you write. In short, they enable you to wrap a certain area of your form in a neatly encapsulated and easily reusable mini-form. In particular, you can drop two or three components onto a frame and then embed the frame inside a form. The frame provides a neatly encapsulated area where the logic associated with a set of components can reside. Furthermore, this enables you to easily reuse those components in multiple applications.

The only drawback of frames that I see is that it takes a certain degree of both imagination and engineering intelligence to understand how and when to use them. However, if you have the experience necessary to properly leverage this tool, it can be very valuable.

## Creating a Frame

After that introduction, you might be expecting frames to be hard to use. Fortunately, that is not the case. Working with frames is a lot like working with forms. If you know how to create and use a form, you know 90% of all you need to know about frames.

Load Kylix and start a new application. Choose File, New, Frame from the Kylix menu. An entity that looks very much like a small form will be added to your application. This object, called a frame, resides in its own unit. By default, your application should now have Unit1 in it, which contains the form, and Unit2 in it, which contains the frame.

Here is the declaration for the frame:

```
TFrame2 = class(TFrame)
private
  { Private declarations }
public
  { Public declarations }
end;
```

Even the declaration for a frame looks a lot like the declaration for a form. The big difference is that it descends from TFrame rather than TForm.

The fact that x and start a the frame has a number in its name proves to be somewhat awkward in many cases. As a result, you might want to give it a new name that does not include a number—in this case, you can call it TPoemFrame.

It is now time to do something with the frame. Just for argument's sake, let's drop a TMemo and a button on the frame. Name the button Longfellow. Double-click the button to create an event handler, just as you would when working with a form. Enter this code in the event handler:

```
procedure TPoemFrame.LongfellowClick(Sender: TObject);
const
```

**4**

**OBJECTS AND INTERFACES**

```
  CR =#10;
var
  S: String;
begin
  S := 'The morning breaks, the steeds in their stalls'+CR+
    'Stomp and neigh, as the hostler calls;' + CR +
    'The day returns, but nevermore' + CR +
    'Returns the traveler to the shore,' + CR +
    'And the tide rises, and the tide falls';
  Memo1.Text := S;
end;
```

On the Component Palette, on the far left, is an icon labeled Frames. Click it and then click your main form. (Don't click the source for your main form—click the form itself.) A dialog box appears that contains a list of all the frames in your project, as shown in Figure 4.4. Select the frame that you created and click OK. Your frame will be inserted into the form, as shown in Figure 4.5.

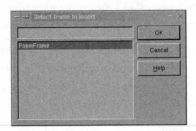

**FIGURE 4.4**

*The Select Frame to Insert dialog box enables you to select a frame that you want to insert into a form.*

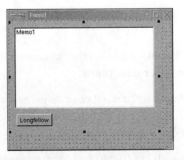

**FIGURE 4.5**

*A simple frame with one button. and a memo on it, inserted into a form.*

At this stage, the declaration for Form1 looks like this:

```
TForm1 = class(TForm)
  PoemFrame1: TPoemFrame;
private
  { Private declarations }
public
  { Public declarations }
end;
```

As you can see, the frame that you created has been inserted into the form, just like a normal component such as a button or a list box. The difference is that this object that you have inserted into your form encapsulates both a series of visual controls and a significant block of code. Listing 4.12, for instance, shows the code for the frame as it now stands.

**LISTING 4.12**   The Complete Code for PoemFrame

```
unit MyFrame;

interface

uses
  SysUtils, Types, Classes,
  QGraphics, QControls, QForms,
  QDialogs, LGradient, QStdCtrls;

type
  TPoemFrame = class(TFrame)
    Longfellow: TButton;
    Memo1: TMemo;
    procedure LongfellowClick(Sender: TObject);
  private
    { Private declarations }
  public
    { Public declarations }
  end;

implementation

{$R *.xfm}

procedure TPoemFrame.LongfellowClick(Sender: TObject);
const
  CR =#10;
```

**4**

**LISTING 4.12**  Continued

```
var
  S: String;
begin
  S := 'The morning breaks, the steeds in their stalls'+CR+
    'Stomp and neigh, as the hostler calls;' + CR +
    'The day returns, but nevermore' + CR +
    'Returns the traveler to the shore,' + CR +
    'And the tide rises, and the tide falls';
  Memo1.Text := S;
end;

end.
```

The point here is that all of Listing 4.12 is encapsulated inside the single declaration in `Form1` that looks like this:

```
PoemFrame1: TPoemFrame;
```

This is the essence of encapsulation. A relatively complex piece of code is reduced to a simple line of code that is easy to understand and manage.

## Reusing Frames

The final trick that you need to learn when using frames is how to reuse them by placing them on the Component Palette. If you manage your frames correctly, you can reuse them in multiple projects. Each time you use the frame, you might make slight improvements to it. These improvements automatically are inherited by the other projects that use the frame. To get access to these improvements, all you have to do is recompile any project that uses the component.

To get started, you need to save your frame to disk. You should consider saving all the frames that you want to reuse in a single directory. That will make it relatively easy for you to maintain the paths to the source files used by your projects. For instance, you might save the frames that you create in a global directory such as the `lunits` directory that ships on the CD that accompanies this book.

After you have saved the frame, right-click it. Select the Add to Palette option. A dialog box pops up like the one shown in Figure 4.6. For now, you can choose the default options in the dialog box. This saves your frame under the name PoemFrameTemplate to a page on the Component Palette named Templates.

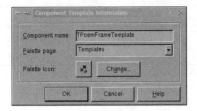

**FIGURE 4.6**
*The dialog box provided by Kylix when you decide to save a frame to the Component Palette.*

At this stage, you are done creating your frame. The next step is to reuse the frame in a second project.

Close the current project and start a new project in Kylix. Open your main form, turn to the Templates page in the Component Palette, and drop your new template onto your form. Now you can run your program and watch the frame in action.

That's all there is to it. Nothing could be simpler.

The frame that you added to your new project is the same frame, in the same directory, as the frame that you originally created. You are not working with a copy of your frame, but with the original frame. Any changes that you make to this frame, therefore, also will be registered in any past or future projects that use the frame. Of course, the changes will not appear until you compile or recompile the code for these other projects.

In this section of the chapter, you learned about frames. In Chapter 7, you will learn about a similar technology known as form inheritance. In most cases, I believe that frames are a superior technology to form inheritance. If possible, use frames in your application and resort to form inheritance only in special circumstances when it obviously solves complex problems for you in a clean and logical manner.

# The Command-Line Compiler

The standalone compiler is useful primarily when you want to compile applications before using them with the standalone debugger. Many C/C++ programmers have an aversion to the IDEs that are supplied with their products. However, there is a very intimate connection between a Pascal program and the Kylix environment. Most programmers probably will find it much simpler to work inside the IDE rather than try to design programs from the command line. However, there are bound to be at least a few independent souls with different ideas, and I'm sure they will be glad for the command-line compiler.

The command-line compiler is called dcc. It is stored in the Kylix bin directory. To run it, you should type **dcc** and then the name of your project file.

---

**C++ AND JAVA**
    **NOTE**

Unlike a standard C++ compiler, but like Java, you do not need to specifically mention the units that are part of your project. If you pass the compiler the name of your DPR file, it will automatically compile any pas files included in that project.

---

The compiler takes many parameters. You can view them by typing the compiler's name with no parameters.

The most important parameter is –u, which allows you to designate the path to where the unit directories are stored:

```
dcc –u/home/ccalvert/kylix/lib:/home/ccalvert/srcpas/lunits prog.dpr
```

Notice that each path to your unit directories is separated by a colon, not by a semicolon as it would be in Windows. It is not legal to write /u rather than –u because the / character in Linux is a path delimiter.

It is often convenient to write an alias stored in your .bashrc file that can help you automatically append the –u option to your compiler:

```
alias dcca –U/home/ccalvert/kylix/lib
```

The /v option to the compiler turns on debug information. As explained in Chapter 7, in the section "Working with Resources," you can use the wrc utility that ships with the open source WINE project to compile resources at the command line.

## Summary

In this chapter, you learned about the syntax for using objects and interfaces. Programming Kylix typically involves using many object-oriented programming techniques. The better you understand this subject, the better you will be at performing your tasks as a Kylix programmer.

Interfaces are one of the most powerful tools available to Kylix programmers. For an example of how to use them in a real-world program, see the section of text under "A Pseudo 3D World," in Chapter 11, "Graphics."

You have now completed your examination of the Object Pascal language. With this material behind you, you are free to begin exploring the advanced features of the IDE, the Kylix interface to lower-level functions, and the structure of the CLX component model. Each of these subjects will be covered in turn in the chapters of the book following this one.

# The Editor and Debugger

*by Charlie Calvert*

## IN THIS CHAPTER

In this chapter, you will learn how to use the editor, manage your projects, and run the debugger. A few other related topics of interest will come up as well, including these:

- The Project Manager
- The Source Code Editor
- The Code Explorer
- The To-Do List
- The Debugger
- Exceptions
- Code Insight

So far in this book, you've learned how to use the visual programming tools, and you've learned about some of the basic and advanced features of the Object Pascal syntax. In this chapter, you learn how to write code inside the IDE, manage your projects, and use the debugger.

## The Source Code Editor and Its Friends

The source code editor is where you write code. Most of the code that you write will appear between the begin..end blocks of methods. You will also use the editor to declare types, constants, variables, uses clauses, and the initialization and finalization sections at the end of a unit. The source code editor is shown in Figure 5.1.

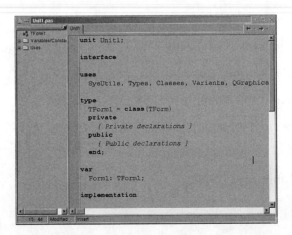

**FIGURE 5.1**

*The editor with source to a default Kylix form shown inside it; here you can see the* interface *and* implementation, *as well as the* uses *clause,* type *section, and* var *section.*

# A Tale of Two Tools: The Editor and the Designer

More takes place in the editor than the mere act of writing code. If you are working on a form or a frame, the editor is in a symbiotic relationship with the Form Designer.

## Influencing the Visual Tools from the Editor

If place components on the Form Designer, the Source Code Editor will reveal code that has been generated as a result. For instance, if you start a new project and then drop down two buttons, an edit control, and a list box, the type declaration for your TForm1 object will show the fruits of your labor. Take a look at the Button1, Button2, Edit1, ListBox1, and procedure Button1Click declarations in Listing 5.1. All the code associated with these elements was generated automatically by actions in the Form Designer. In particular, I double-clicked Button1 to create the Button1Click method.

**LISTING 5.1**  An Example of the Source Code Automatically Generated When You Place Components on a Form in Design Mode

```
unit Main;

interface

uses
  SysUtils, Types, Classes,
  Variants, QGraphics, QControls,
  QForms, QDialogs, QStdCtrls;

type
  TForm1 = class(TForm)
    Button1: TButton;
    Button2: TButton;
    Edit1: TEdit;
    ListBox1: TListBox;
    procedure Button1Click(Sender: TObject);
  private
    { Private declarations }
  public
    { Public declarations }
  end;

var
  Form1: TForm1;
```

**LISTING 5.1**  Continued

```
implementation

{$R *.xfm}

procedure TForm1.Button1Click(Sender: TObject);
begin
  //
end;

end.
```

Conversely, you could write code instantiating methods in the source code editor, and they would show up on the Form Designer. For instance, in Listing 5.2, I manually typed in the declaration and empty implementation for Button2Click.

**LISTING 5.2**  Event Handlers Such as the Button2Click Method, Shown Here, Can Be Entered by Hand in the Editor

```
unit Main;

interface

uses
  SysUtils, Types, Classes,
  Variants, QGraphics, QControls,
  QForms, QDialogs, QStdCtrls;

type
  TForm1 = class(TForm)
    Button1: TButton;
    Button2: TButton;
    Edit1: TEdit;
    ListBox1: TListBox;
    procedure Button1Click(Sender: TObject);
    procedure Button2Click(Sender: TObject);
  private

    { Private declarations }
  public
```

**LISTING 5.2**   Continued

```
  { Public declarations }
end;

var
  Form1: TForm1;

implementation

{$R *.xfm}

procedure TForm1.Button1Click(Sender: TObject);
begin
  //
end;

procedure TForm1.Button2Click(Sender: TObject);
begin
  //
end;

end.
```

To see the results of this action, go to the Form Designer and select Button2. Now open the Object Inspector and turn to the Events page. Drop down the Property Editor for the OnClick event, as shown in Figure 5.2. You will now see that you can assign either Button1Click or Button2Click to this method. In short, the Button2Click method is now visible in the Object Inspector, even though it was created with the editor rather than with the visual tools.

**FIGURE 5.2**

*The* Button1Click *and* Button2Click *methods are visible in the Property Editor for the* OnClick *event.*

**5**

THE EDITOR AND
DEBUGGER

> **NOTE**
>
> You learned a little bit about events in Chapter 1, "Visual Development," in the section "The Object Inspector and Events." However, I think it will be helpful to say a few more words on that subject here. The topic will come up again in various places throughout Part II, "CLX."
>
> The `Button1Click` and `Button2Click` methods are visible in the `OnClick` Property Editor because they have the same signature as all `OnClick` events. In particular, their signature is defined by `TNotifyEvent`, which always takes a single parameter of type `TObject`:
>
> ```
> type TNotifyEvent = procedure (Sender: TObject) of object;
> ```
>
> Any method with this signature can be assigned to an `OnClick` event. Conversely, if you double-click the Property Editor for the `OnClick` event, a method with this signature is created. Technically, a `TNotifyEvent` is a declaration for a pointer to a method. A pointer to a function or a procedure consists of the type name, an equals sign, and a declaration for the function or procedure, minus the name of the function or procedure. A pointer to a method is the same thing as a pointer to a function or procedure, except that you add the `of object` phrase to the end of it.
>
> Note also that the `TNotifyEvent` is not unique to `OnClick` events. For instance, `OnExit` and `OnEnter` events have the same signature. The signature of an event is not designed to be unique, but only to meet the needs of a particular event. For instance, here is the signature for an `OnMouseDown` event on a `TButton` object:
>
> ```
> procedure TForm1.Button1MouseDown(Sender: TObject; Button: TMouseButton;
>    Shift: TShiftState; X, Y: Integer);
> ```
>
> As you can see, this event takes parameters that would naturally be associated with a mouse click. For instance, the last two parameters reveal the X and Y location where the mouse was clicked.
>
> The event that you just saw is a `TMouseEvent`, a type declared in QControls.pas. All `TMouseEvents` take a `TObject`, `TMouseButton`, `TshiftState` parameter and two `Integer` parameters:
>
> ```
> TMouseEvent = procedure(Sender: TObject;
>    Button: TMouseButton; Shift: TShiftState;
>    X, Y: Integer) of object;
> ```
>
> When building components, you will be able to declare your own event types, or you can use existing event types such as `TMouseEvent` and `TNotifyEvent`. You can read more about creating your own events in Chapter 11, "Graphics," in the discussion of the Mandelbrot program in the section "Creating Events and Handling `OnPaint` Methods."

| NOTE | |
|---|---|

> **NOTE**
>
> Another way to change the visual tools from inside the editor is to view an xfm file as text and edit it directly. This subject was covered in Chapter 1, in the section "Editing an XFM File."

## The Project Manager

The main purpose of the Project Manager is to allow you to work easily with large projects that contain the following:

- More than one executable
- More than one shared object
- An executable and one or more shared objects
- Any other combination of shared objects and executables

The Project Manager is easiest to use when docked above the Code Explorer to the left of the Source Code Editor, as shown in Figure 5.3. (The process of docking the window will be explained in more detail later in this discussion.) In this configuration, you can usually reach all the tools that you need with simple motions of the mouse. If you need to start working with a form, you can just press F12 to reach it, or you can press F11 to get the Object Inspector.

**FIGURE 5.3**

*The Project Manager docked above the Code Explorer.*

> **NOTE**
>
> The configuration shown in Figure 5.3 has one drawback: It hides some of the buttons used to control the Project Manager. For instance, you cannot see the Activate button, which is located to the right of the New button.

The Project Manager allows you to add new or existing executables or shared objects to your project. If you go to the File menu and choose New Applications, your current set of projects will be closed and a single application will be started. Use the View menu or some other technique to make sure that the Project Manager is visible.

To add a new application or shared object to a project, simply right-click the root node at the top of the Project Manager. In Figure 5.3, the root node is labeled ProjectGroup1. You are then presented with the option of creating a new project or inserting an existing project. If you choose to create a new application, a modified version of the New Items dialog box will open. (You normally reach this dialog box by selecting File, New.) From the New Items dialog box, you can choose to create an executable, shared object, and so on. If you choose to add an existing project to the Project Manager, you will see an Open File dialog box, and you can browse for the DPR file that you want.

> **NOTE**
>
> It is almost inevitable that, at some point in your programming career, you will select File, New Application when you mean to right-click the root node in the Project and add a new application to the project yourself. The mistake is easy to make. The key point to remember, however, is that if you want to add a new or existing project to your current group, you should not choose File, New. Instead, right-click the root node and work from the pop-up menu.

When you are using the Project Manager, you can reach most of the options available to you by right-clicking with the mouse or by opening the Project menu. You can also browse the tree view control in the Code Explorer, right-clicking when necessary, to see the various options. I will leave it up to you to explore the control.

Some issues about the Project Manager are not entirely intuitive, however. For instance, it is not always obvious which process is currently selected or how to switch from using one process to another.

If you add two or more executables to the Project Manager, notice that one project is high-lighted in bold, as shown in Figure 5.4. The bold print means that a particular project is currently active. To confirm this fact, open the Project menu, where you will see that you can compile either all programs and shared objects, or the currently selected program or shared object. The actual name of the currently selected project will be spelled out in the menu. For instance, if project Foo is currently selected, the menu will give you the option to compile either all projects or project Foo alone.

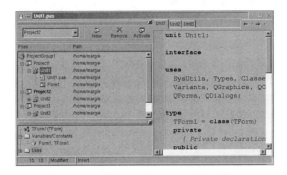

**FIGURE 5.4**
*Three projects seen in the Project Manager. The one in bold is the currently selected project—note the Activate icon on the right and the path listings.*

To select another project, simply double-click it. Alternatively, click once on the project that you want to use and then click the Activate icon that is highlighted in green at the top of the Project Manager. If no icon is highlighted in green, the currently selected program is active.

Yet a third option for switching the selected project is made available by the small black arrow to the right of the green Run button on the default setup for the Debug toolbar. You can see this arrow in Figure 5.5. If you click that small black arrow, you will see a list of projects in the Project Manager. Choose the one you want, and it will become active.

**FIGURE 5.5**
*The Debug toolbar has been pulled free from the IDE. The black arrow to the right of the Run button has been pressed, and a list of projects is visible.*

The Project Manager is an essential tool if you are building multitier applications or applications that consist of at least one application and one or more shared objects. Take the time to learn how to use it, and you can save yourself a good deal of trouble while developing applications.

**5**

**THE EDITOR AND DEBUGGER**

# The Code Explorer

The Code Explorer is designed to help you navigate your code and manipulate the elements found in your units. In particular, you can use this tool to get an overview of the objects, methods, and variables declared and used in any one unit.

This section shows you how to use the Code Explorer and how to use various hotkeys that can help you navigate your code. Overall, the Code Explorer is an easy-to-use tool. However, there are several radically unintuitive things about it, so I ask you to pay special attention for a moment while I show you what the tool can do when set up correctly.

First, let's look at a relatively useless view of the Code Explorer. This is close to the default view, but I'm going to ask you to make a few additional changes. Right-click Code Explorer and choose Properties. The Explorer Options dialog box appears. Make sure that all the Explorer categories are checked, as shown in Figure 5.6. To the right of each category is a little icon that looks like three dots. If you click one of these items, the bottom two dots swing out, to show that this option is expanded. For now, however, I want you to make sure that none of these little icons are in the open position.

## FIGURE 5.6

*The Explorer Options dialog box, with all the Explorer categories checked and none of the fields expanded.*

Click OK in the Explorer Options dialog box, and you are presented with the view in Figure 5.7. At this point, you should be able to see the Classes, Variables/Constants, and Uses folders.

**FIGURE 5.7**

*The Code Explorer showing the Classes, Variables/Constants, and Uses sections completely unexpanded.*

Edit the declaration for TForm so that it looks like this:

```
TForm1 = class(TForm)
private
  FMyInteger: Integer;
  FMyString: String;
public
  procedure Foo;
  procedure Goober;
end;
```

If you now look at the Code Explorer, you will see that it still looks exactly as it does in Figure 5.7. Nothing has changed. The Code Explorer is telling you nothing useful when it is in this state.

Right-click the Code Explorer and choose Properties a second time. This time, make sure that the Private, Protected, Published, Methods, and Classes categories are expanded, as shown in Figure 5.8. Click OK. As shown in Figure 5.9, the Code Explorer now shows you up-front what methods and variables are declared in TForm1.

**FIGURE 5.8**

*In this view, the little icons to the right of the Private, Protected, Published, Methods and Classes categories are all expanded.*

**FIGURE 5.9**

*The Code Explorer, expanded so that you can see the methods and variables in Form1.*

Open the Explorer Options dialog one more time, and turn off the check mark in front of the Private category. If you are like me, you might suppose that you have just made all the private variables disappear from your view of the Code Explorer. This is not the case! You have simply made the *folder* that places private variables in their own category disappear. Take a look at Figure 5.10, and you will see that the Private Folder is gone, but the private variables are still there!

**FIGURE 5.10**

*Turning off the Private category does not make private variables disappear—it makes the Private folder disappear!*

If you uncheck every single check box in the Explorer Categories section, the identifiers Foo, Goober, FMyInteger, and FMyString will still be visible in the Code Explorer. You can't make them go away, no matter what you do. However, you can change whether they are shown in separate folders.

Now type in a new variable. For instance, in the private section of the TForm1, enter **FMyDouble: Double**. Note that you can now see your new entry in the Code Explorer at more or less the same moment that you typed it in.

## Giving the Code Explorer the Look You Want

At this point, you are armed with enough knowledge to start making the Code Explorer do what you want. Of course, each person will have his own idea of what the Explorer should look like. For instance, I sometimes turn off all but the Variables/Constants and Uses categories. I set the Variables/Constants category to expanded, and I leave the Uses folders contracted. While studying this section of the text, you might set up sample uses, type section, and var sections that look like those shown in Listing 5.3.

**LISTING 5.3**  Code That Includes Various Declarations That Can Be Seen in the Explorer

```
uses
  SysUtils, Types, Classes,
  Variants, QGraphics, QControls,
  QForms, QDialogs, QStdCtrls;

type
  TForm1 = class(TForm)
  private
    FMyInteger: Integer;
    FMyString: String;
  public
    procedure Foo;
    procedure Goober;
  end;

  TMyObject = class(TObject)
    procedure Foo;
    procedure Goober;
  end;

var
  Form1: TForm1;
  FDharmaTalk: TWisdom;
  FSermon: TKnowledge;
```

The Code Explorer now looks as it does in Figure 5.11. You can clearly see all the members of TForm1 and TMyObject, and you can see the variables in your program, but the uses clause remains hidden.

**FIGURE 5.11**

*The Code Explorer, when set up correctly, gives you a clear view of your code.*

Add a few more methods to the `TMyObject` class declaration:

```
TMyObject = class(TObject)
  function Peter: TObject;
  function Avalokiteshvara: TComponent;
  function Vishnu: Pointer;
  function Mohammad: Pointer;
end;
```

Notice that the moment you type in a new method, it appears in the Code Explorer. Add variables to the `var` section, and watch the output in the Code Explorer as you type in your code.

Right-click the Code Explorer and choose Properties. Select Show Declaration Syntax, and click OK. Now the Code Explorer will show you the types of your variables and the return values for your functions, as shown in Figure 5.12.

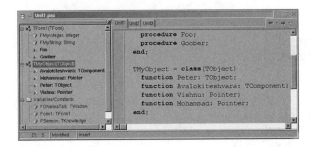

**FIGURE 5.12**
*The Code Explorer showing the types of variables and the return types of functions.*

## Code Generation: Class Completion in the Editor and Explorer

As you have seen, code typed into a class declaration shows up automatically in the Code Explorer. For instance, if you create a new procedure in your form, you can turn to the Code Explorer and see the declaration there.

The opposite is also true. Right-click a section beneath Form1 in the Code Explorer. A menu pops up. Select New from the menu. You will be able to declare a new method or variable. Be sure that you type the complete syntax, including parameters, parentheses, and a final semicolon. For instance, type in this:

```
function Avidya: Pointer;
```

Now go back to the editor and see what you have wrought. Listing 5.4 tells the story.

**LISTING 5.4**   The Avidya Method Shown Here Was Created Inside the Code Explorer

```
unit Main;

interface

uses
  SysUtils, Types, Classes,
  Variants, QGraphics, QControls,
  QForms, QDialogs, QStdCtrls;

type
  TForm1 = class(TForm)
  private
   FMyInteger: Integer;
    FMyString: String;
  public
    procedure Foo;
    procedure Goober;
    function Avidya: Pointer;
  end;

  TMyObject = class(TObject)
    procedure Foo;
    procedure Goober;
    function Vishnu: Pointer;
  end;

var
  Form1: TForm1;
  FSammy: Integer;
  Fred: Integer;
  Sam: TBuddha;

implementation

{$R *.xfm}

function TForm1.Avidya: Pointer;
begin
  Result := nil; // This one line was not generated by the IDE.
end;

end.
```

When you declared the method Avidya in the Code Explorer, not only did the declaration for the method get inserted into class TForm1, but the implementation of the method was added right before the final end statement in the unit. (*Avidya*, sometimes translated as *error*, is the opposite of *Vidya*, and *Vidya* is the Hindu word for *knowledge*. As a result, I thought it appropriate to add the line of code that says Result := nil. All the rest of the code associated with the Avidya method was auto-generated.)

It turns out that there are other ways to automatically insert the outline for the implementation of a method into your code. Suppose that you have declared several methods in a class declaration, as in Listing 5.4. Focus the file in your editor, and press Ctrl+Shift+C. This act automatically sketches out the implementation of all the methods that you declared. To see exactly what I mean, compare Listing 5.4 with Listing 5.5. To convert the one file into the other file, you just press Ctrl+Shift+C. Even the line of code that reads { TMyObject } was inserted automatically.

**LISTING 5.5**   All Methods of TMyObject Were Generated Automatically by Pressing Ctrl+Shift+C

```
unit Main;

interface

uses
  SysUtils, Types, Classes,
  Variants, QGraphics, QControls,
  QForms, QDialogs, QStdCtrls;

type
  TForm1 = class(TForm)
  private
    FMyInteger: Integer;
    FMyString: String;
  public
    procedure Foo;
    procedure Goober;
    function Avidya: Pointer;
  end;

  TMyObject = class(TObject)
    procedure Foo;
    procedure Goober;
    function Vishnu: Pointer;
  end;
```

**LISTING 5.5**   Continued

```
var
  Form1: TForm1;
  FSammy: Integer;
  Fred: Integer;
  Sam: TBuddha;

implementation

{$R *.xfm}

function TForm1.Avidya: Pointer;
begin
  Result := nil;
end;

procedure TForm1.Foo;
begin

end;

procedure TForm1.Goober;
begin

end;

{ TMyObject }

procedure TMyObject.Foo;
begin

end;

procedure TMyObject.Goober;
begin

end;

function TMyObject.Vishnu: Pointer;
begin

end;

end.
```

> **NOTE**
>
> Exactly where you place the cursor when you press Ctrl+Shift+C can make a difference. For instance, if you place it over the declaration for TMyObject, then the methods for TMyObject will be created. If you place it over one of the methods of TForm1, then all the methods for TForm1 will be created. Further experimentation should help you learn more about the best way to position your cursor.

You can also do the opposite of what I described in the last few paragraphs. In particular, you can first type in the implementation for a method and then press Ctrl+Shift+C to have it inserted into the Private section of the declaration for an object.

For instance, start a new project. Go to the implementation section of the unit and declare a simple procedure named Theosophy:

```
procedure TForm1.Theosophy;
begin

end;
```

Now put your cursor anywhere on the top line where your new procedure is declared, and press Ctrl+Shift+C. The declaration for the Theosophy method will be automatically inserted into your unit:

```
TForm1 = class(TForm)
private
  {Private declarations}
  procedure Theosophy; // Autoinserted code
public
  {Public declarations}
end;
```

To move from the declaration for a method to the implementation, or vice versa, simply press Ctrl+Shift+Up arrow or Ctrl+Shift+Down arrow.

## Class Completion: Automatically Implementing Properties

Properties will be addressed in Chapter 10, "Advanced Component Design." However, a few things about properties can and should be addressed in this part of the book.

To automatically implement a property, simply type the core of its declaration, as I have done here for the Dharma property:

```
TForm1 = class(TForm)
private
```

```
  {Private declarations}
  procedure Theosophy;
public
  {Public declarations}
  property Dharma: Integer;
end;
```

Now if you place the cursor over the property named Dharma and press Ctrl+Shift+C, the following code related to this property is generated:

```
property Dharma: Integer read FDharma write SetDharma;

procedure TForm1.SetDharma(const Value: Integer);
begin
  FDharma := Value;
end;
```

You can see the complete source code in Listing 5.6.

**LISTING 5.6**   A Sample Method and Property Auto-generated by Pressing Ctrl+Shift+C in Kylix

```
unit Unit1;

interface

uses
  SysUtils, Types, Classes,
  Variants, QGraphics, QControls,
  QForms, QDialogs;

type
  TForm1 = class(TForm)
  private
    FDharma: Integer;
    procedure Theosophy;
    procedure SetDharma(const Value: Integer);
    { Private declarations }
  public
    { Public declarations }
    property Dharma: Integer read FDharma write SetDharma;
  end;

var
  Form1: TForm1;
```

**Listing 5.6** Continued

```
implementation

{$R *.xfm}

procedure TForm1.SetDharma(const Value: Integer);
begin
  FDharma := Value;
end;

procedure TForm1.Theosophy;
begin
end;

end.
```

The declaration for FDharma, the read and write parts, as well as the setter method for your property, were auto-generated. This technology is referred to as *class completion*.

## The Browser

The browser is the big brother of the Code Explorer. It is based on the same technology as the Code Explorer, and it has many of the same features. However, there are a few differences.

Open up the SamExplorer project found in the Chapter05 directory on your CD. Compile the program, and then select View, Browser from the menu. You will see three buttons at the top of the browser. Each button gives you a different view of the code in your project.

The Globals view on the left is very much like the view in the Code Explorer. In Figure 5.13, you can see the classes and variables/constants from the SamExplorer main unit. Notice that the settings in the browser are the same as those implemented in the previous section, "Giving the Code Explorer the Look You Want." In other words, if you right-clicked in the Code Explorer, chose Properties, and then changed the Show Declaration Syntax option, the changes that you made would appear in both the Code Explorer and the Globals view of the browser.

If you click the Classes button, you see a hierarchical view of the classes in your project, as shown in Figure 5.14. This view is not all that you might like it to be. However, it can be very useful in certain circumstances. Note in particular that if you click the Reference page on the right side of the dialog box, you can see the places where a particular class is referenced in your program. This feature alone can justify including the tool in the product.

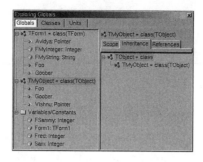

**FIGURE 5.13**
*The Globals view in the browser is much like the view in the Code Explorer.*

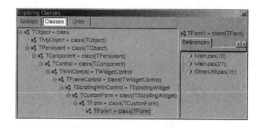

**FIGURE 5.14**
*If you click TForm in the Classes page of the browser for the SamExplorer project, you will see that it appears in both OtherUnit.pas and Main.pas.*

---

> **NOTE**
>
> One trick that I have often employed to make the Browser Classes view more useful is to descend all the custom classes that I create in my own program from a type that I created. For instance, instead of having my classes descend directly from TObject, I create a direct descendant of TObject named TMyObject and then descend as many of my classes as possible from TMyObject. This small extra object layer in my classes is not large enough to be significant in terms of performance in my program, but it can help me better browse the classes that I create. In particular, to see all the simple custom classes in my project, I just need to find one class, named TMyObject, and all my other classes will be listed directly beneath it. You can apply this same principle to other objects that you might need to descend from TPersistant, TComponent, or some other commonly used base class.

5

THE EDITOR AND
DEBUGGER

The Units page of the browser is a lot like the Globals page, except for two significant differences:

- The Units page shows you all the units in your project. Beneath each unit, you can see a similar view to the one in the Code Explorer or the Globals page.
- At the bottom of the Units page is a folder named Used By. When opened, this folder shows what units use the unit you have currently selected.

In big projects, the Used By folder in the browser can contain valuable information. On many different occasions you might need to know what units use another unit. Here is one particular case: Suppose that you have created a unit that you think is no longer useful or that you want to heavily modify. Is it really safe to delete or modify that unit? One glimpse in the browser can answer your questions. This can help you cull dead code rather than leave it in your program "just to be on the safe side." Figure 5.15 shows a view of the Used By section of the browser.

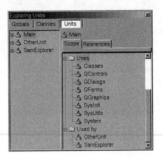

**FIGURE 5.15**

*Open the Units page in the Browser, and you can discover the units that use the currently selected unit—in this case, you can see that two units depend on this one unit.*

More could be said about the browser, but most of its functionality is fairly obvious, and most readers of this book can easily discover it on their own.

## The To-Do List

The To-Do List is a tool that did not seem important to me at first but that, over time, has become a resource that I use on a daily basis. If you want to remind yourself to fix something later, you can just insert a comment into your code at the appropriate place, preceded by TODO::

```
{TODO: Fix this!}
```

Now save your file and select View, To-Do List. Your item will be listed in a To Do Items dialog box, as shown in Figures 5.16 and 5.17.

**FIGURE 5.16**

*The To-Do Items dialog box allows you to set programming chores, assign people to fix them, and give the tasks a priority.*

**FIGURE 5.17**

*The To-Do List dialog box can be docked on the side of the IDE. If you click on an item in the list, you will be taken to the place in the code where the to-do item was inserted.*

If you right-click the To-Do Items dialog box, you will find a pop-up menu with options to add, edit, and delete items. If you add an item directly into the dialog box, it *does not* also appear in your source. In some cases, that is just what you want. In other cases, you want the to-do item next to a piece of code that the item references. If you want the to-do item to appear in your code, then enter it there; otherwise, just enter it in the dialog box.

If you initially placed an item in your source code and you then use the dialog box to edit it, the changes that you make will appear in both the dialog box and your code. For instance, suppose that you entered the following item in your code:

```
{TODO : Need methods for streaming this object's data. }
```

Now you can use the Edit To-Do Item dialog box to assign the task to someone, to give it a priority, and to give it a category, as shown in Figure 5.18.

When you are done using the Edit To-Do Item dialog box, you can look back at your source and see that it looks like this:

```
{TODO 1 -cBack end -oCharlie : Add methods for streaming this object's data. }
```

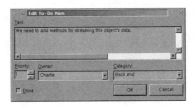

**FIGURE 5.18**

*Use the Edit To-Do Item dialog box to help you properly document your code.*

The 1 at the beginning of the code specifies the item's priority. -cBack end sets the category, and -oCharlie sets the owner. You can add the priority, as well as the -c and -o options, directly in your source. If you open the To-Do dialog box, the changes you made to the source will appear there.

As I said earlier, I initially did not see the importance of the To-Do feature. Now I use it all the time. In particular, it solves the problem of programmers needing to multitask. Suppose that you discover one bug while tracking down a second bug. In such cases, you don't want to break your train of thought and start working on problem A while in the midst of pursuing problem B. The solution is now obvious: Add a To-Do note, and come back to problem A later. This can also help when you are adding a new feature to the program. As you work, you might not want to implement some aspects of this feature immediately because they are too time-consuming. In the normal course of things, you risk forgetting about these features altogether. With a To-Do List, however, you can place a reminder in your code that the feature needs to be implemented.

A benefit that falls out from this process is that the To-Do List gives you something to do when you feel at loose ends or when you can't bring yourself to focus on some particularly knotty problem. Most programmers know that feeling you get when you just can't stand working on a really awful bug, or when you come to work distracted by a personal problem or exhausted from a late night on the town, a late night of hacking, or a late night of serious computing gaming. In such cases, you are often willing to work—it's just that you don't want to work on something too mind-boggling. Well, just open up your To-Do list and look for some mindless task that you can do even in your current state of mind. Fixing even a low-priority bug, or adding even an unimportant feature to your project, is usually a better use of your time than endlessly procrastinating over your mail, or reading *all* the comments to a Slashdot article, or frivolously bothering the programmer in the next office.

## Tool Windows

Tool windows are a set of programming tools, each of which can be docked inside the editor. They are different from toolbars, which cannot be docked anywhere but the main window.

Furthermore, toolbars just provide menu options or speed buttons and don't offer the kind of in-depth debugging services found in tool windows.

The primary window of this kind is the Code Explorer. By default, you will find the Code Explorer nestled along the left side of the editor. The Object Inspector can be docked inside the editor, along with the following debug windows:

- Breakpoints
- CallStack
- Watches
- Threads
- Modules
- CPU
- FPU
- Local Variables
- EventLog

Docking a window in the editor is an intuitive process, but this process is explained briefly here so that you can get a sense of how the process works.

Choose View, Debug Windows and then select the Watch List window. Grab the window by its caption by left-clicking and dragging with the mouse. Move the window around near the bottom of the editor. If you get the window in the right place, a rectangular outline will appear across the bottom of the editor. Your window can be docked in the approximate location drawn by the outline. Simply let go of the left mouse button to complete the operation. When you are done, the editor should look as it does in Figure 5.19.

**FIGURE 5.19**

*The Watch window docked at the bottom of the editor.*

You can try docking the window on the right side of the editor or above the Code Explorer on the left side of the window. When you move the window over the Code Explorer, you will see several different outlines drawn showing the different ways that you can dock the window. It is helpful to try docking in all the places outlined in the IDE. Whether you like the system or not, this is the only hint the IDE gives you on how to best dock your windows. You need to learn to read the messages that the IDE is trying to give you. When it is docked, the Watch List window will have a small move handle on its left side, although it's difficult to see. To undock the window, simply click and drag this handle.

Any of these windows can be docked together into tabbed tool windows. You can have multiple-tabbed tool windows if you want. For instance, you can create one tabbed tool window that contains the Breakpoint and Watch List windows, and another that contains the Object Inspector and Explorer. You can dock tabbed tool windows inside the editor, if you want, using the same process described when docking a single window. Figure 5.20 shows a picture of the Watch List, Call Stack, and Breakpoint windows docked on the bottom of the editor.

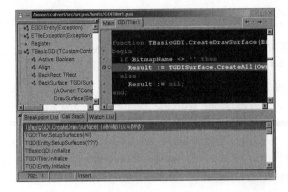

**FIGURE 5.20**

*Docking the Watch List, Call Stack and Breakpoint windows inside the editor. This is a very popular configuration.*

At first, you might struggle to get the windows arranged as you want. You might create tabbed windows and end up with them stacked, or vice versa. To create a tabbed window, drag one window over the other and wait until the black outline that is drawn becomes a rectangle in the middle of the window on which you are going to dock. When that rectangle is right in the middle, with one window docked inside the other, then let go and you will end up with tabbed windows.

## Saving the Desktop and Debug Desktop

When you find an arrangement that you like, you can save this desktop by choosing View, Desktops, Save Desktop. The desktop configuration will then appear under the name you have given it in a drop-down list on the toolbar. (Note that the visibility of this list is toggled. If the list is not visible, right-click the toolbar and select Desktops.) You will probably want to create different desktops for different purposes.

You can also create a debug desktop. This desktop will appear whenever you start debugging an application. For instance, there is no real need for the Watch List window when you are editing your text, but you do need it when you are debugging. As a result, you might decide to include the Watch List window only in a debug desktop.

Successful Kylix programmers usually have at least half a dozen desktops that they switch among, depending on their needs. Don't waste time docking windows repeatedly, if you can help it. Just dock them once and then save your desktop.

# Magic Tools: Code Insight

This section describes one of the most useful services in the Kylix toolbox. It is so important, and so much a regular part of my programming life, that I find myself taking it completely for granted—until I move to another editor where I have to try to make do without it. The three essential tools in the Kylix environment are the editor, the debugger, and Code Insight.

## The Wonders of Code Completion

It is very easy to learn how to use Code Insight:

1. Start a new project.
2. Drop a button on a form.
3. Double-click the button to create an event handler.
4. In the event handler, type **Button1**, followed by a period.
5. Press Ctrl+Spacebar. A list of the methods supported by Button1 will appear in a pop-up window, as shown in Figure 5.21.

Code Insight works not only for the objects found in CLX, but also on any code that you create. To see the technology in action, type the following code:

```
procedure TForm1.Button1Click(Sender: TObject);
var
  S: string;
begin
  Button1.Caption :=
end;
```

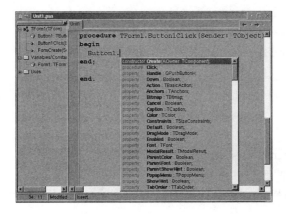

**FIGURE 5.21**
*Code Insight displaying the methods found on* Button1.

Place your cursor after the colon equals (gets) symbol. Press Ctrl+Spacebar. A list of the available string values that are currently in scope will appear. The list will contain objects that themselves have methods that return strings. In the list that you see, you will find S, the string that you declared inside this method. This string will appear in the list even before you press the Compile button. In short, the compiler is compiling your code in the background as you type it, and it knows about variables that you declare before you even save your code to disk!

---

**NOTE**

By now you are surely aware of the speed of the Kylix compiler. However, knowing that the editor can parse your code as you type it helps you to understand the enormous power of this programming environment. This kind of service will not be available for many years for a language like C++. Yes, there is Code Insight in C++ products such as C++ Builder, but it does not respond as quickly as Code Insight in Kylix. Whenever you hear proposals to add features to Object Pascal, such as operator overloading or multiple inheritance, remember that although these elements are valuable at times, they will slow down the compiler. Having a fast compiler is a great advantage when you are working on complex projects.

---

You can sort the code in the Code Completion windows by name or by scope. Simply right-click in the window that pops up to find a menu that lets you select how to sort the code.

Note also that the Code Completion window can be resized with the mouse. Furthermore, you can dynamically filter the options by typing in the window. For instance, if you type the letter

*A*, then all the options in the Code Completion window that do not begin with *A* will disappear. If you type the letters *An*, all the options that do not begin with *An* will disappear.

> **Delphi Note**
>
> The features described in the previous paragraph were not available in Delphi 5. This is one of the few places where Kylix and Delphi 5 differ from one another. This is a feature in Delphi 6.

## The Miracle of Parameter Insight

Other than the fact that we enjoyed them a little too much, we survivors of the 1960s have few regrets. However, if we did have regrets, one of them would raise its head whenever we meet someone in his 20s who can remember all the parameters to every API call that he has ever encountered. Like all aging people, we graying veterans of the flower power years want a memory equalizer: people who are not only younger than us, but who choose safe and more cautious ways to party!

Parameter Insight is such an equalizer. It levels the playing field, making the user, however briefly, the modern equivalent of Mr. Memory. Here is how it works:

1. Start a new project.
2. Drop down a button and double-click it.
3. Scroll up to the area just below the interface, and add the following line of code:

   ```
   uses Xlib;
   ```
4. Scroll back down to the Button1Click method and type in the letters **XCreateWin**. Now press Ctrl+Enter.
5. A Code Completion window pops up, showing that the call XCreateWindow() might be the one you seek.
6. Select XCreateWindow.
7. The method will be inserted in your code, followed by open and close parentheses. Above the parenthesis a list of all 12 parameters to this method should appear. (If it does not appear, make sure that the opening parenthesis is there, and press Ctrl+Shift+Spacebar to conjure it up.)
8. The first parameter will be highlighted in bold print.
9. As you type in each parameter, the editor will highlight the next one in line.

You can see Parameter Insight in action in Figure 5.22.

**5**

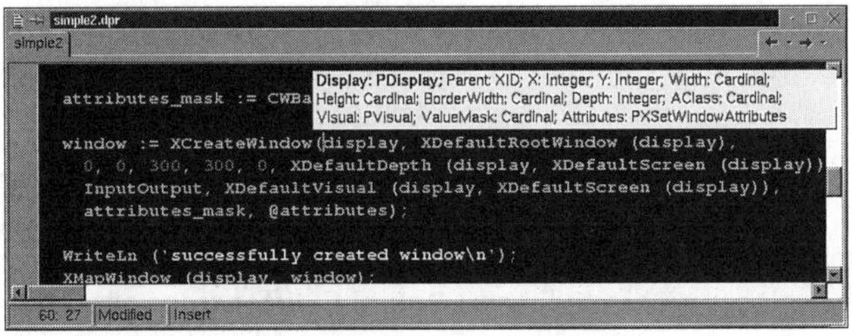

**FIGURE 5.22**

*Parameter Insight showing the parameters of* XcreateWindow.

Parameter Insight works not only for the functions that are built into Linux or that are part of CLX, but also for the parameters to functions that you write. The moment that you type in a valid method, you should be able to see its parameters when you try to call it from some other part of your program. (Of course, the method that you are trying to call must be in scope, or this will not work.)

If you try to use Parameter Insight and nothing happens, then the problem is usually due to errors in your code. Some errors the compiler can work around, but others stop it cold. In such cases, you won't be able to use Parameter Insight until you fix the error.

> **NOTE**
>
> Of course, this can become a Catch-22 situation: You want to use Parameter Insight or Code Insight to fix an error, but you can't use them because of the error itself. This happens a significant percentage of the time—perhaps 20 percent. That is an annoyance, but certainly getting the answer 80 percent of the time is better than always having to look up the information.

## Code Insight: Browsing Your Source

Start a new project, or use an existing project that has a Button1Click method in it. Type in the following code:

```
procedure TForm1.Button1Click(Sender: TObject);
begin
  Button1.Caption :=
    'The mountains and rivers around us are our teacher. -Doan Van Khan c1200'
end;
```

Hold your mouse over Button1 in the expression Button1.Caption, and press the Ctrl key. The identifier Button1 will become highlighted and underlined. Left-click it. Alternatively, you can right-click Button1 and choose Find Declaration from the menu. In either case, you will be taken to the declaration of Button1 at the top of your program:

```
Button1: TButton;
```

Now select the word TButton, and follow the same actions that you performed in the previous paragraph. If you are working with a version of Kylix that comes with the source to CLX, you will be taken to the declaration TButton in QStdCtrls.pas.

Notice that TButton descends from TButtonControl. Follow TButtonControl back to its declaration. You will find that it descends from TWidgetControl. Follow TWidgetControl back to TControl, follow TControl to TComponent, follow TComponent to TPersistent, and finally follow TPersistent to TObject.

At this point, there should be several files open in the editor. Assuming that you started in a unit named Unit1, you should see the following units open: Unit1, QStdCtrls, QControls, Classes, and System.

The next question, of course, is how to retrace your steps.

Look at the top of the editor, and you will see a blue arrow pointing to the left. Click it. You will be taken from System.pas to the code you were browsing in Classes.pas. More clicks will lead you to QControls and then QStdCtrls, and finally back to Unit1.

It is difficult to overemphasize the significance of this technology. We are not just talking about a parlor trick. Using the technology, you can trace back through classes, thereby finding the original declaration for any type you are using. For instance, some ordinal types get declared repeatedly. A type named TMyType might be of type TWord, which might be of type Integer. When you look at TMyType, you want to know the underlying type of the variable. Using code browsing, as described in this section, you can find the true type in a matter of seconds. This is an invaluable tool and one that I use nearly every time I sit down to write code.

## Code Templates Can Make You the Fastest Typist in the World

Kylix does not have a built-in macro or scripting language for use in the editor. However, the Open Tools API provides a number of technologies that come close to meeting the definition of a macro language. The problem with the Open Tools API, however, is that it can be a bit tricky to use and has a significantly circumscribed set of functionality in the first version of Kylix, compared to Delphi 5.

Fortunately, code templates provide a subset of the functionality found in a macro language. Here is how it works:

1. Start a new project and create a `Button1Click` method.

2. Type the word **if** and press Ctrl+J.

3. A window will pop up like the one shown in Figure 5.23.

4. The first item in the list should read: `if Statement ifb`.

5. Select this top item and press Enter.

6. An `if` statement will be inserted into your code.

**FIGURE 5.23**

*The window for selecting a code template. If you select the first item in this list, an `if` statement will be inserted into your program.*

The `if` statement created when you use the top item in the default list of code templates looks like this:

```
if | then
begin

end;
```

After it is inserted, your cursor will be placed between the word `if` and the word `then`, in the place where I have inserted the bar character. (The bar character does not appear in your code—I use it here simply as a place holder.) At that point, you can simply begin typing to insert the logic for your branching code.

If you looked carefully at the options in the Code Templates window, you might have noticed the letters `ifb` after the text that read `if statement`. Those are the key to automatically inserting an `if` statement in your program. Simply type **ifb** and then press Ctrl+J; the `if` statement will be inserted immediately, without forcing you to first select it from a window. This can be an extremely fast way to insert commonly used bits of code.

The two obvious questions at this point can be stated as follows:

- Is there an easy way to find all the possible code templates and their shortcuts?
- Can you add to the list of code templates and create your own shortcuts?

Fortunately, the answer to both these questions is "yes."

Select Tools, Editor Options, Code Insight from the menu. The dialog box shown in Figure 5.24 appears. Take a moment to notice that the other Code Insight features that have been discussed in this text can be configured from this dialog box.

**FIGURE 5.24**
*The dialog box for configuring Code Insight.*

Turn your attention to the bottom part of the dialog box. Here you find a list of the existing code template elements. If you want, browse the list so that you can become familiar with it. On the right of the dialog box, you can see buttons to add, delete, and edit code templates.

In a book of this kind, it is not appropriate for me to discuss this feature any further. All the tools on the dialog box are entirely intuitive, and you can easily discover how they work by following your instincts.

One point that is not obvious, however, is that all the code that you write in code templates ends up in a text file. This text file is found in the .borland directory created when you installed Kylix. If you installed Kylix into your home directory, then the path to Kylix will be /home/*UserName*/Kylix, where *UserName* is your username on the system. The code templates file will be in /home/UserName/.borland/Delphi60dci. You can open this file in an editor and change it, if you want. Sometimes you might find this the simplest way to add, edit, and delete code templates. You can also back up this file or share it with other members of your team.

## Using the Debugger

It is now time to begin focusing on the debugger. This is one of the most important features of Kylix, and one that is worth significant study.

The best way to understand the debugger is to spend some time actually using it. Consider the following procedures:

```
function ShortenFront(S: string; Len: Integer): String;
var
  P: PChar;
```

```
begin
  P := PChar(S);
  Inc(P, Len);
  Result := P;
end;

procedure TForm1.Button1Click(Sender: TObject);
var
  S: String;
begin
  S := Edit1.Text;
  Edit1.Text := ShortenFront(S, 6);
end;
```

These two methods belong to a program on your CD in the Chapter05 directory named BuggyCode. The program has a button and an edit control on it, as shown in Figure 5.25.

**FIGURE 5.25**

*The interface for the Buggy Code program.*

If you type a string in the edit control and then press the button, the program will call the ShortenFront routine, which will shorten the string by six characters, starting at the beginning of the string. For instance, if you type in the string **Hello Fran** and press the button, the program will delete the first six characters from the string and print the word *Fran* in the edit control. However, if you type in a string that was less than six characters long, there will be a problem because the routine will try to delete past the end of the string.

To understand the situation a little better, take a look at the ShortenFront routine in detail. It takes a string and the length that you want to delete from the string as parameters. The basic engine of the program is fairly simple. It uses a device known as *pointer arithmetic* to shorten the string. You can use pointer arithmetic on strings or on any pointer value. It will increment, or move the pointer forward, by *N* times the size of the unit in the pointer type. In this case, it will move forward 1 byte at a time. It uses this size element because it is working with a string, and a string is made up of Chars, and Chars are 1 byte in size.

Here is the key line of code:

```
Inc(P, Len);
```

C and C++ also support pointer arithmetic. In those languages, you generally write `myPointer++` when you want to iterate through the values in a pointer. In Pascal, you use the `Inc` procedure instead of the ++ operator. In C/C++, you can use pointer arithmetic with any type, and in Pascal you can use it only with array types such as strings and a few other types. Pointer arithmetic in all three languages is highly optimized and executes very quickly.

You already know how this code can misfire and why it is going to cause trouble. For the sake of this example, however, it might be useful to pretend that we don't know what is wrong, and then use the debugger to analyze the problem. The point of the exercise, of course, is simply to learn how to use the debugger.

## Stepping Through Code with the Debugger

Start by making the breakpoint window visible at the bottom of your screen, as described in the previous section "Tool Windows." Set up the Kylix editor to focus on line 40 in the program:

```
S := Edit1.Text;
```

Click the mouse in the gutter to the left of this line to create a breakpoint. A red line appears over the text in the editor, as shown in Figure 5.26. Look at the text in the Breakpoint List window to help confirm the location and type of your breakpoint.

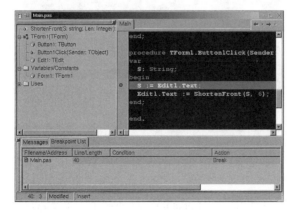

**FIGURE 5.26**

*Placing a breakpoint in the editor.*

Now run the program. Make sure that a piece of text shorter than six characters appears in Edit1. For instance, leave the default text of Edit1 in the control. Now press the button on the form. This triggers the breakpoint and takes you to the line where you set the breakpoint.

Place your mouse over the word Text in Edit1.Text, and hold it there for several seconds. The text that you typed into the Edit control appears in a small pop-up window. Do the same thing with the variable S. At this stage, the variable is empty, so the string appears as two quotes with nothing between them: ' '. The capability to see the contents of a variable when you simply run the mouse over it is called *ToolTip expression evaluation.*

If you are using the default key mapping, you can now press F8 to move to the next line. If you are not using the default key mapping, simply open the Run menu and look for the hot key for the Step Over command, or use the menu item itself. There is also an icon on the Debug toolbar for stepping through your editor with the debugger.

The following line should now be highlighted in blue:

```
Edit1.Text := ShortenFront(S, 6);
```

Now press the F7 key to step into the ShortenFront method. You should end up with the begin statement from the ShortenFront method highlighted in the main window, as shown in Figure 5.27.

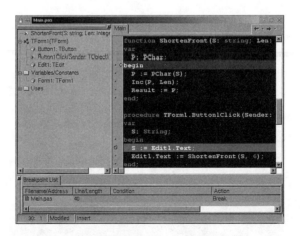

**FIGURE 5.27**
*Stepping through the ShortenFront method with the debugger.*

At this stage, it might be helpful to set up some watches so that you can see the variables in the ShortenFront method. Focus on the Watch List window, which should now be docked at the bottom of your screen. Right-click it and choose Add Watch. In the Expression field, type in the name of the variable that you want to watch, which in this case is S. Press the OK button. Repeat the procedure and add the variable P into the Watch List window. At this stage, you should be able to see both variables in the Watch List window. S should contain the word that you typed in the Edit control, and P should be listed as an inaccessible value, as shown in Figure 5.28. P is inaccessible because it is currently nil and cannot be evaluated, or else it is out of scope as far as the debugger is concerned.

**FIGURE 5.28**
*Viewing variables in the Watch List window.*

## Code That the Debugger Can't Step Through: Optimizations

By default, the compiler has optimizations turned on, to produce the fastest possible code in the executables that you create. When optimizations are turned on, some lines of code and some variables in your program might not be visible when the program is running. These variables or lines of code have been "optimized out" of your program.

If a line has been optimized out, there will be no blue dot in the gutter next to the line. Only lines with the blue dot before them are "live" in the eyes of the debugger. Variables can also be optimized out of your program. In particular, code optimization routines might store variables someplace where the debugger cannot access them at runtime.

As a rule, you can see enough information to step through your program successfully, even with optimizations turned on. However, sometimes this might not be the case. If necessary, you can select Project, Options, Compiler from the menu and turn off optimizations. Now choose Project, Build from the menu. When you again begin stepping though your code, you should find that all the lines of code in your program and all the variables in your program are accessible to you.

If you want a practical example of how optimizations work, you can perform a little trick with your current program. Have the ShortenFront method return the variable S rather than the variable P:

```
function ShortenFront(S: string; Len: Integer): String;
var
  P: PChar;
begin
  P := PChar(S);
  Inc(P, Len);
  Result := S;
end;
```

At this stage, your code is no longer very useful, but you can learn something from making this change. Make sure that optimizations are turned on, and press the Build button. (If you get a message about "Debug session in progress, Terminate?" go ahead and press the OK button.) After you build, the first two lines in this procedure will be optimized out of your program and will not have blue dots in front of them. This has occurred because the compiler sees that you never used the variable P to do anything useful. (In fact, you should even get a hint to this effect in the Messages window.) If you now turn off optimizations and rebuild your program, you will see that the lines are linked in and have blue dots in front of them. You can now step through that code, even though it does not do anything useful. This is a graphic example of what optimization can do in your program. When you are done, don't forget to edit your program so that the method returns the correct value.

Of course, most of the time if a variable or line of code is not visible to the debugger, it is simply out of scope as far as the debugger is concerned, or it is being handled in some special way, such as being placed in a register. So don't jump to conclusions just because you can't see a variable or a line of code in the debugger. But you might want to consider the possibility that the variable is simply not used in your program. In such cases, the compiler will also usually generate a warning at compile time.

## Code That You Can't Step Through: The Linker

If you have turned off optimizations and a line of code is still not available to step through, one of three things has happened:

1. The compiler will sometimes not link in code that it knows you do not call in your program. This is known as *smart linking*, and it is meant to make your program smaller. For instance, if you declare a function or an entire object and then never use that function or object, it might not be linked into your program. If some method in your program accesses the procedure, method, object, or function, then it will not be linked out.

2. Another common problem occurs when you have two copies of a particular file on your machine, and you are looking at the copy that is not linked into your program. This is particularly likely to happen when you are storing source code in multiple directories. In such cases, it is possible to end up with the same source file in two directories. Problems occur if you are looking at the file that is not linked into your program. In particular, it will have no blue dots in front of the lines of code that you believe should be called. Obvious fixes for the problem include deleting one copy of the code, copying the unit into the proper directory, or choosing Project, Options, Directories/Conditionals, and confirming that the Search Path is set up as it should be.

3. The third reason why you might not be able to step through your code is that you either accidentally or purposely turned off debugging. To fix this, pick Tools, Debugger Options and make sure that Integrated Debugging is selected at the bottom left of the Debugger Options dialog box. (In fact, it is useful to turn off the debugger from time to time if you find that it is getting in your way. You need to remember, however, to turn it back on, if necessary.) This might seem like a very obvious suggestion, but in the heat of long debugging sessions, it is easy to become confused. It is also important for me to explicitly state that you can turn debugging on and off if you so desire.

## Watching Your Code in the Watch List Window

I've spent quite a bit of time discussing why code might not be visible to you in the debugger. It is time now to focus once again on the Buggy Code program.

At this stage, assuming that you have your program set up correctly, you should be able to step through the next two lines of your program:

```
P := PChar(S);
Inc(P, Len);
```

The first line assigns the variable S to the PChar that you created. To do this, you simply type-cast the AnsiString as a PChar. After stepping through the code, both the variable S and the variable P should be set to the same value, which is the value that you entered in the edit control. The second line performs the pointer arithmetic.

As you step through the call to Inc, you can see the value of P in the Watch window change. What happens at this stage is undefined, but certainly whatever takes place is likely to tip you off to the fact that it was this line that gave you trouble in your program. Everything was fine until the time you reached this line, and afterward either P was set to an empty string or it was set to a garbage string.

## Inspecting a Variable

The Watch List is by no means the most powerful tool in your arsenal when it comes to inspecting variables. That honor probably belongs to the Inspector.

Run the Buggy Code program again, and this time pause when you get to these lines of code:

```
P := PChar(S);
Inc(P, Len);
```

Double-click the variable Len to select it. Now left-click the highlighted word and drag it down into the Watch List window. When you are done, the variable should appear in the Watch List window, exactly as if you had typed it in rather than dragged it. Now right-click the variable in the Watch List window and choose Inspect from the menu. Alternatively, you could press Ctrl+I. You can achieve the same effect without using the Watch window, by right-clicking the variable Len and choosing Debug, Inspect from the menu. The shortcut for this method is Alt+F5. Yet a third way to get to the same point is to choose Run, Inspect from the menu and then type in the name of the variable that you want to inspect. Whatever means you choose, the end result is that the variable appears in an Inspector window, as shown in Figure 5.29.

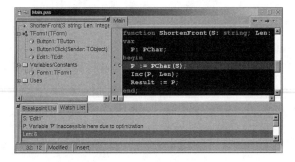

**FIGURE 5.29**

*Using the Inspector to look at a simple integer.*

Notice that there is an ellipses button on the right of the Inspector window. Click that button, and a small edit dialog box appears. In this dialog box you can change the value of the variable Len. In particular, you can change it from 6 to 3, to make your code run correctly.

> **NOTE**
>
> You can change some variables in the Inspector, but you cannot change others. I must confess that I do not know the criteria used to place a variable in one category or another.

The Inspector will do even more wondrous things when you ask it to look at a more complex variable. Use one of the techniques described in this section to bring up the global variable `Form1` in the Inspector. You can now see the data, methods, and properties associated with the variable, as shown in Figure 5.30.

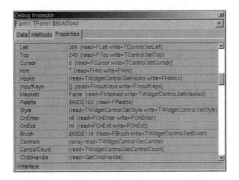

**FIGURE 5.30**

*Inspecting the complex `Form1` object. You can see the current state of all its data, methods, and properties.*

In the Data section, double-click the variable `Button1`. This pops up a new Inspector window showing the data, methods, and properties of the `Button1` object.

## Working with Breakpoints

You can do a number of powerful things with the Breakpoint Editor. In this particular case, the BuggyCode program caused problems when a value with a length smaller than 6 was passed into the program. For the sake of argument, suppose that you still do not know what was wrong with the program, but you suspect that errors occur when a value with a length less than 6 is passed to the `ShortenFront` method.

To confirm this suspicion, you could set up a conditional breakpoint. Conditional breakpoints fire only when certain conditions are met.

Make sure that the Breakpoints window is docked at the bottom of the screen where you can easily find it. Confirm that a breakpoint is set on line 32:

```
P := PChar(S);
```

Right-click the breakpoint in the Breakpoints window. Select Properties to bring up the Source Breakpoint Properties window. In the Condition field, enter **Length(S) < 6**, as shown in Figure 5.31.

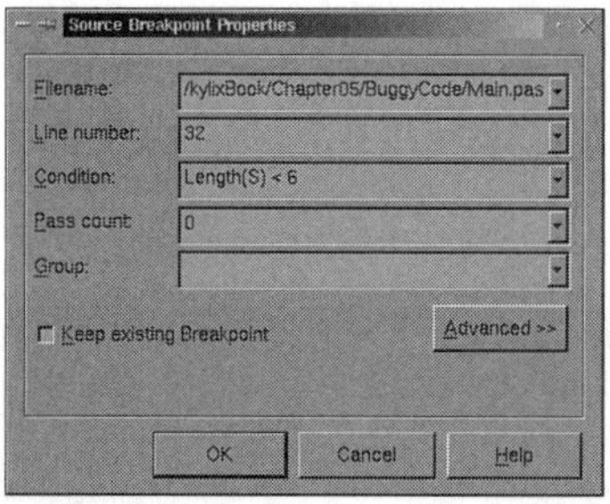

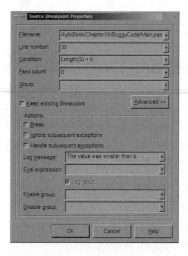

**Figure 5.31**
*The Condition field of the Source Breakpoint Properties window is set to stop only if the length of* s *is smaller than 6.*

Now run the program. If the length of the value that you type into the Edit control is smaller than 6, the breakpoint will be fired. If it is not smaller, the breakpoint will not fire.

Now reopen the Source Breakpoint Properties dialog box, and this time select the Advanced button. The dialog box shown in Figure 5.32 appears. Uncheck the option that says Break. In the Log Message section, type the phrase **The value was smaller than 6**.

**Figure 5.32**
*The Advanced button of the Source Breakpoint Properties dialog box.*

This time, when you run the program, it should not break on the breakpoint. Instead, it will log a message into Event view. To see the message, choose Project, Debug Windows, Event Log from the menu. Scroll through the output in the event log to find the output from the breakpoint.

A lot of information gets written to the event log. To simplify your view, right-click the event log and choose Properties. Now turn off all options except Breakpoint Messages. Now when you run your program, the primary information in the event log will be your custom breakpoint message.

It is also possible to divide your breakpoints into groups. In the Property dialog box for a breakpoint, assign a name to the Group field. Press the Advanced button. Now you will be able to enable or disable an entire group of breakpoints. You can also enable or disable breakpoints by right-clicking the whitespace on the Breakpoint window.

## Using Exceptions to Clean Up Your Code

By this time, you have spent a considerable amount of time looking at the debugger and the Buggy Code program. However, you have not come up with a solution to the problem that you found. There are actually a number of ways to solve the problem, some of which are quite obvious.

Now that you have the problem narrowed down to a particular line of code in your program, it will probably not be very hard to come up with a fix. You might solve the problem by changing both methods so that they look like this:

```
function ShortenFront(S: string; Len: Integer): String;
var
  P: PChar;
begin
  if (Length(S) > Len) then begin
    P := PChar(S);
    Inc(P, Len);
    Result := S;
  end else
    raise Exception.Create('Cannot shorten string: Length larger than
string.');
end;

procedure TForm1.Button1Click(Sender: TObject);
var
  S: String;
begin
  S := Edit1.Text;
  try
    Edit1.Text := ShortenFront(S, 6);
```

```
except
  on E: Exception do
    Edit1.Text := E.Message;
end;
end;
```

Take a look at the new version of the ShortenFront method. It begins by checking to make sure that the string is not shorter than the size by which you want to shorten it. That much is obvious. The question, however, is how best to handle an error condition, if one arises.

You need to communicate back to the user what has gone wrong. There are several ways to do this, but this program elects to raise an exception:

```
raise Exception.Create('Cannot shorten string: Length larger than string.');
```

If the string is the wrong length, the program explicitly raises an exception. An *exception* is a technique used to handle error conditions. The technology does not fix or right the error; instead, it reports the error and backs you out of the whole section of code where the error has occurred.

The moment an exception occurs, the program stops executing your code and unwinds the calls on the stack until it finds the next closest try..except block in your program. Even if you had stepped into 10 different objects and through 15 or 20 different methods, your code would still bounce back out from the place where the error occurred and go directly to the nearest try..except block. If there is no try..except block written in your program, the Application object that is part of CLX itself will catch the exception and report it to the user. However, if that happens, the error message shown to the user might not be pretty, and it would not likely help the user much. The default Kylix exception handler is designed to help you as a programmer, but not to help your user. Although doing so can be dangerous, it is often a good idea to catch the exception before it reaches the outer block. However, it is not a good idea to simply suppress exceptions to make them go away. You should handle the exception properly—and, if you don't know how to handle it, you should pass it on to the Application object.

Like Java, Object Pascal uses exceptions heavily. Not only is this accepted, but it also is actually the preferred way to handle a situation like this.

Here is how to catch an exception:

```
try
  Edit1.Text := ShortenFront(S, 6);
except
  on E: Exception do
    Edit1.Text := E.Message;
end;
```

The keyword try tells the compiler that you are about to enter a block of code that you think might, under certain circumstances, raise an exception. Inside the try block of this program, the ShortenFront method is called. If an exception is raised by the ShortenFront method or by any method that ShortenFront calls, you can catch the exception here in the except block.

Many different kinds of exceptions can be raised. The most generic possible type of exception is encapsulated by the Exception object. Exception is the base class from which all other exception classes descend.

The code in this example declares a variable E to be of type Exception. (This is the only time you can declare a variable in the middle of a method in an Object Pascal program. In all other cases, you must declare the variable in a var section, in a const section, or in a parameter list.)

Assuming that the exception is raised, this code states that Edit1.text should be set to the value of the message for this exception. You passed in the value for this message to its constructor:

```
raise Exception.Create('Cannot shorten string: Length larger than string.');
```

As a result, Edit1.Text will be set to the value "Cannot shorten string: Length larger than string." This might or might not be the best way to handle this kind of error, but it should fairly graphically illustrate how to use exceptions in your own program.

## Declaring Your Own Exception Classes

If you want to create your own Exception class, it's easy enough to do:

```
type
  TMyException = class(Exception);

function ShortenFront(S: string; Len: Integer): String;
var
  P: PChar;
begin
  if (Length(S) > Len) then begin
    P := PChar(S);
    Inc(P, Len);
    Result := S;
  end else
    raise TMyException.Create('Cannot shorten: string too small.');
end;
procedure TForm1.Button1Click(Sender: TObject);
var
  S: String;
begin
  S := Edit1.Text;
```

```
try
  Edit1.Text := ShortenFront(S, 5);
except
  on E: TMyException do
    Edit1.Text := E.Message;
end;
end;
```

Notice that this code is identical to the example shown in the previous section, except that it uses a new exception class named TMyException, which descends from class Exception. When the program raises the exception in the ShortenFront method, it raises an instance of this class of exception rather than a generic Exception class:

```
raise TMyException.Create('Cannot shorten: string too small.');
```

In the except block from the Button1Click method, you should now check for instances of TMyException rather than for instances of Exception.

```
except
  on E: TMyException do
    Edit1.Text := E.Message;
end;
```

This means that if another exception that was not of type TMyException were raised during the call to ShortenFront, it would not be caught by the except block. In fact, this is the best way to handle exceptions that you are not expecting. If you don't know explicitly how to handle an exception, then let it go by.

## The finally Clause and Re-raising Exceptions

Sometimes you want to be sure that code is executed even if an exception is raised. In most cases, this means that you want to use both a try block and a second kind of block, the try..finally block:

```
var
  O: TObject;
begin
  try
    try
      O := TObject.Create;
    except
      on e: exception do begin
```

```
      ShowMessage('Could not create object');
      raise;
    end;
  end;
  finally
    O.Free;
  end;
end;
```

As you can see, the try..except block is nested inside the try..finally block. The line of code O.Free that appears in the finally block is guaranteed to be called, regardless of whether an exception is raised.

---

**NOTE**

The example presented here is not a real-world example. It is meant to be as generic and simple as possible. In particular, it is extremely unlikely that the call to TObject.Create would fail, so normally you would not place it in a try block. Furthermore, in this case you could put the call to O.Free in the try..except block, which means that the finally clause is not necessarily needed in my perhaps overly simplistic example. Here is a second solution to the problem, this time simplifying the code in the except block so that the try..finally block is not needed to ensure that O.Free is called:

```
procedure TForm1.Button1Click(Sender: TObject);
var
  O: TObject;
begin
  try
    O := TObject.Create;
  except
    O.Free;
    raise;
  end;
end;
```

Notice that use of the call raised in the except block. This call re-raises the exception so that it will be handled by the application. If you are not absolutely sure how to handle an exception, it is usually safest to pass it on to the application object, which will handle it correctly.

> **NOTE**
>
> There is obviously a conflict here between your desire to handle exceptions gracefully and the wisdom of passing the exception on to the application object for proper handling. The application object might pop up an ugly message to the user, but it also might know how to handle a problem in a way that will preserve the stability of your program. There are no hard and fast rules in these cases. Certainly you can usually handle exceptions that you raise in your own code, but you have to be careful about entirely suppressing an exception that was raised by CLX.

## Using the CPU Window in the Debugger

As you might recall, in Chapter 3, "Basic Pascal Syntax," in the section "Pointers," I showed you code that looks like this:

```
procedure TForm1.Button1Click(Sender: TObject);
var
  P: Pointer;
  S, Temp: String;
begin
  S := 'Sam';                 // Set S = 'Sam'
  GetMem(P, 10);              // Allocate 10 bytes
  FillChar(P^, 10, 0);        // Zero out all 10 bytes
  Move(S[1], P^, Length(S));  // Move 'Sam' into P^
  SetLength(Temp, 4);         // Make Temp four bytes long
  Move(P^, Temp[1], 1);       // Move S from P to temp
  Inc(PChar(P));              // Make P point to am
  Move(P^, Temp[2], 1);       // Move a from P to temp
  Inc(PChar(P));              // Make P point to m
  Move(P^, Temp[3], 1);       // Move m from P to temp
  Temp[4] := #0;              // Set the null terminator for temp
  Dec(PChar(P), 2);           // Make P point at Sam
  FreeMem(P, 10);             // Free memory allocate for Sam
  Edit1.Text := Temp;
end;
```

Now that you know a little something about the debugger, I will show you more closely exactly how this code works.

As you recall, this program is named Pointers and is found on disk in the Chapter05 directory. Load the program into Kylix. Place a breakpoint on the second line of this method: GetMem(P, 10). Run the program and select the button so that you can reach the breakpoint.

Select View, Debug Windows, CPU from the menu, or press Ctrl+Alt+C. Either action brings up the CPU window, shown in Figure 5.33. Here you can see the actual assembly-level code generated by the Object Pascal compiler.

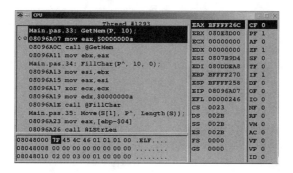

**FIGURE 5.33**
*The CPU view lets you get down to the assembly-level code.*

In the call to `GetMem`, you want to allocate 10 bytes of memory. As a result, the compiler moves the hex value `$0000000a` into eax and then calls the `GetMem` routine:

```
mov eax, $0000000a
call @GetMem
```

Note that the value 10 is passed to `GetMem` in a register. It is never pushed onto the stack. By default, Pascal will always do this with at least the first three parameters to a method, as long as those parameters are all 4 bytes in size. The value of `P` is already in the proper register, so it is not mentioned.

If you want, you can press F7 and step right into the `GetMem` routine. Of course, the code that you see will be meaningful to you only if you have a knowledge of Assembler.

> **NOTE**
>
> The keystrokes that I mention here are the default keystrokes. Some key mappings might use keys other than F7 and F8.

Step through the code of the `Button1Click` method to the beginning of the call to the `FillChar` procedure. Right-click the bottom-left pane in the CPU view. From the pop-up menu that appears, select Goto Address. Enter the value **P** in the dialog box that appears. You are taken to the address of the variable P and are shown a dump of the raw bytes in that area of memory. Now step through the next five lines:

```
mov esi, ebx
mov eax, esi
xor ecx, ecx
mov edx, $0000000a
call @FillChar
```

Rather than step into FillChar with the F7 key, instead step over it with F8. As you step over the call, watch what happens to the area of memory addressed by P: It is zeroed out. For instance, before the call, those 10 bytes of memory will have random values that might look something like this:

```
F8 35 BE 00 10 00 00 00
10 00
```

After the call, the memory will be zeroed out:

```
00 00 00 00 00 00 00 00
00 00
```

Clearly much more could be said about the CPU view. For instance, on the right you can see the current status of the registers on the processor, and you can see the status of the processor flags and the current state of the stack. However, this chapter does not go into this subject in any more depth at this time; instead, you can explore the subject yourself.

## Online Help

Kylix has great online help. You can access it through the menu or through the SpeedBar.

The help is context-sensitive. If you place the cursor over a code fragment that is part of CLX or the Object Pascal language, pressing F1 should automatically bring up help on that subject. For instance, in the Pointers program, if you place the cursor over the word FillChar, all you need do is press F1 to read what the online help has to say about it, as shown in Figure 5.34.

Context-sensitive online help is also available for items in the IDE, including the properties or events in the Object Inspector. Just select a property and press F1 to be taken to a description of it.

Kylix uses a help system called HyperHelp that is fully compatible with the RTF source files used in Windows help projects. You can read more about HyperHelp at http://www.bristol.com/hyperhelp/.

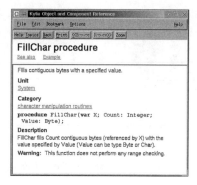

**FIGURE 5.34**

*Place your cursor under a word that you don't know about and then press F1 to get help on it. In this case, the cursor was under the word* FillChar *when F1 was pressed.*

# The Elf Debug Server

When I know a language well enough to use it correctly, it is rarely long before I begin creating programs that are difficult to debug. One of the tools that I used in Windows to help me debug a program is Ray Konopka's fabulous tool CodeSite. CodeSite is produced by Raizes Software, at www.raize.com. If Ray ever ports his tool to Linux, I suggest going out and buying it as soon as possible because it can be an enormous aid to any programmer who is trying to debug a complex application.

Not even a beta of CodeSite was available to me when writing this book, so I was forced to create a poor man's copy of Ray's excellent program. My DebugServer application can accept messages via HTTP from a client. The basic principle of the program is that you write to the server much as you would send debug output to a text file using WriteLn. In fact, you can use one of the units that make up this program as an easy-to-use and automated way of sending debug output to a text file. However, the more powerful technology in the program enables you to send output to the DebugServer itself via HTTP, as shown in Figure 5.35

Because the DebugServer uses HTTP, you can place it on one machine and place the client on a second machine located on the other side of the world.

At this stage, the best thing to do is show you the code for the program. The two key units for the program, ElfDebugHelp.pas and ElfDebugHttp.pas, are both located in the lunits directory found on the CD that accompanies this book. The DebugServer program, shown in Listings 5.7–5.9, is found in the Chapter5 directory from the same CD.

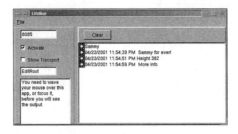

**FIGURE 5.35**

*The output seen in the DebugServer is sent from a client program; this technology lets you view the events of a client program as they occur at runtime.*

**LISTING 5.7**  One of Two Units That Enable You to Send Debug Output from Your Program to a Second Program

```
unit ElfDebugHelp;

////////////////////////////////////////
// Purpose: Aid for debugging programs
// Program: Used by lots of clients, and by ElfDebugServer
// Copyright © 2001 by Charlie Calvert
////////////////////////////////////////


interface

uses
  Qt;

type
  TOutputType = (otStdOut, otFile, otHttp);

  TDBug = class
  private
    FDebugFile: TextFile;
    FHttpHost: String;
    FOutPutMethod: TOutPutType;
    function GetDateTime: string;
```

**LISTING 5.7** Continued

```pascal
public
  constructor Create(AnHttpServer, FileName: string); virtual;
  destructor Destroy; override;
  {$IFDEF MSWINDOWS}
  procedure DumpObject(Obj: TObject);
  {$ENDIF}
  procedure WriteEvent(Description: string; Event: QEventH); overload;
  procedure WriteEvent(Event: QEventH); overload;
  procedure WriteInt(Description: string; Value: Integer);
  procedure WriteStr(Description: string; Value: string); overload;
  procedure WriteStr(Value: string); overload;
published
  property OutPutMethod: TOutPutType read FOutPutMethod write FOutPutMethod;
end;

var
  DBug: TDBug;

implementation

uses
  SysUtils, ElfDebugHttp;

{ TDBug }

constructor TDBug.Create(AnHttpServer, FileName: string);
begin
  FHttpHost := AnHttpServer;
  if FileName = '' then
    AssignFile(FDebugFile, '/tmp/debughelp.txt')
  else
    AssignFile(FDebugFile, FileName);
  Rewrite(FDebugFile);
  CloseFile(FDebugFile);
end;

destructor TDBug.Destroy;
begin
  inherited Destroy;
end;
```

**LISTING 5.7**    Continued

```
{$IFDEF MSWINDOWS}
procedure TDBug.DumpObject(Obj: TObject);
var
  PropList: PPropList;
begin
  WriteStr('ClassName: ', Obj.ClassName);
  GetPropList(Obj, PropList);
  //GetPropList(TypeInfo(Obj.ClassType), );
end;
{$ENDIF}

function TDBug.GetDateTime: string;
begin
  Result := FormatDateTime('c', Now)
end;

procedure TDBug.WriteEvent(Event: QEventH);
begin
  WriteEvent('', Event);
end;

procedure TDBug.WriteEvent(Description: String; Event: QEventH);
var
  S: string;
begin
  case QEvent_type(Event) of
    QEventType_Create: S := 'QEventType_Create';
    QEventType_DragResponse: S := 'QEventType_DragResponse';
    QEventType_DragLeave: S := 'QEventType_DragLeave';
    QEventType_DragEnter: S := 'QEventType_DragEnter';
    QEventType_DragMove: S := 'QEventType_DragMove';
    QEventType_Drop: S := 'QEventType_Drop';
    QEventType_MouseButtonPress: S := 'QEventType_MouseButtonPress';
    QEventType_MouseButtonRelease: S := 'QEventType_MouseButtonRelease';
    QEventType_MouseButtonDblClick: S := 'QEventType_MouseButtonDblClick';
    QEventType_MouseMove: S := 'QEventType_MouseMove';
    QEventType_KeyPress: S := 'QEventType_KeyPress';
    QEventType_KeyRelease: S := 'QEventType_KeyRelease';
    QEventType_FocusIn: S := 'QEventType_FocusIn';
    QEventType_Move: S := 'QEventType_Move';
    QEventType_Resize: S := 'QEventType_Resize';
    QEventType_Wheel: S := 'QEventType_Wheel';
    QEventType_Paint: S := 'QEventType_Paint';
    QEventType_ApplicationPaletteChange: S :=
      'QEventType_ApplicationPaletteChange';
```

**LISTING 5.7**  Continued

```
    QEventType_ParentPaletteChange: S := 'QEventType_ParentPaletteChange';
    QEventType_Show: S := 'QEventType_Show';
    QEventType_Hide: S := 'QEventType_Hide';
  else
    S := 'Unknown: ' + IntToStr(Ord(QEventType(Event)));
  end;
  WriteStr(Description, S);
end;

procedure TDBug.WriteInt(Description: string; Value: Integer);
var
  S: string;
begin
  S := GetDateTime + ' ' + Description + ' ' + IntToStr(Value);
  case FOutPutMethod of
    otFile: begin
      Append(FDebugFile);
      WriteLn(FDebugFile, S);
      CloseFile(FDebugFile);
    end;
    otHttp: SendHttpString(FHttpHost, S);
    otStdOut: WriteLn(S);
  else
    raise Exception.Create('Error in Debug Help WriteInt');
  end;
end;

procedure TDBug.WriteStr(Description: string; Value: string);
var
  S: string;
begin
  S := GetDateTime + ' ' + Description + ' ' + Value;
  case FOutPutMethod of
    otFile: begin
      Append(FDebugFile);
      WriteLn(FDebugFile, S);
      CloseFile(FDebugFile);
    end;
    otHttp: SendHttpString(FHttpHost, S);
    otStdOut: WriteLn(S);
  else
    raise Exception.Create('DebugHelp.WriteStr');
  end;
end;
```

**5**

**THE EDITOR AND
DEBUGGER**

**LISTING 5.7**  Continued

```
procedure TDBug.WriteStr(Value: string);
begin
  WriteStr('', Value);
end;


initialization
  DBug := TDBug.Create('LocalHost', '');
  DBug.OutPutMethod := otHttp;
finalization
  DBug.Free;
end.
```

**LISTING 5.8**  This Unit Provides an HTTP Transport That Allows the Client Being Debugged to Send Information to a Server

```
unit ElfDebugHttp;

/////////////////////////////////////////
// Purpose: Aid in debugging code
// Program: ElfDebugServer, lots of clients
// Copyright © 2001 by Charlie Calvert
/////////////////////////////////////////

interface


uses
  Classes, IdBaseComponent, IdComponent,
  IdTCPConnection, IdTCPClient, IdHTTP;

type
  THttpTalkClient = class(TObject)
  private
    FConnected: Boolean;
    FHttp: TIDHttp;
    FPort: Integer;
    FPortInfo: String;
    FResponse: String;
  protected
    procedure HttpConnected(Sender: TObject);
  public
    constructor Create(AHost: String); virtual;
    destructor Destroy; override;
```

**LISTING 5.8**   Continued

```
    procedure Run(S: string);
    property Port: Integer read FPort write FPort;
    property Response: String read FResponse;
  end;

procedure SendHttpString(Host, S: String);

implementation

uses
  SysUtils;

procedure SendHttpString(Host, S: String);
var
  FHttpTalkClient: THttpTalkClient;
begin
  FHttpTalkClient := THttpTalkClient.Create(Host);
  FHttpTalkClient.Run(S);
  FHttpTalkClient.Free;
end;

{ THttpTalkClient }

constructor THttpTalkClient.Create(AHost: String);
begin
  FConnected := False;
  FHttp := TIdHTTP.Create(nil);
  FPort := 8085;
  with FHttp do begin
    Host := AHost;
    OnConnected := HttpConnected;
    Port := FPort;
    Request.Accept := 'text/html, */*';
    Request.ContentLength := 0;
    Request.ContentRangeEnd := 0;
    Request.ContentRangeStart := 0;
    Request.ProxyPort := 0;
    Request.UserAgent := 'Mozilla/3.0 (compatible; Indy Library)';
  end;
  FPortInfo := 'http://' + AHost + ':' + IntToStr(FPort);
end;
```

**LISTING 5.8**  Continued

```
destructor THttpTalkClient.Destroy;
begin
  if FConnected then
  FHttp.Disconnect;
  FHttp.Free;
  inherited;
end;

procedure THttpTalkClient.HttpConnected(Sender: TObject);
begin
  FConnected := True;
end;

procedure THttpTalkClient.Run(S: string);
var
  ResponseStream: TStringStream;
  List: TStringList;
begin
  ResponseStream := TStringStream.Create('');
  List := TStringList.Create;
  List.Add(S);

  try
    { If you get an exception here, that probably means that
      you don't have the DebugServer running. Sometimes
      you might not want to have the server running. One
      way to handle that situation is to include
      EIDSocketError in the list of "Exception Types to
      ignore in the Tools, Debugger Options, Language Exceptions
      page from the Kylix menu }
    FHttp.Connect;
  except
  end;
  if FHttp.Connected then
    try
      FHttp.Post(FPortInfo, List, ResponseStream);
      FResponse := ResponseStream.DataString;
    finally
      List.Free;
      ResponseStream.Free;
    end;
end;

end.
```

**LISTING 5.9**   The Main Unit from the DebugServer Program

```
unit MainServer;

interface

uses
  SysUtils, Types, Classes,
  Variants, QGraphics, QControls,
  QForms, QDialogs, IdBaseComponent,
  IdComponent, IdTCPServer, IdHTTPServer,
  QStdCtrls, QExtCtrls, QMenus,
  QTypes;

type
  TForm1 = class(TForm)
    HttpServer: TIdHTTPServer;
    Panel1: TPanel;
    ListBox1: TListBox;
    Panel2: TPanel;
    Splitter1: TSplitter;
    Panel3: TPanel;
    EditPort: TEdit;
    CheckBoxActivate: TCheckBox;
    EditRoot: TEdit;
    ClearBtn: TButton;
    ShowTransportCheckBox: TCheckBox;
    MainMenu1: TMainMenu;
    File1: TMenuItem;
    Save1: TMenuItem;
    Open1: TMenuItem;
    N1: TMenuItem;
    Exit1: TMenuItem;
    SaveDialog1: TSaveDialog;
    OpenDialog1: TOpenDialog;
    Memo1: TMemo;
    procedure CheckBoxActivateClick(Sender: TObject);
    procedure HttpServerConnect(AThread: TIdPeerThread);
    procedure HttpServerCommandGet(AThread: TIdPeerThread;
      RequestInfo: TIdHTTPRequestInfo; ResponseInfo: TIdHTTPResponseInfo);
    procedure HttpServerExecute(AThread: TIdPeerThread);
    procedure FormShow(Sender: TObject);
    procedure ListBox1MeasureItem(Control: TWidgetControl; Index: Integer;
      var Height: Integer);
    procedure ListBox1DrawItem(Sender: TObject; Index: Integer;
      Rect: TRect; State: TOwnerDrawState; var Handled: Boolean);
```

**5**

**LISTING 5.9**    Continued

```delphi
    procedure FormDestroy(Sender: TObject);
    procedure HttpServerStatus(axSender: TObject;
      const axStatus: TIdStatus; const asStatusText: String);
    procedure ClearBtnClick(Sender: TObject);
    procedure ShowTransportCheckBoxClick(Sender: TObject);
    procedure Exit1Click(Sender: TObject);
    procedure Save1Click(Sender: TObject);
    procedure Open1Click(Sender: TObject);
  private
    { Private declarations }
    FDebugPlainBitmap: TBitmap;
    FEnableLog: Boolean;
    FShowTransport: Boolean;
    procedure DisplayMessage(S: string);
  public
    { Public declarations }
  end;

var
  Form1: TForm1;

implementation

uses
  LCodeBox;

{$R *.xfm}

procedure TForm1.CheckBoxActivateClick(Sender: TObject);
begin
  HttpServer.Active := True;
end;

procedure TForm1.HttpServerConnect(AThread: TIdPeerThread);
begin
  //ListBox1.Items.Add('Connected');
end;

procedure TForm1.HttpServerCommandGet(AThread: TIdPeerThread;
  RequestInfo: TIdHTTPRequestInfo; ResponseInfo: TIdHTTPResponseInfo);
begin
  if FShowTransport then
  DisplayMessage(Format( 'Command %s %s received from %s on port %d',
```

**LISTING 5.9**   Continued

```
     [RequestInfo.Command, RequestInfo.Document,
     AThread.Connection.Binding.PeerIP,
     AThread.Connection.Binding.PeerPort]));

  DisplayMessage(RequestInfo.UnparsedParams);

  ResponseInfo.ResponseText := 'Sammy';
  ResponseInfo.ResponseNo := 200;
  ResponseInfo.ContentText :=
    '<html><head><title>Info</title></head><body><h1>' +
    ResponseInfo.ResponseText + '</h1></body></html>';
end;

procedure TForm1.HttpServerExecute(AThread: TIdPeerThread);
var
  ErrorString: String;
begin
  ListBox1.Items.Clear;
  if not HTTPServer.Active then begin
    HTTPServer.Bindings.Clear;
    HTTPServer.DefaultPort := StrToIntDef(editPort.text, 8085);
    HTTPServer.Bindings.Add;
  end;

  if not DirectoryExists(EditRoot.text) then
  begin
    ErrorString := Format('Web root folder (%s) not found.',[EditRoot.text]);
    ShowMessage(ErrorString);
    DisplayMessage(ErrorString);
    CheckBoxActivate.Checked := False;
  end else begin
    if CheckBoxActivate.Checked then begin
      try
        HTTPServer.Active := true;
        DisplayMessage(format('Listening for HTTP connections on %s:%d.',
          [HTTPServer.Bindings[0].IP, HTTPServer.Bindings[0].Port]));
      except
        on e: exception do begin
          CheckBoxActivate.Checked := False;
          DisplayMessage(format('Exception %s in Activate. Error is:"%s".',
            [e.ClassName, e.Message]));
        end;
      end;
    end else begin
```

**LISTING 5.9**    Continued

```
        HTTPServer.Active := false;
        // SSL stuff
        HTTPServer.Intercept := nil;
        // End SSL stuff
        DisplayMessage('Stop listening.');
      end;
    end;
{   edPort.Enabled := not acActivate.Checked;
    edRoot.Enabled := not acActivate.Checked;
    cbAuthentication.Enabled := not acActivate.Checked;
    cbEnableLog.Enabled := not acActivate.Checked;
    cbManageSessions.Enabled := not acActivate.Checked; }
end;

procedure TForm1.DisplayMessage(S: string);
begin
  ListBox1.Items.Add(S);
end;

procedure TForm1.FormShow(Sender: TObject);
begin
  CheckBoxActivate.Checked := True;
  FDebugPlainBitmap := TBitmap.Create;
  FDebugPlainBitmap.LoadFromFile(GetStartDir + 'day1.bmp');
end;

procedure TForm1.ListBox1MeasureItem(Control: TWidgetControl;
  Index: Integer; var Height: Integer);
begin
  Height := FDebugPlainBitmap.Height;
end;

procedure TForm1.ListBox1DrawItem(Sender: TObject; Index: Integer;
  Rect: TRect; State: TOwnerDrawState; var Handled: Boolean);
var
  b: tbitmap;
begin
  ListBox1.Canvas.FillRect(Rect);
  ListBox1.Canvas.Draw(Rect.Left, Rect.Top, FDebugPlainBitmap);
  ListBox1.Canvas.TextOut(Rect.Left + FDebugPlainBitmap.Width,
    Rect.Top, ListBox1.Items.Strings[Index]);
end;
```

**LISTING 5.9**   Continued

```pascal
procedure TForm1.FormDestroy(Sender: TObject);
begin
  FDebugPlainBitmap.Free;
end;

procedure TForm1.HttpServerStatus(axSender: TObject;
  const axStatus: TIdStatus; const asStatusText: String);
var
  S: String;
begin
  case axStatus of
    hsResolving: S := 'Resolving';
    hsConnecting: S := 'Connecting';
    hsConnected: S := 'Connected';
    hsDisconnecting: S := 'Disconnecting';
    hsDisconnected: S := 'Disconnected';
    hsText: S := 'Text';
  end;
  ListBox1.Items.Add(S + ' ' + asStatusText);

end;

procedure TForm1.ClearBtnClick(Sender: TObject);
begin
  ListBox1.Clear;
end;

procedure TForm1.ShowTransportCheckBoxClick(Sender: TObject);
begin
  if ShowTransportCheckBox.Checked then
    FShowTransport := True
  else
    FShowTransport := False;
end;

procedure TForm1.Exit1Click(Sender: TObject);
begin
  Close;
end;

procedure TForm1.Save1Click(Sender: TObject);
begin
  if SaveDialog1.Execute then
    ListBox1.Items.SaveToFile(SaveDialog1.Filename);
end;
```

**5**

THE EDITOR AND
DEBUGGER

**LISTING 5.9**   Continued

```
procedure TForm1.Open1Click(Sender: TObject);
begin
  if OpenDialog1.Execute then
    ListBox1.Items.LoadFromFile(OpenDialog1.FileName);
end;

end.
```

To run this program, you need to have both the server and a client going at the same time. I have prepared a client program, available in the DebugServer directory. You can use the client for testing purposes.

Here is the proper way to proceed:

1. Start the server.
2. Start the client.
3. Press the buttons on the client. Output will be sent to the server.
4. At times you might need to wave your mouse over the server or click it before its interface will show the messages that it has already received from the client.

This program uses the Indy Internet components that ship with Kylix. Indy is an open source project. You can download the latest version of the components from http://www.nevrona.com/Indy/.

Nothing in all the realm of contemporary programming is better than open source software. However, it is rarely without its peculiarities. One of the peculiarities of Indy is that it uses exceptions as a means of reporting normal events. This is a valid, if quirky, use of exceptions. Needless to say, you probably normally don't want to see exceptions that announce the completion of ordinary events that are not indicative of any underlying bugs. To suppress Indy's quirky exceptions, add EIDSilentExceptions to the Tools, Debugger Options menu choice. This will suppress all those annoying "Closed Gracefully" exceptions.

> **NOTE**
>
> More information on Indy is available in Chapter 21, "Advanced Web Server Development."

## Services Found in the Debug Help Unit

The best way to use the `ElfDebugHelp` unit is to simply place the ElfDebugHelp file in your uses clause and write output to a text file like this:

```
DBug.WriteStr(MyDescription, MyStringVariable);
```

For instance, you might write this:

```
DBug.WriteStr('In TMyObject''s constructor, user name is invalid.', UserName);
```

An overloaded version of `WriteStr` exists that does not require a description. There are also `WriteInt` and `WriteEvent` methods. The `WriteEvent` method translates some basic QT events into strings:

```
procedure TDBug.WriteEvent(Description: String; Event: QEventH);
var
  S: string;
begin
  case QEvent_type(Event) of
    QEventType_Create: S := 'QEventType_Create';
    QEventType_DragResponse: S := 'QEventType_DragResponse';
    QEventType_DragLeave: S := 'QEventType_DragLeave';
    QEventType_DragEnter: S := 'QEventType_DragEnter';
    QEventType_DragMove: S := 'QEventType_DragMove';
    QEventType_Drop: S := 'QEventType_Drop';
    QEventType_MouseButtonPress: S := 'QEventType_MouseButtonPress';
    QEventType_MouseButtonRelease: S := 'QEventType_MouseButtonRelease';
    QEventType_MouseButtonDblClick: S := 'QEventType_MouseButtonDblClick';
    QEventType_MouseMove: S := 'QEventType_MouseMove';
    QEventType_KeyPress: S := 'QEventType_KeyPress';
    QEventType_KeyRelease: S := 'QEventType_KeyRelease';
    QEventType_FocusIn: S := 'QEventType_FocusIn';
    QEventType_Move: S := 'QEventType_Move';
    QEventType_Resize: S := 'QEventType_Resize';
    QEventType_Wheel: S := 'QEventType_Wheel';
    QEventType_Paint: S := 'QEventType_Paint';
    QEventType_ApplicationPaletteChange: S :=
      'QEventType_ApplicationPaletteChange';
    QEventType_ParentPaletteChange: S := 'QEventType_ParentPaletteChange';
    QEventType_Show: S := 'QEventType_Show';
    QEventType_Hide: S := 'QEventType_Hide';
  else
    S := 'Unknown: ' + IntToStr(Ord(QEventType(Event)));
  end;
  WriteStr(Description, S);
end;
```

**5**

**THE EDITOR AND DEBUGGER**

The WriteEvent method proves important in portions of Chapter 9, "Creating Components." In that chapter, you will start to learn about some of the inner workings of the CLX event model.

## Output from the DebugHelp Unit

The DebugHelp unit can send information via HTTP to the ElfDebugServer, or it can write information to StdOut, or it can send information to a text file. The following enumerated type can be used to determine the type of output you want:

```
TOutputType = (otStdOut, otFile, otHttp);
```

An instance of the TDBug object is created automatically if you include the unit in your program:

```
initialization
  DBug := TDBug.Create('LocalHost', '');
  DBug.OutPutMethod := otHttp;
finalization
  DBug.Free;
end.
```

As you can see, this code defaults to using HTTP. If you want to change the output method, for now you will need to open the ElfDebugHelp unit and manually change the following line of code:

```
DBug.OutPutMethod := otHttp;
```

Here is the WriteInt method from the program:

```
function TDBug.GetDateTime: string;
begin
  Result := FormatDateTime('c', Now)
end;

procedure TDBug.WriteInt(Description: string; Value: Integer);
var
  S: string;
begin
  S := GetDateTime + ' ' + Description + ' ' + IntToStr(Value);
  case FOutPutMethod of
    otFile: begin
      Append(FDebugFile);
      WriteLn(FDebugFile, S);
      CloseFile(FDebugFile);
    end;
    otHttp: SendHttpString(S);
    otStdOut: WriteLn(S);
```

```
  else
    raise Exception.Create('Error in Debug Help WriteInt');
  end;
end;
```

This code first retrieves the current date and time by using the built-in FormatDateTime method found in the SysUtils unit. It manufactures a string consisting of the date and time, the users description, and the integer value that the user wants to display.

If the user wants to output the information to a file, then a file is opened in append mode and the debug string is added to the end of the file. If the user wants to send the information to StdOut, then the WriteLn method is used. If the user wants to send the information to the ElfDebugServer, then the SendHttpString method is used.

Nothing needs to be said about sending information to StdOut. Sending information to a file is a simple matter that is covered in the next section. Sending information to an HTTP server is included in the following section.

## Sending Information to a Text File

The constructor of the TDBug object opens a text file in the tmp directory:

```
// From the private section of TDBug
. . . Code omitted here
. . . FDebugFile: TextFile;
. . . Code omitted here

constructor TDBug.Create(AnHttpServer, FileName: string);
begin
  FHttpHost := AnHttpServer;
  if FileName = '' then
    AssignFile(FDebugFile, '/tmp/debughelp.txt')
  else
    AssignFile(FDebugFile, FileName);
  Rewrite(FDebugFile);
  CloseFile(FDebugFile);
end;
```

In Object Pascal, you use the TextFile type to declare a file designed to hold strings of text. Use the AssignFile method to assign a filename to the TextFile object. Finally, use the ReWrite method to actually create the file. When you are done, use the CloseFile method to clear the text buffers and close the file.

Of course, you can use the WriteLn function to write data to the file after you have opened it:

```
AssignFile(FDebugFile, FileName);
Rewrite(FDebugFile);
WriteLn(FDebugFile, 'Here is data written to a file');
CloseFile(FDebugFile);
```

As shown earlier, you can also use the Append method to open the file for appending:

```
Append(FDebugFile);
WriteLn(FDebugFile, S);
CloseFile(FDebugFile);
```

When using WriteLn, there is no need to translate Integer or floating point types into strings. The WriteLn method does that for you:

```
WriteLn('My String', MyInteger, MyFloat);
```

As you can see, WriteLn takes a variable number of parameters.

---

**NOTE**

In some cases, it is easier to use the TStringList object rather than a TextFile. In particular, the TStringList Add, LoadFromFile, and SaveToFile methods give you all the functionality you need to create an array of strings and then write or read them to or from a disk:

```
var
    MyStringList: IStringList;
begin
    MyStringList := TStringList.Create;
    MyStringList.Add('Burly, dozing humble-bee,');
    MyStringList.Add('Where thou art is clime for me.');
    MyStringList.SaveToFile('/tmp/Emerson.txt');
end;
```

In this case, however, AssignFile is easier to use than a TStringList.

---

That is all there is to say about using TextFiles in Object Pascal. This is a simple technology and one that most readers of this book should be familiar with from other languages or from Delphi itself.

## Sending Information to the HTTP Server

The SendHttpString method mentioned earlier in this text looks like this:

```
procedure SendHttpString(S: String);
var
  FHttpTalkClient: THttpTalkClient;
begin
  FHttpTalkClient := THttpTalkClient.Create();
  FHttpTalkClient.Run(S);
  FHttpTalkClient.Free;
end;
```

As you can see, it simply creates an instance of the THttpTalkClient object and uses its Run method to send the string to the ElfDebugServer.

Because Indy performs the hard work involved with the HTTP protocol, the THttpTalkClient is very straightforward. The constructor for the object creates an instance of the Indy HTTP client. It then provides a few simple lines of code to initialize the Indy object:

```
constructor THttpTalkClient.Create(AHost: String);
begin
  FConnected := False;
  FHttp := TIdHTTP.Create(nil);
  FPort := 8085;
  with FHttp do begin
    Host := AHost;
    OnConnected := HttpConnected;
    Port := FPort;
    Request.Accept := 'text/html, */*';
    Request.ContentLength := 0;
    Request.ContentRangeEnd := 0;
    Request.ContentRangeStart := 0;
    Request.ProxyPort := 0;
    Request.UserAgent := 'Mozilla/3.0 (compatible; Indy Library)';
  end;
  FPortInfo := 'http://' + AHost + ':' + IntToStr(FPort);
end;
```

This line creates the Indy object:

```
  FHttp := TIdHTTP.Create(nil);
```

The next few lines tell the HTTP object the host that it should talk to and the port that it should use. I'm not going to explain this part of the code in detail because it rightfully belongs in the section of the book dedicated to the Web.

Note the last line of code in the constructor, which sets up the `FPortInfo` variable. This variable is used to actually send code to the server:

```
procedure THttpTalkClient.Run(S: string);
var
  ResponseStream: TStringStream;
  List: TStringList;
begin
  ResponseStream := TStringStream.Create('');
  List := TStringList.Create;
  List.Add(S);

  // .. Exception-handling code omitted here
  FHttp.Connect;
  // .. Exception-handling code omitted here
  if FHttp.Connected then
    try
      FHttp.Post(FPortInfo, List, ResponseStream);
      FResponse := ResponseStream.DataString;
    finally
      List.Free;
      ResponseStream.Free;
    end;
end;
```

As you can see, this code uses the `Post` method of the `TIDHttp` object to send information to the server. In particular, the code expects you to wrap up the strings that you want to send in a `TStringList` object. Of course, you can call `List.Add` repeatedly to add as many strings to the `TStringList` object as you want.

## Receiving HTTP Information on the Server

On the server side, you should use the Indy `TIdHttpServer` component to receive messages. I initialize the method in the `HttpServerExecute` method. This method appears to be quite long and complex, but most of this code is simple boilerplate exception handling that I copied from the Indy examples that you can pull off its Web site. The core of the method looks like this:

```
if not HTTPServer.Active then begin
  HTTPServer.Bindings.Clear;
  HTTPServer.DefaultPort := StrToIntDef(editPort.text, 8085);
  HTTPServer.Bindings.Add;
end;
```

Here the port to which the server should listen is established. That is really all you need to do to initialize the server.

Here is how to respond to incoming messages:

```
procedure TForm1.DisplayMessage(S: string);
begin
  ListBox1.Items.Add(S);
end;

procedure TForm1.HttpServerCommandGet(AThread: TIdPeerThread;
  RequestInfo: TIdHTTPRequestInfo; ResponseInfo: TIdHTTPResponseInfo);
begin
  if FShowTransport then
    DisplayMessage(Format( 'Command %s %s received from %s on port %d',
      [RequestInfo.Command, RequestInfo.Document,
      AThread.Connection.Binding.PeerIP,
      AThread.Connection.Binding.PeerPort]));

  DisplayMessage(RequestInfo.UnparsedParams);

  ResponseInfo.ResponseText := 'Sammy';
  ResponseInfo.ResponseNo := 200;
  ResponseInfo.ContentText :=
    '<html><head><title>Info</title></head><body><h1>' +
    ResponseInfo.ResponseText + '</h1></body></html>';
end;
```

The first few lines of this method are essentially dedicated to displaying debug information if the FShowTransport Boolean variable is set to True. The next line shows the user the information sent from the client. At this time, I just use a ListBox for displaying that information via the DisplayMessage method.

Finally, the last few lines of code compose my response back to the client. I sent a meaningless bit of text dedicated to our friend Sammy as the ResponseText. The ResponseNo 200 is simply a constant designating that no errors occurred. The other possible response numbers are listed in the source for MainServer.pas found on the CD that accompanies this book. Finally, the program wraps up the response text in a bit of standard HTML.

## The Owner Draw List Box

As you might have noticed, this server uses an owner draw list box. At this point, the program uses only a few simple icons to decorate the messages that it receives from the client. However, it would obviously be useful to have different kinds of icons for different kinds of messages. For instance, one icon could be associated with error messages, another with warnings, and so on.

5

THE EDITOR AND
DEBUGGER

Here is how to create this owner draw list box:

```
procedure TForm1.ListBox1MeasureItem(Control: TWidgetControl;
  Index: Integer; var Height: Integer);
begin
  Height := FDebugPlainBitmap.Height;
end;

procedure TForm1.ListBox1DrawItem(Sender: TObject; Index: Integer;
  Rect: TRect; State: TOwnerDrawState; var Handled: Boolean);
begin
  ListBox1.Canvas.FillRect(Rect);
  ListBox1.Canvas.Draw(Rect.Left, Rect.Top, FDebugPlainBitmap);
  ListBox1.Canvas.TextOut(Rect.Left + FDebugPlainBitmap.Width,
    Rect.Top, ListBox1.Items.Strings[Index]);
end;
```

Both of these methods are event handlers. In particular, if you drop down a TListBox, you can turn to the Events page in the Object Inspector and create MeasureItem and DrawItem event handlers.

The MeasureItem handler simply returns the size of each item in the list box. The DrawItem method enables you to draw the item that you want displayed in the list box. This would be a difficult job, if not for the fact that the method passes you a TRect record holding the dimensions of the area that you need to fill. The code first fills the entire TRect with the default color. It then uses the Canvas object of the TListBox to draw the bitmap that you created. Finally, it uses the TextOut method of the canvas to draw the text associated with the bitmap.

Here is the code for creating and destroying the bitmap:

```
  FDebugPlainBitmap := TBitmap.Create;
  FDebugPlainBitmap.Free;
```

Further details on using bitmaps, as well as the Draw and TextOut methods of TCanvas, are provided in Chapter 11.

# Summary

This chapter gave you a fairly in-depth look at the editor, the debugger, and related tools. You learned about many advanced features, including Code Insight, the CPU view of the debugger, and the Code Explorer. You should now have a good sense of what the Kylix IDE can do for you. The more you know about the IDE, the more you can do with Kylix.

The next chapter provides some information on how Kylix developers can call to low-level Linux APIs such as those supplied by Xlib. From there, the text moves on to Part II, where you will find an exploration of CLX.

# Understanding the Linux Environment

by Charlie Calvert

## IN THIS CHAPTER

If the greatest fear of a Puritan is that somebody, somewhere is having a good time, then the greatest fear of a Windows programmer is that those people who are having a good time are all using Linux. The purpose of this chapter is to determine just how much fun Linux programmers are having and whether any of us are smart enough to figure out how to have a good time with them!

More specifically, this chapter explains the Linux desktop from a programmer's point of view. It is aimed primarily at programmers new to Linux, or people who have studied Linux only from a user's perspective rather than a programmer's perspective.

Linux culture is considerably more interesting than Windows culture. You have to be something of a business fanatic to really care about the internal politics of Microsoft. There just aren't that many people who wake up wondering what Steve Ballmer said on the previous day. When Microsoft creates a new technology, the only real excitement involves guessing what the marketing department calls it today, and how long it will be until it finally works.

The Linux world, on the other hand, is full of colorful characters, passionate debates, and daring technologies. The key figures in the Linux world are often off on truly quixotic quests that have a high enough probability of failure to keep us interested. In fact, it's arguable that the whole enterprise never should have worked. What do you mean they corralled a group of volunteers together and created an operating system? Come on, we all know it takes big companies like Microsoft or IBM, millions, or in some cases over a billion, dollars to create an operating system! You can't create one for free! Even Sancho Panza could tell you that much. For that matter, the venerable Don's faithful steed Rocinante, if he could talk, could have told us as much!

There is, however, the somewhat disturbing fact that Linux does exist, that it was created for free by volunteers, and that it actually works. The open source movement has also created Web servers, editors, source repositories, and innumerable other pieces of software. Though not perfect, most of these tools are at least as good as their commercial counterparts.

Larger than life programmers with intriguing theories about the computer world often perform all this quixotic coding. Richard Stallman had created an organization with the unlikely name of GNU, dedicated to the absurd goal of creating free software. This is the kind of thing that college sophomores try to do, only to give up on the project withins six months at the outside. Only Stallman started work more than 15 years ago, and his organization changed the face of computing.

But Stallman is not the overlord of the Linux world. Instead, he is but one of many figures. His friend, rival and fellow eccentric Eric Raymond often engages him in loud, passionate conflict. The friendly, reassuring, almost paternal voice of Linux Torvald can also often be heard on the scene. This chapter focuses on the layers of the Linux desktop, including the X Window System, window managers, and widget sets. You will first see an overview of the entire architecture, and then you'll get an analysis of each component. More particularly, the majority of this chapter is dedicated to studying X and teaching you the basics of how to program it using Kylix.

All these characters and all these technologies make appearances in various parts of this book. But now it is time to get started. I'll begin with the Linux desktop, which has special significance to Kylix programmers. Kylix is about creating GUI applications that run on the Linux desktop, so the logical place to begin this series is with the desktop itself. (Don't worry if you are hoping for more information on widgets. The chapters in Part II, "CLX," provide an in-depth look at how to program the widget set using Kylix.)

# Summary of the Linux Environment

Linux is diverse, open, full of interesting experiments, frequently difficult, and at times more than a bit dangerous. Windows is closed, homogenous, restrictive, and fairly safe. Linux is designed to be free and flexible—as a result, it is often difficult to use or understand. Windows is designed to be easy to use, but you lose freedom and flexibility in the course of reaching for this goal.

So Linux is dangerous and Windows is safe. The irony, of course, is that when something does go wrong in Windows, the whole OS can crash or become destabilized. In Linux, it doesn't really matter if the whole GUI crashes to the ground and leaves you back at the command prompt. Nothing will shake the core OS architecture. The GUI might crash, but the servers that you had running in the background will continue running unharmed.

Most programmers will find the Linux environment to be varied, exciting, and full of possibilities. Someone, somewhere is almost certainly pursuing a type of Linux development that you will find attractive. Linux has an open architecture that gives you the freedom to try new ideas; you can pursue your interests in any way that you want.

Kylix is designed to give you entrance into most aspects of Linux development. From my point of view, it is a very exciting prospect, and I have had a great time exploring Linux and learning to leverage it.

# Linux Desktops

From an architectural point of view, the GUI application development environment for Linux is more complex than it is for Windows. In particular, it has three different parts:

1. X
2. The window manager
3. The toolkit or widget setIn Linux terminology, the desktop is the most prominent part of the GUI front end. The launch bar at the bottom of the main window and the taskbar, which appears by default at the top, are part of the desktop. The broad empty space behind these items is also part of the desktop.

The two primary competing desktops available to Linux users are called KDE and GNOME. Figure 6.1 contains a screen shot from the KDE desktop, and Figure 6.2 shows the GNOME desktop. Other desktops, such as Another Level, are also popular, but not to the same degree as KDE or GNOME.

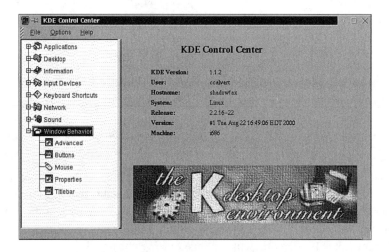

**FIGURE 6.1**
*The standard look of the KDE desktop, with the KDE Control Center open.*

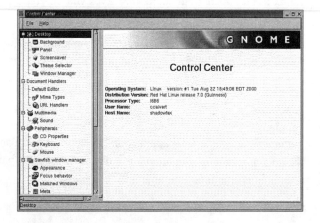

**FIGURE 6.2**
*The standard look of a recent version of the GNOME desktop, with the GNOME Control Center open.*

The purpose of this chapter is to help you understand what these desktops are about and how they are put together. Piece by piece, I will fill in the information that programmers need to understand this technology.

## Anatomy of a Desktop

Unlike the Windows desktop, the Linux desktop is not a single, homogenous entity. Instead, it is made up of several parts:

1. **The X Window System**—This part of the GUI enables you to go into graphics mode and create windows. It handles mouse and keyboard input, and it enables you to print text and show bitmaps. It can also do some fancy networking tricks that will be described later in this chapter. But X can do nothing more than these few vital but not very empowering feats. It takes a while to grasp the restrictions in the X Window System. By itself, X doesn't really take you very far on the road from text mode to a full desktop.

2. **Window managers**—These enable you to arrange windows on the desktop. For instance, layering or tiling windows is handled by the window manager. It also paints the border around a window, adds the icons that decorate the edge of windows, and gives users the ability to maximize or minimize a window. If you put the X Window System and a window manager together, you are still only about a quarter of the way from text mode to a full desktop.

3. **The toolkit or widget set**—Here you'll find the controls that are placed on windows. Buttons and list boxes are examples of tools that are part of the widget set.

4. **The desktop**—Made up of all three of the layers mentioned here, the desktop adds the capability to easily launch programs from a menu and to drop icons on the desktop. Most desktops, such as KDE and GNOME, also come with a suite of tools for performing key system tasks. For instance, most desktops contain tools for editing files, browsing the file system, adding and deleting users, and so on. In short, the creators of the desktop use the first three tools in this list to create a graphical interface to the Linux OS.

It is important to understand that each of these layers can be replaced. None is part of the operating system, and all are designed to conform to public standards. In short, there is more than one window manager, more than one toolkit, and more than one desktop. (Even X itself is replaceable, though the XFree86 implementation of the X Window Standard is extremely popular and all but ubiquitous in the Linux world.)

The diversity represented by the competing window managers, toolkits, and desktops, gives users a considerable degree of choice that is not available on the Windows platform. Programmers are presented with the source to all the pieces of the OS, and they are free to modify them to suit their purposes. In some cases, you can even get your changes folded back into the standard distributions of the OS itself.

However, there is a price to be paid for that freedom and opportunity. In particular, any weak link in the chain can cause problems that are ultimately capable of destabilizing the entire desktop.

Now that you understand the basic facts about the Linux desktop, the next step is to dig into how the Linux environment works. I will begin by examining the X Window System. From there, I will work my way up through the layers until we get back to the desktop.

# X Architectural Overview

This section describes the windowing system used on most Linux machines, including the X client/server model, the X protocol, and X toolkits.

## X History

X was created at the Massachusetts Institute of Technology (MIT). In March 1988, its development was passed from MIT to the X Consortium. You can read about the X Consortium at www.x.org.

Most Linux distributions use an open source implementation of X called XFree86. You can read about XFree86 at www.xfree86.org. The current version of XFree86 at the time of this writing is 6.0.1. You can find out what version you have on your system by typing X -showconfig at a shell prompt.

## The X Window System Name

It is worth taking a few moments to comment on X and its name. Formally, it is called the X Window System. Informally, it is called X. The API that drives X is called the X Library, or Xlib.

X *windows*, with a small "dubya," are the windows created by X. There is no such thing as X *Windows*. "Windows" is a Microsoft trademark, and it is not considered okay to call the X Window System something as common as X Windows.

There have been many versions of X. The current version 11 was created in September 1987, so you will sometimes see X referred to as X11. Multiple releases of X11 also exist, including release 5, which was released in 1991.

## What Is the X Window System?

The X Window System is a piece of software for handling the keyboard mouse and one or more screens. Taken together, these items are called a *display*.

X enables you to create windows shown on a screen. In this sense of the word, a screen is not the same thing as a monitor. In X, there can be multiple windows in one screen, and multiple screens in one display. You can have more than one monitor attached to a single machine, and each monitor can display different windows. In a two-monitor setup, you can move the mouse back and forth freely between the windows displayed on one monitor and the windows displayed on a second monitor.

Displays can also be spread out across a network. For instance, you can sign on to a remote Linux machine and see its X display on your own computer. How X interacts with networks will be discussed more in the section "Networks and the X Client/Server Model."

## Display Types

A typical Linux PC has two kinds of displays. One is the command-line display that runs in text mode. The second kind is a bitmapped graphics display. X is concerned with the latter type of display, although, of course, it is possible to run a command-line view in an X window.

A bitmapped graphics display uses pixels to draw images on the screen, usually using raster graphics. In raster graphics, a single pixel is drawn in the upper-left corner of the screen; then one more pixel is drawn to the right of it, then one more to the right of it, and so on to the end of a line. The operation then moves back to the far left of the screen and draws the next line. The process continues until the bottom of the screen is reached, at which point everything begins again at the top.

Typical resolutions for raster displays on computers are 640×480, 800×600, 1024×768, and so on. In 1024×768 mode, there are 1,024 pixels in each row and 768 rows on the screen—this means that 1024×768, or 786,432, pixels are drawn to fill an entire screen. Today, a typical computer will draw the screen between 60 and 80 times a second.

# Networks and the X Client/Server Model

The X Window System works on a client/server model: The server is X itself (sometimes referred to as an *x-server*), and the client is your program (an *x-client*). In X, there is no direct connection between an application that you create and the display that the user sees; the display of your program is handled by X. As the client, your program makes a contract with X to use its services to display graphics to the user.

In most cases, the connection between your app and the x-server is run over TCP/IP. In a typical scenario, the connection is to LocalHost 127.0.0.1. However, you can attach a server to a remote host. If you are not saying to yourself, "Wow, this is amazing!" then you either don't get it or you are too complacent about computers. The point here is that your application can be running on one computer, and the user interface can exist on an entirely different computer.

## The Slim Pipe Between an X-Server and X-Client

The language spoken over the TCP/IP connection between an x-server and an x-client is called the *X Protocol*. As a rule, you don't have to understand anything about how the X Protocol works, anymore than you have to understand how TCP/IP itself works. These are just services that you can plug in to automatically.

The information sent back and forth over the pipe from the x-server to the x-client are things like mouse down and key down events. The app can send information back to the x-server as well. For instance, it can request that a window be displayed or moved. The x-server and the x-client need not be on the same machine: You could have an x-server on a Windows machine talking to an x-client back on a Linux machine. Or, you could have three terminals of any type that support X servers talking to a single Linux machine.

The problem with this system is that the pipe is small. Sending large chunks of data, such as bitmaps, back and forth can be expensive. Therefore, it is best to avoid sending large chunks of data through this pipe. Big chunks of data typically are loaded by the client and then are sent to the x-server one at a time. The X Server then passes back a handle to the resource. The resource stays on the x-server, and you manipulate it through a handle that is kept in a device context. This scenario should be very familiar to Windows programmers.

## Attaching to a Remote Server

To attach to a remote server, you can telnet to a remote machine and then run a program. X checks an environment variable designating what display you want to use. This variable, named DISPLAY, it lists the hostname and its display. Suppose that you have two machines, called frick and frack. You telnet frick, log in, and then enter the following command:

```
export DISPLAY=frack:0
```

If you now run an X-based program, it will run on frick and display on frack.

By default, the DISPLAY variable is set to :0, meaning the first display of the local host. In this case, the hostname is implicit. You can find out the name of the display on your system by typing **echo $DISPLAY** at the shell prompt. Or, if you prefer, you can see the entire environment for your system by typing **set** at the shell prompt. If you want to scroll through the environment, type **set | less**.

To find out many interesting facts about the current screen, type **xdpyinfo** at the command prompt. xdpyinfo is a utility that provides information on the screen's resolution, dimensions, bit depth, and so on.

> **NOTE**
>
> The format for a server name is host:server.screen. For instance, rohan:0.0 would mean that you wanted to connect to server 0 on the host called rohan and view screen 0. You might need to set information like this in the environment if you were logged on to a remote machine and wanted to run an X program there.

For security reasons, X needs authorization to display on another machine. To give authorization, you run this command:

```
xhost + [remotemachine]
```

For instance, at the frack command prompt, type the following:

```
xhost + frick
```

You can run a complete desktop remotely. For this, you need to run the naked X server with the following command:

```
X -query [remotehost]
```

For example, consider this code:

```
X -query frick
```

## Multiple Displays

You can have more than one display at a time on a single machine. In other words, you can run multiple X servers simultaneously. To see how to do this, let's first have two X displays running on one machine. After you learn how to do that, I'll show how to have a local X display a remote X display on the same machine.

To start two local instances of the X server on a single machine, from X, press Ctrl+Alt+F2 to start a text mode console. After you log in, type the following at the command prompt:

```
startx -- :1
```

This command tells X to run again but this time, on another display ID.

Now you are ready to run a remote X desktop in addition to your local one. Go to a free virtual screen (Ctrl+Alt+F2), as you just did. After logging in, type the following:

```
X :1 -query remotehost
```

After a delay, you should see the login and the desktop.

# Programming X with Kylix

In this section, I'm going to show several X programs. The first is a stripped-down, bare-bones program, shown in Figure 6.3, that simply gets you up and running. Another program that you'll see is a standard Kylix application that queries X to find out about the attributes of the current display. The purpose of this program is to show you how the low-level code found in this chapter relates to standard CLX programming. A final program (see Figure 6.4), available only on this book's CD, is a bit more complete and offers a more in-depth survey of what you can do when programming X. This latter program gives you the capability to handle keyboard input.

**FIGURE 6.3**

*A bare-bones "Hello, world" program written using Xlib.*

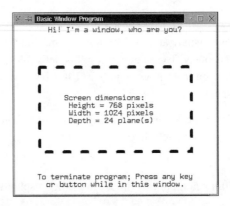

**FIGURE 6.4**

*A somewhat more complex Xlib program that uses bitmaps and fonts and that communicates properly with the window manager—on disk, look for the hello directory.*

Both programs that I will show you do little more than pop up a window and draw a bit of text in it. The second program, however, gives you a few ideas of how to access some of the special features of the X programming environment.

Understanding the Linux Environment

**CHAPTER 6**

301

6

UNDERSTANDING
THE LINUX
ENVIRONMENT

> **NOTE**
>
> Unlike the corresponding situation in Windows, you can find the entire source for Xlib. The best place to look for it is at www.xfree86.org.

The low-level X programs shown in this chapter are extremely atypical examples of how to program with Kylix. They are fairly complex in structure and do not use any of the helpful tools and objects usually employed in a Kylix program. Writing the same kind of program using the Kylix visual tools and CLX would be extremely trivial. However, if you don't use CLX and instead write directly to the X library API, the task of creating a simple GUI program is considerably more difficult.

Here's why I'm showing you these more complex programs:

1. They help you understand X and how it works.

2. They show that Kylix programmers can have access to this kind of low-level functionality if they so desire. Xlib is a very technical API, and being able to access it directly is one of the features that helps set Kylix apart from other programming languages. Usually Xlib is available only to C and C++ programmers. Kylix's capability to execute a line-by-line translation of an Xlib program written in C helps to show the power of the Object Pascal language.

3. Finally, if you understand how X works, you can get a feeling for the capabilities and limitations of a standard Kylix program. All Kylix programs are built on top of X—and if you understand how X works, then you know what you can and cannot do with Kylix. If you know the low-level APIs for a process, then your ability to use a wrapper around that API is significantly improved. In a sense, both Qt and CLX are really nothing more than wrappers around X. As a result, it pays to know a little about how X works.

## Getting Documentation on X

If you are running Red Hat or Mandrake or many other standard distributions, you can get the online docs for XFree86 by downloading a file with a name like XFree86-devel-4.0.1-1.rpm. Remember that you can find the current version number of X on your Red Hat system by typing **rpm -q XFree86**. If you want the version of your X documentation, type **rpm -q XFree86-devel**. If the files are available on your system, pass rpm -qd to find the directories where the docs are stored, or pass -qi to get general information on the release. For instance, type this:

```
rpm -qi XFree86-devel
```

> Finally, you can pass rpm -ql, where l stands for "list". This will give you a list of files in the package.
>
> In general, you will know if the development docs are installed correctly if man gives you an entry when you type **man XCreateWindow**. If man tells you that it knows nothing about XCreateWindow, then XFree86-devel either is not installed on your system or is not installed correctly.
>
> Further documentation for X is not scarce. You can expand your horizons by going to http://www.xfree86.org/support.html, where you will find detailed documentation and an entire book on XFree86. You might also want to purchase the *Xlib Programming Manual, Volume One,* by Adrian Nye, the first in a series of technical books on this subject.

## A "Hello, World" Program in X

This first program, shown in Listing 6.1, makes an end run around a number of the more complex features of an X program. As a result, it is relatively short, weighing in at less than 100 lines.

**Note**

This program must be typed-in nearly entirely by hand. The Kylix IDE will not generate more than the sparest outline of the program for you. If you built the same program in Kylix using CLX and the visual tools, the total number of lines would be much fewer, and you would have had to do almost no typing. As I said, this is an extremely atypical Kylix program.

The program follows the basic structure of a simple console application, although, of course, it runs in a window. By saying this, I mean that it is based on the following very simple program structure:

```
program simple;

begin
end.
```

The begin line is the entry point for the program, just as main() is the entry point for a C program. Execution stops when the code reaches end. The core of the code in the program appears between the begin and end pairs that represent the main block of the program.

Understanding the Linux Environment

**CHAPTER 6**

303

6

UNDERSTANDING
THE LINUX
ENVIRONMENT

Additional functions and procedures can be added between program simple and begin.

The program relies on a big unit called Xlib that contains definitions of the structures, constants, and functions found in the Xlib binary libraries. Of course, these libraries are written in C. As I stated earlier, Kylix can have trouble calling libraries written in C++, but it can call functions written in C. There is no significant difference in performance when calling a function written in C from Object Pascal or from C. In other words, this X program will have essentially the same performance characteristics as the same program written in C.

**LISTING 6.1**   A Simple X Program

```
program Simple2;

{**
  A demo of basic Xlib code with very few
  bells and whistles.

  Copyright  2001 by Charlie Calvert
  $Id: chapter04.html,v 1.3 2001/02/24 21:04:29 ccalvert Exp $
}

uses
  Xlib, SysUtils;

var
  Display: PDisplay;
  Window: TWindow;
  gc: TGC;

procedure DrawMyString(MyString: string);
var
  len: Integer;
begin
  len := Length(MyString);
  XClearWindow (display, window);
  WriteLn ('drawing MyString of length ', len);
  XDrawString (display, window, gc, 10, 100, PChar(MyString), len)
end;


var
  xgcv: XGCValues;
  attributes: XSetWindowAttributes;
  event: XEvent;
```

**LISTING 6.1** Continued

```pascal
  attributes_mask: Integer;
  display_name: PChar;
  done: Integer;
begin
  display_name := nil;

  display_name := XDisplayName(display_name);
  display := XOpenDisplay(display_name);
  if display = nil then  begin
     WriteLn ('could not open display: ', display_name);
     exit;
   end;

  WriteLn( 'successfully opened display ', display_name);

  XSynchronize(display, 1);

  attributes.event_mask := KeyPressMask or
    KeyReleaseMask or ButtonPressMask or
    ButtonReleaseMask or ExposureMask;

  attributes.background_pixel :=
    XBlackPixel(display, XDefaultScreen (display));
  attributes.border_pixel :=
    XBlackPixel(display, XDefaultScreen (display));

  attributes_mask := CWBackPixel or CWBorderPixel or CWEventMask;

  window := XCreateWindow(display,
    XDefaultRootWindow (display),
    0, 0, 300, 300, 0,
    XDefaultDepth(display, XDefaultScreen (display)),
    InputOutput, XDefaultVisual (display, XDefaultScreen (display)),
    attributes_mask, @attributes);

  WriteLn('successfully created window\n');
  XMapWindow(display, window);
  WriteLn('successfully mapped windows\n');

  WriteLn('attempting graphics context creation\n');
  xgcv.foreground := $00FFFFFF;
  xgcv.background := $00000000;
  gc := XCreateGC(display, window, (GCForeground or GCBackground), @xgcv);
  WriteLn('successfully created graphics context');
```

**LISTING 6.1**  Continued

```
done := 0;
while done <> 1 do begin
    XNextEvent (display, @event);

    case (event.xtype) of

      Expose: begin
        if event.xexpose.count <> 0 then
          break;
        DrawMyString('The wondrous world of X!');
      end;

      KeyPress: done := 1;
      ButtonPress: ;
    end;
  end;
  XCloseDisplay (display);
end.
```

Most of the functions in this program are part of Xlib; very few calls are made to native
Object Pascal functions. You can get help on X functions at the command line by typing
**info** *FunctionName* or **man** *FunctionName*. For instance, typing info XDrawString
at the shell command prompt should get you Linux-based help on the XDrawString function.
If these commands don't work, then you either don't have info or man installed, or you don't
have the docs for Xlib installed.

## Obtaining the Display
The first significant call in the Simple2 program looks like this:

```
display_name := XDisplayName(display_name);
```

This function returns the name of the current display.

Usually this name is :0:0. Additional information on displays and display names is presented
earlier in the chapter, in the section "Attaching to a Remote Server."

When you have the name of the display, you can open an instance of it and retrieve a handle to
it:

```
display := XOpenDisplay(display_name);
if display = nil then
begin
  WriteLn ('could not open display: ', display_name);
  exit;
end;
```

In fact, XOpenDisplay can take the name of a display on another machine, as described earlier, in the section "Attaching to a Remote Server."

The variable display that is returned from XOpenDisplay is large and complex:

```
PDisplay = ^Display;
Display = record
  ext_data : PXExtData; { hook for extension to hang data }
  private1 : PXPrivate;
  fd : Longint; { Network socket. }
  private2 : Longint;
  proto_major_version : Longint; { major version of
    server's X protocol }
  proto_minor_version : Longint; { minor version of servers
    X protocol }
  vendor : PChar; { vendor of the server hardware }
  private3 : XID;
  private4 : XID;
  private5 : XID;
  private6 : Longint;
  resource_alloc : TDisplayResourceAllocProc; { allocator
    function }
  byte_order : Longint; { screen byte order, LSBFirst,
    MSBFirst }
  bitmap_unit : Longint; { padding and data requirements }
  bitmap_pad : Longint; { padding requirements on bitmaps }
  bitmap_bit_order : Longint; { LeastSignificant or
    MostSignificant }
  nformats : Longint; { number of pixmap formats in list }
  pixmap_format : PScreenFormat; { pixmap format list }
  private8 : Longint;
  release : Longint; { release of the server }
  private9 : PXPrivate;
```

Understanding the Linux Environment

CHAPTER 6

307

6

UNDERSTANDING
THE LINUX
ENVIRONMENT

```
  private10 : PXPrivate;
  qlen : Longint; { Length of input event queue }
  last_request_read : Cardinal; {number of last read }
  request : Cardinal; { sequence number of last request. }
  private11 : XPointer;
  private12 : XPointer;
  private13 : XPointer;
  private14 : XPointer;
  max_request_size : Cardinal; { maximum number 32 bit words in request }
  db : PXrmHashBucketRec;
  private15 : TDisplayPrivate15Proc;
  display_name : PChar; { "host:display" string used on
 this connect }
  default_screen : Longint; {default screen for operations}
  nscreens : Longint; { number of screens on this server }
  screens : PScreen; { pointer to list of screens }
  motion_buffer : Cardinal; { size of motion buffer }
  private16 : Cardinal;
  min_keycode : Longint; { minimum defined keycode }
  max_keycode : Longint; { maximum defined keycode }
  private17 : XPointer;
  private18 : XPointer;
  private19 : Longint;
  xdefaults : PChar; { contents of defaults from server }
  { there is more code here, but it is private to Xlib }
end;
```

Notice the first two lines of this declaration:

```
PDisplay = ^Display;
Display = record
```

A *record* is the same thing that a C programmer would call a *struct*. A Java programmer would call a record a *class* that has no methods, only data and pointers to functions. In particular, a record differs from a class in that it does not have constructors or destructors, and it does not support inheritance or polymorphism. The declaration shown here says that type Display is a record containing a series of fields such as the fd field, which is of type Longint. Other fields, such as PXExtData, are themselves of type record and represent nested records.

The first line states that PDisplay is a pointer to a record of type Display. In Object Pascal, pointers almost always begin with P, as shown here. A standard nonpointer type usually starts with a T, as in TDisplay. The absence of the T in this particular case is a bit of anomaly and probably results from the translator's attempt to give the Xlib unit a flavor of the X Library itself.

If you recall the xdpyinfo utility mentioned earlier, the body of this structure might begin to come into focus. In particular, most of the information available in the xdpyinfo program appears to be derived from this structure.

## Getting Information on the X Display: An Example

This is a good time to demonstrate how this kind of information applies to a standard Kylix program that uses the Qt library. Listings 6.2 and 6.3 define such a program. As you can see from looking at Figure 6.5, this program shows the user information about the current X display.

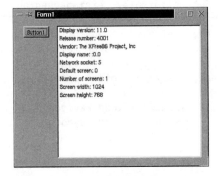

**FIGURE 6.5**

*The output from the xdpyinfoGUI program gives the user insight into the status of the first X display on the system.*

**LISTING 6.2** The dpr File for the xdpyinfoGUI Program Initializes the Kylix Libraries and Launches the Main Form of the Program

```
program xdpyinfoGUI;

uses
  QForms,
  Main in 'Main.pas' {Form1};

{$R *.res}

begin
  Application.Initialize;
  Application.CreateForm(TForm1, Form1);
  Application.Run;
end.
```

Understanding the Linux Environment

**CHAPTER 6**

309

6

UNDERSTANDING
THE LINUX
ENVIRONMENT

**LISTING 6.3**   The Main Form of the xdpyinfoGUI Program Presents the User with Information About the First X Display on the System

```
unit Main;

{ Find out about the XServer from a Kylix program.
  Copyright  2001 by Charlie Calvert
  $Id: chapter06.html,v 1.3 2001/02/24 21:04:29 ccalvert Exp $ }

interface

uses
  SysUtils, Types, Classes,
  QGraphics, QControls, QForms,
  QDialogs, QStdCtrls;

type
  TForm1 = class(TForm)
    Button1: TButton;
    ListBox1: TListBox;
    procedure Button1Click(Sender: TObject);
  private
    { Private declarations }
  public
    { Public declarations }
  end;

var
  Form1: TForm1;

implementation

uses
  Xlib;

{$R *.xfm}

procedure TForm1.Button1Click(Sender: TObject);
var
  display: PDisplay;
begin
  display := PDisplay(Application.Display);
  ListBox1.Items.Add('Display version: ' +
    IntToStr(display.proto_major_version) +  '.' +
    IntToStr(display.proto_minor_version));
```

**LISTING 6.3**   Continued

```
  ListBox1.Items.Add('Release number: ' +
    IntToStr(display.release));
  ListBox1.Items.Add('Vendor: ' + display.vendor);
  ListBox1.Items.Add('Display name: ' +
    display.display_name);
  ListBox1.Items.Add('Network socket: ' +
    IntToStr(display.fd));
  ListBox1.Items.Add('Default screen: ' +
    IntToStr(display.default_screen));
  ListBox1.Items.Add('Number of screens: ' +
    IntToStr(display.nscreens));
  ListBox1.Items.Add('Screen width: ' +
    IntToStr(display.screens.width));
  ListBox1.Items.Add('Screen height: ' +
    IntToStr(display.screens.height));
end;

end.
```

To create this simple program, open Kylix and choose File, New Application. Drop a button and list box down on the main form of the program. Double-click the button to create the `Button1Click` method. Add in the code to the method, as shown in Listing 6.3. Finally, add a uses clause that references the Xlib unit.

Note the code that gives you access to the `Display` record, talked about throughout this section of the text. All Kylix programs initialize a global `Application` object created automatically at program startup. You can view part of this initialization process by looking at Listing 6.2.

If you right-click the `Application.Display` variable in the Kylix editor and choose Find Declaration from the pop-up menu, you are taken to the declaration for this object. This field is a property of type `PDisplay`. In the shipping version of the product, this should be of the same type as the `PDisplay` variable. Unfortunately, in the beta version of the product that I'm working with, it is declared as a pointer and must be typecast to a variable of type `Xlib.PDisplay`:

```
var
  display: PDisplay;
begin
  display := PDisplay(Application.Display);
```

You now hold a pointer to a record. The record is of the same type found in the Simple2 program shown in Listing 6.1. In particular, this is the same type of variable that `XOpenDisplay` returns.

Understanding the Linux Environment
CHAPTER 6

311

6

UNDERSTANDING
THE LINUX
ENVIRONMENT

> **NOTE**
>
> XOpenDisplay is an Xlib call, the kind that a C or C++ programmer would make. Application.Display is a CLX property, the kind accessed by the average Kylix programmer. In the normal course of things, neither a Java programmer nor a Visual Basic programmer would ever get access to a low-level system variable of this type. And if they did get access to it, their language is not designed to allow them to manipulate it properly. In particular, Java and Visual Basic make it difficult for programmers to work with pointers. Object Pascal gives you full access to low-level system functionality while wrapping that access inside a language that's generally no more difficult to use than Java or Visual Basic.

After you have obtained the `Display` variable, the body of `Button1Click` method itself is quite straightforward. It simply accesses features of the `Display` record to create a report for the user. Note that you can access the fields of the object in two different ways:

```
display.screens.height
display^.screens^.height
```

The most recent versions of Object Pascal enable you to access pointers with either dot notation or pointer notation.

In some cases, you might want to call `XSynchronize` immediately after getting the display. This can help when you are debugging:

```
XSynchronize(display, 1);
```

## Creating the Main Window with `XCreateWindow`

It is now time to create the main window of the program. The easy way is to call `XCreateSimpleWindow`; the hard way is to call `XCreateWindow` and explicitly assign the attributes for the window.

Here is the code to create the window:

```
attributes.event_mask := KeyPressMask or KeyReleaseMask or
    ButtonPressMask or ButtonReleaseMask or ExposureMask;

attributes.background_pixel := XBlackPixel (display, XDefaultScreen (display));
attributes.border_pixel := XBlackPixel (display, XDefaultScreen (display));

attributes_mask := CWBackPixel or CWBorderPixel or CWEventMask;
```

```
window := XCreateWindow (display, XDefaultRootWindow (display),
    0, 0, 300, 300, 0, XDefaultDepth (display, XDefaultScreen (display)),
    InputOutput, XDefaultVisual (display, XDefaultScreen (display)),
    attributes_mask, @attributes);
```

XCreateWindow takes 10 parameters.

```
function XCreateWindow(
    Display: PDisplay;        // Connection to X Server
    Parent: TWindow;          // The parent window
    X, Y: Longint;            // X and Y relative to parent
    Width, Height: Cardinal;  // Width and height
    BorderWidth: Cardinal;    // How wide is the border?
    Depth: Longint;           // Number of planes, or bit depth
    AClass :Cardinal;         // The type of window to create
    Visual: PVisual;          // Is it grayscale, true color, etc
    ValueMask: Cardinal;      // What attributes do you want to set?
    Attributes: PXSetWindowAttributes // Actually set the attributes here
): TWindow; cdecl;
```

The first parameter is an old friend to us by now: a pointer to the display. The second parameter is the parent window. In our program, the parent can be obtained fairly simply:

XDefaultRootWindow(display)

The XDefaultRootWindow function returns a copy of the root window on the X display.

The X and Y parameters to XCreateWindow are the coordinates of the top-left edge of the window's border relative to the inner corner of the parent's border. The borderwidth, width, and height parameters are self-explanatory.

The depth is the number of planes in the window. In practice, this is usually the same thing as the bit depth of the pixels in the window. If you have a bit depth of 8, you can have 256 colors or scales of gray in your window. A bit depth of 16 gives you 64K worth of colors. The visual parameter is closely related to the depth. It defines whether a window is using grayscale colors, true color, or various other values. The Simple2 program calls XDefaultVisual to get this value. You could also elect to fill out an XVisualInfo record. For more information, type **man XVisualInfo** at the command prompt.

The class can be InputOutput, InputOnly, or CopyFromParent. An InputOutput window can both display output and receive input. An InputOnly window can only receive input. The concept of an output-only window does not exist because all windows need to receive events of some kind. With the CopyFromParent option, the window inherits its parent class.

Understanding the Linux Environment

**CHAPTER 6**

313

6

UNDERSTANDING
THE LINUX
ENVIRONMENT

The Window attributes are set with the last two parameters of the call to `CreateWindow`. The `ValueMask` parameter lets you specify which attributes you want to set. Here are the allowed values:

```
CWBackPixmap = 1 shl 0;
CWBackPixel = 1 shl 1;
CWBorderPixmap = 1 shl 2;
CWBorderPixel = 1 shl 3;
CWBitGravity = 1 shl 4;
CWWinGravity = 1 shl 5;
CWBackingStore = 1 shl 6;
CWBackingPlanes = 1 shl 7;
CWBackingPixel = 1 shl 8;
CWOverrideRedirect = 1 shl 9;
CWSaveUnder = 1 shl 10;
CWEventMask = 1 shl 11;
CWDontPropagate = 1 shl 12;
CWColormap = 1 shl 13;
CWCursor = 1 shl 14;
```

All these values related to the fields of the following record:

```
PXSetWindowAttributes = ^XSetWindowAttributes;
XSetWindowAttributes = record
  background_pixmap: TPixmap;  { background or None or ParentRelative  }
  background_pixel: Cardinal; { background pixel  }
  border_pixmap: TPixmap; { border of the window  }
  border_pixel: Cardinal; { border pixel value }
  bit_gravity: Longint; { one of bit gravity values  }
  win_gravity: Longint; { one of the window gravity values  }
  backing_store: Longint; { NotUseful, WhenMapped, Always  }
  backing_planes: Cardinal; { planes to be preserved if possible  }
  backing_pixel: Cardinal; { value to use in restoring planes  }
  save_under: Bool; { should bits under be saved? (popups)  }
  event_mask: Longint; { set of events that should be saved  }
  do_not_propagate_mask: Longint;{ set of events that should not propagate  }
  override_redirect: Bool; { boolean value for override-redirect  }
  colormap: TColorMap; { color map to be associated with window  }
  cursor: TCursor; { cursor to be displayed (or None)  }
end;
```

The Simple2 program sets the `background_pixel`, `border_pixel`, and `event_mask` fields of this record. As a result, it sets the `ValueMask` parameter of `XCreateWindow` as follows:

```
attributes_mask := CWBackPixel or CWBorderPixel or CWEventMask;

window := XCreateWindow(display, XDefaultRootWindow (display),
```

```
0, 0, 300, 300, 0, XDefaultDepth (display, XDefaultScreen (display)),
InputOutput, XDefaultVisual (display, XDefaultScreen (display)),
attributes_mask, @attributes);
```

Turning your attention to the last parameter, you can see that the background_pixel and border_pixel properties are fairly self-explanatory:

```
attributes.background_pixel := XBlackPixel (display, XDefaultScreen (display));
attributes.border_pixel := XBlackPixel (display, XDefaultScreen (display));
```

The Simple2 program fills in these values by calling the method XBlackPixel.

The event_mask is also fairly straightforward, but it is so important that I want to take a moment to look at it. Here is the relevant code from Simple2.dpr:

```
attributes.event_mask := KeyPressMask or KeyReleaseMask or
    ButtonPressMask or ButtonReleaseMask or ExposureMask;
```

This field is where you define the kind of events that your window will receive. In other words, this is where you define the Input part of your InputOutput window. In this case, the program asks to receive key presses, key releases, button presses, and button releases, and it also requests notification when the window is made visible to the user. This final value, ExposureMask, corresponds to a program in Windows asking for WM_PAINT messages. In other words, it gets sent whenever the window needs to be repainted. Often, X will repaint the window for you, but if you need to do custom drawing, you can respond to this event. I will explain events in more detail in this portion of this chapter.

Here are the values that you can use to set up the event_mask:

```
NoEventMask = 0;
KeyPressMask = 1 shl 0;
KeyReleaseMask = 1 shl 1;
ButtonPressMask = 1 shl 2;
ButtonReleaseMask = 1 shl 3;
EnterWindowMask = 1 shl 4;
LeaveWindowMask = 1 shl 5;
PointerMotionMask = 1 shl 6;
PointerMotionHintMask = 1 shl 7;
Button1MotionMask = 1 shl 8;
Button2MotionMask = 1 shl 9;
Button3MotionMask = 1 shl 10;
Button4MotionMask = 1 shl 11;
Button5MotionMask = 1 shl 12;
ButtonMotionMask = 1 shl 13;
KeymapStateMask = 1 shl 14;
ExposureMask = 1 shl 15;
VisibilityChangeMask = 1 shl 16;
```

Understanding the Linux Environment

**CHAPTER 6**

315

6

UNDERSTANDING
THE LINUX
ENVIRONMENT

```
StructureNotifyMask    = 1 shl 17;
ResizeRedirectMask     = 1 shl 18;
SubstructureNotifyMask = 1 shl 19;
SubstructureRedirectMask = 1 shl 20;
FocusChangeMask        = 1 shl 21;
PropertyChangeMask     = 1 shl 22;
ColormapChangeMask     = 1 shl 23;
OwnerGrabButtonMask    = 1 shl 24;
```

I'm not going to explain each value in detail, but a glance through this list should give you some sense of the options available to you.

The XCreateWindow function can return the following errors:

| | |
|---|---|
| BadAlloc | Resource or memory cannot be allocated. |
| BadColor | The color map you are trying to use is not defined. |
| BadCursor | No cursor with that name is defined. |
| BadMatch | InputOnly windows don't support the values that you passed. |
| BadMatch | The argument's type and range are good, but other problems exist. |
| BadPixmap | A value for a Pixmap argument does not name a defined Pixmap. |
| BadValue | A numeric value is incorrect. |
| BadWindow | The Window argument is invalid. |

## Creating the Main Window with XCreateSimpleWindow

The primary difference between XCreateWindow and XCreateSimpleWindow is whether the attributes for the window are inherited from the parent window or assigned explicitly. In XCreateSimpleWindow, notice that you do not have to set up the attributes, the visual, or the depth. In short, all the tricky parts of calling XCreateWindow are taken care of for you behind the scenes:

```
BlackColor := XBlackPixel(display, XDefaultScreen (display));
WhiteColor := XWhitePixel(display, XDefaultScreen (display));

window := XCreateSimpleWindow(display, XDefaultRootWindow(display),
  0, 300, 300, 0, BlackColor, WhiteColor);
```

XCreateSimpleWindow takes nine parameters:

```
function XCreateSimpleWindow(
  Display: PDisplay;        // The connection to the X Server
  Parent: TWindow;          // The parent window
  X, Y: Longint;            // Upper left corner relative to parent
  Width, Height: Cardinal;  // Width and height of window, minus border
  BorderWidth: Cardinal;    // Proposed border width
```

```
   Border: Cardinal;        // Border color
   Background: Cardinal     // Background color
): TWindow; cdecl;
```

Listing 6.4 provides an example of a program that calls XCreateSimpleWindow.

**LISTING 6.4**  An X Program That Calls XCreateSimpleWindow Rather Than XCreateWindow

```
program Simple;

{ $Id: simple.dpr,v 1.2 2001/01/20 07:37:57 ccalvert Exp $ }

uses
  Xlib, SysUtils;

const
  CR = Char($A);
  MyString = 'The frost performs its secret ministry';// + CR +
{     'Unhelped by any wind. The owlet''s cry' + CR +
      'Came loud - and hark, again! loud as before.' + CR +
      'The inmates of my cottage, all at rest,' + CR +
      'Have left me to that solitude, which suits' + CR +
      'Abstruser musings: save that at my side'+ CR +
      'My cradled infant slumbers peacefully';
Coleridge
http://etext.lib.virginia.edu/stc/Coleridge/poems/Frost_at_Midnight.html}

var
  Display: PDisplay;
  Window: TWindow;
  gc: TGC;

procedure DrawMyString();
var
  len: Integer;
begin
  len := strlen(MyString);
  XClearWindow (display, window);
  WriteLn ('drawing MyString of length ', len);
  XDrawString (display, window, gc, 10, 100, MyString, len);
end;

var
  xgcv: XGCValues;
  attributes: XSetWindowAttributes;
  event: XEvent;
```

Understanding the Linux Environment

**CHAPTER 6**

317

6

UNDERSTANDING
THE LINUX
ENVIRONMENT

**LISTING 6.4**  Continued

```pascal
    attributes_mask: Integer;
    display_name: PChar;
    done: Integer;
    BlackColor, WhiteColor: Integer;
    WindowNameString: PChar;
    WindowName: XTextProperty;
begin
  WindowNameString := 'Frost at midnight';
  display_name := nil;

  display_name := XDisplayName(display_name);
  display := XOpenDisplay(display_name);
  if display = nil then
    begin
      WriteLn('could not open display: ', display_name);
      exit;
    end;

  WriteLn('successfully opened display ', display_name);

  BlackColor := XBlackPixel(display, XDefaultScreen (display));
  WhiteColor := XWhitePixel(display, XDefaultScreen (display));

  window := XCreateSimpleWindow(display, XDefaultRootWindow(display),
    0, 0, 300, 300, 0, BlackColor, WhiteColor);

  //  XStoreName(display, window, 'Frost at Midnight');
  if XStringListToTextProperty(@WindowNameString, 1, @WindowName) = 0 then
  begin
    Writeln('Structure allocation for window name failed.');
    Halt(1);
  end;

  XSetWMProperties(Display, Window, @WindowName,
    nil, nil, 0, nil, nil, nil);

  WriteLn('successfully created window\n');

  XMapWindow(display, window);

  WriteLn('successfully mapped windows\n');

  WriteLn('attempting graphics context creation\n');
```

**LISTING 6.4** Continued

```
xgcv.foreground := $000000FF;
xgcv.background := $00000000;

gc := XCreateGC (display, window, (GCForeground or GCBackground), @xgcv);

WriteLn('successfully created graphics context');

XSelectInput(display, window,
 KeyPressMask or ExposureMask or ButtonPressMask);

done := 0;
while done <> 1 do begin
  XNextEvent (display, @event);

  case (event.xtype) of
    Expose: begin
      if event.xexpose.count <> 0 then
        break;
      DrawMyString();
    end;

    KeyPress: done := 1;

    ButtonPress: begin
    end;
  end;
end;

XCloseDisplay(display);
end.
```

## The Stacking Order

The windows have been created at this point, but our work is not done. A number of important issues still need careful attention.

Windows appear in a particular order. One window is placed on top of another, and portions of a window might hide all or part of another window. You can control the stacking order of the windows on the desktop. As a rule, new windows appear on the top of the stacking order. When you create a new window, you generally just call XMapWindow:

```
XMapWindow (display, window);
```

Understanding the Linux Environment

**CHAPTER 6**

319

6

UNDERSTANDING
THE LINUX
ENVIRONMENT

Other functions that you can call include `XMapRaised`, `XCirculateSubwindows`, `XConfigureWindow`, and `XRestackWindows`. The first of these calls ensures that your window is mapped in at the top of the hierarchy. You can find out about the rest of the calls by using `man` or `info`.

## Creating the Graphics Context

The graphics context in X is almost identical to the device context in Windows. It helps you draw shapes and bitmaps on a window, and it defines the line width, colors, and fill patterns of the shapes you draw. Here is how Simple2 creates the graphics context:

```
WriteLn ('attempting graphics context creation\n');
xgcv.foreground := $00FFFFFF;
xgcv.background := $00000000;
gc := XCreateGC(display, window, (GCForeground or GCBackground), @xgcv);
WriteLn('successfully created graphics context');
```

The first two parameters of `XCreateGC` are the display itself and the handle that you receive when call `XCreateWindow`. The next parameter is similar to the `ValueMask` parameter in `XCreateWindow`. Use this parameter to specify which values you are going to set in the last parameter. In this case, we "or" in the values `GCForeGround` and `GCBackground`, thereby telling the system that we are going to use the foreground and background fields of the `XGCValues` record passed in the last parameter. After making this call, you get back a handle to the graphics context.

The `DrawMyString` method from the Simple2 program uses the graphics context that you retrieved from the system:

```
procedure DrawMyString(MyString: string);
var
  len: Integer;
begin
  len := Length(MyString);
  XClearWindow (display, window);
  WriteLn ('drawing MyString of length ', len);
  XDrawString (display, window, gc, 10, 100, PChar(MyString), len)
end;
```

Note that `XDrawString` takes the display, the window handle, and the graphics context as parameters. You also need to specify the X and Y locations where the string is to be drawn, as well as the string itself and its length. (Windows programmers should find this call very familiar because it is virtually identical to the `TextOut` call found in the Windows API. The difference is that Windows does not require that you redundantly pass in the display or the window.)

Remember that the call to WriteLn seen in the DrawMyString method writes output to a shell window, not to X. If you want to see this output when running from the IDE, you should start Kylix from the shell prompt, not from the KDE or GNOME menu.

## The Event Loop

The event loop in X looks very similar to the event loop at the bottom of a Windows API application.

The code from the Simple2 application first sets up a loop and then calls XNextEvent to find what is in the event queue. Finally, you perform certain actions based on what you found in the queue:

```
done := 0;
while done <> 1 do begin
    XNextEvent (display, @event);

    case (event.xtype) of

      Expose: begin
        if event.xexpose.count <> 0 then
          break;
        DrawMyString('The wondrous world of X!');
      end;

      KeyPress: done := 1;
      ButtonPress: ;
    end;
  end;
  XCloseDisplay (display);
end.
```

After you break out of the loop, you call XCloseDisplay to shut X down.

Here is the declaration for the XEvent structure that you pass to XNextEvent:

```
PXEvent = ^XEvent;
XEvent = record
case Longint of
  0: ( xtype: Longint );
  1: ( xany: XAnyEvent );
  2: ( xkey: XKeyEvent );
  3: ( xbutton: XButtonEvent );
  4: ( xmotion: XMotionEvent );
  5: ( xcrossing: XCrossingEvent );
  6: ( xfocus: XFocusChangeEvent );
  7: ( xexpose: XExposeEvent );
```

Understanding the Linux Environment

**Chapter 6**

321

6

UNDERSTANDING
THE LINUX
ENVIRONMENT

```
 8: ( xgraphicsexpose: XGraphicsExposeEvent );
 9: ( xnoexpose: XNoExposeEvent );
10: ( xvisibility: XVisibilityEvent );
11: ( xcreatewindow: XCreateWindowEvent );
12: ( xdestroywindow: XDestroyWindowEvent );
13: ( xunmap: XUnmapEvent );
14: ( xmap: XMapEvent );
15: ( xmaprequest: XMapRequestEvent );
16: ( xreparent: XReparentEvent );
17: ( xconfigure: XConfigureEvent );
18: ( xgravity: XGravityEvent );
19: ( xresizerequest: XResizeRequestEvent );
20: ( xconfigurerequest: XConfigureRequestEvent );
21: ( xcirculate: XCirculateEvent );
22: ( xcirculaterequest: XCirculateRequestEvent );
23: ( xproperty: XPropertyEvent );
24: ( xselectionclear: XSelectionClearEvent );
25: ( xselectionrequest: XSelectionRequestEvent );
26: ( xselection: XSelectionEvent );
27: ( xcolormap: XColormapEvent );
28: ( xclient: XClientMessageEvent );
29: ( xmapping: XMappingEvent );
30: ( xerror: XErrorEvent );
31: ( xkeymap: XKeymapEvent );
32: ( pad: array[0..23] of Longint );
end;
```

This is a variant record. Variant records can contain different structures at different times, depending on the kind of event that occurs. You can tell which kind of event occurred by looking at the xtype field. It contains values such as Expose, KeyPress, or ButtonPress.

The various event structures included in this record are too numerous to mention. However, here is one of the most important ones, which you can use as a template for understanding the other structures:

```
PXKeyEvent = ^XKeyEvent;
XKeyEvent = record
  xtype: Longint;   { of event  }
  serial: Cardinal; { # of last request processed by server  }
  send_event: Bool; { true if this came from a SendEvent request  }
  xdisplay: PDisplay;   { Display the event was read from  }
  xwindow: TWindow;     { "event" window it is reported relative to  }
  root: TWindow;        { root window that the event occurred on  }
  subwindow: TWindow;   { child window  }
  time: TTime;          { milliseconds  }
  x: Longint;           { pointer x, y coordinates in event window  }
```

```
    y: Longint;
    x_root: Longint;        { coordinates relative to root  }
    y_root: Longint;
    state: Cardinal;        { key or button mask  }
    keycode: Cardinal;      { detail  }
    same_screen: Bool;      { same screen flag  }
  end;
```

If the xtype field is XKeyPress, the XKeyEvent record will be filled out for you. The
XKeyEvent record contains all the information that you could possibly want to know about an
XKeyEvent. An example of how this works is shown in the Expose event from the Simple2 pro-
gram:

```
    case (event.xtype) of

      Expose: begin
        if event.xexpose.count <> 0 then
          break;
        DrawMyString('The wondrous world of X!');
      end;
```

In this case statement, when the event type is Expose, you can access the event.xexpose
record. In particular, this code checks to see the count field of the record. (You might recall
that Expose messages are similar to WM_PAINT messages in Windows.)

## Summary of Writing a Program in X

Back in the ancient days of DOS programming, when I first came to Borland, the programmers
there made it clear to me that it was not enough to just know the ins and outs of Turbo Pascal.
If I wanted to be really useful, I needed to understand not only the Pascal language, but also
the operating system on which it was constructed.

The longer I stayed at Borland, the more I came to understand the wisdom of this advice.
Knowing a lot about Turbo Pascal helped me in certain familiar situations. But when unique
questions came up, or new technologies emerged, the only way to survive was to understand
not just a set of particulars, but the theory on which those particulars rested. That meant I
needed to understand not just Pascal, but the operating system and the machine itself.

This follows the spirit of that advice from my friends at Borland. Kylix is dependant on both
Xlib and QT, and in the last few pages of this chapter you have been pluming the depths of the
XWindow library.

In the process, you have seen a good deal of detailed information about writing directly to the
Xlib API. As you have seen, this is a complex operation. In fact, I would say that it is at least
as difficult as writing Windows API applications.

Understanding the Linux Environment

**CHAPTER 6**

323

6

UNDERSTANDING
THE LINUX
ENVIRONMENT

In this text, I was able to give you enough detail to get you started on the sea voyage that takes you to the fabled wind-swept shores of Xlib expertise. This knowledge should stand you in good stead when you need to understand exactly how CLX works and why it works that way.

# Window Managers

One of the oddities of the X Window System is that it does not define how windows will be displayed on the screen. For instance, X does not specify whether windows should be tiled or overlapped. It has no policy regarding the types of captions, borders, or other decorative items surrounding a window. All this is in the hands of an x-client called a *window manager*.

## Why Window Managers Were Created

X's lack of policy regarding window management occurred for historical reasons. Possibly a different kind of implementation would have been developed if X were being created today.

When X11 came into being in the late 1980s, there was no consensus on whether tiled or overlapped windows were best. Nor was there a policy governing what kinds of decorative controls, such as minimize and maximize buttons, should adorn a window. Partially as a result of these concerns, the team that created X decided to let an undefined x-client named the window manager handle the problem.

However, other considerations led the X development team to use window managers. For instance, X is designed to run on a truly large variety of client machines. Many of these machines have extreme restrictions on what they are capable of doing. As a result, it was not clear exactly how much X could demand of the windows that it created. By letting the window manager handle these details, the X team could create a single specification that worked on many platforms.

Whether window managers are a good thing or a bad thing is a matter of debate. However, it is true that they add an element of creativity to the X Window System. A variety of third parties have built window managers, and many of them are very visually rich and provide the user with a wide range of options.

## The Power of the Window Manager

Because X leaves so many matters up to the window manager, window managers have a lot of power. When you create a window, you can pass the window manager suggestions on how you would like it to be implemented. For instance, you can suggest that it be a certain size or shape and have a certain stacking order. In the X programming lexicon, these suggestions are called *hints*. You cannot give a window manager a command. Instead, you give it hints about how you would like it to behave.

In theory, you don't know whether the window manager will heed your requests. In practice, at least under KDE or GTK, you can usually assume that the window manager will accommodate your requests. But you can't be sure of it. In fact, you generally have to check to see what the window manager actually did with your requests before you try to draw into a window. For instance, you can't be sure that a window is really the width and height that you requested; as a result, you should check the window's height and width before you use it.

## Changing and Querying Window Managers

By default, under KDE, your window manager is called the K Window Manager (KWM). This follows the traditional naming for window managers, such as twm, which is part of the MIT distribution of X; mwm, which is the Motif Window Manager; and olwm, which is the Open Look Window Manager. Not all window managers follow this naming convention, though. For instance, Enlightenment is the name of a famous window manager often used with GNOME.

# X Toolkits

X toolkits, or widget sets, are one of the most obvious features of a GUI environment. When you launch Linux in graphics mode, you see windows—more importantly, you see the buttons, edit controls, menus, speed bars, and other features of applications. All these things are part of an X toolkit.

Widget sets sit on top of X and its window manager and provide sets of components that the user can manipulate at runtime. As you will read in Part II of this book, Kylix provides an object-oriented framework named CLX that enables you to talk to, create, and control these widgets.

As explained earlier, the two most well-known widget sets in Linux are called Qt and GTK. Both are available on most of the major Linux distributions such as Red Hat or Mandrake.

## Controls, Components, and Widgets

In Windows, items such as buttons, list boxes, and scrollbars are called *controls*. In Linux, they are called *widgets*. Widget stands for "windows gadget."

In Windows, usually only one set of core controls is used to build applications. These controls are created by Microsoft and are built into the operating system. Of course, you can build a single Windows application that does not use any of the core Windows controls. Furthermore, in some cases you can subclass Windows controls so that all instances of them in the environment take on a unique behavior. Nevertheless, in practice and by default, most Windows applications rely primarily on a set of controls hand-crafted in Redmond.

The Linux platform, on the other hand, has multiple widget sets that you can choose from. Most developers on Linux choose to use the Qt widget set created by the Troll Tech company from Norway, or the GTK+ widget set, created by Richard Stallman's GNU organization. These widget sets are sets of classes, like the button class or list box class in Windows. Other widget sets are available, and some of them have a fairly large following. But the majority of Linux developers use either the Troll Tech Qt widget set or the GNU GTK widget set.

You can read about Qt at `http://doc.trolltech.com/index.html`, and you can find more general information about TrollTech at `www.trolltech.com`.

The GTK is a GNU project. You can read about GNU at `www.gnu.org`, and you can read about GTK at `www.gtk.org`.

One of the things that Qt provides that X doesn't is a group of widgets. All X gives you is a bunch of rectangles or bitmaps, and lets you draw on them and blit them back and forth. MIT, which created X, said that it would *not* define policy—things such as buttons and list boxes. So, the plan from the beginning was to have widget sets running on top of X. CLX, when it sits on top of Qt, provides its own API. Kylix does not call the Qt classes directly. (The contract between Borland and TrollTech states that Borland can use Qt to create CLX, but it cannot give its users access to the raw Qt API.)

It is a good thing that Linux provides choices to developers and users. However, it is painful to have to choose whether you belong to the GNU or the TrollTech camp. Borland elected to go with Qt. This decision means that the GUI applications that you create with CLX will use the Qt library.

Fortunately, applications built with Qt will run under GNOME, and applications built with GTK will run under KDE. As a result, Kylix applications will run under both the KDE and the GNOME desktops.

# A Few Words About Desktops

Most Linux users are familiar with their desktops. My purpose here will be simply to tie together some of the information given so far in this chapter.

## The KDE Desktop

KDE stands for the K Desktop Environment. This is meant to be, at least in part, an echo of the initials CDE, the Common Desktop Environment, which is a well-known Unix desktop. The most obvious features of KDE are the panel that appears at the bottom of the default KDE desktop and the taskbar that appears at the top of the default KDE desktop. KDE also comes with a suite of applications and utilities. KDE uses the Qt C++ cross-platform GUI toolkit for development.

KDE comes with its own default window manager. Most people use that window manager whenever they are using KDE. Information about KDE can be accessed at `http://www.kde.org`.

## The GNOME Desktop

The GNOME desktop was developed by the GNU Project. The initials stand for GNU Network Object Model Environment. GNOME supports to various degrees a number of window managers, including Sawfish (until recently called Sawmill), Enlightenment, Window Maker, IceWM, Scwm, and FVWM (version 2.3). Sawmill and Enlightenment are the most popular of these. GNOME provides a dialog box that makes it easy to add new window managers to the desktop or to switch from one window manager to another.

Like KDE, GNOME has a panel at the bottom of the screen in its default desktop. The GTK+ and Glib Libraries form the foundation for the GUI, but GNOME also provides a set of widgets in addition to GTK+.

Because both GNOME and KDE are open source, they are evolving, not static environments. To get more information about GNOME, go to `http://www.gnome.org`.

## Summary

This chapter gave you an overview of the Linux GUI, which you will be programming when using the Kylix visual tools.

You can use Kylix to access all aspects of the Linux operating system, from its front end back to the low-level system calls found in `Libc`. Many of the low-level system calls will be discussed in Part III, "Linux Systems Programming." You can find a discussion of using CLX to program the Linux GUI in Part II of this book, which begins in the next chapter, "CLX Architecture and Visual Development."

# CLX

# PART
# II

## IN THIS PART

# CLX Architecture and Visual Development

*by Charlie Calvert*

## IN THIS CHAPTER

This chapter is dedicated to helping you understand the relationship between CLX and Qt. Here you will find the core background material that will help you create powerful CLX components. Vitally important information on the open source project FreeCLX is also included in this chapter.

This chapter is probably one of the most difficult to understand in the entire book. If you find the going difficult, I will confess that you could probably finish and understand most of the rest of this book without understanding more than a few of the more obvious facts found in this chapter.

The first half of this chapter focuses on explaining how the Kylix team translated the VCL from a Windows-based API into the CLX API that runs on Linux. Or, to state the same thing somewhat differently, the chapter explains how the Kylix team wrapped the Linux Qt API in a visual class library.

People who want to use only the most basic features of Kylix can get away with understanding little or nothing about this subject. Programmers who want to fully understand CLX on a deeper level need to master everything in this chapter. Other readers might want to come to rest somewhere on the continuum between these two extremes.

I personally did not feel comfortable with CLX until I understood the material in this chapter. I just don't like the feeling I get when I don't understand how a system is working. I never feel as though I have things right until I understand why things are done a particular way.

Furthermore, I was not able to solve several programming problems without using the knowledge discussed in this chapter. For instance, see the section on the TElfCompass component that appears in Chapter 11, "Graphics"—in particular, see the section of that chapter called "Changing the World Coordinates." There you will find a concrete example of how I was forced to go beyond what CLX has to offer and instead use the C wrapper around Qt to solve a problem. Learning how to create solutions of that kind is very much what this chapter is all about.

**DELPHI NOTE**

If you are an expert Delphi programmer who wants to make the transition to Kylix, this is probably the key chapter in this book. Absorb what is written here, and you will have most of the information that you need to port even the most complex applications from the Windows VCL to Linux CLX.

Even those who do not have a theoretical turn of mind will probably be interested in the more practical examples found in the second half of this chapter. For instance, the sections "Working with Styles," "Working with Resources," and "Creating Nonrectangular Forms" will have general appeal to everyone. The sections on resources and styles should be of special interest to Delphi programmers because they highlight significant differences from the technologies found in Kylix programs and those found in Windows programs.

All readers of this book should also be sure to see the section of this chapter entitled "Stalking the Elusive CLX Message." It covers key material on how to handle messages in CLX.

The next few chapters of the text first lay the groundwork for building components, and then show you how to go about building components. However, before you build components of your own, you should check to see if there are existing components that you can use. The following link, maintained by Borland itself, can help you find existing components that add to the power of Kylix: `http://www.borland.com/kylix/resources/kylixtools.html`.

## Qt and CLX

Before you can fully understand everything that will be said in the next few chapters, you need to understand the relationship between CLX and Qt. CLX, of course, is the object-oriented library that lies at the heart of Kylix.

By way of review, here is a little bit of doggeral for you:

```
CLX is to Kylix
As MFC is to Visual C++
As GTK is to GNOME
As OWL was to Borland C++;
And even as the first great Windows OOP library,
The original OWL, was to Turbo Pascal
```

In Microsoft Windows, the controls that most people see on the screen are part of the Windows API. In GNOME programming, the controls that most people see are part of the GTK. In KDE programming, the controls that most people see are part of Qt. In other words, Qt has the same relationship to the KDE that GTK has to GNOME: It is the object-oriented library out of which KDE is made. Before the release of Kylix, if you wanted to create a native KDE program, you would have used Qt.

| NOTE |
| --- |

You can read about KDE at `http://www.kde.org`. You can read about Qt at `http://www.trolltech.com`.

Qt is a C++ class library that contains many basic controls such as list boxes, edit controls, buttons, and scrollbars. All the buttons, edit controls, scrollbars, and other basic components that you see in a standard KDE application come from the Qt library.

Because CLX is a wrapper around Qt, and most of the controls on the Kylix Component palette are simply Pascal wrappers around Qt classes. In particular, the Kylix team wrote C wrappers around every single method in the Qt API and then made those calls available to you in a file named Qt.pas. More particularly, the actual C functions appear to be in `libqtintf.so`, a shared object called by all CLX programs. You will learn more about this shared object in Chapter 8, "Packaging and Sharing Code," when looking at the `ldd` utility in the section "Packages and the `LD_LIBRARY_PATH`."

The C wrapper was placed around the Qt C++ API because Object Pascal cannot call certain types of C++ objects directly. There is no difference between a simple C++ object and a simple Object Pascal object. Thus, if you create simple C++ objects with the right compilers, you can call them directly from Object Pascal. However, C++ supports both multiple inheritance and operator overloading, neither of which is supported in the Object Pascal syntax. As a result, Object Pascal does not know what to do with objects that use multiple inheritance. Because multiple inheritance is part of Qt, something had to be done to make the API accessible from Kylix. The particular solution that the Kylix team came up with was simply to wrap C functions around every single Qt method. For instance, the method `QButton:create` became the C function `QButton_create`.

My understanding is that this process was automated. A series of scripts was run against the Qt API, and the result was that a set of C functions was generated that could be called directly from Kylix. I've been told that automating this process ensured that every single public or protected Qt method in every single Qt object has been exposed to Kylix programmers. Nothing was left out because the human element was taken out of the equation: An automated process wrapped the Qt library, thereby ensuring that every method was included, regardless of how trivial it is.

A form of inheritance was built into this process. Methods that `QButton` inherited from `QWidget` tend to be accessed via the `QWidget_XXX` series of functions rather than the `QButton_XXX` series. You pass a handle to `QWidget_XXX` to polymorphically call the correct instance of the object. Thus, you should not jump to conclusions if you think that you have found some method of Qt that does not appear to be available in the Pascal C wrappers. The function is probably there—you just need to learn how to access it. You will learn how later in the text.

If you open Qt.pas, you will find Pascal translations of all the constants and all the objects that are part of Qt. All of these functions and constants are yours to do with as you like. You can create anything that you want with them and distribute them in any way that you want. Borland has already paid TrollTech for the use of these functions. When you bought Kylix, you did your part to help defray the cost of this fee.

Here are some of the functions in Qt.pas:

```
function QWidget_create(parent: QWidgetH; name:
  PAnsiChar; f: WFlags): QWidgetH; cdecl;
procedure QWidget_destroy(handle: QWidgetH); cdecl;
function QWidget_winId(handle: QWidgetH): Cardinal; cdecl;
procedure QWidget_setName(handle: QWidgetH; name: PAnsiChar); cdecl;
```

No great degree of insight is required to see what is happening here. QWidget is the base class for components in Qt. All Qt components descend from QWidget, just as all Object Pascal components descend from TComponent. QWidget_create is obviously a wrapper around the constructor for the Qt QWidget class:

```
QWidget ( QWidget * parent=0, const char * name=0, WFlags f=0 )
~QWidget ()
WId winId () const
void QWidget:setName ( const char * name )
```

The relationship between the methods in the Qt library and the methods in the CLX library is too obvious to need much further explanation. Clearly, QWidget_destroy is the wrapper around QWidget, and QWidget_setName is the wrapper around QWidget:setName.

---

**NOTE**

As mentioned in the previous sidebar, you might search in vain for a method such as QButton_setName. The method is actually available to you, but you need to call it through an odd sort of polymorphism. In particular, you call QWidget_setName and pass the handle to a QButton object. As a result of this action, the QButton_setName method will be called. More on this later.

---

If you want to learn more about the QWidget object, you can go to http://doc.trolltech. com/qwidget.html. Needless to say, this particular page could change over time. However, the simplicity and logical syntax of the name probably means that TrollTech will continue to make the docs for the QWidget object available on a page named QWidget.html, just as the docs for the QButton object are found on http://doc.trolltech.com/qbutton.html. The index for the whole class library is at http://doc.troltech.com/classes.html.

NOTE

The simplicity, logic, and satisfying correctness of the Qt naming scheme for these online docs parallels a general sense of orderliness that pervades much of the Qt API. In the old days, I would have taken one look at the Qt OOP library and said that it had to have come out of Borland. Certainly, the team that put MFC together could have learned from the elegance of the Qt library. But Qt is not a Borland API, and you have to respect the busy trolls in Finland who created this excellent tool. However, if you dig deep enough into Qt, you will start finding problems in its implementation of certain complex classes. For instance, the Kylix team finally gave up on using the limited Qt `TreeView` and `ListView` controls and ended up writing its own controls in Object Pascal. Something similar was done for the `OpenDialog` control. Despite these shortcomings in some of the more complex objects, Qt nevertheless has a pleasing and sensible structure that elegantly shows off many of the best features of object-oriented programming.

Kylix runs only on Linux, and Delphi 6 supports CLX on Windows. However, Qt has a wider range of deployment. Here are the platforms supported by Qt at the time of this writing:

AIX 4.1 or later

BSDI/OS 2.0 or later

DG/UX

FreeBSD 2.1 or later

HP-UX 10.20 or later

Irix 6.x

Linux

NetBSD

OS/2 (with XFree86)

QNX

SCO UNIX

Solaris 2.5.1 or later

Tru64 (Digital UNIX) 4.0 or later

Windows 95

Windows 98

XLib on Windows

Windows NT 4.0 or later

Here are the compilers that Qt tests for compatibility:

Borland C++—Windows 95/98/NT/2000

Comeau C++—Linux

Compaq C++—Tru64 (Digital UNIX), Linux

GCC/egcs—most platforms

Hewlett-Packard aCC—HP-UX

Hewlett-Packard CC—HP-UX

KAI C++—Linux

MipsPRO—Irix

Sun WorkShop/Forte Developer—Solaris

Visual C++—Windows 95/98/NT/2000

IBM xlC—AIX

Qt even comes with a visual programming interface. I have seen screen shots of this tool on the TrollTech Web site, but I have never used it.

There is a free distribution of Qt that you can use for open-source projects on Linux. Various licensing agreements that involve payments are put into effect if you decide not to go the open-source route. None of these licensing agreements, including the open-source license, apply to applications made with Kylix. You can distribute Kylix applications in any manner you like. However, if you include even one direct call to Qt in your Kylix application, then the free Borland license for distributing your applications is void. The calls in Qt.pas, however, are covered by your license. Assuming that you have a legal version of Kylix, you can call into Qt.pas to your heart's content and not worry about license fees.

## FreeCLX

At the time of this writing, it is not clear what files will ship with the open-source version of Kylix that will be released in the summer of 2001. However, it appears certain that the source to Qt.pas will be included in that version. In particular, at the time of this writing, a SourceForge open-source project named FreeCLX has been opened by the Kylix team.

Updates to CLX appear on this site. For instance, you can get the latest version of libqtintf.so.2.2.4.1 from the FreeCLX site. At the time of this writing, various CLX units have been updated on FreeCLX, including DirSel.pas, QComCtrls, Qdialogs, and QStdCtrls.

You can access FreeCLX at `http://sourceforge.net/projects/freeclx/`. Again, this looks like a Web address that will stick around for a while. However, if it is not available, just go to `www.sourceforge.net` and search for freeclx.

You can browse the FreeCLX library online at the previous addresses. If you want more direct access to the library, enter the following at the Linux command prompt:

```
cvs -d :pserver:anonymous@cvs.freeclx.sourceforge.net:/cvsroot/freeclx login
```

When prompted for a password, just press Enter. If you get no confirmation and no errors, then all has gone well and you are signed in.

The files in FreeCLX should be included in your version of Kylix. However, if you are interested in the open source process, here is how to download the source to freeclx:

```
cvs -d \
:pserver:anonymous@cvs.freeclx.sourceforge.net:/cvsroot/freeclx \
checkout freeclx
```

This whole command should appear on one single line. It is broken up into multiple lines just so that it will fit into the text of this book. The backslash at the end of the first two lines should not be included. To make sure that nothing goes wrong, just run the getFreeClx.sh script found in the Chapter07 directory from the CD for this book:

```
%sh getFreeClx.sh
```

When you are prompted for a password, press Enter. FreeCLX will be downloaded into a directory beneath the directory from which you run the script. So, you will need the proper rights to the directory from which you run the script. To get the rights you need, use the Linux utilities chown and chmod, both of which are discussed on my site at http://www.elvenware.com/charlie/linux/LinuxUsers.html. More information can be found at http://www.elvenware.com/charlie/linux/LinuxFAQ.html. If all else fails, just run it from your home directory; that directory should have the rights you need.

FreeCLX is important because it shows what parts of CLX have been given to the open-source community. Fortunately, these include all the key classes discussed in these chapters on CLX, as well as the key database classes. These are now open-source classes, and they can be studied and improved by the Kylix community.

For further information on FreeCLX, check www.borland.com and www.elvenware.com after the release of the open-source version of Kylix. You will not be able to do anything with the source to FreeCLX unless you first have the Kylix compiler. A free version of the Kylix compiler is scheduled to be released in the summer of 2001.

# Qt and Events

We are about to embark on a discussion of events in CLX. There is a complex interrelationship between CLX and Qt when it comes to capturing events. The next few sections of the text are designed to illuminate that discussion.

I will start with a short and very practical section on handling basic events in CLX components. That section will give you an overview of topics that will be examined from many different angles throughout the next few chapters. Specific references to these sections will be given at the end of the next section of this chapter.

When you have a feeling for the clean and simple way messages are handled in a typical CLX component, I'll move into a long section explaining what is going on behind the scenes when messages are generated and captured in a Kylix program. This long section delves deep into both the Qt and the CLX event model. It will appeal primarily to people who want to do serious work with CLX.

## Stalking the Elusive CLX Message

In traditional Windows programming, in many forms of Linux programming, and even in Delphi, programmers handle mouse movements by responding to messages. That is not the Kylix way of doing things. Instead, I suggest that you let CLX respond to the movements of the mouse and then simply override the methods that CLX uses to report these events.

> **NOTE**
>
> In saying that messages are not the CLX way of doing things, I do not mean to imply that CLX provides no support for messages. In particular, see the `TObject.Dispatch` and `TWidgetControl.Broadcast` methods. Also view the discussion of the `EventFilter` method that appears in the later section "The Night CLX Let Me Down: EventFilter Mojo." The `EventFilter` method is also discussed frequently throughout much of the text between the end of this section and the section on `EventFilter` mojo.

If you are creating a component and want to catch mouse move messages, you should use the following method:

```
procedure MouseMove(Shift: TShiftState; X, Y: Integer); override;
```

This method overrides the CLX `MouseMove` method of the `TControl` object. The `MouseMove` method is called whenever the user moves the mouse over a component.

In some components, however, there is no need to know the exact location of the mouse at any one time. Instead, the only events that need to be tracked are those when the mouse passes over the component and when it leaves the component. Fortunately, CLX tracks these events:

```
    procedure MouseEnter(AControl: TControl); dynamic;
    procedure MouseLeave(AControl: TControl); dynamic;
```

These two methods are part of TControl. TControl is in the inheritance tree of TPanel:

```
TObject
TPersistent
TComponent
TControl
TWidgetControl
TCustomControl
TCustomPanel
TPanel
```

Objects such as TComponent, TControl, and TWidgetControl are fairly complex. Only the most experienced Object Pascal programmers can hope to have any a good feeling for all the hundreds of methods in the inheritance tree of an object such as TPanel.

So how can you know that a method such as MouseEnter even exists? Sadly, there is no good answer to that question. Your best bet, really, is to have a good sense of how computers work and how large APIs such as CLX, Qt, and Xlib are put together. If you have a good feeling for these kind of tools, you know that methods such as MouseEnter and MouseLeave have to exist—or, at least, *ought* to exist. Getting a feel for this kind of thing is something that really can come only with experience.

The developers of CLX have been in the programming business a long time, and they have focused for many years on building tools such as Kylix. As a result, they know what methods you, as a programmer, are going to need to create your programs. Furthermore, they see it as their job to surface all the core features of the operating system on which they are building their tool. The end result of this process is that most of the features available in the Linux or Windows GUI should be found somewhere in the CLX API. In short, if an experienced programmer feels that a CLX method ought to exist, it probably does exist. If it doesn't exist, then most of the time there is a good reason for it not to exist. Sometimes, however, oversights do occur. Somehow such oversights, no matter how minor, tend to loom large in our minds. Fortunately, however, they are few and far between.

With Delphi, the job of the Object Pascal development team was fairly straightforward: find and surface as many features of the Windows GUI and underlying operating system as possible. With Kylix, however, that goal is tempered by the desire to get CLX to run on both Windows and Linux. As a result, CLX has a tendency to surface all the key features of the GUI and OS that both Windows and Linux have in common. Clearly, there are limitations in this formula that are not inherent in the Delphi VCL. Nonetheless, you can still expect to find an incredible wealth of tools in CLX. The more time you can spend exploring the resources found in Classes.pas and QControls.pas, the better. There is a wealth of power there, waiting for you to tap it.

> **NOTE**
>
> Classes.pas and QControls.pas contain the classes from which most CLX components descend. In particular, TComponent, TControl, TwidgetControl, and TCustomControl are declared and implemented in these files. The standard CLX components are all declared in QStdCtrls.pas, and additional components are declared in QExtCtrls.pas. If you want to become an expert in CLX, you should begin to live inside these files. Let me add, however, that most programmers don't need to be that much of an expert on CLX to make good use of the product. For instance, lots of expert Object Pascal programmers know a lot about database programming, or Web programming, or graphics programming, and little about the contents of QControls.pas. If you want to be an expert on CLX, though, these files are your primary sources.

Practical examples of all the issues discussed in this section will be given in the next few chapters. For instance, capturing the MouseMove event is discussed in detail in Chapter 11, in the section "Drawing the Rubber Band" in the Mandelbrot example. The MouseEnter and MouseLeave events are discussed in Chapter 9, "Creating Components," in the section "Responding to Messages." A more in-depth discussion of the base classes for CLX controls appears in Chapter 10, "Advanced Component Design," in the section "Building Components from Scratch."

## Qt Signals and Slots

It is now time to begin an in-depth discussion of Qt and its relationship to CLX. Most of the discussion will concern event handling, but many other general topics of discussion will also be included.

In Qt, programmers traditionally do not respond directly to messages. Instead, they work with a *signal and slot mechanism*. Listing 7.1 shows an example of a simple Qt program that uses signals and slots.

**LISTING 7.1**  Using Signals and Slots in a C++ Qt Program

```
#include <qapplication.h>
#include <qslider.h>
#include <qlcdnumber.h>

int main (int argc, char* argv[])
{
  QApplication myapp(argc, argv);
```

**LISTING 7.1** Continued

```
QWidget *mywidget = new QWidget();
mywidget->setGeometry(400, 300, 170, 110);

QSlider* myslider = new QSlider(0, 9, 1, 1, QSlider:Horizontal, mywidget);

myslider->setGeometry(10, 10, 150, 30);

QLCDNumber *mylcdNumber = new QLCDNumber(1, mywidget);
mylcdNumber->setGeometry(60, 50, 50, 50);
mylcdNumber->display(1);

QObject:connect(myslider, SIGNAL(sliderMoved(int)),
  mylcdNumber, SLOT(display(int)));

myapp.setMainWidget(mywidget);
mywidget->show();

return myapp.exec();
}
```

This program pops up a simple window containing a QLCDNumber control and a QSlider control. In CLX, the wrappers around these controls are named TTrackBar and TLCDNumber. You can see what the Qt program looks like in Figure 7.1.

> **NOTE**
>
> A Kylix program named Slider, found on the CD that accompanies this book, has the same physical appearance and acts in the same way as the C++–based Slider program. If you cannot compile the Qt program and run it, you can compile the Kylix program. Doing this might help you understand the discussion of the Qt Slider program.

**FIGURE 7.1**

*The Slider program shows how a slider can be moved back and forth on a form to change the value displayed in the* LCDNumber *control.*

Qt programs usually have an `Application` object, just as most Kylix programs have an `Application` object:

```
QApplication myapp(argc, argv);
```

Most Qt programs also have a window as a background, just as most Kylix programs have a `TForm` object as a background. In Qt, you create this background or form object by instantiating an instance of `QWidget`:

```
QWidget *mywidget = new QWidget();
```

It is a simple matter to create two components:

```
QSlider* myslider = new QSlider(0, 9, 1, 1, QSlider:Horizontal, mywidget);

myslider->setGeometry(10, 10, 150, 30);

QLCDNumber *mylcdNumber = new QLCDNumber(1, mywidget);
mylcdNumber->setGeometry(60, 50, 50, 50);
mylcdNumber->display(1);
```

The constructor for the `QSlider` component takes a minimum value, a maximum value, a step value, a starting value, an orientation, and a parent:

```
QSlider (
  int minValue,
  int maxValue,
  int pageStep,
  int value,
  Orientation,
  QWidget * parent,
  const char * name=0 }
```

Filling in these parameters is a very straightforward process. The only moderately tricky parts are setting the orientation to `Horizontal` and assigning the main widget as the parent. The call to `setGeometry` is identical to the CLX and VCL call to `SetBounds`. Experienced programmers will have seen this kind of thing many times in many different languages and APIs.

This constructor for the `QLCDNumber` control takes a starting value of 1 and the `QWidget` control as a parent. The next call is to `setGeometry`, which, as explained previously, does nothing more than set the bounds, or size, of the component as it appears at runtime.

The following two lines of code provide an introduction to the signal and slot mechanism:

```
mylcdNumber->display(1);

QObject::connect(myslider, SIGNAL(sliderMoved(int)),
  mylcdNumber, SLOT(display(int)));
```

The first line of code is redundant, in that it simply resets the initial value of the QLCDNumber control to 1. This task was already performed in the call to the object's constructor. The call is included here anyway, to draw attention to the display method. In particular, it reappears in the next line of code, which uses signals and slots.

QObject is the base class in Qt, just as TObject is the base class in Object Pascal. QObject has a class or static method named connect. An Object Pascal class method is the same thing as a C++ or Java static method. In particular, you can call a class or static method without first creating an instance of the object to which it belongs. You can see an example of that here. Nowhere in this program is the new operator applied to QObject; you can call connect directly without first instantiating an instance of QObject.

```
QObject::connect(myslider, SIGNAL(sliderMoved(int)),
    mylcdNumber, SLOT(display(int)));
```

**NOTE**

The call to QObject connect and the discussion of class vs. static methods could be confusing to some readers. If you are new to C++, you should focus your attention on the fact that the words QObject and connect are separated by a :: symbol rather than a -> symbol. A discussion of class methods in Object Pascal appears in Chapter 4, "Objects and Interfaces," in the section "Class Methods."

**NOTE**

When I'm hurried or tired, I find it easy to get QObject and QWidget confused. QWidget is the base class for all Qt components. It descends from QObject, which is the base class for all Qt classes. QWidget is the base class for all classes that are also components, and QObject is the base class for all classes, regardless of whether they are also components.

The connect method is used to set up what a Kylix programmer would call an event. The QSlider's sliderMoved method is connected to the QLCDNumber:display method. By associating these two methods, the QSlider component can easily inform the QLCDNumber control that the user has changed the value that should be displayed. In particular, whenever the user moves the thumb of the slider control, the QSlider::sliderMoved method calls the QLCDNumber::display method.

There is nothing special about the `sliderMoved` and `display` methods. They are just ordinary C++ methods that are marked as signals and slots, just as some Kylix methods are marked as being `virtual`. In short, you use a compiler directive to mark the methods as signals and slots, and, after doing that, you can link them together with the `QObject::connect` method. Of course, they won't link properly unless they both pass and accept the same type and number of arguments.

## The Qt Application Object and the Event Loop

Before closing this section of the chapter, let's go back and look at the last few lines of the Qt program:

```
myapp.setMainWidget(mywidget);
mywidget->show();

return myapp.exec();
```

`setMainWidget` is the call that establishes the `QWidget` object as the main "form" of the application. This call asserts that the `mywidget` instance is the window on which the other controls rest. Without this call, your program cannot terminate correctly.

The call to the `show()` method of `QWidget` is self-explanatory. A few words need to be said, however, about the last line in the program.

`myapp` is the Qt application object. The Qt application object is very similar to both the VCL `TApplication` object and the CLX `TApplication` object. In fact, the CLX application object is a glorified—and considerably extended—wrapper around the Qt application object. One of the fields of `TApplication` is an instance of this Qt object, which is created like this:

```
function TApplication.GetAppWidget: QWidgetH;
begin
  if not Assigned(FAppWidget) then
  begin
    FAppWidget := QWidget_create(nil, nil, 0);
    QWidget_setFocusPolicy(FAppWidget, QWidgetFocusPolicy_NoFocus);
  end;
  Result := FAppWidget;
end;
```

As you can see, this method contains a call to `QWidget::create` that is similar to the one in the Slider program.

Here is the event loop that lies at the center of CLX applications:

```
procedure TApplication.HandleMessage;
```

```
begin
  QApplication_processOneEvent(Handle);
  if GetCurrentThreadID = Integer(MainThreadID) then
    CheckSynchronize;
end;
```

As you can see, this call depends on the processOneEvent method of the QApplication object. In short, your CLX applications rest largely on the foundation of the Qt QApplication object.

## Calling Raw Qt Code from Object Pascal

Take a look at the following somewhat absurd program, found on the CD that accompanies this book. It is a rough equivalent in Object Pascal to the C++ program that you have just seen. This is not a CLX program, but it's an Object Pascal program that uses Qt.pas to create and manipulate Qt objects. The program compiles and runs correctly, but the event mechanism does not work properly.

```
program NoClxSlider;

uses
  Qt,
  QForms;

{$R *.res}

var
  myApp: QApplicationH;
  mySlider: QSliderH;
  myWidget: QWidgetH;
  myLcdNumber: QLCDNumberH;
  Hooks: QWidget_hookH;
begin
  Application.Initialize;
  myApp := Application.Handle;
  MyWidget := QWidget_create(nil, nil, 0);
  mySlider := QSlider_create(0, 9, 1, 1, Orientation_Horizontal,
    mywidget, PAnsiChar('Sam'));
  QWidget_setGeometry(mySlider, 10, 10, 150, 30);
  mylcdNumber := QLCDNumber_create(1, mywidget, PAnsiChar('MyLCDNumber'));
  QWidget_setGeometry(myLCDNumber, 60, 50, 50, 50);
  QlcdNumber_display(myLCDNumber, 1);
  QObject_connect(myslider, PAnsiChar('SIGNAL(sliderMoved(int))'),
    mylcdNumber, PAnsiChar('SLOT(display(int))'));
  QApplication_setMainWidget(myApp, myWidget);
  QWidget_show(myWidget);
```

```
    QApplication_exec(myApp);
    QSlider_destroy(mySlider);
    QLCDNumber_destroy(myLCDNumber);
    QWidget_destroy(myWidget);
end.
```

Needless to say, I am not suggesting that you write programs this way. If you want to write this kind of code, you would be better off using C++ and working with the original Qt library, as shown in the C++ version of this program. This Object Pascal example is used only so that you can get some sense of how Qt.pas is structured and what the calls in it mean.

As you can see, an important part of this kind of code development is working with handles to Qt objects. Unlike the situation that prevails in Windows programming, the handles to objects in CLX are not integer values; they're objects. Here are the declarations for several CLX classes that act as handles to Qt objects:

```
    QtH = class(TObject) end;
    QObjectH = class(QtH) end;
    QApplicationH = class(QObjectH) end;
    QWidgetH = class(QObjectH) end;
    QButtonH = class(QWidgetH) end;
    QCheckBoxH = class(QButtonH) end;
    QPushButtonH = class(QButtonH) end;
    QClxBitBtnH = class(QPushButtonH) end;
    QRadioButtonH = class(QButtonH) end;
    QtoolButtonH = class(QButtonH) end;
```

One of the advantages of working with objects as handles is that Object Pascal provides strong type information for each class it creates. This means that the compiler can clearly identify a Hook object as belonging to a particular class of Qt object.

---

**NOTE**

Many readers are no doubt interested in the technical details of how to get the Qt event mechanism working in a CLX program. Code relevant to that subject is shown in the section "CLX, Qt, and the Hook Object."

---

## The Slider Program in CLX

Take a look at Listing 7.2, which contains the CLX version of the Qt program shown in Listing 7.1.

**7**

**CLX ARCHITECTURE**

**LISTING 7.2**  The CLX Version of the Qt Slider Program

```
unit Main;

interface

uses
  SysUtils, Types, Classes,
  QGraphics, QControls, QForms,
  QDialogs, QComCtrls, QStdCtrls;

type
  TForm1 = class(TForm)
    LCDNumber1: TLCDNumber;
    TrackBar1: TTrackBar;
    procedure TrackBar1Change(Sender: TObject);
  private
    { Private declarations }
  public
    { Public declarations }
  end;

var
  Form1: TForm1;

implementation

{$R *.xfm}

procedure TForm1.TrackBar1Change(Sender: TObject);
begin
  LCDNumber1.Value := IntToStr(TrackBar1.Position);
end;

end.
```

To create this program, you simply drop a TLCDNumber and TTrackBar component on a form. The TTrackBar component is on the Common Controls page of the Component Palette. It is stored in ComCtrls.pas.

Use the Object Inspector to create a TrackBar1Change method. In particular, you need to turn to the Events page in the Object Inspector and create an OnChange event handler for the TTrackBar object. To create the handler, you can double-click the whitespace to the right of the OnChange property listing in the Events page of the Object Inspector. The OnChange handler that you create performs the same duty in CLX that the signal and slot mechanism performs in Qt: It connects the events that occur in the TTrackBar control to the display property of the TLCDNumber control.

Of course, you might complain that this TrackBar1Change method appears to connect not to the display property of the TLCDNumber control, but to something known as the value property. Although this complaint is reasonable, a close inspection reveals that it hinges on a purely semantic issue. Here is the SetValue method of TLCDNumber control, as found in the source to CLX:

```
procedure TCustomLCDNumber.SetValue(const Value: AnsiString);
var
  i: Integer;
  ErrorVal: Integer;
  FloatVal: Extended;
  WS: WideString;
begin
  FValue := Value;
  if AutoSize then
    ResizeView;
  if not HandleAllocated then
    Exit;
  Val(FValue, i, ErrorVal);
  if ErrorVal = 0 then
  begin
    QLCDNumber_display(Handle, i);
    Exit;
  end;
  if TextToFloat(PChar(FValue), FloatVal, fvExtended) then
  begin
    QLCDNumber_display(Handle, FloatVal);
    Exit;
  end;
  WS := FValue;
  QLCDNumber_display(Handle, @WS);
end;
```

This method is annoyingly long, but you can see that it all boils down to nothing more than a call to the C wrapper around QLCDNumber::display:

```
QLCDNumber_display(Handle, i);
```

# CLX, Qt, and the Hook Object

In the preceding sections of this chapter, you learned that Qt uses a signal and slot mechanism, and CLX uses an event mechanism. Although it is not usually important to understand how the two are connected, this information might be valuable at times to certain developers. There is no good documentation on this issue, so some of what is included in this section is simply conjecture.

Before getting started, here's an overview of this subject. Qt has a signal and slot mechanism. CLX has an event mechanism. To translate Qt signals and slots into CLX events, the Kylix team created a mechanism known as hooks. Each CLX object type has a hook object. This hook object converts the signals and slot events associated with a particular object into CLX events. It then sends these events to the appropriate CLX control.

The method of a CLX control that receives events can be defined by a developer. Although you can define your own methods for receiving events, most CLX controls already have methods set up to receive events. In particular, there is a CLX method of `TWidgetControl` named `EventFilter` that receives the majority of these events. This method is inherited from `TWidgetControl` by the CLX objects that wrap the Qt objects. Clearly, this means that the `EventFilter` method and other methods like it are important to those who want to dig deeply into the CLX API. `EventFilter` plays much the same role in CLX that the `WndProc` method played in the VCL. This method will be discussed several times in the next few sections of this chapter.

This is a complicated subject, so before going any deeper, it might be worthwhile to lay out the basics again, this time using example objects. Suppose that you have a C++ Qt object, such as `QSlider`, or `QLCDNumber`. You also have an Object Pascal–based CLX object that wraps the Qt object. The question of the moment, of course, is how the CLX object knows when things happen to the Qt object. If a `sliderMoved` event occurs in the Qt `QSlider` object, how does the CLX `TTrackBar` object find out about it?

The answer is that there is an intermediate object, known as a hook object, whose job it is to tell the CLX object when a signal or other event is generated by the Qt object. Kylix programmers do not ever create hook objects. In fact, the details of how hook objects work are hidden, most likely inside the depths of `libqtintf.so`, a shared object for which there is no source.

The class `TWidgetControl`, from which most CLX controls descend, has an instance of a hook object:

```
FHooks: QWidget_hookH;
```

The H in `QWidget_hookH` stands for "handle." But `QWidget_hookH` is not a simple integer value, as in the case of a handle to an object in Windows. Instead, `QWidget_hookH` is an object. It is not a Qt object, but it's a CLX object that descends from `TObject` and adds nothing to it, as you can see from looking at this excerpt from Qt.pas:

```
QObject_hookH = class(TObject) end;
QClxWorkspace_hookH = class(QObject_hookH) end;
```

```
QAccel_hookH = class(QObject_hookH) end;
QToolTip_hookH = class(QObject_hookH) end;
QWidget_hookH = class(QObject_hookH) end;
QButton_hookH = class(QWidget_hookH) end;
QCheckBox_hookH = class(QButton_hookH) end;
QPushButton_hookH = class(QButton_hookH) end;
QRadioButton_hookH = class(QButton_hookH) end;
QToolButton_hookH = class(QButton_hookH) end;
// And on and on this list goes, through most of the CLX objects.
```

You've seen several of these hook objects, so you hopefully can sense that there is one for each of the important CLX classes that wrap a Qt control.

These hook objects get assigned at runtime through a variety of mechanisms, the most important of which is a virtual method named HookEvents:

```
procedure TWidgetControl.HookEvents;
var
  Method: TMethod;
begin
  if FHooks = nil then
  begin
    HandleNeeded;
    FHooks := QWidget_hook_create(Handle);
  end;

  TEventFilterMethod(Method) := MainEventFilter;
  Qt_hook_hook_events(FHooks, Method);

  QObject_destroyed_event(Method) := Self.DestroyedHook;
  QObject_hook_hook_destroyed(FHooks, Method);
end;
```

This method creates an instance of the FHooks object, based on the handle of the CLX control. As mentioned in the previous section on creating Qt programs in Object Pascal, each type of CLX control can be uniquely identified through its handle. Table 7.1, for instance, shows the FHandle declaration or access method for a series of CLX controls.

**TABLE 7.1**  Declarations and Access Methods for CLX Controls

| Object Name | Code Excerpt |
| --- | --- |
| TWidgetControl | FHandle: QWidgetH; |
| TGroupBox | function GetHandle: QGroupBoxH; |
| TLCDNumberControl | function GetHandle: QLCDNumberH; |
| TCustomLabel | function GetHandle: QLabelH; |

**TABLE 7.1** Continued

| Object Name | Code Excerpt |
|---|---|
| TButtonControl | function GetHandle: QButtonH; |
| TCustomCheckBox | function GetHandle: QCheckBoxH; |

Again, all of these QxxxH types end up resolving to an instance of TObject, exactly as shown in the Qxxx_hookH listing shown earlier in this section.

The handle uniquely identifies the kind of hook object that is being created:

```
FHooks := QWidget_hook_create(Handle);
```

After calling the function, you end up with an FHooks object uniquely designed to help relay from Qt to CLX the correct events for a particular type of control.

The next question, then, is, where do these events get sent? Look back at the HookEvents method, and you will see the following code:

```
TEventFilterMethod(Method) := MainEventFilter;
Qt_hook_hook_events(FHooks, Method);
```

The MainEventFilter is a method of TWidgetControl through which all the events that come to CLX are filtered. In practice, however, MainEventFilter just acts as a relay station. Most of the real work is done by the EventFilter method, which is called by MainEventFilter:

```
function TWidgetControl.MainEventFilter(Sender: QObjectH; Event: QEventH):
➥Boolean; cdecl;
var
  Form: TCustomForm;
begin
  try
    if csDesigning in ComponentState then
    begin
      Form := GetParentForm(Self);
      if (Form <> nil) and (Form.DesignerHook <> nil) and
        Form.DesignerHook.IsDesignEvent(Self, Sender, Event) then
      begin
        Result := True;
        Exit;
      end;
    end;
    Result := EventFilter(Sender, Event);
  except
    Application.HandleException(Self);
    Result := False;
  end;
end;
```

Most of the code in this method is not particularly important and applies only at design time, or else it is meant to help handle exceptions. At runtime, the key line to focus on creates the call to `EventFilter`:

```
Result := EventFilter(Sender, Event);
```

One reason that `EventFilter` is called indirectly from this method probably is that the developers wanted to make `EventFilter` virtual and to allow all descendant classes to override it, if they so desired. So, they created `MainEventFilter` as the primary call and had it indirectly call `EventFilter`, which is declared virtual.

The `EventFilter` method will be discussed at some length in the section "The Night CLX Let Me Down: `EventFilter` Mojo." For now, you need to know only that it consists of a long `case` statement. Each section of the `case` statement handles a particular set of events. For instance, keyboard events are handled by one part of the `case` statement, mouse events are handled by another, and so on. In short, it acts much like a `WndProc` does in Windows, or like the event loop you saw in the Xlib programs in Chapter 6, "Understanding the Linux Environment."

`Qt_hook_hook_events` is passed both the `FHooks` object and the method that is designed to receive messages from Qt. We don't know exactly what happens back there in the darkness of `libqtintf.so`, but we can assume that code is written to capture a Qt signal, and that these signals are translated into events that are sent to the `MainEventFilter`, which then passes them on to `EventFilter`, which is the key method that CLX programmers might want to override. This will be discussed at length in the section "The Night CLX Let Me Down: `EventFilter` Mojo."

Of course, some controls end up setting up their own custom methods for handling the hooked events that are sent to them from the land of Qt:

```
procedure TCustomMemo.HookEvents;
var
  Method: TMethod;
begin
  inherited;
  QMultiLineEdit_textChanged_Event(Method) := TextChangedHook;
  QMultiLineEdit_hook_hook_textChanged(QMultiLineEdit_hookH(Hooks), Method);
  QMultiLineEdit_returnPressed_Event(Method) := ReturnPressedHook;
  QMultiLineEdit_hook_hook_returnPressed(QMultiLineEdit_hookH(Hooks), Method);
end;
```

Here you can see code that tells the `hook` object for `QMultiLineEdit` controls that it should send events to the method of `TCustomMemo` named `TextChangedHook`.

It is time now to sum up what we have learned about the CLX hook mechanism. Though the details are murky, certain things are clear. Qt has a signal and slot mechanism. CLX has an event mechanism. To translate Qt signals and slots into CLX events the Kylix team created a mechanism they called hooks. Each CLX object type has a hook object. This hook object converts the signals and slots associated with a particular object into events, and then sends all these events to the `EventFilter` method inherited from `TWidgetControl` by the CLX objects that wrap Qt objects. Clearly, this means that the `EventFilter` method is the key to the kingdom for those who want to dig deeply into the CLX API.

My point in this section on Qt and FreeCLX is not to insist that you delve deeply into the source for Qt, or even that you must dig into the source for CLX. Intermediate-level Kylix programmers don't need to know much about CLX, and they don't need to know anything about Qt. But if you want to clamber up into the guru zone, then you need the additional information found in the CLX and Qt source files.

## The Night CLX Let Me Down: EventFilter Mojo

Astute readers no doubt sense how carefully I'm choosing my words in this section of the book. The issue of paramount importance is simply this: "How good of a job does CLX do of surfacing all the tools needed to make a great program? Are there parts of the operating system that I want to get at, that CLX won't let me reach?"

When speaking of the Delphi VCL, I could fairly confidently answer, "No, there really aren't any important parts of Windows that you can't access using Object Pascal. If the OS surfaces the feature, then you can probably get at it. Sometimes it takes some work, but you can get at it." Although Kylix is clearly more powerful than any other Linux programming language (other than GCC), nevertheless there are some limitations to what it can do.

Let's take a moment, then, to review at least one of the key ways to start pushing CLX aside and getting as close to the metal as possible. If you feel the urge to go beyond the usual CLX API, then here is one of the methods that you want to override:

```
function TWidgetControl.EventFilter(Sender: QObjectH; Event: QEventH): Boolean;
```

This one is the big Kahuna. `EventFilter` gets most of the events that Qt and the OS throws at it. Just opening up `QControls` and looking at the 500+ lines that form the implementation of this method is enough to send any sane programmer running for the safety of the standard CLX APIs. However, some people like to live on the edge. They claim that the air is thinner but cleaner out there.

If you are determined to rip the civilized veneer off CLX and face the raw blast of the Linux GUI, then this is the method to override. Listing 7.3 gives you a sense of what overriding this method looks like in practice.

**LISTING 7.3**  The ClxEvents Program Shows How to Override the `EventFilter` Method for a `TForm`

```
unit Main;

// Copyright  2001 by Charlie Calvert

interface

uses
  SysUtils, Types, Classes,
  Variants, QGraphics, QControls,
  QForms, QDialogs, Qt, QStdCtrls;

type
  TForm1 = class(TForm)
    ListBox1: TListBox;
    procedure FormDestroy(Sender: TObject);
  private
    FMyList: TStringList;
  protected
    function EventFilter(Sender: QObjectH; Event: QEventH): Boolean; override;
  public
    constructor Create(AOwner: TComponent); override;
  end;

var
  Form1: TForm1;

implementation

{$R *.xfm}

{ TForm1 }

constructor TForm1.Create(AOwner: TComponent);
begin
  FMyList := TStringList.Create;
  inherited;
end;

function TForm1.EventFilter(Sender: QObjectH; Event: QEventH): Boolean;
var
  S: string;
  i: Integer;
```

**LISTING 7.3**  Continued

```
begin
  Result := inherited EventFilter(Sender, Event);
  case QEvent_type(Event) of
    QEventType_Create: S := 'QEventType_Create';
    QEventType_DragResponse: S := 'QEventType_DragResponse';
    QEventType_DragLeave: S := 'QEventType_DragLeave';
    QEventType_DragEnter: S := 'QEventType_DragEnter';
    QEventType_DragMove: S := 'QEventType_DragMove';
    QEventType_Drop: S := 'QEventType_Drop';
    QEventType_MouseButtonPress: S := 'QEventType_MouseButtonPress';
    QEventType_MouseButtonRelease: S := 'QEventType_MouseButtonRelease';
    QEventType_MouseButtonDblClick: S := 'QEventType_MouseButtonDblClick';
    QEventType_MouseMove: S := 'QEventType_MouseMove';
    QEventType_KeyPress: S := 'QEventType_KeyPress';
    QEventType_KeyRelease: S := 'QEventType_KeyRelease';
    QEventType_FocusIn: S := 'QEventType_FocusIn';
    QEventType_Move: S := 'QEventType_Move';
    QEventType_Resize: S := 'QEventType_Resize';
    QEventType_Wheel: S := 'QEventType_Wheel';
    QEventType_Paint: S := 'QEventType_Paint';
    QEventType_ApplicationPaletteChange: S :=
➥'QEventType_ApplicationPaletteChange';
    QEventType_ParentPaletteChange: S := 'QEventType_ParentPaletteChange';
    QEventType_Show: S := 'QEventType_Show';
    QEventType_Hide: S := 'QEventType_Hide';
  else
    S := 'Unknown: ' + IntToStr(Ord(QEventType(Event)));
  end;
  if ListBox1 <> nil then begin
    ListBox1.Items.Add(S);
    ListBox1.ItemIndex := ListBox1.Items.Count;
    if FMyList.Count > 0 then begin
      for i := 0 to FMyList.Count - 1 do
        ListBox1.Items.Insert(0, 'Pre Init: ' + FMyList.Strings[i]);
      FMyList.Clear;
    end;
  end else
    if FMyList <> nil then
      FMyList.Add(S);
end;

procedure TForm1.FormDestroy(Sender: TObject);
begin
```

**LISTING 7.3**   Continued

```
  FreeAndNil(FMyList);
  FreeAndNil(ListBox1);
end;

end.
```

When you run this program, it captures every event that is sent to the main form of the program and displays it in a list box. (If you want to capture the events sent to other controls, then override the same method in those controls. They all inherit this method from TWidgetControl.)

> **NOTE**
>
> If you study the FilterEvent method carefully, you will find that it misses the actual creation and destruction of the form. It misses them because it can't properly capture those events from inside the form itself. However, everything else that happens to the form will be captured by this method.

When looking at Figure 7.2, you should notice the QEventType_Move, QEventType_Resize, QEventType_Show, and other messages. Needless to say, all the events that you see named in this program are being caught by CLX. You don't need to catch them here. Instead, you can get at them by accessing methods such as MouseMove, MouseEnter, or MouseLeave, discussed earlier in this chapter. But other events might occur in your application that you need to capture, and the EventFilter method is the way to get at them.

**FIGURE 7.2**
*Many of the key events that occur on a* TForm *object are clearly recorded in the ClxEvent application.*

Needless to say, if you don't call the EventFilter's ancestor, there almost certainly will be trouble in your application:

```
Result := inherited EventFilter(Sender, Event);
```

Note also the case statement at the heart of the ClxEvent program's version of FilterEvent:

```
function TForm1.EventFilter(Sender: QObjectH; Event: QEventH): Boolean;
var
  S: string;
  i: Integer;
begin
  Result := inherited EventFilter(Sender, Event);
  case QEvent_type(Event) of
    QEventType_Create: S := 'QEventType_Create';
    QEventType_DragResponse: S := 'QEventType_DragResponse';
    etc....
```

As you can see, there are lots of constants here. All of them are declared in Qt.pas:

```
QEventType = (
  QEventType_None = 0 { $0 },
  QEventType_Timer = 1 { $1 },
  QEventType_MouseButtonPress = 2 { $2 },
  QEventType_MouseButtonRelease = 3 { $3 },
  QEventType_MouseButtonDblClick = 4 { $4 },
  QEventType_MouseMove = 5 { $5 },
  QEventType_KeyPress = 6 { $6 },
  // Many constants omitted here to preserve our sanity.
  QEventType_User = 1000 { $3e8 },
  QEventType_ClxBase = 1000,
  QEventType_ClxUser = 2000,
  QEventType_ClxUserLimit = 4000);
```

Here you see the declarations for the types of events generated by Qt.

As stated earlier in this chapter, the Qt.pas file contains Object Pascal translations of most of the types used by the public parts of Qt. For instance, if you are looking for the keyboard event constants, you will find them in Qt.pas. They appear as a series of constants beginning with Key_Escape:

```
Key_Escape = 4096 { $1000 };
Key_Tab = 4097 { $1001 };
Key_Backtab = 4098 { $1002 };
etc...
```

A bit more mysterious is the QEventH type declared in the header for EventFilter:

```
QtH = class(TObject) end;
QEventH = class(QtH) end;
```

As you can see, QEventH is actually a direct and unmodified descendant class of type TObject. In Object Pascal, you can't have a case statement on anything but scalar types. As a result, you can't have a case statement on TObject or QEventH. So, what does this case syntax really mean:

```
case QEvent_type(Event) of
```

A moment's contemplation reveals that it can't possibly be a simple type cast. The only scalar number that you can get by typecasting an instance of TObject would be its address, and it makes no sense to have a case statement of the kind shown here on an address. So what is going on?

If you turn to Qt.pas, you see this declaration for QEvent_type:

```
function QEvent_type(handle: QEventH): QEventType; cdecl;
```

The lights should begin to come on. QEvent_type is a function—and not just an ordinary function, but one of the C wrappers around the C++ functions that make up the Qt library. In short, this is really a wrapper around the method found in Qt that appears to have been declared something like this: QEvent:type().

To gain a deeper understanding of what is happening, the next step is go to the TrollTech Web site and take a look at the online Qt documentation. At the time of this writing, the URL needed to access this was http://doc.trolltech.com/qevent.html. There I found the following enumerated type:

```
enum Type { None = 0, Timer = 1, MouseButtonPress = 2, MouseButtonRelease = 3,
MouseButtonDblClick= 4, MouseMove = 5, KeyPress = 6, KeyRelease = 7, FocusIn =
8, FocusOut = 9, Enter = 10, Leave = 11, Paint = 12, Move = 13, Resize = 14,
Create = 15, Destroy = 16, Show = 17, Hide = 18, Close = 19, Quit = 20,
Reparent = 21, ShowMinimized = 22, ShowNormal = 23, WindowActivate = 24,
WindowDeactivate = 25, ShowToParent = 26, HideToParent = 27, ShowMaximized =
28, Accel = 30, Wheel = 31, AccelAvailable = 32, CaptionChange = 33, IconChange
= 34, ParentFontChange = 35, ApplicationFontChange = 36, ParentPaletteChange =
37, ApplicationPaletteChange = 38, Clipboard = 40, Speech = 42, SockAct = 50,
AccelOverride = 51, DragEnter = 60, DragMove = 61, DragLeave = 62, Drop = 63,
DragResponse = 64, ChildInserted = 70, ChildRemoved = 71, LayoutHint = 72,
ShowWindowRequest = 73, ActivateControl = 80, DeactivateControl = 81, User =
1000 }
```

Clearly there is a link between this enumerated type and the Object Pascal QEventType. Further perusal of the TrollTech page shows the method accessed by the QEvent_type function:

**7**

**CLX ARCHITECTURE**

```
QEvent:QEvent ( Type type )Constructs an event object with a type.
QEvent:~QEvent () [virtual]
Destructs the event. If posted, it will be removed from the list of events.
QEvent:Type QEvent:type() const
Returns the event type.
```

This object has a constructor, destructor, and method that returns the type of the event. These types are really an enumerated type, and the mysterious case statement discussed earlier is built around this enumerated type.

If you dig further into the Qt docs, you will see that there is documentation on most of the events:

```
MouseMove - mouse move, QMouseEvent
KeyPress - key press (including e.g. shift), QKeyEvent
KeyRelease - key release, QKeyEvent
FocusIn - widget gains keyboard focus, QFocusEvent
FocusOut - widget loses keyboard focus, QFocusEvent
Enter - mouse enters widget's space
Leave - mouse leaves widget's space
```

Here you can gain enlightening information such as the fact that the MouseMove event occurs when the mouse is moved and that KeyPress events occur when a key is pressed. Well okay, maybe that information is not quite so revelatory. But don't be too quick to judge the TrollTech docs; some of the information is more useful. In particular, you can see that the Enter and Leave events record what happens when the mouse enters or leaves a control.

All of this brings full circle to where we began this section on events. As you recall, you saw two core CLX event methods:

```
procedure MouseEnter(AControl: TControl); override;
procedure MouseLeave(AControl: TControl); override;
```

When I introduced these methods, I said that they record when the mouse enters and leaves the control's "space."

By now, all the mystery should be stripped away from these admirable methods. You know all that there is to know about how CLX gets these events and how they are handled by Qt itself. Furthermore, you have a good idea of where to start looking if you want to dig into the Qt source and find out yet more about what is happening in a Kylix program.

Needless to say, probably no one needs to dig into the Qt source to write a Kylix program. In fact, you probably normally shouldn't even look at the FilterEvents method. Instead, you should just find standard CLX methods such as MouseEnter and MouseLeave, override them, and tap into their power.

However, there is much to be said for understanding how the tools that you use work. In fact, it is your job as an insatiably knowledge-hungry programmer to understand how your tools are put together. Using that knowledge, you can discover the capabilities and limits of your programs. So, by all means, if you have the inclination, dig down into CLX—and perhaps even crack open the code to Qt. If you have the desire to explore, then may the source be with you!

---

**NOTE**

There is more to be said about events. See Chapter 9, and pay special attention to the section "Working with `FilterEvents` in Components."

---

# Working with Styles

In Chapter 4, you encountered owner draw list boxes in the section "The Owner Draw List Box." It turns out that there is a second way to change the appearance of items on your forms. This second technique involves changing the style of the components you use.

You can change the style of your entire application with a single line of code. Here are two examples of what that line might look like:

```
Application.Style.DefaultStyle := dsWindows;

Application.Style.DefaultStyle := dsMotif;
```

The first example makes the style of your application similar to a Windows program, as shown in Figure 7.3. The second example makes your code take on a motif look, as shown in Figure 7.4.

The following constants can change your code in much the same manner as the `dsWindows` and `dsMotif` styles declared in the CLX file Styles.pas:

```
TDefaultStyle = (dsWindows,
                 dsMotif,
                 dsMotifPlus,
                 dsCDE,
                 dsQtSGI,
                 dsPlatinum,
                 dsSystemDefault);
```

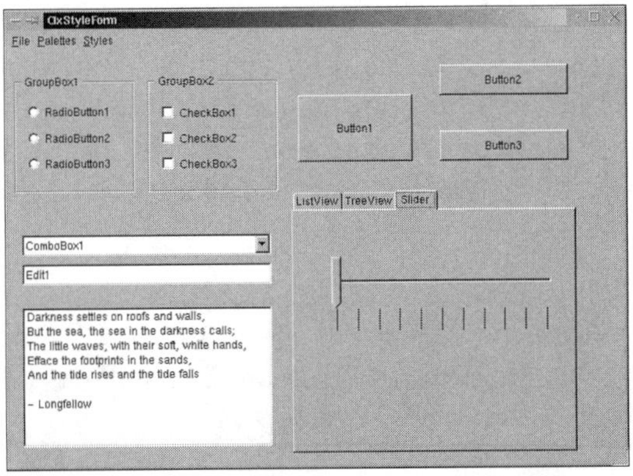

**FIGURE 7.3**

*The Windows look can be seen around the edges of buttons, in check boxes and radio buttons, and in the thumb of the slider component.*

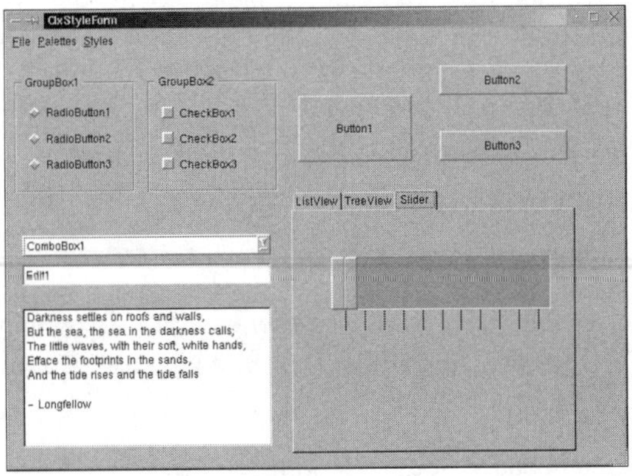

**FIGURE 7.4**

*You can give your program the motif look by changing a single line of code in your program.*

However, you can go beyond the global changes listed in the TDefaultStyle enumerated type. For instance, you can change the look of various components by assigning your own methods to method pointers in the Kylix Application object:

```
Application.Style.BeforeDrawButton := Self.DrawPushButton;
Application.Style.DrawButtonLabel := Self.DrawPushButtonLabel;
Application.Style.DrawButtonMask := Self.DrawButtonMask;
```

This code tells Kylix that it should call your DrawPushButton method instead of relying on the default technique for drawing a button.

For instance, here is a method used for drawing custom check boxes:

```
procedure TForm2.DoDrawRadio(Sender: TObject; Canvas: TCanvas;
  const Rect: TRect; Checked, Down, Enabled: Boolean;
  var DefaultDraw: Boolean);
begin
  DefaultDraw := False;
  Canvas.Brush.Color := clBtnFace;
  Canvas.FillRect(Rect);
  if Checked or Down then
    Canvas.Draw(Rect.Top, Rect.Left, rbbChecked)
  else
    Canvas.Draw(Rect.Top, Rect.Left, rbbUnChecked);
end;
```

rbbChecked and rbbUnChecked are bitmaps created to represent the state of a RadioButton. For instance, the rbbChecked bitmap shows the state of the button when it is pressed, and the rbbUnChecked bitmap shows the state of the button when it is not checked. These bitmaps completely replace the original graphical representation of a check box. The original check box is not shown at all, and instead you see the bitmap that you use in the DoDrawRadio method.

To have Kylix call your DoDrawRadio method, you simply write these lines of code:

```
var
  Size: TSize;
begin
  Size.cx := 20;
  Size.cy := 20;
  Application.Style.DrawRadio := Self.DoDrawRadio;
  Application.Style.RadioSize := Size;
```

Needless to say, you should make Size the same size as the bitmaps that you want to draw.

Figure 7.5 shows a program from the CD that accompanies this book. This program radically changes the look of the form shown in Figures 7.3 and 7.4 through techniques such as the ones I have been discussing.

When looking at Figure 7.5, notice in particular the thumb on the slider and the circular bitmaps drawn at the top of the list view control. You can also see that the check boxes and radio buttons have changed.

The example program shown in Figures 7.3, 7.4, and 7.5 was originally created by a member of the Delphi R&D team about nine months before Kylix shipped. I ended up maintaining the program, and some of what you see on the accompanying CD is now my work, not his. Nevertheless, the original inspiration for the program was not mine, and most of the code was written by someone else.

**7**

**CLX ARCHITECTURE**

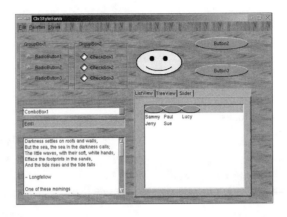

**Figure 7.5**
*Custom styles are used to define the look of the check boxes, radio buttons, sliders, combo boxes, buttons, and other controls in this form.*

Two versions of the program are located on the accompanying CD, one named ClxStyle2 and the other named ClxStyleOld. Both versions are quite similar, although the ClxStyleOld program is probably somewhat more complete. This was the one that I used in the images shown in this chapter. Unfortunately, the program is too long to quote in full here. All the important technical tricks used in the program have already been discussed in this text. The rest of the code consists simply of the implementation of the various changes shown in Figure 7.5. You will probably enjoy opening the programs and experimenting with them. In particular, you should take a look at the menu for the program.

## Working with Resources

The simplest way to work with resources in a Kylix application is to simply include an RC file in your program. Simply choose Project and Add to Project, and add your RC file into your program.

Here is a simple RC file that allows you to add bitmaps to your program:

```
Back BITMAP "BACKIMG1.BMP"
TileMap BITMAP "TILEMAP.BMP"
Monk2 BITMAP "MONK2.BMP"
TileMap2 BITMAP "TILEMAP2.BMP"
TileMap3 BITMAP "TILEMAP3.BMP"
MessageDlg BITMAP "MESSAGEDLG1.BMP"
```

This file is simple enough to make, but it might not run correctly in your copy of Kylix. If it will not compile inside the IDE, you need to get a utility called wrc.

You can get wrc from the Wine project, which is an open-source Windows emulation project available for free from the Web. After installing Wine, by default, wrc will be placed in your /usr/bin directory.

To run wrc, type this:

**wrc -r MyResource.rc**

MyResource.rc might look like this:

```
Sammy BITMAP "Background.bmp"
```

To load the files at runtime, write code that looks like this:

```
Bitmap := TBitmap.Create;
Bitmap.LoadFromResourceName(HInstance, 'Sammy');
```

In this example, Sammy is the name that you gave the resource in your res file. For instance, the identifiers Monk2, TileMap2, and MessageDlg are similar strings from the rc file shown at the beginning of this section.

An example program of this type, named LoadBitmapFromRes, is available in the Chapter07 directory on the CD that accompanies this book. The source for the program is shown in Listing 7.4.

**LISTING 7.4** The LoadBitmapFromRes Program Shows How to Work with Bitmap and String Resources

```
unit Main;

interface

// Here is the sole line in the RC file for this program:
// Sammy BITMAP "background.bmp"

uses
  SysUtils, Types, Classes,
  Variants, QGraphics, QControls,
  QForms, QDialogs, QStdCtrls,
  QButtons;

type
  TForm1 = class(TForm)
    BitBtn1: TBitBtn;
    Edit1: TEdit;
    procedure BitBtn1Click(Sender: TObject);
  private
```

**LISTING 7.4** Continued

```
    { Private declarations }
  public
    { Public declarations }
  end;

var
  Form1: TForm1;

implementation

{$R *.xfm}

resourcestring
  ResString = 'This bitmap and this string were stored in resources';

procedure TForm1.BitBtn1Click(Sender: TObject);
var
  Bitmap: TBitmap;
begin
  Bitmap := TBitmap.Create;
  Bitmap.LoadFromResourceName(HInstance, 'Sammy');
  if Bitmap <> nil then
    Canvas.Draw(10, 10, Bitmap);
  Bitmap.Free;
  Edit1.Text := ResString;
end;

end.
```

Here is the complete text for the .rc file used by this program:

```
Sammy BITMAP "background.bmp"
```

**NOTE**

As this book was about to go to press, a company called SiComponents released a resource compiler for Linux. You should be able to find a link to its tool on the page http://www.sicomponents.com/sircc32.html.

## String Resources

Another type of resource that you might use in your program is a string resource. To create a string resource, you should add a resource string section to your program:

```
resourcestring
  MyString = 'The leaves of memory seemed to make ' +
             'a mournful rustling in the dark.';
```

You can now use this string in your program as you see fit simply by referencing it:

```
ShowMessage(My String);
```

Strings of this type are stored not in your programs memory, but in a file kept on disk. They are accessed one at a time as, or if, you use them in your program. As a result, they are more memory-efficient than string constants, which, by definition, are kept in memory throughout the run of your program. The LoadBitmapFromRes program, which you saw in Listing 7.4, shows an example of using this kind of syntax in a live program.

## Creating Nonrectangular Forms

To wrap up this chapter, I want to show you some of the fun you can have with CLX when you understand how it works. In particular, you'll see a program that uses forms that have unusual shapes:

- Circular
- Octagonal
- Rounded on the edges
- One that is shaped like a truck

At design time, these forms look just like normal Delphi forms. You can add components to them and associated code with those components, exactly as you would a normal Kylix form. Everything about the forms is perfectly  normal, except for the way they appear at runtime. You can see the octagonal and the truck-shaped forms in Figures 7.6 and 7.7.

**FIGURE 7.6**

*A Kylix form that is shaped like a truck. You can drop controls on the form just as if it were a standard form.*

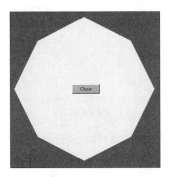

**FIGURE 7.7**

*A Kylix form that has an octagonal shape.*

The technology for creating irregularly shaped controls is built into Qt. In particular, a method of QWidget named setMask provides support for creating transparent or partially transparent windows. All you need to do is create a bitmap that describes the area that you want to be opaque and the area that you want to be transparent. Paint one area in black and the other in white. When you are done, the parts of the bitmap painted black will be transparent. To aid you in this endeavor, the Kylix Qt.pas unit declares a color named clMask that is set to clBlack, and a second color named clNoMask that is set to clWhite.

> **NOTE**
>
> You will learn more about Kylix and colors in Chapter 11. That chapter thoroughly explains the technology behind Kylix constants such as clBlack, clBlue, and clYellow.

## Form Inheritance

Following the lead of the Clock example that ships in the Kylix demos directory, I decided to use form inheritance as the base technology for my transparent forms.

Form inheritance has a somewhat checkered history in the land of Object Pascal. Back in the bad old days, Delphi competed primarily with the omnipresent Visual Basic and a now nearly forgotten product named PowerBuilder. Delphi was so much more powerful than either of these products that it was hard to understand why it was having trouble outselling them. The marketing team leaders talked to developers who chose the competition over Delphi and asked them why they made this seemingly inexplicable decision. In particular, they focused on people who opted for the slow and unwieldy alternative put forward by the makers of

PowerBuilder. An answer that came back frequently from the queried developers was that they enjoyed having the capability to create a form with a few controls on it, and then create other forms based on this first form. This concept was known as *visual inheritance*. Instead of inheriting the code from an object, these forms inherited the visual appearance of another form.

To compete with PowerBuilder, the team come up with a technology called Delphi Form Inheritance. This is not my favorite feature in the Delphi and Kylix product lines. But I have found it very useful a few times, and certainly all Kylix developers should know that it is available.

To learn how to use this technology, first create a new application. By default, your project will be named `Project1`. For the sake of discussion, let's stick with the default name for the project. After creating the project, choose File, New from the menu. In the New Items dialog box, choose the page called Project1. (If your project has a different name, then choose the page with the name of your project.) The main form of your project will be visible on the selected page of the New Items dialog box. Select the form, and select the Inherited radio button at the bottom of the dialog box. Click OK to close the dialog box.

Your project will now have two forms. By default, they will be placed in Unit1.pas and Unit2.pas. The declaration for the form in Unit1 will look like this:

```
TForm1 = class(TForm)
private
  { Private declarations }
public
  { Public declarations }
end;
```

The declaration for the form in Unit2 will look like this:

```
TForm2 = class(TForm1)
private
  { Private declarations }
public
  { Public declarations }
end;
```

As you can see, `TForm2` descends not from `TForm`, but from `TForm1`. As practitioners of OOP, it is easy for us to grasp the basic concept involved in the relationship between the two classes. It is a case of simple inheritance. However, it turns out that this seemingly straightforward syntactical arrangement is actually a bit deceptive. This is one of the very few places in Kylix where a certain amount of hand waving is going on behind the scenes.

Go back into Delphi, and make `Form1` 350 pixels wide and 150 pixels deep. To do this, simply set the `ClientWidth` or `Width` property of `Form1` to 350, and set the `ClientHeight` or `Height` property to 150. Now take a look at Form2. Miraculously, it also is 350 pixels wide and 150 pixels high. It inherited these traits from Form1. Each change that you make to Form1 is being passed on, via visual inheritance, to Form2.

Now drop a button down on Form1. Take a look a look at Form2. It, too, now contains a button.

Arrange the two forms so that you can see them both at the same time. Move the button on Form1 around and about. Notice that the button on Form2 follows the button on Form1.

Now go to Form2 and move the button around. Go back to Form1, and move its button. This time, you will find that the button on Form2 will not follow the button on Form1. What happened? Well, when you moved the button on Form2, you broke the relationship for the Left and Top properties of the button on Form2 with the Top and Left properties of the button back on Form1. You did not totally shatter the relationship between the two components; you only broke the parts of the relationship that depended on the properties that you changed in Form2. In other words, if you resize the button on Form1, the button on Form2 will also resize. But if you move the button on Form2, it will no longer cause the button on Form1 to move.

Perhaps you meant to break the inheritance for the Left and Top properties of the button in Form2. But what if you did not? What if you moved the button on Form2 by accident? Is there a way to correct the situation?

Yes, there is a solution to the broken inheritance problem. In Form2, go to the Object Inspector and click the Left property for the button. Select the option in the menu Revert To Inherited. The Left property for the button in Form2 automatically goes back in sync with the Left property for the button on Form1. Do the same thing for the Top property. The changes to the position of the button on Form1 again are reflected in the position of the button on Form2.

The inheritance relationship between forms can become quite complicated. Form inheritance can be a great thing in some circumstances, but before using it, you should consider whether the well-engineered Kylix frame technology better suits your needs. (Frames were discussed in Chapter 4.)

## Overriding the Initialization of a Widget

The irregularly shaped forms that I have created all inherit certain traits from a base form. In fact, they use true visual form inheritance. However, most of the power stems from simple OOP inheritance, not from visual inheritance.

The base class of these irregularly shaped forms overrides two CLX methods named InitWidget and WidgetFlags. The children of this base class inherit the changes made to these two CLX methods. They also inherit a new method named DrawMask. All the child forms need to do is override this one method. In the method, they define the shape of the mask for their form. For instance, if they draw a circle into the Canvas object passed to this method, they will become circular forms.

But I'm getting ahead of myself. At this point, you need to take a look at the code for the base class and for at least one of the child classes. The base class is shown in Listing 7.5, and the child class for the octagonal form is shown in Listing 7.6.

**LISTING 7.5**   The Base Form from Which All the Nonrectangular Forms Descend

```
unit BaseForm;

interface

uses
  SysUtils, Types, Classes,
  Variants, QGraphics, QControls,
  QForms, QDialogs, Qt, QMenus, QTypes, QStdCtrls;

type
  TBaseClearForm = class(TForm)
    PopupMenu1: TPopupMenu;
    Exit1: TMenuItem;
    procedure Exit1Click(Sender: TObject);
  private
  protected
    procedure DrawMask(ACanvas: TCanvas); virtual;
  public
    procedure InitWidget; override;
    function WidgetFlags: Integer; override;
    { Public declarations }
  end;

var
  BaseClearForm: TBaseClearForm;

implementation

uses Octagon;

{$R *.xfm}

{ TForm1 }


function TBaseClearForm.WidgetFlags: Integer;
begin
```

**LISTING 7.5** Continued

```pascal
    // We don't want to erase before we paint.
    Result := inherited WidgetFlags and not
      Integer(WidgetFlags_WRepaintNoErase);
end;

procedure TBaseClearForm.InitWidget;
var
  QB: QBitmapH;
  QP: QPainterH;
  VCanvas: TCanvas;
begin
  inherited InitWidget;
  // Set up our DrawMask
  QB := QBitmap_create(Width, Height,
    True, QPixmapOptimization_DefaultOptim);
  try
    QP := QPainter_create(QB, Handle);
    try
      VCanvas := TCanvas.Create;
      try
        VCanvas.Start(False);
        VCanvas.Handle := QP;
        DrawMask(VCanvas);
        VCanvas.Stop;
      finally
        VCanvas.Free;
      end;
      QWidget_setMask(Handle, QB);
    finally
      QPainter_destroy(QP);
    end;
  finally
    QBitmap_destroy(QB);
  end;
end;

procedure TBaseClearForm.Exit1Click(Sender: TObject);
begin
  Close;
end;

procedure TBaseClearForm.DrawMask(ACanvas: TCanvas);
begin
  //
end;

end.
```

**LISTING 7.6**  The Code for an Octagonal Form

```
unit Octagon;

interface

uses
  SysUtils, Types, Classes,
  Variants, QGraphics, QControls,
  QForms, QDialogs, Main,
  QMenus, QTypes, QStdCtrls,
  BaseForm;

type
  TOctagonForm = class(TBaseClearForm)
    Button1: TButton;
    procedure Button1Click(Sender: TObject);
  private
    { Private declarations }
  protected
    procedure DrawMask(ACanvas: TCanvas); override;
  public
    { Public declarations }
  end;

var
  OctagonForm: TOctagonForm;

implementation

{$R *.xfm}

procedure TOctagonForm.DrawMask(ACanvas: TCanvas);
var
  pts: array[0..7] of TPoint;
  begin
  pts[0] := Point(64, 64);
  pts[1] := Point(192, 0);
  pts[2] := Point(320, 64);
  pts[3] := Point(384, 192);
  pts[4] := Point(320, 320);
  pts[5] := Point(192, 384);
  pts[6] := Point(64, 320);
  pts[7] := Point(0, 192);
ACanvas.Polygon(pts);
end;
```

**LISTING 7.6**   Continued

```
procedure TOctagonForm.Button1Click(Sender: TObject);
begin
  Close;
end;

end.
```

When examining this code, by far the most important method is the TOctagonForm DrawMask method. That is where the shape for the mask is defined. However, it will help to take a look at a few other methods before you peer into the heart and soul of the DrawMask method.

As I said earlier, the base class for the irregularly shaped form overrides the WidgetFlags and InitWidget methods. Here is the WidgetFlags implementation:

```
function TBaseClearForm.WidgetFlags: Integer;
begin
  // We don't want to erase before we paint.
  Result := inherited WidgetFlags and not
    Integer(WidgetFlags_WRepaintNoErase);
end;
```

As you can see, this method simply sets the flags for the base widget so that the widget will not erase the form before you paint on it. What is important here is merely to note that this method enables you to change certain details about the structure of the underlying widget that will represent your form. If you want to make subtle changes to the appearance of your forms, overriding this method could be one of the options that you pursue.

Another way to change the behavior of a Kylix widget is to override the InitWidget method. In this case, the base form creates a bitmap, which it places in a canvas object, and then allows its children to draw into this bitmap view the good graces of the virtual DrawMask method:

```
procedure TBaseClearForm.InitWidget;
var
  QB: QBitmapH;
  QP: QPainterH;
  VCanvas: TCanvas;
begin
  inherited InitWidget;
  // Setup our DrawMask
  QB := QBitmap_create(Width, Height,
    True, QPixmapOptimization_DefaultOptim);
  try
    QP := QPainter_create(QB, Handle);
    try
```

```
        VCanvas := TCanvas.Create;
        try
          VCanvas.Start(False);
          VCanvas.Handle := QP;
          DrawMask(VCanvas);
          VCanvas.Stop;
        finally
          VCanvas.Free;
        end;
        QWidget_setMask(Handle, QB);
      finally
        QPainter_destroy(QP);
      end;
    finally
      QBitmap_destroy(QB);
    end;
end;
```

The QBitmap, QPainter, and TCanvas objects that you see here are all discussed in depth in
Chapter 11. For now, you need to know only that TCanvas is an abstraction in CLX that represents all the graphical elements in a form or component. For instance, any brushes, bitmaps,
pens, fonts, and other graphical items on your form are wrapped inside the TCanvas object.
The QBitmap and QPainter objects, on the other hand, are part of Qt proper. The canvas ends
up owning and managing these secondary graphical elements. The real work is done by the
QBitmap and QPainter objects, but the TCanvas object manages them and provides you with
an easy way to manipulate these native Qt objects.

Notice, in particular, this chunk of code:

```
        VCanvas := TCanvas.Create;
        try
          VCanvas.Start(False);
          VCanvas.Handle := QP;
          DrawMask(VCanvas);
          VCanvas.Stop;
        finally
          VCanvas.Free;
```

Here you see the canvas being created. A method of TCanvas named Start tells Qt that it
should begin painting. Then, the DrawMask method is called. This is the point at which the base
object hands the act of painting over to the child objects. The child objects then draw onto the
bitmap in the canvas the shape that they want to assume.

When the child forms are done drawing, control passes back to the parent form. The TCanvas
object uses the Stop method to tell Qt that the painting is done. Finally, the TCanvas object
itself is destroyed.

> **NOTE**
>
> This section of the text mentioned the `InitWidget` and `WidgetFlags` methods. One other key method that you can override when initializing a widget is `CreateWidget`.

## Painting the Shape of a Form

The act of actually painting into the `TCanvas` object provided by the base form can be very simple. For instance, consider this trivial implementation of the `DrawMask` method in the `TCircle` object:

```
procedure TCircleForm.DrawMask(ACanvas: TCanvas);
var
  R: TRect;
begin
  R := ClientRect;
  ACanvas.Brush.Color := clMask;
  ACanvas.FillRect(R);
  ACanvas.Brush.Color := clDontMask;
  ACanvas.Ellipse(R);
end;
```

This method is borrowed from the Clock example in the demos directory for Kylix itself. As you can see, it first paints the entire form black, using the `clMask` constant. It then paints a white ellipse in the middle of the form. The ellipse will be visible to the user, but the area around the edges of the ellipse will be completely transparent. The edges will not even respond to mouse clicks. Instead, clicks on the transparent portions of the form will be passed to the underlying forms or programs. For all intents and purposes, this is an elliptical form. It appears round to the eye, and it responds only to mouse clicks in the round part of the form.

You will notice that I don't bother using the `clMask` and `clDontMask` constants in the other `DrawMask` methods:

```
procedure TOctagonForm.DrawMask(ACanvas: TCanvas);
var
  pts: array[0..7] of TPoint;
begin
  pts[0] := Point(64, 64);
  pts[1] := Point(192, 0);
  pts[2] := Point(320, 64);
  pts[3] := Point(384, 192);
  pts[4] := Point(320, 320);
  pts[5] := Point(192, 384);
```

```
  pts[6] := Point(64, 320);
  pts[7] := Point(0, 192);
  ACanvas.Polygon(pts);
end;
```

As far as I can tell, all that is necessary here is the contrast between two colors. Actually defining them as clMask and clDontMask was not necessary in my experiments. Qt will handle the rest. In particular, this example uses the Polygon method of the TCanvas object to draw an octagonal shape defining the perimeter of the form. Each point defines another vertice in the octagon, much like a connect-the-dots drawing for children. All you need to do is define the coordinates of the points that you want the Polygon method to connect.

The truck example uses the same technology as the TOctagon form, except that there are some 256 points in that example. The increase in the number of points is necessary because the truck is a much more complex shape than an octagon. For instance, the truck has round wheels, an angled windshield, and other irregularities that require multiple points to delineate properly.

Hopefully you have enjoyed this little foray into the colorful world of irregularly shaped forms. Using this technology, you can create programs that are shaped like animals, spaceships, TVs, plastic radios, or any number of different items.

Perhaps most importantly, this kind of technology is fun to use. But it also helps to grab users' attention and set them at ease. A funny-looking truck-shaped form can help users loosen up and get over their fear of computers. As experienced developers, we often wrestle with the needs and quirks of users who are intimidated by technology that is all too familiar to us. Sometimes just a little levity can help users approach the program with a spirit of play. Just that simple added touch of imagination can help break the ice. It can help a user approach your program with the same sense of enjoyment that you found in building it.

| **NOTE** |
| --- |
| When building complex forms like the truck example, you will want some help from a graphics program that saves the shapes it creates in a textual format or in a binary format that you can read. That way you don't have to figure out the coordinates by hand; instead, you can get a graphical design program to create the shapes. Then you can simply read the data from the program's output and translate it into Pascal code. |

**7**

**CLX ARCHITECTURE**

# Summary

In this chapter, you learned about the relationship between CLX and Qt. In particular, you saw that CLX is based on a series of C wrappers that encapsulate the entire Qt API. You also learned how the Qt event mechanism is handled inside a CLX application.

Ultimately, the material in this chapter is among the most important sections of this book. Some of it is unquestionably a bit difficult to master. If you get it under your belt, however, you will be well on your way to mastering Kylix.

# Packaging and Sharing Code

*by Charlie Calvert*

CHAPTER

8

## IN THIS CHAPTER

This chapter is the first in a series of three chapters on building components. Components are one of the most important developments in contemporary programming, and there is not an environment on the market that makes them easier to use or create than Kylix.

In this chapter you will build a simple component that changes default settings in an edit control. In the next two chapters you will build a series of increasingly complex components.

Components are placed in a form of shared object called a `package`. Because packages are so centrally important to Kylix development, I am going to spend a considerable portion of this chapter discussing them. In fact, packages represent the main topic of this chapter. The component included in this chapter is designed to teach you just enough about components so you will understand what I mean when I say that packages contain components. A more in-depth discussion of the topic will be included in the next two chapters.

Closely related to the subject of packages is the whole matter of how you build shared objects in Kylix. The very end of this chapter will include a brief section on that important topic.

The information you learn in this chapter depends on your knowledge of the Pascal object model. An understanding of OOP is absolutely essential to developers who want to take full advantage of components. If you do not understand the Pascal object model, nothing that I write in the next three chapters will make any sense. My coverage of objects in Chapter 4, "Objects and Interfaces," is intended as a thorough explication of the Kylix OOP model for experienced programmers who are new to Pascal.

## Component Theory

Kylix components have three outstanding strengths:

- They are native components, built in Object Pascal. This means that you can write, debug, and test your components from inside standard Kylix programs. In short, it's much easier to learn to dig in and really write your own Kylix component than it is to try to understand and write, for instance, Windows-based ActiveX controls. Borland's or Microsoft's wizards can make it fairly easy to create an ActiveX control, but actually understanding the technology is extremely difficult. Furthermore, the curve you are on when learning about CLX controls is continuous. At first, you will probably create fairly simple controls that use only a few easy to understand technologies. As you gain more experience you deepen your knowledge, while staying within the context of the Kylix programming environment. Other component models force you to completely abandon your native programming environment and switch to another language when you want to learn to access advanced component development. This gives Kylix a big advantage over other visual tools that force you to move to C++, (or else use very abstract, highly generalized tools) if you want to build components. It is a bit like getting the advantages of both Visual Basic and Visual C++, all wrapped up in a single product. Or, to put the matter in Linux terms, it is like finding one product that contains the ease of use found in Perl/TCL or Python, and the depth and flexibility found in gcc.

- Kylix components are fully object-oriented, which means you can easily change or enhance existing components by creating descendant objects.

- The components you create in Kylix are small, fast, and light. Furthermore, they can be linked directly into your executables.

You can create Kylix components that do nearly anything, from serial communications, to database access, to multimedia development. There are few, if any, limits in the Kylix component model. Developers who have a strong imagination are often able to do wondrous things with Kylix components.

> **NOTE**
>
> Most publicly available components cost in the range of $50 to $150, though many good ones are given away for free. Some of these tools encapsulate functionality that might cost tens of thousands of dollars to produce in-house. For instance, a good communication library might take a year to build. However, if a company can sell it in volume, it can afford to charge $100 or $200 for the same product. That's a real bargain. And most of these tools are easy to use. Building components is a great way for relatively small third-party companies to make money, and buying components is a great way to save time on big projects. These are ground-breaking tools that are changing everything about the way programs are constructed.

**8**

This book and its CD contain explanations detailing all the prerequisite knowledge component builders need, from a description of Kylix itself, through a description of its language, and on to an overview of its implementation of OOP. From this foundation, it will be easy for you to begin building your own components.

# Creating Descendants of an Existing Component

In this section, you will see how to create a custom TEdit control. The changes made to the standard TEdit component involve tweaking its colors, as well as its font's colors, names, sizes, and styles.

In the next chapter, a very brief portion of the text will show how to make similar changes to other components. The goal is to show how to create a suite of custom controls that you can place on the Component Palette and use for special effects, or to define the look and feel of a certain set of applications belonging to a particular department or company.

With projects like this, it's best to start with one simple example and then move on to one with a larger number of objects. In Listing 8.1, you find the code for a first version of a unit that eventually holds the descendants of TEdit, TPanel, and TLabel controls, as well as a number of other controls. Scan through it, check out its basic structure, and then read on to see my brief discussion of how to use the component editor to put it together. Listing 8.2 contains the source to a program that tests the unit.

**LISTING 8.1**  The Code for a Simple Component Descending from TEdit; This Code Is Found in ElfControlsA.pas in the lunits Directory

```
//////////////////////////////////////
// Purpose: First example of how to create a component
// Project: Elves.dpk
// Copyright  2001 by Charlie Calvert
//
unit ElfControlsA;

interface

uses
  Classes, QGraphics, QControls,
  QStdCtrls;

type
  TElfSmallEditA = class(TEdit)
  private
    { Private declarations }
  protected
    { Protected declarations }
  public
    { Public declarations }
    constructor Create(AOwner: TComponent); override;
  published
    { Published declarations }
  end;

procedure Register;

implementation

constructor TElfSmallEditA.Create(AOwner: TComponent);
begin
```

**LISTING 8.1**  Continued

```
  inherited Create(AOwner);
  Color := clBlue;
  Font.Color := clYellow;
  Font.Name := 'Times New Roman';
  Font.Size := 12;
  Font.Style := [fsBold];
end;

procedure Register;
begin
  RegisterComponents('Elves', [TElfSmallEditA]);
end;

end.
```

**LISTING 8.2**  The Main Form for the TestElvesA.dpr Program Serves as a Test Bed for the ElfControlsA Unit

```
////////////////////////////////////
// Purpose: Test TElfSmallEditA control
// Project: TestElvesA.dpr
// Copyright  2001 by Charlie Calvert
//
unit Main;

interface

uses
  SysUtils, Classes, QGraphics,
  QControls, QForms, QDialogs,
  QStdCtrls;

type
  TForm1 = class(TForm)
    RunTestBtn: TButton;
    procedure RunTestBtnClick(Sender: TObject);
    procedure FormResize(Sender: TObject);
  end;

var
  Form1: TForm1;

implementation
```

**LISTING 8.2**  Continued

```
uses
  ElfControlsA;

{$R *.xfm}

procedure TForm1.RunTestBtnClick(Sender: TObject);
var
  MyEdit: TElfSmallEditA;
begin
  MyEdit := TElfSmallEditA.Create(Self);
  MyEdit.Parent := Self;
  MyEdit.Show;
end;

{-----------------------------------------------------------------
  This code can now be replaced by the Anchors property.
-----------------------------------------------------------------}
procedure TForm1.FormResize(Sender: TObject);
begin
  RunTestBtn.Left := 5;
  RunTestBtn.Top := Height - (RunTestBtn.Height + 10);
end;

end.
```

It's simple to create this unit, test it, and compile it as a component that's merged in with the rest of the tools on the Component Palette. To get started, choose File, New and create a new application. Then select File, New, Component from the first page of the Object Repository. Doing so causes the dialog box shown in Figure 8.1 to appear.

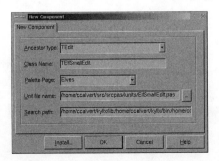

**FIGURE 8.1**

*The New Component dialog box.*

The Component Wizard is a simple code generator that has been integrated into the IDE, using the Tools API. The code generator first asks you for the name of the component you want to create. It then asks you to select the component's parent from a drop-down list. After you have defined the type of component you want to create, you can select the page in the Component Palette where you want it to reside. To follow along with my first example, you should fill in the blanks with this information:

```
Class Name: TElfSmallEdit
Ancestor: TEdit
Palette Page: Elves
```

For your efforts, the Component Wizard churns out the code in Listing 8.3, in which everything is boilerplate except the first line of the class declaration, the global var declaration, and the parameterspassed to the RegisterComponents method.

**LISTING 8.3**  The Standard Boilerplate Output of the Component Wizard

```
unit Unit2;

interface

uses
  SysUtils, Types, Classes,
  QGraphics, QControls, QForms,
  QDialogs, QStdCtrls;

type
  TElfSmallEdit = class(TEdit)
  private
    { Private declarations }
  protected
    { Protected declarations }
  public
    { Public declarations }
  published
    { Published declarations }
  end;

procedure Register;

implementation
```

**LISTING 8.3** Continued

```
procedure Register;
begin
  RegisterComponents('Elves', [TElfSmallEdit]);
end;

end.
```

The Component Wizard starts by giving you a uses clause designed to cover most of the bases you are likely to touch in a standard component:

```
uses
  SysUtils, Types, Classes,
  QGraphics, QControls, QForms,
  QDialogs, QStdCtrls;
```

You may, of course, need to add additional units to this list, but it should handle most situations fairly cleanly.

The next step is to provide a basic class declaration, in which the name and parent are filled in with the choices you specified in the Component Wizard dialog. Default scoping directives are placed in the code for your convenience, and you can delete any portion of them that you don't think you'll need:

```
type
  TElfSmallEdit = class(TEdit)
  private
    { Private declarations }
  protected
    { Protected declarations }
  public
    { Public declarations }
  published
    { Published declarations }
  end;
```

## Two-Way Tools

Borland calls Kylix a *two-way tool*. Two-way tools allow you to edit code either visually or manually. In other words, you can often make changes to your source either in a visual tool or in a text editor.

You can't do everything visually, but you can always do everything in the editor. Perhaps someday we will be able to do everything with the visual tools if we want.

The current state of the art, however, still leaves hand-written code triumphant as the most powerful and flexible tool available. But there is an ever growing number of tasks that can be done more efficiently with the visual tools.

Two-way tools are important because it means that there is nothing hidden from you, no secret bits of information stored where you can't find them. If you want to change the name of your component, you can just use the text editor - or the visual tools: It's up to you! There are no secret cookies being stored behind the scenes.

This concept is true of all facets of Kylix programming. All you need to compile the programs is the source code. Even the XFM files that define the forms can be saved and edited as source, if you simply right-click on them and choose Text xfm from the menu.

A lot of functionality for an object is defined in the classes from which it descends. For instance, the TElfSmallEdit control derives a lot of capability from the TEdit control. However, the source to the TEdit controls ships with most versions of Kylix. In fact, it is stored as part of an Open Source project on SourceForge, as explained in Chapter 7, "CLX Architecture and Qt," in the section called "FreeCLX."

There aren't any big secrets here. As far as I can tell, all of the source to the CLX is available, and it is all written in Object Pascal. For instance, all the source for Kylix's component technology is freely available. Even the part that is not written in Object Pascal, the Qt library, still has its source freely available from www.trolltech.com.

For some reason, I have not been able to find the source to the C wrapper around the Qt API. I don't know why that code is not provided, but the reasons may involve the contract between Borland and TrollTech. If there were any other missing pieces, it would seem to me that they must be very obscure, and not particularly important. However, the latest versions of this file in binary form are available on SourceForge as libqtintf.

**8**

Before you can place a component on the Component Palette, you must first register it with the system:

```
procedure Register;
begin
  RegisterComponents('Elves', [TElfSmallEdit]);
end;
```

Registering a class makes it known to the Kylix Component Palette when the relevant unit is compiled into the Kylix component library. The Register procedure has no impact on programs compiled with this unit. Unless your program calls the Register procedure (which it should *never* do), the code for the Register procedure never even appears in your executable.

## Saving Your Work

After using the Component Wizard, you should save your work. In particular, you need to save both the test project you created, and then the component itself. Proceed as you normally would by creating a directory for the project and saving Main.pas and TestElvesA.dpr inside it. The new unit that you created, however, should not be saved into the same directory, but should be placed in a separate directory, such as the lunits directory where LCodeBox.pas is stored. You likely want a single path that leads to all related files of this type. If you have all of your components in different subdirectories you will end up with a library path that is long and unwieldy.

> **NOTE**
>
> The lunits directory is where I store the code that needs to be shared among the programs that come on the CD that accompanies this book. After installing the code off the CD, you can follow my suggestion and use that directory if you like. Of course, you can also feel free to place the component in another directory of your own choosing, or even in the kylix/lib directory, if that is what you want. The point is not really that you place it in any one particular directory, but that you create a directory for all your shared code.

Because your component will appear on the Component Palette, it is now going to come into play as part of Kylix itself. The directory where you place your component should be on the library path for the Kylix environment. If Kylix cannot find a unit in your current directory, it searches in this directory for your files. You can set that path by choosing Tools, Environment Options, Library, Library Path from the Kylix menu. Click on the ellipses (...) button next to the library path edit control. A dialog box appears. Type the path into the dialog box, or browse for the path to the directory where you stored your component. Now click on the Add button to add your path to the list of Kylix library paths. When you are done, close all the dialog boxes you opened by clicking the OK button.

I don't want you to place this component on the Component Palette quite yet. Instead, just set up the library path and add the unit you created to your main form's uses clause. It's best not to open up the Project Manager and make this class a part of your project. If you add the class to your project, the path to it becomes hard-coded into your DPR file, which may cause problems later on. Instead, just set up the library path as described previously. If you do that, the compiler will have no trouble locating the unit.

# Defining the Features of Your Component

The goal of the component you are creating is to give the TEdit control a new set of default behaviors. In particular, the control will automatically appear with certain new colors and certain fonts. These changes would be easy to make into a component without going to the trouble of creating your own descendant component. So in that sense, this exercise is not particularly enlightening. On the other hand, the point of this exercise is not to create a powerful new component, but instead to show you how to begin creating your own components. The act of changing the default values for a component is a good exercise if your goal is to learn how the component technology works. Then, once you have the basics under your belt, this text will move on to showing more powerful component creation features.

To get started, you need to override the Create constructor and change the fonts inside of it. To declare the method, write the following in your class declaration:

```
TElfSmallEdit = class(TEdit)
public
  constructor Create(AOwner: TComponent); override;
end;
```

Notice that in this declaration I have removed the private, published, and protected directives created by the Component Wizard. I removed the extra scoping directives simply to keep the amount of code you need to look at as small and straightforward as possible.

The Create method for TElfSmallEdit is declared as public. If you think about the process of creating a component dynamically, you will see in a moment that the constructor has to be public. This is one method that must be exposed to all users. Furthermore, it would make no sense to place the method in the published section because you would not want the constructor to appear in the Object Inspector. (In fact, the constructor does not belong, and could not be displayed, in the Object Inspector. As a result, it simply makes no sense to place the constructor in the published section.)

Create is passed a single parameter of type TComponent, which is a base class that encapsulates the minimum functionality needed to be an owner of another component. In particular, whatever form you place a component on usually will be the owner of that component. However, the owner does not have to be a form. For instance, it could be a TPanel. In fact, any CLX control has the built in capability to act properly as the owner of another control. Finally, use the override directive to specify that this is a virtual method that you want to redefine.

C++ AND JAVA
NOTE

Constructors do not have to be declared as virtual, but in most cases it makes sense to declare them that way. As noted earlier, the Pascal language is unlike C++ and Java in that the ancestor constructor for a class is not automatically called. To call the ancestor constructor for an Object Pascal class, you must explicitly use the inherited keyword.

The implementation of the Create constructor is simple:

```
constructor TElfSmallEdit.Create(AOwner: TComponent);
begin
  inherited Create(AOwner);
  Color := clBlue;
  Font.Color := clYellow;
  Font.Name := 'Times New Roman';
  Font.Size := 12;
  Font.Style := [fsBold];
end;
```

The code first calls the inherited Create, passing in the variable AOwner. As stated earlier, the owner of a component will often, though not always, be the form on which the component is to be displayed. In other words, the user will drop the component onto a form, and that form will become the owner of the component. In such a case, AOwner is a variable that points at the form. CLX uses it to initialize the Owner property, which is one of the fields of all components.

The owner of a control is responsible for destroying the control. This takes place when the owner itself is being destroyed. If you dispose a control yourself, be sure to set it to nil, or else you risk raising an exception when the control's owner tries to destroy it. Most of the time, however, you do not need to worry about destroying the control and can just let the owner take over that job.

**NOTE**

The ultimate owner of all forms and components in your program is the Application object. This object is created and destroyed automatically by CLX. When the Application object is destroyed, it will destroy the objects it owns, which will in turn destroy the objects they own. As a result, you generally do not need to worry about destroying components. If you do elect to explicitly destroy them, you might want to use the FreeAndNil procedure found in the SysUtils unit. This routine automatically calls Free on your object, and then sets it to nil.

The next step is to define the color and font that you want to use. To do so, use the `Style` property of the `TFont` object. `Font.Style` is defined as follows:

```
TFontStyle = (fsBold, fsItalic, fsUnderline, fsStrikeOut);
TFontStyles = set of TFontStyle;
```

The first line says that `TFontStyle` is an enumerated type containing the elements `fsBold`, `fsItalic`, `fsUnderline`, and `fsStrikeout`. `fsBold` is equivalent to zero, `fsItalic` to 1, and so on. `TFontStyle` is a set containing the elements of the `TFontStyle` enumerated type.

If you want to add the underline and bold style to the text in the `edit` control, write the following:

```
Font.Style := [fsBold, fsUnderline];
```

This code says that `Font.Style` is a set containing the elements `fsBold` and `fsUnderline`. Needless to say, any font with these styles appears both bold and underlined. If you want to then add the italic style at runtime, write:

```
Font.Style := Font.Style + [fsItalic];
```

Here the plus symbol (+) is used as the set operator for a union.

## Testing the Component

At this stage, the code is ready to go on the Component Palette. However, most of the time when you write components, you should test them first to see whether they work. That way you don't run the risk of adding a potentially buggy component to Kylix itself.

To test the new class, first add the name of the unit you are testing to the `uses` clause of the main form of your test program. Drop a button on the program's main form, and create an `OnClick` handler:

```
procedure TForm1.Button1Click(Sender: TObject);
var
  MyEdit: TElfSmallEdit;
begin
  MyEdit := TElfSmallEdit.Create(Self);
  MyEdit.Parent := Self;
  MyEdit.Show;
end;
```

This code creates the component and shows it on the main form. `Self`, of course, is the way that `TForm1` refers to itself from inside one of its own methods. The owner of the new component is `Form1`, which will be responsible for disposing of the component when finished with it. As mentioned earlier, this happens automatically. You never need to worry about disposing of a visible component shown on a form.

C++ AND JAVA
NOTE
There is no significant difference between Self in Object Pascal and this in C++ or Java. Quite literally, the two keywords have the same meaning, and generally the same usage, in all three languages.

The parent of the component is also Self, which in this case resolves to Form1. The Parent variable is used by X when it is trying to decide how to display the form on the screen. If you place a panel on a form and drop a button on the panel, the owner of that button may be the form or the panel, but the parent is the panel. Ownership determines when and how the component is deallocated, and parental relationships determine where and how the component is displayed. Ownership is fundamentally a Kylix issue, whereas parental relationships are primarily a concern of X itself, and of the window manager. Ownership is about memory allocation; parental authority is about where a component is displayed.

I want to emphasize that this process of creating a control dynamically like this is useful primarily when you are testing your controls. In particular, it helps prevent you from adding a buggy, access-violation creating component to the Component Palette. If you put a really unstable component on the Component Palette, you can destabilize the whole Kylix environment. As a result, I suggest creating a test platform for your component before you place it on the Component Palette. In the next section, I will show you how to place a component on the Component Palette so that it acts like a normal control of the kind that ship with Kylix.

You should now run your project, click on the button and see what happens. Furthermore, you should use the debugging technologies described in Chapter 5, "The Editor and Debugger," to step through your code and see exactly how it works.

## Packages: Placing a Component on the Component Palette

After running the program and testing the component, the next step is to put it up on the Component Palette. This involves working with something called a package. In this section of the chapter I will say a few words about packages, and then I will tell you the simple steps required to build your own packages.

### What Is a Package?

A *package* is a special kind of shared library that can contain one or more components, objects, or functions. Its primary benefit is to allow you to wrap up components in a library and share them with multiple programs. Packages originally emerged out of the Delphi team's desire to create a good way to store objects in a Windows DLL. During development, they began to take on a larger and more complex role. All of the functionality of Packages on Windows has been moved over to Kylix, with the only difference being the largely syntactical distinction between putting the components in a shared object rather than a DLL. From the casual user's point of view, there are few differences between a shared object and a DLL, so the technology has essentially come over unchanged from the Windows world.

> **NOTE**
>
> In saying that the technology is unchanged, I do not mean that a Windows-based technology is being used in Linux. Kylix packages are real native Linux shared objects. They have no Windows code in them, and no reliance on Windows code. The Kylix team did a lot of hard work to make sure that packages in Linux appeared the same way to the user as packages in Windows. My only point is simply that shared objects and DLLs are, from the casual user's perspective, equivalent technologies. They perform the same role in Linux and Windows, even if many of the implementation details of the two technologies vary. For instance, Linux shared objects can be relocated in memory in a manner that is rarely seen in Windows. But that was the Kylix team's problem, and should not be something we normally need to think about as Kylix developers. Certainly we never need to think about such matters when building packages.

A package has the letters BPL as a preface to its name. As a rule, you want to place packages in a directory that is on your path, such as the lunits directory discussed earlier in this chapter.

Packages can reduce the size of the average Kylix program from four or five hundred KB to less than 25KB. Of course, all that missing weight has to go somewhere, and at least one core CLX package is more than a megabyte in size. However, that file can be used by multiple executables. As a result, if you have more than one program that shares the package, the sum total of your files is smaller than if you used normal executables.

Kylix gives you the choice to use packages or to build normal executables. By default, you create normal executables.

You can choose Project, Options, Packages to decide whether you want to include packages with any particular executable. As a rule, you should always choose to build your projects with packages because it saves disk space. However, packages are somewhat more difficult to work with and to distribute than simple executables. In particular, you need to distribute both the executable and the package, and you must ensure that the package is on the LD_LIBRARY_PATH. As a result, you might choose not to use them under certain circumstances, particularly if you are new to Kylix, or new to Linux.

## Packages and the `LD_LIBRARY_PATH`

`LD_LIBRARY_PATH` is a Linux environment variable that the system uses when checking for libraries. Most shared objects used by the system are stored in `/usr/lib`. Files placed in this directory will automatically be accessible to the system, and you need do nothing special to access them. However, you might not want to place your libraries there. To set the library path, go to the command prompt and type

`export LD_LIBRARY_PATH=$LD_LIBRARY_PATH:`*`/THE/PATH/TO/MY/LIBS`*

where you fill in the path to your libraries. For instance, you might type:

`export LD_LIBRARY_PATH=$LD_LIBRARY_PATH:/home/ccalvert/myLibs.`

If you want, you can place the code to export your `LD_LIBRARY_PATH` in your `.bash_profile` file, which is, on most Linux distributions, a hidden file in your home directory. The `.bash_profile` script should be run once when you first sign in to the system. If you prefer, you can place it in the `.bashrc` script, which is run each time you open a shell. Placing it in this second file is not recommended because it can lead to the creation of very long and repetitious `LD_LIBRARY_PATH`s.

> **NOTE**
>
> To see hidden files on your system, type **ls -la** at the command prompt. The a parameter, passed to `ls`, tells the utility to show all files, including hidden files. Hidden files always begin with a period. Other than the fact that you don't normally see them, there is no real difference between a hidden file and a normal file. For instance, you can edit and save them in the same editor using the same techniques that you use to access normal files.

As explained in the readme from the CD that accompanies this book, Kylix needs to set up its own library path. This can be accomplished manually by running the `kylixpath` bash script that was placed on your hard drive when you installed Kylix. To find this file, type **locate kylixpath** or **slocate kylixpath** at the command prompt. If that fails, go the root directory on your hard drive and type **find . -iname kylixpath**. `locate` and `slocate` rely on a database of programs on your hard drive, so they run fairly quickly. `Find` literally searches across your hard drive, so it takes a while to run. `slocate` is the secure version of `locate`. The database used by `slocate` and `locate` is created automatically on Red Hat 7 and later versions. If you need to build the database yourself, become root and run `slocate` with the -u option:

```
% su
% slocate -u
```

As stated earlier, it is usually a good idea to call the `kylixpath` script from inside your `.bash_profile` or `.bashrc` file. For instance, my `.bash_profile` file contains the following line:

```
source /home/ccalvert/bin/kylixpath > /dev/null
```

I pump the output from `kylixpath` to the null device so that I don't have to look at it every time I sign on. However, you might want to run the command a few times on its own from the command prompt, making sure that you understand the output from the program.

You should study the `kylixpath` script to see exactly how Kylix sets up its paths. That information can be quite useful to you, and can serve as an example of how to write your own scripts. The `librarysimple` project on the CD that accompanies this book also has some accompanying scripts that might help you work with this aspect of Kylix programming.

If you want to know what libraries a Kylix program depends on, type **ldd** *MyExecutable* at the command prompt, where *MyExecutable* is the name of your Kylix program. Here is the output from running `ldd` on the ClxStyle2 program that ships on the CD that accompanies this book:

```
/lib/libNoVersion.so.1 => /lib/libNoVersion.so.1 (0x40018000)
libqtintf.so => /home/ccalvert/kylix/bin/libqtintf.so (0x4001a000)
libX11.so.6 => /usr/X11R6/lib/libX11.so.6 (0x401ac000)
libpthread.so.0 => /lib/libpthread.so.0 (0x4027a000)
libdl.so.2 => /lib/libdl.so.2 (0x40290000)
libc.so.6 => /lib/libc.so.6 (0x40294000)
libqt.so.2 => /home/ccalvert/kylix/bin/libqt.so.2 (0x403bd000)
/lib/ld-linux.so.2 => /lib/ld-linux.so.2 (0x40000000)
libXext.so.6 => /usr/X11R6/lib/libXext.so.6 (0x40a54000)
libSM.so.6 => /usr/X11R6/lib/libSM.so.6 (0x40a62000)
libICE.so.6 => /usr/X11R6/lib/libICE.so.6 (0x40a6b000)
libjpeg.so.62 => /usr/lib/libjpeg.so.62 (0x40a82000)
libstdc++-libc6.1-1.so.2 => /usr/lib/libstdc++-libc6.1-1.so.2 (0x40aa1000)
libm.so.6 => /lib/libm.so.6 (0x40ae4000)
```

What you are looking at is the output from the program when packages are turned off. As a result, you see primarily Linux libraries, such as `libc`, the C library, and `libm`, the math library. Notice also `libqt`, which is the Qt library on which CLX is based. `libqtintf` appears to be the C wrapper around the Qt library. It is this wrapper that is used by CLX.

Now let's compile the same program with packages turned on and then run `ldd` against it:

```
/lib/libNoVersion.so.1 => /lib/libNoVersion.so.1 (0x40018000)
bplvisualclx.so.6 => /home/ccalvert/kylix/bin/bplvisualclx.so.6 (0x4001a000)
libqtintf.so => /home/ccalvert/kylix/bin/libqtintf.so (0x40288000)
bplbaseclx.so.6 => /home/ccalvert/kylix/bin/bplbaseclx.so.6 (0x4040c000)
libdl.so.2 => /lib/libdl.so.2 (0x405a3000)
```

```
libpthread.so.0 => /lib/libpthread.so.0 (0x405a6000)
libc.so.6 => /lib/libc.so.6 (0x405bc000)
libX11.so.6 => /usr/X11R6/lib/libX11.so.6 (0x406e5000)
libqt.so.2 => /home/ccalvert/kylix/bin/libqt.so.2 (0x407b3000)
/lib/ld-linux.so.2 => /lib/ld-linux.so.2 (0x40000000)
libXext.so.6 => /usr/X11R6/lib/libXext.so.6 (0x40e4a000)
libSM.so.6 => /usr/X11R6/lib/libSM.so.6 (0x40e58000)
libICE.so.6 => /usr/X11R6/lib/libICE.so.6 (0x40e62000)
libjpeg.so.62 => /usr/lib/libjpeg.so.62 (0x40e79000)
libstdc++-libc6.1-1.so.2 => /usr/lib/libstdc++-libc6.1-1.so.2 (0x40e98000)
libm.so.6 => /lib/libm.so.6 (0x40eda000)
```

Notice the following lines:

```
bplvisualclx.so.6 => /home/ccalvert/kylix/bin/bplvisualclx.so.6 (0x4001a000)
bplbaseclx.so.6 => /home/ccalvert/kylix/bin/bplbaseclx.so.6 (0x4040c000)
```

These are your Kylix packages that contain your components.

While you are at it, you might want to run ls  -l on the executables you create with packages, and without packages. For instance:

```
-rwxrwxr-x  1 ccalvert ccalvert    37964 Mar 19 09:16 ClxStyleForm2
-rwxrwxr-x  1 ccalvert ccalvert   595560 Mar 19 10:04 ClxStyleForm2
```

As you can see, there is a difference of one half a megabyte between the size of a file compiled with packages and the size of a file compiled without packages. On the other hand, the packages themselves are not small, so this system only works to your benefit if you are creating at least two different Kylix applications.

## Packages and the Component Palette

If you want to place a component on the Component Palette, you must create a package. All the Kylix components shown on the Component Palette are stored in packages. The components stored on the Component Palette can be linked directly into your programs. Just because the Component Palette uses packages, that doesn't mean your executable has to use them. In particular, notice the DCU files in the Kylix LIB directory. These DCU files contain components that can be linked directly into your program.

The most important package is called bplvisualclx.so.6. You can't do much with Kylix without using that package because it contains all the core components. Most of the other packages are optional. In particular, if you are not doing database programming, you might select Components, Install Components from the Kylix menu and remove the database components. The IDE loads more quickly and has a smaller footprint without them installed.

You can create packages that contain discrete sets of functionality. For instance, if you create a suite of multimedia components, it would make sense to put them in their own package. Clever programmers can create small packages that contain only the components used by their program. Furthermore, you can update a particular program's behavior simply by creating a new version of one of your packages.

You can browse the contents of existing installed Kylix packages. To do so, choose Components, Install Packages from the Kylix menu. Select the Components button when a package you are interested in is highlighted. A list of the components in that package will be displayed in a dialog box. Obviously you can also use the Install Packages menu selection to add or remove existing packages from Kylix. You can also temporarily disable a particular package by removing the check from the box at the left of the package name.

One final benefit of packages should be mentioned at least briefly. If you are working over the Internet, you can supply your customers with a few key CLX packages, such as `bplvisualclx`. If you then build your programs with packages, they will be very small, and can be sent over the Internet in just a few seconds.

## Creating Packages

You can create a package by choosing Components, Install Components, and then selecting the Into New Component page. Now you can browse across your hard drive for the `ElfControlsA.pas` file, and allow Kylix to build the package for you automatically in the background. However, I am going to recommend that you use a second, somewhat more complex technique, because it allows you to have better control over the process of creating a package.

To get started with this second technique, choose File, New, Package from the Kylix menu. This opens the Package Editor and creates a new file called `Package1.dpk`, shown in Listing 8.4 and Figure 8.2. Save this package under the name `Elves.dpk` in the `lunits` directory. (If you don't want to overwrite the version of `Elves.dpk` that I supply, call the package `MyElves.dpk`, or some other name of your choosing.) To view the source to the package, right-click on the word Contains in the Package Editor and choose View Source from the menu.

To add a unit to the package, you can manually edit the Uses clause yourself, or else click on the Add button at the top of the Package Editor. If you click on the Add button, you will be prompted to browse for the files you want to include in the package. You should also choose Tools, Environment Options, Library and make sure the `lunits` directory where `ElfControlsA.pas` is stored has been added to your library path.

**8**

PACKAGING AND
SHARING CODE

**FIGURE 8.2**

*The Kylix Package Editor with one file added to it called* ElfControlsA.pas.

**LISTING 8.4**  A Simple Kylix Package Containing the TElfSmallEditA Component in the Unit Called ElfControlsA.pas

```
package Elves;

{$R *.res}
{$ALIGN 8}
{$ASSERTIONS ON}
{$BOOLEVAL OFF}
{$DEBUGINFO ON}
{$EXTENDEDSYNTAX ON}
{$IMPORTEDDATA ON}
{$IOCHECKS ON}
{$LOCALSYMBOLS ON}
{$LONGSTRINGS ON}
{$OPENSTRINGS ON}
{$OPTIMIZATION ON}
{$OVERFLOWCHECKS OFF}
{$RANGECHECKS OFF}
{$REFERENCEINFO ON}
{$SAFEDIVIDE OFF}
{$STACKFRAMES OFF}
{$TYPEDADDRESS OFF}
{$VARSTRINGCHECKS ON}
{$WRITEABLECONST OFF}
{$MINENUMSIZE 1}
{$IMAGEBASE $400000}
{$DESCRIPTION 'My Elves Unit'}
{$IMPLICITBUILD OFF}

requires
  baseclx,
  visualclx;
```

**LISTING 8.4**   Continued

```
contains
  ElfControlsA in 'ElfControlsA.pas';

end.
```

Once you have created a package and added the units that contain your components to it, you can simply click the Compile and Install buttons at the top of the package editor in order to install your component on the Component Palette.

If you want, you can also click the Options button and enter in a descriptive string, and add other options that might be of interest to you, as shown in Figure 8.3. As usual, you can do any of the things in source code that you can do in the Project Options dialog box. For instance, if you look at the end of Listing 8.4, you can see that it is a simple matter to enter the description for a unit by hand. Needless to say, whether you do it by hand, or do it via the dialog box, the result is the same. Furthermore, changes made by hand are seen in the dialog box, and vice versa.

**FIGURE 8.3**
*The Project Options dialog box for a package.*

> **NOTE**
>
> If you right-click on the word Contains in the package manager, you can choose Build from the pop-up menu. If your code begins doing things that make no sense at all, you may find that it helps to perform a build rather than a simple compile.

## Design Time and Runtime Packages

In the Project Options dialog box you may have noticed that you can mark a package as Designtime Only, Runtime Only, or both. You might want to distribute runtime-only packages to users. They will not be able to open a runtime-only package in the Kylix IDE, and hence will not be able to steal your components and use them in their own programs.

Most design time-only packages rely on runtime-only packages. In particular, they take runtime-only packages and add features such as component editors to them. These editors, and other IDE-based features, make it easy for programmers to manipulate a component via the Object Inspector and Form Designer. I discuss how to create these features in Chapter 10, "Advanced Component Design."

Because I almost always give away the source to my components, I have never had reason to specifically create either design time or runtime packages. As a result, I almost always mark my components as both. However, if I were in the business of selling components, (rather than the business of giving them away), I would consider this an important feature.

## Icons: Working with DCR Files

In Chapter 10, in the section called "Creating Icons for Components," I will explain how to make the DCR files that contain the bitmaps displayed in the Component Palette. For now all you need to know is that a DCR file is a special kind of resource, and that you can add these DCR files directly to a package file or to a unit that contains your component source. Here is an example of package that includes several DCR files:

```
package Elves;

{$R *.RES}
{$R 'Fileiter.dcr'}
{$R 'Gradient.dcr'}
{$R 'Ftp1.dcr'}
```

You can add as many units and DCR files to a package as you want. When you want to edit an existing DPK file, just choose File, Open from the menu, and browse for files with a DPK extension.

## Simultaneously Opening a Package and a Project

You can keep the Package Editor open at the same time as you have another project open. If the ElfControlsA.pas file is linked into your current project, any changes you make to the control will be reflected in your project the first time you compile your project. However, these changes will not make it into the component you use at design time until you rebuild the package that contains the component. For instance, if you add a new published property to a component, you can use it in the code of your program right away, but it won't show up in the object inspector until you rebuild the package that contains it. As a result, you sometimes want to keep both the package and the DPK file open at the same time in a single project group so that you can easily recompile them both.

> **NOTE**
>
> Being able to open a project and a DPK file at the same time is a good feature. However, there are times when it can cause a certain amount of confusion if you are not fully cognizant of the fact that both projects are open. As a result, I often close the standard Kylix project that I am working on, and then open the DPK file. That way, I don't accidentally end up with two projects open at the same time when I don't really intend to be in that state.

## The requires Clause

Some packages use other packages. For instance, the TElfSmallEdit control descends from the TEdit control, which is stored in bplvisualclx. This means that the Elves.dpk file requires that bplvisualclx be used so that it will know about TEdit controls and how to use them. This dependency is why there is a requires clause in your package:

```
requires
  baseclx,
  visualclx;
```

## Registering Components

After you have created a component and installed it, you can create a new program and drop your component on its main form. In particular, you should look for a new component page called Elves. This page exists because we specified that our component should be placed on a page called Elves:

```
procedure Register;
begin
  RegisterComponents('Elves', [TElfSmallEditA]);
end;
```

After you find your new component and drop it on a form, you will find that you have created a tool that works exactly like the components that come preinstalled with Kylix. In the next chapter, I will dig further into the subject of components, explaining exactly how you can access all their most important features.

# Exploring a Package at Runtime

Because packages are so important to Kylix developers, I want to show you a program that will allow you to browse the contents of a package at runtime. In particular, the packageCracker program that I am about to show you will allow you to open up a package, find out key information about its structure, and also explore all the units included in the package. You can see an instance of the packageCracker program in Figure 8.4.

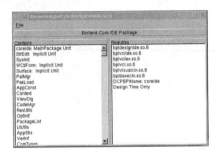

## FIGURE 8.4

*The* packageCracker *program exploring the* bplcoreide *package, which contains that unit out of which the IDE itself is made.*

Despite the esoteric nature of the program, the structure of packageCracker is actually quite straightforward. In particular, it takes advantage of a single powerful Kylix routine called GetPackageInfo. You can see the entire program in Listing 8.5.

**LISTING 8.5**  The packageCracker Program Allows You to Open a Package and See Its Insides

```
unit main;

// Copyright  2001 by Charlie Calvert

interface

uses
  SysUtils, Classes, QGraphics,
  QControls, QForms, QDialogs,
  QStdCtrls, QComCtrls, QExtCtrls,
  QMenus, QTypes;

type
  TForm1 = class(TForm)
```

**LISTING 8.5**  Continued

```pascal
    Panel1: TPanel;
    DescriptionLabel: TLabel;
    Panel2: TPanel;
    RequiresListBox: TListBox;
    RequiresLabel: TLabel;
    Splitter1: TSplitter;
    Panel3: TPanel;
    ContainsListBox: TListBox;
    ContainsLabel: TLabel;
    MainMenu1: TMainMenu;
    File1: TMenuItem;
    Open1: TMenuItem;
    N1: TMenuItem;
    Exit1: TMenuItem;
    OpenDialog1: TOpenDialog;
    Splitter2: TSplitter;
    procedure FormResize(Sender: TObject);
    procedure FormShow(Sender: TObject);
    procedure Open1Click(Sender: TObject);
  private
    { Private declarations }
  public
    { Public declarations }
  end;

var
  Form1: TForm1;

implementation

uses
  Libc, LCodeBox;

var
  FPackageName: string;

{$R *.xfm}

procedure ShowInfo(const Name: string; NameType: TNameType;
  Flags: Byte; Param: Pointer);
var
  UnitInfo: string;
  ufMainPackage: Byte;
```

**LISTING 8.5**   Continued

```
begin
  UnitInfo := '';
  ufMainPackage := ufMainUnit or ufPackageUnit;
  if Flags and ufMainPackage <> 0 then
    UnitInfo := UnitInfo + 'MainPackage Unit'
  else begin
    if Flags and ufMainUnit <> 0 then
      UnitInfo := UnitInfo + 'Main Unit ';
    if Flags and ufPackageUnit <> 0 then
      UnitInfo := UnitInfo + 'Package Unit ';
  end;
  if Flags and ufWeakUnit <> 0 then
    UnitInfo := UnitInfo + ' Weak Unit ';
  if Flags and ufOrgWeakUnit <> 0 then
    UnitInfo := UnitInfo + ' OrgWeak Unit ';
  if Flags and ufImplicitUnit <> 0 then
    UnitInfo := UnitInfo + ' Implicit Unit ';

  if UnitInfo <> '' then
    UnitInfo := ': ' + UnitInfo;
  if NameType = ntContainsUnit then
    Form1.ContainsListBox.Items.Add(Name + UnitInfo)
  else if NameType = ntRequiresPackage then
    Form1.RequiresListBox.Items.Add(Name)
  else if NameType = ntDcpBpiName then
    Form1.RequiresListBox.Items.Add('DCPBPIName: ' + Name);

end;

function ModuleCracker(PackageName: string): Boolean;
var
  Flags: Integer;
  ModuleDesc: string;
  PackageModule: HModule;
begin
  Result := True;
  Form1.RequiresListBox.Clear;
  Form1.ContainsListBox.Clear;
  try
    ModuleDesc := GetPackageDescription(PChar(FPackageName));
  except
    on E: EPackageError do begin
      Form1.Caption :=
        'Not a package, or I can''t find packages this file depends on.';
```

**LISTING 8.5**  Continued

```
      Form1.DescriptionLabel.Caption := E.Message;
      Exit;
    end;
  end;
  PackageModule := HMODULE(dlOpen(PChar(FPackageName), PkgLoadingMode));

  GetPackageInfo(PackageModule, nil, Flags, ShowInfo);
  if ModuleDesc <> '' then begin
    Form1.DescriptionLabel.Caption := ModuleDesc;
    if Flags and pfDesignOnly = pfDesignOnly then
      Form1.RequiresListBox.Items.Add('Design Time Only');
    if Flags and pfRunOnly = pfRunOnly then
      Form1.RequiresListBox.Items.Add('Run Time Only');
  end;
  dlclose(Pointer(PackageModule));
end;

procedure TForm1.FormResize(Sender: TObject);
begin
  Panel2.Width := (Width div 2) - (Splitter1.Width div 2);
end;

procedure TForm1.FormShow(Sender: TObject);
begin
  FPackageName := '';
  FormResize(nil);
end;

procedure TForm1.Open1Click(Sender: TObject);
var
  Home: String;
begin
  Home := GetEnvironmentVariable('HOME');
  OpenDialog1.InitialDir := HOME + '/kylix/bin';
  if OpenDialog1.Execute then begin
    Caption := OpenDialog1.FileName;
    FPackagename := OpenDialog1.FileName;
    ModuleCracker(FPackageName);
  end;
end;

end.
```

When first opened, the program presents a blank face to the user. To get it rolling, you need to choose File, Open from the menu. An OpenDialog will appear, and by default it should take you to the Kylix bin directory where you can begin browsing the packages that come with Kylix:

```
Home := GetEnvironmentVariable('HOME');
OpenDialog1.InitialDir := HOME + '/kylix/bin';
if OpenDialog1.Execute then begin
  Caption := OpenDialog1.FileName;
  FPackagename := OpenDialog1.FileName;
  ModuleCracker(FPackageName);
end;
```

The first line uses the Object Pascal GetEnvironmentVariable routine to retrieve the user's home directory. It then appends that string '/kylix/bin' to the home directory. In most cases, this will take you to the directory where your Kylix packages are installed. However, if you did not install your version of Kylix under your home directory, you may want to change this code.

If all goes well, the OpenDialog will allow you to browse your kylix/bin directory for bpl files. Pick one that seems interesting to you, and begin browsing it. For instance, you might find it interesting to explore bplbaseclx.

> **NOTE**
>
> The act of browsing packages can occasionally have a dark side. In particular, if you open an invalid package, or a package that depends on another package that the packageCracker program can't find, you might find packageCracker tending to raise an exception or two. However, if you limit your browsing to the /kylix/bin directory, all should go well in most circumstances.

## Getting Inside a Package at Runtime

The ModuleCracker routine first calls the CLX routine GetPackageDescription to retrieve a description of the package:

```
ModuleDesc := GetPackageDescription(PChar(FPackageName));
```

After getting the description of a package, the next step is to actually open it. To do this, I use the same routine I would use were I to open a standard shared object. In fact, packages are nothing more than shared objects.

Here is the routine you would use to open a shared object:

```
PackageModule := HMODULE(dlOpen(PChar(FPackageName), PkgLoadingMode));
```

This is the same routine that a C++ programmer would use to open a shared object. In Windows, you would do the same thing by calling LoadLibrary. The dlOpen routine returns a handle to a shared object.

After opening the module, the code calls GetPackageInfo to explore its contents:

```
GetPackageInfo(PackageModule, nil, Flags, ShowInfo);
```

Here is the declaration for GetPackageInfo:

```
procedure GetPackageInfo(Module: HMODULE; Param: Pointer;
  var Flags: Integer; InfoProc: TPackageInfoProc);
```

This routine takes the handle to a package in its first parameter. The second parameter defines a bit of optional user-defined data. For instance, you could pass in a component in this field. After the call is complete, the Flags parameter will contain constants designating various traits of the package. The final parameter is a callback function that you define. CLX will repeatedly call your callback function with information about the contents of the package. For instance, it will call the function once for each unit that the package contains or relies upon.

When the callback function is called, it is passed parameters that describe the actual contents of the package. By parsing these parameters, the routine can list all the units it contains, and it can tell whether the package is marked as design time, runtime, or both.

For instance, consider this code fragment:

```
ufMainPackage := ufMainUnit or ufPackageUnit;
if Flags and ufMainPackage <> 0 then
  UnitInfo := UnitInfo + 'MainPackage Unit'
else begin
  if Flags and ufMainUnit <> 0 then
    UnitInfo := UnitInfo + 'Main Unit ';
  if Flags and ufPackageUnit <> 0 then
    UnitInfo := UnitInfo + 'Package Unit ';
end;
```

If the Flags parameter passed to the callback function is set to both ufMainUnit and ufPackageUnit, the unit referenced in the Name parameter of the callback is the Main unit in the package. In short, it is the same type of unit shown in Listing 8.4.

If you explore this program in more depth, you will soon see that it harvests a wealth of information from CLX, and then shares it with the user. Object Pascal is a very type-rich language.

As a result, this kind of introspective exploration of its parts is not at all unusual. You will see other examples of this kind of exploration in the sections of this book that explore Run Time Type Information (RTTI).

# Creating a Shared Object

Packages are rather complex shared objects. It is not, however difficult to build simple shared objects. In Listings 8.6 and 8.7, I show you a very simple example of how to create your own shared objects.

**LISTING 8.6** A Simple Shared Object; The Code for Creating the Object Is Identical to the Code for Creating a DLL in Windows

```
library simple;

function Add(x: Integer; y: Integer): Integer;
begin
  Result := x + y;
end;

function GetNine: Integer;
begin
  result := 9;
end;

function Square(x: Integer): Integer;
begin
  Result := x * x;
end;

exports
  Add,
  GetNine,
  Square;

begin
end.
```

**LISTING 8.7** The Test Program for the Simple Shared Object

```
program test;

const
  libsimple='libsimple.so';
```

**LISTING 8.7**   Continued

```
function GetNine: Integer; external libsimple name 'GetNine';
function Square(x: Integer): Integer; external libsimple name 'Square';
function Add(x: Integer; y: Integer): Integer; external libsimple name 'Add';

var
  i: Integer;

begin
  WriteLn(GetNine);
  Write('Enter a number: ');
  ReadLn(i);
  WriteLn(Square(i));
  WriteLn('2 + the number you entered = ', Add(2, i));
  ReadLn;
end.
```

The code for this program is found in the Chapter08/SimpleLibrary directory on the CD that accompanies this book.

To run this program, first open the library, simple.dpr, in the IDE. Click the Compile button to compile it. Now open up the test.dpr program and compile it. Test.dpr is a console application, so you can probably best run it from a shell prompt. But before you can run it, you will need to set up your LD_LIBRARY_PATH, as described in the text and note that follow the next few paragraphs.

All shared objects begin with the keyword library:

```
library simple;
```

This signature is followed by one or more procedures, functions, objects, or methods that you want to place in your library. For instance, the simple shared object I have created has routines in it with names like Square and Add.

Any of the routines that you want to export from the library should be listed in the exports clause:

```
exports
  Add,
  GetNine,
  Square;
```

That is all you need to do to create a shared object.

Now you can just click the Compile button and you are nearly finished. I say nearly finished because you will also want to create a directory known by the system or listed on your

`LD_LIBRARY_PATH`. Use this directory to house your shared objects. In the `kylixpath` script mentioned earlier in this chapter, the developers of Kylix have placed a `lib` directory which is usually located directly off your home directory. For instance, it is listed as `/home/ccalvert/lib` on my system. If you create this directory, and then place your completed shared objects in this directory, they should, by default, be on the `LD_LIBRARY_PATH` created when you run the `kylixpath` shell script.

Go to a shell, move to the appropriate directory, and type **./test**. This will run the test program, which is a console application.

---

**NOTE**

In most cases, if you want to run a Kylix program from the command line, you will need to be sure that the `kylixpath` script has been run first. If you do not do this, the system will report that it cannot find certain libraries that your program relies upon. In short, you need to make sure that `LD_LIBRARY_PATH` is set up correctly, or else make sure that your `/etc/ld.so.conf` file is set up and configured correctly as explained in your Linux documentation.

In the simple library directory, I have added some scripts that may help you set things up correctly on your system. In particular, the following script, called `setLibraryPath.sh`, adds the current directory to your `LD_LIBRARY_PATH`:

```
#! /bin/bash
CurDir=$PWD
echo Before you ran this script the lib path was $LD_LIBRARY_PATH
echo Your currernt directory is $CurDir
LD_LIBRARY_PATH=$LD_LIBRARY_PATH:$CurDir
echo After running this script, the lib path is: $LD_LIBRARY_PATH
```

Remember to type **source setLibraryPath.sh** when running this script. If you don't include the word `source`, or a period, the script will affect the shell session in which it runs, and not your current shell.

---

Shared objects can consist of many files. To use multiple files in your library, all you need to do is create additional units, and then list them in the `uses` clause for your main library file. In most cases, you want to have only one `exports` clause, and that should be in the main library file. You can, however, export routines that are declared and implemented in other units.

For instance, you can add a `uses` clause to the simple library:

```
library simple;

uses
  otherUnit in 'otherUnit.pas';
```

```
function Add(x: Integer; y: Integer): Integer;
begin
  Result := x + y;
end;
```

```
// Additional unchanged code omitted here.
```

Then you can create your new unit:

```
unit otherUnit;

interface

procedure Foo;

implementation

procedure Foo;
begin
  WriteLn('Sam');
end;

end.
```

Finally, you can export the unit from the library:

```
exports
  Add,
  Foo,
  GetNine,
  Square;
```

This exports clause appears at the bottom of simple.dpr, exactly as it does in Listing 8.6. The only difference is that now the routine Foo, which is declared and implemented in otherUnit.pas, is also being exported.

As you will learn in the next section, there is nothing at all tricky about importing this new routine into your program:

```
function GetNine: Integer; external libsimple name 'GetNine';
function Square(x: Integer): Integer; external libsimple name 'Square';
function Add(x: Integer; y: Integer): Integer;
  external libsimple name 'Add';
procedure Foo; external libsimple name 'Foo';
```

The new version of the library, with the Foo routine added, is available in the simpleLib2 directory found on the CD that accompanies this book.

## Calling Library Routines from a Kylix Program

If you want to call a routine found in a shared object, there are two ways to proceed. The first technique I will show in this section of the chapter, and the second technique in the next section of this chapter, entitled "Loading a Shared Object Dynamically." Of the two techniques, the most commonly used, by far, is the one shown in this section.

Here is the code you need to write in order to access a routine declared in a shared object:

```
const
  libsimple='libsimple.so';

function GetNine: Integer; external libsimple name 'GetNine';
function Square(x: Integer): Integer; external libsimple name 'Square';
function Add(x: Integer; y: Integer): Integer;
  external libsimple name 'Add';
```

This block of code begins by declaring a constant containing the name of the library where the routines are stored. As you can see, this constant is used in the declaration for each imported function. You could, if you so desired, simply write the name out once for each routine, rather than declaring the constant. However, that is an error prone process, especially if you ever decide to change the name of the library.

When declaring the routines, first write out their signature exactly as it is declared in the shared object:

```
function GetNine: Integer;
```

Next, add the word external, followed by the name of the library, the word name, and the name of the routine itself:

```
function GetNine: Integer; external libsimple name 'GetNine';
```

Once you have taken these steps, you are free to call the routines exactly as you would were they listed in your present source file:

```
  WriteLn(GetNine);
  Write('Enter a number: ');
  ReadLn(i);
  WriteLn(Square(i));
  WriteLn('2 + the number you entered = ', Add(2, i));
```

## Loading a Shared Object Dynamically

There are cases when you want to have complete control over when a library is loaded and when it is unloaded. Here is a routine that shows how to do this particular programmer's dance in Linux:

```
procedure TForm1.Button1Click(Sender: TObject);
type
  TFunc = function (c: Integer): Integer; cdecl;
var
  lib: Pointer;
  MyFunc: TFunc;
begin
//   dlopen(Filename: PChar; Flag: Integer): Pointer;
  try
    lib := dlopen('libc.so.6', RTLD_NOW );
    if lib <> nil then begin
     // dlsym = GetProcAddress
      MyFunc := dlsym(lib,'isupper');
      if @MyFunc <> nil then begin
        if MyFunc(Ord('A')) <> 0 then
          ListBox1.Items.Add('Yes')
        else
          ListBox1.Items.Add('No');
      end;
    end;
  finally
    dlclose(lib);
  end;
end;
```

You are already familiar with the dlOpen and dlClose routines used to access a shared object.
The other key routine in this sample is called dlSym, and it is used to access a particular function from the library you have opened.

---

**NOTE**

The code samples shown here access the libc library that ships with every version of
Linux. However, the version of this library changes over time. There is some chance
that libc.so.6 is not on your system, but instead a file with a name like libc.so.7,
or some other similar value. If you have trouble with this routine, look in the /lib
directory for the name of the libc library on your system. In any case, if you find the
library, you can be sure that it will have the isupper routine in it.

---

You can find the LoadLib program from which this code fragment was taken in the
Chapter08/loadLib directory on the CD that accompanies this book. A somewhat fancier version of this program is in the LoadLib2 directory. You might want to run both programs. The
first has code that is easier to understand, but the second provides an example more likely to
mirror the kind of code you would use in a real-world program rather than a demo program.

# Summary

In wrapping up this subject, let me just add that many programmers are confused by packages when they first see them. I suggest doing whatever you can to alleviate this situation: Build your own packages, experiment with packages, and spend as much time in the Package Editor as you possibly can.

If it helps, build a few shared objects so that you can begin to sense how libraries are put together. For me, the key to understanding a technology is to grasp the theory behind it, and then work through a few simple examples that I can use to prove to myself that my theoretical understanding is correct. Once I begin to feel comfortable with a technology, I usually find it possible to move on to more complex examples with a relative degree of grace.

Packages are a powerful tool, but you can't use them unless you understand them. I've explained how they work in the last few pages, but to really come to terms with them, you have to get your hands dirty creating your own packages. My suggestion is to start doing so immediately, and to dedicate some significant periods of time to becoming familiar with this whole process. The next two chapters will certainly provide you numerous opportunities to hone your skills.

# Creating Components

*by Charlie Calvert*

## IN THIS CHAPTER

This chapter continues the study of CLX and the art of building visual components. More specifically, the components built in this chapter fall into three categories:

- The first group is a set of TEdit, TLabel, and TPanel descendants that show how to change default colors, captions, and fonts.

- The members of the second group are compound components that consist of multiple inherited or aggregated components. This section of the chapter covers building components that consist of several different child components; that is, it shows how to group components together to form new components. Specific examples shown in this book include a panel that comes with two radio buttons and a panel that can host an arbitrary number of check boxes.

- As a bonus, I will show you two controls that you might find useful in your day-to-day programming work. One is a colorful and interactive panel descendant component, the other a compound component that combines a label and an edit control that work together as a single unit. This latter component, presented at the end of the chapter, is used in several other places throughout this book. In the next chapter, I develop other useful controls such as a clock and a nonvisual component that knows how to iterate through subdirectories. You can use the latter control to build programs that search for files, delete all files with a certain extension, and so on.

Components are one of the most important topics in Kylix programming. If you don't understand and use components, you are missing one of Kylix's best features. This chapter is designed to show you the basics, and to go further by teaching you a few of the non-trivial subtleties involved in this topic. In the next chapter, you will take the subject further by looking at several advanced components.

**NOTE**

This chapter contains a lot of information useful to Delphi developers who are porting applications from Windows to Linux. In particular, you will learn how to handle keydown, mousedown, and resizing events, and you will learn how to ensure that your control receives special keystrokes such as the arrow keys. Of special interest is the material presented in the first half of this chapter.

**JAVA, C++, AND VB NOTE**

This chapter covers properties. If you are new to Object Pascal, you will want to pay special attention to these important sections of the chapter.

# Working with Messages

In this section of the chapter you are going to learn about working with messages in CLX. In particular, you will see two components. The first component is a useful component that you might include in your own programs. It shows a simple, and very common, way to handle messages in CLX programs. The second component is designed solely to show you how to do some fairly esoteric things with components. This second component is based on information provided in Chapter 7, "CLX Architecture and Qt."

## Simple Messages: A Useful Control

The component you are about to create reacts when the user waves his mouse over it. You have probably seen this type of thing on a Web page, where the words "roll over" are often associated with similar controls or bitmaps. Using this technique, the portions of the form where the user is currently waving the mouse seem to come alive, as if responding to the user's thoughts by perking up and shining brightly.

My CLX version of this type of component is called TE1fGlowPanel. I'm going to show you a very simple version of this component at the beginning of this chapter. I will offer a rewrite of the component near the end of this chapter, and then again near the end of the next chapter. Each rewrite will add new features culled from the lessons learned in the intervening text. Hopefully you will find the whole process entertaining, as few fields of study in the art of programming are quite as marvelous or thrilling as the act of building components.

> **NOTE**
>
> Besides the TE1fGlowPanel, this chapter and the next consist of many small sample components. That way you will have many easy to understand components that focus in on specific issues. I usually find that multiple small examples are easier to understand than one large block of code. The problem with large examples is that it is hard to focus in on the parts relevant to a particular problem.

**9**

CREATING
COMPONENTS

Listing 9.1 contains the source to the first version of the TE1fGlowPanel component. Notice that I append an A to the control name so it will not be confused with later versions. Figure 9.1 shows a test bed for the component. You can use this latter program to confirm that your unit is working properly.

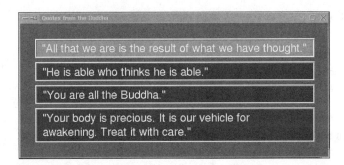

**FIGURE 9.1**

*The* colorForm *program, found in the chap09 directory on the CD that accompanies this book, shows the way the* TE1fGlowPanels *light up when the mouse is passed over them.*

**LISTING 9.1**  The Source for the First Version of the TE1fGlowPanel

```
unit ELFGlowPanelA;

// Copyright © 2001 by Charlie Calvert

interface

uses
  SysUtils, Classes, QGraphics,
  QControls, QForms, QDialogs,
  QExtCtrls;

type
  TElfGlowPanel = class(TPanel)
  protected
    procedure MouseEnter(AControl: TControl); override;
    procedure MouseLeave(AControl: TControl); override;
  public
    constructor Create(AOwner: TComponent); override;
  end;

procedure Register;

implementation

uses
  LCodeBox;

procedure Register;
```

**LISTING 9.1**  Continued

```
begin
  RegisterComponents('Elves', [TElfGlowPanel]);
end;

{ TGlowPanel }

constructor TElfGlowPanel.Create(AOwner: TComponent);
begin
  inherited Create(AOwner);
  BevelInner := bvLowered;
  BevelWidth := 2;
  Color := 6579200;
  ParentColor := False;
  Font.CharSet := fcsLatin1;
  Font.Color := clYellow;
  Font.Height := 24;
  Font.Name := 'Arial';
  Font.Pitch := fpVariable;
  Font.Style := [];
end;

procedure TElfGlowPanel.MouseEnter(AControl: TControl);
begin
  inherited;
  Color := RGB(0, 200, 200); // See LCodeBox for RGB
end;

procedure TElfGlowPanel.MouseLeave(AControl: TControl);
begin
  inherited;
  Color := RGB(0, 100, 100); // See LCodeBox for RGB
end;

end.
```

When scanning the source to this control, you should perceive that it responds to events. In particular, it responds to the movement of the mouse. When the user waves the mouse over the component, it changes the color it is showing.

Notice the constructor for the control:

```
constructor TElfGlowPanel.Create(AOwner: TComponent);
begin
```

```
    inherited Create(AOwner);
    BevelInner := bvLowered;
    BevelWidth := 2;
    Color := 6579200;
    ParentColor := False;
    Font.CharSet := fcsLatin1;
    Font.Color := clYellow;
    Font.Height := 24;
    Font.Name := 'Arial';
    Font.Pitch := fpVariable;
    Font.Style := [];
end;
```

This code is similar to what you saw in the previous chapter. The color, the font, and a few of the other properties of the control are tweaked to give it a particular look and feel. It turns out that the colors you choose when working with this component are very important. If you don't choose the right colors, the control ends up looking horrible. In this constructor, I set the stage for using one set of colors that work fairly well together. An enhanced version of the component would offer the user more choices by providing multiple sets of colors.

## Responding to Messages

Besides the constructor, TElfGlowPanel consists of two methods that change the way the control looks when the mouse moves over it:

```
    procedure MouseEnter(AControl: TControl); override;
    procedure MouseLeave(AControl: TControl); override;
```

Both of these methods use the override directive.

In particular, the first method brightens the shade of color in the control when the mouse wanders across its domain:

```
    Color := RGB(0, 200, 200); // This color is brighter
```

The second method returns the control to its original color:

```
    Color := RGB(0, 100, 100); // This color is darker
```

### A Linux Version of the RGB Function

RGB is not a native CLX function. Instead, it is a method in the LCodeBox unit that ships with this book:

```
    function RGB(Red: Integer; Green: Integer; Blue: Integer): TColor;
    begin
```

```
      Result := QColorColor(QColor_create(Red, Green, Blue));
  end;
```

As you can see, the QColor object that is part of the C++ Qt library is used in CLX programming for creating colors. However, the act of converting a Qt color object into a native Delphi TColor type is a bit painful and unfamiliar to some users. As a result, I wrap it in a custom function called RGB.

Let's look at the RGB function in more depth. QColor is a Qt object, and create is the constructor for this object. QColor_create is therefore a C wrapper around the constructor for this C++ object.

QColorColor is a function from QGraphics.pas that looks like this:

```
  function QColorColor(Color: QColorH): TColor;
  begin
    Result := QColor_red(Color) or (QColor_green(Color) shl 8) or
      (QColor_blue(Color) shl 16);
  end;
```

QColor_red, QColor_green, and QColor_blue are functions in Qt.pas. Each one returns an integer value. The end result is an integer value such as $FF0000.

I find all of this painful to think about, so I just wrap it up in a function called RGB, which converts the standard red, green, and blue components of a color into a native Delphi TColor type. Functions like RGB appear in many other commonly used APIs. For most programmers, it should have a familiar, if not downright cozy, feel. In short, my hope is that it is easier to use than the calling QColorColor on the QColor_create function.

For now, that is all I'm going to say about the TElfGlowPanel. It is a simple component that demonstrates an easy-to-understand technique for adding significant improvements to the behavior of the standard TPanel component.

## Working with FilterEvents in Components

In Chapter 7, there is a long discussion of events that culminates in the section titled "The Night CLX Let Me Down: EventFilter Mojo." The component shown in this section has a strong kinship to the discussion of events provided in Chapter 7. In fact, it is arguable that this component would have made a nice addition to Chapter 7. However, I could not include a full component in Chapter 7 because I had not yet discussed the basic facts about how a component works. By now, however, you are prepared to learn about how events can be filtered in a component.

Rather than rehashing the subject matter covered in Chapter 7, I'll ask you to turn back to that section of the text if you feel that the significance of the material shown in this section is somehow evading you. I believe, however, that the code shown in TElfEventListBox has great significance to people who really want to understand how CLXs works, and who want to solve some of the more complicated programming problems that can arise when working with CLX events.

The component shown in Listing 9.2 demonstrates how to set up your own event filters and event handlers for a control. This control both overrides FilterEvent and also creates a local version of the FilterEvent method called MainEvent. You can switch back and forth between the two events by commenting and uncommenting lines of code in the component.

The program sends debug output to an HTTP server called DebugServer, which is found in the chap05 directory on the CD that comes with this book. The DebugServer is discussed in Chapter 5, "The Editor and Debugger," in the section near the end of the chapter titled "The Elf Debug Server."

The ElfEventListBox is tested in the TestElfEventListBox program found in the Chapter09 directory on the CD that accompanies this book. You can adjust what output is sent to the server and then study the results.

**LISTING 9.2**  The ElfEventListBox Component Is Designed Simply to Show You What Happens When You Start Hooking Events in a CLX Application

```
//////////////////////////////////////////
// Purpose: Show how to use FilterEvents in a component
// Program: The test bed is called TestElfEventListBox
// Copyright © 2001 by Charlie Calvert
//
unit ElfEventListBox;


interface

{ This object sends output to the program DebugServer program
  found in the Chapter05 directory. DebugServer should be running at the same
➥time this component is used.
  Furthermore, make sure the initialization section in
  ElfDebugHelp has the debug output to otHttp. }

uses
  SysUtils, Types, Classes,
  QGraphics, QControls, QForms,
  QDialogs, QStdCtrls, Qt;
```

**LISTING 9.2**  Continued

```pascal
type
  TElfEventListBox = class(TListBox)
  private
  protected
    procedure HookEvents; override;
    function EventFilter(Sender: QObjectH; Event: QEventH): Boolean; override;
    function MainEventFilter(Sender: QObjectH; Event: QEventH): Boolean; cdecl;
    procedure ListViewChanged(); cdecl;
    { Protected declarations }
  public
    { Public declarations }
  published
    { Published declarations }
  end;

procedure Register;

implementation

uses
  ElfDebugHelp, ElfDebugHttp;

procedure Register;
begin
  RegisterComponents('Elves', [TElfEventListBox]);
end;

{ TElfEventListBox }

function TElfEventListBox.EventFilter(Sender: QObjectH;
  Event: QEventH): Boolean;
begin
  //  DBug.WriteEvent('FilterEvent', Event);
  Result := Inherited EventFilter(Sender, Event);

end;

procedure TElfEventListBox.HookEvents;
var
  Method: TMethod;
begin
  inherited;
  TEventFilterMethod(Method) := MainEventFilter;
  Qt_hook_hook_events(Hooks, Method);
```

9

**LISTING 9.2**  Continued

```
  QListBox_selectionChanged_Event(Method) := ListViewChanged;
  QListBox_hook_hook_selectionChanged(QListBox_hookH(Hooks), Method);
end;

procedure TElfEventListBox.ListViewChanged;
begin
  Items.Add('Changed');
end;


function TElfEventListBox.MainEventFilter(Sender: QObjectH;
  Event: QEventH): Boolean;
begin
  DBug.WriteEvent('MainEvent', Event);
  Result := EventFilter(Sender, Event);
end;

end.
```

This component overrides the HookEvent method to change the way events are processed by this component. The major point of the component is simply to show how to use the HookEvent method.

In particular, the new HookEvent method in the component does two things:

- It converts the MainEventFilter method into the primary event filter for the component. Events will now be sent to this method, and not to the EventFilter method in TCustomListBox.

- It also changes the method that handles selection change events for the component. In particular, it makes sure that each time the selection of an item in the list box is changed, the ListViewChanged method is called.

Having accomplished these ends, the component does little else. In fact, it actually ends up sending all the events that reach the MainEventFilter method back to the original TCustomListBox.EventFilter method that CLX uses by default. The point of the component is simply to show you how to use the HookEvent method to change the way a component passes on events.

Here is the key code in the program, as it appears in the HookEvent method:

```
var
  Method: TMethod;
begin
```

```
TEventFilterMethod(Method) := MainEventFilter;
Qt_hook_hook_events(Hooks, Method);
```

The first line sets the variable Method up as a pointer to the MainEventFilter routine. The second line tells clicks that it should send all the list box events to the MainEventFilter method.

Here is an excerpt from the events for the MainEventFilter method:

```
04/01/2001 11:06:25 PM FilterEvent QEventType_Move
04/01/2001 11:06:25 PM FilterEvent QEventType_Resize
04/01/2001 11:06:25 PM FilterEvent QEventType_Show
04/01/2001 11:06:25 PM FilterEvent Unknown: 57176
04/01/2001 11:06:25 PM FilterEvent QEventType_Paint
04/01/2001 11:06:25 PM FilterEvent QEventType_Paint
04/01/2001 11:06:25 PM FilterEvent QEventType_FocusIn
04/01/2001 11:06:27 PM FilterEvent Unknown: 62524
04/01/2001 11:06:27 PM FilterEvent QEventType_KeyPress
04/01/2001 11:06:29 PM FilterEvent QEventType_Paint
04/01/2001 11:06:29 PM FilterEvent QEventType_Paint
04/01/2001 11:06:29 PM FilterEvent Unknown: 62720
```

As you can see, all the key events that occur to the list box are passed on to this method.

I am not going to say anything else about filtering events in this chapter. I ask you to remember that a more in-depth discussion of this subject matter is provided in Chapter 7. The code I show here simply expands on the material in Chapter 7 by showing how it relates to components. In particular, it shows you how to use the HookEvents method.

## Extending the Elves Unit

Now that you have deeper insight into the way CLX works, it's time to put that knowledge to work in a more varied set of examples. The code I'm going to show you now continues the project started in the previous chapter. In particular, it is time to build a series of CLX controls that exercise the power of the Kylix environment. When building these controls, there is no need to root around under the hood as we did when exploring the TElfGlowPanel. Instead, you can use the basic capabilities of the CLX library, much as a programmer would when using the VCL.

It's time now to create a second version of the Elves unit, containing a new edit control, along with two labels and two panels. The additional edits and labels show how quickly you can build on an idea or object when you understand where you're headed. One of the panels shows how you can get rid of the occasionally annoying label that always shows up in the middle of a panel, and the other shows how you can create a single component that contains other components. Specifically, it shows how to create a panel that already comes equipped with two radio buttons. Once you understand how that works, you will see how to make a more useful control that contains a variable number of check boxes.

The code for the new version of the `ElfControls` unit is shown in Listing 9.3, and its test bed appears in Listing 9.4.

**Listing 9.3**  The Second Version of the `ElfControls` Unit Contains Three Compound Components, such as a Descendant of the Glow Panel that Comes Equipped with a Resizable List of Radio Buttons

```
////////////////////////////////////////
// Purpose: Examples of how to create simple components
// Project: Elves.dpk
// Copyright © 2001 by Charlie Calvert
//
unit ElfControls;

{-----------------------------------------------------------------------

  This file contains some very simple components. Though
  some of them are useful, the intent of this file is just
  to provide examples used to teach how to build components.

  Since I use a radio button and check boxes as subcomponents
  in some of these examples, I must register the TRadioButton
  and TCheckBox components in the initialization section for
  this unit.
-----------------------------------------------------------------------}
interface

uses
  Classes, Types, QGraphics,
  QControls, QDialogs, QStdCtrls,
  QExtCtrls, ElfGlowPanelA;

const
  ElfTextColor = TColor($FFFFAA);
  ElfBackColor = TColor($AAAA7F);

  //
  // ElfBackColor = TColor($9696AA);

  // Brown and Yellow
  // ElfTextColor = TColor(clYellow);
  // ElfBackColor = TColor($7FAAAA);


type
  TELFSmallEdit = class(TEdit)
  public
```

**LISTING 9.3**   Continued

```pascal
    constructor Create(AOwner: TComponent); override;
  end;

  TELFBigEdit = class(TELFSmallEdit)
  public
    constructor Create(AOwner: TComponent); override;
  end;

  TELFSmallLabel = class(TLabel)
  public
    constructor Create(AOwner: TComponent); override;
  end;

  TELFBigLabel = class(TELFSmallLabel)
  public
    constructor Create(AOwner: TComponent); override;
  end;

  TELFKeyCheckBox = class(TCheckBox)
  protected
  public
    constructor Create(AOwner: TComponent); override;
  published
    property OnKeyDown;
  end;

  TELFEmptyPanel = class(TPanel)
  public
    constructor Create(AOwner: TComponent); override;
  published
    property OnKeyDown;
  end;

  { This object makes a panel act like a button }
  TELFMousePanel = class(TELFEmptyPanel)
  private
    function XYWithinClient(P: TSmallPoint): Boolean;
  protected
    procedure MouseDown(Button: TMouseButton; Shift: TShiftState;
      X, Y: Integer); override;
    procedure MouseUp(Button: TMouseButton; Shift: TShiftState;
      X, Y: Integer); override;
    procedure KeyDown(var Key: Word; Shift: TShiftState); override;
  public
```

**LISTING 9.3**  Continued

```
    constructor Create(AOwner: TComponent); override;
  end;

  TELFLabelPanel = class(TELFEmptyPanel)
  private
    FLabel: TLabel;
    FPanel: TPanel;
    function GetLabelStr: string;
    procedure SetLabelStr(S: string);
  protected
    procedure TextChanged; override;
  public
    constructor Create(AOwner: TComponent); override;
  published
    property LabelStr: string read GetLabelStr write SetLabelStr;
  end;

  TELFRadio2Panel = class(TELFEmptyPanel)
  private
    FRadio1: TRadiobutton;
    FRadio2: TRadioButton;
    function GetRadio1Caption: string;
    function GetRadio2Caption: string;
    procedure SetRadio1Caption(const Value: string);
    procedure SetRadio2Caption(const Value: string);
  protected
    procedure Resize; override;
  public
    constructor Create(AOwner: TComponent); override;
    property Radio1: TRadioButton read FRadio1;
    property Radio2: TRadioButton read FRadio2;
  published
    property Radio1Caption: string read GetRadio1Caption write
➥SetRadio1Caption;
    property Radio2Caption: string read GetRadio2Caption write
➥SetRadio2Caption;
  end;

  TCheckArray = Array of TCheckBox;

  TELFCheckPanel = class(TELFGlowPanelA)
  private
    FCheckArray: TCheckArray;
    FCaptions: TStrings;
```

**LISTING 9.3**   Continued

```
    function CreateCheck(Index: Integer): TCheckBox;
    procedure SetCaptions(const Value: TStrings);
    procedure CaptionsChange(Sender: TObject);
    procedure MakeButtons(NumButtons: Integer);
    procedure ClearButtons;
  protected
    procedure Resize; override;
  public
    constructor Create(AOwner: TComponent); override;
    destructor Destroy; override;
    function GetCheckBoxes: TCheckArray;
  published
    property Captions: TStrings read FCaptions write SetCaptions;
  end;

procedure Register;

implementation

uses
  SysUtils, LCodeBox;

constructor TELFSmallEdit.Create(AOwner: TComponent);
begin
  inherited Create(AOwner);
  Color := ElfBackColor;
  Font.Color := ElfTextColor;
  Font.Name := 'Times New Roman';
  Font.Size := 12;
  Font.Style := [fsBold];
end;

constructor TElfBigEdit.Create(AOwner: TComponent);
begin
  inherited Create(AOwner);
  Font.Size := 24;
  Width := 170;
end;

constructor TElfSmallLabel.Create(AOwner: TComponent);
begin
  inherited Create(AOwner);
  Color := ElfBackColor;
  Font.Color := ElfTextColor;
```

**LISTING 9.3**  Continued

```pascal
  Font.Name := 'Times New Roman';
  Font.Size := 12;
  Font.Style := [fsBold];
end;

constructor TElfBigLabel.Create(AOwner: TComponent);
begin
  inherited Create(AOwner);
  Font.Size := 24;
end;

constructor TElfKeyCheckBox.Create(AOwner: TComponent);
begin
  inherited;
  InputKeys := InputKeys + [ikArrows];
end;

constructor TElfEmptyPanel.Create(AOwner: TComponent);
begin
  inherited Create(AOwner);
  ControlStyle:= ControlStyle - [csSetCaption];
end;

{ --- TMousePanel --- }

constructor TElfMousePanel.Create(AOwner: TComponent);
begin
  inherited Create(AOwner);
  BevelInner := bvRaised;
  BevelWidth := 2;
end;

procedure TElfMousePanel.KeyDown(var Key: Word; Shift: TShiftState);
begin
  if ssAlt in Shift then
    ShowMessage('The alt key was pressed');
end;

function TElfMousePanel.XYWithinClient(P: TSmallPoint): Boolean;
begin
  Result := (P.X < ClientWidth) and (P.Y < ClientHeight);
end;
```

**LISTING 9.3**  Continued

```
procedure TElfMousePanel.MouseDown(Button: TMouseButton; Shift: TShiftState;
    X, Y: Integer);
begin
  BevelInner := bvLowered;
//  if csCaptureMouse in ControlStyle then
//    SetMouseGrabControl(Self);
end;

procedure TElfMousePanel.MouseUp(Button: TMouseButton; Shift: TShiftState;
    X, Y: Integer);
var
 AOnClick: TNotifyEvent;
begin
  BevelInner := bvRaised;
  inherited;
  SetMouseGrabControl(nil);
  AOnClick := OnClick;
  if Assigned(AOnClick) then
    if XYWithinClient(SmallPoint(x, y)) then
      OnClick(Self);
end;

{ --- TLabelPanel --- }

constructor TElfLabelPanel.Create(AOwner: TComponent);
const
  ATop = 4;
  Aleft = 5;
  ABevelWidth = 2;
begin
  inherited Create(AOwner);

  ParentFont := False;
  BevelInner := bvRaised;
  BevelWidth := ABevelWidth;

  FLabel := TLabel.Create(Self);
  FLabel.Parent := Self;
  FLabel.ParentFont := False;
  FLabel.Left := ALeft;
  FLabel.Top := ATop;
  Flabel.Caption := 'ALabel';
  FLabel.Width := 50;
  FLabel.Show;
```

**LISTING 9.3** Continued

```
  FPanel := TPanel.Create(Self);
  FPanel.Parent := Self;
  FPanel.Top := ATop;
  FPanel.BevelInner := bvRaised;
  FPanel.BevelWidth := ABevelWidth div 2;
  FPanel.Height := Height - (2 * ATop);
  FPanel.Left := FLabel.Width + (FPanel.BevelWidth);
  FPanel.Width := Width - FPanel.Left - (FPanel.BevelWidth * 4);
  Caption := 'FPanel';
  FPanel.ParentFont := False;
  FPanel.Show;
end;

pocedure TElfLabelPanel.TextChanged;
begin
  inherited;
  FPanel.Caption := Caption;
end;

function TElfLabelPanel.GetLabelStr: string;
begin
  Result := FLabel.Caption;
end;

procedure TElfLabelPanel.SetLabelStr(S: string);
var
  Extent: TSize;
begin
  FLabel.Caption := S;
  Extent := Canvas.TextExtent(S);
  FPanel.Left := Extent.cx;
  FPanel.Width := Width - FPanel.Left - (BevelWidth * 2);
  Font.Color := Color;
end;

{ --- TRadio2Panel ---}

constructor TElfRadio2Panel.Create(AOwner: TComponent);
begin
  inherited Create(AOwner);
  Width := 175;
  Height := 60;
```

**LISTING 9.3**   Continued

```
  FRadio1 := TRadioButton.Create(Self);
  FRadio1.Parent := Self;
  FRadio1.Caption := 'Radio1';
  FRadio1.Left := 20;
  FRadio1.Top := 10;
  FRadio1.Show;

  FRadio2 := TRadioButton.Create(Self);
  FRadio2.Parent := Self;
  FRadio2.Caption := 'Radio2';
  FRadio2.Left := 20;
  FRadio2.Top := 32;
  FRadio2.Show;
end;

function TElfRadio2Panel.GetRadio1Caption: string;
begin
  Result := Radio1.Caption;
end;

function TElfRadio2Panel.GetRadio2Caption: string;
begin
  Result := Radio2.Caption;
end;

procedure TElfRadio2Panel.SetRadio1Caption(const Value: string);
begin
  Radio1.Caption := Value;
end;

procedure TElfRadio2Panel.SetRadio2Caption(const Value: string);
begin
  Radio2.Caption := Value;
end;

// In Windows, this was caused by a wm_size message
procedure TElfRadio2Panel.ReSize;
begin
  inherited;
  if FRadio1 <> nil then
    FRadio1.Width := Width - (FRadio1.Left + 15);
  if FRadio2 <> nil then
    FRadio2.Width := Width - (FRadio2.Left + 15);
end;
```

**9**

**CREATING COMPONENTS**

**LISTING 9.3**  Continued

```pascal
procedure Register;
begin
  RegisterComponents('Elves', [TElfSmallEdit, TElfBigEdit, TElfMousePanel,
    TElfSmallLabel, TElfBigLabel, TElfKeyCheckBox, TElfEmptyPanel,
    TElfRadio2Panel, TElfLabelPanel, TElfCheckPanel]);
end;

{ TElfCheckPanel }
constructor TElfCheckPanel.Create(AOwner: TComponent);
begin
  inherited;
  FCaptions := TStringList.Create;
  TStringList(FCaptions).OnChange := CaptionsChange;
  Width := 175;
  Height := 50;
end;

procedure TElfCheckPanel.ClearButtons;
var
  i: Integer;
begin
  for i := 0 to High(FCheckArray) do
    if FCheckArray[i] <> nil then
      FreeAndNil(FCheckArray[i]);
end;

procedure TElfCheckPanel.MakeButtons(NumButtons: Integer);
var
  i: Integer;
begin
  ClearButtons;
  Height := (5 + (20 * NumButtons)) + 15;
  if High(FCheckArray) <> NumButtons then
    SetLength(FCheckArray, NumButtons);
  for i := 0 to NumButtons - 1 do
    FCheckArray[i] := CreateCheck(i);
end;

function TElfCheckPanel.CreateCheck(Index: Integer): TCheckBox;
var
  C: TCheckBox;
begin
  C := TCheckBox.Create(Self);
  Font.Size := 12;
```

**LISTING 9.3**   Continued

```
  Font.Color := clBlack;
  C.Parent := Self;
  C.Caption := FCaptions[Index];
  C.Name := 'Check' + IntToStr(Index);
  C.Left := 20;
  C.Top := 5 + (20 * Index);
  C.Show;
  Result := C;
end;

destructor TElfCheckPanel.Destroy;
begin
  FCaptions.Free;
  inherited;
end;

procedure TElfCheckPanel.CaptionsChange(Sender: TObject);
begin
  MakeButtons(FCaptions.Count);
end;

procedure TElfCheckPanel.Resize;
begin
  inherited;

end;

procedure TElfCheckPanel.SetCaptions(const Value: TStrings);
begin
  FCaptions.Assign(Value);
end;

function TElfCheckPanel.GetCheckBoxes: TCheckArray;
begin
  Result := FCheckArray;
end;

initialization
  RegisterClasses([TRadioButton, TCheckBox]);
end.
```

**LISTING 9.4**   The Test Bed for the `ElfControls` Unit

```
//////////////////////////////////////
// Purpose: Test components from the ElFControls unit
// Project: TestElves.dpr
// Copyright © 1998..2001 by Charlie Calvert
//
unit Main;

interface

uses
  SysUtils, Classes, QGraphics,
  QControls, QForms, QDialogs,
  QExtCtrls, ElfControls, QStdCtrls,
  QComCtrls, QMenus, QTypes,
  ElfGlowPanelA, ElfLabelEdit;

type
  TForm1 = class(TForm)
    PageControl1: TPageControl;
    TabSheet1: TTabSheet;
    TabSheet2: TTabSheet;
    MainMenu1: TMainMenu;
    CreateControlsonTabSheet11: TMenuItem;
    TabSheet3: TTabSheet;
    Button1: TButton;
    ElfLabelEdit1: TElfLabelEdit;
    ELFMousePanel1: TELFMousePanel;
    ELFKeyCheckBox1: TELFKeyCheckBox;
    ELFCheckPanel1: TELFCheckPanel;
    ELFBigEdit1: TELFBigEdit;
    ELFSmallLabel1: TELFSmallLabel;
    ELFSmallEdit1: TELFSmallEdit;
    ELFBigLabel1: TELFBigLabel;
    Memo1: TMemo;
    Exit1: TMenuItem;
    CreateControlsonTabSheet1: TMenuItem;
    procedure CreateControlsonTabSheet11Click(Sender: TObject);
    procedure CCRadio2Panel1Resize(Sender: TObject);
    procedure Button1Click(Sender: TObject);
    procedure Exit1Click(Sender: TObject);
  private
    { Private declarations }
  public
    { Public declarations }
  end;
```

**LISTING 9.4**  Continued

```
var
  Form1: TForm1;

implementation

{$R *.xfm}

{ -------------------------------------------------------------------------
  This method shows an example of how to test a component before you
  place it on the Component Palette. This is always a good idea since
  you may have problems with your component that cause it to generate
  access violations. Since your component becomes part of the Delphi
  itself, access violations in the component can cause instability
  in the IDE. Hence it is often a good idea to test it like this
  first, before compiling it as a component.
  ------------------------------------------------------------------------- }
procedure TForm1.CreateControlsonTabSheet11Click(Sender: TObject);
var
  MyEdit: TElfBigEdit;
  Radio2Panel: TElfRadio2Panel;
begin
  MyEdit := TElfBigEdit.Create(Self);
  MyEdit.Parent := Tabsheet1;
  MyEdit.Text := 'Inheritance!';
  MyEdit.Left := 10;
  MyEdit.Top := 10;
  MyEdit.Width := 200;
  MyEdit.Show;

  Radio2Panel := TElfRadio2Panel.Create(Self);
  Radio2Panel.Parent := TabSheet1;
  Radio2Panel.Left := MyEdit.Left;
  Radio2Panel.Top := MyEdit.Height + MyEdit.Top + 5;
  Radio2Panel.Width := MyEdit.Width;
  Radio2Panel.Radio1Caption := 'Kylix';
  Radio2Panel.Radio2Caption := 'Development';
  Radio2Panel.Radio1.Checked := True;
  Radio2Panel.BevelWidth := 3;
  Radio2Panel.Show;
end;


{ -------------------------------------------------------------------------
  I'm responding to this method just so you can see that OnResize
  events are being handled properly.
  ------------------------------------------------------------------------- }
```

**9**

**CREATING
COMPONENTS**

**LISTING 9.4**   Continued

```
procedure TForm1.CCRadio2Panel1Resize(Sender: TObject);
begin
  //
end;

procedure TForm1.Button1Click(Sender: TObject);
var
  CheckBoxes: TCheckArray;
  S: String;
  i: Integer;
begin
S := '';
  CheckBoxes := ElfCheckPanel1.GetCheckBoxes;
  for i := 0 to ElfCheckPanel1.Captions.Count - 1 do
    if CheckBoxes[i].Checked = True then
      S := S + IntToStr(i + 1) + ' ';
  ShowMessage(S);
end;

procedure TForm1.Exit1Click(Sender: TObject);
begin
  Close;
end;


end.
```

The TestElves program shown here takes some of the key controls from the new
ElfControls.pas unit through their paces. It is very similar to the test bed that you created for
the ElfControlsA.pas unit, only it is a bit more complex.

The TestElves program has a page control on its main form. One page of this control contains
a button that allows you to dynamically create an instance of a component for testing, as
explained in the previous chapter in the section called "Creating Descendants of an Existing
Component." The second page contains actual copies of the controls as they appear when
dropped from the Component Palette. As a result, this program does not load properly unless
you update the Elves.dpk file to contain not only ElfControlsA.pas, but also
ElfControls.pas.

# The Art of Naming CLX Components

If you have two units on your system, both of which contain instances of TElfSmallEdit, it's probably best to uninstall the first instance before trying to install the new instance. Or, you can do as I have done here, and name one version of the control TElfSmallEditA, and the second version TElfSmallEdit. If you don't do this, you may have two files on your system, one called ElvesControlsA.pas and the second called ElvesControls.pas. Both might contain an instance of TElfSmallEdit. Under such circumstances you have to use the Component, Install, Remove menu option to remove the first version of TElfSmallEdit before replacing it with a second version. If you have only one version of TElfSmallEdit, and you just want to update it, there is no need to remove the first instance before installing the updated instance.

The subject matter in the last paragraph also explains why I call my control TElfSmallEdit, rather than simply TSmallEdit. The problem is that there are many developers creating controls, and the chance of a name collision is fairly large. If you append, for instance, your initials before the name of each control you create, the chance of a name collision becomes much smaller. This is not a perfect system, and it is not guaranteed to work, but it certainly improves the odds of things working out correctly.

## The `TElfBigEdit` and `TElfEmptyPanel` Controls

When you've created a component that does something you like, it's easy to create children of it. Class TElfBigEdit descends from TElfSmallEdit:

```
TElfBigEdit = class(TElfSmallEdit)
```

It inherits its font nearly unchanged from TSmallEdit, except that it sets Font.Size to 24, a nice hefty figure that helps the control live up to its name:

```
constructor TElfBigEdit.Create(AOwner: TComponent);
begin
  inherited Create(AOwner);
  Font.Size := 24;
end;
```

This elegant syntax is a good example of how OOP can save you time and trouble while still allowing you to write clear code.

The label controls shown in this code work in exactly the same way the edit controls do, except that they descend from TLabel rather than from TEdit. The TElfEmptyPanel component rectifies one of the petty issues that sometimes annoy me: Every time you put down a panel, it gets a caption. Most of the time, the first thing you do is delete the caption so you can place other controls on it without creating a mess!

Once again, you can change `TPanel` by overriding its constructor. This time, all you need to do is set the `ControlStyle` property:

```
constructor TElfEmptyPanel.Create(AOwner: TComponent);
begin
  inherited Create(AOwner);
  ControlStyle:= ControlStyle - [csSetCaption];
end;
```

Here are the available options for the `ControlStyle` property:

```
TControlStyle = set of (csAcceptsControls, csCaptureMouse,
    csDesignInteractive, csClickEvents, csFramed, csSetCaption, csOpaque,
    csDoubleClicks, csFixedWidth, csFixedHeight, csNoDesignVisible,
    csReplicatable, csNoStdEvents, csDisplayDragImage, csActionClient,
    csMenuEvents, csNoFocus);
```

This book is not the proper place for describing these options in depth. However, they are documented in the online help.

All of these controls are trivial to create. That is however, also their great virtue. Once you understand what a component is and how to go about creating it, it is easy to start building up whole suites of your own components.

## Creating Compound Components

The next new component in this version of the `ElfControls` unit enables you to drop down a panel that comes equipped with two radio buttons. This makes a single control out of a set of components that are often combined. You could create other controls that contained three, four, or more radio buttons. Or, you could even create a panel that would populate itself with a specific number of radio buttons.

The declaration for this new radio button is still fairly simple, but considerably more complex than the declarations you have seen so far:

```
TElfRadio2Panel = class(TElfEmptyPanel)
private
  FRadio1: TRadiobutton;
  FRadio2: TRadioButton;
  function GetRadio1Caption: string;
  function GetRadio2Caption: string;
  procedure SetRadio1Caption(const Value: string);
  procedure SetRadio2Caption(const Value: string);
protected
  procedure WmSize(var Message: TMessage); message wm_Size;
```

```
public
  constructor Create(AOwner: TComponent); override;
  property Radio1: TRadioButton read FRadio1;
  property Radio2: TRadioButton read FRadio2;
published
  property Radio1Caption: string read GetRadio1Caption write
➥SetRadio1Caption;
  property Radio2Caption: string read GetRadio2Caption write
➥SetRadio2Caption;
  end;
```

I will explain the WmSize handler in just one moment, and then after that I will talk about the Radio1Caption and Radio2Caption properties. For now, I want to concentrate on the Radio1 and Radio2 properties.

The actual radio buttons themselves are declared as private data, and access to them is given by the Radio1 and Radio2 properties. This is the way that Kylix performs something called *aggregation*, which is an alternative to multiple inheritance. After declaring these two components as private data and exposing them as properties, you have essentially allowed the TPanel object to inherit the functionality of two radio controls. In other words, it now does everything that a panel does, such as having a border and bevel 3D look, plus everything that you can do with two radio buttons. For all intents and purposes, this is the same thing as multiple inheritance, but it is cleaner, and much less troublesome.

Modifying a property of these radio buttons doesn't require write access to the radio button property, so you don't need to add a write clause. The following statement performs one read of RP.Radio1 and one write to the Caption property of that radio button:

```
RP.Radio1.Caption := 'hello'
```

You don't want write access to the radio button properties, either, because that would allow the user to assign them garbage (or nil). It's a different matter to give the user read and write action to the Caption property of the TRadioButton, since that does no harm. But if they assigned nil or garbage to Radio1 itself, then there could be trouble.

The Create method for the Radio2Panel begins by setting the width and height of the panel:

```
constructor TElfRadio2Panel.Create(AOwner: TComponent);
begin
  inherited Create(AOwner);
  Width := 175;
  Height := 60;

  FRadio1 := TRadioButton.Create(Self);
  FRadio1.Parent := Self;
  FRadio1.Caption := 'Radio1';
```

**9**

```
  FRadio1.Left := 20;
  FRadio1.Top := 10;
  FRadio1.Show;

  FRadio2 := TRadioButton.Create(Self);
  FRadio2.Parent := Self;
  FRadio2.Caption := 'Radio2';
  FRadio2.Left := 20;
  FRadio2.Top := 32;
  FRadio2.Show;
end;
```

The next step is to create the first radio button. Notice that the code passes `Self` as the owner, and sets the parent to the panel itself. The rest of the code in the `Create` method is too trivial to merit comment.

The reason the control sports a `ReSize` handler is simply that the two `RadioControls` have captions that can stick out over the end of the control, creating an unsightly mess. By handling `ReSize` events, you can be sure that these two captions never stick out over the end of the panel:

```
procedure TElfRadio2Panel.ReSize;
begin
  inherited;
  if FRadio1 <> nil then
    FRadio1.Width := Width - (FRadio1.Left + 15);
  if FRadio2 <> nil then
    FRadio2.Width := Width - (FRadio2.Left + 15);
end;
```

The code that controls the widths of the radio buttons is fairly trivial. However, it might be worth talking for a moment about the whole idea of handling `ReSize` events.

---

**NOTE**

In Windows, programmers often handled this same kind of event by responding to wm_Size messages:

```
    procedure WmSize(var Message: TMessage); message wm_Size;
```

This routine would be called every time Windows sends a wm_Size message to the program. Needless to say, this will occur when the control is being resized; for instance, it will be called at program startup. In Qt programming, however, you do not respond to wm_Size messages. Instead, Qt will handle events using its own Signal and Slot mechanism.

In Kylix programming, this kind of event is usually handled by creating an `OnResize` handler. However, I don't want to create an `OnResize` handler for this object because the user of the component may want to create one of their own. Kylix events are simply method pointers pointing at a particular method, and they can't point at two methods at the same time. To avoid a conflict, I override the CLX `ReSize` method, which is the method CLX uses when it responds to `OnResize` events. In particular, the CLX class called `TWinControl` handles these events. `TPanel`, and thus `TElfRadio2Panel`, both descend from `TWinControl`. This means I need to call the inherited `ReSize` handler, or else my control will not work properly. As you can see, the first line of my handler does call inherited, and this means that the event is handled properly, and the user's `OnResize` events will also be called.

I'm almost through describing this control, but it happens there is one last tricky issue that needs to be covered. At the very end of the unit, the `TRadioButton` class is registered:

```
RegisterClasses([TRadioButton]);
```

Registering the `TRadioButton` control would normally occur when you drop an instance of the component on a form. However, the user may never explicitly drop a `TRadioButton` on the form. Dropping the `TElfRadio2Panel` does not automatically create the same effect, as it will cause the `TElfRadio2Panel` to be registered, but would not automatically register a `TRadioButton` object. In particular, the `TRadioButton` is simply created in the constructor for `TElfRadio2Panel`, and is therefore never officially registered with the system. As a result, the safe thing to do is register the component explicitly, as I do here.

When it comes time to test out the `TElfRadio2Panel` object, you can write the following code in the test-bed program to take it through its paces:

```
procedure TForm1.CreateControlsonTabSheet11Click(Sender: TObject);
var
  MyEdit: TElfBigEdit;
  Radio2Panel: TElfRadio2Panel;
begin
  MyEdit := TElfBigEdit.Create(Self);
  MyEdit.Parent := Tabsheet1;
  MyEdit.Text := 'Inheritance!';
  MyEdit.Left := 10;
  MyEdit.Top := 10;
  MyEdit.Width := 200;
  MyEdit.Show;

  Radio2Panel := TElfRadio2Panel.Create(Self);
  Radio2Panel.Parent := TabSheet1;
  Radio2Panel.Left := MyEdit.Left;
  Radio2Panel.Top := MyEdit.Height + MyEdit.Top + 5;
```

```
    Radio2Panel.Width := MyEdit.Width;
    Radio2Panel.Radio1Caption := 'Kylix';
    Radio2Panel.Radio2Caption := 'Development';
    Radio2Panel.Radio1.Checked := True;
    Radio2Panel.BevelWidth := 3;
    Radio2Panel.Show;
end;
```

Here, `Radio2Panel` is declared to be of type `TElfRadio2Panel`. Note that each of the radio buttons that belong to the panel act exactly as you would expect a normal radio button to act, only you have to qualify them differently before you access them. Furthermore, you can access the bevel property of `TPanel` to give your control a fancy 3D look, as shown in Figure 9.2.

**FIGURE 9.2**

*The* `TElfRadio2Panel` *control can use the* `BevelInner`, `BevelOuter`, *and* `BorderWidth` *properties of the* `TPanel` *control to create a fancy 3D look.*

## Creating Published Properties of a Component

A published property of a component appears in the `published` section of the class declaration:

```
TElfRadio2Panel = class(TElfEmptyPanel)
    ... // Code omitted here
published
    property Radio1Caption: string read GetRadio1Caption write SetRadio1Caption;
    property Radio2Caption: string read GetRadio2Caption write SetRadio2Caption;
end;
```

These two published properties will now appear in the Object Inspector. That is the purpose of declaring a property as `published`: it makes it visible in the Object Inspector. In particular, Kylix adds extra runtime type information to these properties so that the IDE can read that information at design time and expose the values of these properties to the user.

If you want, you can surface `Radio1` and `Radio2` as published properties of `TElfRadio2Panel`. However, when you first do so, they will have no property editors available because Kylix has no built-in property editors for `TRadioButtons`. To build your own, you can refer to the discussion of the `Clock` component and some key portions of the Tools API found in the next chapter.

A second, simpler way exists to work around the lack of a default editor. Specifically, you can create custom properties for each of the properties of an aggregated control that you want to surface. In this case, I create properties for the `Radio1Caption` and `Radio2Caption` properties. Both of these properties have `read` and `write` clauses designed to give you automatic access to the `Caption` property of the underlying radio button control:

```
function TElfRadio2Panel.GetRadio1Caption: string;
begin
  Result := Radio1.Caption;
end;

procedure TElfRadio2Panel.SetRadio1Caption(const Value: string);
begin
  Radio1.Caption := Value;
end;
```

As you can see, these are very simple methods that just expose the underlying `Radio1.Caption` property inside the Object Inspector.

> **NOTE**
>
> Remember that when you are declaring properties like this, much of the grunt work can be performed by Kylix. All you need do is declare the properties themselves:
>
> ```
> property Radio1Caption: string read GetRadio1Caption write
> ➥SetRadio1Caption;
> ```
>
> Once you've done this, you can press Ctrl+Shift+C and Kylix will automatically create the declaration and outline for the implementation of the `GetRadio1Caption` and `SetRadio1Caption` methods. In this case you will still have to fill in the single line of each implementation, but the header and `begin..end` pair for the methods is generated automatically.

I should perhaps add that there is nothing wrong with asking the user to write `Radio1.Caption` instead of giving him a `Radio1Caption` property. The only reason I am creating this property is simply so that it can be exposed easily in the Object Inspector itself.

## A Note on Streaming Properties

Before closing this section, I'd like to add some additional notes about how Kylix handles streaming chores. The good news is that most of the time, you do not have to concern yourself with streaming the properties for a component. Kylix handles most streaming chores automatically. In particular, it automatically streams `published` properties that are simple types. Furthermore, many commonly used complex types already have property editors that ship with

**9**

**CREATING COMPONENTS**

Kylix. For instance, the Font property of a TEdit control is not a simple type. In fact, it is an object with many complex properties. However, you do not need to worry about streaming Font properties because Kylix already has built-in code to handle that task. There are only limited circumstances under which you must explicitly stream the fields of your object.

If a property type is a TComponent or descendant, the streaming system assumes it must create an instance of that type when reading it in. In other words, if you place a TComponent or descendant object on a form, Kylix automatically tries to stream that component when you close or open a form at design time. In particular, it streams the information into the *.xfm file for your form. All forms have these .xfm files, and their purpose is to hold the streamed information that describes your form. For instance, if you set the Width property of your form to 400, that information will automatically be streamed out to the .xfm file for your form.

What all this boils down to is that you don't have to worry about writing custom code to stream the Radio1Caption and Radio2Caption properties into an XFM file. That chore is taken care of for you automatically by the system. The only time you would have to start streaming a property would be if you declared it to be of some type, such as a record, that Kylix did not already know. In that case you would have to build your own property editor. In general, such cases are very rare, and you can usually assume that Kylix will handle the streaming for you automatically.

Automatic streaming of properties may not be big news to some readers. However, back in the bad old days of DOS and the TurboVision library, everyone had to do their own streaming, which proved to be a non-trivial, and error prone process. We all owe a note of thanks to the Borland Object Pascal team for implementing this feature for us so that we could be spared a great deal of pain and trouble. Kylix would not be nearly as easy to use if we had to stream our own properties!

## A Second Compound Component

Now that you know how to make compound components, let's create a second one that will be both a bit more complex, and also significantly more useful in a real life situation. The TElfCheckPanel provides a group of check boxes that are easy to construct and easy to use together as a single unit.

The TElfCheckPanel component is much like the TRadioGroup component found on the Standard page of the Component Palette. It also resembles the TCheckListBox component from the Additional page of the Component Palette.

Figure 9.3 shows how you can click on the Captions property of the TElfCheckPanel to enter a list of captions for your check boxes. After you enter the list, you can click the green Run button from the Kylix toolbar, or choose the Run command from the Run menu, and see your component in action, as shown in Figure 9.4.

**FIGURE 9.3**

*To create the check boxes in the* TElfCheckPanel *you simply fill in the* Captions *property for the check boxes you want to create.*

**FIGURE 9.4**

*At runtime, you can see the components you created in the* Captions *property editor.*

TElfCheckPanel is a descendant of TElfGlowPanel. As a result, it responds automatically when the user waves the mouse over it. By inheriting the properties of TElfGlowPanel, the TElfCheckPanel component illustrates the principle of inheritance. More importantly, it shows how the strongly OOP-based nature of CLX helps you leverage the power of OOP in your components. Not all component libraries are truly object oriented. One of the great strengths of CLX is that its components are also true objects.

The TElfCheckPanel is part of the ElfControls unit. However, Listing 9.5 shows you only the code that relates to TElfCheckPanel.

**LISTING 9.5**  The TElfCheckPanel Component Maintains a User-defined List of TCheckBoxes on Top of a TElfGlowPanel

```
unit ElfControls;

interface

uses
  Classes, Types, QGraphics,
  QControls, QDialogs, QStdCtrls,
  QExtCtrls, CCGlowPanelA;
```

**LISTING 9.5**  Continued

```pascal
type
  // Declaration for other controls omitted here

  TElfCheckPanel = class(TElfGlowPanelA)
  private
    FCheckArray: TCheckArray;
    FCaptions: TStrings;
    function CreateCheck(Index: Integer): TCheckBox;
    procedure SetCaptions(const Value: TStrings);
    procedure CaptionsChange(Sender: TObject);
    procedure MakeButtons(NumButtons: Integer);
    procedure ClearButtons;
  protected
    procedure Resize; override;
  public
    constructor Create(AOwner: TComponent); override;
    destructor Destroy; override;
    function GetCheckBoxes: TCheckArray;
  published
    property Captions: TStrings read FCaptions write SetCaptions;
  end;

implementation

// implementation for other control omitted here

{ TElfCheckPanel }

constructor TElfCheckPanel.Create(AOwner: TComponent);
begin
  inherited;
  FCaptions := TStringList.Create;
  TStringList(FCaptions).OnChange := CaptionsChange;
  Width := 175;
  Height := 50;
end;

procedure TElfCheckPanel.ClearButtons;
var
  i: Integer;
begin
  for i := 0 to High(FCheckArray) do
    if FCheckArray[i] <> nil then
      FreeAndNil(FCheckArray[i]);
end;
```

**LISTING 9.5** Continued

```
procedure TElfCheckPanel.MakeButtons(NumButtons: Integer);
var
  i: Integer;
begin
  ClearButtons;
  Height := (5 + (20 * NumButtons)) + 15;
  if High(FCheckArray) <> NumButtons then
    SetLength(FCheckArray, NumButtons);
  for i := 0 to NumButtons - 1 do
    FCheckArray[i] := CreateCheck(i);
end;

function TElfCheckPanel.CreateCheck(Index: Integer): TCheckBox;
var
  C: TCheckBox;
begin
  C := TCheckBox.Create(Self);
  Font.Size := 12;
  Font.Color := clBlack;
  C.Parent := Self;
  C.Caption := FCaptions[Index];
  C.Name := 'Check' + IntToStr(Index);
  C.Left := 20;
  C.Top := 5 + (20 * Index);
  C.Show;
  Result := C;
end;

destructor TElfCheckPanel.Destroy;
begin
  FCaptions.Free;
  inherited;
end;

procedure TElfCheckPanel.CaptionsChange(Sender: TObject);
begin
  MakeButtons(FCaptions.Count);
end;

procedure TElfCheckPanel.Resize;
begin
  inherited;

end;
```

**LISTING 9.5** Continued

```
procedure TElfCheckPanel.SetCaptions(const Value: TStrings);
begin
  FCaptions.Assign(Value);
end;

function TElfCheckPanel.GetCheckBoxes: TCheckArray;
begin
  Result := FCheckArray;
end;

initialization
  RegisterClasses([TRadioButton, TCheckBox]);
end.
```

Clearly the most interesting part of this component involves the act of creating new check boxes at design time by simply typing entries into an edit control. How does the component convert these simple text entries into actual instances of the TCheckBox component?

To understand what is happening it is best to start at the beginning, with the component's constructor:

```
constructor TElfCheckPanel.Create(AOwner: TComponent);
begin
  inherited;
  FCaptions := TStringList.Create;
  TStringList(FCaptions).OnChange := CaptionsChange;
  Width := 175;
  Height := 50;
end;
```

As you can see, the first thing the component does is create an instance of the TStringList object called FCaptions. A TStringList object can be thought of as little more than a glorified linked list of strings. Among its many useful traits is the capability to hold an object associated with each string, as well as provide routines for maintaining the list.

Whenever items are added or deleted from the TStringList, it produces an OnChange event. The OnChange event for this object is set to the CaptionsChange method, which in turn calls the MakeButtons method.

```
procedure TElfCheckPanel.CaptionsChange(Sender: TObject);
begin
  MakeButtons(FCaptions.Count);
end;
```

```
procedure TElfCheckPanel.MakeButtons(NumButtons: Integer);
var
  i: Integer;
begin
  ClearButtons;
  Height := (5 + (20 * NumButtons)) + 15;
  if High(FCheckArray) <> NumButtons then
    SetLength(FCheckArray, NumButtons);
  for i := 0 to NumButtons - 1 do
    FCheckArray[i] := CreateCheck(i);
end;
```

The `TElfCheckPanel` object maintains an array of `TCheckBoxes` called `FCheckArray`:

```
TCheckArray = Array of TCheckBox;
FCheckArray: TCheckArray;
```

The `MakeButtons` method only gets called when the user adds items to the `FCaptions` `TStringList` object. In one second, I will explain how items get added to that list. But first, let's clear up the issue of what happens in the `MakeButtons` method.

The first thing `MakeButtons` does is call `ClearButtons` to empty out this array of check boxes:

```
procedure TElfCheckPanel.ClearButtons;
var
  i: Integer;
begin
  for i := 0 to High(FCheckArray) do
    if FCheckArray[i] <> nil then
      FreeAndNil(FCheckArray[i]);
end;
```

As you learned in Chapter 3, "Basic Pascal Syntax," the `High` function returns the high end of the range of items in a dynamic array. As a result, you do not need to keep track of how many items are in the array. You can change the number of items at any time, and retrieve the current number of items from the `High` function. `ClearButtons` simply iterates from 0 to the number of items in the `FCheckArray`. Along the way, it checks to make sure that all the items in the list have been deleted and set to nil.

The `MakeButtons` method is passed a single parameter that tracks the number of items in the `FCaptions` list:

```
procedure TElfCheckPanel.CaptionsChange(Sender: TObject);
begin
  MakeButtons(FCaptions.Count);
end;
```

**9**

MakeButtons uses this parameter to ensure that the FCheckArray has room to hold one TCheckBox object for each item the user entered in the FCaptions array:

```
if High(FCheckArray) <> NumButtons then
  SetLength(FCheckArray, NumButtons);
```

The technique of using the SetLength function to resize an array was covered in Chapter 3. Here you can see it put to good use.

The last lines in the MakeButtons function actually create the instances of the TCheckBox object:

```
for i := 0 to NumButtons - 1 do
  FCheckArray[i] := CreateCheck(i);
```

The CreateCheck method is the longest in the component, but it is also one of the most obvious:

```
function TElfCheckPanel.CreateCheck(Index: Integer): TCheckBox;
var
  C: TCheckBox;
begin
  C := TCheckBox.Create(Self);
  Font.Size := 12;
  Font.Color := clBlack;
  C.Parent := Self;
  C.Caption := FCaptions[Index];
  C.Name := 'Check' + IntToStr(Index);
  C.Left := 20;
  C.Top := 5 + (20 * Index);
  C.Show;
  Result := C;
end;
```

There is a lot of code here, but all that really happens is that an instance of the TCheckBox object is created, and then its basic properties are filled in by the most obvious and intuitive manner possible. Note in particular, however, the line that assigns the check box caption property to the currently indexed item of the FCaptions array.

By now you have seen how the MakeButtons method quickly and efficiently disposes of the old array of check boxes and creates a new array. There is, however, one line left in the method that has not been covered:

```
Height := (5 + (20 * NumButtons)) + 15;
```

This line sets the height of the entire TElfGlowPanel on which the list of check boxes resides. In particular, it makes sure the TElfGlowPanel is just tall enough to hold all the check boxes.

(This line of code could be improved by using the TextHeight routine in the TCanvas object to calculate the current height of the font used for the caption of the TCheckBoxes.)

The only secret the TElfCheckPanel has left to conceal is how it gets the information typed in the Captions property into the FCaptions string list. Foregoing an appeal to the component's modesty, let's also take a moment to explore that topic by examining the SetCaptions method:

```
procedure TElfCheckPanel.SetCaptions(const Value: TStrings);
begin
  FCaptions.Assign(Value);
end;
```

This method is passed an instance of the TStrings object. TStringList descends from TStrings. As a result, through the principles of polymorphism, you are allowed to assign an instance of the TStrings object to an instance of the TStringList object. That is, in fact, exactly what the SetCaptions method does. The question, then, is where does the TStrings object come from?

The SetCaptions method is assigned to the FCaptions property, which is of type TStrings:

```
property Captions: TStrings read FCaptions write SetCaptions;
```

This declaration for the Captions property ensures that the SetCaptions method is called whenever the user edits the Captions property. Furthermore, the property editor for the Captions property allows the user to create a TStrings object. When the user is done creating the object, the instance of the TStrings object that the user created is then assigned to the FCaptions TStringList object.

> **NOTE**
>
> Some readers might be wondering why the Captions property behaves as it does. In particular, when you click on the Captions property, an ellipsis (...) button appears. If you click on the button, a dialog opens that contains a TMemo control. You can use this control to enter the captions of the TCheckBox objects that you want to create. It happens that the TMemo control holds its list of lines of text in an object of type TStrings. When you are done entering your list of strings in the memo control, you close the dialog. The list you have created is then assigned to the TStringList object. The question, of course, is how the property editor for the Captions property learned the fancy trick of popping open a dialog that contains a memo control. Now that you understand the issue at hand, I'm going to have to tell you that the answer is in Chapter 10, "Advanced Component Design." In particular, that chapter will describe how to create both property and component editors. While reading about that subject, you will learn how to teach a property editor to pop up a dialog that contains other controls such as a TMemo.

**9**

**CREATING COMPONENTS**

It has taken me a moment to explain the `TElfCheckPanel`. However, the code for the component itself is actually quite short. One of the remarkable things about CLX is its capability to allow you to create powerful components with relatively few lines of code. Furthermore, the Object Pascal syntax is so clean, easy to read, and logical, that even complex components are easy to write, use, and understand.

## Creating a Combined `TLabel` and `TEdit` Component

By this time you have enough knowledge in your head to start making real components that will be of some genuine use in your own programs. To help you get started, I'll show a `TElfLabelEdit` component. This control combines a label and an edit control into one component, as shown in Figure 9.5. This control is one I use all the time, as it automates the boring task of placing a label and edit control on a form, and laboriously lining them up correctly. The source for the control is shown in Listing 9.6.

**FIGURE 9.5**

*A `TElfLabelEdit` component combines a label control and an edit control into one entity.*

---

**LISTING 9.6**    The Source for the `TElfLabelEdit` Control

```
/////////////////////////////////////
// Purpose: An edit control and label control that work as one unit.
// Project: Elves.dpk
// Copyright © 1998..2001 by Charlie Calvert
//
unit ElfLabelEdit;

{-------------------------------------------------------------------
  This is an edit control and a label control that work as
  one unit. It should be part of the ElfControls.dpk file
  and is stored in Elves page of the Component Palette.
-------------------------------------------------------------------}

interface
```

**LISTING 9.6**   Continued

```
uses
  SysUtils, Types, Classes,
  QGraphics, QControls, QForms,
  QDialogs, QStdCtrls, Qt;

type
  TTextType = (ttNone, ttInset, ttEmbossed);
  TLabelType = (ltTop, ltBottom, ltLeft, ltRight);

  { I never could figure out the CLX label component,
    so I inherit directly from TCustomControl. }
  TElfLabel = class(TCustomControl)
  private
    FTextType: TTextType;
    procedure SetTextType(const Value: TTextType);
    function TextWidth(S: string): Integer;
    function GetLabelText: WideString;
  protected
    procedure DoDrawText(var Rect: TRect; Flags: Longint);
    procedure Paint; override;
  public
    constructor Create(AOwner: TComponent); override;
  published
    property TextType: TTextType read FTextType write SetTextType;
  end;

  TElfLabelEdit = class(TCustomControl)
  private
    FEdit: TEdit;
    FLabelGap: Integer;
    FGap: Integer;
    FLabel: TElfLabel;
    FLabelType: TLabelType;
    function GetEditText: string;
    function GetLabelText: string;
    procedure SetLabelText(const Value: string);
    procedure SetEditText(const Value: string);
    function GetEditReadOnly: Boolean;
    function GetEditVisible: Boolean;
    function GetLabelVisible: Boolean;
    function GetTextType: TTextType;
    procedure SetEditReadOnly(const Value: Boolean);
    procedure SetPositionBottom;
    procedure SetPositionLeft;
```

9

CREATING
COMPONENTS

**LISTING 9.6**   Continued

```
    procedure SetPositionRight;
    procedure SetPositionTop;
    procedure SetEditVisible(Value: Boolean);
    procedure SetGap(Value: Integer);
    procedure SetLabelType(Value: TLabelType);
    procedure SetLabelVisible(Value: Boolean);
    procedure SetTextType(const Value: TTextType);
    function GetEditColor: TColor;
    procedure SetEditColor(const Value: TColor);
  protected
    procedure Resize; override;
    procedure FontChanged; override;
    procedure ShowingChanged; override;
  public
    constructor Create(AOwner: TComponent); override;
    property Edit: TEdit read FEdit write FEdit;
    property CSCLabel: TElfLabel read FLabel write FLabel;
  published
    property EditColor: TColor read GetEditColor write SetEditColor;
    property EditReadOnly: Boolean read GetEditReadOnly write SetEditReadOnly;
    property EditText: string read GetEditText write SetEditText;
    property EditVisible: Boolean read GetEditVisible write SetEditVisible;
    property Font;
    property Gap: Integer read FGap write SetGap;
    property LabelPosition: TLabelType read FLabelType write SetLabelType;
    property LabelText: string read GetLabelText write SetLabelText;
    property LabelTextType: TTextType read GetTextType write SetTextType;
    property LabelVisible: Boolean read GetLabelVisible write SetLabelVisible;
  end;

procedure Register;

implementation

procedure Register;
begin
  RegisterComponents('Elves', [TElfLabelEdit, TElfLabel]);
end;

{ TLabelEdit }

// This was a cmFontChanged message handler
// Check out the BroadCast and NotifyControls methods
// of TWidgetControl
```

**LISTING 9.6**   Continued

```pascal
procedure TElfLabelEdit.FontChanged; //
begin
  inherited;
  case LabelPosition of
    ltTop: begin
      FEdit.Top := FLabel.Top + FLabel.Height + 5;
      Height := FEdit.Top + FEdit.Height + 5;
    end;
  end;
end;

constructor TElfLabelEdit.Create(AOwner: TComponent);
begin
  inherited Create(AOwner);
  FGap := 5;
  FLabelGap := 2;
  Width := 200;
  Height := 50;

  FLabel := TElfLabel.Create(Self);
  FLabel.Parent := Self;
  FLabel.Caption := 'Temp';

  FEdit := TEdit.Create(Self);
  FEdit.Parent := Self;

  FLabelType := ltTop;
  FLabel.Visible := True;
  FEdit.Visible := True;
end;

function TElfLabelEdit.GetEditReadOnly: Boolean;
begin
  Result := FEdit.ReadOnly;
end;

function TElfLabelEdit.GetEditText: string;
begin
  Result := FEdit.Text;
end;

function TElfLabelEdit.GetEditVisible: Boolean;
begin
  Result := FEdit.Visible;
end;
```

**LISTING 9.6** Continued

```pascal
function TElfLabelEdit.GetLabelText: string;
begin
  Result := FLabel.Caption;
end;

function TElfLabelEdit.GetLabelVisible: Boolean;
begin
  Result := FLabel.Visible;
end;

function TElfLabelEdit.GetTextType: TTextType;
begin
  Result := FLabel.TextType;
end;

procedure TElfLabelEdit.SetEditReadOnly(const Value: Boolean);
begin
  FEdit.ReadOnly := Value;
end;

procedure TElfLabelEdit.SetEditText(const Value: string);
begin
  FEdit.Text := Value;
end;

procedure TElfLabelEdit.SetEditVisible(Value: Boolean);
begin
  FEdit.Visible := Value;
end;

procedure TElfLabelEdit.SetGap(Value: Integer);
begin
  FGap := Value;
  Self.RePaint;
end;

procedure TElfLabelEdit.SetLabelText(const Value: string);
begin
  FLabel.Caption := Value;
end;

procedure TElfLabelEdit.SetLabelType(Value: TLabelType);
```

**LISTING 9.6**   Continued

```
begin
  FLabelType := Value;
  case FLabelType of
    ltBottom: SetPositionBottom;
    ltLeft: SetPositionLeft;
    ltRight: SetPositionRight;
    ltTop: SetPositionTop;
  end;
  Self.RePaint;
end;

procedure TElfLabelEdit.SetLabelVisible(Value: Boolean);
begin
  FLabel.Visible := Value;
end;

procedure TElfLabelEdit.SetPositionBottom;
begin
  FEdit.Left := FGap;
  FEdit.Top := FGap;
  FEdit.Width := Width - (FGap * 2);
  FLabel.Left := FEdit.Left;
  FLabel.Top := FEdit.Top + FEdit.Height + FGap;
  FLabel.Width := FLabel.Canvas.TextWidth(FLabel.Text) + FLabelGap;
  FLabel.Height := 15;
end;

procedure TElfLabelEdit.SetPositionLeft;
begin
  FLabel.Left := FGap;
  FLabel.Top := FGap;
  FLabel.Width := FLabel.Canvas.TextWidth(FLabel.Text) + FLabelGap;
  FLabel.Height := 15;

  FEdit.Left := FLabel.Width + FGap;
  FEdit.Top := FLabel.Top;
  FEdit.Width := Width - FEdit.Left - FGap;
end;

procedure TElfLabelEdit.SetPositionRight;
begin
  FLabel.Width := Canvas.TextWidth(FLabel.Text) + FLabelGap;
  FEdit.Left := FGap;
  FEdit.Top := FGap;
  FEdit.Width := Width - FLabel.Width - FGap;
```

**LISTING 9.6**  Continued

```pascal
    FLabel.Left := FEdit.Width + FGap;
    FLabel.Top := FEdit.Top;
    FLabel.Width := FLabel.TextWidth(FLabel.Text) + FLabelGap;
    FLabel.Height := 15;

end;

procedure TElfLabelEdit.SetPositionTop;
begin
  FLabel.Left := FGap;
  FLabel.Top := FGap;
  FLabel.Width := FLabel.Canvas.TextWidth(FLabel.Text) + FLabelGap;
  FLabel.Height := 15;

  FEdit.Left := FLabel.Left;
  FEdit.Top := FLabel.Top + FLabel.Height + FGap;
  FEdit.Width := Width - (FGap * 2);
end;

procedure TElfLabelEdit.SetTextType(const Value: TTextType);
begin
  FLabel.TextType := Value;
end;

procedure TElfLabelEdit.ShowingChanged;
begin
  inherited;
  if (csDesigning in ComponentState) then
    LabelPosition := FLabelType;
end;

procedure TElfLabelEdit.Resize;
begin
  inherited;
  if FEdit <> nil then
    FEdit.Width := Width - (FEdit.Left + 5);
end;

{ TElfLabel }

constructor TElfLabel.Create(AOwner: TComponent);
begin
  inherited;
  FTextType := ttInset;
end;
```

**LISTING 9.6** Continued

```
function TElfLabel.GetLabelText: WideString;
begin
  //For compatibility. Not used by Qt Label.
  Result := Caption;
end;

procedure TElfLabel.DoDrawText(var Rect: TRect; Flags: Integer);
var
  Text: string;
  HighColor: TColor;
  LowColor: TColor;
  SaveColor: TColor;
  ThreeDRect: TRect;
begin
  Text := GetLabelText;
  if not Enabled then begin
    Canvas.Font.Color := clBtnHighlight;
    Canvas.TextOut(0, 0, Text);
    Canvas.Font.Color := clBtnShadow;
    Canvas.TextOut(1, 1, Text);
  end else begin
    case FTextType of
      ttInset: begin
        HighColor := clBtnHighLight;
        LowColor := clBtnShadow;
      end;

      ttEmbossed: begin
        HighColor := clBtnShadow;
        LowColor := clBtnHighLight;
      end;

      else begin
        HighColor := clBtnShadow;
        LowColor := clBtnHighLight;
      end;
    end;

    if TextType in [ttInset, ttEmbossed] then begin
      SaveColor := Canvas.Font.Color;

      // Draw One Way
      Canvas.Font.Color := HighColor;
      Canvas.TextOut(0, 0, Text);
```

9

CREATING
COMPONENTS

**LISTING 9.6**   Continued

```
      // Draw the Other Way
      ThreeDRect := Rect;
      Canvas.Font.Color := LowColor;
      Canvas.TextOut(2, 2, Text);

      Canvas.Font.Color := SaveColor;
    end;

    // Draw Regular
    Canvas.TextRect(Rect, 1, 1, Text);
  end;
end;

procedure TElfLabel.SetTextType(const Value: TTextType);
begin
  FTextType := Value;
  Invalidate;
end;

function TElfLabel.TextWidth(S: string): Integer;
begin
  Result := Canvas.TextWidth(S);
end;

procedure TElfLabel.Paint;
var
  R: TRect;
begin
  inherited;
  R := BoundsRect;
  DoDrawText(R, 0);
end;

function TElfLabelEdit.GetEditColor: TColor;
begin
  Result := Edit.Color;
end;

procedure TElfLabelEdit.SetEditColor(const Value: TColor);
begin
  Edit.Color := Value;
end;

end.
```

This object is a good deal like the `Radio2Panel` control, only considerably more useful. Consider the following declaration:

```
TElfLabelEdit = class(TCustomControl)
  private
    FEdit: TEdit;
    FLabelGap: Integer;
    FGap: Integer;
    FLabel: TElfLabel;
    FLabelType: TLabelType;
    function GetEditText: string;
    function GetLabelText: string;
    procedure SetLabelText(const Value: string);
    procedure SetEditText(const Value: string);
    function GetEditReadOnly: Boolean;
    function GetEditVisible: Boolean;
    function GetLabelVisible: Boolean;
    function GetTextType: TTextType;
    procedure SetEditReadOnly(const Value: Boolean);
    procedure SetPositionBottom;
    procedure SetPositionLeft;
    procedure SetPositionRight;
    procedure SetPositionTop;
    procedure SetEditVisible(Value: Boolean);
    procedure SetGap(Value: Integer);
    procedure SetLabelType(Value: TLabelType);
    procedure SetLabelVisible(Value: Boolean);
    procedure SetTextType(const Value: TTextType);
    function GetEditColor: TColor;
    procedure SetEditColor(const Value: TColor);
  protected
    procedure Resize; override;
    procedure FontChanged; override;
    procedure ShowingChanged; override;
  public
    constructor Create(AOwner: TComponent); override;
    property Edit: TEdit read FEdit write FEdit;
    property CSCLabel: TElfLabel read FLabel write FLabel;
  published
    property EditColor: TColor read GetEditColor write SetEditColor;
    property EditReadOnly: Boolean read GetEditReadOnly write SetEditReadOnly;
    property EditText: string read GetEditText write SetEditText;
    property EditVisible: Boolean read GetEditVisible write SetEditVisible;
    property Font;
```

```
    property Gap: Integer read FGap write SetGap;
    property LabelPosition: TLabelType read FLabelType write SetLabelType;
    property LabelText: string read GetLabelText write SetLabelText;
    property LabelTextType: TTextType read GetTextType write SetTextType;
    property LabelVisible: Boolean read GetLabelVisible write SetLabelVisible;
  end;
```

You can see that this control aggregates one custom designed label and one edit control. It has three key properties:

- One for reading and writing the caption of the label.

- One for reading and writing the caption of the edit control.

- One for changing the font of the label and edit control. Notice that I don't have to declare the get and set methods for the Font control. This is because the Font control is inherited from TCustomControl by way of TControl, and all I have to do here is surface it as a published property. In TControl, the Font property is declared as protected, which means it will not show up in the Object Inspector. My code here says only that I want the property to be visible to the user in the Object Inspector.

This control is superficially similar to the TElfRadio2Panel. The big difference here is that this control descends from something called TCustomControl, rather than from a known control such as TPanel. This means that TElfLabelEdit doesn't inherit the fancy border and bevel technology found in an panel control. On the other hand, it doesn't carry the baggage associated with a TPanel control either. Not that a TPanel control is all that bulky, but it has properties that this control doesn't need, such as a bevel and border, so why include them?

All TElfLabelEdit really directly inherits is the capability to be a visual component that can have width and height, and can be stored on the Component Palette. This is exactly what you need in this case, while TPanel would be overkill.

It turns out that there are several different base classes like TCustomControl that you can descend from if you want to create a control that has only generic component-based technology, without having any specific functionality such as you find in a TEdit or a TPanel. I descended TElfSmallEdit from TEdit because I wanted to inherit the capabilities of an edit control, and I inherited to TElfRadioPanel from TPanel because I wanted to inherit the bevel and border capabilities of TPanel. I inherited TElfLableEdit from TCustomControl because all I really wanted was a control that had width and height, and that could be placed on the Component Palette.

> **NOTE**
>
> As I imply in the last few paragraphs, there is actually a bit more to the story of `TCustomControl` than I cover in this chapter. However, I want to cover the nitty gritty aspects of this subject in the next chapter, where I will have more room to maneuver, and when your mind is fresh and ready for a new topic. For now, all you really need to know is that you can create a component by descending from `TCustomControl`, and in the next chapter I will explain the details of this rather involved subject.
>
> I should add, however, that descending from `TCustomControl` gives a component very little overhead compared to what you find when you create an ActiveX control. Even the best ActiveX controls tend to be a bit bulky, while `TCustomControl` is really a very lightweight ancestor.

Here is the constructor for this control:

```
constructor TElfLabelEdit.Create(AOwner: TComponent);
begin
  inherited Create(AOwner);
  FGap := 5;
  FLabelGap := 2;
  Width := 200;
  Height := 50;

  FLabel := TElfLabel.Create(Self);
  FLabel.Parent := Self;
  FLabel.Caption := 'Temp';

  FEdit := TEdit.Create(Self);
  FEdit.Parent := Self;

  FLabelType := ltTop;
  FLabel.Visible := True;
  FEdit.Visible := True;
end;
```

As you can see, this method creates both a label and an edit control, assigns them a width and height, some default text values, and then makes them visible. In this case I make the controls visible by setting the `Visible` property to `True`, which is much the same as calling their `Show` method. Notice that I do not hard code in the values for the edit control, but rather let it be defined by values assigned to the label control.

Like the TElfRadio2Panel, this control responds to resizing events:

```
procedure TElfLabelEdit.Resize;
begin
  inherited;
  if FEdit <> nil then
    FEdit.Width := Width - (FEdit.Left + 5);
end;
```

The effect of this code is to ensure that the edit control is always more or less the same width as the underlying TCustomControl. That way, when the user resizes the entire component, the edit control follows suit in a logical and well-behaved manner.

Somewhat more complex is the behavior that occurs when you change the font of the control. The font of the TCustomControl is automatically transferred to the edit and label controls because they have TCustomControl as an owner. In particular, they all respond to a Qt font changed message that gets propagated by the owner up the tree to the children.

When the font inside these controls is changed, they might no longer be arranged correctly on the form. That is why my descendant of TCustomControl responds to these messages and makes the appropriate changes to the appearance of the control:

```
procedure TElfLabelEdit.FontChanged; //
begin
  inherited;
  case LabelPosition of
    ltTop: begin
      FEdit.Top := FLabel.Top + FLabel.Height + 5;
      Height := FEdit.Top + FEdit.Height + 5;
    end;
  end;
end;
```

In particular, notice that I adjust the location of the edit control and the bottom of the entire control so that they can accommodate the new font size. This code works if the font is being made either larger or smaller.

The TElfLabelEdit control is one that I find incredibly useful. There is something in my constitution that does not enjoy messing around with forms and ensuring that all their controls are the right height and width. This simple control eliminates a good deal of the petty work required in such situations, and it ensures that each edit and label pair will be lined up exactly right, to the pixel.

## Changing the Position of the Label

The label in the label edit control can appear on the top of the edit control, to its right, to its left, and below it. This concept is captured in the TLabelEdit enumerated type, and in the LabelPosition property:

```
TLabelType = (ltTop, ltBottom, ltLeft, ltRight);
property LabelPosition: TLabelType read FLabelType write SetLabelType;
```

Kylix automatically knows how to translate an enumerated type into a drop-down list that appears in the Object Inspector. Figure 9.6 shows how this works in practice. The point here is that you don't need to do anything more than declare an enumerated type as a property in the published section to take advantage of this feature.

**FIGURE 9.6**

*The drop-down property editor bfor the* LabelPosition *property of the* TElfLabelEdit *control automatically shows the members of the enumerated type* TLabelEdit.

The following bit of code shows how to handle user interaction with the LabelPosition property:

```
procedure TElfLabelEdit.SetLabelType(Value: TLabelType);
begin
  FLabelType := Value;
  case FLabelType of
    ltBottom: SetPositionBottom;
    ltLeft: SetPositionLeft;
    ltRight: SetPositionRight;
    ltTop: SetPositionTop;
  end;
  Self.RePaint;
end;
```

9

CREATING
COMPONENTS

```
procedure TElfLabelEdit.SetPositionLeft;
begin
  FLabel.Left := FGap;
  FLabel.Top := FGap;
  FLabel.Width := FLabel.Canvas.TextWidth(FLabel.Text) + FLabelGap;
  FLabel.Height := 15;

  FEdit.Left := FLabel.Width + FGap;
  FEdit.Top := FLabel.Top;
  FEdit.Width := Width - FEdit.Left - FGap;
end;

procedure TElfLabelEdit.SetPositionTop;
begin
  FLabel.Left := FGap;
  FLabel.Top := FGap;
  FLabel.Width := FLabel.Canvas.TextWidth(FLabel.Text) + FLabelGap;
  FLabel.Height := 15;

  FEdit.Left := FLabel.Left;
  FEdit.Top := FLabel.Top + FLabel.Height + FGap;
  FEdit.Width := Width - (FGap * 2);
end;


procedure TElfLabelEdit.SetPositionRight;
begin
  // Code omitted which is much like SetPositionTop or SetPositionLeft
end;

procedure TElfLabelEdit.SetPositionBottom;
begin
  // Code omitted which is much like SetPositionTop or SetPositionLeft
end;
```

The SetLabelType method gets called because it is the write portion of the declaration for the LabelPosition property:

```
property LabelPosition: TLabelType read FLabelType write SetLabelType;
```

The FGap field shown in the code is set to a constant used to set up the border around the label. The other key fact you need to know about the label, however, is how wide it should be. You can get this kind of information from the Canvas.TextWidth and Canvas.TextHeight properties that belong to the label itself:

```
FLabel.Width := FLabel.Canvas.TextWidth(FLabel.Text) + FLabelGap;
```

The Canvas property of a control encapsulates the concept of drawing on a surface. In Windows, the TCanvas object was a wrapper around the GDI. It allows you to do things like work with fonts, draw rectangles, ellipsis, and other shapes, and work with bitmaps. You will learn all about the Canvas object in Chapter 11, "Graphics." As far as this label control is concerned, the only key point you have to absorb at this time is that the Canvas object is inherited from TCustomControl. If you made TComponent the ancestor for this control, it would not have a TCanvas object built into it.

> **NOTE**
>
> In some cases, you might want to create controls that use their parent's canvas object in order to save the memory associated with creating a canvas for a particular control. You will learn more about this subject in Chapter 10.

## ElfLabelEdit and Compatibility with Windows

I originally wrote the ElfLabelEdit for use in Windows. In that first version, I responded to Windows messages. When rewriting the control for Linux, I switched many of my Windows response methods to CLX response methods. For instance, I stopped responding to WM_FONTCHANGED and/or CM_FONTCHANGED messages, and began overriding the standard CLX FontChanged method. I also did work to enhance the 3D feature of the Label control.

After making these changes in Linux, I copied some of this code back to my Windows machine. The changes looked harmless, and I was not expecting trouble. However, a major problem occurred in Delphi 5 because of the following line of code in my constructor:

```
LabelPosition := ltTop;
```

This line of code is not in the version of the control you have. I had to remove it because it was causing the SetPositionTop method to be called in Windows before the control was properly constructed. In particular, I got an error message saying that I was trying to work with a control that had no parent. The fix to the problem was to add in the ShowingChanged method, which is in the version of code that ships with this book.

My point here, of course, is that in Linux the control did have a parent at an early stage in its development, while in Windows it did not. This shows that there can be subtle incompatibilities between the code you write for Linux and the code you write for Windows. Please note that I was not testing the control under CLX for Windows, but under the VCL. Furthermore, I am currently talking about component development, and not application development. Subtle problems like this are more likely to arise when you try to create cross-platform components, rather than cross-platform applications.

## 3D Text Labels

You may have noticed that the label control used by the TElfLabelEdit component has a 3D appearance. The TElfLabel can be drawn in three different ways:

```
TTextType = (ttNone, ttInset, ttEmbossed);
```

The actual code for drawing the control looks like this:

```
procedure TElfLabel.DoDrawText(var Rect: TRect; Flags: Integer);
var
  Text: string;
  HighColor: TColor;
  LowColor: TColor;
  SaveColor: TColor;
  ThreeDRect: TRect;
begin
  Text := GetLabelText;
  if not Enabled then begin
    Canvas.Font.Color := clBtnHighlight;
    Canvas.TextOut(0, 0, Text);
    Canvas.Font.Color := clBtnShadow;
    Canvas.TextOut(1, 1, Text);
  end else begin
    case FTextType of
      ttInset: begin
        HighColor := clBtnHighLight;
        LowColor := clBtnShadow;
      end;

      ttEmbossed: begin
        HighColor := clBtnShadow;
        LowColor := clBtnHighLight;
      end;

      else begin
        HighColor := clBtnShadow;
        LowColor := clBtnHighLight;
      end;
    end;
```

```
    if TextType in [ttInset, ttEmbossed] then begin
      SaveColor := Canvas.Font.Color;

      // Draw One Way
      Canvas.Font.Color := HighColor;
      Canvas.TextOut(0, 0, Text);

      // Draw the Other Way
      ThreeDRect := Rect;
      Canvas.Font.Color := LowColor;
      Canvas.TextOut(2, 2, Text);

      Canvas.Font.Color := SaveColor;
    end;

    // Draw Regular
    Canvas.TextRect(Rect, 1, 1, Text);
  end;
end;
```

If you study this code, you will see that the text of the control is actually drawn twice. One time it is drawn in a lighter shade than the other time. Furthermore, each time it is drawn at a slightly different offset. The end effect is that the text appears to have a shadow behind it, as if it were slightly elevated from the page. For instance, the text might be drawn once in light gray color at a slight offset of one or two pixels from the standard position for the text. The second time it is drawn in standard black, directly over the location where the text would normally appear. The end result is that the black text appears to have a light gray shadow behind it, and slightly offset, as if the light were coming in from an angle and casting a shadow. This is a very old technique, similar to the one used to create the drop shadow on buttons and other 3D controls. Once you have the code for doing this kind of thing, you can use it in many different places in your programs.

> **TIP**
>
> Other useful components can be found in the `chapter09` and `lunits` directories on the CD that accompanies this book.

## Summary

In this chapter, you have learned about building components. Specifically, you learned:

- How to create components that change an ancestor's default settings. For instance, you created `TEdit` descendants with new default colors and fonts.

- How to create compound components that consist of multiple inherited or aggregated components.
- How to create packages and how to install components.
- How to create your own published properties.
- How to respond to Windows and VCL messages.

There is no denying that the basics of component development in Kylix are quite simple. However, some readers might be thinking that there were a few tricks I performed in this chapter that required a bit of background understanding of how the CLX is put together, such as knowing about the `MouseDown` and `Resize` events.

In fact, component development can get a little tricky at times; the more you know about the CLX and Qt, the better you will be at it. However, there are quite a few tricks you can pull without having deep knowledge. Furthermore, component development is a field that you can expand into once you start to find the basics of Kylix development a bit too easy.

# Advanced Component Design

*by Charlie Calvert*

## IN THIS CHAPTER

This chapter continues the exploration of CLX components. Tools and technologies covered in this chapter include

- Exploring properties.
- Creating clock components that can be dropped on a form then stopped and started at will.
- Creating custom event handlers for your controls.
- Creating tools built on top of abstract component base classes such as `TWinControl`, `TCustomControl`, `TComponent`, and `TGraphicControl`. These are the classes you descend from if you want to build your own components from the bottom up.
- Working with component templates to create quick and dirty compound components.

Besides core component creation topics, this chapter also covers two related topics:

*Property editors* are used to edit the properties of components. The classic examples are the common dialog boxes that pop up when you edit the `Color` or `Font` properties that belong to most visible components. The drop down lists and string editing capabilities found in the Object Inspector are also property editors.

*Component editors* are associated not with a single property, but with an entire component. An example is the editor that pops up when you double-click on a `TMainMenu` component.

The property editors and component editors are related to a broader topic called the Tools API. The Tools API consists of a series of interfaces to the Kylix IDE that allow you to build wizards, interfaces to version control systems, and similar utilities. The API for property editors, component editors, and the Tools API are kept in the `../kylix/source/toolsapi` directory. The full Delphi API is not readily available in the first version of Kylix, but certain readily available portions of it can, and will, be examined.

This chapter is one of the key places where you can learn to take the basic tools found in every copy of Kylix and use them to build powerful systems. Kylix is a fabulous resource waiting for people to come along and unlock its secrets. This chapter contains some of the keys you need to fully utilize all the capabilities of this wonderful tool.

## Properties

Before you can go much further with Kylix, you need to have a good understanding of properties. In particular, as you begin to develop components, you will begin to use and create your own properties. To do so effectively requires a full understanding of this surprisingly complex topic.

Properties provide several advantages:

- They give you the power to hide data. Using properties, you can conceal from the user of your object the actual way that you are storing data. This gives you the freedom to change that storage mechanism if you so wish.

- If you write a component and place it in the Component Palette, its published properties appear in the Object Inspector.

- Some properties can be made available at design time, while variables are only available at runtime.

- Properties can have side effects such as not only setting the value of a private variable such as FWidth, but also physically changing the width of the object that appears on the screen.

- Property access methods can be declared virtual, which gives them more flexibility than simple variables.

## Declaring Properties

In the next few pages I am going to discuss the simple object shown in Listing 10.1.

**LISTING 10.1**   A Simple Object with a Few Properties

```
type
  TWidget = class(TObject)
  private
    FCol: Integer;
    FRow: Integer;
    FQuantity: LongInt;
    FBoxSize: LongInt;
    FMaxQuantity: LongInt;
    FDescription: string;
    function GetQuantity: string;
    procedure SetQuantity(S: string);
  protected
    function GetName: string; virtual;
  public
    constructor Create; virtual;
    procedure Sell(Amount: LongInt); virtual;
    procedure Stock; virtual;
    procedure Paint; virtual;
    property Quantity: string read GetQuantity write SetQuantity;
    property Col: Integer read FCol write FCol;
    property Row: Integer read FRow write FRow;
  end;
```

**LISTING 10.1**   Continued

```
implementation

constructor TWidget.Create;
begin
  inherited Create;
  FBoxSize := 5;
end;

function TWidget.GetQuantity: string;
begin
  Result := 'Quantity: ' + IntToStr(FQuantity);
end;

procedure TWidget.SetQuantity(S: string);
begin
  FQuantity := StrToInt(S);
end;

function TWidget.GetName: string;
begin
  result := StripFromFront(ClassName, 1);
end;

procedure TWidget.Sell(Amount: LongInt);
begin
  if Amount = 0 then
    FQuantity := FQuantity - FBoxSize
  else
    FQuantity := FQuantity - Amount
end;

procedure TWidget.Stock;
begin
  FQuantity := FQuantity + FBoxSize;
end;

procedure TWidget.Paint;
begin
  GotoXY(FCol, FRow);
  Write('* ' + GetName);
end;
```

Consider the following three properties:

```
public
  property Quantity: string read GetQuantity write SetQuantity;
  property Col: Integer read FCol write FCol;
  property Row: Integer read FRow write FRow;
```

The two numeric properties shown here are simple tools that do nothing more than hide data and lay the groundwork for their use inside the Object Inspector:

```
property Col: Integer read FCol write FCol;
```

The declaration starts with the keyword `property` followed by the name of the property. Every property must be declared as having a certain type, which in this case is `Integer`.

Most properties can be both read and written. The `read` directive for the `Col` property states that the value to be displayed is `FCol` and the value to write is `FCol`. In short, the following code sets the private field of `TWidget` called `FCol` to the value 2, and sets `i` to the value of `FCol` (again, 2):

```
var
  i: Integer;
begin
  MyWidget.Col := 2;
  i := MyWidget.Col;
end;
```

The reasons for doing this are two-fold:

- To hide data so that it is protected.
- To create a syntax that allows properties to be shown in the Object Inspector. Of course, you won't see these values in the Object Inspector until you metamorphose the object into a component.

The `Col` and `Row` properties provide what is called *direct access*; they map directly to the internal storage field. As a result, the runtime performance of accessing data through a direct-access property is exactly the same as accessing the private field directly.

The `Col` and `Row` examples represent the simplest possible case for a property declaration. The `Quantity` property presents a few variations on these themes:

```
property Quantity: string read GetQuantity write SetQuantity;
```

Rather than reading a variable directly, `Quantity` returns the result of a private function:

```
function TWidget.GetQuantity: string;
begin
  Result := 'Quantity: ' + IntToStr(FQuantity);
end;
```

**10**

ADVANCED
COMPONENT
DESIGN

`SetQuantity`, on the other hand, enables you to change the value of the `FQuantity` variable:

```
procedure TWidget.SetQuantity(S: string);
begin
  FQuantity := StrToInt(S);
end;
```

`GetQuantity` and `SetQuantity` are examples of access methods. Just as the internal storage for direct access variables begins by convention with the letter F, access methods usually begin with either "Set" or "Get." This is, however, simply a convention. Unlike the case in the Java world, there is no technical benefit derived from following this convention. It is simply a convenience useful during program maintenance.

Take a moment to consider what is happening here. To use the `Quantity` property, you need to use the following syntax:

```
var
  S: string;
begin
  S := W.Quantity;
  W.Quantity := '25';
end;
```

In the preceding code, `S` is set to a string that might look like `'Quantity: 10'` or `'Quantity: 25'`. Note that when you are writing to the `FQuantity` property, you *don't* write:

```
W.Quantity('25');
```

Instead, you use the simple, explicit syntax of a direct assignment. Kylix automatically translates the assignment into a function call that takes a parameter. C++ buffs will recognize this as a limited form of operator overloading.

If there were no properties, the previous code would look like this:

```
var
  S: string;
begin
  S := W.GetQuantity;
  W.SetQuantity('25');
end;
```

Instead of remembering one property name, this second technique requires you to remember two, and instead of the simple assignment syntax, you must remember to pass a parameter. Although it is not the main purpose of properties, it should now be obvious that one of their benefits is that they provide a clean, easy-to-use syntax.

> **NOTE**
>
> The Quantity property differs from the Sell and Stock methods because it changes FQuantity directly, rather than adding to or subtracting from it.

## Viewing Properties in the Object Inspector

As declared, the Col, Row, and Quantity properties I have been discussing appear in the public section of an object. If they were part of a component, and if they were moved to the published section of an object, they could be seen from inside the Object Inspector at design time:

```
published
  property Quantity: string read GetQuantity write SetQuantity;
  property Col: Integer read FCol write FCol;
  property Row: Integer read FRow write FRow;
```

There is no rule that says which properties should be declared in the published or public sections. In fact, properties often appear in public sections, but there is little reason for them to be in private sections, though they do make occasional appearances in protected sections. In this case, all the properties appear in the public section because TWidget is not a descendant of TComponent.

> **NOTE**
>
> A read-only property has a read clause but no write clause. Since read-only properties cannot be edited, it makes little sense to place them in the published section of an object. As a result, published properties should usually be declared with both read and write clauses. Read-only properties, however, frequently appear in public and protected sections.

The most important feature of properties is that they can appear in the Object Inspector. However, properties are useful in and of themselves, even in objects that do not ever appear as components. The $64,000 question, of course, is just how useful the property syntax is in a program. Java, for instance, opted not to develop property syntax. Tools such as JBuilder simply key off the get and set parts of Java getter and setter methods to develop properties that appear in the JBuilder version of the Object Inspector. In other words, if JBuilder sees methods called getWidth or setWidth, it will place a property called Width in the JBuilder Inspector. Most other Java development environments follow this same pattern. Debating the

**10**

relative merits of getters and setters versus properties is a matter for language lawyers. For my part, however, I believe that properties are a powerful and useful part of Object Pascal, and those languages that don't support them are the poorer for their absence. I'm not implying that Java or C++ are crippled languages, only that I believe they would be better off if they supported Kylix style properties.

# More on Properties

Kylix provides support for five different types of properties:

- Simple properties are declared to be integers, characters, or strings.
- Enumerated properties are declared to be of some enumerated type. When shown in the Object Inspector, you can view them with a drop-down list. The Position property from TForm is an enumerated type. Range types, such as the Cursor property, are treated in a similar fashion.
- Set properties are declared to be of type Set. The Anchors property from TForm is an example of this type of property. You can only choose one enumerated value at a time, but you can combine several values in a property of type Set.
- Object properties are declared to be of some object type, such as the Items property from the TListBox component, which is declared to be of type TStrings.
- Array properties are like standard arrays, but you can index on any type, even a string.

The PropTest program in Listing 10.2 gives an example of each of the five types of properties. It also gives the TStringList object a fairly decent workout. The program itself is only minimally useful outside the range of a purely academic setting such as this book.

**LISTING 10.2**   The Main Unit for the Proptest Program

```
unit Main;

{ Program copyright © 1996..2001 by Charles Calvert }
{ Project Name: PROPTEST }

{ This sample program shows how to use some
  of the basic features of properties. }

interface

uses
  SysUtils, Classes, QGraphics,
  QControls, QForms, QDialogs,
  QStdCtrls;
```

**LISTING 10.2**   Continued

```delphi
type
  TForm1 = class(TForm)
    bCreateObjects: TButton;
    ListBox1: TListBox;
    ListBox2: TListBox;
    procedure bCreateObjectsClick(Sender: TObject);
  private
    { Private declarations }
  public
    { Public declarations }

  end;

var
  Form1: TForm1;

implementation

uses
  MyObj1;

{$R *.xfm}

procedure TForm1.bCreateObjectsClick(Sender: TObject);
var
  M: TMyProps;
  Ch: Char;
  i: Integer;
begin
  M := TMyProps.Create(Self);
  M.Parent := Self;
  M.SimpleProp := 25;
  M.EnumProp := teEnum;
  M.SetProp := [teEnum, teSet];
  M.StrArrayProp['Jones'] := 'Sam, Mary';
  M.StrArrayProp['Doe'] := 'John, Johanna';
  ListBox1.Items.Add(M.StrArrayProp['Doe']);
  ListBox1.Items.Add(M.StrArrayProp['Jones']);
  for i := 0 to M.ObjectProp.Count - 1 do
    ListBox2.Items.Add(M.ArrayProp[i]);
  //Ch := M.Default1;
end;

end.
```

**10**

ADVANCED
COMPONENT
DESIGN

**LISTING 10.3**   The Unit Containing the Object Used by the Proptest program.

```
unit MyObj1;

{ Program copyright © 1996..2001 by Charles Calvert }
{ Project Name: PROPTEST }

interface

uses
  Classes, QForms, QControls,
  QStdCtrls, QGraphics, SysUtils;

type
  TEnumType = (teSimple, teEnum, teSet, teObject, teArray);
  TSetProp = set of TEnumType;

  TCouple = class(TObject)
    Husband: string;
    Wife: string;
  end;

  TMyProps = class(TCustomControl)
  private
    FSimple: Integer;
    FEnumType: TEnumType;
    FSetProp: TSetProp;
    FObjectProp: TStringList;
    FDefault1: Char;
    function GetArray(Index: integer): string;
    function GetStrArray(S: string): string;
    procedure SetStrArray(Index: string; S: string);
  protected
    procedure Paint; override;
  public
    constructor Create(AOwner: TComponent); override;
    destructor Destroy; override;
    property ArrayProp[i: integer]: string read GetArray;
    property StrArrayProp[i: string]: string read GetStrArray write
SetStrArray;
  published
    property SimpleProp: Integer read FSimple write FSimple;
    property EnumProp: TEnumType read FEnumType write FEnumType;
    property SetProp: TSetProp read FSetProp write FSetProp;
    property ObjectProp: TStringList read FObjectProp write FObjectProp;
    property Default1: Char read FDefault1 write FDefault1 default '1';
  end;
```

**LISTING 10.3**   Continued

```
implementation

uses
  LCodeBox;

constructor TMyProps.Create(AOwner: TComponent);
begin
  inherited Create(AOwner);
  Width := 100;
  Height := 100;
  Left := (TForm(AOwner).ClientWidth div 2) - (Width div 2);
  Top := (TForm(AOwner).ClientHeight div 2) - (Height div 2);
  FObjectProp := TStringList.Create;
  Default1 := '1';
end;

destructor TMyProps.Destroy;
var
  i: Integer;
begin
  for i := 0 to FObjectProp.Count - 1 do
    FObjectProp.Objects[i].Free;
  FObjectProp.Free;
  inherited Destroy;
end;

procedure TMyProps.Paint;
begin
  Canvas.Brush.Color := clBlue;
  inherited Paint;
  Canvas.Rectangle(0, 0, Width, Height);
  Canvas.TextOut(1, 1, 'FSimple: ' + IntToStr(FSimple));
  Canvas.TextOut(1, Canvas.TextHeight('Blaise'), GetArray(0));
  Canvas.TextOut(1, Canvas.TextHeight('Blaise') * 2, FObjectProp.Strings[1]);
end;

function TMyProps.GetArray(Index: integer): string;
begin
  Result := FObjectProp.Strings[Index]
end;

function TMyProps.GetStrArray(S: string): string;
var
  Couple: TCouple;
```

**LISTING 10.3** Continued

```
begin
  Couple := TCouple(FObjectProp.Objects[FObjectProp.IndexOf(S)]);
  Result := Couple.Husband + ', ' + Couple.Wife;
end;

function GetHusband(S: string): string;
begin
  Result := StripLastToken(S, ',');
end;

function GetWife(S: string): string;
begin
  Result := StripFirstToken(S, ',');
end;

procedure TMyProps.SetStrArray(Index: string; S: string);
var
  Couple: TCouple;
begin
  Couple := TCouple.Create;
  Couple.Husband := GetHusband(S);
  Couple.Wife := GetWife(S);
  FObjectProp.AddObject(Index, Couple);
end;

end.
```

The structure of the Proptest program is simple. There is a main form with a button on it. If you click the button, you instantiate an object of type TMyProps. TMyProps has five properties, one for each of the major types of properties. These properties have self-explanatory names:

```
property SimpleProp;
property EnumProp;
property SetProp;
property ObjectProp;
property ArrayProp;
```

Before exploring these properties, I should mention that TMyProps is descended from the native Kylix object called TCustomControl. TCustomControl is intelligent enough to both display itself on the screen and store itself on the Component Palette. It has several key methods and properties already associated with it, including a Paint method and Width and Height fields. (You will learn more about TCustomControl in the next section of this chapter, "Building Components from Scratch.")

Because TCustomControl is so intelligent, it is easy to use its Paint method to write values to the screen:

```
procedure TMyProps.Paint;
begin
  Canvas.Brush.Color := clBlue;
  inherited Paint;
  Canvas.Rectangle(0, 0, Width, Height);
  Canvas.TextOut(1, 1, 'FSimple: ' + IntToStr(FSimple));
  Canvas.TextOut(1, Canvas.TextHeight('Blaise'), GetArray(0));
  Canvas.TextOut(1, Canvas.TextHeight('Blaise') * 2,
                 FObjectProp.Strings[1]);
end;
```

Note that you do not need to explicitly call the Paint method. CLX calls it for you whenever the object needs to paint or repaint itself. This means that you can hide the window behind others, and it will repaint itself automatically when it is brought to the fore. Inheriting functionality that you need from other objects is a big part of what OOP is all about.

The first three properties of TMyProps are extremely easy to understand:

```
property SimpleProp: Integer read FSimple write FSimple;
property EnumProp: TEnumType read FEnumType write FEnumType;
property SetProp: TSetProp read FSetProp write FSetProp;
```

These are direct access properties that simply read to and write from a variable. You can use them with the following syntax:

```
M.SimpleProp := 25;
M.EnumProp := teEnum;
M.SetProp := [teEnum, TeSet];
```

The syntax for using the ObjectProp property is similar to the examples shown previously, but it is a bit harder to fully comprehend the relationship between an object and a property:

```
property ObjectProp: TStringList
  read FObjectProp write FObjectProp;
```

ObjectProp is of type TStringList, which is a descendant of the TStrings type used in the TListBox.Items property or the TMemo.Lines property. I use TStringList instead of TStrings because TStrings is essentially an abstract type meant for use only in limited circumstances. For general purposes, you should always use a TStringList instead of a TStrings object. (In fact, neither TListBox nor TMemo actually uses variables of type TStrings. They actually use descendants of TStrings, just as I do here. The point is that all of these types can be used polymorphically because they all descend from TStrings.)

> **NOTE**
>
> A TStringList has two possible functions. You can use it to store a simple list of strings, and you can also associate an object with each of those strings. To perform the latter task, call AddObject(), passing a string in the first parameter and a TObject descendant in the second parameter. You can then retrieve the object by passing in the string you used in the call to AddObject().
>
> TStringLists do not destroy the objects that you store in them. It is up to you to deallocate the memory of any object you store on a TStringList.
>
> If you want a simple list object that doesn't have all this specialized functionality, use a linked list or the versatile TList object that ships with Kylix.

After making the declaration for ObjectProp shown earlier, you can now use it as if it were a simple TStringList variable. This can sometimes be a bit inconvenient, however. For instance, the following syntax retrieves an object that is associated with a string:

```
S := 'StringConstant';
MyObject := FObjectProp.Objects[FObjectProp.IndexOf(S)]
```

Furthermore, you must be sure to allocate memory for the FObjectProp at the beginning of TMyProps's existence, and you must dispose of that memory in the TMyProps destructor:

```
constructor TMyProps.Create(AOwner: TComponent);
begin
  inherited Create(AOwner);
  FObjectProp := TStringList.Create;
  ...
end;

destructor TMyProps.Destroy;
begin
  for i := 0 to FObjectProp.Count - 1 do
    FObjectProp.Objects[i].Free;
  FObjectProp.Free;
  inherited Destroy;
end;
```

The key point is that TMyProps.Destroy is called automatically whenever the form is freed. You should almost never explicitly call Destroy on any object, though in objects that have no parent there are frequent occasions when you will explicitly call Free, which in turn calls Destroy.

Finally, you must also allocate memory for each object you place in a TStringList. That is, you must create not only a TStringList, but you must also create each object you pass to the TStringList.AddObject routine. When you are done with those objects, you must destroy them:

```
for i := 0 to FObjectProp.Count - 1 do
    FObjectProp.Objects[i].Free;
```

There is nothing you can do about the necessity of allocating and deallocating memory for an object of type TStringList. You can, however, use array properties to simplify the act of accessing it, and to simplify the act of allocating memory for each object you store in it. Proptest shows how this can be done. Specifically, it entertains the concept that you are creating a list for a party to which only married couples are being invited. Each couple's last name is stored as a string in a TStringList, and their first names are stored in an object that is stored in the TStringList in association with the last name. In other words, Proptest calls AddObject with the last name in the first parameter and an object containing their first names in the second parameter. This sounds complicated at first, but array properties can make the task trivial from the user's point of view. (In this case, I mean the user of the object, not the user of the program.)

In the Proptest program, I store a simple object with two fields inside the TStringList:

```
TCouple = class(TObject)
  Husband: string;
  Wife: string;
end;
```

Note that this object looks a lot like a simple record. In fact, I would have used a record here, except that TStringLists expect TObject descendants, not simple records. (Actually, you can sometimes get away with storing non-objects in TStringLists, but I'm not going to cover that topic in this book.)

As described earlier, it would be inconvenient to ask consumers of TMyObject to allocate memory for a TCouple object each time they needed to be used. Instead, Proptest asks the user to pass in first and last names in this simple string format:

```
'HusbandName, WifeName'
```

Proptest also asks them to pass in the last name as a separate variable. To simplify this process, I use a string array property:

```
property StrArrayProp[i: string]: string read GetStrArray write SetStrArray;
```

Notice that this array uses a string as an index, rather than a number!

**10**

Given the StrArrayProp declaration, the user can write the following code:

```
M.StrArrayProp['Jones'] := 'Sam, Mary';
```

This is a simple, intuitive line of code, even if it is a bit unconventional. The question, of course, is how can Kylix parse this information?

If you look at the declaration for StrArrayProp, you can see that it has two access methods called GetStrArray and SetStrArray. SetStrArray and its associated functions look like this:

```
function GetHusband(S: string): string;
begin
  Result := StripLastToken(S, ',');
end;

function GetWife(S: string): string;
begin
  Result := StripFirstToken(S, ',');
end;

procedure TMyProps.SetStrArray(Index: string; S: string);
var
  Couple: TCouple;
begin
  Couple := TCouple.Create;
  Couple.Husband := GetHusband(S);
  Couple.Wife := GetWife(S);
  FObjectProp.AddObject(Index, Couple);
end;
```

Note the declaration for SetStrArray. It takes two parameters. The first one is an index of type string, and the second is the value to be stored in the array. So, 'Jones' is passed in as an index, and 'Sam, Mary' is the value to be added to the array.

SetStrArray begins by allocating memory for an object of type TCouple. It then parses the husband's and wife's names from the string by calling two token-based functions from the LCodeBox unit that ships with this book. Finally, a call to AddObject is executed. When the program is finished, you must be sure to deallocate the memory for the TCouple objects in the Destroy method:

```
destructor TMyProps.Destroy;
var
  i: Integer;
begin
  for i := 0 to FObjectProp.Count - 1 do
    FObjectProp.Objects[i].Free;
  FObjectProp.Free;
  inherited Destroy;
end;
```

The twin of SetStrArray is GetStrArray. This function retrieves a couple's name from the TStringList whenever the user passes in a last name. The syntax for retrieving information from the StrArray property looks like this:

```
S := M.StrArrayProp['Jones'];
```

In this case, S is assigned the value 'Sam, Mary', which are the Jones' first names. Once again, note the remarkable fact that Kylix enables us to use a string as an index in a property array.

The implementation for GetStrArray is fairly simple:

```
function TMyProps.GetStrArray(S: string): string;
var
  Couple: TCouple;
begin
  Couple := TCouple(FObjectProp.Objects[FObjectProp.IndexOf(S)]);
  Result := Couple.Husband + ', ' + Couple.Wife;
end;
```

The code first retrieves the object from the TStringList, and then performs some simple hand waving to re-create the original string passed in by the user. Obviously, it would be easy to add additional methods that retrieved only a wife's name, or only a husband's name.

I'm showing you this syntax not because I'm convinced that you need to use TStringLists and property arrays in exactly the manner shown here, but because I want to demonstrate how properties can be used to conceal an implementation and hide data from the user. For instance, you could later change the way the object stores the first and last names without ever having to change to interface to your object.

The last two properties declared in this program show how to use important property types, and they also demonstrate how properties can be used to reduce relatively complex operations to a simple syntax that looks like this:

```
M.StrArrayProp['Doe'] := 'John, Johanna';
S := M.StrArrayProp['Doe'];
```

Consumers of this object don't need to know that I am storing the information in a TStringList, and they won't need to know if I change the method of storing this information at some later date. As long as the interface for TMyObject remains the same—that is, as long as I don't change the declaration for StrArrayProp—I am free to change the implementation at any time.

There is one other array property used in this program that should be mentioned briefly:

```
property ArrayProp[i: integer]: string read GetArray;
```

**10**

ADVANCED
COMPONENT
DESIGN

ArrayProp uses the traditional integer as an index. However, note that this array still has a special trait not associated with normal arrays: It is read only! Because no write method is declared for this property, it cannot be written to; it can be used only to query the TStringList that it ends up addressing:

```
function TMyProps.GetArray(Index: integer): string;
begin
  Result := FObjectProp.Strings[Index]
end;
```

You can call ArrayProp with this syntax:

```
S := M.ArrayProp[0];
```

This is an obvious improvement over writing the following:

```
S := M.FObjectProp.Strings[0];
```

Creating a simple interface for an object may not seem important at first, but in day-to-day programming a simple, clean syntax is invaluable. For instance, the Proptest program calls ArrayProp in the following manner:

```
for i := 0 to M.ObjectProp.Count - 1 do
  ListBox2.Items.Add(M.ArrayProp[i]);
```

In this case, it's very helpful that the call to GetArray is so simple. It would not be as much fun if you had to complicate matters further by writing this line:

```
ListBox2.Items.Add(M.FObjectProp.Strings[0]);
```

---

**NOTE**

Astute readers might be noticing that Kylix is flexible enough to enable you to improve even its own syntax. For instance, if you wanted to, you could create a list box descendant that enables you to write this syntax:

```
ListBox2.AddStr(S);
```

instead of

```
ListBox2.Items.Add(S);
```

The techniques you are learning in these chapters on CLX will prove to be the key to enhancing Kylix so that it becomes a custom-made tool that fits your specific needs and tastes.

If you bury yourself in the Kylix source code, eventually you might notice the `default` directive, which can be used with properties:

```
property Default1: Char read FDefault1 write FDefault1 default '1';
```

Looking at this syntax, you would tend to think that this code automatically sets `FDefault1` to the value `'1'`. However, this is not its purpose. Rather, it tells Kylix whether this value needs to be streamed when a form file is being written to disk. If you make `TMyProp` into a component, drop it onto a form, and save that form to disk, Kylix explicitly saves that value if it is not equal to 1, but skips it if it is equal to 1.

An obvious benefit of the `default` directive is that it saves room in DFM files. Many objects have as many as 25, or even 50, properties associated with them. Writing them all to disk would be an expensive task. As it happens, most properties used in a form have default values that are never changed. The `default` directive merely specifies that default value, and Kylix thus knows whether to write the value to disk. If the property in the Object Inspector is equal to the default, Kylix just passes over the property when it's time to write to disk. When reading the values back in, if the property is not explicitly mentioned in the `xfm` file, the property retains the value you assigned to it in the component's constructor.

> **NOTE**
>
> The property is never assigned the default value by Kylix. You *must* ensure that you assign the default values to the properties as you indicated in the class declaration. This must be done in the constructor. A mismatch between the declared default and the actual initial value established by the constructor will result in lost data when streaming the component in and out.
>
> Similarly, if you change the initial value of an inherited `published` property in your constructor, you should also reassert/redeclare (partial declaration) that property in your descendant class declaration to change the declared default value to match the actual initial value.
>
> The `default` directive does nothing more than give Kylix a way of determining whether it needs to write a value to disk. It never assigns a value to any property. You have to do that yourself in your constructor.

Of course, there are times when you want to assign a property a default value at the moment that the object it belongs to is created. These are the times when you wish the `default` directive did what its name implies. However, it does not now, and never will, perform this action. To gain this functionality you must use the constructor, as shown in the `Proptest` application:

```
constructor TMyProps.Create(AOwner: TComponent);
begin
```

```
inherited Create(AOwner);
Width := 100;
Height := 100;
FDefault1 := 1;
...
```

Here, the Width and Height properties are set by default to 100. (As explained in the second paragraph of the preceding note, you need to be careful that you check to see whether a published property is declared as default.)

The Proptest program is obviously not meant to perform any useful function, but instead explores the world of properties from a syntactical point of view. Even the example of storing a couple's names in a TStringList is implemented primarily for the sake of exploring the syntax involved. It was just a fortuitous coincidence that it ended up yielding a fairly efficient, if idio-syncratic, solution to a real-life problem.

After reading this section, it should be clear that array properties represent one of the most powerful and flexible aspects of Kylix programming. I don't think it's stretching things to say that array properties provide the same kind of breakthrough flexibility that some people feel operator overloading brings to C++. Kylix array properties always provide a clean, easy-to-read syntax that hides object data and implementations.

# Building Components from Scratch

The previous chapter focused on creating descendants of existing components. Now it's time to explore in depth the subject of creating entirely new components.

The main idea to grasp here is that there are a handful of abstract classes from which new components may descend. The term "abstract" can have a specific technical meaning, but here I am using it to refer to any object that exists only so that you can create descendants of it. In short, the following objects have built-in functionality that all components need to access, but you would never want to instantiate an instance of any of them:

- TWidgetControl is the base control for all classes that encapsulate Qt objects. Descendants of this class exist inside their own window, and can receive input focus. All TWidgetControl descendants have a handle. This handle points to the underlying Qt object, and can be used to access that object directly. Many components of this type actu-ally descend from TFrameControl, which is in turn a descendant of TWidgetControl. Other base classes that descend from TWidgetControl include TButtonControl and TCustomListBox.

- A descendant of TWidgetControl called TCustomControl is the base class from which many programmer-designed controls descend. It provides the developer with a Canvas and a Paint method. If you want to draw the display of your new component, you should inherit from TCustomControl.

- `TGraphicControl` exists outside of the `TWidgetControl` hierarchy that makes up most of CLX. It is for components that don't need to receive input focus, don't need to contain other components, and don't need a handle. These controls draw themselves directly on their parent's surface, thereby saving resources. Not having a window handle eliminates a lot of management overhead, and that translates into faster display updates. In short, `TGraphicControls` exist inside their parent's window, rather than having their own window like a `TWidgetControl` descendant. They use their parent's handle and their parent's device context. They still have `Handle` and `Canvas` fields that you can access, but they actually belong to their parent. `TSplitter`, `TPaintBox`, and `TShape` objects are examples of this type of component. `TGraphicControl` and `TWidgetControl` both descend directly from `TControl`.

- `TComponent` enables you to create nonvisual components. If you want to make a tool such as the `TTable`, `TQuery`, `TOpenDialog`, or `TTimer` devices, this is the place to start. These components reside on the Component Palette, but they perform internal functions that you access through code, rather than appearing to the user at runtime.

Here are two loosely defined rules, made to be broken, which you can follow when trying to decide when to create a `TWidgetControl` or `TGraphicControl` descendant:

- Create a `TWidgetControl` or `TCustomControl` descendant whenever the user needs to directly interact with a visible control.

- If the user doesn't need to interact with a visible component, create a `TGraphicControl` descendant.

To get a "handle" on the issues involved here, you should place a `TShape` or `TBevel` control on a form and run the program. Clicking or attempting to type on these controls produces no noticeable result. These components don't ever receive the focus. Now place a `TEdit` control on the form. It responds to mouse clicks, gets the focus, and you can type in it. `TEdit` controls are descendants of `TWidgetControl`, and `TShape` is a descendant of `TGraphicControl`.

---

**NOTE**

I should add one caveat to the rules about `TGraphicControl` explained previously. In one limited sense, the user can interact with `TGraphicControls`. For instance, they do receive mouse messages, and you can set the mouse cursor when the mouse flies over them. They just can't receive keyboard-input focus. If an object can't receive focus, it usually seems inert to the user. Note, however, that in Kylix the seemingly inert `TLabel` control, for reasons that entirely escape me, descends from `TWidgetControl`. `TSplitter`, on the other hand, can interact with the user, and yet it descends from `TGraphicControl`. As you can see, the rules I am trying to lay down here are not hard and fast. Nonetheless, they can provide a general guideline for you.

If you are having trouble deciding whether you want to descend from TWidgetControl or TCustomControl, you should always go with TCustomControl. It has a real Paint method, and some other functionality that is useful when creating a component of your own. If for some odd reason you wanted to wrap an existing Qt control inside a CLX object, you should start with TWinControl. Most Kylix components that follow this path begin by creating intermediate custom objects, so that TEdit's hierarchy looks like this:

```
TControl
TWigetControl
TCustomEdit
TEdit
```

TListBox's hierarchy looks like this:

```
TWidgetControl
TFrameControl
TCustomListBox
TListBox
```

Of course, Kylix wraps all the major Qt controls for you, so you won't need to perform this operation unless you are working with a specialized third-party control of some sort. And even then, it is not at all clear to me that you would have all the tools you need to create the event handlers for your custom Qt control.

The difference between TCustomEdit and TEdit is that TCustomEdit does not publish any of its properties, while TEdit does publish its properties. The reason for this is to give you a chance to create your own TEdit control with just the properties you want to see in the Object Inspector.

NOTE

The issue addressed in the previous paragraph is one of the "hip" facts that all Object Pascal programmers are supposed to know if they want to be one of the in crowd. The direct descendants of TEdit and TPanel that I created in the previous chapter are, in the eyes of many Kylix developers, very lame and salty. Indeed, these people are correct. If you want to create a phat component, you should descend from TCustomEdit, not from TEdit.

Following are the declarations for TGraphicControl and TCustomControl:

```
TGraphicControl = class(TControl)
private
  FCanvas: TCanvas;
```

```
protected
  procedure Paint; virtual;
  procedure PaintRequest; override;
  property Canvas: TCanvas read FCanvas;
public
  constructor Create(AOwner: TComponent); override;
  destructor Destroy; override;
end;


TCustomControl = class(TWidgetControl)
private
  FCanvas: TCanvas;
  procedure UpdateMask;
protected
  procedure BoundsChanged; override;
  procedure CreateWidget; override;
  procedure Painting(Sender: QObjectH; EventRegion: QRegionH); override;
  function EventFilter(Sender: QObjectH; Event: QEventH): Boolean; override;
  procedure Paint; virtual;
  procedure MaskChanged; override;
  procedure DrawMask(Canvas: TCanvas); virtual;
  property Canvas: TCanvas read FCanvas;
public
  constructor Create(AOwner: TComponent); override;
  destructor Destroy; override;
  procedure Invalidate; override;
end;
```

You can see that these are fairly simple objects. Notice in particular that they mostly just add painting capabilities to their parent controls. If you went back one step further in the hierarchy to TControl or TWidgetControl, you would see huge objects. For instance, the declaration for TControl is nearly 250 lines long (not the implementation, mind you, just the type declaration).

I'm showing you this source code because component builders should work directly with the source, rather than using the online help or the DOCs. For simple jobs, it's easy to create your own components without the source. However, if you have a big project, you have to use the source, Luke. May the source be with you!

# The Clock Component

It's now time  to build a relatively sophisticated component from the ground up. The controls from the ElfClock unit (shown in Figure 10.1) are little clocks that you can pop onto a form, and activate and deactivate at will. You can start the clock running, and then tell it to stop by changing the value of a Boolean property called Running.

**FIGURE 10.1**
*The TTestClockComponent sample program shows off the various kinds of clocks made in the chapter.*

When constructing class TElfClock (pronounced Tee Elf Clock), the first thing that needs to be decided is whether the clock is going to descend from TWidgetControl or TGraphicControl. It turns out that TElfClock is not built on top of any particular Qt control, and it does not need to get the focus, so it does not need to descend from TWidgetControl. In fact, it is a perfect candidate for a TGraphicControl descendant.

Of course, you could use TCustomControl as the parent of TElfClock. In fact, making that change would not force you to change any other line besides the class declaration in the code for that component.

Later in this chapter, you will see that the component, shown in Listing 10.4, also contains a special property editor, as well as a simple component editor. As you will see, neither of these tools is inherently difficult to build. Listing 10.5 contains the main form for a program that can be used to test the clock component.

**LISTING 10.4**  The Code for the Clock Component Should Be Kept in the Units Subdirectory where You Store CodeBox and Other Utility Units

```
unit ElfClock;

{ Program copyright © 1995..2001 by Charles Calvert }
{ Project Name: Elves.dpk }

interface

uses
  SysUtils, Classes, QGraphics,
  QControls, QForms, QStdCtrls,
  QExtCtrls, QDialogs;

type
  TElfClock = class(TGraphicControl)
```

**LISTING 10.4**   Continued

```
private
  FTimer: TTimer;
  FRunning: Boolean;
  procedure SetRunning(Run: Boolean);
protected
  procedure OnTimer(Sender: TObject);
  procedure Paint; override;
public
  constructor Create(AOwner: TComponent); override;
published
  property Running: Boolean read FRunning write SetRunning;
end;


TElfColorClock = class(TElfClock)
private
  FFaceColor: TColor;
protected
  procedure Paint; override;
  procedure SetFaceColor(NewColor: TColor); virtual;
public
  constructor Create(AOwner: TComponent); override;
published
  property Color;
  property FaceColor: TColor read FFaceColor write SetFaceColor;
end;


TClockStyle = (csEllipse, csRectangle);


TElfFancyClock = class(TElfColorClock)
private
  FClockStyle: TClockStyle;
  FBevelWidth: Integer;
  FBorderWidth: Integer;
  procedure DrawBorder;
  procedure SetBevelWidth(const Value: Integer);
  procedure SetBorderWidth(const Value: Integer);
protected
  procedure Paint; override;
public
  constructor Create(AOwner: TComponent); override;
published
  property BevelWidth: Integer read FBevelWidth write SetBevelWidth;
  property BorderWidth: Integer read FBorderWidth write SetBorderWidth;
  property ClockStyle: TClockStyle read FClockStyle write FClockStyle;
  property Font;
 end;
```

**LISTING 10.4** Continued

```
procedure Register;

implementation

uses
  LCodeBox, Types;

procedure Register;
begin
  RegisterComponents('Elves', [TElfClock, TElfColorClock, TElfFancyClock]);
end;

{--------------------------------------------------------------------------}
{ TClock ------------------------------------------------------------------}
{--------------------------------------------------------------------------}

constructor TElfClock.Create(AOwner: TComponent);
begin
  inherited Create(AOwner);
  Width := 100;
  height := 100;
  FTimer := TTimer.Create(Self); // Destroyed automatically
  FTimer.OnTimer := OnTimer;
  FTimer.Interval := 250;
end;

procedure TElfClock.Paint;
begin
  Canvas.Ellipse(0, 0, Width, Height);
end;

procedure TElfClock.SetRunning(Run: Boolean);
begin
  if Run then begin
    FTimer.Enabled := True;
    FRunning := True;
  end else begin
    FRunning := False;
    FTimer.Enabled := False;
  end;
end;

procedure TElfClock.OnTimer(Sender: TObject);
var
```

**Listing 10.4**  Continued

```
  S: string;
  x,y, TextWidth, TextHeight :Integer;
  SaveColor: TColor;
begin
  S := GetTimeString;
  TextWidth := Canvas.TextWidth(S);
  TextHeight := Canvas.TextHeight(S);
  x := (Width div 2) - (TextWidth div 2);
  y := (Height div 2) - (TextHeight div 2);
  SaveColor := Canvas.Pen.Color;
  Canvas.Pen.Color := Canvas.Brush.Color;
  Canvas.Rectangle(x, y, x + TextWidth, y + TextHeight);
  Canvas.Pen.Color := SaveColor;
  Canvas.TextOut(x, y, S);
end;


{-----------------------------------------------------------------------}
{ TColorCLock ----------------------------------------------------------}
{-----------------------------------------------------------------------}

constructor TElfColorClock.Create(AOwner: TComponent);
begin
  inherited Create(AOwner);
  FFaceColor := clGreen;
end;



procedure TElfColorClock.Paint;
begin
  Canvas.Brush.Color := FFaceColor;
  inherited Paint;
end;

procedure TElfColorClock.SetFaceColor(NewColor: TColor);
begin
  FFaceColor := NewColor;
  Invalidate;
end;

{-----------------------------------------------------------------------}
{ TFancyCLock ----------------------------------------------------------}
{-----------------------------------------------------------------------}
```

**10**

**ADVANCED
COMPONENT
DESIGN**

**LISTING 10.4**   Continued

```
constructor TElfFancyClock.Create(AOwner: TComponent);
begin
  inherited Create(AOwner);
  FBevelWidth := 1;
  FBorderWidth := 1;
end;

procedure TElfFancyClock.DrawBorder;
var
  R: TRect;
begin
  R := Rect(0, 0, Width, Height);
  Frame3D(Canvas, R, clBtnHighLight, clBtnShadow, FBevelWidth);
  R := Rect(FBorderWidth, FBorderWidth, Width - FBorderWidth,
    Height - FBorderWidth);
  Frame3D(Canvas, R, clBtnHighLight, clBtnShadow, FBevelWidth);
end;

procedure TElfFancyClock.Paint;
var
  Gap: Integer;
begin
  Canvas.Font.Name := Font.Name;
  Canvas.Font.Size := Font.Size;
  Canvas.Font.Color := Font.Color;
  Canvas.Brush.Color := FFaceColor;
  case FClockStyle of
    csEllipse: begin
      Canvas.Pen.Color := Font.Color;
      Canvas.Pen.Width := FBevelWidth;
      Gap := (FBevelWidth + FBorderWidth);
      Canvas.Ellipse(FBevelWidth + Gap, FBevelWidth + Gap,
        Width - FBevelWidth - Gap, Height - FBevelWidth - Gap);
      Canvas.Ellipse(FBorderWidth + Gap, FBorderWidth + Gap,
        Width - FBorderWidth - Gap, Height - FBorderWidth - Gap);
      DrawBorder;
      end;
    csRectangle: begin
      Canvas.Rectangle(0, 0, Width, Height);
      DrawBorder;
    end;
  end;
end;
```

**LISTING 10.4**   Continued

```
procedure TElfFancyClock.SetBevelWidth(const Value: Integer);
begin
  FBevelWidth := Value;
  Invalidate;
end;

procedure TElfFancyClock.SetBorderWidth(const Value: Integer);
begin
  FBorderWidth := Value;
  Invalidate;
end;

end.
```

**LISTING 10.5**   The Test Bed for the Clock Component Is Stored in the CLOCK3 Subdirectory

```
//////////////////////////////////////
// Purpose: Test the TColorClock component
// Project: ClockTestBed.dpr
// Copyright © 1998..2001 by Charlie Calvert
//
unit Main;

interface

uses
  SysUtils, Classes, QGraphics,
  QControls, QForms, QDialogs,
  QStdCtrls, ElfClock;

type
  TForm1 = class(TForm)
    CreateBtn: TButton;
    RunClockBtn: TButton;
    ColorsBtn: TButton;
    ColorDialog1: TColorDialog;
    procedure CreateBtnClick(Sender: TObject);
    procedure RunClockBtnClick(Sender: TObject);
    procedure ColorsBtnClick(Sender: TObject);
  private
    FMyClock: TElfColorClock;
```

**LISTING 10.5**   Continued

```
public
  { Public declarations }
end;

var
  Form1: TForm1;

implementation

{$R *.xfm}

procedure TForm1.CreateBtnClick(Sender: TObject);
begin
  FMyClock := TElfColorClock.Create(Self);
  FMyClock.Parent := Self;
end;

procedure TForm1.RunClockBtnClick(Sender: TObject);
begin
  FMyClock.Running := not FMyClock.Running;
end;

procedure TForm1.ColorsBtnClick(Sender: TObject);
begin
  if ColorDialog1.Execute then
    FMyClock.FaceColor := ColorDialog1.Color;
end;

end.
```

This ClockTestBed program is a small executable designed to check out the status of the simplest of the clock components. To run this program, you should first press the button that creates the clock and makes it visible on the form. The next logical step is to start the clock running; then, if you'd like, you can also change its color. You get an Access Violation if you click on the latter two buttons before pushing the first. The problem is that it is an error to call a method or property of the TElfClock object before the object itself has been created. To prevent this from happening, you could enable or disable the second two buttons.

## Understanding TElfClock

The code for the clock components uses inheritance, virtual methods, and properties. TElfClock has two pieces of private data:

```
FTimer: Integer;
FRunning: Boolean;
```

One is an identifier for the timer, and the other is a Boolean value that specifies whether the clock is running.

The TTimer component ships with Kylix and appears on the Component Palette. However, this component creates an instance of the object manually: you never use the visual tools at all. Here are some basic facts you need to know to use a TTimer component:

- When you want to start a timer, set the TTimer.Enabled property to True.
- To stop a timer, set Enabled to False.
- The OnTimer event will call a method in your program at specified intervals.
- The TTimer.Interval property defines the length of time between calls to the timer, measured in milliseconds.

A typical call to create the timer looks like this:

```
FTimer := TTimer.Create(Self); // Destroyed automatically
FTimer.OnTimer := OnTimer;
FTimer.Interval := 250;
FTimer.Enabled := True;
```

The value 250 assigned to the Interval property specifies that the timer is called once every 250 milliseconds, or once every quarter second.

Timer events are sent to your window by way of the OnTimer event:

```
procedure TElfClock.OnTimer(Sender: TObject);
```

The response to this event is a simple procedure that calls TextOut, and gets the time from a function in the LCodeBox unit called GetTimeString:

```
procedure TElfClock.OnTimer(Sender: TObject);
var
  S: string;
  x,y, TextWidth, TextHeight :Integer;
  SaveColor: TColor;
begin
  S := GetTimeString;
  TextWidth := Canvas.TextWidth(S);
  TextHeight := Canvas.TextHeight(S);
  x := (Width div 2) - (TextWidth div 2);
  y := (Height div 2) - (TextHeight div 2);
  SaveColor := Canvas.Pen.Color;
  Canvas.Pen.Color := Canvas.Brush.Color;
  Canvas.Rectangle(x, y, x + TextWidth, y + TextHeight);
```

**10**

ADVANCED
COMPONENT
DESIGN

```
  Canvas.Pen.Color := SaveColor;
  Canvas.TextOut(x, y, S);
end;
```

Notice that I use the `TextWidth` and `TextHeight` functions from the `TCanvas` object in the `QGraphics` unit to calculate the distance the text will extend both horizontally and vertically. My goal is to ensure that the center of the text string lies as close as possible to the center of the control.

The calls to enable and disable the timer are managed primarily through a property called `Running`:

```
property Running: Boolean read FRunning write SetRunning;
```

The write mechanism, a procedure called `SetRunning`, is a fairly straightforward tool:

```
procedure TElfClock.SetRunning(Run: Boolean);
begin
  if Run then begin
    FTimer.Enabled := True;
    FRunning := True;
  end else begin
    FRunning := False;
    FTimer.Enabled := False;
  end;
end;
```

If the user sets the `Running` property to `True`, this procedure is executed and a `FTimer.Enabled` is set to `True`. If the user sets `Running` to `False`, `FTimer.Enabled` is set to `False`, and the clock immediately stops functioning.

## The Clock `Paint` Method

Before leaving this description of the `TElfClock` object, I should briefly mention the `Paint` method:

```
procedure TElfClock.Paint;
begin
  Canvas.Ellipse(0, 0, Width, Height);
end;
```

This procedure is called whenever the circle defining the circumference of the clock needs to be repainted. You never have to check for this circumstance, and you never have to call `Paint` directly. Kylix relies on the underlying system to keep an eye on the `TElfClock` window. If it needs to be painted, Kylix automatically sends an `OnPaint` event, which in turn calls the `Paint` method shown here.

> **NOTE**
>
> When writing components, sometimes it's easiest if you can get right down to the underlying Qt or Xlib level, or as near to it as you would like to get. The FilterEvent technology shown in the previous two chapters can help you get down to that level, on the rare occasions when you have a need for that kind of thing.

## The TElfColorClock Component

The TElfColorClock component is a descendant of TElfClock that adds color to the control. I made TElfColorClock a separate object, rather than just adding color to TElfClock, for two different reasons (both of which are related to design):

- You might want to create a descendant of TElfClock that doesn't have color, or that implements color differently than TElfColorClock does. By creating two objects, one called TElfClock and the other called TElfColorClock, I enable programmers to have the greatest amount of freedom when creating descendants. This principle has only minimal weight in a simple object such as TElfClock, but it can become extremely important when you are developing large and complex hierarchies. In short, be careful of building too much functionality into one object!

- TElfClock and TElfColorClock also provide another example of inheritance, and vividly demonstrate how this technology can be utilized to your advantage.

TElfColorClock declares a private data store called FFaceColor that is of type TColor. Users can set the FColor variable by manipulating the FaceColor property:

```
property FaceColor: TColor read FFaceColor write SetFaceColor;
```

SetFaceColor is a simple procedure that sets the value of FFaceColor, and calls the CLX function Invalidate, which is inherited from TControl:

```
procedure TElfColorClock.SetFaceColor(NewColor: TColor);
begin
  FFaceColor := NewColor;
  Invalidate;
end;
```

In this case you can call either the CLX Validate function or InvalidateRect, which is inherited from TWidgetControl. Just to be sure this makes sense, it's worth taking a paragraph or two to provide a refresher course on InvalidateRect. Here is the declaration for the routine:

```
procedure InvalidateRect(Rect: PRect; Erase: Bool);
```

InvalidateRect forces a window to completely redraw itself if the first parameter is set to nil. If the second parameter is set to False, the background of the redrawn portions of the control is not erased before redrawing. The first parameter is a pointer to a TRect record that can be used to define the area that you want to redraw. As you might have guessed, calls to the native Kylix function called Invalidate end up calling InvalidateRect.

## The Child is Father of the Man

An interesting, and somewhat humorous, feature of TControl and TWidgetControl is that they are, due to a fluke of Object Pascal syntax, simultaneously parents of each other. In particular, TControl's Parent property is of type TWidgetControl, and yet TControl is itself the parent of TWidgetControl in the CLX object hierarchy. This statement appears to fly in the face of logic. In fact, it may sound more like an episode from Robert Graves' book *I, Claudius,* than something from a work on Linux programming. There is, however, an explanation.

In the CLX object hierarchy, TWidgetControl descends from TControl. Hence, in one sense of the word, TControl is the "parent," with a small "p," of TWidgetControl. However, the Parent, with a big "P," property of TControl is of type TWidgetControl. Thus, in another sense of the word, TWidgetControl is the Parent of TControl. This is how it is possible for TControl.Invalidate to depend on TWidgetControl.InvalidateRect, even though—in one sense of the word—TControl is the parent of TWidgetControl. In particular, the ability to pre-declare an object in Pascal makes it possible to have a child object be a property of its parent.

See the section called "Scoping Issues with Classes that Reference One Another," in Chapter 4, "Objects and Interfaces," for an explanation of this subject. If none of this makes any sense to you, I would not be concerned, as it is not a terribly important point. However, if you are able to follow this admittedly convoluted, though not erroneous, logic, you are well on your way to getting a good grasp of Object Pascal syntax, and of the architecture of the CLX hierarchy.

Calls to Invalidate naturally force calls to the TColorClick.Paint method:

```
procedure TElfColorClock.Paint;
begin
  Canvas.Brush.Color := FFaceColor;
  inherited Paint;
end;
```

Paint sets the brush associated with the window's device context to the color specified by the user; then it calls the Paint method defined in TElfClock.

Notice that I also surface the `Color` property of `TControl`:

`property Color;`

Back in the source for `TControl`, found in `Controls.pas`, you can find the original declaration for this property in the `protected` section of the class declaration. All I'm doing here is surfacing the property in the `Published` section so it appears in the Object Inspector.

The `Color` property defines the background color of the form, while the face color defines the color of the clock face. If you want the clock face to appear to be drawn directly on the surface of the parent control, just leave `Color` at its default value or set it to the color of its parent.

## Creating a Fancy Clock

The fancy clock takes the color clock and makes it more appealing by giving the user a choice of fonts. The object also adds a border and bevel, and it allows the user to draw the face as either a rectangle or an ellipse:

```
TClockStyle = (csEllipse, csRectangle);
TElfFancyClock = class(TElfColorClock)
private
  FClockStyle: TClockStyle;
  FBevelWidth: Integer;
  FBorderWidth: Integer;
  // Code omitted here
published
  property BevelWidth: Integer read FBevelWidth write SetBevelWidth;
  property BorderWidth: Integer read FBorderWidth write SetBorderWidth;
  property ClockStyle: TClockStyle read FClockStyle write FClockStyle;
  property Font;
end;
```

All this would seem like a fairly complicated process, but it ends up being fairly simple to do if you just take advantage of the code found in the CLX.

Adding font support, for instance, would seem to be a very difficult operation, given the nature of fonts. However, the CLX allows you to give the user complete control over the font by just adding two words to your program:

`property Font;`

Adding this code to the `published` section of your object surfaces the `Font` property declared in the object's ancestry. It also automatically brings along the font editor. The font editor appears as part of the Object Inspector, as shown in Figure 10.2.

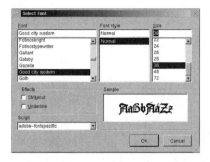

**FIGURE 10.2**

*The property editor for fonts is used by default for all* published *properties declared to be of type* TFont.

Besides the new TFont property, the TElfFancyClock component gives the user two different looks for the clock, one oval and the other rectangular, as shown earlier in Figure 10.1. The TClockStyle enumerated type gives the component a way to track the user's choice:

```
TClockStyle = (csEllipse, csRectangle);
```

At this stage all you need to know is that the user has the choice of either of these options. In just a moment, I will show the new paint method. It's in the paint method that the implementation of these two options is developed. You might also note that Kylix automatically creates a property editor that gives the user a drop-down list for choosing these new properties, as shown in Figure 10.3.

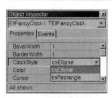

**FIGURE 10.3**

*Kylix automatically creates a drop-down list to act as the property editor for the* ClockStyle *property.*

The BevelWidth and BorderWidth are the last two properties added to the TElfFancyClock object. The set and get methods for the BevelWidth and BorderWidth properties look just as you would expect:

```
procedure TElfFancyClock.SetBevelWidth(const Value: Integer);
begin
  FBevelWidth := Value;
  Invalidate;
end;
```

```
procedure TElfFancyClock.SetBorderWidth(const Value: Integer);
begin
  FBorderWidth := Value;
  Invalidate;
end;
```

The complicated code appears in the `paint` method:

```
procedure TElfFancyClock.Paint;
var
  Gap: Integer;
begin
  Canvas.Font.Name := Font.Name;
  Canvas.Font.Size := Font.Size;
  Canvas.Font.Color := Font.Color;
  Canvas.Brush.Color := FFaceColor;

  case FClockStyle of
    csEllipse: begin
      Canvas.Pen.Color := Font.Color;
      Canvas.Pen.Width := FBevelWidth;
      Gap := (FBevelWidth + FBorderWidth);
      Canvas.Ellipse(FBevelWidth + Gap, FBevelWidth + Gap,
        Width - FBevelWidth - Gap, Height - FBevelWidth - Gap);
      Canvas.Ellipse(FBorderWidth + Gap, FBorderWidth + Gap,
        Width - FBorderWidth - Gap, Height - FBorderWidth - Gap);
      DrawBorder;
      end;
    csRectangle: begin
      Canvas.Rectangle(0, 0, Width, Height);
      DrawBorder;
    end;

  end;
end;
```

The `paint` method begins by setting the font of the object's canvas to the font chosen by the user. The next line sets the `FaceColor`, exactly like the code found in the `TElfColorClock` object.

A case statement is then set up to draw either a rectangle or an ellipse, depending on the user's needs:

```
    case FClockStyle of
    csEllipse: begin
      // DrawEllipse
    csRectangle: begin
      // DrawRectangle
      end;
```

The rectangle style does a fairly good job of drawing a bevel and a border that look reasonably professional. The ellipse code was a bit harder to implement, and I ended up fudging things a bit. In particular, I draw two ellipses, one inside the other. This gives the impression that there is a border, then a space, then a bevel. I simply create the width of the bevel by changing the width of the pen used to draw the circumference of the ellipse.

Both the rectangle and ellipse styles call the `DrawBorder` method:

```
procedure TElfFancyClock.DrawBorder;
var
  R: TRect;
begin
  R := Rect(0, 0, Width, Height);
  Frame3D(Canvas, R, clBtnHighLight, clBtnShadow, FBevelWidth);
  R := Rect(FBorderWidth, FBorderWidth, Width - FBorderWidth,
    Height - FBorderWidth);
  Frame3D(Canvas, R, clBtnHighLight, clBtnShadow, FBevelWidth);
end;
```

`DrawBorder` lets a routine called `Frame3D` do most of its work. `Frame3D` is a public function from CLX found in the `ExtCtrls.pas` unit. It is the same routine the Kylix controls use to create 3D effects, and overall it works quite well. In particular, it uses the `InflateRect` call from the `QGraphics` unit to create a 3D bevel or border that has the right kind of corners. The lesson to learn here is that the CLX has a lot of good routines hidden away in its back corners. The more you know the CLX, the easier it will be to create your programs.

That's all I'm going to say about `TElfClock`, `TElfColorClock`, and `TElfFancyClock`. Overall, these are fairly simple components, interesting primarily because they show you how to go about constructing your own controls from scratch. This kind of exercise lies very much at the heart of Kylix's architecture, and I expect some readers will be spending most of their time engaged almost exclusively in the business of building components.

## Creating Icons for Components

The icon associated with a component and placed in the Component Palette is defined in a file with a .dcr extension. If you do not provide this file, Kylix uses the icon associated with the object's parent. If there is no icon anywhere in the component's ancestry, a default icon with a box, pyramid, and oval is used.

A .dcr file is a resource file with the extension changed from RES to DCR. The resource file contains a bitmap resource with the same name as your component. For instance, the bitmap resource in a DCR file for a TColor component would have a resource ID of TColor. The resource should be approximately 24×24 pixel bitmap that can be edited in any paint program, such as the famous Linux Gimp editor.

Create an RC file listing your bitmap, and compile it, as explained in Chapter 7, "CLX Architecture and Visual Development," in the section titled "Working with Resources." Just take the .res file that wrc produces, and rename it to have a .dcr extension.

Listing 10.6 shows the contents of the Elves.rc file from the lunits directory on the CD that accompanies this book. You should compile this file with the wrc program from the Open Source Wine project. Listing 10.7 shows a shell script that I use to first compile the rc file, and then rename the resulting .res file to a file with a .dcr extension.

**LISTING 10.6**   The Elves.rc File which Defines the List of Bitmaps Shown in the Elves Page of the Component Palette

```
TElfLabelEdit BITMAP "elflabeledit.bmp"
TElfLabel BITMAP "elflabel.bmp"
TElfClock BITMAP "elfclock.bmp"
TElfFancyClock BITMAP "elffancyclock.bmp"
TElfColorClock BITMAP "elfcolorclock.bmp"
```

**LISTING 10.7**   This Shell Script will Compile Elves.rc and Rename the Resulting .res File to Elves.dcr

```
#! /bin/bash

#wrc comes with the freely downloaded open source project called Wine
wrc -r elves.rc
mv elves.res Elves.dcr
```

Once you have your .dcr file, you should include it at the top of Elves.dpk:

```
package Elves;

{$R *.res}
{$R 'Elves.dcr'}
{$ALIGN 1}
{$ASSERTIONS ON}
{$BOOLEVAL OFF}
{$DEBUGINFO ON}
... Many lines of code omitted here
```

**10**

# The Tools API: Property Editors and Component Editors

Just creating a component is often only half the battle. You also want to make the component easy to use. One way to do this is to create a well-designed component with an intuitive interface. However, sometimes you need to give the user help by designing custom property editors or component editors. The next few pages of this chapter show how to proceed.

Before we move on, I think it is important to make sure that everyone knows what it is I am talking about. If you drop a TMainMenu component from the Standard page of the Component Palette on a form, you can double-click on it to bring up a component editor. You can use this component editor to modify the TMainMenu component itself. In particular, you can use it to add, delete, and edit menu items.

If you double-click on the Font property of a TEdit control, you will open a property editor. Needless to say, a property editor is used to edit the properties of a component. Even the simple properties, such as a Caption or Text property, have property editors. In those cases, the visible part of the property editor is just the simple edit control that is embedded in the Object Inspector itself.

Listings 10.8 through 10.11 show the component and property editors that accompany the TElfClock component. Over the next few pages you will have chance to get a good look at this code. The discussion should provide the knowledge you need to begin adding helpful design time features to your own components.

**LISTING 10.8**  The Design Time Code for Adding a Property Editor and Component Editor to the Clock

```
unit ElvesDesignCode;

interface

uses
  ElfClock, DesignIntf, DesignEditors,
  ClxEditors;

type
  TElfClockEdit = class(TComponentEditor)
    procedure Edit; override;
  end;

  TElfColorNameProperty = class(TColorProperty)
  public
```

**LISTING 10.8**   Continued

```
    function GetAttributes: TPropertyAttributes; override;
    procedure Edit; override;
  end;

procedure Register;

implementation

uses
 QGraphics, ColorPicker1,  ClockEditor1;

procedure Register;
begin
  RegisterComponentEditor(TElfFancyClock, TElfClockEdit);
  RegisterPropertyEditor(TypeInfo(TColor),
    TElfClock, 'Color', TElfColorNameProperty);
end;
{--------------------------------------------------------------------}
{ TClockEdit --------------------------------------------------------}
{--------------------------------------------------------------------}

procedure TElfClockEdit.Edit;
var
  ClockEditor: TClockEditor;
begin
  ClockEditor := TClockEditor.Create(nil);
  ClockEditor.BackColor := TElfFancyClock(Component).Color;
  ClockEditor.FaceColor := TElfFancyClock(Component).FaceColor;
  ClockEditor.FontColor := TElfFancyClock(Component).Font.Color;
  ClockEditor.ShowModal;
  TElfFancyClock(Component).Color := ClockEditor.BackColor;
  TElfFancyClock(Component).FaceColor := ClockEditor.FaceColor;
  TElfFancyClock(Component).Font.Color := ClockEditor.FontColor;
  ClockEditor.Free;
end;


{--------------------------------------------------------------------}
{ TColorNameProperty ------------------------------------------------}
{--------------------------------------------------------------------}

function TElfColorNameProperty.GetAttributes;
begin
  Result := [paMultiSelect, paValueList, paDialog];
end;
```

**10**

ADVANCED
COMPONENT
DESIGN

**Listing 10.8**  Continued

```
procedure TElfColorNameProperty.Edit;
var
  S: String;
  ColorPicker: TColorPicker;
begin
  S := '';
  ColorPicker := TColorPicker.Create(nil);
  ColorPicker.ShowModal;
  S := ColorToString(ColorPicker.ColorChoice);
  ColorPicker.Free;
  SetValue(S);
end;

end.
```

**Listing 10.9**  A Property Editor for the Clock Unit

```
////////////////////////////////////////
// Purpose: Allow the user to pick a color
// Project: Elves.dpk
// Copyright © 1998 to 2001 by Charlie Calvert
//
unit ColorPicker1;

interface

uses
  SysUtils, Classes, QGraphics,
  QControls, QForms, QDialogs,
  QStdCtrls, QButtons, QExtCtrls,
  HackedColorGrd;

type
  TColorPicker = class(TForm)
    ColorGrid1: TColorGrid;
    Bevel1: TBevel;
    BitBtn1: TBitBtn;
    BitBtn2: TBitBtn;
    procedure BitBtn1Click(Sender: TObject);
  private
    FColorChoice: TColor;
    { Private declarations }
  public
```

**LISTING 10.9**   Continued

```
  property ColorChoice: TColor read FColorChoice;
end;

var
  ColorPicker: TColorPicker;

implementation

{$R *.xfm}

procedure TColorPicker.BitBtn1Click(Sender: TObject);
begin
  FColorChoice := ColorGrid1.ForegroundColor;
end;

end.
```

**LISTING 10.10**   A Component Editor for the Clock Unit

```
//////////////////////////////////////
// Purpose: A component editor the clock unit
// Project: Elves.dpk
// Copyright © 1998..2001 by Charlie Calvert
//
unit ClockEditor1;

interface

uses
  SysUtils, Classes, QGraphics,
  QControls, QForms, QDialogs,
  QExtCtrls, QStdCtrls, QButtons;

type
  TClockEditor = class(TForm)
    Panel1: TPanel;
    GroupBox1: TGroupBox;
    Backgroundbtn: TButton;
    FaceColorBtn: TButton;
    FontColorBtn: TButton;
    BGShape: TShape;
    FaceShape: TShape;
    FontShape: TShape;
```

**10**

**LISTING 10.10**   Continued

```
    ColorDialog1: TColorDialog;
    BitBtn1: TBitBtn;
    BitBtn2: TBitBtn;
    procedure BackgroundbtnClick(Sender: TObject);
    procedure FaceColorBtnClick(Sender: TObject);
    procedure FontColorBtnClick(Sender: TObject);
  private
    FBackColor: TColor;
    FFaceColor: TColor;
    FFontColor: TColor;
    procedure SetBackColor(Value: TColor);
    procedure SetFaceColor(Value: TColor);
    procedure SetFontColor(Value: TColor);
  public
    property BackColor: TColor read FBackColor write SetBackColor;
    property FaceColor: TColor read FFaceColor write SetFaceColor;
    property FontColor: TColor read FFontColor write SetFontColor;
    { Public declarations }
  end;

var
  ClockEditor: TClockEditor;

implementation

{$R *.xfm}

procedure TClockEditor.BackgroundbtnClick(Sender: TObject);
begin
  if ColorDialog1.Execute then
    BackColor := ColorDialog1.Color;
end;

procedure TClockEditor.FaceColorBtnClick(Sender: TObject);
begin
  if ColorDialog1.Execute then
    FaceColor := ColorDialog1.Color;
end;

procedure TClockEditor.FontColorBtnClick(Sender: TObject);
begin
  if ColorDialog1.Execute then
    FontColor := ColorDialog1.Color;
end;
```

**LISTING 10.10**   Continued

```
procedure TClockEditor.SetBackColor(Value: TColor);
begin
  FBackColor := Value;
  BGShape.Brush.Color := Value;
end;

procedure TClockEditor.SetFaceColor(Value: TColor);
begin
  FFaceColor := Value;
  FaceShape.Brush.Color := Value;
end;

procedure TClockEditor.SetFontColor(Value: TColor);
begin
  FFontColor := Value;
  FontShape.Brush.Color := Value;
end;

end.
```

**LISTING 10.11**   The Source for the Design Time Package that Holds the `TElfClock` Component and Property Editors

```
package ElvesDesignTime;

{$R *.res}
{$ALIGN 8}
{$ASSERTIONS ON}
{$BOOLEVAL OFF}
{$DEBUGINFO ON}
{$EXTENDEDSYNTAX ON}
{$IMPORTEDDATA ON}
{$IOCHECKS ON}
{$LOCALSYMBOLS ON}
{$LONGSTRINGS ON}
{$OPENSTRINGS ON}
{$OPTIMIZATION ON}
{$OVERFLOWCHECKS OFF}
{$RANGECHECKS OFF}
{$REFERENCEINFO ON}
{$SAFEDIVIDE OFF}
{$STACKFRAMES OFF}
{$TYPEDADDRESS OFF}
```

**10**

**ADVANCED COMPONENT DESIGN**

**LISTING 10.11** Continued

```
{$VARSTRINGCHECKS ON}
{$WRITEABLECONST OFF}
{$MINENUMSIZE 1}
{$IMAGEBASE $400000}
{$IMPLICITBUILD OFF}

requires
  baseclx,
  visualclx,
  designide,
  GDITiles,
  Elves;

contains
  ClockEditor1 in 'ClockEditor1.pas' {ClockEditor},
  ColorPicker1 in 'ColorPicker1.pas' {ColorPicker},
  ElvesDesignCode in 'ElvesDesignCode.pas';

end.
```

# Design Time Code Versus Runtime Code

There are two types of code associated with a component. The code that makes up the component itself is called *runtime code*. The code that creates the property editors and component editors that are seen at design time is called *design time code*. In Kylix, you should place all the runtime code for your components in one package, and the design time code for your components in a separate package.

There are three different reasons why you should care about design time packages and runtime packages:

- If you place both the runtime and design time code for your components in the same package, and you distribute your package with your program, other programmers can use your components for free. Giving them a package with your design time code in it gives them all they need to use your components in their own programs. If you don't want to give your components away, you will want to place your design time code in a separate package that you never give to the users of your program. To run your program, they need only the runtime package.

- Separating your runtime code and your design time code helps you organize your source in much the same way that OOP itself helps you organize your source. In short, it is a form of encapsulation. My runtime code is in this neat little package, and here, wrapped up in its own nice little package, is my design time code! All kidding aside, this is the thing that I like the most about design time and runtime packages.

- The final reason you should care about packages is that in the first shipping versions of Kylix, many of the components you create will not compile correctly if you don't divide your code into runtime and design time packages. I do not know if this was intended by the developers or not, but the end result is that you have to divide many components into design time and runtime packages if you want to use them at all!

---

**NOTE**

In the first shipping versions of Kylix, if you try to compile many types of design time code into your project, you will get an error about not being able to find const.pas. In a package, you can correct this problem by adding designide into the requires clause of your package:

```
requires
    baseclx,
    visualclx,
    designide,
    GDITiles,
    Elves;
```

This clause says that the clock package requires the presence of baseclx, visualclx, designide, and two packages that I ship with this book, called GDITiles and Elves. The package requires these other packages because it relies on code that is compiled into these packages.

---

## The State of Tools API on Kylix

There are several different categories of services found in the Tools API. Each is accessible through a separate set of routines. These APIs enable you to write code that can be linked directly into the Kylix IDE. Specifically, you can link your tools into packages, the same way you link in components. Here is a list of the Tools APIs that are relevant to Kylix:

- Component editors
- Property editors
- Editor interfaces

Other parts of the Tools API are a bit problematic in the first versions of Kylix. For instance, there are sections of the Tools API designed to help you create wizards, or manage the debugger, or work with version control systems. Other APIs are represented by the following objects: IOTAMenuWizard, IOTARepositoryWizard, IOTAFormWizard, and IOTAProjectWizard.

**10**

**ADVANCED COMPONENT DESIGN**

At the time this book was written, not all of these subsystems were working. I will discuss some of these interfaces and issues related to them in the next section, "The Tools API and Wine."

I will show you how to use the component and property editor interfaces. There is an example of how to use the Editor interface in the Kylix demo directory.

Needless to say, most people will never use the Tools API. However, it will be important to a small minority of developers, and its existence means that everyone will be able to buy or download tools that extend the functionality of the IDE.

## The Tools API and Wine

As stated in the introduction to this book, Kylix is a true Linux compiler. The IDE, however, is a port of the Delphi 5 IDE to Windows. It runs on top of Wine. As such, all the code that becomes part of the IDE itself must be written using the VCL, and cannot use CLX. Therefore, if you want to create a wizard that has visual features for use in Kylix, you must create it in Delphi 5, and then compile it in Linux. Your wizard must not contain any CLX code, and it must use the packages vcl and designide in its requires clause. I do not intend to document this—um—process in this book. However, Object Pascal guru and talented author Ray Lischner has written about the process in an article that appears on the http://community. borland.com Web site. Here is the relevant URL: http://community.borland.com/ article/0,1410,27205,00.html.

The following URL points to Ray's own site, where you might be able to find additional information: http://www.tempest-sw.com/opentools/.

The portions of the Kylix IDE that have to do with the property editors and the form designer do not use the VCL. Instead, they were rewritten in CLX. As a result, you can write real property and component editors in CLX, and they will work fine inside the IDE.

## The Tools API and Interfaces

The Tools API is based largely on a set of interfaces. These interfaces establish the conventions on which this technology is based. In many cases, Borland provides default implementations of these interfaces. This means that you can use the default implementation of the interface you need just as you would use any other class. However, if you want, you can implement the interface yourself, thereby getting the opportunity to customize the code as you please.

I will admit to being quite confused when I first saw the interfaces for the Tools API. I believe, however, that this confusion stemmed primarily from the fact that the Tools API was almost entirely undocumented. In practice, the technology is not difficult, but it got a reputation of being hard simply because no one knew how it worked. I found that understanding this technology was a very simple, but not particularly intuitive, process.

## Property Editors

The Tools API for creating property editors is perhaps the most commonly used interface into the heart of the IDE. When you first use Kylix and start becoming familiar with the Object Inspector, you are bound to think that it is a static element that never changes. However, you can change the functionality of the Object Inspector by adding new property editors to it.

As mentioned earlier, property editors control what takes place on the right side of the Properties page of the Object Inspector. In particular, when you click on the Color property of a TEdit, you can select a new color from a drop-down list, from a common dialog box, or by typing in a new value. In all three cases, you are using a property editor.

If you want to create a new property editor, you should create a descendant of TPropertyEditor, a class declared in DesignEditors.pas, from the ../kylix/source/toolsapi directory. Here is the declaration for the property editor associated with the TElfColorClock component:

```
TElfColorNameProperty = class(TColorProperty)
public
  function GetAttributes: TPropertyAttributes; override;
  procedure Edit; override;
end;
```

The DesignEditors unit depends on DesignIntf.pas. DesignIntf declares a set of interfaces, and DesignEditors provides a default implementation for these interfaces.

The DesignEditors unit is unusual in that it is very carefully documented by the developer who created it. For instance, here are excerpts from that unit describing the two methods I call in my descendant of TPropertyEditor:

```
Edit: Called when the '...' button is pressed or the property is double-
clicked. This can, for example, bring up a dialog to allow the editing the
component in some more meaningful fashion than by text (e.g. the Font
property).
```

```
GetAttributes: Returns the information for use in the Object Inspector to be
able to show the appropriate tools.  GetAttributes returns a set of type
TPropertyAttributes:
```

I won't quote further, for fear of sounding like I'm plagiarizing. The point, however, is that these entries were written by the developers, and they extensively document this important interface to the core code inside the heart of the IDE. Here are declarations for Edit and GetAttributes, as well as the other key functions in the IProperty interface:

```
IProperty = interface
    ['{7ED7BF29-E349-11D3-AB4A-00C04FB17A72}']
    procedure Activate;
    function AllEqual: Boolean;
    function AutoFill: Boolean;
    procedure Edit;
    function HasInstance(Instance: TPersistent): Boolean;
    function GetAttributes: TPropertyAttributes;
    function GetEditLimit: Integer;
    function GetEditValue(out Value: string): Boolean;
    function GetName: string;
    function GetComponentValue: TComponent;
    procedure GetProperties(Proc: TGetPropProc);
    function GetPropInfo: PPropInfo;
    function GetPropType: PTypeInfo;
    function GetValue: string;
    procedure GetValues(Proc: TGetStrProc);
    procedure Revert;
    procedure SetValue(const Value: string);
    function ValueAvailable: Boolean;
  end;
```

Once again, all these methods are at least superficially documented inside DesignIntf.PAS. You should study that file carefully if you want to learn more about creating complex property editors.

If you wanted, you could create your own implementation of the IProperty interface. When you were done, you would have a custom property editor that could be shown in the Object Inspector. However, all that work is not necessary in this case because Borland provides a serviceable one in DesignEditors.pas called TPropertyEditor. Here is the first line of the declaration for that class:

```
TPropertyEditor = class(TBasePropertyEditor, IProperty)
```

The actual implementation of TPropertyEditor is very long. Delving into it would be an appropriate task for a book dedicated to the Tools API, but it would probably be a bit much for this book. The TBasePropertyEditor is an easier subject to tackle. Here is its declaration from DesignIntf.pas:

```
  TBasePropertyEditor = class(TInterfacedObject)
  protected
```

```
  procedure Initialize; virtual; abstract;
  procedure SetPropEntry(Index: Integer; AInstance: TPersistent;
    APropInfo: PPropInfo); virtual; abstract;
public
  constructor Create(const ADesigner: IDesigner; APropCount: Integer);
virtual;
  end;
```

TInterfacedObject was discussed in Chapter 4. As you can see, both Initialize and SetPropEntry are virtual abstract methods that must be overridden by the class that descends from this class. In this case, that is TPropertyEditor. So one of the duties of TPropertyEditor is to implement these methods. The constructor looks like this:

```
constructor TBasePropertyEditor.Create(const ADesigner: IDesigner;
  APropCount: Integer);
begin
  inherited Create;
end;
```

As you can see, the constructor does nothing.

---

**NOTE**

By now, most normal human beings would be getting a bit frustrated. Here TBasePropertyEditor has three methods, two of which are abstract, and the third doesn't do anything! Why bother to declare the class at all? Well, the likely reason is that it establishes the convention for creating all classes that implement that IProperty interface. If you want to create a property editor, it is suggested that you create a class with a constructor that looks like this, and two procedures that implement the Initialize and SetPropEntry methods.

I'll confess that all this is bit rich for my blood. I feel a little bit as though we need a Scott Meyers to come along and adjudicate all this for us, as if we were working in C++. In fact, Danny Thorpe plays much the same role in Object Pascal development that Scott Meyers plays in the world of C++ development. My only complaint is that if I want C++, I'll go use C++. Object Pascal is meant to be a bit less opaque.

---

At this stage, you are almost ready to see what is up in the TColorProperty class itself. Here is the remaining bit of the hierarchy that gets you from TPropertyEditor to TColorProperty:

```
TOrdinalProperty = class(TPropertyEditor)
  function AllEqual: Boolean; override;
  function GetEditLimit: Integer; override;
end;
```

```
TIntegerProperty = class(TOrdinalProperty)
public
  function GetValue: string; override;
  procedure SetValue(const Value: string); override;
end;

TColorProperty = class(TIntegerProperty)
public
  procedure Edit; override;
  function GetAttributes: TPropertyAttributes; override;
  function GetValue: string; override;
  procedure GetValues(Proc: TGetStrProc); override;
  procedure SetValue(const Value: string); override;
end;
```

Both TOrdinalProperty and TIntegerProperty are relatively trivial objects. For instance, here is the GetEditLimit method:

```
function TOrdinalProperty.GetEditLimit: Integer;
begin
  Result := 63;
end;
```

This method defines the length of the string you can type into the edit control used to implement this property editor. For instance, if you are in an Integer base property editor such as the Width field, you can enter a total of up to 63 characters.

Here you are seeing the good side of the Tools API. If you want to change the length of the string you can type in this control, all you need to do is override this simple method, and then return a new value. That is exactly what OOP is designed to do. Once you get beyond the surface complexity of the Tools API, much of it is quite elegant.

The GetValue and SetValue methods of TIntegerProperty are also admirably straightforward and serviceable. Here, for instance, is the GetValue method:

```
function TIntegerProperty.GetValue: string;
begin
  with GetTypeData(GetPropType)^ do
    if OrdType = otULong then // unsigned
      Result := IntToStr(Cardinal(GetOrdValue))
    else
      Result := IntToStr(GetOrdValue);
end;
```

This method simply converts the integer value contained in this property into a string that can be displayed in an edit control. Needless to say, SetValue reverses the process. Again, the clarity and power of these methods are excellent examples of what it means to write good object-oriented code. The creator of the Tools API knows OOP inside out. As a result, he makes you master some theory before you can use his tools. However, once you get past the theory, the results are quite pleasing.

In order to create a flexible, polymorphic hierarchy, the `SetValue` method requests that you convert the value you have edited into string. Therefore, the `SetValue` method for strings, integers, floats, and even `TColor` properties all have the same declaration. Needless to say, underneath, the `SetValue` method must convert the string back into an integer, float, `TColor` object, or what have you.

By this time, you should be able to begin to guess what some of the methods of `TColorProperty` might look like. Here, for instance, is the `GetValue` method:

```
function TColorProperty.GetValue: string;
begin
  Result := ColorToString(TColor(GetOrdValue));
end;
```

This is trivial code. In fact, most of the code in `TColorProperty` is not much more complicated than this. Once you begin to grasp this, you can see that the act of actually implementing the raw interfaces declared in `DesignIntf.pas` is not really as formidable a task as it might have at first appeared. However, there is little reason for doing so, since the implementations in `DesignEditors` and `ClxEditors` will meet the needs of most developers.

The `Edit` method of `TColorPropertyEditor` is the one you want to override to change the way a property editor actually edits data:

```
procedure TElfColorNameProperty.Edit;
var
  S: String;
begin
  S := '';
  InputQuery('New Color', 'Enter Color', S);
  SetValue(S);
end;
```

In this case, I am creating a substitute for the `TColorDialog` that pops up when you click on the ellipsis icon in Object Inspector. I am, of course, replacing a fancy dialog box with a simpler one that asks the user to enter a string such as `"clBlue"` or `"clGreen"`. The point, however, is that you are learning how to create your own property editors.

In a more complex example, you might open a form that allowed the user to make extensive changes to a property. This is what I do in the `TElfColorClock` component. In particular, I create a dialog box that has a `TColorGrid`, two bevels, and two `BitBtns` in it, as shown in Figure 10.4.

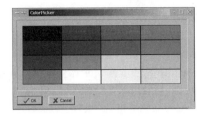

**FIGURE 10.4**

*The property editor for the* Color *property of the* TElfColorClock *and its descendants.*

This is still probably not as fancy a dialog box as the one used by the CLX, but it serves as a good example of how to create your own custom component editors.

Here is what the TElfColorNameProperty.Edit method looks like that launches this dialog box:

```
procedure TElfColorNameProperty.Edit;
var
  S: String;
  ColorPicker: TColorPicker;
begin
  S := '';
  ColorPicker := TColorPicker.Create(nil);
  ColorPicker.ShowModal;
  S := ColorToString(ColorPicker.ColorChoice);
  ColorPicker.Free;
  SetValue(S);
end;
```

The code creates an instance of the TColorPicker dialog box, shows it to the user, and then makes use of the color the user chose.

SetValue, called at the end of this procedure, is another method of TPropertyEditor. You saw an example of this kind of method earlier in this section. In this particular case, the ColorToString and StringToColor methods from the Graphics.pas CLX unit help to make this task relatively simple.

The GetAttributes method is a way of defining what types of property editors you want to have associated with TElfColorNameProperty:

```
function TElfColorNameProperty.GetAttributes;
begin
  Result := [paMultiSelect, paValueList, paDialog];
end;
```

A property editor that has the `paMultiSelect` flag remains active even if the user has selected more than one component of that type. For instance, you can select 10 edit controls and change all their fonts in one step. Kylix allows you to do that because `TEdit`s have their `paMultiSelect` flag set.

The `paValueList` flag dictates that the property editor drops down a list of values from an enumerated or set type when the user clicks the arrow button at the far right of the editor. This functionality is built into Kylix, and you need only set the flag to have it be supported by your property editor.

Finally, `paDialog` states that the property editor pops up a dialog box. Because the `Edit` function shown earlier uses either an `InputQuery` or the `TColorPicker` dialog box, I have decided that this flag should be set. Ultimately, the `paDialog` flag does little more than assure that the ellipsis button appears at the right of the property editor.

---

> **NOTE**
>
> When you choose both `paDialog` and `paValuelist` in a single component, the property editor button always winds up being a combo drop-down list button. In other words, the dialog button is obscured, even though the functionality is still present. See, for instance, the `Color` property of a `TForm` or `TEdit`.

## More on Registering Your Component and Component Editors

You must register property editors with the system before compiling them into packages:

```
procedure Register;
begin
  ...
  RegisterPropertyEditor(TypeInfo(TColor),
    TElfClock, 'Color', TColorNameProperty);
end;
```

The declaration for `RegisterPropertyEditor` looks like this:

```
procedure RegisterPropertyEditor(PropertyType: PTypeInfo;
  ComponentClass: TClass; const PropertyName: string;
  EditorClass: TPropertyEditorClass);
```

Here is what the various parameters mean:

- PropertyType. The first parameter passed to this function states the type of data handled by the editor. In this case, it is TColor. Kylix uses this information as the first in a series of checklists that determine which properties should be associated with this editor.

- ComponentClass. The second parameter further qualifies which components will use this editor. In this case, I have narrowed the range down to TElfClock and its descendants. If I had written TComponent instead of TElfClock, or if I had set this parameter to nil, all properties of type TColor would start using that editor. What this means is that you could build a new editor for fonts or colors, install it on a customer's system, and it would work with all properties of that type. In other words, you don't have to create a component in order to write an editor for it. Furthermore, some of the fanciest component packs that you can buy include new editors of this type. After you install the new component pack, you get new, improved versions of the editors for some of the common Kylix properties. At this time, most of these fancy component packs work only in Delphi, but hopefully some of these will have been converted to Kylix, or new component packs will have been developed.

- PropertyName. The third parameter limits the scope to properties with the name passed in this string. If the string is empty, the editor is used for all properties that get passed the first two parameters.

- EditorClass. This parameter defines the class of editor associated with the properties defined in the first three parameters. This is where you specify the new property editor that you created.

If you want to find out more about this function, refer to the comments in DesignIntf.

While I'm at it, I'm going to add a few more words about registering components in general. To add the clock components to the Component Palette, you must first register them:

```
procedure Register;
begin
  RegisterComponents('Elves', [TElfClock, TElfColorClock, TFancyClock]);
  ...
end;
```

Here, I specify that the TElfClock, TFancyClock, and TElfColorClock objects should be placed in a page on the Component Palette called Elves.

The second parameter to `RegisterComponents` takes an array of type
`TComponentClass`:

```
procedure RegisterComponents(const Page: string;
  ComponentClasses: array of TComponentClass);
```

Kylix supports open-arrays, which means that you do not have to declare how many
members are going to be included in an array. Instead, you only need to declare the
type of members that will go in the array, as shown earlier. Furthermore, when creating these arrays, you can build them on-the-fly rather than having to declare an array
variable. To do this, type an open bracket and then enter the members of the array
separated by commas. To close the array, type a closing bracket. For more information, see the discussion of arrays in Chapter 3, "Basic Pascal Syntax," or look up *Open-
Array Construction* in the online help.

## Component Editors

When you have seen how to build property editors, it is easy to understand component editors.
These tools are descendants of `TComponentEditor`, just as property editors are descendants of
`TPropertyEditor`:

```
TElfClockEditor = class(TComponentEditor)
  procedure Edit; override;
end;
```

The simplest possible `TClock` component would have an editor that pops up a dialog box specifying a copyright:

```
procedure TElfClockEditor.Edit;
begin
  ShowMessage('Clock copyright © 2001 Charlie Calvert');
end;
```

This technology, of course, is not likely to make your users feel as though they are being cod-
dled, but it gets you started working with these useful tools.

A more interesting component editor would pop up a custom Kylix form, such as the one
shown in Listing 10.10, and found in the book's CD in the file called ClockEditor1.pas. This
dialog box is designed to let you see the colors for the main elements of the control, as shown
in Figure 10.5. Needless to say, it would not be hard to improve on this component editor by
dropping down a `TTabbedNotebook` and adding mechanisms for setting most of the properties
of the control.

## FIGURE 10.5

*The minimalist component editor for the* TElfColorClock *component.*

You can access a component editor by double-clicking on a component. Here is the code that gets executed when you double-click:

```
procedure TElfClockEdit.Edit;
var
  ClockEditor: TClockEditor;
begin
  ClockEditor := TClockEditor.Create(nil);
  ClockEditor.BackColor := TElfFancyClock(Component).Color;
  ClockEditor.FaceColor := TElfFancyClock(Component).FaceColor;
  ClockEditor.FontColor := TElfFancyClock(Component).Font.Color;
  ClockEditor.ShowModal;
  TElfFancyClock(Component).Color := ClockEditor.BackColor;
  TElfFancyClock(Component).FaceColor := ClockEditor.FaceColor;
  TElfFancyClock(Component).Font.Color := ClockEditor.FontColor;
  ClockEditor.Free;
end;
```

The code first creates an instance of the object. It then assigns default values to all the fields the user is going to edit. Finally it shows the dialog box, and then retrieves the users' input.

The key property in the TComponentEditor class is called Component. It is an instance of the underlying component for which you are writing a component editor. To access the component, you need only typecast the Component property:

```
TElfFancyClock(Component).Color := ClockEditor.BackColor;
```

This line of code changes the Color property of the component. Making the change this way has the exact same effect as making the change in the Object Inspector. This is merely a second way of getting at the properties of the component at design time.

The Register method for TElfClockEditor looks like this:

```
procedure Register;
begin
    ...
```

```
RegisterComponentEditor(TElfClock, TElfClockEditor);
  ...
end;
```

The declaration for this procedure looks like this:

```
procedure RegisterComponentEditor(ComponentClass: TComponentClass;
  ComponentEditor: TComponentEditorClass);
```

The first parameter specifies the class with which the editor is associated, and the second parameter specifies the class of the editor.

In this section, you have been introduced to property editors and component editors. These examples are important primarily because they help focus your attention on DesignIntf.pas, ClxEditors.pas, and DesignEditors.pas, which are three of the group of several files that ship with Kylix that define the Tools API. If you want to extend the Kylix IDE, you should get to know all the files in that directory.

## Some Notes on Component Maintenance

Over the years, I have found problems with the CompDirs program that owed their origin to bugs in the TFileIterator component. When I found one of those bugs, or suspected its existence, I could take TFileIterator out of the CompDirs program and create a simple test bed. For instance, I could just shut down the relatively complex CompDirs program, and test the component inside something simple like FindAllW, or a program custom-made to stress the part of the component that I thought might not be working correctly. Inside these custom test beds, I could usually find the problem fairly quickly and fix it. Then I could go back to the CompDirs program and see if everything was working correctly.

My point in the last paragraph is simply that components help you structure programs so that they can be easily maintained. It is a terrible mistake to bind an object into a program so that it can't be easily tested on its own. Components not only make it difficult for you to make that kind of mistake, but they also make it particularly easy to test an object in a new environment. In short, components can help you write well-ordered, proper, object-oriented code. They make it easy, or least easier, for you to maintain your code.

## Component Templates

I've already shown you traditional compound components and frames. Component templates are a third way to bring multiple components together and reuse them.

Component templates are so simple to use that I will only say a few brief words about them. However, these are important words, as this technology can be very useful under certain circumstances.

To create a component template, drop a button and an edit control on a form. Associate a method with the button that places some text in the edit control:

```
procedure TForm1.SampleBtnClick(Sender: TObject);
begin
  SampleEdit.Text :=
    'The greatest thing in the world is to ' +
    'know how to be one's own self. - Montaigne'
end;
```

Now select both of the controls on the form with the mouse and choose Component, Create Component Template from the Kylix menu. You will be asked to give your creation a name and an optional icon. Click on the OK button to finish the operation.

At this stage a new page, called, by default, Templates, will be added to the Component Palette. This page is usually placed way over on the far right, where you need to scroll over to see it. On this page will be the new component that you just created. This component will be a combination of the button and edit control. Even the source code you wrote will remain associated with this control, and will be re-created exactly as you wrote it in your form if you reuse the component. To see this action, create a new project and drop your new component template on it, just as you would any other control.

The great advantage of component templates is their ease of use. The disadvantage is that they don't effectively support basic OOP principles such as encapsulation, inheritance, or polymorphism. For instance, the code you write ends up in the form you drop the component on, rather than tucked away in a separate object. This is not necessarily a bad thing, but it violates the principle of encapsulation. It is also difficult to share components created in this manner with other developers. Nevertheless, this is a powerful and easy to use technology.

## Summary

In this chapter you had a chance to broaden your knowledge of Kylix component creation. In particular, you saw

- Which controls to descend from if you want to create a control from scratch.
- How to add functionality not available in an ancestor object. For instance, the TElfColorClock object does things that TElfClock does not.
- How to build up controls from scratch so that they can add new functionality to the programming environment. For instance, the TElfClock component brings something entirely new to Kylix programming that does not exist in any other component that ships with the product.

- Something about the Tools API, and specifically about the art of making property editors and component editors.

- How to create a component template.

In many ways, I wish I could explore this topic in even more depth, but a book like this has only so much room for exploring even the most interesting subjects.

# Graphics

*by Charlie Calvert*

## IN THIS CHAPTER

Creating graphics elements in CLX programs is the subject of this chapter. While reading about this subject you will see

- A Mandelbrot program that allows you to save pictures of the screen to a file.
- A game engine that creates a very old-fashioned pseudo-3D maze, similar to the kind used back in the early 1990s. This implementation of the game engine uses a classic design pattern called Abstract Factory.

Before you can learn about these tools, however, you need to first learn how the major objects in QGraphics.pas are put together. In particular, you will learn about the TCanvas, TBrush, TPen, and TBitmap objects.

## The Major Objects Found in QGraphics.pas

Graphics programming using native APIs is often quite complex. Kylix employs object-oriented programming techniques to simplify the task.

Graphics programming in Kylix uses CLX. This object-oriented library allows you to draw shapes, text, and bitmaps. CLX also provides control over items such as colors, line thickness, fonts, and shading.

Nearly all of the key objects related to graphics programming with Kylix are stored in QGraphics.pas. The only real exceptions are declarations for basic types, such as the TRect structure, or various Qt objects, which are inherited from other units. The core code that you need to understand, however, is located in QGraphics.pas.

Table 11.1 presents a list of the key objects in the QGraphics unit. The most important object shown here is TCanvas, followed closely by TBrush, TBitmap, and TPen. You can think of a TCanvas object as both owning and encapsulating all the other objects, such as pens and brushes.

**TABLE 11.1**  The Most Important Objects Found in the QGraphics Unit

| Object | Description |
| --- | --- |
| TCanvas | This is the basic graphics object used to wrap the Qt graphics system. It is used to paint fonts, pictures, and shapes on a form or other surface. |
| TBrush | This object designates the color or pattern that fills the interior of shapes. |

**TABLE 11.1** Continued

| Object | Description |
|---|---|
| TPen | This object draws lines and designates the color of the outline of shapes. |
| TPicture | This is a generalized, high-level CLX container for "pictures" such as bitmaps or icons. |
| TBitmap | The CLX wrapper around bitmaps. It descends not from TPicture, but TGraphic. |
| TIcon | The CLX wrapper around icons. It descends not from TPicture, but TGraphic. |
| TGraphicsObject | This is the base class for TBrush, TFont, and TPen. |
| TFont | An object for manipulating the font used when drawing text. |

The primary burden of this chapter is to explain the most important of these objects. Once you have a sense of how they work, you will be free to have some fun with them in your own programs.

> **NOTE**
>
> Throughout this chapter, I often talk about blting or blitting a bitmap or other graphical object to the screen. I believe the word *blt*, pronounced *blit*, is an abbreviation for "blasting bits" to the screen. If you want to draw a bitmap on the screen, most programmers would refer to the operation as blitting the picture to the screen. A method called BitBlt is used to perform this operation in a number of different languages and APIs on both Linux and Windows. As a result, the term "to blt" has entered most programmers' lexicon.

# The TCanvas Object

All forms, and many components, have a canvas. The TCanvas object functions much like a canvas does in the real world. It provides the surface on which graphics objects can be painted.

Frequently, the TCanvas object is used with a component. To visualize how this is done, open up Kylix and drop a button and an image component on the form. Double-click on the button and insert code that looks like this:

```
procedure TForm1.Button1Click(Sender: TObject);
begin
  Image1.Canvas.Brush.Color := clRed;
  Image1.Canvas.Rectangle(10,10,100,100);
end;
```

When you run the program, a red rectangle will be painted on the canvas.

It is important to notice that you cannot access a property such as Brush directly from the component. It is not valid to write:

```
Image1.Brush.Color
```

Trying to access the Brush property directly does not work because the Canvas object is aggregated into Image1. The Canvas object is not brought in through multiple inheritance.

The form, like other objects, has a canvas. If you are accessing a form's canvas from inside the form, you do not need to specify that the canvas belongs to that form. To illustrate this, change the internal code for the procedure above so that it reads as follows:

```
procedure TForm1.Button1Click(Sender: TObject);
begin
  Canvas.Brush.Color := clRed;
  Canvas.Rectangle(10,10,100,100);
end;
```

This code paints directly on the surface of the form itself. Though usually not necessary, it would not have been wrong to write

```
Form1.Canvas.Brush.Color := clRed;
Form1.Canvas.Rectangle(10,10,100,100);
```

Table 11.2 shows several methods of the TCanvas object that all CLX programmers should know.

**TABLE 11.2**    Key Methods of the TCanvas Object

| Method | Description |
| --- | --- |
| Arc | Draw an arc |
| Chord | Draw a closed figure showing the intersection of a line and an ellipse |
| CopyRect | Copy an area of one canvas to another, see Draw |
| Draw | Draw a bitmap or other graphic on a canvas, see CopyRect |
| Ellipse | Draw an ellipse |
| FillRect | Fill a rectangle |

**TABLE 11.2**   Continued

| Method | Description |
|---|---|
| FloodFill | Fill an enclosed area |
| FrameRect | Draw a border around a rectangle |
| LineTo | Draw a line |
| MoveTo | Draw a line |
| Pie | Draw a pie-shaped object |
| Polygon | Draw a multisided object |
| Polyline | Connect a set of points on the canvas |
| Rectangle | Draw a rectangle |
| RoundRect | Draw a rectangle with rounded corners |
| StretchDraw | Same as Draw, but stretches the object to fill an area |
| TextHeight | The height of the string on the current font |
| TextOut | Output text |
| TextRect | Output text in a defined area |
| TextWidth | The width of a string in the current font |

The Canvas object also has a series of useful properties, including all those shown in Table 11.3. Note that most of the items listed in Table 11.3 are class properties, including the key Brush and Pen properties.

**TABLE 11.3**   Key Properties of the TCanvas Object

| Property | Description |
|---|---|
| Brush | Defines the interior of a shape such as an ellipse. If you draw a rectangle, the brush defines the color and texture of the area inside the border of the rectangle. |
| CopyMode | Describes the methodology for blitting one bitmap into another. This includes masking, various Boolean operations, and blitting pure colors such as white or black. |
| Font | Defines the font used when drawing text. |
| Pen | Defines the outline of shapes and the character of lines. |
| PenPos | The current position of the pen, equivalent to MoveTo. |
| ClipRect | The area of the screen that needs to be repainted in a paint operation. Also ensures that you do not try to paint outside the bounds of a component. |

**TABLE 11.3**  Continued

| Property | Description |
|----------|-------------|
| Handle | Use this property when you want to call into the low raw Qt calls that lie behind the CLX library. |
| LockCount | The number of threads that have a lock on the paint surface. |
| StartCount | Every time a painting operation begins, CLX will call a Qt method called Start. This count shows how many simultaneous calls there are to this procedure at any one time. |
| TextAlign | Is the text aligned to the left, the top, or center? |

# Drawing Using Qt

Some of the properties of the Canvas object cry out for some explanation. In fact, it is difficult to fully understand what is happening in the QGraphics unit if you don't understand the Qt graphics objects that it encapsulates.

Consider the following short method from the PainterTest program found on the CD that accompanies this book:

```
procedure TForm1.RawPaintButtonClick(Sender: TObject);
var
  Painter: QPainterH;
  Brush: QBrushH;
  Color: QColorH;
begin
  Painter := QPainter_create();
  QPainter_begin(Painter, Form1.GetPaintDevice);
  Color := QColor_create(0, 0, 255);
  Brush := QBrush_create(Color, BrushStyle_SolidPattern);
  QPainter_setBrush(Painter, Brush);
  QPainter_drawEllipse(Painter, 10, 10, 100, 100);
  QPainter_end(Painter);
  QColor_destroy(Color);
  QBrush_destroy(Brush);
  QPainter_destroy(Painter);
end;
```

This method draws a blue ellipse to the screen. None of the calls, and none of the variables used in the method, are part of CLX. Instead, the whole method depends on the raw Qt API.

A painter object is what you use in Qt when you want to paint a two-dimensional object to the screen. When you begin a painting operation, you first call the begin method of QPainter:

```
QPainter_begin(Painter, Form1.GetPaintDevice);
```

A PaintDevice is the surface on which the QPainter object paints. Every paintable surface has such a device. Behind the scenes, CLX usually calls a Qt method called QWidget_to_QPaintDevice to obtain the device associated with particular control.

The RawPaintButtonClick method also contains calls to create a Qt Color and a Brush object:

```
Color := QColor_create(0, 0, 255);
Brush := QBrush_create(Color, BrushStyle_SolidPattern);
```

The brush is assigned to the QPainter object so that any shapes drawn by the painter will be filled with the brush passed to it:

```
QPainter_setBrush(Painter, Brush);
```

At this stage you are finally ready to paint an ellipse to the screen:

```
QPainter_drawEllipse(Painter, 10, 10, 100, 100);
```

The only chore left at this point is to clean up the mess you have created:

```
QPainter_end(Painter);
QColor_destroy(Color);
QBrush_destroy(Brush);
QPainter_destroy(Painter);
```

All of this jiving around ends up accomplishing nothing more than what you have already seen in this Button1Click method:

```
procedure TForm1.Button1Click(Sender: TObject);
begin
  Image1.Canvas.Brush.Color := clRed;
  Image1.Canvas.Rectangle(10,10,100,100);
end;
```

In one case I call Rectangle rather than Ellipse, but in effect the two methods are identical. Clearly it is much easier to use the CLX wrapper around the Qt API whenever possible.

## Changing the World Coordinates

Both the CLX and VCL graphics classes are very powerful. Indeed, the CLX QGraphics unit and the VCL Graphics unit are virtually identical. From a user's point of view, the only differences between them involve some Windows-specific code for drawing metafiles that is absent from QGraphics. I like the Object Pascal graphics classes a lot, and use them all the time.

Their virtue is their simplicity and ease of use. Their facility stems from the fact that they omit covering certain corner cases that can greatly complicate certain graphics operations. In particular, the CLX and VCL graphics classes tend to fall down when you start changing the screen coordinate system, mapping mode, or view port.

A component called TElfComps found in the lunits directory draws a simple compass to the screen, as shown in Figure 11.1. This compass might be useful in a game, or in any program where you want to point to the east, west, north, or south. The CompassTest program from this book's CD illustrates how to use the component.

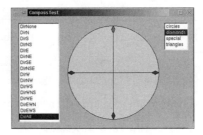

**FIGURE 11.1**

*The compass component allows you to point to the north, east, south, or west.*

The standard Qt and CLX coordinate system starts in the upper-left of the screen and gets larger as you move to the right along the x-coordinate or down the page along the y-coordinate. If you think for a moment about a compass, however, it soon becomes clear that its coordinate system does not begin in the upper-left of the screen, but rather in the center of the component itself.

Qt, like most complete graphical APIs, allows you to move the coordinate system from the left corner of the screen if you so desire. Here is the code from the TElfComps component that changes the nature of the coordinate system:

```
procedure TCompassBase.SetItUp(Painter: QPainterH);
begin
  SetUpSizes;
  Painter := Canvas.Handle;
  QPainter_save(Painter);
  QPainter_setWindow(Painter, -FSizes.HalfSqrSize, -FSizes.HalfSqrSize,
    FSizes.HalfSqrSize, FSizes.HalfSqrSize);
  QPainter_setViewport(Painter, 0, 0, FSizes.hMid, FSizes.VMid);
end;
```

The usual explanations of this kind of thing involve an opaque parlance about projects, matrices, and transformations. I'm not sure, however, that I'm fully equipped to pull it off with much panache. As a result, I will simply say that `SetWindow` defines the coordinates for the window, stating that the far left and top of the window have a logical value defined by minus `FSizes.HalfSqrSize`. The far right and bottom of the window both have the logical coordinate `FSizes.HalfSqrSize`. The actual value of `HalfSqrSize` is not really germane to this discussion. For the sake of argument, let's say it is 25, but it could be any other number. This statement says that the far left of the window will, from the internal point of view of the component, be considered to be at -25, -25, and the bottom right coordinate will be at +25, +25. 0, 0 will be right in the middle. These numbers have nothing to do with the actual size of the component. They are just logical coordinates. If the component were two light-years across, the bottom right corner of the coordinate would still be at +25, +25. The size of one unit will stretch or shrink depending on the actual size of the component. The coordinate system defined by `SetWindow` will stay the same regardless of the actual size of the window as defined by `SetViewPort`.

`SetViewPort` describes the same window as `SetWindow`, but it speaks in terms of actual device coordinates. Suppose `SetWindow` and `SetViewPort` were passed these coordinates:

```
QPainter_SetWindow(Painter, -50, -50, 50, 50);
QPainter_SetViewport(Painter, 0, 0, 100, 100);
```

In this case, each unit defined by `SetWindow` would be equal to one. If `SetViewPort` were defined to be 1,000 pixels in size, each unit defined by the `setWindow` could be thought of as being 10 actual units in size.

Internally, however, the component would never have to be concerned about the actual size or location of the window. It thinks of itself as always being 100 units in length, with its top-left corner at -50, -50, its bottom right at 50, 50, and its center at 0, 0.

The coordinate system described in the previous paragraph is perfect for our compass. In particular, the compass needs to be able to pick up on clicks of the mouse in order to change the direction in which it points:

```
Function FindUserChoice(X,Y: Integer): Char;
var
  Ch: Char;
begin
  Ch := '0';
  if (X >= 0) and (Y >= 0) then begin
    if X >= Y then Ch := 'E'
    else Ch := 'S';
  end
  else
```

```
if (X >= 0) and (Y <= 0) then begin
  if X >= Abs(Y) then Ch := 'E'
  else Ch := 'N';
end
else
if (X <= 0) and (Y <= 0) then begin
  if X >= Y then Ch := 'N'
  else Ch := 'W'
end
else
if (X <= 0) and (Y >= 0) then begin
  if Abs(X) >= Y then Ch := 'W'
  else Ch := 'S'
end;
FindUserChoice := Ch;
end;
```

This method determines whether the user clicked in the north, south, east, or west coordinate of the compass. Because the compass is set up to regard point 0, 0 as its center, the code shown here is always going to work regardless of the size or location of the component.

Clearly the SetViewport and SetWindow methods make it easy for us to create the compass component. They are not, however, part of CLX graphics classes. To use them, I was forced to step outside of CLX and go directly to the Qt API.

In other components that I have built, moving outside the CLX API and changing the coordinate system has on very rare occasions flustered the entire CLX encapsulation of the graphical API, and forced me to abandon CLX altogether. In those cases, I was forced to use the underlying API for all my graphics calls.

In my opinion, these rare occasions when the CLX graphics classes fail to do what we want do not provide sufficient reason to drop the API altogether. In fact, the CLX graphics classes can save you hours of work, and can provide an excellent means of creating very sophisticated cross-platform graphics that have good performance characteristics.

These graphics classes are great. Over the next few pages I'm going to show how they work, and then I will provide a few real-world examples to show that they are very fast and very powerful.

## The TColor Type

Almost all the graphics objects use the TColor type. The palette system allows you to define three different colors, Red, Green, and Blue. Each color has 255 different shades. It is convenient to define colors using the RGB function, found in the LCodeBox unit that comes on the CD that accompanies this book:

```
Canvas.Brush.Color := RGB(255,0,0);   {Red}
Canvas.Brush.Color := RGB(0,255,0);   {Green}
Canvas.Brush.Color := RGB(0,0,255);   {Blue}
```

By using the various combinations available, with choices from 0 to 255 in each color, you can create many different colors:

```
RGB(255,0,255);    {Purple}
RGB (255,255,0);   {Yellow}
RGB(127,127,127);  {Grey}
```

CLX also provides a series of constants that specify certain colors. For instance `clBlack` is defined as the color produced by this code:

```
RGB(0,0,0);
```

You will find a whole series of these colors in `QGraphics.pas`, including `clBlack`, `clMaroon`, `clGreen`, `clOlive`, `clNavy`, `clPurple`, `clTeal`, `clGray`, `clSilver`, `clRed`, `clLime`, `clBlue`, `clFuchsia`, `clAqua` and `clWhite`.

Probably the easiest way to start working with colors is by using the `TColorDialog` provided by Kylix. Open an application and add a Color dialog box, a `TPaintBox`, and a button to the form. Double-click on the button and fill in code so that the event code looks like this:

```
procedure TForm1.Button1Click(Sender: TObject);
begin
  if ColorDialog1.Execute then begin
    PaintBox1.Canvas.Brush.Color := ColorDialog1.Color;
    PaintBox1.Canvas.Rectangle(0, 0, PaintBox1.Width, PaintBox1.Height);
  end;
```

You can choose pre-mixed colors or you can also create custom colors with various RGB settings. An example of this type of program is found in the `ColorProgram` directory found on the CD that accompanies this book.

You can view the pre-set colors available for your use in programming in Kylix by accessing the color property for an object in the Object Inspector. For example, if you access the color property for `Form1`, you will be able to see your choices. If you set the color property of your form through the Object Inspector, you will be setting the color of the brush property of the form's canvas.

## Brushes

When you are setting the color of a shape, the interior of the shape will be set to the color of the brush for the canvas. You can set both the color and the style of the brush. The brush styles include the following:

- bsSolid: A solid color

- bsClear: Transparent

- bsHorizontal: Horizontal lines

- bsVertical: Vertical lines

- bsFDiagonal: Forward diagonal lines

- bsBDiagonal: Backward diagonal lines

- bsCross: Intersecting vertical and horizontal lines

- bsDiagCross: Intersecting diagonal lines in both directions

The program shown in Listing 11.1 will allow you to play with the various brush styles that are available to you.

**LISTING 11.1**    BrushStyles1

```
/////////////////////////////////////////
// Purpose: Show how to use Brush Styles
// Program: BrushStyles1
// Copyright © 2001 by Charlie Calvert and Margie Calvert
//
unit Main;

interface

uses
  SysUtils, Classes, QGraphics,
  QControls, QForms, QDialogs,
  QExtCtrls, QStdCtrls, QButtons, QTypes;

type
  TForm1 = class(TForm)
    RadioGroup1: TRadioGroup;
    Timer1: TTimer;
    PaintBox1: TPaintBox;
    procedure RadioGroup1Click(Sender: TObject);
    procedure FormCreate(Sender: TObject);
    procedure Timer1Timer(Sender: TObject);
    procedure FormClose(Sender: TObject; var Action: TCloseAction);
  private
    FChangeBy: Integer;
    procedure ShowBrush(MyBrushStyle: TBrushStyle);
  end;
```

**LISTING 11.1**   Continued

```
var
  Form1: TForm1;

implementation

uses
  TypInfo;

{$R *.xfm}

procedure TForm1.ShowBrush(MyBrushStyle: TBrushStyle);
begin
  PaintBox1.Canvas.Brush.Color := clWhite;
  PaintBox1.Canvas.Rectangle(0,0,PaintBox1.width, PaintBox1.height);
  PaintBox1.Canvas.Brush.Color := clBlue;
  PaintBox1.Canvas.Brush.Style := MyBrushStyle;
  PaintBox1.Canvas.Rectangle(0,0,PaintBox1.width, PaintBox1.height);
end;

procedure TForm1.RadioGroup1Click(Sender: TObject);
begin
  ShowBrush(TBrushStyle(RadioGroup1.ItemIndex));
end;

procedure TForm1.FormCreate(Sender: TObject);
var
  i: Integer;
  TypeData: PTypeData;
begin
  FChangeBy := 1;
  TypeData := GetTypeData(TypeInfo(TBrushStyle));
  for i := 0 to TypeData.MaxValue do
    RadioGroup1.Items.Add(GetEnumName(TypeInfo(TBrushStyle), i));
end;

procedure TForm1.Timer1Timer(Sender: TObject);
begin
  if RadioGroup1.ItemIndex >= RadioGroup1.Items.Count - 1 then
    FChangeBy := -1;
  if RadioGroup1.ItemIndex < 1 then
    FChangeBy := 1;
  RadioGroup1.ItemIndex := RadioGroup1.ItemIndex + FChangeBy;
  RadioGroup1Click(nil);
end;
```

**LISTING 11.1**   Continued

```
procedure TForm1.FormClose(Sender: TObject; var Action: TCloseAction);
begin
  Timer1.Enabled := False;
end;
end.
```

This program uses a radio group component and an image component. To set up the radio group, you will need to set the Items property of the radio group on the property page in the Object Inspector.

You could, of course, use the Items property of the TRadioGroup object to fill in the values for the pen modes. However, there is an easier way to proceed that will also have the virtue of automatically updating itself should the Object Pascal team decide to change the TBrushStyle value. Here is how to add the brush styles to the radio group at runtime:

```
procedure TForm1.FormCreate(Sender: TObject);
var
  TypeData: PTypeData;
  i: Integer;
begin
  TypeData := GetTypeData(TypeInfo(TPenMode));
  for i := 0 to TypeData.MaxValue do
    RadioGroup1.Items.Add(GetEnumName(TypeInfo(TPenMode), i));
end;
```

This method uses the TypInfo unit, discussed in Chapter 4, "Objects and Interfaces," in the section called "RTTI and Floating Point Types." It first retrieves the type data for TPenMode in order to learn how many different enumerate values there are in this type. It then calls GetEnumName for each possible enumerated value. The end result is that you hold a series of strings such as pmBlack, pmWhite, and so on.

The radio group should show a radio button for each brush style. Double-click the radio group and fill in the line of code in the stub provided by Kylix for the TForm1.RadioGroup1Click event:

```
ShowBrush(TBrushStyle(RadioGroup1.ItemIndex));
```

Once you have created the program, you can run it and view the different brush styles that are available. A timer in the program selects each item in turn, thereby allowing you to view all the possible styles without straining your mouse finger.

The TBrush object also has a Bitmap property. If you set the Bitmap property to a small external bitmap image, you can use the bitmap to create a pattern for the brush. See the

BitmapBrush program on the CD that accompanies this book for an example of how this works. Here is the key method from that program:

```
procedure TForm1.PaintColors(BitmapName: String);
var
  MyBitmap: TBitmap;
begin
  MyBitmap := TBitmap.Create;
  MyBitmap.LoadFromFile(BitmapName);
  Canvas.Draw(25, 35, MyBitmap);
  Canvas.Brush.Bitmap := MyBitmap;
  Canvas.Rectangle(0, 0, Width, Height);
  MyBitmap.Free;
end;
```

You are likely to use only one method for the TBrush object, and that is called Assign. It is used when you wish to copy the characteristics of one brush to another.

## Pens

When you draw a shape, the outline of the shape will be set by the pen currently assigned to the canvas. For instance, if you draw a rectangle the color and style of the center of the rectangle will be defined by the color of the brush, and the color and thickness of the outline of the rectangle will be defined by the pen.

The pen also has styles that can be set, but they only apply if the pen width is kept to one pixel. Among the pen styles are:

- psSolid: A solid line
- psClear: A transparent line
- psDot: A dotted line
- psDashDot: A line composed of dashes and dots
- psDashDotDot: A line composed of sequences of one dash and two dots
- psInsideFrame: A solid line that can use a dithered color

To get a sense of how the pen styles may be changed, take a look at this short method that uses the RGB function from LCodeBox:

```
procedure TForm1.BitBtn1Click(Sender: TObject);
begin
  Canvas.Brush.Color := RGB(0,0,0);
  Canvas.Pen.Color := clTeal;
  Canvas.Pen.Style := psDot;
```

```
    Canvas.Brush.Style := bsHorizontal;
    Canvas.Rectangle(10,10,100,100);
end;
```

By changing the pen styles, you will change the appearance of the outline of the rectangle. Notice in particular the act of changing the color of the pen, and the style of the pen:

```
    Canvas.Pen.Color := clTeal;
    Canvas.Pen.Style := psDot;
```

Needless to say, the psDot property causes the outline of the rectangle to appear as a series of dots.

The TPen object has two other properties that are very useful: Width and Mode. The Width property allows you to set the width in pixels of the line drawn by the pen. The Mode property gives you a range of Boolean options for determining how the pen color and the color of the Canvas mix. The color of the pen will be combined with the color of the canvas in different ways depending on the value of TPen.Mode. For instance, the pen color could completely overwrite the underlying canvas color, in which case the pen color could be unchanged. Or it could blend in completely with the underlying canvas color, in which case the border will be invisible. In between are various states in which the pen color and the underlying canvas color are combined to yield new colors. One of the features of the PenMode property will play an important role in the rubber banding trick that is outlined later in the chapter in the section titled "Drawing the Rubber Band."

The PenMode program, found in Listing 11.2, will give you a chance to experiment with the TPen Mode, Width, and Color properties.

**Listing 11.2**   The Main Unit from the PenMode Program Found in the Chapter 11 Directory on the CD that Accompanies this Book

```
unit Main;

// Show off the pen modes
// This program is based on code originally written by Jeff Cottingham
// Copyright © 2001 by Charlie and Margie Calvert

interface

uses
  SysUtils, Classes, QGraphics,
  QControls, QForms, QDialogs,
  QStdCtrls, QButtons, QExtCtrls,
  QImgList, QComCtrls, QTypes;
```

**LISTING 11.2**   Continued

```
type
  TForm1 = class(TForm)
    RadioGroup1: TRadioGroup;
    PaintBox1: TPaintBox;
    ToolBar1: TToolBar;
    ToolButton1: TToolButton;
    ImageList1: TImageList;
    Timer1: TTimer;
    ToolButton2: TToolButton;
    ColorDialog1: TColorDialog;
    ToolButton3: TToolButton;
    procedure RadioGroup1Click(Sender: TObject);
    procedure ToolButton1Click(Sender: TObject);
    procedure FormShow(Sender: TObject);
    procedure Timer1Timer(Sender: TObject);
    procedure ToolButton2Click(Sender: TObject);
    procedure ToolButton3Click(Sender: TObject);
    procedure FormCreate(Sender: TObject);
  private
    FChangeBy: Integer;
    FPenColor: TColor;
    FBrushColor: TColor;
    procedure DrawStuff(AWidth, AHeight: Integer;
      ACanvas: TCanvas; MyPenMode: TPenMode);
    { Private declarations }
  public
    { Public declarations }
  end;

var
  Form1: TForm1;

implementation

uses
  TypInfo;

{$R *.xfm}

procedure TForm1.DrawStuff(AWidth, AHeight: Integer;
  ACanvas: TCanvas; MyPenMode: TPenMode);
const
  XGap = 25;
  YGap = 25;
```

**LISTING 11.2** Continued

```
var
  x: integer;
  y: integer;
  i: integer;
  XSize, YSize: Integer;
begin
  x := 0;
  y := 0;
  ACanvas.Brush.Color := FBrushColor;
  ACanvas.Rectangle(0,0, AWidth, AHeight);
  ACanvas.Pen.Color := FPenColor;
  ACanvas.Pen.Width := 2;
  ACanvas.Pen.Mode := MyPenMode;

  YSize := AHeight div YGap;
  for i := 0 to YSize do begin
    ACanvas.moveTo(0, y);
    ACanvas.LineTo(AWidth, y);
    inc(y,25);
  end;

  XSize := AWidth div XGap;
  for i := 0 to XSize do begin
    ACanvas.MoveTo(x, 0);
    ACanvas.LineTo(x, AHeight);
    inc(x, XGap);
  end;

  ACanvas.MoveTo(0,0);
  ACanvas.LineTo(AWidth, AHeight);
  ACanvas.MoveTo(AWidth, 0);
  ACanvas.LineTo(0, AHeight);

  ACanvas.Ellipse(0, 0, AWidth, AHeight);
end;

procedure TForm1.RadioGroup1Click(Sender: TObject);
begin
  DrawStuff(PaintBox1.Width, PaintBox1.Height, PaintBox1.Canvas,
    TPenMode(RadioGroup1.ItemIndex));
end;

procedure TForm1.ToolButton1Click(Sender: TObject);
begin
  Close;
end;
```

**LISTING 11.2** Continued

```pascal
procedure TForm1.FormShow(Sender: TObject);
begin
  FPenColor := clGreen;
  FBrushColor := clBlue;
  RadioGroup1.ItemIndex := 0;
  RadioGroup1Click(nil);
  FChangeBy := 1;
end;

procedure TForm1.Timer1Timer(Sender: TObject);
begin
  if RadioGroup1.ItemIndex >= RadioGroup1.Items.Count - 1 then
    FChangeBy := -1;
  if RadioGroup1.ItemIndex < 1 then
    FChangeBy := 1;
  RadioGroup1.ItemIndex := RadioGroup1.ItemIndex + FChangeBy;
  RadioGroup1Click(nil);
 end;

procedure TForm1.ToolButton2Click(Sender: TObject);
begin
  if ColorDialog1.Execute then
    FBrushColor := ColorDialog1.Color;
end;

procedure TForm1.ToolButton3Click(Sender: TObject);
begin
  if ColorDialog1.Execute then
    FPenColor := ColorDialog1.Color;
end;

procedure TForm1.FormCreate(Sender: TObject);
var
  TypeData: PTypeData;
  i: Integer;
begin
  TypeData := GetTypeData(TypeInfo(TPenMode));
  for i := 0 to TypeData.MaxValue do
    RadioGroup1.Items.Add(GetEnumName(TypeInfo(TPenMode), i));
end;


end.
```

When you run this program, it draws a series of patterns on the main form that illustrate all the major pen modes. A timer drives the program at one second intervals. When the timer fires, the pen mode is changed, and the scene is redrawn. After watching the program for a few seconds, you will see at least one possible effect of each of the possible pen mode settings on a series of different graphical objects. The program provides other services, such as the capability to change the colors displayed in the scene. You can see a screenshot of the program in Figure 11.2.

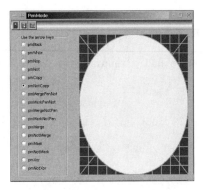

**Figure 11.2**

*The PenMode program provides an ever-changing hallucinatory display of colors and patterns.*

It is important to understand that the effect of applying a particular pen mode to the picture will vary depending on the current state of the picture. Because this program always goes through the pen modes in the same order, you will not necessarily get a sense of how this works.

Curious programmers should feel free to tweak the PenMode program to their heart's content. If you are interested in pen modes, you might want to change several aspects of the way the program works. For instance, making changes to DrawStuff method can help you see exactly what effect pen modes have on the act of drawing a line.

## Creating the PenMode Application

To create the core of this application, drop a TRadioGroup, TPaintBox, and TTimer component onto a new form. The buttons in the radio group will be filled out at runtime according to the scheme outlined above in the BrushStyles1 program. They will reflect the various possible values of the TPenMode property. These include: pmBlack, pmWhite, pmNop, pmNot, pmCopy, pmNotCopy, pmMergePenNot, pmMaskPenNot, pmMergeNotPen, pmMaskNotPen, pmMerge, pmNotMerge, pmMask, pmNotMask, pmXor, and pmNotXor.

The pen modes are an enumerated type, and therefore their place in sequence can be used to call them. That is, pmBlack corresponds to 0, pmWhite to 1, pmNop to 2, and so on. The code in the TForm1.RadioGroup1Click procedure capitalizes on the fact that the radio group items can be identified with the ordinal values from 0 to 14. The heavy lifting is done in the line of code that reads:

```
DrawStuff(PaintBox1.Width, PaintBox1.Height, PaintBox1.Canvas,
    TPenMode(RadioGroup1.ItemIndex));
```

The RadioGroup1.ItemIndex (which counts out the radio group buttons from 0 to 14) is type-cast as TPenMode. By doing this, we have linked the radio group button 0 to TPenMode 0, which is pmBlack, and radio group button 1 to TPenMode 1, which is pmWhite, and so on up the list. Because we can do this, we can link the appropriate radio button to the right pen mode with one line of code.

The DrawStuff procedure takes a TPenMode, which we have called MyPenMode, as a parameter. In the body of the procedure, we set the pen mode for our canvas as MyPenMode. The for loops in this code simply create a grid of lines that will fit the default size of the image component which you place on the form. The appearance of the grid will change as the pen mode controls the interface between the background color and the color of the grid drawn by the TPen object.

The pen modes can be visualized as Boolean operations involving the color of the pen (P) and the color of the canvas destination color (D). Depending on the mode that is called, the background can turn to the inverse of background color, "not D," or the pen color can turn to the inverse of pen color, "not P." In some modes, intersecting areas of the pen will be colored differently. Again, you will see a practical use for this technology while examining the discussion of rubber banding in the section that deals with the Mandelbrot set.

## Fonts

Printing out a string from the canvas object is quite easy. You simply write:

```
Form1.Canvas.TextOut(1,1,'This canvas can talk.');
```

However, it is likely that you will want to control the appearance of your text. For this, you will need to manipulate the font properties. The TFont object has 10 key properties: Color, Handle, FontPen, Height, Name, Pitch, PixelsPerInch, Size, Style, and CharSet. The Handle property provides a handle to the underlying QFont object, while the FontPen provides a handle to the underlying QPen object. The Pitch defines whether the characters all have the same width.

> **NOTE**
>
> The PixelsPerInch property should be familiar to many Kylix users because that is the one you must change when converting Delphi forms to Kylix forms. In particular, you want to change the default Windows value of 96 PixelsPerInch to 75 PixelsPerInch. This will make the fonts and components on your Delphi forms appear correctly in Kylix programs.

To get a sense of how to set some of the font properties, create an application and drop a button onto your form. Double-click on the button to create an event procedure and fill in code so that it appears like this:

```
procedure TForm1.BitBtn1Click(Sender: TObject);
var
  MyFontStyle: TFontStyles;
begin
  MyFontStyle := [fsBold, fsItalic];
  Canvas.Font.Style := MyFontStyle;
  Canvas.Font.Name := 'Arial';
  Canvas.Font.Color := clRed;
  Canvas.Font.Size := 36;
  Canvas.TextOut(2,2,'This is mine.');
end;
```

In this code, we created a variable of the FontStyles data type. There is a set of four different styles that can be used with this data type: fsBold, fsItalic, fsUnderline, and fsStrikeOut. Any or all of these styles may be used at the same time. In this case, we decided to use fsBold and fsItalic. We assigned our font style MyFontStyle to the canvas, chose Arial as the font name we wished to use, clRed as the font color, and 36 pixels as the font size. We then created a string which the canvas could draw at coordinates of x = 2, y = 2 on the main form of the program.

An easy way to work with fonts is to use the font dialog box provided by Kylix. To use this tool, drop a TFontDialog component on your form and also drop a button on your form. Double-click the button to create an event:

```
procedure TForm1.Button1Click(Sender: TObject);
begin
  if FontDialog1.execute then
    Canvas.Font := FontDialog1.Font;
  Canvas.TextOut(1,1,'This is a test.');
end;
```

The Font dialog box allows you to choose the font's name, style, size, color, and effects.

# Drawing Shapes

The canvas object makes drawing shapes quite easy. The basic formula is illustrated by the Rectangle method.

```
Canvas.Rectangle(0,0,100,100);
```

The first two parameters in this method give the x- and y- coordinates on the screen for the top-left corner of the shape. The third parameter gives the length in pixels for the width of the rectangle, and the fourth parameter gives the length in pixels for the height of the rectangle. The ellipse follows similar rules. To draw a line, you will need to specify the x- and y-coordinates for the beginning of the line and the x- and y-coordinates for the end of the line.

The DrawShape1 program on this book's CD demonstrates these basic shapes: the rectangle, the ellipse, and the line. You will find the code for the program in Listing 11.3.

**LISTING 11.3** The Code for the DrawShape1 Program

```
////////////////////////////////////////
// Purpose: Simple paint program
// Program: RealDrawShape.pas
// Copyright © 2001 by Charlie & Margie Calvert
//
unit Main;

interface

uses
  SysUtils, Classes, QGraphics,
  QControls, QForms, QDialogs,
  QStdCtrls, QExtCtrls;

type
  TForm1 = class(TForm)
    Edit1: TEdit;
    Edit2: TEdit;
    Edit3: TEdit;
    Edit4: TEdit;
    Image1: TImage;
    ColorDialog1: TColorDialog;
    FontDialog1: TFontDialog;
    Edit5: TEdit;
    RadioGroup1: TRadioGroup;
    Label1: TLabel;
    Label2: TLabel;
```

**LISTING 11.3** Continued

```
    Label3: TLabel;
    Label4: TLabel;
    BrushColorImage: TImage;
    PenColorImage: TImage;
    Label5: TLabel;
    Label6: TLabel;
    procedure RadioGroup1Click(Sender: TObject);
    procedure BrushColorImageClick(Sender: TObject);
    procedure PenColorImageClick(Sender: TObject);
    procedure FormShow(Sender: TObject);

  private
  procedure DrawShape();
    procedure DrawColorImage(Image: TImage; Color: TColor);
    { Private declarations }
  public
    { Public declarations }
  end;

var
  Form1: TForm1;

implementation

{$R *.xfm}

uses
  LCodeBox;

procedure TForm1.DrawShape();
var
  w : integer;
  x : integer;
  y : integer;
  z : integer;
  p : integer;

begin
  w := StrToInt(Edit1.Text);
  x := StrToInt(Edit2.Text);
  y := StrToInt(Edit3.Text);
  z := StrToInt(Edit4.Text);
  p := StrToInt(Edit5.Text);
```

**LISTING 11.3**  Continued

```pascal
  Image1.Canvas.Brush.Color := clWhite;
  Image1.Canvas.Rectangle(0,0,Image1.Width, Image1.Height);
  Image1.Canvas.Pen.Width := p;

  Image1.Canvas.Brush.Color := BrushColorImage.Canvas.Brush.Color;
  Image1.Canvas.Pen.Color := PenColorImage.Canvas.Brush.Color;

  case RadioGroup1.ItemIndex of
    0: Image1.Canvas.Rectangle(w,x,y,z);
    1: Image1.Canvas.Ellipse(w,x,y,z);
    2: begin
      Image1.Canvas.MoveTo(w,x);
      Image1.Canvas.LineTo(y,z);
    end;
  end;
end;


procedure TForm1.RadioGroup1Click(Sender: TObject);
begin
  DrawShape();
end;

procedure TForm1.DrawColorImage(Image: TImage; Color: TColor);
begin
  Image.Canvas.Brush.Color := Color;
  Image.Canvas.Rectangle(0, 0, Image.Width, Image.Height);
end;

procedure TForm1.BrushColorImageClick(Sender: TObject);
begin
  if ColorDialog1.Execute then
    DrawColorImage(BrushColorImage, ColorDialog1.Color);
end;

procedure TForm1.PenColorImageClick(Sender: TObject);
begin
  if ColorDialog1.Execute then
    DrawColorImage(PenColorImage, ColorDialog1.Color);
end;
```

**LISTING 11.3** Continued

```
procedure TForm1.FormShow(Sender: TObject);
begin
  DrawColorImage(BrushColorImage, RGB(170, 170, 255));
  DrawColorImage(PenColorImage, RGB(85, 170, 255));
  DrawShape();
end;

end.
```

The output from this program is shown in Figure 11.3. It provides rudimentary beginnings of a simple paint program.

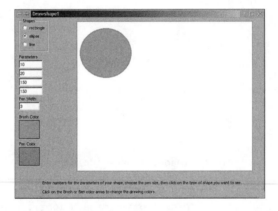

**FIGURE 11.3**

*The RealDrawShapes program allows you to work with some basic methods for drawing lines or shapes.*

The four edit controls on the main form allow you to set the parameters for the shapes. In the DrawShape method, the four integers culled from these controls are used to define the coordinates of each shape:

```
case RadioGroup1.ItemIndex of
  0: Image1.Canvas.Rectangle(w,x,y,z);
  1: Image1.Canvas.Ellipse(w,x,y,z);
  2: begin
    Image1.Canvas.MoveTo(w,x);
    Image1.Canvas.LineTo(y,z);
  end;
end;
```

A fifth edit control allows you to set the pen width. This program uses two color dialog boxes, which allow you to set the color of the shape and the color of the line around it.

The radio group is at the heart of this program. To set up the radio group correctly, you will need to set the items property of RadioGroup1 in the Object Inspector. If you click on the ellipses button for the Items property editor in the Object Inspector, and then type the name of each shape on a separate line, Kylix will set up and label the radio buttons for you. The ItemIndex for each radio button will be set for you automatically, starting with zero for the first button.

The case statement triggered by the radio buttons contains the code that actually draws the shapes. If the ItemIndex of the radio group is 0, a rectangle is drawn, if it is 1, an ellipse is drawn, and if it is 2, a line is drawn.

To create the TForm1.RadioGroup1Click procedure, you will start by double-clicking on RadioGroup1 when you are in design view. Kylix will create the code stub in which you can call the DrawShape procedure.

If you wish, you can add more edit controls and more shapes so that you can play with shapes that require more parameters using this program.

> **NOTE**
>
> The shape drawing methods that most often cause people confusion are the Polygon and Polyline methods of the TCanvas object. The technique for using these methods is demonstrated at the end of Chapter 7, "CLX Architecture and Visual Development," in the section called "Painting the Shape of a Form."

This is the end of the section that describes the core functionality of the CLX graphics unit. The rest of the chapter shows advanced examples of how to use these powerful tools in more sophisticated programs. A few new objects are explored in these sections. For instance, the TBitmap object will be examined at length in several sections of the text.

## The Mandelbrot Example

The TestElfMandel program found on the CD that accompanies this book gives you a chance to see the Kylix graphic system in action. This program includes a component that draws the classic Mandelbrot set. Using the mouse, you can zoom in repeatedly on parts of the set that interest you. A rubber banding technique is used to help you draw a rectangle around the area you want to investigate. The program has a built-in feature that allows you to save screen shots of the pictures you make, and it does a fair job of repainting the pictures you create if you switch away from its main window.

A screen shot of the program is shown in Figure 11.4. Listings 11.4 and 11.5 contain the code for the program. The first listing shows the code to the component that draws the Mandelbrot set. The second listing shows the program that saves screen shots of the completed drawings, and that also handles the repainting.

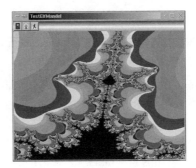

**FIGURE 11.4**

*The TestElfMandel program allows you to have some fun zooming in on, and taking pictures of, the Mandelbrot set.*

**LISTING 11.4** The `TElfMandy` Component Draws the Mandelbrot Set if You Click and Drag on It or Call Its `Run` Method

```
//////////////////////////////////////////
// Purpose: Draw the Mandlebrot set
// Component: TElfMandy
// Copyright © 2001 by Charlie Calvert
//
unit ElfMandy;

interface

uses
  QForms, QControls, Types,
  Classes;

type
  TElfMandy = class(TCustomControl)
  private
    FDragging: Boolean;
    FDrawnOnce: Boolean;
```

**LISTING 11.4** Continued

```
     FDepth: Integer;
     FXRange: Double;    // The width and height of the
     FYRange: Double;    // Mandlebrot plane. Starts at 3.
     FScrOrgX: Integer;
     FScrOrgY: Integer;
     FScrMaxX: Integer;
     FScrMaxY: Integer;
     FBaseOrgX: Double;
     FBaseOrgY: Double;
     FOldRect: TRect;
     FQuitDrawing: Boolean;
     FOnPaint: TNotifyEvent;
     FOnBeginDraw: TNotifyEvent;
     FOnEndDraw: TNotifyEvent;
     function Distance(X, Y: Double): Double;
     procedure Calculate(X, Y: Double;
       var XIter, YIter: Double);
     function GetColor(Steps: Integer): Integer;
     procedure GetOriginsandWidths(var XOrg, YOrg, XMax, YMax: Double);
  public
     constructor Create(AOwner: TComponent); override;
     procedure SetBoundary(ScrX, ScrY, ScrX1, ScrY1: Integer);
     procedure SetMouseDownPos(ScrX, ScrY: Integer);
     procedure SetMouseUpPos(ScrX1, ScrY1: Integer);
     function Run: Boolean;
     property QuitDrawing: Boolean read FQuitDrawing write FQuitDrawing;
     procedure Paint; override;
     procedure MouseDown(Button: TMouseButton; Shift: TShiftState;
       X, Y: Integer); override;
     procedure MouseMove(Shift: TShiftState; X, Y: Integer); override;
     procedure MouseUp(Button: TMouseButton; Shift: TShiftState;
       X, Y: Integer); override;
     procedure Resize; override;
  published
     property Align;
     property Depth: Integer read FDepth write FDepth;
     property Canvas;
     property OnPaint: TNotifyEvent read FOnPaint write FOnPaint;
     property OnEndDraw: TNotifyEvent read FOnEndDraw write FOnEndDraw;
     property OnBeginDraw: TNotifyEvent read FOnBeginDraw write FOnBeginDraw;
  end;

procedure Register;
```

**LISTING 11.4**   Continued

```
implementation

uses
  QGraphics;

procedure Register;
begin
  RegisterComponents('Elves', [TElfMandy]);
end;

constructor TElfMandy.Create(AOwner: TComponent);
begin
  inherited Create(AOwner);
  FXRange := 3;
  FYRange := 3;
  FBaseOrgX := -2.25;
  FBaseOrgY := -1.5;
  Width := 25;
  Height := 25;
end;

procedure TElfMandy.GetOriginsandWidths(var XOrg, YOrg, XMax, YMax: Double);
var
  VOrgX,
  VOrgY,
  VMaxX,
  VMaxY: Double;
  XPercent, YPercent,
  MaxXPercent, MaxYPercent: Double;
begin
  VOrgX := FScrOrgX;
  VOrgY := FScrOrgY;
  VMaxX := FScrMaxX;
  VMaxY := FScrMaxY;
  XPercent := VOrgX / Width;
  YPercent := VOrgY / Height;
  MaxXPercent := VMaxX / Width;
  MaxYPercent := VMaxY / Height;
  XOrg := (XPercent * FXRange) + FBaseOrgX;
  YOrg := (YPercent * FYRange) + FBaseOrgY;
  XMax := (MaxXPercent * FXRange) + FBaseOrgX;
  YMax := (MaxYPercent * FYRange) + FBaseOrgY;
  FBaseOrgX := XOrg;
  FBaseOrgY := YOrg;
```

**LISTING 11.4**  Continued

```pascal
  FXRange := XMax - XOrg;
  FYRange := YMax - YOrg;
end;

function TElfMandy.Distance(X, Y: Double): Double;
begin
  if (X <> 0.0) and (Y <> 0.0) then
    Result := Sqrt(Sqr(X) + Sqr(Y))
  else if X = 0.0 then
    Result := Abs(Y)
  else
    Result := Abs(X);
end;

procedure TElfMandy.Calculate(X, Y: Double;
                          var XIter, YIter: Double);
var
  XTemp, YTemp: Double;
begin
  XTemp := Sqr(XIter) - Sqr(YIter) + X;
  YTemp := 2 * (XIter * YIter) + Y;
  XIter := XTemp;
  YIter := YTemp;
end;

// Steps won't be larger than FDepth.
function TElfMandy.GetColor(Steps: Integer): Integer;
const
  TopVal= 16777215; // RGB(255,255,255)
var
  Variation: Double;
  Val: Integer;
begin
  Variation := TopVal / FDepth;
  Val := Round(Variation * Steps);
  Result := Val;
end;

procedure TElfMandy.SetBoundary(ScrX, ScrY, ScrX1, ScrY1: Integer);
begin
  FScrOrgX := ScrX;
  FScrOrgY := ScrY;
  FScrMaxX := ScrX1;
  FScrMaxY := ScrY1;
end;
```

**LISTING 11.4**   Continued

```
procedure TElfMandy.SetMouseDownPos(ScrX, ScrY: Integer);
begin
  FScrOrgX := ScrX;
  FScrOrgY := ScrY;
end;

procedure TElfMandy.SetMouseUpPos(ScrX1, ScrY1: Integer);
begin
  FScrMaxX := ScrX1;
  FScrMaxY := ScrY1;
  Run;
end;

function TElfMandy.Run: Boolean;
var
  i, j, Steps: Integer;
  XStep, YStep, XPos, YPos, XOrg, YOrg: Double;
  XMax, YMax, XIter, YIter: Double;
  Done: Boolean;
  R: TRect;
begin
  if Assigned(OnBeginDraw) then
    OnBeginDraw(Self);
  Result := False;
  R := BoundsRect;
  R.Top := 0;
  InvalidateRect(R, True);
  if FDepth < 1 then FDepth := 50;
  GetOriginsAndWidths(XOrg, YOrg, XMax, YMax);
  XStep := (XMax - XOrg) / Width;
  YStep := (YMax - Yorg) / Height;
  for i := 0 to Width do
    for j := 0 to Height do begin
      XPos := XOrg + i * XStep;
      YPos := YOrg + J * YStep;
      XIter := 0.0;
      YIter := 0.0;
      Steps :=0;
      Done := False;
      repeat
        Calculate(XPos, YPos, XIter, YIter);
        Inc(Steps);
        if Distance(XIter, YIter) >= 2.0 then
          Done := True;
```

**LISTING 11.4** Continued

```
        if Steps = FDepth then
          Done := True;
      until Done;
      if Steps < FDepth then begin
        //Canvas.PutPixel(Canvas.Handle, i, j, GetColor(Steps));
        Canvas.Pen.Color := GetColor(Steps);
        Canvas.DrawPoint(i, j);
      end;
      Application.ProcessMessages;
      if FQuitDrawing then Exit;
  end;
  if Assigned(OnEndDraw) then
    OnEndDraw(self);
  Result := True;
end;

procedure TElfMandy.MouseDown(Button: TMouseButton; Shift: TShiftState; X,
  Y: Integer);
begin
  inherited;
  FDragging := True;
  SetMouseDownPos(X, Y);
end;

procedure TElfMandy.MouseUp(Button: TMouseButton; Shift: TShiftState; X,
  Y: Integer);
begin
  FDragging := False;
  FDrawnOnce := False;
  inherited;
  SetMouseUpPos(X, Y);
end;

procedure TElfMandy.Resize;
begin
  inherited;
  SetBoundary(0, 0, Width, Height);
end;

{** It's probably just late at night, but it seems to
    me that the Mandelbrot set is more interesting if
    I leave the Pen Mode as pmNotXor. }
procedure TElfMandy.MouseMove(Shift: TShiftState; X, Y: Integer);
//var
```

**LISTING 11.4**   Continued

```
// SaveStyle: TPenMode;
begin
  if FDragging = True then begin
  //  SaveStyle := Canvas.Pen.Mode;
    Canvas.Pen.Mode := pmNotXor;
    if FDrawnOnce = True then
      Canvas.Rectangle(FOldRect);
    FOldRect := Rect(FScrOrgX, FScrOrgY, X, Y);
    Canvas.Rectangle(FScrOrgX, FScrOrgY, X, Y);
//    Canvas.Pen.Mode := SaveStyle;
    FDrawnOnce := True;
  end;
end;

procedure TElfMandy.Paint;
begin
  inherited;
  if Assigned(OnPaint) then
    OnPaint(self);
end;

end.
```

**LISTING 11.5**   The TestElfMandel Program Shows How to Save an Area of the Screen to a Bitmap

```
unit Main;

interface

uses
  SysUtils, Types, Classes,
  Variants, QGraphics, QControls,
  QForms, QDialogs, ElfMandy,
  QStdCtrls, QComCtrls, QImgList;

type
  TForm1 = class(TForm)
    ElfMandy1: TElfMandy;
    ToolBar1: TToolBar;
    ToolButton1: TToolButton;
    ToolButton2: TToolButton;
    ImageList1: TImageList;
```

**LISTING 11.5**   Continued

```
    ToolButton3: TToolButton;
    SaveDialog1: TSaveDialog;
    procedure Button1Click(Sender: TObject);
    procedure ToolButton2Click(Sender: TObject);
    procedure ToolButton3Click(Sender: TObject);
    procedure ElfMandy1Paint(Sender: TObject);
    procedure FormCreate(Sender: TObject);
    procedure FormDestroy(Sender: TObject);
    procedure ElfMandy1RunDone(Sender: TObject);
    procedure ElfMandy1BeginDraw(Sender: TObject);
  private
    { Private declarations }
    FBitmap: TBitmap;
    FBitRect: TRect;
    FMandyDrawing: Boolean;
    procedure SnapPicture;
  public
    { Public declarations }
  end;

var
  Form1: TForm1;

implementation

uses
  Qt;

{$R *.xfm}
{$R startpicture.res}

procedure TForm1.Button1Click(Sender: TObject);
begin
  ElfMandy1.Run;
end;

procedure TForm1.ToolButton2Click(Sender: TObject);
begin
  Close;
end;
```

**LISTING 11.5**    Continued

```
procedure TForm1.ToolButton3Click(Sender: TObject);
begin
  SnapPicture;
  SaveDialog1.InitialDir := '/tmp';
  if SaveDialog1.Execute then begin
    FBitmap.SaveToFile(SaveDialog1.FileName);
  end;
end;

procedure TForm1.ElfMandy1Paint(Sender: TObject);
begin
  if (FMandyDrawing <> True) and (FBitmap <> nil) then
    ElfMandy1.Canvas.CopyRect(Rect(0, 0, ElfMandy1.Width, ElfMandy1.Height),
      FBitmap.Canvas, Rect(0, 0, ElfMandy1.Width, ElfMandy1.Height));
end;

procedure TForm1.FormCreate(Sender: TObject);
begin
  FBitmap := TBitmap.Create;
  FBitmap.LoadFromResourceName(HInstance, 'StartPixs');
end;

procedure TForm1.FormDestroy(Sender: TObject);
begin
  FBitmap.Free;
end;

procedure TForm1.ElfMandy1RunDone(Sender: TObject);
begin
  FMandyDrawing := False;
  SnapPicture;
end;

procedure TForm1.SnapPicture;
begin
  FBitmap.Width := ElfMandy1.Width;
  FBitmap.Height := ElfMandy1.Height;
  FBitRect := Rect(0, 0, ElfMandy1.Width, ElfMandy1.Height);
  //BitBlt(QPaintDeviceH(FBitmap.Handle), 0, 0, QPaintDeviceH(Canvas.Handle),
  //  0, 0, Width, Height, RasterOp_CopyROP, False);
  FBitmap.Canvas.CopyRect(FBitRect, ElfMandy1.Canvas, FBitRect);
end;
```

**LISTING 11.5** Continued

```
procedure TForm1.ElfMandy1BeginDraw(Sender: TObject);
var
  B: TBitmap;
begin
  FMandyDrawing := True;
  B := TBitmap.Create;
  B.Width := ElfMandy1.Width;
  B.Height := ElfMandy1.Height;
  ElfMandy1.Canvas.CopyRect(Rect(0, 0, ElfMandy1.Width, ElfMandy1.Height),
    B.Canvas, Rect(0, 0, ElfMandy1.Width, ElfMandy1.Height));
  B.Free;
end;

end.
```

If the truth were to be fully told, my interest in the Mandelbrot set itself would probably be best characterized as primarily aesthetic. Which is just as well, as this is a book on programming, not on mathematics. A few things, however, can be said on this subject, without crossing waters that are too deep and treacherous.

Though the math theory involved is moderately complicated, the basic idea behind the Mandelbrot set is fairly simple. The eponymous creator of this set gave us a particular formula that involves complex numbers, that is, numbers with a real and an imaginary part. The imaginary part involves the square root of a negative number. Such values are said not to exist, and hence are called imaginary.

You plug values into the formula given to us by Mr. Mandelbrot. Many of these values cause the formula to iterate indefinitely in a small range or to produce values that fall outside a defined range. In particular, the numbers either remain smaller than 2, or they get larger than 2 and then keep getting larger. Any number fed into the formula that generates a result larger than 2 is said to have escaped from the set. A certain group of numbers, however, yield finite results in a narrow range smaller than 2. Ironically, these numbers, the ones that stay in the Mandelbrot set, are not of interest to us. In fact, our program stops calculating after any particular number has failed to escape the set within a given number of iterations. This does not mean the number will never escape, only that it did not escape within, for instance, 50 iterations of the formula.

The program is particularly interested in the number of iterations of the formula required to assign, however tentatively, an identity to any particular number. If a number escapes the set after only two or three iterations, it is assigned one color, and if it escapes the set later, it is assigned another color. Those that don't escape are shown in black. (The value itself has no effect on the color. It is the number of iterations it has gone through that is important.) Because black areas aren't very interesting to look at, we are interested in the values that escape the set, and in particular, we are interested in how long it took them to escape the set. It is the fascinating patterns created by assigning colors to these different escape times that make the set so aesthetically pleasing.

---

**NOTE**

Throughout much of the rest of this discussion I will often refer to the user's desire to "zoom in on a section of the Mandelbrot set." Technically, the user usually desires to zoom in not on the Mandelbrot set itself, but on those values that escape from the set, or some combination of values that have and have not escaped the set. Nonetheless, I find it easiest to say that the user is zooming in on the set, rather than belaboring the point that the user is zooming in on at least some values that have escaped from the set. Hopefully you will find this conceit more helpful than bothersome or misleading.

---

If you want to learn more about the math that generates these extraordinary pictures, you might go to www.google.com, where you can look up the word Mandelbrot and tune into the cacophony of informed and uninformed voices pontificating on this subject. After considerable searching, I finally found one site that seems to make at least a reasonable attempt to explain the subject in clear English: http://www.olympus.net/personal/dewey/mandelbrot.html.

The results produced by iterating the Mandelbrot equation are simply astounding. I am amazed that the quite ordinary process of iterating over values produced by a relatively simple mathematical formula should yield such varied, frequently sinuous, occasionally symmetrical, at other times chaotic, results.

It is also amazing that drilling down into the set yields no final stopping point, but only the continued discovery of further layers of complexity. It is as if one started opening up a set of Russian dolls and found that there was no end to the process. No matter how small one doll might be, it can be opened to reveal yet another smaller, but perfectly rendered, doll inside it. Of course, our program works with numbers that yield only a certain level of detail, so the set appears to resolve into a set of smooth curves if you drill into it deeply enough. My understanding, however, is that this is not the true end of the complexity of the set, but only an artifact of the formulas and hardware used to calculate the results.

## Drawing the Mandelbrot Set

**11**

Coming down from the clouds to a much more practical point of view, one of the highlights of this program are the lines of code used to actually draw the points calculated by the Mandelbrot equation:

```
Canvas.Pen.Color := GetColor(Steps);
Canvas.DrawPoint(i, j);
```

The `GetColor` function calculates an RGB value based on the number of iterations the formula has gone through. For instance, a value that escaped the set in four iterations would be assigned one color, while a value that escaped within 25 iterations would be assigned a second color, and one that did not escape within the maximum number of iterations would be assigned a third color. The chosen color is assigned to the current pen, which is in turn used when the `DrawPoint` method of the canvas paints a pixel to the screen. The color of the pixel is defined by the current color of the pen. The end result is that a fabulous image is drawn to the screen, each pixel of which is based on the time it took a value to escape from the Mandelbrot set.

One pixel at a time, the program covers the entire surface of the `TElfMandy` component. The actual size of the component is configurable, and will differ according to the whims of the user.

## Drawing the Rubber Band

One of the interesting features of the `TElfMandy` component is that it allows you to use the mouse to draw a rectangle around the portion of the Mandelbrot set on which you want to zoom in. Because the rectangle gets bigger and smaller in an elastic manner as you move the mouse, this technique is known as *rubber banding*.

There are three steps in this process. When the user clicks the mouse down on the `TElfMandy` component, a variable called `FDragging` is set to `True`:

```
procedure TElfMandy.MouseDown(Button: TMouseButton; Shift: TShiftState;
  X, Y: Integer);
begin
  inherited;
  FDragging := True;
  SetMouseDownPos(X, Y);
end;
```

When the mouse is lifted up, the variable is set to `False`. In between those two times, the mouse is moved by the user, and the rectangle drawn to the screen shrinks and expands as if it were a rubber band. Needless to say, the relevant code is handled by the response to the `MouseMove` event:

```
procedure TElfMandy.MouseMove(Shift: TShiftState; X, Y: Integer);
begin
  if FDragging = True then begin
    Canvas.Pen.Mode := pmNotXor;
    if FDrawnOnce = True then
      Canvas.Rectangle(FOldRect);
    FOldRect := Rect(FScrOrgX, FScrOrgY, X, Y);
    Canvas.Rectangle(FScrOrgX, FScrOrgY, X, Y);
    FDrawnOnce := True;
  end;
end;
```

The most important line of code sets the pen mode of the canvas to pmNotXor. This mode will alternately draw and erase the rectangle that you apply to the canvas. The first time you draw in this mode, a rectangle is drawn to the screen. Drawing a second time in this mode to the same location will erase the rectangle, revealing what lies beneath it. This capability to reveal what was hidden beneath the triangle is the magic of the pmNotXor mode.

The first time the MouseMove method is called after the user begins dragging the mouse, there is no rectangle to erase. As a result, the program only draws the rectangle to the screen once on the first pass:

```
if FDrawnOnce = True then
  Canvas.Rectangle(FOldRect);
FOldRect := Rect(FScrOrgX, FScrOrgY, X, Y);
Canvas.Rectangle(FScrOrgX, FScrOrgY, X, Y);
FDrawnOnce := True;
```

The component does, however, save the location to which the rectangle was drawn in a variable called FOldRect, which is global to the entire object. A rectangle is then drawn starting at the place where the mouse began dragging, and extending to the current location of the mouse. That is, in most cases, the upper-left corner is where the user first clicked, and the bottom-right is where the mouse currently resides. Finally, the FDrawnOnce variable is set to true, thereby ensuring that two rectangles will be drawn on the next pass. The first rectangle is drawn to erase the previous rectangle, and the second establishes the new location of the mouse.

Once the users have found the portion of the Mandelbrot set that they wish to focus on, they lift up the mouse:

```
procedure TElfMandy.MouseUp(Button: TMouseButton; Shift: TShiftState; X,
  Y: Integer);
begin
  FDragging := False;
  FDrawnOnce := False;
  inherited;
  SetMouseUpPos(X, Y);
end;
```

This code sets both the `FDragging` and `FDrawOnce` variables to false. The end result of this action is that the `MouseMove` call does not execute any of the program's code until the user has again begun dragging the mouse. At that time, the value of the `FDrawnOnce` variable assures that only one rectangle is drawn on the first pass.

> **NOTE**
>
> Some readers might notice that I do not ever erase the rectangle drawn on the user's last pass through the `MouseMove` method before lifting the mouse button. It is not necessary to make this erasure because the entire surface of the component is about to be redrawn in order to show the new area of focus.

After all this hand-waving is completed, the program then goes on to the serious business of actually drawing the details of the newly defined area of the Mandelbrot set. In short, it iterates once again over dear old Mr. Mandelbrot's oft-traversed equation, but this time feeds it a different set of values.

## `TBitmap`: Taking a Picture of the Mandelbrot Set

One of the more interesting aspects of the TestElfMandel program is its capacity to capture the contents of the completed Mandelbrot pictures and then save them to a file. It turns out that Kylix makes this process extremely simple:

```
procedure TForm1.SnapPicture;
begin
  FBitmap.Width := ElfMandy1.Width;
  FBitmap.Height := ElfMandy1.Height;
  FBitRect := Rect(0, 0, ElfMandy1.Width, ElfMandy1.Height);
  FBitmap.Canvas.CopyRect(FBitRect, ElfMandy1.Canvas, FBitRect);
end;
```

`FBitmap` is a variable of type `TBitmap`. The code to create an instance of this variable is very straightforward:

```
FBitmap := TBitmap.Create;
```

The Kylix `TBitmap` component has its own built-in `TCanvas` object. To begin using this object, you can set the width and height of the bitmap that you want to create:

```
  FBitmap.Width := ElfMandy1.Width;
  FBitmap.Height := ElfMandy1.Height;
```

After you have done this, you have a fully functional bitmap object at your disposal. In other words, using these properties does more than merely set the width and height of the component; you are actually creating an empty bitmap of this width and height. You could, for instance, begin drawing on the bitmap's canvas in order to create pictures of your own design:

```
FBitmap.Canvas.Ellipse(10, 10, 25, 25);
```

However, this is not the course of action that our program wants to pursue. Instead, the TestElfMandel program simply copies the current contents of the TElfMandy component to the bitmap:

```
 FBitmap.Canvas.CopyRect(FBitRect, ElfMandy1.Canvas, FBitRect);
```

Ah, the glory of a well-designed object library at work! The CopyRect function simply copies an area of one TCanvas object to a defined area in another TCanvas object. Never mind that one is the TCanvas of a form or component, and the other is the TCanvas of a TBitmap object. That is not important, as CLX takes care of any such underlying details!

> **NOTE**
>
> You could just as easily copy the contents of a TForm or TFrame object to a TBitmap. In fact, you can copy the surface of any component that has a TCanvas object to a TBitmap object or to any other component that has a TCanvas. Third-party developers can even create new components that have canvases. For instance, it would be nice to have a TOpenGL object that sported a TCanvas. The overriding theme in this case is that the CLX component architecture and the CLX OOP architecture interact in ways that make Kylix components much more powerful than components from other, less OOP-centric, development environments.

Before closing this section, I should point out that the TCanvas.Draw method can also be used to draw a TBitmap or other graphics object onto a TForm, TFrame, or any other object that contains a TCanvas. The difference between the Draw and CopyRect methods is that the former allows you to work with specific areas of the target and source bitmaps, while the latter simply blits the entire source component at a specified x and y location in the target canvas. Here is the declaration for TCanvas.Draw:

```
procedure Draw(X, Y: Integer; Graphic: TGraphic);
```

Needless to say, TBitmap is a descendant of TGraphic. Hence, according to the rules of polymorphism, you can pass a TBitmap to the Draw method:

```
Form1.Canvas.Draw(10, 10, MyBitmap);
```

# Creating Events and Handling `OnPaint` Methods

**11**

When the user asks to save a screenshot from the program, a dialog box opens asking the user to specify the name of the file to which the screenshot should be saved. This dialog box correctly opens directly on top of the TestElfMandel program. As a result, the contents of the picture of the Mandelbrot set is erased by the Save File dialog box. After the dialog box closes, the users sees a primarily white window in place of his beautiful drawing.

Fortunately, there is a simple way to correct this problem. The solution involves two steps:

1. A screen shot of the Mandelbrot picture must be taken.
2. The screen shot needs to be blitted over the white surface left by the Open File dialog box.

To make this work, you need to know when to save the picture of the completed Mandelbrot drawing. The TElfMandy component makes this possible by firing an event after the drawing is complete. Here are the parts of the component that make this possible:

```
TElfMandy = class(
  FOnPaint: TNotifyEvent;
  FOnBeginDraw: TNotifyEvent;
  // Code omitted here
  property OnEndDraw: TNotifyEvent read FOnEndDraw write FOnEndDraw;
  property OnBeginDraw: TNotifyEvent read FOnBeginDraw write
  // Code omitted here
end;

function TElfMandy.Run: Boolean;
var
  i, j, Steps: Integer;
  XStep, YStep, XPos, YPos, XOrg, YOrg: Double;
  XMax, YMax, XIter, YIter: Double;
  Done: Boolean;
  R: TRect;
begin
  if Assigned(OnBeginDraw) then
    OnBeginDraw(Self);
  // Code omitted here
  if Assigned(OnEndDraw) then
    OnEndDraw(self);
  Result := True;
end;
```

As you recall, TNotifyEvent is declared thusly:

```
type TNotifyEvent = procedure (Sender: TObject) of object;
```

In short, it is an event handler of the most common type, similar to an OnClick event. Including the OnEndDraw and OnBeginDraw properties in the declaration of TElfMandy guarantees that the Event page in the Object Inspector for this component includes these two programmer-defined events.

The TElfMandy.Run method checks to see if the user has used the Object Inspector to create handlers for the OnBeginDraw and OnEndDraw events. If he or she has, the methods are called.

Here is the OnEndDraw handler for the TestElfMandy Program:

```
procedure TForm1.ElfMandy1RunDone(Sender: TObject);
begin
  FMandyDrawing := False;
  SnapPicture;
end;
```

As you can see, this method calls the SnapPicture method that you have just finished contemplating. If the user then obscures the component with the Save dialog box or some other window, the program will automatically be notified by the operating system. CLX translates this notification into an OnPaint event, which the TestElfMandel program handles in the following manner:

```
procedure TForm1.ElfMandy1Paint(Sender: TObject);
begin
  if (FMandyDrawing <> True) and (FBitmap <> nil) then
    ElfMandy1.Canvas.CopyRect(Rect(0, 0, ElfMandy1.Width, ElfMandy1.Height),
      FBitmap.Canvas, Rect(0, 0, ElfMandy1.Width, ElfMandy1.Height));
end;
```

The code first checks to make sure that the component is not currently in the process of drawing the Mandelbrot picture. This is necessary because the act of drawing the set causes repaint messages to be sent to the control. If it is not currently drawing, and if the FBitmap variable is not set to nil, the CopyRect method is used to blit the contents of the FBitmap variable back into the TElfMandy component from which the picture originally came. All this churning about is hardly noticed by the user: he merely sees that the component still appears as it did before it was obscured. This is what the user expects, and so all seems right with the world. Indeed, this same sort of thing happens behind the scenes on a regular basis when the user moves windows around in an environment such as X or Microsoft Windows. In short, every window that gets obscured must be repainted by CLX or the OS each time it is revealed to the user. It is just that, in this case, it is up to us to repaint it.

> **NOTE**
>
> The TElfMandy component could be improved by keeping a bitmap that serves as a backup copy of the drawing. This backup bitmap could be automatically blitted to the screen, thus saving us the trouble that we have gone to in the TestElfMandel program.

## LoadResource: Creating the Opening Scene

If you have run the TestElfMandel program, you will notice that it first appears with a fully drawn copy of the Mandelbrot set on its surface. Needless to say, it could not calculate the set that quickly. Instead, it is simply loading a bitmap that is bound into the program's executable. This process was explained in Chapter 7 in the section called "Working with Resources."

That is all I'm going to say about the Mandelbrot program. The beautiful pictures this program creates provided a good backdrop for a discussion of some key Kylix technologies, such as working with bitmaps, painting individual pixels, and working with the Boolean-based painting technologies that make rubber banding possible.

# A Pseudo-3D World

Those of us who have been around for awhile recall the old pseudo-3D engines that drove classic role-playing games such as Eye of the Beholder, the early Might and Magic games, and the somewhat more obscure game called Dungeon Hack. The technology behind these games was not really very complicated, at least by today's standards. As a result, it might be fun to create an old-fashioned pseudo-3D engine of this type.

A real 3D engine creates worlds that you can walk into and walk around. In these worlds, you can choose whatever perspective on a scene you want and it still looks relatively real. If there is a chair sitting in the middle of the room, you can walk around the chair and view it from many different angles.

In a pseudo-3D world such as the one we are about to create, you can only look at scenes from certain predefined positions. Objects tend to be simple and two dimensional, and the world you walk through has very carefully prescribed boundaries.

Figure 11.5 shows the CityMap gaming engine, which gives you a view of a classic pseudo three-dimensional dungeon. None of the rooms in this dungeon are larger than a certain size, and things in the distance tend to fade off very quickly into a dense fog. In short, it's quite primitive when compared to the engines that power a game like Unreal or Quake. Nonetheless, it is a real gaming engine, and there are many intelligent people who still spend many long hours wandering around worlds like this.

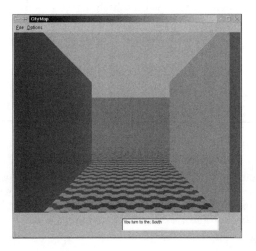

**FIGURE 11.5**

*A typical view of a scene generated by the CityMap gaming engine.*

The game engine is, of course, loaded with code that shows how to use the Kylix graphics system. Furthermore, on Win32 platforms, or if you use the Wine engine, this same code can be compiled to use DirectDraw rather than the standard platform graphics engine. To make the switch from X to DirectDraw, you only need to change one line of code in the program. The tricks that make this possible involve patterns that use Interfaces. They are useful enough that I will cover them briefly near the end of the discussion of this gaming engine.

## The Architecture of a Pseudo-3D World

When walking through a maze, you do not ever see the whole maze at any one time. Instead, your view is limited to a very small segment of the maze. The maze used in this game is made up entirely of right angles. Furthermore, the walls in the maze are made up of blocks of a specified size. For instance, let's posit that each block is four feet square. If the person trapped in the maze saw a wall that was 16 feet long, it would be made up of four, four foot segments of wall. Given the regular nature of the maze, and the rigidly defined size of the wall segments, it is possible to posit that the user can never see more than 16 segments of wall at any one time. The question is, which 16 segments?

Figure 11.6 shows a group of 16 wall segments that make up the entire field of view that a person in the maze could see at any one time. Given this configuration, the user would be trapped, and would have nowhere to go. His only hope would be that the view behind him would be more open. Figure 11.7, on the other hand, shows an open alley in the maze, down which the user can proceed. From the user's point of view, the configuration of walls shown in Figure 11.7 looks like the scene shown in Figure 11.8.

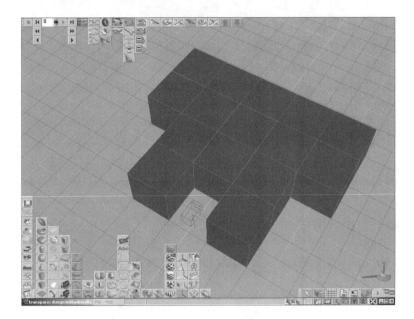

**FIGURE 11.6**

*A view of the maze from up above in which all 16 visible wall segments are in place.*

As you can see, the difference between Figures 11.6 and 11.7 is that some of the 16 wall segments are unoccupied in the second picture. The whole basis of the gaming engine is that any one view of the maze will be made of some combination of empty or full wall segments laid out in a symmetric pattern before the user.

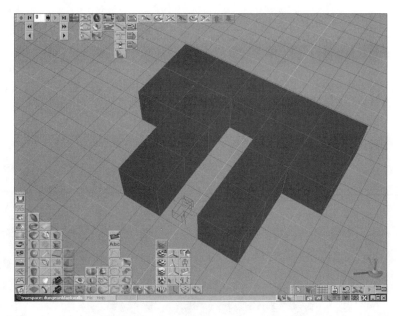

**FIGURE 11.7**

*A view of the maze from above in which an alley is open before the user.*

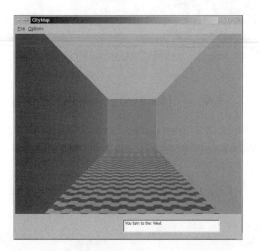

**FIGURE 11.8**

*A view from the user's perspective of the same alley shown in Figure 11.5.*

The maze itself can be defined as a two dimensional array of integers. Any member of the array that has a zero in it is open, and any member of the array that has 1 in it is closed, that is, it contains a wall segment:

```
 5 11
10 14
1 1 1 1 1 1 1 1 1 1
1 0 0 0 0 0 0 0 0 1
1 0 0 0 1 1 0 1 1 1
1 0 0 0 1 0 0 0 0 1
1 0 0 0 1 1 1 0 1 1
1 0 0 0 0 1 0 0 0 1
1 1 1 1 0 1 0 1 0 1
1 0 0 0 0 0 0 0 0 1
1 1 1 1 1 1 1 1 0 1
1 0 0 1 3 1 0 0 0 1
1 0 0 0 0 0 0 1 0 1
1 0 1 1 1 1 1 1 0 1
1 0 0 0 0 0 0 0 0 1
1 1 1 1 1 1 1 1 1 1
```

The top two rows in this array have only two elements in them. The first two elements define the user's current position in the array, that is, column 5, row 11. The second two numbers define the size of the array, which is 10 by 14.

The user, of course, never sees the whole array at any one time. Instead, she sees only a segment of the array, with blocks in it. Each block is numbered 1 through 16, as follows:

```
{          7  12                    1  2  3
    1  4   8  13       12 13 14 15 16      4  5  6
    2  5   9  14        7  8  9 10 11   7  8  9 10 11
    3  6  10  15           4  5  6      12 13 14 15 16
          11  16           1  2  3
}
```

The three groups of numbers shown here depict the user's view when he or she is facing first east, then north, and finally south. Position 2, of course, is where the user is located. It will never, one most sincerely hopes, contain a block. If it did, the laws of physics would cause irreparable harm to our main character.

The first two rows of the 16 blocks that make up the user's view of the maze are three in number. The last two rows are five in number. The first two rows are so small because the game sports the conceit that the user cannot turn his or her head to the right or left. The user is always looking directly ahead. If the user wants to see what is to her right or left, she must turn her whole body in that direction.

From the user's limited perspective, the blocks in the first positions of the first two rows are outside her field of view. She simply is not allowed to turn her head to look at them. As a result these blocks never need to be drawn.

## Creating Graphics for the Game

Once upon a time, the graphics for a game of this sort would have been difficult to create. However, even the relatively inexpensive grades of tools available to programmers and artists in this day are more than sufficient to create the art that you need.

The key point to grasp is that all the elements in your art need to be laid out very precisely. You need to have a tool that allows you to define blocks for your wall that are of very precise dimensions, and you need to be able to place them in precise locations. Neither the dimensions nor the locations of the wall segments need to be particularly complex; they just need to be absolutely precise.

Unfortunately, I have been using the same tools for this kind of work for many years. As a result, I have no sense at all of what the market has to offer. I lay out the walls for the maze in TrueSpace, from Caligari. I then use that program's built-in Python scripting engine to take pictures of each of the 16 blocks in quick succession. I then take these pictures into Paint Shop Pro from Jasc Software. (My wife Margie is becoming an expert on the Linux graphic's program called the Gimp, which Margie and I used exclusively in the production of the screenshots for this book. The Gimp is a very powerful tool, and is easily the equal of most Windows-based graphics programs.)

Finally, I store all the pictures I have created in a single Kylix DLL. I then look in the array defining my maze, and place the pictures of each of the included 16 wall segments in the 16 spaces arrayed before the viewer. I start in the back, and move toward the front. If the back row has three zeroes and two ones, I leave the zero positions blank, and snag the bitmaps of the two included segments of the wall. I then move on to the next row, and then the next, and so on, until all four rows have been painted.

Some users may see ways to optimize this system. I do not, however, let it trouble me if some of the wall segments in the back are completely obscured by wall segments in the front. The simple truth is that video cards today can blit 16 bitmaps of almost any reasonable size and shape to the screen so quickly that no human being can sense any delay at all as the process takes place. It is, for all practical purposes, instantaneous. As a result, there is no need for further optimizations unless you want to begin upgrading the capabilities of the engine. In such a case, the calculation to figure out which blocks really need to be painted would probably be less expensive than actually painting the blocks.

# Double Buffering and Surfaces

Most graphics engines in this day and age support the concept of a surface. A surface represents a bitmap or some other two dimensional graphical element. In this game engine, there is a surface that represents the background for the whole maze, and then 15 more surfaces, one for each of the visible wall segments in the maze. Finally, there is something called a back surface or back buffer. The back surface provides the core technology you need for implementing a powerful technology known as *double buffering*.

> **NOTE**
>
> I use the terms *back surface* and *back buffer* interchangeably in this text.

The idea behind double buffering is to emulate as closely as possible the frame-based techniques used in celluloid movies. Double buffering simply shows the users a series of still pictures at a rate sufficiently hurried as to give the illusion of fluid motion or animation.

> **NOTE**
>
> Amazingly enough, as I write this text, the first digital—as contrasted with celluloid—movies are being shown in movie theaters. The world is changing as we speak! My understanding, however, is that digital movies are still founded on a frame-based technology.

Double buffering allows you to compose a frame offscreen and then flip it in front of the viewer. While the viewer is absorbing this information, you compose another scene and then flip it to the screen. For instance, you might start out with the first frame showing a ball at the far left of the screen; then, to create the illusion of movement, you can move the ball from left to right a few pixels each frame. With each slight change of position, you flip a new picture in front of the users. You are showing a series of static pictures of a ball, but the users perceive this as animated motion.

The average movie flips new images to the screen at a rate of approximately 25 frames per second. These rates are so rapid that the human eye never detects the presence of individual frames but instead sees a convincing illusion of true motion. If you move a ball across the screen at rates close to 25 frames per second, the users will think they are seeing not a series of still pictures of a ball, but an actual movie of a ball moving through space. Depending on the quality of your code, modern computers are capable of performing at rates much higher than 25 frames per second, even without the aid of tools such as DirectX or OpenGL.

Our gaming engine does not try to depict fluid motion, but it still presents a series of fully composed scenes to the user. In the heat of a game, the user may want to change his viewpoint several times a second. For this game engine to work, the viewpoint needs to change as quickly and seamlessly as possible. Double buffering can help you achieve this effect.

---

## Finding the Best Design for your Application

I should perhaps mention that when I first started creating animations, I got it into my head that it was foolish to compose an entire buffer and flip it to the screen. This seemed like a wasteful operation to me, and I was determined to make all my changes directly on the screen, so as not to needlessly consume resources.

It turned out that my approach was entirely wrong headed, particularly when I tried to create relatively sophisticated effects. Over time, I found that it was very hard to hide from a user the changes you make directly on the screen. The act of blotting out one portion of the screen, and then painting something in near to it, created very messy artifacts that were easy to see, even when done as efficiently as possible. This kind of sleight of hand should almost always be done on a back buffer, out of sight of the user. Then when you flip the picture to the screen, the user sees only a fully composed image.

Everyone knows that John Carmack's Quake is used as a benchmark to measure the capability of a video card to do page flipping, which is just another term for double buffering. If this technology is good enough for John Carmack, then it is very likely that it is good enough for you.

If you are still unconvinced, you should consider that many modern graphical subsystems guarantee that page flips will occur in sync with a screen refresh. I've never met anyone who could see a 72Mhz screen refresh actually taking place. If a picture is refreshed at that rate, the user will not be able to consciously detect the instant when you blit an image to the screen.

Experience has taught me that no matter what I say, some readers will be determined to try to make changes to the area of the screen the user is actually looking at. Though there are indeed some occasions when this type of thing is appropriate, the vast majority of time you want to compose your images offscreen, and then flip them in front of the user. So if you really want to try writing directly to the screen, go ahead, and if you get frustrated, come back and try double buffering. You'll be amazed at how quickly it solves seemingly intractable problems.

---

The technology used in our game engine allows you to create a back buffer, draw to it, and then flip it to the visible area in your video memory. On today's computers, the operation is very fast. As a result, you can use this technology to perform very smooth animations.

This game engine has one graphical surface called the back surface. While the user is viewing the primary surface, the program blits, if necessary, the background and all 15 visible wall segments to the back surface. When the time comes, this back surface is blitted into the primary surface, and becomes visible to the user.

Different graphics systems will use different technologies to represent a surface. In our game engine, each surface will be represented by a TBitmap object wrapped up in a custom object of our own making. If you want to switch to a new technology, such as OpenGL or DirectX, all you need to do is wrap a DirectX or OpenGL surface inside a custom Kylix object. Then you can simply swap in the new technology and swap out the old. As I will explain later in this chapter, examples of actually doing this with DirectX are available on the CD that accompanies this book. To understand exactly how this works, however, you need to start looking at the actual code for the game engine.

## The Core Code for the Gaming Engine

The code for this game is quite long, and I don't suspect most readers really want to look through it all in printed form. As a result, I will focus on a few key units that provide the most important features of the gaming engine.

Listings 11.6 through 11.9 show the core code for the gaming engine. It turns out that even a relatively simple gaming engine like this one has its complexities and disciplines. I would enjoy describing them in some detail, but there is not enough room. As a result, I'm going to focus on the graphics code relevant to this chapter, and also on some interesting code that relies on a classic pattern involving interfaces that makes it easy to plug in multiple back ends such as DirectX or OpenGL.

**LISTING 11.6** The Definition for the Interfaces that Drive the Graphics Engine

```
/////////////////////////////////////////
// Purpose: Declare interfaces so one can switch back ends
// Program: CityMap
// Copyright © 2001 by Charlie Calvert
//
unit DrawInterfaces;

interface

uses
  Types, QForms;
```

**LISTING 11.6** Continued

```
type
  ISimpleSurface = interface
    function GetRealSurface: Pointer;
  end;

  IDrawTools = interface
    function BackGroundBlits: Boolean;
    procedure BltIntoBackSurface(x, y: Integer;
      Surface: ISimpleSurface; R: TRect);
    procedure BltPrimary(R, R1: TRect);
    procedure BltWorkSurface(x, y: Integer; R: TRect);
    procedure DestroyObjects;
    procedure DrawText(X, Y: Integer; S: String);
    procedure DoOneFlip;
    function CreateNewSurface(AName: String): ISimpleSurface;
    function GetActive: Boolean;
    function GetFullScreen: Boolean;
    function GetSizeX: Integer;
    function GetSizeY: Integer;
    function GetUsePalette: Boolean;
    procedure Initialize(Form: TForm; BackGroundMapStr: PChar;
      TransColor: Integer; DllName: PChar);
    function InitObjects: Boolean;
    procedure Restore;
    procedure SetActive(Value: Boolean);
    procedure SetFullScreen(Value: Boolean);
    procedure SetSizeX(Value: Integer);
    procedure SetSizeY(Value: Integer);
    procedure SetUsePalette(Value: Boolean);
    property Active: Boolean read GetActive write SetActive;
    property SizeX: Integer read GetSizeX write SetSizeX;
    property SizeY: Integer read GetSizeY write SetSizeY;
    property UsePalette: Boolean read GetUsePalette write SetUsePalette;
    property FullScreen: Boolean read GetFullScreen write SetFullScreen;
  end;

function GetDrawTools: IDrawTools;
function GetDelphiTools: IDrawTools;
implementation

uses
  NativeGraphicsCode;

function GetDrawTools: IDrawTools;
```

**LISTING 11.6** Continued

```
begin
  // Uncomment this line and add DirectDrawCode to uses clause to get
  // DirectX support in Windows or under Wine
  // Result := TComDrawDirect.Create;
end;

function GetDelphiTools: IDrawTools;
begin
  Result := TDelphiDraw.Create;
end;

end.
```

**LISTING 11.7** The NativeGraphicsCode Unit Contains the Code that Implements the Interfaces Shown in DrawInterfaces.pas

```
/////////////////////////////////////////
// Purpose: Draw graphics to the screen
// Program: CityMap
// Copyright © 2001 by Charlie Calvert
//
unit NativeGraphicsCode;

interface

uses
  Types, QForms, QGraphics,
  DrawInterfaces, Qt;

type
  TSimpleSurface = class(TInterfacedObject, ISimpleSurface)
  private
    FName: String;
    FSurface: TBitmap;
  public
    constructor Create(AName: String);
    function GetRealSurface: Pointer;
    property Surface: TBitmap read FSurface write FSurface;
  end;

  TDelphiDraw = class(TInterfacedObject, IDrawTools)
  private
```

**LISTING 11.7**   Continued

```
    FActive: Boolean;
    FBackgroundMap: String;
    FBackSurface: TBitmap;
    FDLLName: String;
    FForm: TForm;
    FFullScreen: Boolean;
    FHandle: QOpenScrollViewH;
    FPrimarySurface: TCanvas;
    FSizeX: Integer;
    FSizeY: Integer;
    FTransColor: Integer;
    FUsePalette: Boolean;
    FWorkSurface: TBitmap;
    procedure GetBitmapFromDLL(Bitmap: TBitmap; BitmapName: String);
public
    function BackGroundBlits: Boolean;
    procedure BltIntoBackSurface(x, y: Integer;
      Surface: ISimpleSurface; R: TRect);
    procedure BltPrimary(R, R1: TRect);
    procedure BltWorkSurface(x, y: Integer; R: TRect);
    procedure DestroyObjects;
    procedure DrawText(X, Y: Integer; S: String);
    procedure DoOneFlip;
    function CreateNewSurface(AName: String): ISimpleSurface;
    function GetActive: Boolean;
    function GetFullScreen: Boolean;
    function GetSizeX: Integer;
    function GetSizeY: Integer;
    function GetUsePalette: Boolean;
    procedure Initialize(Form: TForm; BackGroundMapStr: PChar;
      TransColor: Integer; DllName: PChar);
    function InitObjects: Boolean;
    procedure Restore;
    procedure SetActive(Value: Boolean);
    procedure SetFullScreen(Value: Boolean);
    procedure SetSizeX(Value: Integer);
    procedure SetSizeY(Value: Integer);
    procedure SetUsePalette(Value: Boolean);
    property Active: Boolean read GetActive write SetActive;
    property SizeX: Integer read GetSizeX write SetSizeX;
    property SizeY: Integer read GetSizeY write SetSizeY;
    property UsePalette: Boolean read GetUsePalette write SetUsePalette;
    property FullScreen: Boolean read GetFullScreen write SetFullScreen;
  end;
```

**LISTING 11.7** Continued

```
implementation

uses
  QDialogs, SysUtils;

{ TDelphiDraw }

function TDelphiDraw.BackGroundBlits: Boolean;
begin
  FBackSurface.Canvas.Draw(0, 0, FWorkSurface);
  Result := True;
end;

procedure TDelphiDraw.BltIntoBackSurface(x, y: Integer;
  Surface: ISimpleSurface; R: TRect);
var
  RealSurface: TBitmap;
begin
  RealSurface := TBitmap(Surface.GetRealSurface);
  FBackSurface.Canvas.Draw(x, y, RealSurface);
end;


procedure TDelphiDraw.BltPrimary(R, R1: TRect);
begin
  FPrimarySurface.Draw(0, 0, FBackSurface);
end;


procedure TDelphiDraw.BltWorkSurface(x, y: Integer; R: TRect);
begin
  FBackSurface.Canvas.Draw(x, y, FWorkSurface);
end;

function TDelphiDraw.CreateNewSurface(AName: String): ISimpleSurface;
var
  Surface: TSimpleSurface;
  Bitmap: TBitmap;
begin
  Bitmap := TBitmap.Create;
  Surface := TSimpleSurface.Create(AName);
  GetBitmapFromDLL(Bitmap, AName);
  Surface.Surface := Bitmap;
  Result := Surface;
end;
```

**LISTING 11.7**   Continued

```
procedure TDelphiDraw.DestroyObjects;
begin
  FreeAndNil(FPrimarySurface);
  FreeAndNil(FWorkSurface);
  FreeAndNil(FBackSurface);
end;

procedure TDelphiDraw.DoOneFlip;
begin

end;

procedure TDelphiDraw.DrawText(X, Y: Integer; S: String);
begin
  FWorkSurface.Canvas.TextOut(X, Y, S);
end;

function TDelphiDraw.GetActive: Boolean;
begin
  Result := FActive;
end;

procedure TDelphiDraw.GetBitmapFromDLL(Bitmap: TBitmap; BitmapName: String);
var
  Lib: THandle;
begin
  Lib := 0;

  if FDllName <> '' then begin
    // Load library maps to dlOpen in sysutils.pas
    Lib := LoadLibrary(PChar(FDllName));
    if Lib < 32 then begin
      ShowMessage('Cound not find or load library: ' + FDLLName);
      Exit;
    end;
  end;

  Bitmap.LoadFromResourceName(Lib, BitmapName);

  FreeLibrary(Lib);
end;

function TDelphiDraw.GetFullScreen: Boolean;
```

**LISTING 11.7** Continued

```delphi
begin
  Result := FFullScreen;
end;

function TDelphiDraw.GetSizeX: Integer;
begin
  Result := FSizeX;
end;

function TDelphiDraw.GetSizeY: Integer;
begin
  Result := FSizeY;
end;

function TDelphiDraw.GetUsePalette: Boolean;
begin
  Result := FUsePalette;
end;

procedure TDelphiDraw.Initialize(Form: TForm; BackGroundMapStr: PChar;
  TransColor: Integer; DllName: PChar);
begin
  FHandle := Form.Handle;
  FForm := Form;
  FDllName := DllName;
  FActive := False;
  FTransColor:= TransColor;              // Transparent color
  FBackGroundMap := BackGroundMapStr;  // Name of background bitmap
end;

function TDelphiDraw.InitObjects: Boolean;

  function MakeSurface(x, y: Integer): TBitmap;
  var
    Surface: TBitmap;
  begin
    Surface := TBitmap.Create;
    Surface.Width := x;
    Surface.Height := y;
    Result := Surface;
  end;
```

**LISTING 11.7**   Continued

```
begin
  FPrimarySurface := FForm.Canvas; // MakeSurface(FSizeX, FSizeY);
  FBackSurface := MakeSurface(FSizeX, FSizeY);
  FWorkSurface := MakeSurface(FSizeX, FSizeY);
  GetBitmapFromDLL(FWorkSurface, FBackgroundMap);
  FActive := True;
  Result := True;
end;

procedure TDelphiDraw.Restore;
begin

end;

procedure TDelphiDraw.SetActive(Value: Boolean);
begin
  FActive := Value;
end;

procedure TDelphiDraw.SetFullScreen(Value: Boolean);
begin
  FFullScreen := Value;
end;

procedure TDelphiDraw.SetSizeX(Value: Integer);
begin
  FSizeX := Value;
end;

procedure TDelphiDraw.SetSizeY(Value: Integer);
begin
  FSizeY := Value;
end;

procedure TDelphiDraw.SetUsePalette(Value: Boolean);
begin
  FUsePalette := Value;
end;

{ TSimpleSurface }

constructor TSimpleSurface.Create(AName: String);
begin
  FName := AName;
end;
```

**LISTING 11.7**   Continued

```
function TSimpleSurface.GetRealSurface: Pointer;
begin
  Result := FSurface;
end;

end.
```

**LISTING 11.8**   The DrawRoot2 Unit Contains the Code for Actually Painting the Maze to the Screen

```
/////////////////////////////////////////
// Purpose: Run the graphics engine
// Program: CityMap
// Copyright © 2001 by Charlie Calvert
//
unit DrawRoot2;

interface

uses
  SysUtils, QForms, Globals,
  Creatures01, MzTown, DrawInterfaces;

const
  MaxMapRows = 12;
  MaxMapCols = 21;
  WorldBackGround = 'Back';
  CityBackGround = 'City';

type
  TSide = (ExtLeft, Left, Center, Right, ExtRight);

  TCityBoard = class(TObject)
  private
    FDrawTools: IDrawTools;
    FDDSBackExtLeft: ISimpleSurface;
    FDDSBackLeft: ISimpleSurface;
    FDDSBackCenter: ISimpleSurface;
    FDDSBackRight: ISimpleSurface;
    FDDSBackExtRight: ISimpleSurface;
    FDDSMidExtLeft: ISimpleSurface;
    FDDSMidLeft: ISimpleSurface;
    FDDSMidCenter: ISimpleSurface;
```

**LISTING 11.8**   Continued

```
    FDDSMidRight: ISimpleSurface;
    FDDSMidExtRight: ISimpleSurface;
    FDDSForeLeft: ISimpleSurface;
    FDDSForeCenter: ISimpleSurface;
    FDDSForeRight: ISimpleSurface;
    FDDSFrontLeft: ISimpleSurface;
    FDDSFrontRight: ISimpleSurface;
    FForm: TForm;
    FMazeTown: TMazeTown;
    function BackGroundBlits: Boolean;
    procedure DrawPlace(DlgForm: TForm; X, Y, Value: Integer);
    procedure DrawWallSegment(DlgForm: TForm; WallNum, Value: Integer);
    function GetActive: Boolean;
    function GetFullScreen: Boolean;
    procedure SetActive(const Value: Boolean);
    procedure SetFullScreen(const Value: Boolean);
  public
    constructor Create; virtual;
    procedure DestroyObjects;
    procedure DoOneFlip;
    procedure DrawDebug(DlgForm: TForm);
    procedure DrawScene(DlgForm: TForm);
    function HandlePanel: Boolean;
    procedure Initialize(Form: TForm; BackGroundMapStr: PChar;
      TransColor: Integer; DllName: PChar);
    function InitObjects: Boolean;
    procedure Move(Value: Integer);
    procedure Restore;
    property Active: Boolean read GetActive write SetActive;
    property DrawTools: IDrawTools read FDrawTools write FDrawTools;
    property FullScreen: Boolean read GetFullScreen write SetFullScreen;
    property MazeTown: TMazeTown read FMazeTown;
  end;


implementation

uses
  Classes, Types, QGraphics,
  QDialogs, Qt;

{ --- TCityBoard --- }

{ The first Row
```

**LISTING 11.8**   Continued

```
New FrontWall.bmp
FrontLeft, 0, 0, 54, 384
FrontRight 54, 0, 108, 384}


{ 1= Left
  3= Right
  4= ForeLeft
  5= ForeCenter
  6= ForeRight
  7= MidExtLeft
  8= MidLeft
  9= MidCenter
  10= MidRight
  11= MidExtRight
  12= BackExtLeft
  13= BackLeft
  14= BackCenter
  15= BackRight
  16= BackExtRight}
function TCityBoard.BackGroundBlits: Boolean;
var
  R: TRect;

  function GetFrontPos(Pos: TSide): TRect;
  begin
    case Pos of
      Left: Result := Rect(0, 0, 49, 480);
      Right: Result := Rect(0, 0, 49, 480);
    end;
  end;

  { The second row
    New ForeWall
    ForeLeft 0, 0, 187, 384
    ForeRight 187, 0, 374, 384 }
  function GetForePos(Pos: TSide): TRect;
  begin
    case Pos of
      Left: Result := Rect(0, 0, 213, 480);
      Center: Result := Rect(0, 0, 542, 480);
      Right: Result := Rect(0, 0, 213, 480);
    end;
  end;
```

**LISTING 11.8**   Continued

```
{ The Third Row
  New MidWall.bmp
  MidLeft 0, 0, 232, 268
  MidRight 232, 0, 463, 268
  MidCenter  464, 0, 733, 268 }
function GetMidPos(Pos: TSide): TRect;
begin
  case Pos of
    ExtLeft: Result := Rect(0, 0, 121, 214);
    Left: Result := Rect(0, 0, 254, 214);
    Center: Result := Rect(0, 0, 214, 214);
    Right: Result := Rect(0, 0, 254, 214);
    ExtRight: Result := Rect(0, 0, 121, 214);
  end;
end;

{ The Back Row
  -----------
  New BackRow.bmp
  ``````````````
  BackExtLeft 0, 0, 121, 181
  BackLeft 428, 0, 630, 181
  BackCenter 235, 2, 428, 181
  BackRight 630, 0, 832, 181
  BackExtRight 121, 0, 235, 181 }
function GetBackPos(Pos: TSide): TRect;
begin
  case Pos of
    ExtLeft: Result := Rect(0, 0, 175, 132);
    Left: Result := Rect(0, 0, 151, 132);
    Center: Result := Rect(0, 0, 132, 132); { 18? X 179 }
    Right: Result := Rect(0, 0, 151, 132);
    ExtRight: Result := Rect(0, 0, 175, 132);  { 121 * 179 }
  end;
end;

begin
  FDrawTools.BackGroundBlits;

  {============================================================================}
  {== BACK ROW ================================================================}
  {============================================================================}
```
```

**LISTING 11.8** Continued

```pascal
if FMazeTown.CurrentView[Ord(ptBackExtLeft)].Value = 1 then begin
  R := GetBackPos(ExtLeft);
  FDrawTools.BltIntoBackSurface(0, 174, FDDSBackExtLeft, R);
end;

if FMazeTown.CurrentView[Ord(ptBackLeft)].Value = 1 then begin
  R := GetBackPos(Left);
  FDrawTools.BltIntoBackSurface(121, 174, FDDSBackLeft, R);
end;

if FMazeTown.CurrentView[Ord(ptBackExtRight)].Value = 1 then begin
  R := GetBackPos(ExtRight);
  FDrawTools.BltIntoBackSurface(465, 174, FDDSBackExtRight, R);
end;

if FMazeTown.CurrentView[Ord(ptBackRight)].Value = 1 then begin
  R := GetBackPos(Right);
  FDrawTools.BltIntoBackSurface(368, 174, FDDSBackRight, R);
end;

if FMazeTown.CurrentView[Ord(ptBackCenter)].Value = 1 then begin
  R := GetBackPos(Center);
  FDrawTools.BltIntoBackSurface(254, 174, FDDSBackCenter, R);
end;

{==============================================================================}
{== MID ROW ===================================================================}
{==============================================================================}

if FMazeTown.CurrentView[Ord(ptMidExtLeft)].Value = 1 then begin
  R := GetMidPos(ExtLeft);
  FDrawTools.BltIntoBackSurface(0, 133, FDDSMidExtLeft, R);
end;

if FMazeTown.CurrentView[Ord(ptMidLeft)].Value = 1 then begin
  R := GetMidPos(Left);
  FDrawTools.BltIntoBackSurface(0, 133, FDDSMidLeft, R);
end;

if FMazeTown.CurrentView[Ord(ptMidExtRight)].Value = 1 then begin
  R := GetMidPos(ExtRight);
  FDrawTools.BltIntoBackSurface(519, 133, FDDSMidExtRight, R);
end;
```

**LISTING 11.8**  Continued

```pascal
if FMazeTown.CurrentView[Ord(ptMidRight)].Value = 1 then begin
  R := GetMidPos(Right);
  FDrawTools.BltIntoBackSurface(386, 133, FDDSMidRight, R);
end;

if FMazeTown.CurrentView[Ord(ptMidCenter)].Value = 1 then begin
  R := GetMidPos(Center);
  FDrawTools.BltIntoBackSurface(213, 133, FDDSMidCenter, R);
end;


{============================================================================}
{== FORE ROW ================================================================}
{============================================================================}

if FMazeTown.CurrentView[Ord(ptForeLeft)].Value = 1 then begin
  R := GetForePos(Left);
  FDrawTools.BltIntoBackSurface(0, 0, FDDSForeLeft, R);
end;

 if FMazeTown.CurrentView[Ord(ptForeRight)].Value = 1 then begin
  R := GetForePos(Right);
  FDrawTools.BltIntoBackSurface(427, 0, FDDSForeRight, R);
end;

if FMazeTown.CurrentView[Ord(ptForeCenter)].Value = 1 then begin
  R := GetForePos(Center);
  FDrawTools.BltIntoBackSurface(49, 0, FDDSForeCenter, R);
end;


{============================================================================}
{== FRONT ROW ===============================================================}
{============================================================================}

if FMazeTown.CurrentView[Ord(ptFrontLeft)].Value = 1 then begin
  R := GetFrontPos(Left);
  FDrawTools.BltIntoBackSurface(0, 0, FDDSFrontLeft, R);
end;

{ Two is where you are standing, so you don't do that one. }

if FMazeTown.CurrentView[Ord(ptFrontRight)].Value = 1 then begin
  R := GetFrontPos(Right);
  FDrawTools.BltIntoBackSurface(591, 0, FDDSFrontRight, R);
end;
```

**LISTING 11.8** Continued

```pascal
    Result := True;
end;

constructor TCityBoard.Create;
begin
  inherited Create;
  FDrawTools := GetDelphiTools;
  FDrawTools.SizeX := PageWidth;
  FDrawTools.SizeY := PageHeight;
  FDrawTools.UsePalette := False;
  FMazeTown := TMazeTown.Create(East);
end;

procedure TCityBoard.DoOneFlip;
var
  R, R1: TRect;
begin
  if not FDrawTools.FullScreen then begin
    BackGroundBlits;
    R := FForm.BoundsRect; // Was call to GetWindowRect
    R1 := Rect(0, 0, FDrawTools.SizeX, FDrawTools.SizeY);
    FDrawTools.BltPrimary(R, R1);
  end;
end;


procedure TCityBoard.DestroyObjects;
begin
  FDDSBackExtLeft := nil;
  FDDSBackLeft := nil;
  FDDSBackCenter := nil;
  FDDSBackRight := nil;
  FDDSBackExtRight := nil;

  FDDSMidExtLeft := nil;
  FDDSMidLeft := nil;
  FDDSMidCenter := nil;
  FDDSMidRight := nil;
  FDDSMidExtRight := nil;

  FDDSForeLeft := nil;
  FDDSForeCenter := nil;
  FDDSForeRight := nil;
```

**LISTING 11.8** Continued

```pascal
    FDDSFrontLeft := nil;
    FDDSFrontRight := nil;
    FDrawTools.DestroyObjects;
end;

function TCityBoard.HandlePanel;
var
  R: TRect;
begin
  case FMazeTown.Direction of
    North: R := Rect(575, 480, 640, 545);
    South: R := Rect(575, 545, 640, 610);
    East:  R := Rect(575, 610, 640, 675);
    West:  R := Rect(575, 675, 640, 740);
  end;
  FDrawTools.BltWorkSurface(23, 401, R);
  Result := True;
end;

procedure TCityBoard.Initialize(Form: TForm; BackGroundMapStr: PChar;
  TransColor: Integer; DllName: PChar);
begin
  FForm := Form;
  FDrawTools.Initialize(Form, BackGroundMapStr, TransColor, DLLName);
end;

function TCityBoard.InitObjects: Boolean;
begin
  FDrawTools.InitObjects;
  Result := False;
  if not FDrawTools.Active then Exit;
  FDDSBackExtLeft := FDrawTools.CreateNewSurface('BackExtLeft');
  FDDSBackLeft := FDrawTools.CreateNewSurface('BackLeft');
  FDDSBackCenter := FDrawTools.CreateNewSurface('BackCenter');
  FDDSBackRight := FDrawTools.CreateNewSurface('BackRight');
  FDDSBackExtRight := FDrawTools.CreateNewSurface('BackExtRight');

  FDDSMidExtLeft := FDrawTools.CreateNewSurface('MidExtLeft');
  FDDSMidLeft := FDrawTools.CreateNewSurface('MidLeft');
  FDDSMidCenter := FDrawTools.CreateNewSurface('MidCenter');
  FDDSMidRight := FDrawTools.CreateNewSurface('MidRight');
  FDDSMidExtRight := FDrawTools.CreateNewSurface('MidExtRight');
```

LISTING 11.8 Continued

```
    FDDSForeLeft := FDrawTools.CreateNewSurface('ForeLeft');
    FDDSForeCenter := FDrawTools.CreateNewSurface('ForeCenter');
    FDDSForeRight := FDrawTools.CreateNewSurface('ForeRight');

    FDDSFrontLeft := FDrawTools.CreateNewSurface('FrontLeft');
    FDDSFrontRight := FDrawTools.CreateNewSurface('FrontRight');

    Result := True;
end;

procedure TCityBoard.DrawWallSegment(DlgForm: TForm;
  WallNum: Integer; Value: Integer);
var
  C: TCanvas;
begin
  C := DlgForm.Canvas;
  case WallNum of
     1: C.TextOut(200, 125, IntToStr(Value));
     2: C.TextOut(230, 125, IntToStr(Value));
     3: C.TextOut(260, 125, IntToStr(Value));
     4: C.TextOut(200, 100, IntToStr(Value));
     5: C.TextOut(230, 100, IntToStr(Value));
     6: C.TextOut(260, 100, IntToStr(Value));
     7: C.TextOut(175, 75, IntToStr(Value));
     8: C.TextOut(200, 75, IntToStr(Value));
     9: C.TextOut(225, 75, IntToStr(Value));
    10: C.TextOut(250, 75, IntToStr(Value));
    11: C.TextOut(275, 75, IntToStr(Value));
    12: C.TextOut(175, 50, IntToStr(Value));
    13: C.TextOut(200, 50, IntToStr(Value));
    14: C.TextOut(225, 50, IntToStr(Value));
    15: C.TextOut(250, 50, IntToStr(Value));
    16: C.TextOut(275, 50, IntToStr(Value));
  end;
end;

procedure TCityBoard.DrawDebug(DlgForm: TForm);
var
  i: Integer;
  WallSegment: TWallSegment;
begin
  DlgForm.Canvas.Brush.Color := clGray;
  DlgForm.Canvas.Rectangle(170, 40, 287, 150);
  for i := 1 to 16 do begin
```

**LISTING 11.8**  Continued

```delphi
    WallSegment := FMazeTown.CurrentView[i];
    DrawWallSegment(DlgForm, i, WallSegment.Value);
  end;
end;

procedure TCityBoard.DrawPlace(DlgForm: TForm; X, Y, Value: Integer);
const
  Size: Integer = 10;
begin
  case Value of
    0: DlgForm.Canvas.Brush.Color := clBlue;
    1: DlgForm.Canvas.Brush.Color := clYellow;
    2: DlgForm.Canvas.Brush.Color := clGreen;
  else
    DlgForm.Canvas.Brush.Color := clWhite;
  end;
  X := X * Size;
  Y := Y * Size;
  DlgForm.Canvas.Rectangle(X, Y, X + Size, Y + Size);
end;

procedure TCityBoard.DrawScene(DlgForm: TForm);
var
  i, j, Value: Integer;
  Map: TMapPointList;
begin
  Map := FMazeTown.MapList;
  BackGroundBlits;
  for i := 1 to Map.MaxRows do
    for j := 1 to Map.MaxCols do begin
      Value := FMazeTown.GetWallSegment(j, i);
      DrawPlace(DlgForm, j, i, Value);
    end;
  DrawPlace(DlgForm, FMazeTown.XSpot, FMazeTown.YSpot, 3);
end;

function TCityBoard.GetFullScreen: Boolean;
begin
  Result := FDrawTools.FullScreen;
end;
```

**LISTING 11.8** Continued

```pascal
procedure TCityBoard.Move(Value: Integer);
begin
  case Value of
    Key_Right: FMazeTown.Key(Key_Right);
    Key_Left: FMazeTown.Key(Key_Left);
    Key_Down: FMazeTown.Key(Key_Down);
    Key_Up: FMazeTown.Key(Key_Up);
  end;
  DoOneFlip;
end;

function TCityBoard.GetActive: Boolean;
begin
  Result := FDrawTools.GetActive;
end;

procedure TCityBoard.Restore;
begin
  FDrawTools.Restore;
  {TODO: Check out restore }
end;

procedure TCityBoard.SetActive(const Value: Boolean);
begin
  FDrawTools.Active := Value;
end;

procedure TCityBoard.SetFullScreen(const Value: Boolean);
begin
  FDrawTools.FullScreen := Value;
end;

initialization
{  AssignFile(F, 'c:\info.txt');
  ReWrite(F);
  WriteLn(F, 'Initialization'); }
finalization
{   CloseFile(F); }
end.
```

**LISTING 11.9** The MzTown Unit Manages the Data Structures that Define the Maze through Which the User Walks

```
/////////////////////////////////////////
// Purpose: Data structures for defining the maze
// Program: CityMap
// Copyright © 1996..2001 by Charlie Calvert
//
unit MzTown;

{ This unit runs a city or maze; }

{ 1= FrontLeft
  2= Center // Never used, It's where you are standing
  3= FrontRight
  4= ForeLeft
  5= ForeCenter
  6= ForeRight
  7= MidExtLeft
  8= MidLeft
  9= MidCenter
  10= MidRight
  11= MidExtRight
  12= BackExtLeft
  13= BackLeft
  14= BackCenter
  15= BackRight
  16= BackExtRight }
{         7  12                    1  2  3
    1  4  8  13      12 13 14 15 16    4  5  6
    2  5  9  14    7  8  9  10 11    7  8  9  10 11
    3  6  10 15       4  5  6       12 13 14 15 16
          11 16       1  2  3
}

{ Here's what a city map looks like:

      5 11
      10 14
      1 1 1 1 1 1 1 1 1 1
      1 0 0 0 0 0 0 0 0 1
      1 0 0 0 1 1 0 1 1 1
      1 0 0 0 1 0 0 0 0 1
      1 0 0 0 1 1 1 0 1 1
      1 0 0 0 0 1 0 0 0 1
      1 1 1 1 0 1 0 1 0 1
```

**11**

**LISTING 11.9**  Continued

```
      1 0 0 0 0 0 0 0 1
      1 1 1 1 1 1 1 0 1
      1 0 0 1 3 1 0 0 1
      1 0 0 0 0 0 1 0 1
      1 0 1 1 1 1 1 0 1
      1 0 0 0 0 0 0 0 1
      1 1 1 1 1 1 1 1 1
  }

interface

uses
  Creatures01, Qt;

type
  TDirection = (North, East, South, West);
  TPositionType = (ptNone, ptFrontLeft, ptFrontCenter, ptFrontRight,
    ptForeLeft, ptForeCenter, ptForeRight, ptMidExtLeft, ptMidLeft,
    ptMidCenter, ptMidRight, ptMidExtRight, ptBackExtLeft,
    ptBackLeft, ptBackCenter, ptBackRight,  ptBackExtRight);

  TWallSegment = record
    X, Y: Integer;
    Value: Integer;
  end;

  TCityPlaceAry = array[1..16] of TWallSegment;

  TMazeTown = class
  private
    FMapList: TMapPointList;
    FMazeFile: string;
    FDirection: TDirection;
    FXSpot, FYSpot: Integer;
    FCurrentView: TCityPlaceAry;
    FViewChanged: Boolean;
    function CheckForwardMove: Boolean;
    function GetNewDir(K: ShortInt): TDirection;
    function GetDirectionString: String;
    function GetCityPlace(X, Y: Integer): TWallSegment;
  public
    constructor Create(Dir: TDirection);
    destructor Destroy; override;
    procedure FillOutCurrentView;
```

**LISTING 11.9** Continued

```
    function GetWallSegment(X, Y: Integer): Integer;
    procedure Move(Direction: TDirection);
    procedure Key(vKey: Word);
    procedure SetCurrentView(Offset: Integer; Value: Integer);
    property CurrentView: TCityPlaceAry read FCurrentView;
    property Direction: TDirection read FDirection write FDirection;
    property DirectionStr: String read GetDirectionString;
    property ViewChanged: Boolean read FViewChanged;
    property MapList: TMapPointList read FMapList;
    property XSpot: Integer read FXSpot;
    property YSpot: Integer read FYSpot;
  end;

implementation

uses
  LCodeBox;

{const
  FTownAry: TTownAry =
    ((1,1,1,1,1,1,1,1,1,1),
     (1,0,0,0,0,0,0,0,0,1),
     (1,0,0,0,1,1,0,1,1,1),
     (1,0,0,0,1,0,0,0,0,1),
     (1,0,0,0,1,1,1,0,1,1),
     (1,0,0,0,0,1,0,0,0,1),
     (1,1,1,1,0,1,0,1,0,1),
     (1,0,0,0,0,0,0,0,0,1),
     (1,1,1,1,1,1,1,1,0,1),
     (1,0,0,1,0,1,0,0,0,1),
     (1,1,0,0,0,0,0,1,0,1),
     (1,1,1,1,1,1,1,1,1,1)
    ); }


constructor TMazeTown.Create(Dir: TDirection);
begin
  inherited Create;
  FDirection := Dir;
  FMapList := TMapPointList.Create;
  FMazeFile := GetStartDir + 'maze1.txt';
  FMapList.ReadText(FMazeFile);
  FXSpot := FMapList.StartX;
  FYSpot := FMapList.StartY;
  FillOutCurrentView;
end;
```

**LISTING 11.9**   Continued

```
destructor TMazeTown.Destroy;
begin
  FMapList.WriteText(FMazeFile, FXSpot, FYSpot);
  FMapList.Free;
  inherited Destroy;
end;

procedure TMazeTown.SetCurrentView(Offset: Integer; Value: Integer);
var
  View: TWallSegment;
begin
  View := FCurrentView[OffSet];
  FMapList.Tiles[View.X, View.Y] := Value;
end;

function TMazeTown.GetWallSegment(X, Y: Integer): Integer;
begin
  Result := FMapList.Tiles[X, Y];
end;

{ Fill out a record describing a location in a city. }
function TMazeTown.GetCityPlace(X, Y: Integer): TWallSegment;
var
  C: TWallSegment;
begin
  C.X := X;
  C.Y := Y;
  if (X <= 0) or (X > FMapList.MaxCols) or
     (Y <= 0) or (Y > FMapList.MaxRows) then
    C.Value := -1
  else
    C.Value := FMapList.Tiles[X, Y];
  Result := C;
end;

procedure TMazeTown.FillOutCurrentView;
begin
  case FDirection of
    North: begin
      FCurrentView[1] := GetCityPlace(FXSpot - 1, FYSpot);
      FCurrentView[2] := GetCityPlace(FXSpot, FYSpot);
      FCurrentView[3] := GetCityPlace(FXSpot + 1, FYSpot);
      FCurrentView[4] := GetCityPlace(FXSpot - 1, FYSpot - 1);
      FCurrentView[5] := GetCityPlace(FXSpot, FYSpot - 1);
```

**Listing 11.9**  Continued

```
    FCurrentView[6] := GetCityPlace(FXSpot + 1, FYSpot - 1);
    FCurrentView[7] := GetCityPlace(FXSpot - 2, FYSpot - 2);
    FCurrentView[8] := GetCityPlace(FXSpot - 1, FYSpot - 2);
    FCurrentView[9] := GetCityPlace(FXSpot, FYSpot - 2);
    FCurrentView[10] := GetCityPlace(FXSpot + 1, FYSpot - 2);
    FCurrentView[11] := GetCityPlace(FXSpot + 2, FYSpot - 2);
    FCurrentView[12] := GetCityPlace(FXSpot - 2, FYSpot - 3);
    FCurrentView[13] := GetCityPlace(FXSpot - 1, FYSpot - 3);
    FCurrentView[14] := GetCityPlace(FXSpot, FYSpot - 3);
    FCurrentView[15] := GetCityPlace(FXSpot + 1, FYSpot - 3);
    FCurrentView[16] := GetCityPlace(FXSpot + 2, FYSpot - 3);
  end;

  East: begin
    FCurrentView[1] := GetCityPlace(FXSpot, FYSpot - 1);
    FCurrentView[2] := GetCityPlace(FXSpot, FYSpot);
    FCurrentView[3] := GetCityPlace(FXSpot, FYSpot + 1);
    FCurrentView[4] := GetCityPlace(FXSpot + 1, FYSpot - 1);
    FCurrentView[5] := GetCityPlace(FXSpot + 1, FYSpot);
    FCurrentView[6] := GetCityPlace(FXSpot + 1, FYSpot + 1);
    FCurrentView[7] := GetCityPlace(FXSpot + 2, FYSpot - 2);
    FCurrentView[8] := GetCityPlace(FXSpot + 2, FYSpot - 1);
    FCurrentView[9] := GetCityPlace(FXSpot + 2, FYSpot);
    FCurrentView[10] := GetCityPlace(FXSpot + 2, FYSpot + 1);
    FCurrentView[11] := GetCityPlace(FXSpot + 2, FYSpot + 2);
    FCurrentView[12] := GetCityPlace(FXSpot + 3, FYSpot - 2);
    FCurrentView[13] := GetCityPlace(FXSpot + 3, FYSpot - 1);
    FCurrentView[14] := GetCityPlace(FXSpot + 3, FYSpot);
    FCurrentView[15] := GetCityPlace(FXSpot + 3, FYSpot + 1);
    FCurrentView[16] := GetCityPlace(FXSpot + 3, FYSpot + 2);
  end;

  {$ifDef LookingFromAbove}
  South: begin
    FCurrentView[1] := GetCityPlace(FXSpot - 1, FYSpot);
    FCurrentView[2] := GetCityPlace(FXSpot, FYSpot);
    FCurrentView[3] := GetCityPlace(FXSpot + 1, FYSpot);
    FCurrentView[4] := GetCityPlace(FXSpot - 1, FYSpot + 1);
    FCurrentView[5] := GetCityPlace(FXSpot, FYSpot + 1);
    FCurrentView[7] := GetCityPlace(FXSpot + 1, FYSpot + 1);
    FCurrentView[8] := GetCityPlace(FXSpot - 1, FYSpot + 2);
    FCurrentView[9] := GetCityPlace(FXSpot, FYSpot + 2);
    FCurrentView[10] := GetCityPlace(FXSpot + 1, FYSpot + 2);
    FCurrentView[11] := GetCityPlace(FXSpot + 2, FYSpot + 2);
```

**LISTING 11.9**  Continued

```pascal
    FCurrentView[12] := GetCityPlace(FXSpot - 2, FYSpot + 3);
    FCurrentView[13] := GetCityPlace(FXSpot - 1, FYSpot + 3);
    FCurrentView[14] := GetCityPlace(FXSpot, FYSpot + 3);
    FCurrentView[15] := GetCityPlace(FXSpot + 1, FYSpot + 3);
    FCurrentView[16] := GetCityPlace(FXSpot + 2, FYSpot + 3);
  end;

West: begin
    FCurrentView[1] := GetCityPlace(FXSpot, FYSpot - 1);
    FCurrentView[2] := GetCityPlace(FXSpot, FYSpot);
    FCurrentView[3] := GetCityPlace(FXSpot, FYSpot + 1);
    FCurrentView[4] := GetCityPlace(FXSpot - 1, FYSpot - 1);
    FCurrentView[5] := GetCityPlace(FXSpot - 1, FYSpot);
    FCurrentView[6] := GetCityPlace(FXSpot - 1, FYSpot + 1);
    FCurrentView[7] := GetCityPlace(FXSpot - 2, FYSpot - 2);
    FCurrentView[8] := GetCityPlace(FXSpot - 2, FYSpot - 1);
    FCurrentView[9] := GetCityPlace(FXSpot - 2, FYSpot);
    FCurrentView[10] := GetCityPlace(FXSpot - 2, FYSpot + 1);
    FCurrentView[10] := GetCityPlace(FXSpot - 2, FYSpot + 2);
    FCurrentView[12] := GetCityPlace(FXSpot - 3, FYSpot - 2);
    FCurrentView[13] := GetCityPlace(FXSpot - 3, FYSpot - 1);
    FCurrentView[14] := GetCityPlace(FXSpot - 3, FYSpot);
    FCurrentView[15] := GetCityPlace(FXSpot - 3, FYSpot + 1);
    FCurrentView[16] := GetCityPlace(FXSpot - 3, FYSpot + 2);
  end;

{$else}
South: begin
    FCurrentView[1] := GetCityPlace(FXSpot + 1, FYSpot);
    FCurrentView[2] := GetCityPlace(FXSpot, FYSpot);
    FCurrentView[3] := GetCityPlace(FXSpot - 1, FYSpot);
    FCurrentView[4] := GetCityPlace(FXSpot + 1, FYSpot + 1);
    FCurrentView[5] := GetCityPlace(FXSpot, FYSpot + 1);
    FCurrentView[6] := GetCityPlace(FXSpot - 1, FYSpot + 1);
    FCurrentView[7] := GetCityPlace(FXSpot + 2, FYSpot + 2);
    FCurrentView[8] := GetCityPlace(FXSpot + 1, FYSpot + 2);
    FCurrentView[9] := GetCityPlace(FXSpot, FYSpot + 2);
    FCurrentView[10] := GetCityPlace(FXSpot - 1, FYSpot + 2);
    FCurrentView[11] := GetCityPlace(FXSpot - 2, FYSpot + 2);
    FCurrentView[12] := GetCityPlace(FXSpot + 2, FYSpot + 3);
    FCurrentView[13] := GetCityPlace(FXSpot + 1, FYSpot + 3);
    FCurrentView[14] := GetCityPlace(FXSpot, FYSpot + 3);
    FCurrentView[15] := GetCityPlace(FXSpot - 1, FYSpot + 3);
    FCurrentView[16] := GetCityPlace(FXSpot - 2, FYSpot + 3);
  end;
```

**LISTING 11.9**   Continued

```
    West: begin
      FCurrentView[1] := GetCityPlace(FXSpot, FYSpot + 1);
      FCurrentView[2] := GetCityPlace(FXSpot, FYSpot);
      FCurrentView[3] := GetCityPlace(FXSpot, FYSpot - 1);
      FCurrentView[4] := GetCityPlace(FXSpot - 1, FYSpot + 1);
      FCurrentView[5] := GetCityPlace(FXSpot - 1, FYSpot);
      FCurrentView[6] := GetCityPlace(FXSpot - 1, FYSpot - 1);
      FCurrentView[7] := GetCityPlace(FXSpot - 2, FYSpot + 2);
      FCurrentView[8] := GetCityPlace(FXSpot - 2, FYSpot + 1);
      FCurrentView[9] := GetCityPlace(FXSpot - 2, FYSpot);
      FCurrentView[10] := GetCityPlace(FXSpot - 2, FYSpot - 1);
      FCurrentView[11] := GetCityPlace(FXSpot - 2, FYSpot - 2);
      FCurrentView[12] := GetCityPlace(FXSpot - 3, FYSpot + 2);
      FCurrentView[13] := GetCityPlace(FXSpot - 3, FYSpot + 1);
      FCurrentView[14] := GetCityPlace(FXSpot - 3, FYSpot);
      FCurrentView[15] := GetCityPlace(FXSpot - 3, FYSpot - 1);
      FCurrentView[16] := GetCityPlace(FXSpot - 3, FYSpot - 2);
    end;
    {$endif}
  end;
end;

function TMazeTown.CheckForwardMove: Boolean;
var
  X, Y: Integer;
begin
  X := FXSpot;
  Y := FYSpot;
  case FDirection of
    North: Dec(Y);
    South: Inc(Y);
    East: Inc(X);
    West: Dec(X);
  end;
  if FMapList.Tiles[X, Y] <> 1 then begin
    FXSpot := X;
    FYSpot := Y;
    FViewChanged := True;
    Result := True
  end else begin
    FViewChanged := False;
    Result := False;
  end;
end;
```

**LISTING 11.9**   Continued

```pascal
function TMazeTown.GetNewDir(K: ShortInt): TDirection;
var
  NewDir: ShortInt;
begin
  NewDir := Ord(FDirection) + K;
  if NewDir = -1 then NewDir := 3;
  if NewDir = 4 then NewDir := 0;
  if NewDir = 5 then NewDir := 1;
  GetNewDir := TDirection(NewDir);
end;

procedure TMazeTown.Key(vKey: Word);
var
  NewDir: TDirection;
  Temp: TDirection;
begin
  case vKey of
    Key_Up: NewDir := FDirection;
    Key_Left: NewDir := GetNewDir(-1);
    Key_Right: NewDir := GetNewDir(1);
    Key_Down: begin
      Temp := FDirection;
      NewDir := GetNewDir(2);
      Move(NewDir);
      Move(NewDir);
      FDirection := Temp;
      FillOutCurrentView;
      Exit;
    end;
  else
    NewDir := FDirection;
  end;
  Move(NewDir);
end;

procedure TMazeTown.Move(Direction: TDirection);
begin
  case Direction of

    North: begin
      if FDirection = North then
        CheckForwardMove
      else begin
        FDirection := North;
```

**LISTING 11.9** Continued

```
          FViewChanged := True;
        end;
      end;

    West: begin
      if FDirection = West then
        CheckForwardMove
      else begin
        FDirection := West;
        FViewChanged := True;
      end;
    end;

    East: begin
      if FDirection = East then
        CheckForwardMove
      else begin
        FDirection := East;
        FViewChanged := True;
      end;
    end;

    South: begin
      if FDirection = South then
        CheckForwardMove
      else begin
        FDirection := South;
        FViewChanged := True;
      end;
    end;
  end;
  if ViewChanged then
    FillOutCurrentView;
end;

function TMazeTown.GetDirectionString: String;
var
  S: String;
begin
  case Direction of
    East: S := 'East';
    West: S := 'West';
    North: S := 'North';
    South: S := 'South';
```

**LISTING 11.9** Continued

```
  else
    S := 'Unknown';
  end;
  Result := S;
end;

end.
```

The key to understanding this gaming engine is to understand the two interfaces declared in the DrawInterfaces.pas unit. These interfaces are called ISimpleSurface and IDrawTools. Here is the entire declaration for ISimpleSurface, and the key parts of the declaration for IDrawTools:

```
ISimpleSurface = interface
  function GetRealSurface: Pointer;
end;

IDrawTools = interface
  function BackGroundBlits: Boolean;
  procedure BltIntoBackSurface(x, y: Integer;
    Surface: ISimpleSurface; R: TRect);
  procedure BltPrimary(R, R1: TRect);
  procedure BltWorkSurface(x, y: Integer; R: TRect);
  procedure DestroyObjects;
  procedure DrawText(X, Y: Integer; S: String);
  function CreateNewSurface(AName: String): ISimpleSurface;
  // code omitted here.
end;
```

ISimpleSurface has one method called GetRealSurface that returns a pointer. A pointer is among the most generic ways of addressing memory that Object Pascal has to offer. A pointer can address any object or syntactical element you can place in memory. As a result, the declaration for ISimpleSurface doesn't really say much about what kind of object GetRealSurface returns. It might return a TBitmap, or it might return an IDirectDrawSurface. The specifics do not matter to the ISimpleSurface interface.

IDrawTools has several key methods that allow you to do all the things you need to do when it comes time to paint surfaces to the screen or the back buffer. In particular, BltIntoBackSurface is a method that allows you to blit an instance of ISimpleSurface into the back buffer. Depending on your implementation of the IDrawTools interface, this might involve blitting a bitmap into another bitmap, or blitting a direct draw surface into another direct draw surface. Again, the IDrawTools interface in general, and BltIntoBackSurface method in particular, don't really care what you are doing behind the scenes. They just define a standard method for the act of blitting one surface into the back surface. You can use this method to blit the background, and each of the 15 wall segments, into the back surface. When you are done, the back surface contains the image you want to show to the user.

The `BltPrimarySurface` method allows you to blit the back surface into the primary surface. In our case, this usually means blitting the bitmap that represents the back surface into the `TCanvas` object that represents the primary surface. The `TCanvas` object, of course, is usually the `TForm` object that the viewer is actually looking at. As a result, after the call to `BltPrimarySurface`, the user is actually looking at the scene you created.

There is another method that might catch your eye called `BltWorkSurface`. This blits a scratch pad surface called `WorkSurface` into the back surface. To be frank, most of the code that I have that uses the `WorkSurface` could probably be safely removed from the program, and replaced with code that uses the `BackSurface`. I suspect that such a process would enhance the performance of my object. Nonetheless, the extra `WorkSurface` object can prove useful in some projects. I suppose I have included it in this program, at least in part out of force of habit.

Another key method of the `IDrawTools` interface is `CreateNewSurface`. If you pass this method the name of a bitmap that you have stored on disk or in a resource, `CreateNewSurface` will create a surface that encapsulates your bitmap. For instance, you could pass the name of one of the 15 bitmaps that make up the wall segments to this method. It would then create a surface that contained this bitmap. When you wanted to blit that segment of the wall to the back surface, you would simply pass the surface you created to the `BltIntoBackSurface` method.

Though I have omitted it from the interface to `IDrawTools`, another method commonly used in this kind of object might be called `CreateBlankSurface`. This object would create a surface that contains no bitmap. The `MakeSurface` procedure shown in the next section provides the same functionality as the hypothetical `CreateBlankSurface` method currently under discussion.

The most important point to grasp about all these methods is that they are generic enough to contain either native graphics libraries such as X or GDI, or more complex graphics libraries such as DirectX or OpenGL. This entire discussion is leading us slowly to the point where it will be clear how you can use these interfaces to allow you to swap in different back ends while leaving the code of your program virtually unchanged.

## Implementing `ISimpleSurface` and `IDrawTools`

Here is the code for implementing the `CreateNewSurface` method when you are simply using the native Kylix graphics tools:

```
function TDelphiDraw.CreateNewSurface(AName: String): ISimpleSurface;
var
  Surface: TSimpleSurface;
  Bitmap: TBitmap;
begin
  Bitmap := TBitmap.Create;
  Surface := TSimpleSurface.Create(AName);
  GetBitmapFromDLL(Bitmap, AName);
  Surface.Surface := Bitmap;
  Result := Surface;
end;
```

This code begins by creating a TBitmap object, as discussed in the section of this chapter called "TBitmap:Taking a Picture of the Mandelbrot Set." I then create an instance of the TSimpleSurface object that implements the ISimpleSurface interface. I will discuss this implementation in one moment.

> **NOTE**
>
> If you need a review of interfaces, turn to the discussion of them found in Chapter 4.

GetBitmapFromDLL reads a bitmap from a resource, as discussed in Chapter 7 in the section called "Working with Resources":

```
procedure TDelphiDraw.GetBitmapFromDLL(Bitmap: TBitmap;
  BitmapName: String);
var
  Lib: THandle;
begin
  Lib := 0;
  if FDllName <> '' then begin
    Lib := LoadLibrary(PChar(FDllName));
    if Lib < 32 then begin
      raise Exception.Create('Could not find or load library: ' + FDLLName);
        end;
  end;
  Bitmap.LoadFromResourceName(Lib, BitmapName);
  FreeLibrary(Lib);
end;
```

In this particular case, I call methods with the names LoadLibrary and FreeLibrary. As many readers will know, methods with these names are part of the Microsoft Windows API. However, Kylix implements wrappers around these methods in the SysUtils.pas unit. By using them here, I am able to write cross-platform code. In short, when compiled in Linux, LoadLibrary calls `dlopen`. When compiled in Windows, `LoadLibrary` maps to the Windows API function called `LoadLibrary`.

> **NOTE**
>
> A discussion of working with shared objects and calling `dlopen` is provided in several parts of Chapter 8, "Packaging and Sharing Code," including the section called "Loading a Shared Object Dynamically."

Here is the code that creates the `PrimarySurface`, `BackSurface`, and `WorkSurface`:

```
function TDelphiDraw.InitObjects: Boolean;

  function MakeSurface(x, y: Integer): TBitmap;
  var
    Surface: TBitmap;
  begin
    Surface := TBitmap.Create;
    Surface.Width := x;
    Surface.Height := y;
    Result := Surface;
  end;

begin
  FPrimarySurface := FForm.Canvas;
  FBackSurface := MakeSurface(FSizeX, FSizeY);
  FWorkSurface := MakeSurface(FSizeX, FSizeY);
  GetBitmapFromDLL(FWorkSurface, FBackgroundMap);
  FActive := True;
  Result := True;
end;
```

The `PrimarySurface` is simply assigned to the canvas for the main form in the application. Neither the `BackSurface` nor the `WorkSurface` need to contain a predefined bitmap, so they are each composed simply of empty `TBitmap` objects with a canvas set equal in width and height to the main form of the application. Contrast these surfaces with the surfaces that contain pictures of the various segments of the wall. Those surfaces load bitmaps into memory. The `BackSurface` and `WorkSurface` don't hold any particular bitmap; rather, they become temporary homes to nearly all the bitmaps used in this program.

> **NOTE**
>
> Notice that the MakeSurface procedure shown here corresponds to the hypothetical
> CreateBlankSurface method discussed at the end of the last section. You might also
> be interested in the fact that MakeSurface is a nested procedure that appears inside
> the declaration for the InitObjects method. Nested procedures are one of the inter-
> esting features of Object Pascal that has received short shrift in this book. Frankly, I
> have a mixed opinion of nested procedures because they can cause problems if not
> used judiciously. The CLX source, however, is rife with instances of this syntax.

If you look in the long DrawRoot2.pas unit shown in Listing 11.8, you will see that there is a
method that creates each of the surfaces that contain the bitmaps representing the wall segments:

```
FDDSBackExtLeft := FDrawTools.CreateNewSurface('BackExtLeft');
FDDSBackLeft := FDrawTools.CreateNewSurface('BackLeft');
FDDSBackCenter := FDrawTools.CreateNewSurface('BackCenter');
FDDSBackRight := FDrawTools.CreateNewSurface('BackRight');
FDDSBackExtRight := FDrawTools.CreateNewSurface('BackExtRight');

FDDSMidExtLeft := FDrawTools.CreateNewSurface('MidExtLeft');
FDDSMidLeft := FDrawTools.CreateNewSurface('MidLeft');
FDDSMidCenter := FDrawTools.CreateNewSurface('MidCenter');
FDDSMidRight := FDrawTools.CreateNewSurface('MidRight');
FDDSMidExtRight := FDrawTools.CreateNewSurface('MidExtRight');

FDDSForeLeft := FDrawTools.CreateNewSurface('ForeLeft');
FDDSForeCenter := FDrawTools.CreateNewSurface('ForeCenter');
FDDSForeRight := FDrawTools.CreateNewSurface('ForeRight');

FDDSFrontLeft := FDrawTools.CreateNewSurface('FrontLeft');
FDDSFrontRight := FDrawTools.CreateNewSurface('FrontRight');
```

As you recall, the names passed into the CreateNewSurface method represent the name of the
resource that contains the bitmap that depicts each particular wall segment. Here is the declaration for the relevant part of the RC file for the resource:

```
BackExtLeft BITMAP "BackExtLeft.bmp";
BackLeft BITMAP "BackLeft.bmp";
BackCenter BITMAP "BackCenter.bmp";
BackRight BITMAP "BackRight.bmp";
BackExtRight BITMAP "BackExtRight.bmp";
```

```
MidExtLeft BITMAP "MidExtLeft.bmp"
MidLeft BITMAP "MidLeft.bmp"
MidCenter BITMAP "MidCenter.bmp"
MidRight BITMAP "MidRight.bmp";
MidExtRight BITMAP "MidExtRight.bmp"

ForeLeft BITMAP "ForeLeft.bmp"
ForeCenter BITMAP "ForeCenter.bmp"
ForeRight BITMAP "ForeRight.bmp"
```

Once again, the technology for creating these resources was discussed in the section of Chapter 7 that I have just alluded to.

Here is the actual implementation of BltIntoBackSurface:

```
procedure TDelphiDraw.BltIntoBackSurface(x, y: Integer;
  Surface: ISimpleSurface; R: TRect);
var
  RealSurface: TBitmap;
begin
  RealSurface := TBitmap(Surface.GetRealSurface);
  FBackSurface.Canvas.Draw(x, y, RealSurface);
end;
```

As you can see this code retrieves a TBitmap from the ISimpleSurface object. It then uses the Draw method of the TCanvas object to blit the bitmap into the back surface.

## ISimpleSurface: Creating a Plug-and-Play Back End

Here is the entire declaration and implementation of the TSimpleSurface object that defines the all-important GetRealSurface method:

```
TSimpleSurface = class(TInterfacedObject, ISimpleSurface)
private
  FName: String;
  FSurface: TBitmap;
public
  constructor Create(AName: String);
  function GetRealSurface: Pointer;
  property Surface: TBitmap read FSurface write FSurface;
end;

constructor TSimpleSurface.Create(AName: String);
begin
  FName := AName;
end;
```

```
function TSimpleSurface.GetRealSurface: Pointer;
begin
  Result := FSurface;
end;
```

As you can see, the object is little more than a thin wrapper around a `TBitmap`. If you were using DirectX, this object would be little more than a thin wrapper around `IDirectDrawSurface`. The code itself may be simple, but the degree of abstraction it provides makes it possible to easily switch back and forth between an implementation that depends on native graphics objects and DirectX graphics objects.

In particular, look at this code from `DrawInterfaces.pas`:

```
function GetDrawTools: IDrawTools;
function GetDelphiTools: IDrawTools;
implementation

uses
  NativeGraphicsCode;

function GetDrawTools: IDrawTools;
begin
  // Uncomment this line and add DirectDrawCode to uses clause to get
  // DirectX support in Windows or under Wine
  // Result := TComDrawDirect.Create;
end;

function GetDelphiTools: IDrawTools;
begin
  Result := TDelphiDraw.Create;
end;
```

If the developer wants to use DirectDraw in her program, she can call `GetDrawTools`. If she wants to use the native graphics tools, she can call `GetDelphiTools`. In Linux, it is necessary for me to comment out the code that implements `GetDrawTools`. I do this because most Linux systems do not support DirectX. On Windows, however, I can leave the code uncommented if I wish.

> **NOTE**
>
> The DirectX implementation of the back end for this graphics engine is found in the directory called DirectX which is nested beneath the CityMap directory on the CD that accompanies this book. There is no room to discuss that code in this text, but you can examine it if you are interested.

The key point to grasp here is that the entire body of your program needs to be changed by only one line if you want to switch from DirectX to native graphics code. In particular, in one case you could call GetDelphiTools, and in the other case you would call get GetDrawTools.

Here is the beginning of the declaration for the TCityMap object in DrawTools.pas:

```
TCityBoard = class(TObject)
private
  FDrawTools: IDrawTools;
  FDDSBackExtLeft: ISimpleSurface;
  FDDSBackLeft: ISimpleSurface;
```

As you can see, FDrawTools is declared to be of type IDrawTools, and not of any specific object type. In short, it is an interface, and not a class. Throughout the program, however, you can use it just as if it were an object:

```
FDrawTools.BackGroundBlits;
```

```
  if FMazeTown.CurrentView[Ord(ptBackExtLeft)].Value = 1 then begin
    R := GetBackPos(ExtLeft);
    FDrawTools.BltIntoBackSurface(0, 174, FDDSBackExtLeft, R);
  end;
```

If FDrawTools points to the DirectX implementation, BltIntoBackSurface will call the DirectX code. If it points at the implementation shown in this chapter, it calls either native X code or GDI code.

Here is the method that assigns a value to FDrawTools:

```
constructor TCityBoard.Create;
begin
  inherited Create;
  FDrawTools := GetDelphiTools;
  FDrawTools.SizeX := PageWidth;
  FDrawTools.SizeY := PageHeight;
  FDrawTools.UsePalette := False;
  FMazeTown := TMazeTown.Create(East);
end;
```

The only line in the whole program that needs to change to switch from one back end to the other is the line that includes the call to GetDelphiTools. In particular, it could be changed to read GetDirectXTools. The pattern I have implemented here is a very clean way to swap one back end for another.

## Drawing the Wall Segments in the Right Location

At this stage, you have all the tools you need to create the game engine. The only thing missing is an explanation of where to blit which bitmaps and when.

The `MzTown.pas` unit defines the maze through which the user walks. Suppose the user is at a particular X and Y location in the maze. What the programmer needs to know now is which of the 15 wall segments before the user should be painted, and which should be left blank. For instance, if the user is facing north, the scene will, conceptually, look like this:

```
12 13 14 15 16
 7  8  9  10 11
    4  5  6
    1  2  3
```

The question of the moment is whether or not positions 4, 5, 6, and so on contain ones or zeros. Is there a wall segment at each position, or is it blank? Here is the code from `MzTown.pas` that answers the question for a user facing north from the x, y location defined by `FXSpot` and `FYSpot`:

```
procedure TMazeTown.FillOutCurrentView;
begin
  case FDirection of
    North: begin
      FCurrentView[1] := GetCityPlace(FXSpot - 1, FYSpot);
      FCurrentView[2] := GetCityPlace(FXSpot, FYSpot);
      FCurrentView[3] := GetCityPlace(FXSpot + 1, FYSpot);
      FCurrentView[4] := GetCityPlace(FXSpot - 1, FYSpot - 1);
      FCurrentView[5] := GetCityPlace(FXSpot, FYSpot - 1);
      FCurrentView[6] := GetCityPlace(FXSpot + 1, FYSpot - 1);
      FCurrentView[7] := GetCityPlace(FXSpot - 2, FYSpot - 2);
      FCurrentView[8] := GetCityPlace(FXSpot - 1, FYSpot - 2);
      FCurrentView[9] := GetCityPlace(FXSpot, FYSpot - 2);
      FCurrentView[10] := GetCityPlace(FXSpot + 1, FYSpot - 2);
```

```
    FCurrentView[11] := GetCityPlace(FXSpot + 2, FYSpot - 2);
    FCurrentView[12] := GetCityPlace(FXSpot - 2, FYSpot - 3);
    FCurrentView[13] := GetCityPlace(FXSpot - 1, FYSpot - 3);
    FCurrentView[14] := GetCityPlace(FXSpot, FYSpot - 3);
    FCurrentView[15] := GetCityPlace(FXSpot + 1, FYSpot - 3);
    FCurrentView[16] := GetCityPlace(FXSpot + 2, FYSpot - 3);
  end;
```

If you look at this code carefully, you will see that it reaches out to all 16 possible locations for
the wall by adding or subtracting a number between 3 and –3 to the current x, y location.
GetCityPlace checks to make sure the request for a value at a particular location in the array
is within bounds, and then returns the value from that part of the array:

```
function TMazeTown.GetCityPlace(X, Y: Integer): TWallSegment;
var
  C: TWallSegment;
begin
  C.X := X;
  C.Y := Y;
  if (X <= 0) or (X > FMapList.MaxCols) or
     (Y <= 0) or (Y > FMapList.MaxRows) then
    C.Value := -1
  else
    C.Value := FMapList.Tiles[X, Y];
  Result := C;
end;
```

If the code is out of bounds, that is, if it is beyond the end of beginning of the array, the
method returns minus one. Otherwise it returns either zero or one.

After calling the FilloutCurrentView method, you know what sections of the wall need to be
drawn to the screen and what sections can be left blank. Here is how to translate that information into something the user can actually see:

```
{=============================================================================}
{== BACK ROW ================================================================}
{=============================================================================}

  if FMazeTown.CurrentView[Ord(ptBackExtLeft)].Value = 1 then begin
    R := GetBackPos(ExtLeft);
    FDrawTools.BltIntoBackSurface(0, 174, FDDSBackExtLeft, R);
  end;

  if FMazeTown.CurrentView[Ord(ptBackLeft)].Value = 1 then begin
    R := GetBackPos(Left);
    FDrawTools.BltIntoBackSurface(121, 174, FDDSBackLeft, R);
  end;
```

```
if FMazeTown.CurrentView[Ord(ptBackExtRight)].Value = 1 then begin
  R := GetBackPos(ExtRight);
  FDrawTools.BltIntoBackSurface(465, 174, FDDSBackExtRight, R);
end;

if FMazeTown.CurrentView[Ord(ptBackRight)].Value = 1 then begin
  R := GetBackPos(Right);
  FDrawTools.BltIntoBackSurface(368, 174, FDDSBackRight, R);
end;

if FMazeTown.CurrentView[Ord(ptBackCenter)].Value = 1 then begin
  R := GetBackPos(Center);
  FDrawTools.BltIntoBackSurface(254, 174, FDDSBackCenter, R);
end;
```

The chunk of code you are looking at draws the back row of the four rows that make up the visible portion of the maze. The code first checks to see if the value at a particular location is equal to one, that is, if it is occupied by a section of the wall. If it is, a method called GetBackPos is called to retrieve the location on the screen where that section of the wall belongs:

```
function GetBackPos(Pos: TSide): TRect;
begin
  case Pos of
    ExtLeft: Result := Rect(0, 0, 175, 132);
    Left: Result := Rect(0, 0, 151, 132);
    Center: Result := Rect(0, 0, 132, 132);
    Right: Result := Rect(0, 0, 151, 132);
    ExtRight: Result := Rect(0, 0, 175, 132);
  end;
end;
```

Calculating the correct values to return from this function was one of the more painful and laborious parts of creating this program. I used some features of Paint Shop Pro that are outside the scope of this book to ease the task. Once you know where the bitmap belongs, you can call the BltIntoBackSurface method to blit it to the BackSurface:

```
FDrawTools.BltIntoBackSurface(254, 174, FDDSBackCenter, R);
```

Needless to say, once all the wall segments have been blitted to the BackSurface, the BackSurface is blitted into the PrimarySurface, and the user can finally see what lies before them in the maze.

In this discussion of the game engine, I have left out a number of details. However, you should by now have a general sense of how the engine works. With this information, you could, if you were so inclined, go on to create a very large and very complex game which relied entirely on the graphics information provided in this chapter.

# Summary

You have just finished reading about the basics of using graphics in Kylix applications. In particular, you have learned about the TBrush, TCanvas, TPen, TBitmap, and related objects. You have also had a chance to see this graphics system in action in a simple paint program, an implementation of the Mandelbrot set, and a simple game engine. I'm afraid I could go on for several hundred more pages showing you other game engines, and even a few fully implemented games that I have put together at one time or another. However, space does not permit me to follow that course, so I will have to save that information for another time.

There are, however, some other games and tools by friends and fellow Kylix engineers that are included only on the CD for this book. If you are interested in this subject, you can load them up into Kylix and begin to play with them.

This is the last chapter in the book that I am going to write. From here on out I will turn you over to the sure hands of John Kaster, Bob Swart, and Erik Bock.

# Linux Systems Programming

## IN THIS PART

# Console Applications, Memory Management, and File I/O in Kylix

*By Paul Freitas*

## IN THIS CHAPTER

Kylix is a wonderful tool for developing GUI applications. Well, it isn't all dropping components onto forms, unfortunately. Sometimes you still have to write code to perform common operations like memory management and file input/output.

To underscore that point, we'll start by going back to basics. You'll examine how you can use Kylix to write console applications. More importantly, you'll see that there are good reasons why you might want to write console applications once in a while, and when they might be appropriate for your projects.

You'll also take a look at memory management in Kylix. You're fortunate that Kylix uses Object Pascal, which makes memory management simple in many cases. Still, there are times when you need to use pointer-based memory management. You'll take a look at how to do that in Kylix programs.

Finally, you'll take a look at file input/output operations in great detail. You'll learn how to write text, typed, and untyped files using traditional Pascal operations. Also, you'll learn how to use a streaming object, TFileStream, to do these things in a simpler more object-oriented way. You'll take a closer look at Linux files, and see that some of their properties, like access permissions, require special handling in Kylix.

## Console Applications

Kylix is a powerful tool for building applications with graphical user interfaces. It can enormously simplify and accelerate the process of developing a GUI for your project. That's probably the main reason you are learning to use Kylix; so you can rapidly develop applications that are user-friendly and easy to use. One of the main weaknesses of Linux is that it lacks these kinds of tools. Kylix was meant to help developers bridge the gap.

If you develop applications with a GUI long enough, it's easy to forget that there is another way. Kylix also lets you build console applications, which launch from a command line. Standard output is to a terminal or, more commonly in the age of windowing environments, a terminal window in a window manager. Console applications can use files for input and output as well, although they are still quite limited in their appeal. They seem so primitive that you might be asking yourself why, with good GUI development tools like Kylix available, you would want to develop one?

In spite of their limitations, console applications can still be quite useful. For example, they tend to be leaner and faster than GUI applications. In a GUI application, it isn't unusual for most of the source code to consist of GUI-related routines, which results in larger, less efficient executables. Console applications lack that overhead, so they tend to be faster. For high-performance scientific computing, most work is still done using console applications.

Console apps have other uses as well. There are times when window managers aren't available; You can still run a console application when your X server has crashed, or when you're logging into your Linux system using a slow Internet connection. Console applications are easy to use in scripts. Last but not least, console applications let you focus on your project instead of your interface. Even with a rapid application development tool like Kylix, there's still nothing faster to develop than a console application.

Fortunately, Kylix lets you make console applications in addition to the usual CLX-based applications. To develop a new console application, follow these steps:

1. Launch Kylix.
2. Select File, New to display the New Items dialog box.
3. Select Console Application.

An editor appears, similar to the one shown in Figure 12.1. Note that the project is much simpler than a Kylix CLX project.

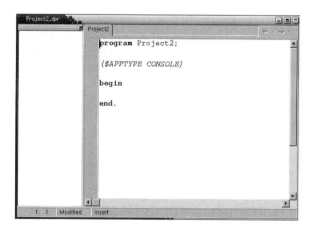

**FIGURE 12.1**
*The editor for a console application.*

## Console Development

Console application development is often standard Pascal programming, like you might have learned in an introductory programming class. Write your code directly in your project's .dpr file. For the most part, your code should be procedural instead of object-oriented. You can use simple objects, such as TStringList, which do not require access to the event stream or to any CLX-derived components.

The developers of Kylix have assumed that your console applications will be simple, procedural Pascal code, so they disabled the Use Unit command on the Kylix File menu. You can still use other units in your code, however. To do so, add a uses statement to your program before the var statement in your application source code. List all the units you use separated by commas. SysUtils, Classes, and Libc are some units that you may find useful, even without access to the event stream. See Listings 12.1 and 12.2 in the "File I/O in Kylix" section of this chapter for examples.

## Running the Console Application

To run your console application, you have several choices. You will eventually want to run your application from a command line, of course. To do so, compile your application from the Project menu. Now you can start your console application from any command line. Note that you won't have debugging tools available if you don't launch your application from within Kylix.

You can also simply select Run, Run from Kylix's menus, as you would for any other Kylix application. You will then have access to all of Kylix's debugging tools. The problem with this method is that you won't see any screen output if you started Kylix from a menu. To avoid this problem, start Kylix from a command line in a terminal window using the command startkylix. All screen output from your program will appear in the terminal window you used to run Kylix.

## Memory Management

If you are an experienced C or C++ programmer, you know exactly how difficult memory management can be. Improper memory management can cause memory leaks, loss of data or application crashes. The Object Pascal used in Kylix is certainly no different. In this section, you review the basics of memory management in Kylix programs.

Your Kylix applications will, of course, be Linux programs. All memory management tasks will be handled ultimately by routines in the glibc libraries, which you may not want to use directly. The glibc routines tend to be very low-level. Also, if you ever want to port your Kylix application to Windows through Delphi, you cannot use the glibc routines because they are unavailable in Windows. That is why Kylix has encapsulated the glibc routines in its own Object Pascal routines, which are more simple and portable.

# Variables and Data Structures

In this discussion of Kylix memory management, let's start with the basics: variables. Local variables are allocated on the application stack, so memory management will be handled automatically. Arrays, strings, and records all fall into this category, so you don't have to worry about explicitly allocating and deallocating memory for them. Global variables behave the same way.

Oftentimes you will want to use a data structure in multiple parts of an application. In these situations, it is generally more useful to create the structure in the program heap. Heap memory is managed differently than stack memory. Structures in the heap must be explicitly allocated and deallocated. They are referenced in the application by pointers, which indicate where to find the structure itself in memory.

To create a dynamic variable, which is a variable in the heap, use the New command, which has the following syntax:

```
procedure New(var P: Pointer);
```

Let's take a look at an example. Suppose you have defined the following structures:

```
type
  TName = record
    First: String[32];
    Last: String{32};
    Middle: String[32];
  end;
  PName = ^TName;
```

The type TName is a data type that you can use to store a person's name. The PName type is a pointer to a TName structure. In the following code, a TName is allocated on the heap, and a pointer is assigned to the PName variable P:

```
var P: PName;
begin
  ...
  New(P);
  ...
end;
```

To access the information in the structure referenced by the pointer, you can dereference it using the caret (^) operator after the pointer. For example, P^.First can be used to access the First field of the TName structure.

Memory structures in the heap will persist until they are explicitly deallocated or the application itself terminates. To deallocate a heap structure, you can use the `Dispose` command. `Dispose(P)` would deallocate the memory assigned to the `TName` structure defined previously.

# Objects

Objects in Kylix programs are generally created on the heap, but in a different manner than dynamic variables and data structures. First, let's take a look at a typical object declaration in a var statement:

```
anObject: TObject;
```

If you are a C or C++ programmer, you might think that `anObject` is an object in the stack, and that the declaration also allocates memory for the object. In some other object-oriented Pascal implementations, that would be true as well. In Kylix, however, `anObject` is really a pointer to an as-yet-undefined object in the heap. Calling a constructor method for the object type allocates the memory.

The constructor method for most objects is called `Create`. There can be multiple constructors for an object, which may or may not have the same name. The names for different constructors will generally start with the word `Create`. To define an object the correct way, you can use the following call:

```
anObject := TObject.Create;
```

Constructors often have parameters, and there may be multiple constructors for an object with different names and parameter lists. Be sure to check the syntax for the specific objects you are using.

By making pointers the default reference type for objects, Borland's Object Pascal makes pointer use almost completely transparent. Most programmers use pointers for objects anyway, so why should your code be cluttered by needless dereference operators? Another nice feature is that you won't have to puzzle over the correct reference syntax for properties and methods. There is one small price you'll have to pay, however. Because Kylix doesn't have a garbage-collection mechanism built in, you will have to deallocate memory yourself.

Memory deallocation is handled by an object's destructor method, which is usually called `Destroy`. Although that's where most of the work is actually done, it is important to note that *you should never call `Destroy` directly!* `Destroy` always tries do deallocate object memory, even if the memory has already been deallocated or was never allocated to begin with. Calling an object's `Destroy` method could cause a program error, and possibly even crash the application.

To remove an object from the heap, call the object's Free method. Free calls Destroy, but only after it checks to see that the object does in fact exist in the heap. For a properly designed and debugged object, it is always safe to call the Free method.

For most Kylix users, that's all you need to know about memory management. There are other routines for memory management (including direct calls to glibc memory management routines) which a few programmers may find useful under obscure circumstances. To learn more about other Object Pascal techniques, please refer to Borland's *Object Pascal Language Reference* and their Kylix *Developer's Guide*. For information on Linux memory management, you can start by reading the Linux online documentation for malloc, the Linux memory allocation function.

# File I/O in Kylix

Whatever kind of application you develop, chances are very good that it will use some kind of file for input, output, or both. In this section, you will learn how to use Kylix for file input/output (I/O) operations.

Pascal programs can use three basic kinds of files. *Text files* are files that contain data in a text format. Their filenames often end with .txt, but not always. Script files, HTML files, and Pascal source code are other examples of text files. The contents of a text file can be read by a human being using Linux utility programs like cat and emacs. *Untyped files*, or binary files, use special file formats, and are generally only intelligible to programs that are designed to understand them. Untyped files can be more compact than text files. An MP3 audio recording and a JPEG image, if written by a Pascal program, are examples of untyped files.

The text and binary (untyped) file concepts are common to most programming languages and operating systems. The third file type that may be found in Pascal programs is called a *typed file*, or *file of record*. Typed files are generated from Pascal record structures containing simple data types such as fixed-length strings and integers. More complicated data types with variable lengths, such as variants, objects, or even long (ANSI) strings, cannot be output to a typed file; an untyped file must be used instead.

Text, typed, and untyped files are not different to the Linux operating system. There are no special filename extensions that denote each kind of file. Instead, these files differ in how the information they contain was written by a Pascal program. Text files contain output formatted so that it can be edited using any text editor. Typed and untyped files lack that kind of formatting; they are instead a more direct copy of what is stored in a computer's memory. A floating point number written to a text file could be read easily by a human, but the same number written to a typed or untyped file would appear as a short, nonsensical set of characters (if it could be read at all).

# Traditional Pascal File Operations

To learn more about file I/O operations using traditional Pascal methods, let's start with the workhorse of Linux file types: the text file. The first step in any file operation is opening the file. Your program will need an internal reference to the text file it uses. That reference is a variable of type TextFile or Text. (For simplicity, we'll use the TextFile type exclusively.) You can associate your file variable with a real file by using the AssignFile procedure. Here's an example:

```
var aTextFile: TextFile;
...
AssignFile(aTextFile, 'readme.txt');
```

Here AssignFile associates aTextFile with the file readme.txt.

Note that AssignFile does not actually open the file; it just creates an internal name for it. There are three ways to open a text file using standard Pascal operations. To open a file for writing, use the Rewrite procedure. Rewrite will create a new text file if one with the given name does not exist; if a file does exist, Rewrite will replace it with a new, empty file. Using the previous example, Rewrite(aTextFile) would open the file readme.txt. For read-only access to a text file, use the procedure Reset. Use Append to add text to the end of an existing file.

## Writing to Text Files

To write to a text file, people generally use the standard Pascal functions Writeln and Write. Writeln writes a single line of text, complete with a line feed. Text written subsequently will appear on a different line. Write performs the same action, but without a line feed. Both procedures have the same syntax. The first argument is a reference to your opened text file. Subsequent arguments (separated by commas) define the text to be written. For example, Writeln(aTextFile, 'Hello!') writes the text "Hello!" to the text file defined by aTextFile. Reading is accomplished using the Readln and Read procedures, also standard Pascal functions. Their syntax is exactly the same as Writeln and Write.

In short, once you have defined your text file using AssignFile, all text file operations follow the procedures defined in any standard Pascal textbook. Once you are finished with your text file, you can use the CloseFile routine to close the file. So, to close aTextFile, you would call CloseFile(aTextFile).

## Writing to Typed or Untyped Files

For typed or untyped files, you can open a file using AssignFile and Rewrite or Reset. You can call these functions the same way you would call them for a text file. Reset works a bit differently than it does for text files; it opens typed and untyped files with read-write access instead of read-only access. Also, again like text files, you close typed and untyped files using `CloseFile`.

As you saw earlier, typed files are associated with Pascal data structures or records. Here is an example of a record that you could use to store data in a company phone directory:

```
TEmployee = record
  FirstName: string[32];
  LastName: string[32];
  Extension: Integer;
end;
```

To define a file variable for a typed file, you define it as a file of a particular record type. You could define a file variable for a company phone directory as:

```
aPhoneDirectory: File of TEmployee;
```

So, using the information we just defined, here's an example of how you could read an employee entry from a directory file named `directory.txt`:

```
var
  EmployeeInfo: TEmployee;
  Directory: File of TEmployee;
begin
  AssignFile(Directory, 'directory.txt');
  Reset(Directory);
  Read(Directory, EmployeeInfo);
  CloseFile(Directory);
end;
```

Notice how simple it is to read an entire employee record. Even though there are many fields in the record, the whole structure can be read with one `Read` statement. Likewise, it can be written with a single `Write` statement. In other file types, you would need to define a procedure for reading and writing the data in the record. With a typed file, you don't need to worry about those details.

Now let's look at untyped files. When you declare your file variable, you declare it as type `File`. Here's an example:

```
var anUntypedFile: File;
```

As you saw earlier, you can open an untyped file with `Reset` or `Rewrite`, exactly as you would for any other file type. For untyped files, there is an extra, optional parameter in the parameter list for these functions that controls the record size. For example, `Reset(anUntypedFile,1)` uses a record size of one byte, and is useful for obtaining information from a file one byte at a time. If you omit the final parameter, `Reset` or `Rewrite` will use a default record size of 128. (We'll get back to the topic of record sizes shortly.)

**12**

Instead of `Read` and `Write`, untyped files use `BlockRead` and `BlockWrite` for data transfers. They have the following syntax:

```
procedure BlockRead(var F: File; var Buf; Count: Integer[; var AmtTransferred:
    Integer]);
procedure BlockWrite(var F: File; var Buf; Count: Integer[; var AmtTransferred:
    Integer]);
```

(The square brackets around the last parameter indicate that it is optional.) F is the file variable, and `Buf` is a buffer where the transferred data is stored. `AmtTransferred` is an indicator of how much data is transferred. If `AmtTransferred` is equal to `Count`, the transfer was successful. If it is less than `Count`, an amount of data less than an entire record size was transferred.

`Count` indicates how much data is to be transferred. The unit of count is the record size used in the `Reset` or `Rewrite` call. Let's take a look at an example:

```
var
   anUntypedFile: File;
   aBuffer: array[1..23] of byte;
   recordsRead: Integer;
...
begin
   ...
   Reset(anUntypedFile,23);
   BlockRead(anUntypedFile,aBuffer,1,recordsRead);
   ...
end;
```

Here, of `Read` and `Write`, untyped files the `BlockRead` procedure attempts to read one record size (which is 23 bytes of data) from the file into `aBuffer`. If it is successful (for example, it reads all 23 bytes without reaching the end of the file first) `recordsRead` will be equal to 1. If not, it will be 0.

You could have chosen the record size differently to achieve the same result. Oftentimes it makes more sense to use a record size of 1 than any other number. It's not unusual to write multiple types of records to the same file; they probably won't all be the same size. Here's how you could have read the same information using a record size of one byte:

```
   Reset(anUntypedFile,1);
   BlockRead(anUntypedFile,aBuffer,23,recordsRead);
```

Sometimes you will want to read or write information from a specific location in a typed or untyped file. For example, you may want to read the third record in the file. To perform operations like these, you need to be able to reset the file pointer to the right location. You can do that by using the `Seek` command. For example, `Seek(anUntypedFile,2)` sets the file pointer to the third record in the file. (The first record's position is 0.)

If you want to of Read and Write, untyped files know the number of records in a typed or untyped file, use the FileSize command on the file variable. Because Append is only available for text files, a common use for the FileSize command is to use it within Seek to reposition the file pointer to the end of the file. In the earlier sample code, Seek(anUntypedFile,FileSize(anUntypedFile)) would set the file pointer to the end of the file, allowing you to append information to the file.

## File I/O Using TFileStream

TFileStream is a class designed to simplify file input/output operations. It lets you handle file operations on a much higher level. Instead of performing I/O operations yourself using the low-level commands described previously, you simply send your information to the TFileStream object and let it handle the details for you. TFileStream lets you make short work of file I/O.

Earlier you learned the three Pascal file types: text, typed, and untyped. To many programmers, especially those who have used languages other than Pascal, those distinctions may seem artificial. If so, TFileStream may be better adapted to your way of thinking. TFileStream has no mechanism for specifying a file type; basically, all files are treated as untyped files. This has consequences for text files, as we'll discuss later.

To open a file and make it ready for input or output, all you have to do is create an instance of a TFileStream object. The parameters you provide when you create the object define how the file should be opened. Let's take a look at the constructor for TFileStream:

```
constructor Create(const filename: string; Mode: Word);
```

The first parameter is the filename of the file you want to use. The second parameter contains an open mode and a share mode connected together by a logical or operation. The resulting Word dictates how the file can be used by your application and by other applications. The open modes and share modes are shown in Tables 12.1 and 12.2.

**TABLE 12.1** TFileStream Open Modes

| Value | Meaning |
| --- | --- |
| fmCreate | Creates a new file with the given name if none exists. If the file does exist, the file will open in write mode. |
| fmOpenRead | Opens the file in read-only mode. |
| fmOpenWrite | Opens the file in write-only mode. Existing contents will be replaced. |
| fmOpenReadWrite | Opens the file in read-write mode; contents will be modified rather than replaced. |

**TABLE 12.2**  `TFileStream` Share Modes

| Value | Meaning |
|---|---|
| `fmShareCompat`, `fmShareExclusive` | No other application can open the file. |
| `fmShareDenyWrite` | Other applications can read the file, but they cannot write to it. |
| `fmShareDenyRead` | Other applications can write to the file, but they cannot read from it. |
| `fmShareDenyNone` | Other applications can have unrestricted access to the file. |

The following sample code opens a file called `afile`. The opening application has write access; all other programs are forbidden from accessing the file until the file is closed:

```
var aFileStream: TFileStream;
...
aFileStream := TFileStream.Create('afile', fmWrite or fmShareExclusive);
```

To read and write to a `TFileStream` object, use the `TFileStream` object's `Read` and `Write` methods. They have the following syntax:

```
function Read(var Buffer; Count: Longint): Longint;
function Write(const Buffer; Count: Longint): Longint;
```

`Buffer` is a pointer to the memory location that is the source or destination of the read or write operation. `Count` indicates how many bytes should be read or written. The `Read` and `Write` functions return an integer that indicates how many bytes were actually transferred in the operation. If the value returned is less than `Count` in a read operation, that indicates that the end of the file was reached before all the requested data was read. In a write operation, a smaller returned value can indicate that the volume has no more space available.

To set the value of `Count` properly, you can determine the size of any variable, data structure, or object type using the `SizeOf` function. For example, `SizeOf(Double)` returns the value 8; `Double` is an eight-byte floating point number type.

`Read` and `Write` return a count of how many bytes were actually read or written. You may not need this information. If so, you can call the `ReadBuffer` and `WriteBuffer` procedures instead, which have the same parameters but don't return a value.

### `TFileStream` Properties and Method

There are several properties of `TFileStream` that contain useful information. Reading and writing in a file usually happens at a location indicated by a pointer called the file pointer. As bytes are read from or written to the file, the file pointer is incremented. The value of the file pointer is stored in the `TFileStream`'s `Position` property. The size of the stream, which is also the length of the file referenced by the `TFileStream` object, is stored in the `TFileStream`'s `Size` property.

`TFileStream` provides a method, `Seek`, which allows you to set the file pointer anywhere in the file you like. Here's the syntax for `Seek`:

```
function Seek(Offset: Longint; Origin: Word): Longint;
```

`Offset` is a number of bytes to move the pointer from the file pointer position indicated by the `Origin` parameter. The possible values of `Origin` are shown in Table 12.3.

**TABLE 12.3** Possible Values of the `Origin` Parameter of the `TFileStream.Seek` Method

| Value | Meaning |
|---|---|
| soFromBeginning | Offset is measured from the beginning of the file. |
| soFromCurrent | Offset is measured from the current file pointer position. |
| soFromEnd | Offset is measured from the end of the file |

Note that `Offset` is of type `Longint`; it can have positive or negative values. This allows you to move the file pointer forwards or backwards from the location specified by `Origin`. Of course, not all values are allowable in all circumstances. The allowable values are determined by the value of `Origin`. If `Origin` is `soFromBeginning`, `Offset` can only be 0 or positive. If `Origin` is `soFromEnd`, `Offset` must be 0 or negative.

It is often a good idea to set the file pointer explicitly using `Seek` before an operation. Multiple objects may use the same `TFileStream` object; it may not be safe to make any assumptions about the value of the file pointer.

## Writing to Text Files

Because `TFileStream` doesn't care what Pascal file type you are using, you can use it to write to ordinary text files. A good way to do this is to assemble each line of the file into a string variable, and then use `Write` or `WriteBuffer` to write the string to the file. The only catch is that you must be careful to use Pascal strings appropriately in the write operation.

Pascal `string` types are not merely null-terminated character strings, the way they are in languages like C. Instead, a Pascal `string` is a data structure consisting of three things: a size, a reference count, and a pointer to the actual string of characters. Let's say your string is called `aString`. You can obtain the length of `aString` by calling `Length(aString)`. To obtain a pointer to the characters in the string, you can call `PChar(aString)^`. Note the dereference operator at the end of the call.

If you're used to null-terminated strings, you might naively think to write a string to a file this way:

```
aFileStream.WriteBuffer(aString,Length(aString)); // DON'T DO THIS!
```

This is incorrect because aString is not merely a pointer, the way it is for other string types. Instead, the WriteBuffer command should be done this way:

```
aFileStream.WriteBuffer(PChar(aString)^,Length(aString));
```

## Line Feeds

There is one more matter you will need to consider: line feeds. Pascal strings don't include the necessary line breaks by default. You can append a Linux line feed character to the end of a string by adding a #10, like this:

```
aString := 'Hello, world!'+#10;
```

Listing 12.1 contains a simple console application that writes two lines of text to a file called theFile.txt. The program is a good summary for many of the concepts we've covered in this chapter so far.

**LISTING 12.1**    Writing a Simple Text File with TFileStream

```
program Project1;

{$APPTYPE CONSOLE}
uses
        Classes,SysUtils;
var
        aString: string;
        aFileStream: TFileStream;
begin
        aFileStream := TFileStream.Create('theFile.txt',fmCreate or
        ⮡fmShareExclusive);
        // Assemble a string, complete with a line feed.
        aString := 'Hello, world!'+#10;
        // Write the string.
        aFileStream.WriteBuffer(PChar(aString)^,Length(aString));
        // Write it again, just to see the line terminations.
        aFileStream.WriteBuffer(PChar(aString)^,Length(aString));
        // Done! Close the file.
        aFileStream.Free;
end.
```

# Specifics of Linux Files

Many Kylix users are experienced Windows developers. There are many differences between files in Linux and Windows file systems, some of which may be important in your application. In this section you will review some basic characteristics of files in Linux file systems.

## Users and Groups

Linux, like its ancestor Unix, is a true multi-user operating system. All files are marked as owned by a user and a group on their system. *User* generally refers to a human being who can log in to the system. A *group* is a collection of users and/or other groups. Groups can be created by the system administrator or any other user who has superuser access to the system. In addition to user and group, Linux files also have a third ownership category called *other*, which simply refers to any user or group not contained in the user or group ownerships.

Linux files also have a set of *access permission types* for each of the three ownership categories, which are *read*, *write*, and *execute*. If a group has read access permission, for example, then any user in that group has permission to read the file. All the access permissions for all the owner categories are independent, and can be set separately.

You can see the specific user and group owners of a file, as well as the access permissions, in a terminal window using the `ls -l` command. Here's what `ls -l` returned for the file `theFile.txt`, which was created using the console application presented at the end of the last section:

```
-rw-r--r--   1 pfreitas users        28 Aug 18 16:45 theFile.txt
```

The first character in the listing would be d if the item was a directory; it isn't, so a hyphen (-) appears instead. The next nine characters denote access permissions. The first three flags are user permissions, the next three are group permissions, and the last three are other permissions. An r indicates read permission, w indicates write permission, and x indicates execute permission. In this particular case, all users have read access to `theFile.txt`. Only the owner has write permission, and no user has execute permission. Later in the output of `ls -l` you see two names, `pfreitas` and `users`. These are the names of the user and group (respectively) that own the file.

When a Kylix application creates a file, it will use a set of default permissions contained in the global variable `FileAccessRights`. In Kylix, file permissions are stored in a variable of integer type. These integers can be constructed using the constants defined in the `Libc` unit and shown in Table 12.4.

**12**

CONSOLE
APPLICATIONS

**TABLE 12.4**  Kylix Constants (Defined in the Libc Unit) that Can Be Used to Set File Permissions

| Constant | Meaning |
|----------|---------|
| S_IRUSR | Owning user has read access. |
| S_IWUSR | Owning user has write access. |
| S_IXUSR | Owning user has execute access. |
| S_IWGRP | Group owner has write access. |
| S_IXGRP | Group owner has execute access. |
| S_IROTH | Others have read access. |
| S_IWOTH | Others have write access. |
| S_IXOTH | Others have execute access. |
| S_IRWXU | Owning user has all accesses. |
| S_IRWXG | Group owner has all accesses. |
| S_IRWXO | Others have all accesses. |

To create an integer for a set of permissions, simply or the appropriate constants together. Let's say you want to create a file that gives the owning user and group read and execute access, but no access to others. Here's how you could construct an appropriate permission integer:

```
var permissions: Integer;
...
begin
  ...
  permissions := S_IRUSR or S_IXUSR or S_IRGRP or S_IXGRP;
  ...
end;
```

Note that the last three constants in the table are constructed from the other constants. They are not strictly necessary, but they are sometimes convenient. For example, if you wanted to give the owner of a file all permissions, you could do it like this:

```
  permissions := S_IRUSR or S_IWUSR or S_IXUSR;
```

It's a lot simpler to use S_IRWXU instead:

```
  permissions := S_IRWXU;
```

## I/O Calls

Kylix was developed to be compatible with Delphi, a Windows application development tool. To ensure cross-platform compatibility, Kylix file I/O calls were made to match the Delphi calls. The developers of Kylix aren't dummies, of course; they knew about the Linux file ownerships and permissions I outlined above. In many cases they overloaded, or created multiple versions of, the file I/O methods to incorporate Linux-specific features.

For example, the definition of the `Create` method for `TFileStream` is overloaded. You already looked at one version. The other one has an extra parameter that lets you set the rights for newly created files. The second definition of the constructor has the following syntax:

```
constructor Create(const filename: string; Mode: Word; Rights: Cardinal);
```

To set the `Rights` parameter, you can use the technique outlined earlier. (`Cardinal` is an integer type.)

Let's take a look at how this capability can be used. Listing 12.2 shows a console application that creates a BASH script file called `listall`. The script file is created with read and execute permission for all users, plus write permission for the owner. You can execute the script file from a terminal window to return the result of an `ls -la` command. It lists all files in the current directory, including hidden files (ones whose filenames start with a period). It also displays all owners and permissions.

**LISTING 12.2**  Writing a Simple BASH Shell Script File with `TFileStream`

```
program MakeScript;

{$APPTYPE CONSOLE}
uses
  SysUtils,Classes,Libc;

var
        aString: string;
        aFileStream: TFileStream;
        Rights: Cardinal;
begin
        // First, let's set the rights. User gets all rights,
        // everyone else gets read and execute access.
        Rights := S_IRWXU or S_IRGRP or S_IXGRP or S_IROTH or S_IXOTH;
        // Create the script file with the rights we just defined.
        aFileStream := TFileStream.Create('listall',fmCreate or
                fmShareExclusive,Rights);
        // Assemble the first line of the file, which specifies the shell type.
        aString := '#!/bin/bash'+#10;
        // Write the first line of the script file.
        aFileStream.WriteBuffer(PChar(aString)^,Length(aString));
        // Now set up the line that does the work.
        aString := 'ls -la'+#10;
```

**LISTING 12.2**  Continued

```
      // Write the second line of the script file.
      aFileStream.WriteBuffer(PChar(aString)^,Length(aString));
      // Done! Close the file.
      aFileStream.Free;
end.
```

## Using `glibc` Commands

Experienced Linux programmers and C programmers may feel somewhat unhappy at this point. In this chapter, you've learned the basics of Kylix file I/O, but all the methods you've learned have been specific to either Kylix or Object Pascal. Linux's glibc (also known as libc) libraries have many file-related commands with which you may already be comfortable. The commands can also be very powerful, allowing you a greater degree of control than you can get with the techniques covered in this chapter.

Obviously, we haven't covered everything there is to know about Kylix file I/O. Many topics are simply beyond the scope of this book. Still, there is one last bit of information we'd like you to have. You can use many of the `glibc` commands directly in your Kylix programs.

Take a look at the `Libc.pas` file in the Kylix source code. (It's in the `source/rtl/linux` directory of your Kylix directory.) Open the file in Kylix and expand the Procedures item in the explorer. If you're an experienced Linux developer, you'll see many of the glibc methods you've come to know and love. If you're new to Linux, many of these methods may seem unfamiliar. To learn more about them, take a look at their man pages. Also, there are many books available that cover general Linux programming in greater detail than we do here.

Kylix is not just a tool for porting Delphi applications to Linux. It is a true Linux development tool that lets you access all the powerful features of the Linux operating system. Be sure to take advantage of that capability when you need it.

## Summary

In this chapter, you've learned how to use Kylix to write console applications and how to do file I/O operations using traditional Pascal operations and the `TFileStream` object. You've also learned how Kylix can manipulate some special features of Linux filesystems, such as access permissions. Lastly, you saw that you can use Kylix to directly access functions in the glibc libraries.

# Processes and Threads

*By Paul Freitas*

## IN THIS CHAPTER

Sometimes we all wish we could do two things at once. It's impossible for us to write code for an upcoming project deadline and drive the kids to soccer practice at the same time. (Hopefully you've never even tried!) We do our best to multitask, but in reality we can only do one thing at a time. That's life.

Of course, computers aren't alive, are they? Unlike humans, they're pretty good at multitasking. Computers running Kylix applications can be exceptionally good. Kylix applications have all the advantages of Linux, a true multitasking operating system, coupled with specially designed BaseCLX classes to handle multithreaded applications. If you run a Kylix application on a machine with multiple processors, it literally can do two things at once. Or more.

In this chapter, you're going to examine the two basic methods of multitasking: processes and threads. You'll start with a basic description of how Linux handles processes, threads and scheduling. Next, you'll examine how you can use special thread classes in your Kylix applications to increase your application's efficiency. Lastly, you'll take a look at how you can use traditional Linux multiprocessing instead of multithreading, and learn a little about how processes can communicate with one another.

# Methods of Application Execution in Linux

Let's start with some elementary definitions. Computers are used for a wide range of purposes, such as retrieving e-mail, serving Web pages, and performing elaborate scientific calculations. You can break down these larger applications into smaller operations, such as writing to disk, reading information from memory, and so on. You can describe these simpler operations as *tasks*. Basically, people write programs to perform tasks.

On a Linux system, a program occupies a place in the operating system referred to as a *process*. You can think of a process as being an encapsulation of a piece of program code, plus the memory needed for the program to work. A program stored in the filesystem is like a blueprint for a house; the process is like a house built from that blueprint. Linux is a true multitasking operating system, so there are multiple processes in the operating system at any given time.

You can get a list of all the running processes on a Linux system by executing the command ps ux from a command line. Try it on a seemingly idle machine, and you may see hundreds of processes. To see how process priorities evolve in time, try running the top program in a terminal window. Leave it running, and watch what happens as you do other things, like check your e-mail or compile code. You'll see how busy the task scheduler can be. Fortunately, the scheduler is a well-established piece of software that won't require your attention.

Each process has its own set of characteristics, such as

- A state of execution, which is often called the *context* of the process. A process can be running, waiting, or stopped, for example.

- A working directory.

- A set of access rights, or *credentials*, that help determine which files and directories the process can access.

- An allocation of memory and other system resources.

The most important process is called the *kernel*. One of its many duties is *scheduling*: deciding which of the existing processes gets to use actual processor time next, and how long it gets to run before it must stop and let the next process run. These quantities of CPU time are referred to as *time slices*. Generally speaking, time slices are so small that the computer is effectively doing multiple things at once, even if it has only one processor, because it is constantly switching tasks. (Of course, many systems have multiple CPUs, so they literally can do multiple things at once.)

Most processes have their own memory allocations, which are not directly accessible by other processes. To share information, independent processes must write files to the filesystem. Processes can *signal* each other by sending a very short message. The process receiving the signal is responsible for knowing how to respond to the signal. When multiple independent processes are used to perform parts of a common task, we call that *multiprocessing*.

Multiprocessing is not the only way to perform multitasking, nor is it necessarily the best way. Because processes all have separate memory allocations, which we'll refer to here as *memory spaces*, passing information between processes can be quite complicated. To use multiprocessing for a given task, you might need to write a lot of code for interprocess communication, which can be cumbersome and unnecessary. Still, multiprocessing can be a good way to make independently written programs work together with a minimum of effort.

Sometimes it's better for tasks to share the same memory space. Writing code becomes much simpler because both tasks can refer to the same variables and objects. This second method of multitasking is known as *multithreading*. The tasks in a multithreaded application are known as *threads*. Each thread of an application is treated as a separate process by the kernel, so threads have many of the same advantages as processes.

Kylix gives you access to all of the Linux system calls that govern process management and interprocess communication. If you want a multiprocessing application, Kylix will certainly let you build one. At the end of this chapter you will learn the basics of multiprocessing. It can be more difficult to learn and more cumbersome to implement in Kylix than multithreading, however.

Before we discuss multiprocessing, you will learn multithreading. Kylix has components that make writing multithreaded applications easy. Most developers will find multithreading just as helpful as multiprocessing, and much easier to work with besides. If multithreading doesn't suit your needs, you still have the option to multiprocess.

13

PROCESSES AND
THREADS

# Kylix Threads

Every Kylix application has at least one thread, the *main CLX thread*, which handles all of the basic application functions. For example, the main CLX thread is responsible for drawing all of the windows in your application. To add extra threads, Kylix uses *thread objects*, which are descendants of the TThread object.

The basic method for making a multithreaded application involves first identifying the different tasks an application needs to perform. These tasks are each encapsulated in a subclass of TThread, one for every type of task that will be performed. To launch a new thread, simply define a thread object of the appropriate type somewhere in your application and call its constuctor.

Let's examine an example of multithreaded development in greater detail. The first step in the process is to create a new thread class. Fortunately, Kylix makes it simple: select New, Thread Object from the File menu. Enter a name for your thread in the New Thread Object dialog box. For example, if you want your thread to be called TSortingThread, enter that name in the dialog box and click OK. (Note that Kylix won't automatically prefix the object name with a capital T. It's still a good idea to use one anyway.)

Kylix will automatically generate some simple source code for your thread class. Here is an example:

```
unit Unit2;

interface

uses
  Classes;

type
  TSortingThread = class(TThread)
  private
    { Private declarations }
  protected
    procedure Execute; override;
  end;

implementation

{ TSortingThread }

procedure TSortingThread.Execute;
```

```
begin
  { Place thread code here }
end;

end.
```

Of course, this isn't a very useful thread in its current form. Its `Execute` method contains only comments, so it does nothing. To make this class useful, you need to enter some instructions in the `Execute` procedure to perform the actual task.

You can enter any kind of code you want in the `Execute` procedure, as if it's a program by itself. For example, let's say you have encapsulated some data in a global object called `MyData`. Let's also assume that the object has its own sorting method called `Sort`. To call the sorting method in your thread, you could write `Execute` to look like this:

```
procedure TSortingThread.Execute;
begin
  MyData.Sort;
end;
```

Sorting will take place in your `TSortingThread` thread instead of the main CLX thread.

To start your thread of execution, all you need to do is create it by calling its constructor, `Create`, with `False` as its only argument. For example, you might have the following code appear in your application:

```
var aSortedThread: TSortedThread;
...
aSortedThread := TSortedThread.Create(False);
```

When the constructor method is reached, the new execution thread starts, which is called a *child thread*. Program execution also continues in the thread that created the child thread (called the *parent thread*). Both threads will execute independently now.

You can temporarily stop thread execution at any time. Call the child thread's `Suspend` procedure to pause its execution. You can resume execution later with the `Resume` method.

Sometimes you will want to create an execution thread, but not have it actually do anything right away. Perhaps your thread object is created in another object's `Create` method, but it doesn't have the data it needs to perform any actions right away. In that case, you will want to create the thread but hold off on execution until the data is available. To do so, create the thread in a suspended state like this:

```
aSortedThread := TSortedThread.Create(True);
```

When you are ready to start thread execution, call the thread object's `Resume` method.

If your thread requires special initialization, override the Create method to include it. For instance, threads can be programmed to free themselves automatically after their Execute method terminates. You can control this behavior through the object's FreeOnTerminate property. One way you can set FreeOnTerminate is by overriding the constructor like this:

```
constructor TSortedThread.Create(CreateSuspended: Boolean);
begin
  inherited Create(CreateSuspended);
  FreeOnCreate := True;
end;
```

## Memory Access by Threads

The main advantage of multithreading over multiprocessing is that all the threads of an application share one global memory space. Shared data is generally stored in global variables, which can be used freely by all threads of the application. Global memory is easy for application developers to reference, without the need for the elaborate constructs that would be needed in a multiprocessing application.

A multithreaded application will have global and local variables, like any other application. Applications with threads have another option called *thread-local variables*. These variables can only be accessed within a specific thread. If you think of a thread as being an application within an application, then thread-local variables are like global variables within that application. To declare a thread-local variable, simply use the threadvar keyword (instead of the var keyword) in the unit where your thread source code resides. Accessing thread-local variables can be much slower than accessing fields of your thread object, however.

> **NOTE**
>
> If you are considering creating a thread-local variable, try adding a field to your thread object instead.

## Synchronization Errors and Thread Safety

Multithreaded applications do have some unique problems. For example, imagine that a multi-threaded application is performing calculations on a large array. What if one thread writes information to the array at the same time another thread is reading from it? It is possible that the second thread will read the array incorrectly, receiving some array values prior to the first thread's operations and some values afterwards. In multithreaded development, you must guard against these kinds of synchronization errors.

Not all data is subject to synchronization errors, however. A *thread-safe object* is one that was specifically designed to allow access by multiple threads. Many of the objects commonly used in Kylix applications are thread-safe, including the following:

- DataCLX objects
- Graphics objects such as TFont, TBitmap, and TPen, when used with the TCanvas locking mechanism described later
- dbDirect database components (provided that the vendor's client library is thread-safe)
- The TThreadList list class, which replaces the thread-unsafe TList class

Unfortunately, visual CLX objects are not thread-safe. All visual CLX objects run from the main CLX thread; all calls to these objects must come from that thread to avoid synchronization problems. This includes data-aware components, even if the data components they refer to (like database components) are thread-safe. If you work extensively with threads, there's a good chance you'll discover other objects that aren't thread-safe.

Clearly, some form of access control is needed. Kylix provides you with a number of mechanisms to prevent synchronization errors, including the following:

- The thread object's Synchronize method (to protect visual CLX objects)
- Critical section objects
- The multi-read exclusive-write synchronizer

## Using a Thread Object's Synchronize Method

To access visual CLX objects in a thread-safe manner, use the thread object's Synchronize method. The parameter of the Synchronize method is a procedure defined within your own thread object. To use Synchronize, follow these steps:

1. Identify sequences of visual CLX instructions that need to be called from the main CLX thread.
2. Encapsulate each set of instructions in a single procedure defined in your thread object. Your procedure should be exactly that; a Pascal procedure, as opposed to a function. Also, it should have no parameters.
3. Call the Synchronize method on your container procedure.

As an example, let's take a look at a function that draws a line between points A and B on a canvas contained in the paintBox object (which is a TPaintBox-type object). In a single-threaded application, you might write the routine this way:

```
// Global variables.
var
```

```
  A, B: TPoint;
  paintBox: TPaintBox;

procedure TObjectInMainCLXThread.DrawALine;
begin
  // Set A and B.
  A := Point(10,10);
  B := Point(20,10);
  // Set the pen color.
  paintBox.Canvas.Pen.Color := clBlack;
  // Draw the line.
  aPaintBox.Canvas.PolyLine([A,B]);
end;
```

Now, if you were to move this method directly into a thread object, it wouldn't be thread-safe because it makes direct calls to a visual CLX component. The calls that cause problems are those related to the aPaintBox object. Let's move them into a container procedure in your hypothetical thread object, TSortedThread:

```
procedure TSortedThread.DrawLineCalls;
begin
  // Set the pen color.
  aPaintBox.Canvas.Pen.Color := clBlack;
  // Draw the line.
  aPaintBox.Canvas.PolyLine([A,B]);
end;
```

Now, here's the DrawALine method with an appropriate call to Synchronize:

```
procedure TSortedThread.DrawALine;
begin
  // Set A and B.
  A := Point(10,10);
  B := Point(20,10);
  // Do the visual CLX calls in a Synchronized container procedure.
  Synchronize(DrawLineCalls);
end;
```

## Critical Sections

Aside from your visual CLX objects, there may be other parts of your application that require protection. It is a common practice, for example, to use global variables for storage in multithreaded applications. They can be protected through the consistent use of objects called *critical sections*.

A critical section is an object of type TCriticalSection. Critical section objects are special in that only one thread can access them at a time. They are very simple objects, but they do have several methods which can help you guard against synchronization errors. Their Acquire and Enter methods can be used to ensure that only one thread can access a protected area until the Release or Leave method is called. (Note that Acquire and Enter perform exactly the same function, as do Release and Leave. From now on, we will refer only to the Acquire and Release methods.)

Here is an example of how you can use critical sections. Let's say that you have a customer record (aCustomerRecord) of type TCustomerRecord that may be prone to synchronization problems. Here, you create a critical section at the same time the customer record is created:

```
var
  aCustomerRecord: TCustomerRecord;
  LockACustomerRecord: TCriticalSection;
```

Now imagine that you want to write a routine to change the record's Address and City fields (which we'll assume are strings). To make these changes in a thread-safe way, you call the critical section's Acquire method to signal that aCustomerRecord is being used by a thread. After you make your changes, release the customer record for use by other threads by calling the critical section's Release method:

```
// Stop other threads from using the data until we're finished changing it.
LockACustomerRecord.Acquire;
// Now change the data.
aCustomerRecord.Address := '1017 Fourth Street';
aCustomerRecord.City := 'Woodland';
// Finally, release the data for other threads to use.
LockACustomerRecord.Release;
```

It is important to understand that the critical section does not actually block threads from accessing the protected information. In the previous example, if you become careless and try to change aCustomerRecord's Address field without first using the critical section's Acquire method, the critical section will do nothing to prevent the change. If Acquire is called first, however, and if the critical section is used consistently throughout the application, only one thread can access the data at a time.

## Multi-Read Exclusive-Write Synchronizers

Critical sections are an excellent method for protecting memory from synchronization errors, but they do have some drawbacks. Critical sections prevent a thread from accessing memory in use by another thread. Although this type of locking is very safe, it can hurt system performance because it prevents all types of access, not just dangerous types.

Synchronization errors can be summarized very simply: one thread is reading memory while another thread is writing to it. Should multiple threads be prevented from *reading from* the same memory address? Generally no, because read operations alone can't cause synchronization errors.

Kylix has an object called a *multi-read exclusive-write synchronizer* that solves this problem. It allows any number of threads to read from protected memory, provided that no threads are writing to it. If a thread is writing to a protected area, all other threads are forced to wait on their read/write operations until the writing thread is finished. Also, write operations are forced to wait until all current read operations are finished. By using multi-read exclusive-write synchronizers instead of critical sections, you can significantly increase application performance.

You can use multi-read exclusive-write synchronizers almost as you would use a critical section. Create a TMultiReadExclusiveWriteSynchronizer object to accompany your protected data. Whenever a thread needs read access to the data, start by calling the synchronizer's BeginRead method. When the read operation is finished, call EndRead. Call BeginWrite before any write operation, and EndWrite afterwards.

## Locking Mechanisms

Critical sections and multi-read exclusive-write synchronizers can prevent synchronization errors from occurring, but only if they are used regularly and consistently. It is often a good idea to encapsulate protected data custom object types that also contain a critical section or synchronizer. Encapsulating data this way gives the resulting object a *locking mechanism.*

Some Kylix objects already have their own locking mechanisms that can make them thread-safe. For example, TCanvas has a Lock method that will prevent threads from drawing to the canvas until the Unlock method is called. Any thread that locks the canvas can use it exclusively until that same thread unlocks it. Other threads will wait until Unlock is called before they proceed with their own operations. With the locking mechanism on TCanvas, drawing objects such as TPen, TBrush, TFont, and TPicture become thread-safe.

The thread-safe list object TThreadList has its LockList and UnlockList methods that work much the same way as TCanvas' Lock and Unlock methods.

## Thread Completion and Termination

Threads don't last forever, of course. There are three conditions that can cause a thread to stop functioning:

- Application termination
- Thread completion
- Thread termination: the thread is terminated by an action in another thread

Application termination is when the application that spawned the thread terminates. The thread stops executing automatically and all its resources are returned to the operating system. All the work of terminating the thread and freeing its memory is done by the operating system itself, which leaves little for the developer to do to support termination. The developer must ensure that if the application does terminate, no critical work done by the thread is lost in the termination process, which is largely a matter of careful design.

*Thread completion* is when the thread finishes the work it was designed to do. When a thread's Execute method completes, the thread's work is finished, and it will terminate operation. Any data contained in the thread will remain there until the thread object is freed, which may happen automatically if FreeOnTerminate is set to True.

> **NOTE**
>
> Be careful how you set FreeOnTerminate if there's a possibility the thread will complete its work before its data can be passed to other threads in your application.

A thread can also be terminated explicitly by another thread. To stop a thread's execution externally, call its Terminate method. Terminate causes the thread's Terminated property to be set to True. It is the developer's responsibility to periodically check Terminated to see if the thread should terminate, and if so take appropriate action.

Many threads are designed to operate until terminated. For example, Web server applications often spawn a separate thread to listen for connection requests. When the listening thread receives a connection request (from a Web browser, for example), it dispatches the request information it receives to another thread to be handled. It then returns to listening. The listening thread never finishes its work; it continues to operate until it is terminated externally.

Here is an example that shows how a listening thread in a Web server application might have its Execute method written:

```
TListeningThread.Execute;
begin
  while not Terminated do
    ListenForConnectionRequests;
end;
```

This is a fairly typical example of how a thread checks to see if it has been terminated. The while loop will continue indefinitely until the thread's Terminate method is called. Once that happens, execution passes out of the while loop and the Execute method completes.

**13**

PROCESSES AND
THREADS

When thread completion or termination occurs, the application generates an OnTerminate event. An OnTerminate event handler is a good place to perform miscellaneous closing operations before the thread is freed. One interesting thing to note about OnTerminate event handlers is that they will be executed in the application's main CLX thread, not in the thread that has been terminated. Many synchronization errors are less likely to occur in an OnTerminate event handler.

When you write an OnTerminate event handler, be aware that any thread-local variables you have declared will not be available. Execution of the OnTerminate event handler occurs in the main CLX thread; thread-local variables in the thread that has terminated cannot be accessed outside that thread.

## Debugging Multithreaded Applications

Multithreaded applications have unique problems when it comes to debugging. There are multiple threads of execution, so developers need to have a list of all the executing threads in an application and their status at any given moment. If a program stops at a breakpoint, it is often important to know which of the running threads encountered the breakpoint. Kylix includes a tool called the Thread Status view that can give this kind of information.

To see the Thread Status view, select View, Debug Windows, Threads. The view should appear as shown in Figure 13.1.

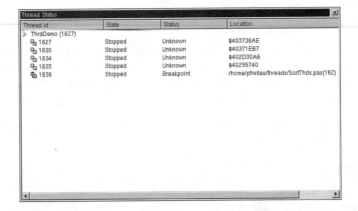

**FIGURE 13.1**
*The Thread Status view during a debugging session.*

The figure shows the contents of the Thread Status view during a typical debugging session. A breakpoint was set in one of the thread objects of the application being debugged, and the application ran until it encountered the breakpoint. The thread that encountered the breakpoint

(1636) is marked by an icon with a green arrow on top. Information about the state, status, and location of all the threads is also given.

The Thread Status view offers several tools that can help during debugging. To see the tools, right-click on a specific thread. You can view a thread's source code, for example, or change the active thread. Also, if your application has spawned other processes, you can obtain information about those processes or even terminate them.

## Final Thoughts on Threads

As you can see, Kylix offers a number of tools and code objects that simplify multithreaded application development. For many rapid application development tasks, multithreading is the easiest way to take advantage of Linux's multitasking capabilities in your Kylix projects. Multithreaded Kylix applications are often easily ported to Windows operating systems through Delphi, which can be quite an advantage over other Linux development tools. Multithreading may offer you all the multitasking solutions you need.

# Linux Processes Control and Interprocess Communication

Kylix was designed to excel at multithreaded applications. Unfortunately, not all tasks can be performed by multithreading. For example, a Kylix programmer may want to execute a program that isn't part of his Kylix project. He may not even have the source code available. In cases like this, multiprocessing can be very useful. We will now examine how you can use Kylix to perform basic multiprocessing operations.

The techniques we will examine in this section are not specific to Kylix; they can be used in any Linux programming environment. All of the calls used in multiprocessing are Linux glibc calls. Kylix doesn't provide any new routines; it just provides an Object Pascal interface to the routines in the Linux glibc libraries.

> **NOTE**
>
> Kylix applications that use multithreading are easy to port to Windows because Delphi uses most of the same objects and methods. Multiprocessing applications use Linux-specific methods, and will be much harder to port.

Linux process control and interprocess communication are by no means new subjects. This section is merely meant to be an introduction to the topic, not an in-depth discussion. For more details, there are a number of useful references available to you, including the following:

- Books on general Linux programming
- The Linux man pages, for API documentation of the glibc routines mentioned here
- The Kylix unit Libc.pas (in your Kylix installation's source/rtl/linux directory), which tells you the Object Pascal calling conventions for the Linux routines
- Web pages, newsgroups, FAQs, HOWTOs, and many other sources available through the Internet

## Creating New Processes

You can think of a running application as a user of the system like any other. Your application can be used to launch other processes in the operating system. Basically, a Linux process can do anything you yourself could do from a command line. Linux processes generally have the user and group permissions of the user who launched them. (They can have superuser privileges as well, regardless of who launched them, if they are installed properly by a root user. This generally isn't a good idea for security reasons.)

### Launching a Process with fork

You can launch a new process by calling the Linux glibc fork command. The new process, which you can call the *child process*, is an exact copy of the process that created it (the *parent process*). The calling syntax for fork in an Object Pascal program is as follows:

```
function fork: pid_t;
```

where pid_t is a Linux process ID number type, basically an integer.

Because fork creates a clone of the application that called it, the function returns a value in both processes. The values are different, which allows the programmer to decide whether the execution is in the parent or the child process. If the returned value is 0, the process is the child process. If the value is positive, the process is the parent process, and the returned value is the child's process ID. There is one other possible value, which is –1. That means an error occurred, and the fork failed to create a new process.

Let's look at an example of a fork operation to get a better understanding for what it does. Imagine this code segment runs as a console application:

```
var result: pid_t;
begin
  result := fork;
  case result of
```

```
    -1: WriteLn('Error occurred!');
    0:  WriteLn('written by the child');
    else
      WriteLn('written by the parent');
  end;
end.
```

The `result := fork;` command creates a new process. Both processes are running the same program at exactly the same line. At first they each contain the same information except for the value of `return`. In the child process, `return` has a value of zero, so it prints the phrase "written by the child" to standard output and exits. Meanwhile, in the parent process, the value of `result` is a valid process ID number. It writes "written by the parent" to standard output instead, and then it also exits.

Duplicating an application this way is perhaps the simplest way to multiprocess. There are several problems with simple duplication, however. If you are writing a Kylix GUI application, duplication will cause errors in the window manager. Both the parent and the child processes will be attempting to manipulate the same windows in the operating system, which is what causes the errors. More importantly, duplication limits you to the use of only one program. Most Linux systems are full of useful programs written and supported by others. You could try to incorporate the source code of these programs into your own application, but most Linux applications aren't even written in Object Pascal. Porting external source code into your application is tedious at best.

There are easier and better ways to use other programs in your Kylix application using some basic Linux glibc library calls. The basic process is as follows:

1. Use `fork` to create a child process.
2. Replace your Kylix application in the child process with another program.

## Replacing Applications with `exec` Functions

You have already seen how to use `fork` to create a child process. To purge your Kylix application from the child process and replace it with another program, use one of the `exec` family of functions (`execl`, `execlp`, `execle`, `execv`, `execve`, and `execvp`) just after calling `fork`.

The `exec` functions all perform the same operation, running another program. They differ only in which arguments are specified, and how they are specified. All `exec` functions start with an Object Pascal `PChar` parameter that specifies the program to run. Other parameters to the function may include command-line arguments and environment settings for the program. All the `exec` functions return an integer, but that only matters if the call fails. If the call succeeds, execution passes to the new program, so the return value is irrelevant—it can never be checked.

Parameters passed to the exec functions can take one of two forms. They can be either a single null-terminated string (C/C++ type char *, Object Pascal type PChar) or a list of null-terminated strings (Object Pascal type PPChar). Specifying a PChar parameter is straightforward. PPChar types are a bit more complicated. Start by creating a one-dimensional array of PChar variables. The array should have a size one greater than the number of elements in the array. The first element should be indexed to zero, and the last should be empty. To set the value of the PPChar being passed into the exec function, simply obtain the address of the array using the @ operator.

Here is an example of a call to execv involving two arguments:

```
var
  programName: PChar;
  argArray: array [0..2] of PChar;
  programArgs: PPChar;
  forkResult: pid_t;
  execResult: Integer;
begin
  argArray := ('arg1','arg2',nil);
  programArgs := @argArray;
  programName := 'TheProgram';
  forkResult := fork;
  case forkResult of
  -1: WriteLn('Error occurred!')
  0: // Execution is in the child process.
  begin
    // Replace this program with the other program.
    execResult := execv(programName, programArgs);
    // If execution gets here, then the child failed
    // to launch the new program. Complain and kill the
    // child process.
    WriteLn('New process failed!');
    _Exit(-1);
  end;
  // Parent execution continues here.
  ...
end;
```

## Signaling or Killing a Process

Our final topic of this section is signaling. Processes are a bit like guided missiles; after they have been launched, they require no further attention from the user. Still, the parent process may depend on the results of the child process to decide its own actions. What if the child fails to complete its work and the parent needs the results?

Linux has a number of signaling methods that you can use to check on the status of a process. The wait4 function can be used to examine the status of child processes. The integer result returned by wait4 can be fed into the WIFEXITED, WIFSIGNALED, and WIFSTOPPED functions to find out if the process being examined exited normally or was terminated or stopped (respectively).

More generally, processes can send signals to one another using the kill function. You probably expected kill to be used to terminate processes, and you are certainly right. Strangely enough, kill is not just a termination mechanism; it is the standard Linux messaging call. The kill function takes two arguments. The first is the pid_t of the process being signaled. The second argument is the message being sent.

There are many possible messages that can be sent. Processes can terminate one another (provided they have appropriate permissions to do so) by sending the message SIGTERM. A process can stop another process with the SIGSTOP message, and start it up again with the message SIGCONT. There are many other messages possible, but these are some of the most common and useful signals.

Signaling can be a very powerful tool, but to go into greater detail on this topic is beyond the scope of this work. There are many general works on Linux programming with more information on this topic.

## Summary

In this chapter, you have seen how to use two different multitasking methods in Kylix. Multithreading is a powerful, cross-platform technique that relies on Kylix TThread objects. Multithreading allows developers to share data easily between tasks, while also providing all the necessary protections against synchronization errors. Multithreading may be the best option for new applications that have little or no existing source code.

Kylix can also be used for traditional Linux multiprocessing operations, using all the standard Linux routines. Multiprocessing lacks the shared memory structures offered by multithreading, so communication between processes can be more difficult. Still, multiprocessing can save development time by allowing developers to use programs outside their current project. Developers with previous Linux multiprocessing experience can apply their knowledge easily in Kylix development.

**13**

**PROCESSES AND THREADS**

# DataCLX

**PART**

**IV**

## IN THIS PART

# DataCLX Basics

*By John Kaster*

## IN THIS CHAPTER

This chapter introduces you to DataCLX and dbExpress, cross-platform technologies that provide database connectivity for Kylix and future versions of Delphi and C++ Builder, which all contain dbExpress and DataCLX.

# DataCLX Architecture

The DataCLX components are cross-platform data-access components written in Object Pascal. These components wrap up calls to the dbExpress components, which are written in ANSI C++ (for instant portability to other platforms). The dbExpress components interact with various SQL servers and were designed specifically to leverage the features of SQL. Using SQL greatly simplifies the interface for database management, so only a few components are required to wrap up data-centric operations. In fact, Borland actually provides more DataCLX components than you really need to use. Three of the DataCLX components (TSQLTable, TSQLQuery, and TSQLStoredProc) exist purely for migration from existing Delphi and C++ Builder applications.

The dbExpress components abstract the interface to various SQL Servers, allowing developers to write an application that can work with any ANSI SQL-92–compliant server while still allowing applications to support the advanced features that a specific server vendor might support. More detail on the dbExpress components is provided in Chapter 16, "Data Access Layer."

# Data Access

The DataCLX components provide properties, functions, and methods that simplify database application programming. All database-management system features can be accessed through the DataCLX components, including connecting to a database, retrieving data, performing updates, and handling metadata management.

## Connecting to a Database

To connect to a database, you use a TSQLConnection component. The SQL connection component has properties for specifying the name of the database, a username, a password, a role, and a variety of other parameters for controlling how you connect to the database.

Let's start using the components by creating a new database application. Select File, New Application from the Kylix menu to create a new application with a blank form.

Next, select the dbExpress tab on the component palette and drop a TSQLConnection component onto the form. Then select the ConnectionName property in the Object Inspector. Click on the drop-down arrow and select IBLocal as the connection name. Notice that the DriverName property is automatically set to InterBase because IBLocal is configured as an InterBase database connection. Several other properties of the component are also set, based on the configuration information that already exists for this connection.

Set the LoginPrompt property to False. The username and password are already defined for this InterBase connection, so you don't need to type them again. If you leave LoginPrompt set to True, every time you activate the database connection, you'll have to type in the username and password, which can get very tiresome. Of course, you can require a login prompt for the users of your application when it is completed by setting the LoginPrompt property back to True.

You might be wondering where the username and password properties are stored because they are not immediately visible in the Object Inspector. The Params property contains the user name, password, role, and all the other parameters for this connection as a list of name/value pairs in this TStrings object. You can see all the values by clicking on the ellipses for this property in the Object Inspector. The Params property editor makes it easy to change any of the values that already exist, as you can see in Figure 14.1.

**FIGURE 14.1**

Params *property editor.*

If you want to add parameters that are not listed, simply type them here as new lines. When you close the editor window, you will be prompted to save these values. If you choose to save them, those new values will be saved into the string list, and the next time you bring up the Params property editor, the new values will be listed.

Before you go on, you need to make sure that you can actually connect to the database. Try to set the Connected property to True in the Object Inspector. If you get an error, your database name isn't pointing to a valid InterBase database. This is easy to fix. Right-click on the TSQLConnection component and select the Edit Connection Properties menu item. Modify the Database property to point to the employees.gdb file, as shown in Figure 14.2.

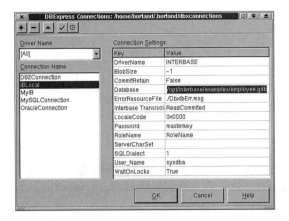

**FIGURE 14.2**

*The Connections editor.*

> If you don't know where the employees.gdb file is, you can use find . -name
> employee.gdb from the root directory. On many InterBase installs, this file is
> /usr/local/interbase/examples/employee.gdb.

After you have successfully tested the connection to the database, you can disconnect again, if you want, because the dataset component that you're using next will turn the connection back on when you need it.

## Retrieving Data

Drop a TSQLClientDataset connection onto the form. Set the DBConnection property to the name of the SQLConnection that you already have on the form. It should be called SQLConnection1 unless you renamed it. (If you had more than one, you'd get a list of all of them in the drop-down list.)

You'll use the CommandText property to tell the component how to retrieve data. By default, the CommandType property is set to ctQuery, so the property editor will display an ellipsis that brings up the CommandText property editor when you click it. This editor assists you in building SQL select statements. If the database is available, the editor automatically retrieves the list of tables defined in the database. This list is displayed in the upper-left list box of the property editor.

Directly beneath the list of tables is the list of fields for the currently selected table. If you select a different table, the field list is immediately updated to display the fields for this table. You will also notice that an asterisk (*) is in the field list. This is to make it convenient to select all fields in your SQL statement. You can use the information in these two list boxes as a guide for writing your SELECT statement, or you can actually write the SELECT statement using them. In this case, you'll do the latter.

Select the Employee table and either double-click it or click the Add Table to SQL button. Either way, you will see the text Select from EMPLOYEE. To finish the select statement, highlight the asterisk and either double-click it or click the Add Field to SQL button. Your property editor should look something like Figure 14.3.

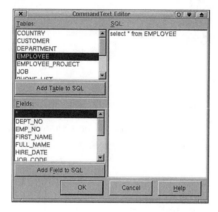

**FIGURE 14.3**
*CommandText Property Editor.*

Click OK to set the CommandText property to this select statement. Now you can test the retrieval of data from the dataset by setting the Active property to True. The entire dataset should be retrieved quickly. You can deactivate the dataset again, if you want.

# Data Control

You've set up your connection to the database and have even retrieved data from a table. Now you need to use some data controls to actually display the data on your form.

## Displaying Data with Visual Data Controls

A TDataSource component is used to abstract the communication between data controls and data access components. So, go to the Data Access tab of the Component Palette, drop a TDataSource onto the form, and set its DataSet property to SQLClientDataSet1.

Next, go to the Data Controls tab and drop a `TDBNavigator` and `TDBGrid` component onto the form. You want to communicate with the `SQLClientDataset` via the `DataSource` that you just dropped. You can set the `DataSource` property for both components by holding down the Shift key and clicking them, and then setting the property. If the dataset is inactive, the form should now look something like Figure 14.4.

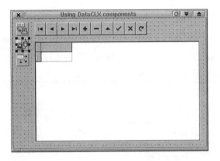

**FIGURE 14.4**

*Inactive data.*

You can now activate the dataset to see the data in the `Employee` table by setting the `Active` property of `SQLClientDataSet1` to `True`. The actual data from the table will appear in the grid, as shown in Figure 14.5.

**FIGURE 14.5**

*Active data.*

When you first load the data into the grid, the headings for the columns are simply the names of the fields. In the case of this dataset, the headings are reasonably clear because the names of the fields are pretty easy to understand, but this might not always be the case. Fortunately, the DataCLX components enable you to change the display properties of the grid very easily. The text displaying as the heading for a field is determined by the `DisplayLabel` property of the data field. By default, the `DisplayLabel` of the field is the same as its name in the dataset. To change the display labels of the fields, you need to make the fields persistent first.

Naturally, there is an easy way to do this. Let's bring up the Component Editor menu for the dataset, shown in Figure 14.6, by right-clicking the component on the form.

**FIGURE 14.6**
*Dataset Component Editor menu.*

You can see many special options for this dataset. The menu option that you're interested in right now is Fields Editor. (Don't worry, we'll cover the other menu options later.) When the Fields Editor appears, no fields are currently listed because no persistent fields have been defined. You can quickly add them by right-clicking in the list box to bring up the Fields Editor menu, shown in Figure 14.7.

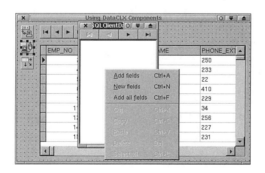

**FIGURE 14.7**
*Fields Editor menu.*

Select the Add All Fields menu option, and all the fields in the dataset will be made persistent (that is, a TField object will be defined for each one in both the form and the source code). Now you can see that all the fields in the dataset are available in the list box, as shown in Figure 14.8.

**FIGURE 14.8**
*The Fields Editor.*

When the fields are persistent, you can modify the properties of any or all of them by selecting one or more in the Fields Editor list box and modifying its properties in the Object Inspector. For this example, you'll set the values for the display labels listed in Table 14.1.

**TABLE 14.1** Display Label Values

| Field Name | Display Label |
| --- | --- |
| EMP_NO | Emp # |
| FIRST_NAME | First Name |
| LAST_NAME | Last Name |
| PHONE_EXT | Phone |
| HIRE_DATE | Hired |

As you change each of the display labels, the heading for its column in the grid immediately updates (just consider it more fun with Borland's two-way tools). Now the grid looks like Figure 14.9.

This looks better, but when you run the application, you now notice that the default size of the HIRE_DATE field is much too wide (see Figure 14.10).

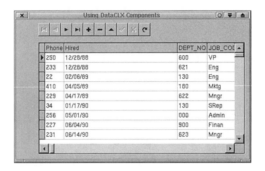

**FIGURE 14.9**

*Grid with new display labels.*

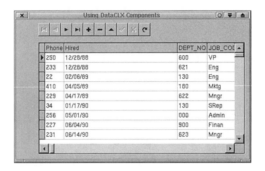

**FIGURE 14.10**

*Grid with wide hire date.*

To improve the appearance, you can use the Fields Editor to edit the `DisplayWidth` property of the `HIRE_DATE` field to set its size to 10. You can see this change immediately reflected in the IDE.

Now you want to remove the job-related fields from the grid. To do so, select the `JOB_CODE`, `JOB_GRADE`, and `JOB_COUNTRY` fields in the Fields Editor list at the same time by Shift-clicking them and setting their visible property to `False`. Now the grid no longer displays these fields, although they're still in your dataset.

Manipulating the field properties demonstrates how the grid can use the persistent fields that you have defined for the dataset for controlling the display of data in the grid. You can further refine the appearance of the grid by using its Columns Editor to change the default display order of the columns. Bring it up by right-clicking the grid and selecting the Columns Editor menu option from the component editor menu.

When no columns are defined for the grid, the field properties in the dataset are used to automatically create them. When all the columns are defined, only those columns will be displayed in the grid, and the visibility value of the field that the column uses will now be overridden by the column definition. You can add column definitions for all fields in the dataset by right-clicking the Columns Editor and selecting Add All Fields. Figure 14.11 shows reordered column definitions; the FIRST_NAME and LAST_NAME columns are moved to the end of the list, and the FULL_NAME field appears second. Now the columns in the grid will be displayed in that order.

**FIGURE 14.11**
*Grid columns defined.*

Hopefully, this exercise gives you a feel for how you can access data and control its display and navigation. Let's talk now about how this process works underneath the surface.

# Typical Data Flow

Data access in Kylix has two distinct modes of operation. The first and most obvious, because of all the visual data-aware components, is interactive modification and viewing of the data. The second is forward-only movement through a dataset, for publishing or reporting purposes.

## Interactive Data Manipulation

dbExpress was designed with Borland's TClientDataSet technology in mind. ClientDataSets are exactly what the name implies: data sets that are used in client-side applications. This feature greatly increases the scalability and responsiveness of your database client applications. Some of the things that you can do with ClientDataSets are listed here:

- Persist data as either XML or binary files on the client side
- Manipulate all the data in memory for fast runtime performance
- Deploy an application with zero configuration, for instant setup and simple application distribution

- Use ANSI 92 SQL syntax for instant filtering and aggregation on the client side
- Find data with partial matches and no case sensitivity for instant incremental searching
- Create nested tables that will internally maintain master-detail relationships
- Scale a local table-based system to dbExpress to support a SQL database engine
- Import any SQL query result from dbExpress directly into a local MyBase XML table
- Support all popular data types, including BLOBs and Oracle's Abstract Data Types (ADTs)
- Track all data changes automatically on the client side for every insert, update, and delete without writing any code
- Generate optimized SQL update statements automatically when you want to apply those data changes back to your SQL server

The logic for all of these features is contained in a shared object called `libmidas.so`. `TClientDataSet` is one of the components used to wrap up this logic in a convenient format so that you can reach new levels of flexibility in your database applications. `ClientDataSets` are very cool technology; we'll explore them more in Chapter 15.

## MyBase Storage Format

The storage format for `ClientDataSet` files is called MyBase™. MyBase has both XML and binary formats for its files, which can also be used to store "briefcase" files that are snapshots of the current state of data being manipulated on the client side. Even pending changes to the data can be stored in these files, so totally disconnected data operations are completely supported with MyBase files.

Because all data changes are tracked locally, a persistent connection to the source database is never required. You need only an active database connection while retrieving the data for the `ClientDataSet`. If you're loading the data from a local MyBase table, you never need to activate a database connection until you apply the updates using the `TClientDataSet.ApplyUpdates` method.

## Data Flow

Here's the high-level view of the default data flow with `ClientDataSets`:

1. Activate the `ClientDataSet` (or related component) to retrieve the data based on the options set in the `CommandText` and `CommandType` properties. If you are not already connected to the database, this will automatically happen.
2. Disconnect from the database.
3. Make changes to the data in the client application using DataCLX components or code.

**14**

**DATACLX BASICS**

4. Call the `ApplyUpdates` method, which will automatically reconnect you to the database.

5. All changes to the data will be packaged up into a delta packet.

6. Each record of the delta packet will be analyzed, and the appropriate SQL command to reflect these changes will be issued.

7. Disconnect from the database.

This is generally what occurs. If an exception occurs, the client will be notified. Otherwise, the data will be synchronized. There can be a lot more to the data flow than this. DataCLX surfaces events for customization of the process every step of the way.

## Data Publishing

By "data publishing," we mean simply producing reports, Web pages, form letters, or some other data that is accessed in read-only mode; no updates are made to the data in the database. The process for data publishing is simpler because it is a one-way process. The data is only retrieved; no updates go back to the database engine.

In many cases, you can continue to use `ClientDataSets` for publishing data as well as data manipulation. However, sometimes you have a very large result set that you don't want to load into memory in a `ClientDataSet`. In this case, you would ordinarily use a `TSQLDataSet` component, which uses a unidirectional read-only cursor to retrieve data from a SQL command, starting at the first row in the result set and moving forward (only) from there until you reach the end of the result set.

In this case, a persistent connection to the database is required because data rows will be retrieved on demand.

The typical data flow for this process is one-way (it is possible to issue SQL commands to update data in the database, but usually you use a `ClientDataSet`) and occurs similar to the following:

1. Activate the `SQLDataSet` (or related component). This activates the database connection, if it is currently closed, and retrieves the first record of the result set.

2. Move forward through the result set, using either the `MoveBy` or `Next` methods of the dataset. (You can also use a `TDBNavigator` component for this, if you want, as long as you move only forward. If you try to move backward, an exception will occur.)

3. Continue until you reach the end of the result set.

4. Close the dataset.

That's about all that happens when retrieving data from the database with a unidirectional cursor. Borland chose to implement dbExpress using unidirectional cursors because they are faster and more lightweight than bidirectional cursors, and the `ClientDataSets` provide bidirectional functionality for applications that require it.

# Configuring the Server

The various database engines available on Linux are configured in different ways. Some (such as PostgreSQL and MySQL) are included in the major Linux distributions. Others, such as InterBase, can be downloaded from a Web site and then installed using either an RPM or a setup utility on the product CD. If you are running your database server on the same machine on which you run Kylix, you need to make sure that the database server has been started before you can connect to it. If the database server is not on your machine, you will probably need a client on your machine to access it. Make sure that you install the client and start it before trying to connect to the database server.

Depending on the stock-keeping unit (SKU) of your copy of Kylix, you will have at least two of these drivers. In Kylix 1.0, the Desktop Developer SKU includes dbExpress drivers for InterBase and MySQL. The Server Developer SKU in Kylix 1.0 adds dbExpress drivers for IBM DB2 and Oracle 8i to what you get in Desktop Developer. Borland is working on additional database drivers for future releases, so you may have more drivers in your SKU by the time you read this.

When you install Kylix, some text configuration files are created in the .borland directory for that user. These text files are formatted like INI-style files. If you used the allsetup.sh file provided on the CD for this book, you have a /usr/local/kylix/.borland directory. When you run Kylix for the first time as a different user, a .borland folder will be created and the files in the original Kylix configuration directory will be duplicated there. You can then customize your specific connection information for that user. This way, if you want to do development with multiple "personalities"—where your database work is Oracle-centric or InterBase-centric, for example—you can simply create a new user and run Kylix as that user, setting up all your database configuration information for that specific personality.

However, we're getting a bit ahead of ourselves. You will find additional detailed database configuration notes for InterBase, MySQL, DB2, and Oracle on the CD included with this book. Let's look now at the default connection options installed by Kylix.

## Connecting to InterBase

InterBase is Borland's own SQL database engine that distinguishes itself in vertical market and embedded systems. It is a full-featured ANSI SQL-92–compliant database engine that supports advanced features such as multiple transactions, stored procedures, triggers, generators, advanced data types, and versioning. It also happens to be my favorite database engine because

**14**

the API for it is exactly the same on every platform that it supports. (It supports a lot of platforms.) You can find more information on InterBase at `http://www.borland.com/interbase/`.

The default InterBase connection is called IBLocal, which happens to be the same name as the BDE (Borland Database Engine) SQL Links alias for InterBase that is provided with versions of Delphi on the Windows platform. It is a nickname for local InterBase connections.

I used the IBLocal connection described earlier to provide the overview of DataCLX. As mentioned there, you can right-click the `TSQLConnection` component that you drop onto the form to point to the location of your InterBase database (a .gdb file), if you don't have the location currently set. When Kylix is installed, the value for the database is set to database.gdb, which is a nonexistent database.

To connect to InterBase, you need to have the InterBase client installed on your machine. The InterBase client can be installed by running the setup program included in your copy of InterBase.

> **NOTE**
>
> One of the example databases is employee.gdb, which is usually in one of two locations. See the earlier note on connecting to a database for suggestions on where it might be. If you are connecting to another machine, you preface the machine/server name in front of the file reference. For example, jfkylix:/ibdata/codecentral.gdb would point to the server machine jfkylix and the file codecentral.gdb in the ibdata directory.

After you specify the correct location of an InterBase database, you simply need to set the `Connected` property of the component to `True` in the Object Inspector and start connecting your dataset-based components to it, as you did in the first section of this chapter. You'll use additional data-aware components in the next few chapters.

## Connecting to MySQL

At the time of this writing, MySQL is probably the most popular SQL engine available for Linux. Most Linux distributions include an installation utility for MySQL. The initial version of Kylix shipped with support for MySQL 3.22.30. If you have a later version of MySQL, you should check the Borland Web site for updates to the MySQL dbExpress driver, at `http://www.borland.com/devsupport/kylix/`.

The dbExpress driver for MySQL uses the C API for MySQL, so you will need to install the MySQL client to communicate with a MySQL database. At the time this chapter was published, the MySQL 3.22.32 RPM binaries are at `http://www.mysql.com/downloads/mysql-3.22.html`.

MySQL databases are aliased, so you don't refer to a specific file location—you refer to a name for the database that you or your database administrator set up. When your MySQL client is installed, you can take the following steps to connect to the MySQL server:

1. Choose File, New Application.
2. Drop a `TSQLConnection` onto the form from the dbExpress tab of the Component Palette.
3. Set the `ConnectionName` property to `MySQLConnection`.
4. Edit the connection properties to point to the appropriate database name.
5. Drop a `TSQLClientDataset` onto the form.
6. Click on the ellipses for the `CommandText` property and use the `CommandText` editor to build your SQL statement.

## Connecting to DB2

The steps for installing DB2, both the server and the client, are much more involved than those for installing InterBase or MySQL. For details, refer to the IBM DB2 Web site, at `http://www.ibm.com/db2/`. The initial Kylix release was tested with the DB2 Version 6.x and 7.1 CLI libraries for Linux.

Like MySQL, DB2 uses a database name for a specific database rather than a filename. You will need to know your DB2 database name to connect to the database. When you have your DB2 configuration working, you can connect to a DB2 database by taking steps similar to the following:

1. Choose File, New Application.
2. Drop a `TSQLConnection` onto the form from the dbExpress tab of the Component Palette.
3. Set the `ConnectionName` property to `DB2Connection`.
4. Edit the connection properties to point to the appropriate database name.
5. Drop a `TSQLClientDataset` onto the form.
6. Click on the ellipses for the `CommandText` property, and use the `CommandText` editor to build your SQL statement.

## Connecting to Oracle

As always, Borland has excellent support for Oracle's advanced features, and dbExpress is an excellent way to get to Oracle data. Because the Oracle Call Interface (OCI) changes drastically even in point revisions, it is important to note that Borland tested Kylix with versions 8.1.5 and 8.1.6 of the OCI client libraries. Like MySQL and DB2, Oracle databases are also set up as a database name, not a physical file location. You can connect to an Oracle database as follows:

1. Choose File, New Application.
2. Drop a TSQLConnection onto the form from the dbExpress tab of the Component Palette.
3. Set the ConnectionName property to OracleConnection.
4. Edit the connection properties to point to the appropriate database name.
5. Drop a TSQLClientDataset onto the form.
6. Click on the ellipses for the CommandText property, and use the CommandText editor to build your SQL statement.

## Summary

This chapter covered the basics of using DataCLX, the data-aware components you can use when building GUI applications in Kylix. We also talked briefly about the data access architecture and how to connect to various database engines. This chapter introduces the concepts that will be explored in the following chapters on using data-aware components with Kylix, the data access layer, and a real-world database application.

# Working with Data-Aware Components

By John Kaster

## IN THIS CHAPTER

This chapter gets programmers up to speed on using the DataCLX and the Visual CLX data-aware components. It will update current Delphi users with the structure and use of the new cross-platform data-aware components and will get new Kylix programmers familiar with the basic architecture of all of Kylix's data-aware components.

## TSQLConnection

When we start talking about the data-aware components provided by Kylix, it makes the most sense to start by talking about the database connection components because you usually need a database connection before doing anything with a dataset. Kylix introduces the TSQLConnection component, which is a DataCLX component. As mentioned in the previous chapter, DataCLX components are those data-aware components that deal with the data access layer of database programming; retrieval and modification of data in the persistent datastore.

This connection component descends from TCustomConnection, which is the base class of the "connection" components Borland provides. TCustomConnection became the common ancestor for all database-like connections in Delphi 5, including Borland's remote connectivity options like CORBA, DCOM and Web connections. This change was made after a very productive lunch conversation I had with Mark Edington and another Borland engineer who worked on the connectivity components for Delphi 5, in which I was complaining about the lack of a common ancestor for all connection components.

By having a common ancestor for all types of dataset-based connections, Borland makes it very easy to migrate a single-tier (database and application on the same machine) or two-tier application (also called client/server, where the database is running on a machine other than the application) to a multi-tier or distributed database application, where your connection to the database is remote, usually by being brokered through an application server.

---

### DataSnap

DataSnap™ (formerly part of Borland MIDAS) is the term Borland uses for the technology that enables remote database connectivity for Delphi and C++ Builder applications. Unfortunately, DataSnap components do not ship with the initial product releases for Kylix. I hope you will see them soon, perhaps even by the time you have purchased this book. When these DataSnap components are available for Kylix, they will function almost identically to those already provided for Delphi and C++ Builder.

One additional connectivity option you should see when they are available for Kylix will be SOAP-based connections. SOAP support is already available with Delphi 6 on Windows. CORBA, Socket, and Web (HTTP/HTTPS) connectivity should also be supported for Kylix. DCOM will not be a supported protocol for Kylix because DCOM isn't native to the Linux platform and is not supported for Linux by Microsoft.

Before Delphi 5, it was very difficult to write a complete database engine replacement for the Borland Database Engine (BDE). (The BDE is still provided with the Windows versions of Delphi and C++ Builder.) The TDatabase component was BDE-specific, and there was no base ancestor from which you could query connection-based information. This made it difficult to write components that would work with *any* database connection. Because Borland introduced support for additional database engines in Delphi 5 (with native components that specifically supported Borland's InterBase API and Microsoft's ADO), it was important to enable components to work with an abstract connection component, just like components could work generically with any dataset by using the abstract dataset component. Once TCustomConnection was available, many complete database engine replacements became available from third parties because the same data-aware components that worked with BDE connections could then be made to work with ADO, InterBase, or other types of connections with very little effort. By setting the stage in Delphi 5, it was much easier to produce another set of database connectivity components that would work with Borland's new cross-platform database access layer, dbExpress.

The components in Kylix that begin with "TSQL" are all DataCLX components that facilitate using dbExpress. These components include TSQLConnection, TSQLDataSet, TSQLMonitor, TSQLTable, TSQLQuery, TSQLStoredProc, and TSQLClientDataset.

A TSQLConnection component communicates via dbExpress classes with a specific database in a one-tier or two-tier environment. The minimum values required for this component are a connection name (available connections are normally contained in your dbxconnections file), a username, and a password. With this information, you can get a connection to a SQL database and retrieve or update data. Other options can include your SQL role name, SQL dialect, and so on.

Perhaps the diagram in Figure 15.1 (stolen from my Kylix seminar slides) will help explain what I'm talking about. We'll discuss more of what's in this diagram later on.

The TSQLConnection component makes calls to the dbExpress SQLConnection class, which is discussed in detail in Chapter 16, "Data Access Layer." TSQLConnection will handle making and ending connections to a specific database. Information like your identity, connection options, and database location are all specified as parameters for this component. Once you have specified the values for a specific database connection (usually stored in the dbxconnections file), you can simply set the Connected property to True to connect, or False to disconnect from the database.

When you set the connected property to True, the TSQLConnection DataCLX component will initialize the needed structures and make the calls to the dbExpress SQLConnection class to open a connection to the specified database. If an error occurs while attempting to connect or at any time during the communication with the database server, the component will handle it elegantly, raising an exception describing the problem so you can quickly and easily fix it, rather than providing a cryptic error number code (or core dump).

**15**

WORKING WITH
DATA-AWARE
COMPONENTS

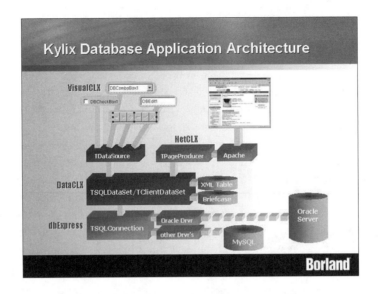

**FIGURE 15.1**

*Database application architecture.*

## TSQLConnection Properties

In most cases, you simply need to drop a TSQLConnection component, set the ConnectionName property to the appropriate name, and set the Connected property to True. When I'm writing a new database application, I always set the LoginPrompt property to False first, so I never have to type in the username or password to connect to the database during development of the application.

When you set the ConnectionName, you will notice that several other component properties, such as DriverName, GetDriverFunc, LibraryName, and VendorLib, are all automatically assigned to corresponding values specified in the dbxconnections file for that connection name. You can override these settings after they are initialized by selecting the ConnectionName, but your changes will be overridden if you select a different connection name again. If you want to make changes to those properties permanent for that connection, you should right-click on the TSQLConnection connection component and use the component editor to save those changes back to the configuration file.

Once you have a connection to the database by setting some of the published properties (those you see in the Kylix Object Inspector), you may be interested in looking at some of the public properties of this component because it can provide a tremendous amount of information about the database you are using.

For example, the `DataSets` property is an indexed property that gives you access to any datasets currently active that are using that specific SQL connection. The `ActiveStatements` property tracks the number of statements that are active with a specific SQL connection. You may need to monitor this property if your application supports many simultaneous operations on a database, but you have a finite limit of simultaneous statements that can be supported by your database engine. The `ActiveStatements` value, which is a `LongWord`, is actually incremented in `TCustomSQLDataSet.CheckStatement` and decremented in `TCustomSQLDataSet.FreeStatement`, so whenever you query this read-only property, you are getting the current value. It does not need to be refreshed because it is always kept up-to-date by the datasets using a specific connection. You can compare the value of this property to `MaxStatementsPerConn`, which indicates the maximum number of statements the database connection will support, based on information provided by the driver.

These two statement properties are used in conjunction with the `AutoClone` property, which controls whether or not to automatically clone a connection to a database when the maximum number of statements has been reached. The `TSQLConnection` component can handle this for you automatically and clone your connection, making a secondary connection that will still be managed internally. However, this cloned connection would use additional resources, so you may decide to implement a "throttle" on your application by turning off `AutoClone` and controlling the number of active statements yourself. When `AutoClone` is turned off, activating too many statements will raise an exception, so you want to be sure to control this behavior yourself as gracefully as you can.

Another important property for database programming is the boolean `TransactionsSupported` property, which indicates whether the database engine you are connected to supports transactions. If transactions are not supported, the `StartTransaction`, `RollBack`, and `Commit` methods do nothing. Let's talk some more about what the methods of this component can do if they are enabled.

## TSQLConnection Methods

The simplicity of setting a few properties and connecting to a database with this component is deceptive. There are literally dozens of methods for this component, all designed to make it easier to work with a specific SQL database connection. There are methods for querying the state of the connection, retrieving information about the connection, issuing commands to the connection, and finding out its capabilities.

In most applications, you won't need to call any methods at all. You'll simply set some component properties and your application will be up and running. However, there will be times when you will want to do more than simply connect to the database and find out some additional information about it. These methods allow you to override the default ways of

**15**

communicating with your SQL database, and support customizing your communication process in an incremental fashion.

## TSQLConnection Events

The events for this control provide notifications for connecting, disconnecting, and logging in to the database server. With these events, you can control and log all access to the database from your application. Let's build a sample application that shows how these events can be used. Follow these steps:

1. Choose File, New Application.
2. Set the Caption of the form to TSQLConnection Component.
3. Drop a TSQLConnection from the dbExpress tab and set its ConnectionName property to IBLocal (which should be configured to point to an existing InterBase database file by now).
4. Drop a TStatusBar from the Common Controls tab on the form and set its SimplePanel property to True.
5. Drop a TButton on the form and set its Caption property to Connect.
6. Drop a TLabel on the form and set its Caption property to LoginParams.
7. Drop a TMemo on the form and set all its Anchor properties to True, and resize it to fit from side to side and along the bottom of the form, above the status bar.

The form should now look something like Figure 15.2.

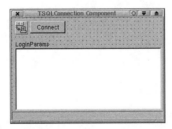

**FIGURE 15.2**
TSQLConnection *test application form.*

Now you need to hook up the events. You can create the routines for the event-specific code by selecting the Event tab and double-clicking on the event names. Kylix will automatically write the declarations and begin and end code for you, and position you in the editor ready to write code. Do this for each event, and also double-click on the button and write the following code:

```
procedure TForm1.SQLConnection1AfterConnect(Sender: TObject);
begin
  StatusBar1.SimpleText := 'Connected to '
    + SQLConnection1.ConnectionName;
end;


procedure TForm1.SQLConnection1AfterDisconnect(Sender: TObject);
begin
  StatusBar1.SimpleText := 'Disconnected from '
    + SQLConnection1.ConnectionName;
end;


procedure TForm1.SQLConnection1BeforeConnect(Sender: TObject);
begin
  StatusBar1.SimpleText := 'Connecting to '
    + SQLConnection1.ConnectionName;
end;


procedure TForm1.SQLConnection1BeforeDisconnect(Sender: TObject);
begin
  StatusBar1.SimpleText := 'Disconnecting from '
    + SQLConnection1.ConnectionName;
end;


procedure TForm1.Button1Click(Sender: TObject);
const
  Captions: array[boolean] of string = ('Connect', 'Disconnect');
begin
  SQLConnection1.Connected := not SQLConnection1.Connected;
  Button1.Caption := Captions[SQLConnection1.Connected];
end;


procedure TForm1.SQLConnection1Login(Database: TSQLConnection;
LoginParams: TStrings);
begin
  Memo1.Lines.Assign(LoginParams);
end;
```

Now run the application and click the Connect button. After connecting, you should see the information in Figure 15.3, which all occurs because of the events you've just hooked.

Click the same button (that now says Disconnect) and you will see the status bar is now updated and the button caption has changed, indicating that you are no longer connected to the database (see Figure 15.4).

**15**

WORKING WITH
DATA-AWARE
COMPONENTS

**FIGURE 15.3**

*Connected to* IBLocal.

**FIGURE 15.4**

*Disconnected from* IBLocal.

## TSQLDataSet

TSQLDataSet is a descendant of TCustomSQLDataSet, which is the common ancestor for all datasets that talk to dbExpress drivers. All of the dataset components in DataCLX except for TSQLClientDataSet use unidirectional, read-only cursors. If you want to get persnickety, TSQLDataSet and TClientDataSet (discussed later) are the only dataset components you really need to provide a fully functional database application. The other components are provided purely for your convenience, either for setting up simple database applications or for porting existing Delphi applications to DataCLX components. I'll explain more when I talk about each DataCLX component.

TCustomSQLDataSet descends from TDataSet, which is the common ancestor for all dataset components available in Kylix 1 and Delphi 6. This means that if you design your own code or components correctly, you could write applications that will work with any dataset component. Because the DataCLX components are the only explicitly cross-platform components Borland provides, however, it might be a good idea to keep the code simpler and just use them.

TSQLDataSet is the only dataset component you need to use when fetching data from the database server. It has all of the functionality that the other unidirectional datasets provide. The property `CommandType` indicates the operating mode for the `CommandText` property. When you set `CommandType` to `ctQuery`, the `CommandText` property must be a SQL command. If `ctStoredProc` is used, `CommandText` is the name of a stored procedure. If `ctTable` is used, `CommandText` is the name of a table (basically, it just means "select * from <CommandText>").

One of the coolest things about the `CommandType` property of `TSQLDataSet` is the way it causes the `CommandText` property editor to change behavior. If `CommandType` is `ctQuery`, the `CommandText` property editor will display an ellipse that opens a SQL command editor when you click on it. If `CommandType` is `ctStoredProc`, the `CommandText` property editor becomes a drop-down list that contains the names of all the stored procedures in the database indicated in your `TSQLConnection`. If it's `ctTable`, all the standard tables (non-system tables) in the database are listed in a drop-down for the `CommandText` property.

You can see how this works by using a `TSQLConnection` that points to your `IBLocal` connection. If you are using `employee.gdb`, it contains stored procedures and tables that will get listed in the `CommandText` property editor when you switch command types.

I'll be using `TSQLDataSet` in some sample usage patterns a little later, so we'll wait for step-by-step instructions until then.

## TSQLQuery

This component is provided purely to ease the process of porting an existing application that uses a `TQuery` (a BDE SQL dataset component found in Delphi) or similar component to a DataCLX-based application. `TSQLQuery` descends from `TCustomSQLDataSet`, and its constructor sets the `CommandType` property for the component to `ctQuery`. The `CommandType` property is also not a published property for `TSQLQuery`. Furthermore, the `CommandText` property is replaced by the SQL property, which basically does the same thing as `CommandText`. Since `TSQLDataSet` does everything `TQuery` does, I won't be talking about it any further.

## TSQLStoredProc

Like `TSQLQuery`, this component is intended to make porting existing Delphi applications to DataCLX easier. Its constructor sets `CommandType` to `ctStoredProc`, and leaves this property unpublished as well. Because `TSQLDataSet` supports everything this component does, I'm not going to spend any time on this one, either.

## TSQLTable

As with the two components I just mentioned, `TSQLTable` is provided for porting ease from existing Delphi source code. It publishes many more properties than the other two porting components because it replicates as much of the Delphi `TTable` component as possible, which is designed for manipulating local/desktop database files. Since dbExpress and the DataCLX components are specifically for processing dynamic SQL commands, you should definitely replace calls to `TTable`s with `TSQLDataSet`s during the porting process whenever possible.

# TClientDataset

`TClientDataset` is the component that implements MyBase™ dataset features. It is based on technology Borland used to call MIDAS. MIDAS has now been split into two different marketing groups: MyBase, and DataSnap. MyBase is the data-manipulation and `TClientDataSet` functionality, and DataSnap is the remote connectivity over standard wire protocols (like DCOM, IIOP, TCP/IP, HTTP/HTTPS, SOAP/XML, and so on) and offers support for distributing your data with Web services. Kylix 1.0 Server Developer and Desktop Developer do not include the DataSnap components. If you want to find out more about them, see the information on Delphi at either `http://www.borland.com/delphi/` or `http://community.borland.com/delphi/`.

This component has some of the following features:

- Local datasets in either XML or binary format
- Completely memory-based for fast runtime performance
- Zero configuration for instant setup and simple application distribution
- Small footprint, less than 300k
- ANSI 92 SQL Syntax for live filtering and data aggregation
- Linkable tables for master-detail relationships
- Import any SQL query result from dbExpress into a local MyBase table
- Update dbExpress tables with MyBase data
- Supports all popular data types including Blobs and ADTs
- Supports calculated and aggregate fields
- Instant client-side indexing on any scalar data type
- Tracks all data changes (inserts, deletes, updates) to data on the client side for full client-side database operations
- Interactive data reconciliation error handling
- Support for parameterized queries

I'm sure there are more features I'm forgetting, but some of what `TClientDataSet` can do will come out as we do some examples later in this chapter.

# TClientDataSet Properties

This component has a lot of properties, so we'll just talk about a few of the more commonly used ones here, and explore many of the others later on in this chapter. The `Active` property controls whether the data in the `TClientDataSet` is loaded into memory. To load the data into memory so you can work with it, you either point to a `TDataSetProvider` component or use a MyBase dataset file. To use a `TDataSetProvider`, you assign the `ProviderName` property to the name of an available `TDataSetProvider`. So, for example, you might take the following steps (we're going to re-use the components we'll set up in this example, so there are a few more steps listed here than are actually required):

1. Choose File, New Application.

2. Name the form FormUsingData.

3. Choose File, New, DataModule (we'll be re-using this data module for other examples).

4. Name the `DataModule` dmIBLocal. The caption for the data module should be updated.

5. Drop a `TSQLConnection` on dmIBLocal, and name it dbIBLocal.

6. Drop a `TSQLDataSet` on dmIBLocal, and name it sqlEmployees. Then assign its `SQLConnection` to dbIBLocal.

7. Click on the ellipses for `CommandText` and specify `select * from EMPLOYEES` as your SQL statement.

8. Drop a `TDataSetProvider` from the Data Access tab on the Component Palette, set its `Name` to prvEmployees, and assign its `DataSet` property to sqlEmployees.

9. Drop a `TClientDataSet` from the same tab, set its `Name` to cdsEmployees, and assign its `ProviderName` to prvEmployees, which will be available in the drop-down.

10. Drop at `TDataSource` from the same tab, set its `Name` to dsEmployees, and assign its `DataSet` property to cdsEmployees.

11. Save this unit as dIBLocal.pas.

The data module should look something like Figure 15.5 when you're done.

Now that you've hooked up the `ClientDataSet` to a `SQLDataSet` via a `DataSetProvider`, you can populate all the data you want to work with on the client side by setting the `Active` property to `True`. Once the dataset is active, you can use any data-aware control to manage or view the data by talking to `dsEmployees`, which abstracts your relationship to the dataset (and would allow you to change the dataset you're using without re-writing any of your client data access code that talks to the data source).

**15**

WORKING WITH
DATA-AWARE
COMPONENTS

**FIGURE 15.5**

*The base* dmIBLocal *data module.*

The steps you've just taken are what you would use to manipulate any dbExpress-supported database interactively. You can load any data that can be represented as a result set into a client dataset. This includes the results from executing stored procedures. I should also mention that you can set the dbIBLocal.Connected property to False now that you've loaded the data on the client side. You won't need to connect again until you want to post the changes you'll make on the client side to the server.

TClientDataSet supports keeping a "briefcase" file copy of the data you've pulled from your SQL server locally with the FileName property. This property was introduced in Delphi 4, as a result of a conversation I had with one of our R&D people after doing one of my Delphi tours. It basically is a convenient way of making a Get/Set property that results in calls to the ClientDataSet methods LoadFromFile and SaveToFile. It makes briefcase file mode much more convenient—you simply need to specify the name of the file to use for briefcase mode, and everything else is handled for you automatically. When you start the application, if thecomponent finds the file specified in FileName, it will load the data from it. When you close the application, the current state of the data will be written back out to the filename specified. All you need to do to briefcase-enable your database application is specify a name for the MyBase file.

If your dataset is somewhat large (1,000 records or more), you may want to let the user see some data quickly, and then load the rest of the data from the SQL database on demand (that is, when the user scrolls down in the result set). The PacketRecords property controls how many records to get at a specific time. When it's set to –1 (negative one), it loads the entire result set all at once. If you set it to 0 and activate the dataset, it will load the metadata information for the dataset, but no data rows. When you set it to some value greater than zero, it will load that number of rows of data at a time. When you use a value greater than zero, you must have your TSQLConnection component active to support loading the data on-demand. Simply navigating beyond the data that's currently loaded will cause the ClientDataSet to fetch the next <PacketRecords> rows from the server.

As I mentioned earlier, this component supports client-side indices. You can create an index on any scalar field type (numeric, date, character, boolean) simply by setting the

IndexFieldNames property. For example, you could set the IndexFieldsNames property for cdsEmployees to last_name;first_name and this would set the display order of the data to be alphabetical by last name, and then first name. Whenever you set an index value, it changes the display order of the data only. The storage order of the dataset remains the same.

We'll discuss more properties of TClientDataSet when we do some sample usage patterns.

## TClientDataSet Methods

Specifying a semicolon-delimited list of fields in the IndexFieldNames property is the easiest way to set the display order for an index. However, if you want to support both ascending and descending fields in the same index, or create multiple display orders that you can change at run-time and select by name, you would want to use the AddIndex method to create another TIndexDef for the dataset. Here's the declaration for this method:

```
procedure AddIndex(const Name, Fields: string; Options: TIndexOptions;
  const DescFields: string = ''; const CaseInsFields: string = '';
  const GroupingLevel: Integer = 0);
```

By passing these values, you can specify the name and settings for an index on the dataset. A few years ago, I created a component called TClientDataSetGrid, which is a TDBGrid descendant that allows the end-user of your application to change the display order of a ClientDataSet simply by clicking or Shift+clicking on the columns in a grid. Go back to the blank form you just created, and drop a TClientDataSetGrid component down on the form. Then, do the following:

1. Choose File, Use Unit, dIBLocal.
2. Set the Grid's Anchor properties all to True and resize it so it takes up most of the form, leaving a little space at the top of the form.
3. Select the dmIBLocal data module, and set cdsEmployees.Active to True.
4. Choose Run, Run.
5. Click on the LAST_NAME column in the grid, and then Shift+click on the FIRST_NAME column.

You should see something similar to Figure 15.6.

Note the numbers and the arrows in the column headers indicate the order the fields occur in the index, and whether they're ascending or descending. This behavior is supported by using and re-using the same TIndexDef (the name defaults to SortGrid) repeatedly, by extracting its current settings and knowing what values need to be set. Look at the SortGrid procedure in CSDBGrid.pas for complete details.

15

WORKING WITH
DATA-AWARE
COMPONENTS

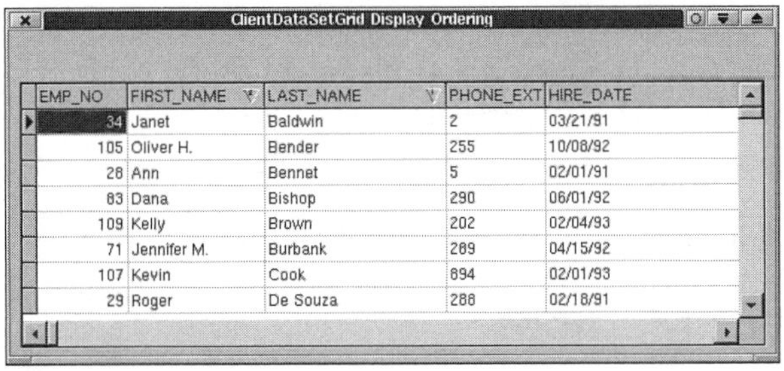

**FIGURE 15.6**

ClientDataSetGrid *in Last_Name, First_Name order.*

---

**NOTE**

The TClientDataSetGrid component is provided on the CD-ROM included with this book. Follow the instructions on the CD for installing the custom components discussed in this book to get it installed into your Kylix IDE.

---

After you've pulled the data to the client side, you can work with the data locally until you decide you want to apply those changes back to your SQL database. Then you'd simply call the ApplyUpdates method for the ClientDataSet, and your changes get written back to your SQL database with optimized SQL statements that only update the data that must be updated, based on the changes that are automatically tracked by ClientDataSet components. These changes are represented in a delta packet, which is a special datapacket that indicates what kind of update each record contains. This value is one of the following TUpdateKind values:

- UpdateKind—Description.
- ukModify—Edited values in the record. Only those values that have changed are included in this record. Unchanged values are NULL. When this value is specified, the previous record in the delta had no UpdateKind value set, which means it is the original record with the scalar values initially retrieved from the database. This unmodified record is used to determine reconciliation errors.
- ukDelete—This record should be deleted. If a primary key field has been identified for the dataset, only that key value will be used for generating the delete statement.
- ukInsert—New record. All values will be written to the new row after it has been created.

Delta packets even support master-detail records, where updates, deletions, and insertions will be performed in the order required to maintain the relationships among the records. If you need to process an entire delta packet in one of the `TDataSetProvider` events (which we'll discuss later), it's good to know that for modified records, the modified record is preceded by the unmodified record with all original data values (except for any blob fields) so the reconciliation process can detect reconciliation errors. There are two cases where you might experience a reconciliation error, and both of them mean that someone else modified the record between the time you retrieved the data and the time you're applying your update. If the record has been deleted (it is no longer found), or some of the data values in the record have changed, you will get a reconciliation error when you call `ApplyUpdates`. If you want to gracefully handle the reconciliation error in the client application, you can add a reconciliation error dialog box to your application:

1. Select File, New, Dialogs, Reconcile Error Dialog box (follow the instructions in the comments at the top of the unit).

2. Save it as `fReconcileErr.pas`.

3. Select `dmIBLocal` and use the unit `fReconcileErr`.

4. Select `cdsEmployees` and double-click on the `OnReconcileError` event in the object inspector.

5. Use CodeInsight to help you write the following line of code for that event:

   ```
   Action := fReconcileError.HandleReconcileError(DataSet, UpdateKind, E);
   ```

Now your client application is set to gracefully handle reconciliation errors that might occur when applying updates to the dataset. You can test the reconciliation error handling by running two different copies of the client application and changing the same record in the different client instances, and then applying updates. If you go back to the main form for the application (`fUsingData`) you can set up your current GUI interface to do this test and simulate multiple users making changes to the data:

1. Drop a `TDBNavigator` on the form and set its `DataSource` property to `dmIBLocal.dsEmployees`.

2. Drop a `TActionList` component on the form and double-click on it to open the ActionList editor.

3. Create a new action and set its `Caption` to &Apply.

4. Double-click on the action's `OnExecute` event and set the event-handling code to

   ```
   dmIBLocal.cdsEmployees.ApplyUpdates(-1);
   ```

5. Double-click on the action's `OnUpdate` event and set the event-handling code to

   ```
   Action1.Enabled := dmIBLocal.cdsEmployees.ChangeCount > 0;
   ```

6. Drop a button on the form and assign its `Action` to Action1. With this action, the Apply button will only be enabled when there are actually changes to be applied to the dataset. Implementing code like this will process all errors (if any occur) before returning.

7. Compile the project.

8. From a command shell, run three instances of this executable with `./UsingData &`. You may need to use `source kylixpath` in your `Kylix/bin` directory to set up your path correctly.

9. In the first instance of the application, set the first employee record's `FIRST_NAME` to "Alec" and post it to the client dataset by pressing the checkmark in the navigator component to post the record locally and click the Apply button to apply the update back to the database.

10. Set the second instance of this record to "William" and click the checkmark on the navigator to post the record locally.

11. Set the third instance to "Steve" and post the change locally.

12. Then, click the Apply button in the second instance (the one that has "William"), and you'll see the reconciliation error dialog box shown in Figure 15.7. (If you were running it from the IDE with integrated debugging turned on, you'd see the exception raised in the IDE first.)

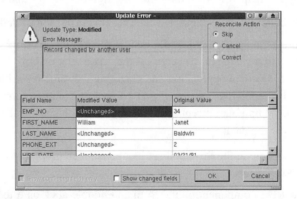

**FIGURE 15.7**
*Update Error dialog box.*

13. If you want to see only the fields that have changed, check Show Changed Fields, as shown in Figure 15.8.

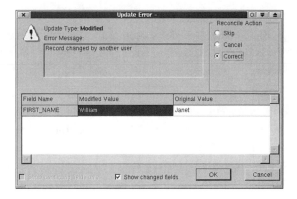

**FIGURE 15.8**
*Only changed fields dialog box.*

14. Select Correct as your reconcile action and click OK. Your change will be accepted.

15. Click Apply on the third instance, and you'll see that it also will open the reconciliation error dialog box.

This should be enough on `TClientDataSet` to set up the background for some additional usage cases we'll detail later on.

## TDataSetProvider

A `ClientDataSet` uses a `TDataSetProvider` to provide data from a dataset and resolve updates to that dataset or directly to its database server. This component encapsulates the logic needed for retrieving that data and resolving updates to that database. It can be used to build datapackets that have nested datasets (master/detail information), and it can also be used to process a datapacket before a `ClientDataSet` receives it, and for massaging a delta packet before applying those updates back to the database. This component and its events give you almost complete control over the data providing and resolving process. Dan Miser has written an article that is available on the Borland Community Web site called "Using ClientDataSets as a replacement for cached updates" that goes into extensive detail on many of the specialized things you can do with `ClientDataSets` and `DataSetProviders`. It can be found at `http://community.borland.com/article/0,1410,22571,00.html`. There is also additional information on this subject at `http://community.borland.com/delphi/distcomp/`.

There are two properties I want to discuss here that greatly enhanced the performance and capabilities of the provider/resolver model. First, set the `Options` property values `poIncFieldProps` and `poPropogateChanges` to `True`. The first value of the enumerated set, `poIncFieldProps`, will pass the constraints for any persistent fields you create down to the

ClientDataSet that received the datapacket from the provider. The second, poPropogateChanges, will do a "reverse" delta after updates are made in a BeforeUpdateRecord event on the DataSetProvider and reflect those changes back to the client automatically. This is my preferred technique for handling things like server-generated keys and other changes along those lines.

The second property is the UpdateMode for the data that is being resolved. Set it to upWhereKeyOnly, so the SQL where clause that gets generated for finding the original record will only use the key value for the data to match, rather than all the original values when performing an update. You can use the SQL Monitor form you'll create later to see how this streamlines the SQL update statement.

Now you need to set your primary key field for the dataset provider update mode you just selected:

1. Right-click (or double-click) on sqlEmployees and open the Fields Editor.
2. Right-click on the Fields Editor and select Add All Fields.
3. Delete the field FULL_NAME.
4. Select EMP_NO.
5. Set the ProviderFlag pfInKey to True.
6. Right-click on cdsEmployees and open the Fields Editor (if cdsEmployees is active, deactivate it).
7. Right-click on the Fields Editor and select Add All Fields.

Many of the examples later in this chapter will show how you can use DataSetProviders.

## TSQLClientDataSet

Most CLX components are "lean and mean," designed to be used in conjunction with other components for very discrete functions. TSQLClientDataSet doesn't conform to this generality because it was designed specifically for access to simple dbExpress result sets where all the features of Borland's MyBase technology except for nested master-detail data and TDataSetProvider events might be needed. The introduction of the component was prompted by two things: The many demonstrations I've provided for Kylix since we first started talking about it more than two years ago, and the unidirectional read-only cursor the other TCustomSQLDataSet descendants provide.

Unlike TClientDataset, TSQLClientDataSet is not designed for use with a TDataSetProvider. It is a "super component" derived from TCustomClientDataSet. It has a TDataSetProvider and TSQLDataSet internally, to make it easier to set up two-tier applications without requiring so many components. It can be an expensive shortcut, but it's often useful when you're working with a single table in a two-tier application.

If you want to develop an application that will support remote connections for datasets in the future (when this feature is released for Kylix) or TDataSetProvider events, you should not use a TSQLClientDataSet because you'll be packaging up the data twice. Use instead a TSQLDataSet with a TDataSetProvider and hook it up to a TClientDataSet.

We'll be using TSQLClientDatasets later on in this chapter. Because the component is basically a wrapped up TClientDataSet, we'll just move on for now and you'll pick up more capabilities as you use this component.

## TSQLMonitor

Some other database access engines allow you to see exactly what's going on with your communication to a database. However, you may not have the capability to turn on this monitoring or tracing in your own application. This often greatly reduces an application's usefulness because you might have to wade through thousands (literally) of calls to the database engine to find the one or two calls you're really interested in. dbExpress surfaces a monitoring feature that will allow you to trace the communications you make with any of the database engines dbExpress supports. This feature is provided in Kylix with the TSQLMonitor component.

This component provides great granularity by allowing you to specify a distinct SQLConnection to monitor, and turn that connection on and off in your own application. Let's set up a SQL Monitoring window for your current application:

1. Choose File, New Form.
2. Set the caption to SQL Monitor.
3. Choose File, Use Unit, dIBLocal.
4. Name the form component FormSQLMonitor and save the form as fSQLMonitor.pas.
5. Drop a TSQLMonitor on the form and set its SQLConnection property to dmIBLocal.dbIBLocal.
6. Drop a TStatusBar on the form and set SimplePanel to True.
7. Drop a TCheckBox at the top right of the form, and resize it so its Width is about 250 or so.
8. Drop a TPanel underneath it, size it to take up the remainder of the form, set BevelOuter to bvNone, clear its Caption, and set its Anchor properties to True.
9. Drop a TListBox on the panel and set its Align property to alLeft.

10. Drop a TSplitter on the panel. (If you don't have the most recent version of CLX, you may nccd to sct its Width property to 3 if it's currently 100.)

11. Drop a TMemo on the panel, and set its Align property to alClient, and its ScrollBars property to ssAutoBoth.

The form should look something like Figure 15.9.

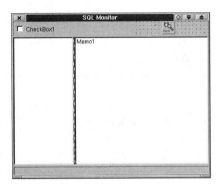

**FIGURE 15.9**
*SQL Monitor window.*

Next, let's set the caption for the monitoring check box in the FormCreate event to indicate the SQLConnection you're tracing:

1. Double-click on the form itself (where the form's grid is still displayed).

2. Set the FormCreate event code to:

```
if Assigned(SQLMonitor1.SQLConnection) then
  CheckBox1.Caption := '&Monitor '
    + SQLMonitor1.SQLConnection.ConnectionName
else
  CheckBox1.Enabled := False;
SQLMonitor1.Active := CheckBox1.Checked;
```

Now you're ready to hook up the trace log event.

3. Double-click on the SQLMonitor OnLogTrace event, and put in the following code:

```
ListBox1.Items.Add(Format('Cat:%d, Len:%d, Client:%d',
  [CBInfo.eTraceCat,
  CBInfo.uTotalMsgLen,
  CBInfo.ClientData]));
StatusBar1.SimpleText := Format('%d log entries',
  [SQLMonitor1.TraceCount]);
```

This code will populate the list box with some diagnostic data on every trace event. Let's assign the text of a specific trace to the Memo control whenever the user selects an item in the list box.

4. Double-click on `ListBox1`.

5. In its `OnClick` event, put the following code:

```
if ListBox1.ItemIndex > -1 then
    Memo1.Text := SQLMonitor1.TraceList[ListBox1.ItemIndex];
```

Save all your changes. Because this is already part of the current project and is automatically created, you can simply create a menu option on the main form to show the SQL Monitor window by using that unit and calling `FormSQLMonitor.Show`. You may also want set up a button to activate and deactivate the `ClientDataSet` to see what SQL statements get executed.

# Normal Dataset Usage Patterns

Now that you've had a brief (Honestly, there's a lot more we could cover than this!) overview of the data-access components in Kylix, you can start looking at some specific examples of how you can use these components for everyday data operations.

## Queries

Let's go back to your data module and create a couple of simple query components that will give you some lookup tables.

Drop a `TSQLClientDataset` on the data module, name it sqlDepartments, and set its `DBConnection` to dbIBLocal and its `CommandText` to select * from department.

## Lookup Fields

Now you'll use this `sqlDepartments` to create a lookup field for `cdsEmployees`. You'll also remove a field that you'll be replicating as a calculated field a little later:

1. Right-click (or double-click) on `sqlEmployees` and open the Fields Editor.

2. Right-click on the Fields Editor and select Add All Fields.

3. Delete the field `FULL_NAME`.

4. Right-click on `cdsEmployees` and open the Fields Editor (if `cdsEmployees` is active, de-activate it).

5. Right-click on the Fields Editor and select Add All Fields.

6. Press Ctrl+N for a new field.

7. Set the Name to Department, the Type to String, the Size to 40, and the Field Type to Lookup. Set the Key Fields to DEPT_NO, the Lookup Dataset to sqlDepartments, Lookup Keys to DEPT_NO, and Result Field to DEPARTMENT, as shown in Figure 15.10.

**FIGURE 15.10**

*Department Lookup field.*

8. Click OK. You will see the Department field now as one of your persistent fields. The grid will automatically recognize this as a lookup field. Because you now have this lookup field, it's no longer necessary to see the DEPT_NO field when you can see the name of the department instead. So let's replace the DEPT_NO field with Department in the grid.

9. Select DEPT_NO and set Visible to False.

10. Move Department up above DEPT_NO by using Ctrl+Up arrow in the Fields Editor. (You might have to deselect the other fields as you move it if your version of the dialog box, depending on whether your ScrollLock key is on and the window manager you're using. Some have problems with moving the field around in the list.)

11. Set sqlDepartments.Active to True.

12. Run the application again. If you have to, activate cdsEmployees first if you didn't make that Connect button I talked about earlier.

13. Scroll to the right until you see the Department column, and select one of the Department cells.

14. Click on the cell again, and it will switch you into edit mode, where you will automatically be provided with a drop-down list.

15. Click the drop-down arrow, and you should see something similar to Figure 15.11.

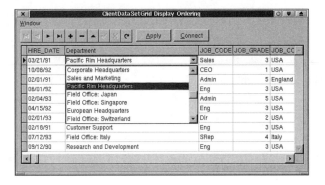

**FIGURE 15.11**
*Department lookup ComboBox.*

## Parameterized Queries

You'll use a parameterized query to set up a master-detail relationship for cdsEmployees. You want to see all the projects for each employee:

1. Drop a TDataSource on the data module, name it dsEmpMaster, and set its DataSet to sqlEmployees.

2. Drop a TSQLDataSet on the data module, name it sqlEmpProj, set its SQLConnection to dbIBLocal, and its CommandText to

   select * from EMPLOYEE_PROJECT where EMP_NO = :EMP_NO.

3. Set sqlEmpProj.DataSource to dsEmpMaster.

The :EMP_NO value is a parameter value for this query. You can assign the value for this parameter by using either of the following parameter references:

sqlEmpProj.Params[0].Value := 1;

or

sqlEmpProj.Params.ParamByName('EMP_NO').Value := 1;

which would be a slightly "safer" method of referencing the parameter in case the parameter list changes in the future.

## Master/Detail Relationships

Because you are setting the DataSource property, the value for :EMP_NO will automatically be determined. Whenever the value is needed to retrieve data from the dataset, the current EMP_NO field value from sqlEmployees will be used. Because you started using persistent fields for cdsEmployees by adding the lookup field, you now need to explicitly add this field to your persistent field list:

1. Select cdsEmployees and set Active to False if it isn't already.

2. Open its Fields Editor, right-click, select Add Fields or press Ctrl+A, and add sqlEmpProj.

3. Set Active to True (if you're so inclined).

4. Select sqlEmpProj and set DisplayLabel to Projects.

5. Run the application again and scroll to the rightmost column in the grid. You should see something like Figure 15.12.

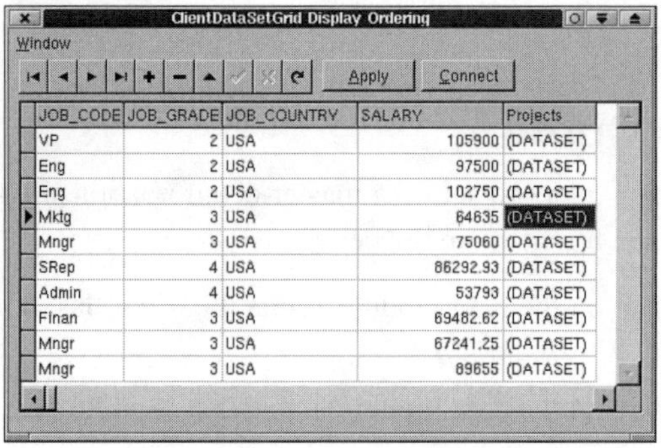

**FIGURE 15.12**

*Detail data column.*

If you select one of the Projects cells and click on the ellipses, another data grid will appear that contains employee numbers and project IDs for the employees. If you use the navigator component, you will notice that the detail information gets automatically updated in this pop-up data grid. Figure 15.13 shows the values I have for employee Leslie Johnson.

**FIGURE 15.13**

*Detail data grid.*

## Customizing Detail Grids

Nested datasets are a very powerful feature of TClientDataSet, but you would certainly want to make that pop-up grid information a little friendlier as well. For example, you don't even need to show the project ID if you can show the name of the project instead. Kylix is flexible enough to support this as well. Let's go back and do a little more work in the data module:

1. Drop a TSQLClientDataSet on the data module, name it sqlProjects, and set DBConnection to dbIBLocal and CommandText to select * from PROJECT.

2. Drop a TClientDataset on the data module, name it cdsProjDetails, set DataSetField to cdsEmployeessqlEmpProj, and open the Fields Editor.

3. Add all fields, select PROJ_ID, and set Visible to False.

4. Press Ctrl+N to add a new field. Set Name to Project, Type to String, Size to 40, Field Type to Lookup, Key Fields to PROJ_ID, Dataset to sqlProjects, Lookup k\Keys to PROJ_ID, and Result Field to PROJ_NAME. Click OK.

The next time you pop-up the grid, you will not see the PROJ_ID column, but you will see the name of each project, as shown in Figure 15.14.

**FIGURE 15.14**

*Customized detail data grid.*

## Calculated Fields

As mentioned previously, TClientDataSet also supports calculated fields. You'll create two new calculated fields for this employee information so you can conveniently browse through it in the grid. One will be the employee's full name as an internally calculated field, and the other will be the employee's monthly salary as a calculated field.

### Internally Calculated Fields

An internally calculated field can be used in a client-side index, and its data gets stored and retrieved with a ClientDataSet file. Internally calculated fields are only available for ClientDataSets. Follow these steps:

1. Right-click on `cdsEmployees` and open the Fields Editor.

2. Press Ctrl+N to add a new field. Set `Name` to `FullName`, `Type` to `String`, `Size` to `40`, and `Field Type` to `InternalCalc`.

3. Click OK.

4. Double-click on the `cdsEmployees` `OnCalcFields` event and put in the code

```
cdsEmployeesFullName.Value := DataSet.FieldByName('LAST_NAME').Value
    + ', '  + DataSetFieldByName('FIRST_NAME').Value;
```

or

```
cdsEmployeesFullName.AsString := cdsEmployeesLAST_NAME.AsString
    + ', ' + cdsEmployeesFIRST_NAME.AsString;
```

Either code statement will end up doing the same thing. The second version of the code will be faster because it doesn't do field lookups and it's calling `AsString` instead of `Value`.

### Normal Calculated Fields

You'll now add that calculated field to `cdsEmployees` (which will make it an internally calculated field) and also add the monthly salary calculated field:

1. Double-click on `cdsEmployees` if you can't see the fields editor.

2. Press Ctrl+N to add a new field. Set `Name` to `Monthly`, `Type` to `Currency`, and `Field Type` to `Calculated`. Click OK

3. Double-click on `cdsEmployees` `OnCalcFields` event if you're not already there in the editor, and add the following code:

```
cdsEmployeesMonthly.Value := cdsEmployeesSalary.Value / 12;
```

Now that you've created these two calculated fields, you can compare the differences between internally and externally calculated fields beyond the fact that internally calculated fields can be used in a client-side index and normal calculated fields cannot.

## Local Incremental Searching

A few years ago, I created a "helper" component that chains the event handlers for an edit box and a combo box to provide incremental searching of `ClientDataSets`. The component is called `TDBFieldComboLocator`, and is included on the CD for this book. The property `CaseInsensitive` toggles case insensitive searching for the values typed into the edit box. The `ComboBox` property points to the `TCustomComboBox` descendant that will be filled with the searchable field names. `DataSource` points to the data source of the dataset to use. `EditControl` indicates the `TCustomEdit` descendant that will be used for incremental searching as its value changes. `PartialKey` toggles recognition of partial keys in the search. The following steps will set up the components you need to provide this feature in your application:

1. Select the main form.

2. Resize the grid to have enough room between the navigator and the top of the grid to drop a TEdit and a TComboBox.

3. Drop a TEdit on the left side of the form below the navigator.

4. Drop a TComboBox to the right of the edit box.

5. Drop a TDBFieldComboLocator, set ComboBox to ComboBox1, DataSource to dmIBLocal.dsEmployees (not dsEmpMaster!), and EditControl to Edit1.

If you run the application now, you can select any field that is "locatable" in the combo box, and start typing in the value you want to find in the edit box. Obviously, it works best with string values because partial matches make the most sense there, but it will work with any indexable field type. The following code is what provides the incremental search behavior:

```
function FieldLocateValue(const Field : TField; sText : string = '') : variant;
begin
  Result := Null;
  try
    if sText = '' then
      sText := Field.asString;
    if Field is TStringField then
      Result := sText
    else if (Field is TIntegerField) or (Field is TLargeIntField) then
      Result := StrToInt(sText)
    else if Field is TNumericField then
      Result := StrToFloat(sText)
    else if Field is TDateField then
      Result := StrToDate(sText)
    else if Field is TTimeField then
      Result := StrToTime(sText)
    else if Field is TDateTimeField then
      Result := StrToDateTime(sText);
  except
    Result := Null;
  end;
end;

procedure TDBFieldComboLocator.LocateField;
var
  Value : Variant;
  Field : TField;
begin
  Field := ActiveField;
  Value := FieldLocateValue(Field, FEditControl.Text);
  if Value <> Null then
```

```
      FDataLink.DataSet.Locate(Field.FieldName, Value,
        FLocateOptions);
end;

procedure TDBFieldComboLocator.EditChange(Sender: TObject);
var
  Field: TField;
  sText: string;
begin
  if Assigned(FEditChange) then
    FEditChange(Self);
  Field := ActiveField;
  sText := FEditControl.Text;
  if PartialKey and Assigned(Field) and (sText <> '')
    and (FieldLocateValue(Field, sText) <> Null) then
    LocateField;
end;
```

I'm including `LocateField` and `FieldLocateValue` here so you can see all of the logic for the incremental search in one place. By looking at `FieldLocateValue`, you can also determine the limitations for what fields are locatable by my component. `LocateField` actually makes the call to the `Locate` method for the dataset, which is what can provide case insensitive and partial key matches on any scalar field on a `ClientDataSet`. For example, set your ComboBox field to `LAST_NAME` and start typing in a last name in either upper or lowercase. As you type, you will see the data pointer moving through the grid to the record matching what you're typing.

---

> **NOTE**
>
> This component uses a technique I call *event chaining*, which will intercept the events that might be set for the edit box and combo box to make the calls to the `EditChange` and `ComboBoxChange` events that make these standard components appear data-aware. In nearly all situations, this is fine. However, when you set the event via code instead of through the object inspector, it is possible to break this incremental search functionality. The best way to implement this would be to implement a listener pattern for the two events, but I haven't found the time to do that yet. This caveat also applies to the next component I'm talking about, `TDBFilterCombo`.

# Local Filtering

Another "helper" component I wrote at the same time as TDBFieldCombo that works in a similar fashion is TDBFilterCombo. This component will hook up a TCustomEdit control and a TButtonControl descendant to a DataSource to allow editing and toggling of local filters on the dataset. One of the features of this component makes it a little easier to build the filter by creating a pop-up menu that provides a menu of the fieldnames in the dataset. This functionality is encapsulated in TDBFieldMenu, which can be found in DBFldLoc.pas, the same unit as TDBFieldCombo and TDBFilterCombo.

Let's set up a filtering dialog box for this dataset as well:

1. Drop a TEdit to the right of the combo box you've already dropped.
2. Drop a TCheckBox to the right of that.
3. Drop a TDBFieldComboLocator, set CheckBox to CheckBox1, DataSource to dmIBLocal.dsEmployees (not dsEmpMaster!), and EditControl to Edit2.

If a filter is currently active, the edit box you connect to will automatically contain the expression for that filter, and the check box will be checked. You can edit the filter expression in the edit box, and turn the filter on and off by checking and unchecking the checkbox at runtime. An example I often use with this dataset is setting the filter to EMP_NO > 100 and EMP_NO < 100 and turning the filter on and off to see how quickly it works. The filter expression can be any valid comparison operator supported by ANSI SQL 92, including LIKE, AND, NOT, and OR.

# Bookmarks

Bookmarks provide a unique identifier for any record in a ClientDataSet. With bookmarks, you can build a list of individual records to process, or "push" a value to return to when operating on multiple records in a dataset, by saving the current record's bookmark, and then assigning the current bookmark to the dataset to that value later on. The bookmark list is currently a little too tightly bound to a TDBGrid or descendant, but you can still use a TBookMarkList very effectively for processing distinct records of a result set.

Let's see how:

1. Add the DB unit to the Uses clause in your interface section of your main form so the TDataSet type will be available for us to use.
2. Add the dbclient unit to the Uses clause in your implementation section of your main form.
3. Put this code in the implementation section of the unit (or get it off the CD included with the book in the UsingData.dpr project):

```
type
  TBoolFunc = function(DataSet: TDataSet) : boolean of object;

function GridIterate( { Run through the selected rows for a grid }
  Grid : TDBGrid;      { Grid to iterate through }
  Test : TBoolFunc;    { Function to call for each iteration }
  RePos : boolean = True { Restore dataset position }
  ) : integer;
var
  cds    : TCustomClientDataSet;
  iRows,
  iRow : integer;
  sMark : TBookMarkStr;
  DataSet : TDataSet;
begin
  cds      := nil;
  Result   := 0;
  iRows    := Grid.SelectedRows.Count;
  DataSet := Grid.DataSource.DataSet;
  if RePos then
    sMark := DataSet.BookMark;
  try
    if DataSet is TCustomClientDataSet then
    begin
      cds := TCustomClientDataSet.Create( nil );
      cds.CloneCursor( TClientDataSet( DataSet ), False, True );
      DataSet := cds;
    end;
    DataSet.DisableControls;
    if iRows > 0 then
    begin
      for iRow := 0 to iRows - 1 do
      begin
        DataSet.BookMark := Grid.SelectedRows[ iRow ];
        if Test(DataSet) then
          Inc( Result );
      end; { for each row }
    end { multiple rows }
    else if Test(DataSet) then
      Inc( Result );
  finally
    if Repos then
      DataSet.BookMark := sMark;
```

```
      DataSet.EnableControls;
      cds.Free;
    end; { with Dataset/finally }
  end; { GridIterate() }
```

This might look like a lot of code, but it's not really that complicated. The GridIterate routine will return the number of records processed by the test routine you'll be passing to it that matches the definition you provide for TBoolFunc. Of course, you need to enable marking records in the dataset, and it would be a good idea to show how many records are marked. Let's do that next:

1. Drop a TStatusBar on the form, and set SimplePanel to True.

2. Select ClientDataSetGrid1 and set the Options subproperty dbMultiSelect to True to enable selecting multiple records in the grid.

3. Double-click on the OnMouseUp event and edit the code to look like the following:

```
procedure TFormUsingData.ClientDataSetGrid1MouseUp(Sender: TObject;
  Button: TMouseButton; Shift: TShiftState; X, Y: Integer);
begin
  StatusBar1.SimpleText := Format('%d row(s) selected',
    [ClientDataSetGrid1.SelectedRows.Count]);
end;
```

4. Now, let's add the code for the routine to process the marked records in your selection set. In the public section of FormUsingData, type

```
function GridAdd(DataSet: TDataSet): boolean;
```

5. Press Ctrl+Shift+C (or whatever key you've set for CodeCompletion™, because some window managers use this keystroke), and edit the code to look like this:

```
function TFormUsingData.GridAdd(DataSet: TDataSet): boolean;
begin
  NameList := NameList + #10 + DataSet.FieldByName('FullName').asString;
  Result := True;
end;
```

6. Drop a button on the form, set its Caption to &Select, and double-click on it.

7. Add the following code:

```
procedure TFormUsingData.Button3Click(Sender: TObject);
begin
  NameList := '';
  GridIterate(ClientDataSetGrid1, GridAdd);
  ShowMessage(NameList);
end;
```

Now you can run this and see how it works. You'll connect and select multiple records, so it looks something like Figure 15.15.

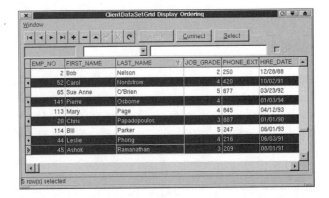

**FIGURE 15.15**

*Selecting multiple records in the grid.*

When you click the Select button now, the message will display the names of all the people you've selected (see Figure 15.16).

**FIGURE 15.16**

*Showing the selected names.*

## Using Stored Procedures

Stored procedures are a very powerful solution for improving performance and functionality of a SQL database application. The only caution I have about using them is that the language for writing stored procedures is not consistent across multiple database servers. This means that the more you invest in stored procedure code for your database application, the more you are tied to one specific SQL server implementation.

This doesn't mean that you should never use stored procedures. It just means that you must use them wisely in your applications if you plan on supporting more than one database engine. Personally, I use InterBase unless I absolutely have to use a different database engine, so I rarely run into problems with having to migrate stored procedure code. Because I'm most familiar with InterBase, you have it provided to you with Kylix, and we're already using an

InterBase database in this chapter, I'm going to use it for writing the stored procedure as well. You'll add another form to your existing application to make this a little easier:

1. Choose File, New, Form or click the New Form button on the Kylix toolbar.

2. Name it FormCommandText and set the Caption to CommandText Editor.

3. Drop a TMemo on the form and set all four Anchor properties to True. Then set ScrollBars to ssAutoBoth, WordWrap to False, and size it to take up most of the form.

4. Drop a TButton on the form and set its caption to OK.

5. Declare Connection: TSQLConnection; in the public section of the form interface.

6. Double-click on the button, and add the following code:

```
if not Connection.Connected then
   Connection.Connected := True;
Connection.ExecuteDirect(Memo1.Text);
```

7. Save this file as fCommandText.pas.

8. To add this CommandText editor to the main form Window menu, choose File, Use Unit, fCommandText.

9. Double-click on the main menu component on the main form to open the menu editor.

10. Add another submenu item under the Window menu and set its Caption to &Command Text Editor.

11. Double-click on it and enter the code:

```
FormCommandText.Connection := dmIBLocal.dbIBLocal;
FormCommandText.Show;
```

12. Run the application, open the command text window, and enter the following command:

```
create generator emp_gen;
```

Click OK.

13. Replace the command with:

```
set generator emp_gen to 145;
```

Click OK. This will set it to the highest employee number you should have in your dataset.

14. Replace the command with:

```
create procedure new_empid
returns (emp_id integer)
as begin
   emp_id = gen_id(emp_gen, 1);
end
```

Click OK.

**15**

WORKING WITH
DATA-AWARE
COMPONENTS

You've now created the generator and the stored procedure to provide you with a sequence generated employee ID.

---

**NOTE**

Jeff Overcash, of TeamB and InterBaseExpress fame, has posted a Linux version of IBConsole to CodeCentral (`http://codecentral.borland.com`). IBConsole does far more than this trivial little command text editor does. You will probably find it very useful to have if you do any work with InterBase on Linux.

---

Close the application and select the data module. What you want to do now is use that stored procedure to generate IDs for new employee records on demand:

1. Drop a TSQLDataSet on the data module. Name it sqlNewID, set CommandType to ctStoredProc, and select NEW_EMPID.

2. Click on the Params ellipses and you'll see one parameter named EMP_ID.

3. Select EMP_ID and you'll see that its DataType is ftInteger.

This shows that you've successfully created the stored procedure. The next step is using it for generating new employee IDs when the records are being created, not before then. You'll finish the steps for using this stored procedure now.

## Client-Side Temporary Keys

A typical database problem with auto-generated keys is supporting the client-side creation of new records without worrying about key conflicts when the data is passed to the server. One conventional way of solving this problem is by reserving ranges of keys for each specific person to use when creating new records. As you can imagine, this can be a huge maintenance problem as well as a hassle for the people entering the data. ClientDataSets and DataSetProvider events can make this process much easier.

The technique I usually use also reserves a "range" of values for a primary key field, but every client instance can use the same range because their connection to the database is processed uniquely. I use negative values for this range. Let's set up your reservation system:

1. Put the following code in the implementation section of your data module:

```
var
   KeyValue: integer = 0;
```

You'll use this as the starting point for the data value and decrement it every time you add a new record. If you want to get fancy and save your `ClientDataSet` as a MyBase file, you can modify this value in the `AfterOpen` event for the `ClientDataSet` so it's set to whatever your lowest negative value is.

2. Double-click on the `cdsEmployees AfterInsert` event, and enter the following code:

```
Dec(KeyValue);
cdsEmployeesEMP_NO.AsInteger := KeyValue;
```

This will provide a unique key for every new employee record you provide. The last step is customizing values for newly inserted records when you're applying those updates to the database.

3. Double-click on the `prvEmployees BeforeUpdateRecord` event. Enter the following code:

```
if UpdateKind = ukInsert then
begin
  sqlNewID.ExecSQL;
  DeltaDS.FieldByName('EMP_NO').NewValue :=
    sqlNewID.Params.ParamValues['EMP_ID'];
end;
```

Save these changes and run the application. Create a few records and you'll see how the employee ID value is a new negative number each time. If you save the changes, the stored procedure will be called to generate a unique employee ID for every new record, and the changes that occur in the `BeforeUpdateRecord` event will be propagated back to the `ClientDataSet`.

## Aggregate Fields

Aggregate fields are a very underused feature of `ClientDataSet` technology. This is probably due to a lack of examples that show how to use them. Aggregate fields are calculated on-the-fly on the client side, meaning that as you add records or change information in a dataset, the values calculated in the aggregate fields are immediately adjusted without requiring the fetching of additional data from the server, or even applying the data updates to the server. The changes to the data are all tracked on the client side, and the aggregate field will reflect those changes. The recalculation of the values of the aggregate field is performed whenever the record buffer is updated. This update can occur on posting of edited changes, or record changes.

Setting up aggregate fields can be a little involved, so this example will be kept as simple as possible. It will demonstrate the concept, and cover the steps you need to implement aggregate fields in your own applications. Follow these steps:

1. Create a new application.

2. Drop a `TClientDataSet` and set its `FileName` value to `items.xml`. This is a MyBase table containing sample line items for a series of orders.

3. Drop a `TDataSource` and set its `DataSet` value to `ClientDataSet1`.

4. Drop a `TDBNavigator` and `TDBNavigator` and set their `DataSource` value to `DataSource1`.

5. Double-click on the `ClientDataSet1.IndexDefs` property and set its `Fields` value to `OrderNo`.

6. Double-click on `ClientDataSet1` and create a new field. Specify its `Type` as `Aggregate` and its `Field Type` as `Aggregate`, and name it TotQty. Set its `Expression` value to `Sum(Qty)`, its `GroupingLevel` value to `1`, and its `IndexName` value to `ClientDataSet1Index1`, and set `Active` to `True`.

7. Drop a `TLabel` on the form and set its `Caption` value to `# of Parts`.

8. Drop a `TDBEdit` on the form and set its `DataSource` value to `DataSource1` and its `DataField` value to `TotQty`.

9. Set `ClientDataSet1.AggregatesActive` to `True` and `Active` to `True`.

If you now run the application and scroll to different orders, you will see the value of the `TotQty` field change. If you edit any of the `Qty` values, you will see the `TotQty` summary field value change whenever you post the record change.

Aggregate fields require a client-side index. The grouping level controls the precision of the value to use. A grouping level of zero basically ignores the index and produces a calculation for all values in the index. Other grouping levels will break at each field level in the index. In this case, because there is only one field in the index, a grouping level greater than 1 would do nothing different. However, if you were to create an index on a different table that might have `Country;State;Zip` as its `Fields` value, you could get aggregates at all three levels of this dataset.

The current implementation of aggregate fields understands `Sum`, `Count`, `Avg`, `Min`, and `Max`. See your Kylix help on aggregate fields for more details on how to specify aggregate field expressions.

## Summary

In this chapter, we covered a large amount of information on the data access components in Kylix. The techniques shown here can be used in any Kylix database application, and some of them have never been documented before. The main components you will be using when configuring your data access are `TSQLConnection`, `TSQLDataSet`, `TDataSetProvider`, and `TClientDataSet`. You will see some of the techniques described in this chapter, and these components, in Chapters 16, "Data Access Layer" and 17, "Creating a Real-World Application."

# Data Access Layer

*by John Kaster*

## IN THIS CHAPTER

The Kylix project provided Borland an opportunity to produce a next generation data access solution for its native code development products (currently, Kylix, Delphi, and C++ Builder). The Kylix project dictated a cross-platform solution. It was also a time to address the assumptions made about how developers write database applications today. One primary decision was made based on an observation of the market; the vast majority of database development done today and in the near future will be done with SQL database engines. Another decision was dictated by the existence of native code provider/resolver technology that was always intended as a cross-platform and language independent solution.

## Goals of the Data Access Layer

Borland has a long history of writing database access engines. The goals of this new data access layer were prompted by the lessons learned in writing and supporting these other driver technologies, like the Borland Database Engine and SQL Links, Microsoft's ADO, JDBC, and other database driver technology that has come and gone. In short, the goals for this new data access layer were:

- Maximize data access speed
- Provide platform independence
- Provide easy deployment
- Minimize size and resource usage
- Provide a common interface to process SQL and stored procedures efficiently
- Make driver development easy and extensible
- Provide access to database specific features

dbExpress™ and DataCLX™ are the result of these goals. Let's talk briefly about each of these goals before diving in to more detail.

## Maximize Data Access Speed

Data access is maximized with two different technologies. First, the dbExpress set of C++-based SQL database access classes are designed to place the raw data processing burden on the SQL server, where it belongs. The cursors returned by dbExpress are read-only, unidirectional cursors, which are the fastest and lightest weight cursors you can use with a SQL engine.

Data caching is another technique for improving data access speed. DataCLX employs client-side connection pooling and data caching through the use of Borland's ClientDataSet technology to provide client-specific data operations exclusively on the client side, reducing network and server load on the database engine. dbExpress provides datapackets to ClientDataSets for client-side processing. Changes to the data are tracked in the ClientDataSet, which will make requests (based on delta packets) back to the dbExpress engine, which will resolve these changes back to the database engine by dynamically generating optimized SQL statements for the data resolution.

## Provide Platform Independence

The initial dbExpress drivers were written in C++ on the Solaris platform because Borland had plans to provide DataSnap server access there. When Borland decided to start the Kylix project, the dbExpress drivers were ported from Solaris to Linux (in a matter of a few days) and testing on the Linux platform was begun. Because the Kylix IDE was still being developed while DataCLX was being developed, the drivers were then ported to the Windows platform (in a few hours) so DataCLX could be developed with Delphi while the Kylix IDE was being enhanced.

From the start, dbExpress has proven that it is indeed a platform-independent database driver implementation:

- It runs on Solaris.
- It runs on Linux and is available with Kylix.
- It runs on Windows and is available with Delphi 6 and future releases of C++ Builder.

Another aspect of platform independence is the configuration information. dbExpress uses INI-style text files because text files are available on any platform Borland may choose to support with dbExpress in the future.

## Provide Easy Deployment

Unlike ODBC, ADO, or the BDE, dbExpress drivers are designed to work totally independently of each other. If you want to deploy an application that only talks to Oracle, the only dbExpress driver you have to deploy with your application is the Oracle driver. In fact, in Delphi 6, you can even link the dbExpress driver directly into your application. Expect to see this in the future for Kylix.

This design requirement greatly reduces the versioning problems other database engines provide. Configuration is also very easy because you can use text configuration files (or not), and also set the configuration options directly in the DataCLX components for your application. It is also easy to simply provide a dialog box to end users during installation allowing them to point to the location of the database files or server.

## Minimize Size and Resource Usage

The dbExpress drivers are very small and lightweight. They don't cache data unnecessarily. They place the data-processing burden on the database server, where it belongs. Data caching is implemented in the DataCLX components, which are not a "black box" you cannot control. You can easily control in your application exactly how much data is cached on the client side, greatly reducing the overall memory and resource requirements for your application.

## Provide a Common Interface to Process SQL and Stored Procedures Efficiently

The dbExpress classes allow you to write to one set of APIs in your application (the dbExpress API) to process a wide variety of SQL and stored procedure implementations. For example, InterBase, Oracle, and DB2 all have different ways of processing stored procedures. Rather than having to write three different implementations, you only need to talk to dbExpress classes that will do the communication for you, and the dbExpress calling interface will always be the same no matter what database engine you're using in your application.

An important feature this capability provides is being able to switch backend database servers in your application with little or no source code changes in your application.

## Make Driver Development Easy and Extensible

The dbExpress drivers are explicitly designed to support ANSI SQL 92 compatible database engines, and use Dynamic SQL as the data processing language for talking to these drivers, which greatly simplifies the task of creating a database driver. However, the dbExpress classes support extensions on the default types, structures, and values that can be used, which leave dbExpress wide open for custom extensions to SQL servers, such as Oracle's abstract data types and specialized stored procedure processing.

## Provide Access to Database Specific Features

Various database engines have features that are of crucial importance to developers who standardize on those databases. For example, InterBase has support for multiple transactions and multiple result sets from stored procedures. Oracle has complex data types. To be successful, a database access engine must provide the capability to use vendor-specific database features. By making the dbExpress drivers extensible, Borland has accomplished this and already provides the crucial vendor-specific features developers need when talking to their favorite databases.

# The Big Picture

The image in Figure 16.1 (stolen from my Kylix seminar slides) represents the architecture of a normal database application with Kylix.

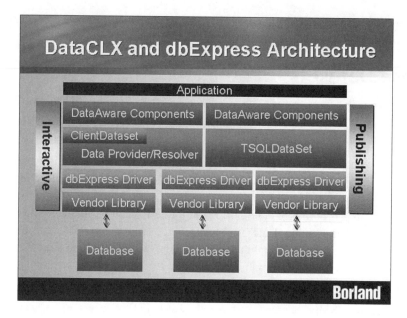

**FIGURE 16.1**

*DataCLX/dbExpress architecture.*

There are two sides to every story, and implementing a database application with Kylix is no exception. For the interactive side, where you want to provide bidirectional scrolling and GUI-client based manipulation of the data by using data-aware components, you would use a `ClientDataSet` to implement a provider/resolver mechanism for retrieving data, tracking the changes to it, and updating the database.

The publishing side might involve generating results from millions of records. Ordinarily, I would recommend writing stored procedures or queries that will allow you to do the bulk of your database processing on the server. However, there are those few cases where you might actually need to manipulate a few million records on the client side (perhaps for publishing to a bunch of pages on a Web site). In this case, you would want to retrieve those records with a `TSQLDataSet` or other unidirectional dataset and publish the data or perform calculations on it in a forward-only fashion.

At the dbExpress driver layer, each separate box indicates a single dbExpress driver. For example, the first could be InterBase, the second Oracle, and the third DB2. The first vendor library would be the InterBase API, the second Oracle's OCI, and the third DB2's CLI. The databases pointed to would be one or more databases of each vendor library.

The dbExpress drivers and vendor libraries are listed in separate boxes because each dbExpress driver works totally independently of any other.

# MyBase Datasets

The `TClientDataset` component uses a datapacket format Borland has dubbed MyBase™. The file format can be expressed both as a binary stream and XML. It is the same format used for Delphi 5's ClientDataSet briefcase files.

The datapacket contains all the information required to have a stateless multi-tier database server. It is a self-contained, self-describing packet that is platform and language independent, making it ideal for cross-platform, cross-language distributed database applications. MyBase datasets come from part of the technology Borland formerly called DataSnapMulti-tier Distributed Application Services (DataSnap) for Delphi 3 (where it was introduced) through 5. For Kylix and future versions of Delphi and C++ Builder, MyBase will be used to refer to the datapacket format, and DataSnap™ will be used to refer to the remote connectivity options that can be used with MyBase datasets.

The initial releases of Kylix (Server Developer and Desktop Developer) do not include the remote connectivity components of DataSnap. Remote connectivity via CORBA, HTTP, TCP/IP, and SOAP will be available in a later Kylix release.

The MyBase dataset contains several distinct pieces that are required to support the features needed to do rich client-side data manipulation while minimizing connectivity to the database server. Let's talk briefly about those features.

## Formats (Binary and XML)

MyBase (`ClientDataSet`) datapackets can be stored in either a binary format or a specialized XML format. Delphi 6 and future releases of Kylix and C++ Builder provide the capability to convert this specialized XML document into any format for which you might have an XML schema or other type of XML Document Object Model definition.

The binary format is, of course, more compact than the verbose text format dictated by XML. For best performance, you should use the binary format when making briefcase files, requesting datapackets from a database, or sending delta packets back to the database. XML will always take extra time to process because the datapacket will need to be parsed, and the datapackets will be larger, in most cases substantially larger than the binary equivalent.

# Metadata

MyBase datasets contain metadata that describes the structure of the data contained in the data-packet. Each MyBase datapacket is required to contain this information because each packet is self-describing to support stateless operation. We'll use a sample MyBase dataset in XML format to illustrate the next few sections. (It was created by using cdsEmployees from the UsingData project in Chapter 15, "Working with Data-Aware Components." You right-click on the component and save it as an XML datapacket.) Although the datapacket is a little long, I think it helps to see the pieces in one place before discussing each individual part; see Listing 16.1.

**LISTING 16.1**  XML Datapacket for cdsEmployees

```
<?xml version="1.0" standalone="yes"?>
<DATAPACKET Version="2.0">
  <METADATA>
    <FIELDS>
      <FIELD attrname="EMP_NO" fieldtype="i2" required="true">
        <PARAM Name="PROVFLAGS" Value="7" Type="i4" Roundtrip="True"/>
      </FIELD>
      <FIELD attrname="FIRST_NAME" fieldtype="string" required="true"
      WIDTH="15"/>
      <FIELD attrname="LAST_NAME" fieldtype="string" required="true"
      WIDTH="20"/>
      <FIELD attrname="PHONE_EXT" fieldtype="string" WIDTH="4"/>
      <FIELD attrname="HIRE_DATE" fieldtype="SQLdateTime"
      required="true"/>
      <FIELD attrname="DEPT_NO" fieldtype="string" required="true"
      SUBTYPE="FixedChar" WIDTH="3"/>
      <FIELD attrname="JOB_CODE" fieldtype="string" required="true"
      WIDTH="5"/>
      <FIELD attrname="JOB_GRADE" fieldtype="i2" required="true"/>
      <FIELD attrname="JOB_COUNTRY" fieldtype="string" required="true"
      WIDTH="15"/>
      <FIELD attrname="SALARY" fieldtype="fixed" required="true" DECIMALS="2"
      WIDTH="15"/>
      <FIELD attrname="sqlEmpProj" fieldtype="nested">
        <FIELDS>
          <FIELD attrname="EMP_NO" fieldtype="i2" required="true">
            <PARAM Name="PROVFLAGS" Value="7" Type="i4" Roundtrip="True"/>
          </FIELD>
          <FIELD attrname="PROJ_ID" fieldtype="string" required="true"
          SUBTYPE="FixedChar" WIDTH="5">
            <PARAM Name="PROVFLAGS" Value="7" Type="i4" Roundtrip="True"/>
          </FIELD>
```

**LISTING 16.1** Continued

```
        </FIELDS>
        <PARAMS PRIMARY_KEY="1 2" LCID="0"/>
      </FIELD>
    </FIELDS>
    <PARAMS MD_FIELDLINKS="11 1 1" DEFAULT_ORDER="1" PRIMARY_KEY="1"
    LCID="0"/>
  </METADATA>
  <ROWDATA>
    <ROW EMP_NO="2" FIRST_NAME="Bob" LAST_NAME="Nelson" PHONE_EXT="250"
    HIRE_DATE="00:00:000019880028" DEPT_NO="600" JOB_CODE="VP"
    JOB_GRADE="2" JOB_COUNTRY="USA" SALARY="105900.00">
      <sqlEmpProj>
      </sqlEmpProj>
    </ROW>
    <ROW EMP_NO="4" FIRST_NAME="Bruce" LAST_NAME="Young" PHONE_EXT="233"
    HIRE_DATE="00:00:000019880028" DEPT_NO="621" JOB_CODE="Eng"
    JOB_GRADE="2" JOB_COUNTRY="USA" SALARY="97500.00">
      <sqlEmpProj>
        <ROWsqlEmpProj EMP_NO="4" PROJ_ID="VBASE"/>
        <ROWsqlEmpProj EMP_NO="4" PROJ_ID="MAPDB"/>
      </sqlEmpProj>
    </ROW>
    ... (many more data rows go here)
  </ROWDATA>
</DATAPACKET>
```

In the METADATA declaration of the datapacket, all the field definitions for the datapacket are defined. You will notice there is actually a nested FIELDS declaration that contains an additional set of field definitions. This is the detail table of the master/detail relationship, contained in a nested field type. In this example, the nested field is called sqlEmpProj. This is important because of the actual row data that gets transferred with the datapacket (as you can see in the ROWDATA section).

Immediately following the definition of the datapacket structure is the actual data from the dataset. The declaration begins with ROWDATA, and then immediately jumps into the definition of the data for each row. You can see that the nested dataset can contain multiple rows in its own section.

You may wonder why it was necessary to declare a field for the nested data rows. Good question! The answer is quite reasonable; you need to name the nested structure because you may have more than one type of nested dataset in your datapacket. For example, you may have items contained inside the project's dataset (perhaps named sqlProjTasks) and a history list of accomplishments for the employee that is another nested dataset for the employee table itself (perhaps named sqlEmpAccomp).

As you can readily see, you can quickly produce a very large datapacket by having multiple levels of master/detail relationships. If you design your client interface so only one customer record is retrieved at a time, having multiple nested datasets may result in a highly usable interface. If your client interface allows multiple customer records to be retrieved at once, and they contain a number of orders, and these orders contain a number of items, your datapacket is going to become large; as a result, the person using the client application may have to wait a little while for the datapacket to load and be displayed. You may want to use the PacketRecords property of the ClientDataSet to provide a partial view of the data in your application and fetch additional records on demand.

## Constraints

In the sample datapacket in Listing 16.1, the following element definition

```
<FIELD attrname="SALARY" fieldtype="fixed" required="true"
  DECIMALS="2" WIDTH="15"/>
```

contains some data constraints, like specifying that this field must be assigned a value (required="true"), it has two decimal points, and its overall data width is 15 characters. If you look through the datapacket, you can see additional examples, as well.

## Data

The ROWDATA section in Listing 16.1 contains the data values for the rows in the dataset. The data in these rows must conform to that defined in the METADATA section.

## Field Types

Various field types are defined in this datapacket example, such as integer, string, datetime, floating point, and nested dataset fields. Any field type Kylix supports can be contained in the datapackets processed by ClientDataSets, including the abstract data types you would find in Oracle.

## Special Fields

As mentioned in Chapter 15, you can also have special field types like calculate, internally calculated, lookup, and aggregate fields in your ClientDataSet.

### Nested Data Sets

In Listing 16.1, sqlEmpProj is a nested dataset. This is a special field type that actually contains multiple rows of an additional dataset. This data is retrieved by the provider based on the master/detail relationships defined with multiple datasets and datasources. See Chapter 15 for examples. This data is populated for each master record and attached as a nested dataset as part of that master record's data. This provides great encapsulation of information for a specific master record.

## Deltas

The delta packet contains all the information needed to update the SQL database engine in a stateless fashion. In other words, the datapacket and client are stateful, maintaining all the information the server will require to update the data for any specific record currently on the server. Let's consider the following delta packet:

```
<DATAPACKET Version="2.0" >
  <METADATA>
    <FIELDS>
      <FIELD attrname="CustNo" fieldtype="r8" />
      <FIELD attrname="Company" fieldtype="string" WIDTH="30" />
      <FIELD attrname="Addr1" fieldtype="string" WIDTH="30" />
      <FIELD attrname="Addr2" fieldtype="string" WIDTH="30" />
      <FIELD attrname="City" fieldtype="string" WIDTH="15" />
      <FIELD attrname="State" fieldtype="string" WIDTH="20" />
      <FIELD attrname="Zip" fieldtype="string" WIDTH="10" />
      <FIELD attrname="Country" fieldtype="string" WIDTH="20" />
      <FIELD attrname="Phone" fieldtype="string" WIDTH="15" />
      <FIELD attrname="FAX" fieldtype="string" WIDTH="15" />
      <FIELD attrname="TaxRate" fieldtype="r8" />
      <FIELD attrname="Contact" fieldtype="string" WIDTH="20" />
      <FIELD attrname="LastInvoiceDate" fieldtype="dateTime" />
      <FIELD attrname="CustOrderTable" fieldtype="nested" >
        <FIELDS>
          <FIELD attrname="OrderNo" fieldtype="r8" />
          <FIELD attrname="CustNo" fieldtype="r8" required="true" />
          <FIELD attrname="SaleDate" fieldtype="dateTime" />
          <FIELD attrname="ShipDate" fieldtype="dateTime" />
          <FIELD attrname="EmpNo" fieldtype="i4" required="true" />
          <FIELD attrname="ShipToContact" fieldtype="string" WIDTH="20" />
          <FIELD attrname="ShipToAddr1" fieldtype="string" WIDTH="30" />
          <FIELD attrname="ShipToAddr2" fieldtype="string" WIDTH="30" />
          <FIELD attrname="ShipToCity" fieldtype="string" WIDTH="15" />
          <FIELD attrname="ShipToState" fieldtype="string" WIDTH="20" />
          <FIELD attrname="ShipToZip" fieldtype="string" WIDTH="10" />
          <FIELD attrname="ShipToCountry" fieldtype="string" WIDTH="20" />
          <FIELD attrname="ShipToPhone" fieldtype="string" WIDTH="15" />
          <FIELD attrname="ShipVIA" fieldtype="string" WIDTH="7" />
          <FIELD attrname="PO" fieldtype="string" WIDTH="15" />
```

```
        <FIELD attrname="Terms" fieldtype="string" WIDTH="6" />
        <FIELD attrname="PaymentMethod" fieldtype="string" WIDTH="7" />
        <FIELD attrname="ItemsTotal" fieldtype="r8" SUBTYPE="Money" />
        <FIELD attrname="TaxRate" fieldtype="r8" />
        <FIELD attrname="Freight" fieldtype="r8" SUBTYPE="Money" />
        <FIELD attrname="AmountPaid" fieldtype="r8" SUBTYPE="Money" />
      </FIELDS>
      <PARAMS DEFAULT_ORDER="2" PRIMARY_KEY="1" LCID="1033" />
    </FIELD>
  </FIELDS>
  <PARAMS MD_FIELDLINKS="14 1 2" LCID="1033" DATASET_DELTA="1"/>
</METADATA>
<ROWDATA>
  <ROW CustNo="9841" Company="Neptune's Trident Supply" Addr1="PO Box 129"
  City="Negril" State="Jamaica" Country="West Indies" Phone="778-897-3546"
  FAX="778-897-6643" TaxRate="0" Contact="Louise Franks"
  LastInvoiceDate="19951101T06:32:05000" RowState="1" >
    <CustOrderTable/>
  </ROW>
  <ROW Addr1="PO Box 129-A" RowState="8" >
    <CustOrderTable/>
  </ROW>
  <ROW CustNo="9841" Company="Neptune's Trident Supply"
  Addr1="PO Box 129-A" City="Negril" State="Jamaica" Country="West Indies"
  Phone="778-897-3546" FAX="778-897-6643" TaxRate="0"
  Contact="Louise Franks" LastInvoiceDate="19951101T06:32:05000"
  RowState="64" >
    <CustOrderTable>
      <ROWCustOrderTable OrderNo="1045" CustNo="9841" SaleDate="19881016"
      ShipDate="19881017" EmpNo="36" ShipVIA="FedEx" Terms="FOB"
      PaymentMethod="Credit" ItemsTotal="787.8" TaxRate="0" Freight="0"
      AmountPaid="787.8" RowState="1" />
      <ROWCustOrderTable AmountPaid="799.9" RowState="8" />
    </CustOrderTable>
  </ROW>
  <ROW CustNo="9841" Company="Neptune's Trident Supply"
  Addr1="PO Box 129-A"
  City="Negril" State="Jamaica" Country="West Indies" Phone="778-897-3546"
  FAX="778-897-6643" TaxRate="0" Contact="Louise Franks"
  LastInvoiceDate="19951101T06:32:05000" RowState="64" >
    <CustOrderTable>
      <ROWCustOrderTable OrderNo="1145" CustNo="9841" SaleDate="19940117"
      ShipDate="19940117" EmpNo="144" ShipVIA="FedEx" Terms="FOB"
      PaymentMethod="Credit" ItemsTotal="4229.8" TaxRate="0" Freight="0"
      AmountPaid="4229.8" RowState="1" />
      <ROWCustOrderTable AmountPaid="4229.84" RowState="8" />
```

```
    </CustOrderTable>
   </ROW>
  </ROWDATA>
</DATAPACKET>
```

The METADATA section is actually identical to the datapacket in Listing 16.1, except for the additional parameter DATASET_DELTA = "1" in the second PARAMS section of the metadata. This value indicates that this is a delta packet. Some additional rows of data follow the metadata. These rows identify the changes made to the data since it was originally sent to the client by the server. Table 16.1 describes the changes we made to the data so you can see how the delta packet retains only the information needed for the resolver to correctly handle conflict resolutions while still providing the information needed to make the data changes.

**TABLE 16.1** Delta Packet Data Changes

| Change | Data Row | Field | Original Value | New Value |
|--------|----------|-------|----------------|-----------|
| 1 | CustNo 9841 | Addr1 | PO Box 129 | PO Box 129-A |
| 2 | Order 1045 for CustNo 9841 | AmountPaid | 787.8 | 799.9 |
| 3 | Order 1145 for CustNo 9841 | AmountPaid | 4229.8 | 4229.84 |

For every change to a data row, the original contents of the row are passed back to the server for two reasons. First, if a primary key is not available for that row, the row will be matched based on all these values. Second, it makes graceful conflict resolution possible. For example, you may have grabbed a set of data from the server in the morning, and made changes to it over the course of a day. While you were making the changes, someone else also updated one of the same records on the server, so your original record is out of date. If your original row is not passed back to the server, it is difficult to determine the origin of the conflicts in the data.

## Return to Sender

By passing back the original contents of the row you received to the server, an intelligent dialog box can automatically be provided to the user by hooking up a TReconcilePageProducer component to your XML Broker. This dialog box shows

- The data currently on the server
- The data you originally retrieved
- The changes you made to your original data

You can then choose what to do with each specific conflict, either leaving it alone, applying your modifications, editing it, and so forth.

The second part of the packet for the data row is the actual change to the data. In this section, only the changed fields are listed, along with a RowState flag indicating what to do with the values in that row. If multiple fields are changed for the same record, they will be listed in this section of the datapacket.

Table 16.2 lists the RowState values and what they mean.

**TABLE 16.2**   RowState Definitions

| RowState *Value* | *Meaning* |
| --- | --- |
| 1 | Original record |
| 2 | Deleted record |
| 4 | Inserted record |
| 8 | Updated record |
| 64 | Detail updates |

Also, notice that the value of the datapacket for the customer row changes after the first delta data row because the data will have been changed by then.

# Database Connectivity

Now that we've covered the provider/resolver mechanism in TClientDataSet, we will start talking in more detail about dbExpress, which provides the actual SQL database connectivity with Kylix. However, before we get into that in more detail, I'd like to make a quick digression for those Delphi or C++ Builder developers who are familiar with the BDE and compare dbExpress to the BDE.

## dbExpress Versus BDE

dbExpress is capable of processing queries and stored procedures like the Borland Database Engine (BDE). BDE is a feature-rich, bulkier client whereas dbExpress is simpler, easy to implement, and best suits the DataSnap provider and resolver model.

Database intensive applications should use queries or stored procedures to get to the data. Opening tables through BDE not only consumes client resources but also locks up server resources. dbExpress eliminates the concept of opening tables, and clients are recommended to use SQL queries with better selectivity for optimized data-access.

Unlike the BDE, dbExpress returns only unidirectional cursors and therefore does no caching. The DataSnap ClientDataSet can be used for caching, and scrolling, indexing, and filtering on the result set.

The BDE caches metadata so that they can be readily available for future requests. dbExpress does no metadata caching, and the design time metadata access interface is implemented using the core data-access interface.

The BDE's runtime performance with SQL databases is affected by the internal query generation for navigation, blob access, and metadata retrieval. dbExpress executes only queries requested by the user, thereby optimizing database access by not introducing any extra queries.

dbExpress manages a record buffer or a block of record buffers internally, and provides clients with individual field values. BDE on the other hand uses a client-allocated record buffer and this may be error-prone as the client might pass an insufficient or a corrupted record buffer.

Among the other differences from the BDE, dbExpress has no concept of live queries, cached updates, schema creation support, heterogeneous query processing, batch-move, and so on.

dbExpress also addresses the following issues we currently have with the BDE:

- Complexity involved with BDE configuration, BDE deployment, and adapting to a new data source.
- Runtime resource overheads from caching blobs and metadata, and loading BDE configuration.
- Performance.

## dbExpress Abstraction

The four core classes in dbExpress are SQLDriver, SQLConnection, SQLCommand, and SQLCursor. SQLMetaData is the metadata access interface that's built on the core classes. All of the classes have methods to set and get runtime properties that clients can use to take advantage of database specific features or fine tune data access.

Some of the benefits of dbExpress over previous data access driver technology Borland supported are

- Support for multiple transactions (with Oracle 8i and InterBase).
- Support for stored procedures returning cursors.
- Support for BLOB output parameters in stored procedures.
- Support for static linking database applications into a standalone exe.

- No internal 64K limit on the record buffer.
- Support for abstract types in SQL and stored procedures (Oracle 8i only).
- Support for IN/OUT parameters in SQL using RETURNING clause (Oracle 8i only).
- Support for unidirectional cursors with no caching.
- Better performance and less resource usage.
- No limitation on the number of client application instances, only limited by the system resources and any restriction on the underlying vendor client library.
- As long as the vendor client is thread safe, dbExpress drivers will be thread safe.

## SQLDriver

SQLDriver does database-specific initialization like loading the vendor client, initializing the environment and allocating necessary handles and gets a SQLConnection object. Listing 16.2 is the declaration for the SQLDriver object.

**LISTING 16.2** SQLDriver Declaration

```
abstract COMINTF SQLDriver
{
   virtual INT32 GCCSTDC QueryInterface( GUID riid, ppVOID ppv ) = 0;
   virtual UINT32 GCCSTDC AddRef( ) = 0;
   //Destructs the SQLDriver object
   virtual UINT32 GCCSTDC Release( ) = 0;
   //Gets a new SQLConnection object
   virtual SQLResult GCCSTDC getSQLConnection (
      ppSQLConnection ppConn) = 0;
   //Set/Get options for database driver level properties
   virtual SQLResult GCCSTDC setOption (
      eSQLDriverOption  eDOption,
      INT32             lValue )  = 0;
   virtual SQLResult GCCSTDC getOption (
      eSQLDriverOption  eDOption,
      pINT32            plValue,
      INT16             iMaxLength,
      pINT16            piLength )  = 0;

};
```

## SQLConnection

SQLConnection implementation takes care of establishing a connection to a database, gets a SQLCommand object for query and stored procedure processing, gets a SQLMetaData object for metadata retrieval and handles transactions. Listing 16.3 shows the declaration for SQLConnection.

**LISTING 16.3** SQLConnection Declaration

```
abstract COMINTF SQLConnection
{

    virtual INT32 GCCSTDC QueryInterface( GUID riid,  ppVOID ppv ) = 0;
    virtual UINT32 GCCSTDC AddRef( ) = 0;
    //Destructs the SQLConnection object
    virtual UINT32 GCCSTDC Release( ) = 0;

    //Attach to a database server
    virtual SQLResult GCCSTDC connect (
       pCHAR pszServerName,
       pCHAR pszUserName,
       pCHAR pszPassword ) = 0;

    //Detach from a database server
    virtual SQLResult GCCSTDC disconnect () = 0;

    //Destructs the SQLConnection object

    //Gets a new SQLCommand object
    virtual SQLResult GCCSTDC getSQLCommand (
       pp3QLCommand ppComm) = 0;

    //Gets a new SQLMetaData object
    virtual SQLResult GCCSTDC getSQLMetaData (
       ppSQLMetaData ppMeta) = 0;

    //Set/Get options for database connection level properties
    virtual SQLResult GCCSTDC setOption (
       eSQLConnectOption eCOption,
       INT32             lValue ) = 0;

    virtual SQLResult GCCSTDC getOption (
       eSQLConnectOption eCOption,
       pINT32            plValue,
       INT16             iMaxLength,
       pINT16            piLength ) = 0;

    //Transaction support
    virtual SQLResult GCCSTDC beginTransaction(
       UINT32 ulTrasnID );
```

**LISTING 16.3**   Continued

```
virtual SQLResult GCCSTDC commit(
   UINT32 ulTrasnID );

virtual SQLResult GCCSTDC rollback(
   UINT32 ulTrasnID );

//Error handling
virtual SQLResult GCCSTDC getErrorMessage (
   pBYTE pszError ) = 0;

virtual SQLResult GCCSTDC getErrorMessageLen (
   pUINT16 puErrorLen ) = 0;

};
```

## SQLCommand

SQLCommand provides methods for processing a query or a stored procedure and returns a
SQLCursor object if available. It also supports executing a prepared query multiple times with
parameter binding, and returning multiple cursors from a stored procedure. Listing 16.4 shown
its declaration.

**LISTING 16.4**   SQLCommand Declaration

```
abstract COMINTF SQLCommand
{
   virtual INT32  GCCSTDC QueryInterface( GUID riid, ppVOID ppv ) = 0;
   virtual UINT32 GCCSTDC AddRef( ) = 0;
   //Destructs the SQLCommand object
   virtual UINT32 GCCSTDC Release( ) = 0;

   //Set/Get options for command level properties
   virtual SQLResult GCCSTDC setOption (
      eSQLCommandOption eSOption,
      INT32             lValue ) = 0;

   virtual SQLResult GCCSTDC getOption (
      eSQLCommandOption eSOption,
      pINT32            plValue,
      INT16             iMaxLength,
      pINT16            piLength )  = 0;

   //Set/Get methods for parameter binding support
   virtual SQLResult GCCSTDC setParameter (
```

**LISTING 16.4**   Continued

```cpp
        UINT16      uParameterNumber,
        STMTParamType ePType,
        UINT16      uLogType,
        UINT16      uSubType,
        INT32       lMaxPrecision,
        INT32       lMaxScale,
        UINT32      ulLength,
        pVOID       pBuffer,
        BOOL        bIsNull ) = 0;

    virtual SQLResult GCCSTDC getParameter (
        UINT16  uParameterNumber,
        pVOID   pData,
        UINT32  ulLength,
        pINT32  plInd ) = 0;

    //Prepare and cxecute SQL and stored procedure
    virtual SQLResult GCCSTDC prepare (
        pCHAR pszSQL ) = 0;

    virtual SQLResult GCCSTDC execute (
      ppSQLCursor ppCur) = 0;

    //Direct execution of query or stored procedure or DDL
    //No parsing will be done
    virtual SQLResult GCCSTDC executeImmediate (
        pCHAR pszSQL,
        ppSQLCursor ppCur) = 0;

    //A new SQLCursor object will be returned if there is another result set
    //available from a stored procedure execution
    virtual SQLResult GCCSTDC  getNextCursor (
        ppSQLCursor ppCur);

    //Number of rows affected as a result of INSERT/DELETE/UPDATE
    virtual SQLResult GCCSTDC getRowsAffected (
        pINT32 plRows) = 0;

    //Free resources used for parameter binding
    virtual SQLResult GCCSTDC close () = 0;

    //Error handling
    virtual SQLResult GCCSTDC getErrorMessage (
        pBYTE pszError ) = 0;
```

**LISTING 16.4**   Continued

```
virtual SQLResult GCCSTDC getErrorMessageLen (
   pUINT16 puErrorLen ) = 0;

};
```

## SQLCursor

SQLCursor holds data and metadata with respect to the executed query or stored procedure and has methods to get individual field values. Listing 16.5 is the declaration for SQLCursor.

**LISTING 16.5**   SQLCursor Declaration

```
abstract COMINTF SQLCursor
{
   virtual INT32  GCCSTDC  QueryInterface( GUID riid, ppVOID ppv ) = 0;
   virtual UINT32 GCCSTDC  AddRef( ) = 0;
   //Destructs the SQLCursor object
   virtual UINT32 GCCSTDC  Release( ) = 0;

   //Error handling
   virtual SQLResult GCCSTDC getErrorMessage (
      pBYTE pszError );

   virtual SQLResult GCCSTDC getErrorMessageLen (
      pUINT16 puErrorLen );

   //Metadata access methods
   virtual SQLResult GCCSTDC getColumnCount (pUINT16 puColumns) = 0;

   virtual SQLResult GCCSTDC getColumnNameLength (
      UINT16   uColumnNumber,
      pUINT16 puLen ) = 0;

   virtual SQLResult GCCSTDC getColumnName (
      UINT16  uColumnNumber,
      pCHAR   pColumnName) = 0;

   virtual SQLResult GCCSTDC getColumnType (
      UINT16   uColumnNumber,
      pUINT16 puType,
      pUINT16 puSubType ) = 0;

   virtual SQLResult GCCSTDC getColumnLength (
      UINT16   uColumnNumber,
      pUINT32 pulLength ) = 0;
```

**LISTING 16.5**  Continued

```
virtual SQLResult GCCSTDC getColumnPrecision (
    UINT16 uColumnNumber,
    pINT16 piPrecision ) = 0;

  virtual SQLResult GCCSTDC getColumnScale (
     UINT16 uColumnNumber,
     pINT16 piScale ) = 0;

  virtual SQLResult GCCSTDC isNullable (
     UINT16 uColumnNumber,
     pBOOL  pbNullable ) = 0;

  virtual SQLResult GCCSTDC  isAutoIncrement (
     UINT16 uColumnNumber,
     pBOOL  pbAutoIncr ) = 0;

  virtual SQLResult GCCSTDC isReadOnly (
     UINT16 uColumnNumber,
     pBOOL  pbReadOnly ) = 0;

  virtual SQLResult GCCSTDC isSearchable(
     UINT16 uColumnNumber,
     pBOOL  pbSearchable ) = 0;

  virtual SQLResult GCCSTDC isBlobSizeExact(
     UINT16 uColumnNumber,
     pBOOL  pbBlobExactSize );

  //Fetch the next record or the next set of records
  virtual SQLResult GCCSTDC  next() = 0;

  //Data access methods
  virtual SQLResult GCCSTDC getString (
     UINT16 uColumnNumber,
     pCHAR  pData,
     pBOOL  pbIsNull );

  virtual SQLResult GCCSTDC getShort (
     UINT16 uColumnNumber,
     pINT16 pData,
     pBOOL  pbIsNull );

  virtual SQLResult GCCSTDC getLong (
     UINT16 uColumnNumber,
```

**16**

**LISTING 16.5**   Continued

```
      pINT32 pData,
      pBOOL  pbIsNull );

  virtual SQLResult GCCSTDC getDouble (
     UINT16 uColumnNumber,
     pDFLOAT  pData,
     pBOOL  pbIsNull );

  virtual SQLResult GCCSTDC getBcd (
     UINT16 uColumnNumber,
     pFMTBcd  pData,
     pBOOL  pbIsNull );

  virtual SQLResult GCCSTDC getTimeStamp (
     UINT16           uColumnNumber,
     pSQLLTIMESTAMP  pData,
     pBOOL            pbIsNull );

  virtual SQLResult GCCSTDC getTime (
     UINT16      uColumnNumber,
     pINT32      pData,
     pBOOL       pbIsNull );

  virtual SQLResult GCCSTDC getDate (
     UINT16      uColumnNumber,
     pINT32      pData,
     pBOOL       pbIsNull );

  virtual SQLResult GCCSTDC getBytes (
     UINT16      uColumnNumber,
     pBYTE       pData,
     pBOOL       pbIsNull );

  virtual SQLResult GCCSTDC getBlobSize (
     UINT16  uColumnNumber,
     pUINT32 pulLength,
     pBOOL   bIsNull );

  virtual SQLResult GCCSTDC getBlob (
     UINT16 uColumnNumber,
     pVOID  pData,
     pBOOL  bIsNull,
     UINT32 ulLength );

};
```

## SQLMetaData

The SQLMetaData interface defines the various database metadata that can be obtained on an opened database connection. The getSQLMetaData() method from a SQLConnection object will return a SQLMetaData object. SQLMetaData provides only the metadata needed by DataSnap, Kylix, Delphi, and C++ Builder data-access components. There are numerous other database metadata properties skipped to make the implementation simpler. However, most of these can be surfaced using get and set options on the SQLMetaData object and without changing the interface. Listing 16.6 is the declaration interface definesfor the SQLMetaData class.

**LISTING 16.6** SQLMetaData Declaration

```
abstract COMINTF SQLMetaData
{
    virtual INT32 GCCSTDC  QueryInterface( GUID riid, ppVOID ppv ) = 0;
    virtual UINT32 GCCSTDC AddRef( ) = 0;
    //Destructs the SQLMetaData object
    virtual UINT32 GCCSTDC Release( ) = 0;

    //Set/Get options for database metadata properties
    virtual SQLResult GCCSTDC  setOption (
        eSQLMetaDataOption  eMOption,
        INT32               lValue ) = 0;

    virtual SQLResult GCCSTDC  getOption (
        eSQLMetaDataOption  eDOption,
        pINT32              plValue,
        INT16               iMaxLength,
        pINT16              piLength ) = 0;

    //Get Object list
    virtual SQLResult GCCSTDC  getObjectList (
        eSQLObjectType eObjType,
        ppSQLCursor    ppCur) = 0;

    //Get Table list
    virtual SQLResult  GCCSTDC  getTables (
        pCHAR pszTableName,
        UINT32 uTableType,
        ppSQLCursor ppCur) = 0;

    //Get Procedure list
    virtual SQLResult GCCSTDC  getProcedures (
        pCHAR pszProcName,
        UINT32 uProcType,
        ppSQLCursor ppCur) = 0;
```

**LISTING 16.6** Continued

```
//Get Column metadata for a given table
virtual SQLResult  GCCSTDC  getColumns (
   pCHAR pszTableName,
   pCHAR pszColumnName,
   UINT32 uColType,
   ppSQLCursor ppCur) = 0;

//Get Parameter metadata for a given Stored Procedure
virtual SQLResult  GCCSTDC getProcedureParams (
   pCHAR pszProcName,
   pCHAR pszParamName,
   ppSQLCursor ppCur) = 0;

//Get Index info associated with a given table
virtual SQLResult GCCSTDC  getIndices (
   pCHAR pszTableName,
   UINT32 uIndexType,
   ppSQLCursor ppCur) = 0;

//Error handling
virtual SQLResult GCCSTDC getErrorMessage (
   pBYTE pszError );
virtual SQLResult GCCSTDC getErrorMessageLen (
   pUINT16 puErrorLen );

}; interface defines
```

### SQLMetaData Methods

For all of the methods described in the following sections, a search pattern can be specified for catalog name and schema name by setting the eMetaCatalogName and eMetaSchemaName properties by calling setOption().

### *Search Pattern*

A search pattern can be specified to constrain results returned from the following methods and can contain the following characters, based on the standard SQL wildcard characters:

- An underscore (_) represents any single character.

- A percentage (%) represents a sequence of one or more character.

- An escape character, when preceded to the underscore or the percentage characters allows them to be used as literal characters in search patterns.

- A sequence of two escape characters will allow the escape character to be used as a literal character in search patterns.

Database-specific escape characters can be obtained from a SQLMetaData object by calling getOption(eMetaSQLEscapeChar).

### getObjectList()

```
getObjectList(
  eSQLObjectType eObjType,
  ppSQLCursor ppCur)
```

Given an eSQLObjectType, this method returns a SQLCursor with a list of available objects in the database.

Columns in the returned cursor are

| Column | Type |
|---|---|
| 1.RECNO | fldINT32 |
| 2.CATALOG_NAME | fldZSTRING |
| 3.SCHEMA_NAME | fldZSTRING |
| 4.OBJECT_NAME | fldZSTRING |

Cursor columns are ordered by the object name (OBJECT_NAME).

### getTables()

```
getTables(
  pCHAR pszTableNamePattern,
  UINT32 uTableType,
  ppSQLCursor ppCur)
```

Given an eSQLTableType, this method returns a SQLCursor with a list of tables or views or synonyms, and so on, in the database. One or more eSQLTableType can be ORed and passed in uTableType to get a list of more than one table type. A search pattern for the table name can also be specified in the first argument. If it is NULL, no criteria will be used in the search.

Columns in the returned cursor are

| Column | Type |
|---|---|
| 1.RECNO | fldINT32 |
| 2.CATALOG_NAME | fldZSTRING |
| 3.SCHEMA_NAME | fldZSTRING |
| 4.TABLE_NAME | fldZSTRING |
| 5.TABLE_TYPE | fldINT32 |

Cursor columns are ordered by the table name (TABLE_NAME).

**getProcedure()**
```
getProcedures (
  pCHAR pszProcNamePattern,
  UINT32 uProcType,
  ppSQLCursor ppCur)
```

Given an eSQLProcType, this method returns a SQLCursor with a list of procedures, functions, and so on in the database. One or more eSQLProcType can be ORed and passed in uProcType to get a list of more than one stored procedure type. A search pattern for the procedure name can also be specified in the first argument. If it's NULL, no criteria will be used in the search.

Columns in the returned cursor are

| Column | Type |
| --- | --- |
| 1.RECNO | fldINT32 |
| 2.CATALOG_NAME | fldZSTRING |
| 3.SCHEMA_NAME | fldZSTRING |
| 4.PROC_NAME | fldZSTRING |
| 5.PROC_TYPE | fldINT32 |
| 6.IN_PARAMS | fldINT16 |
| 7.OUT_PARAMS | fldINT16 |

Cursor columns are ordered by the procedure name (PROC_NAME).

**getColumns()**
```
getColumns (
  pCHAR pszTableName,
  pCHAR pszColumnNamePattern,
  UINT32 uColType,
  ppSQLCursor ppCur)
```

Given a table name, this method returns a SQLCursor with a list of columns in the table. A search pattern to filter certain column names can also be specified in the second parameter. One or more eSQLColType can be ORed and passed in uColType to get a list of more than one specific column types like RowId.

Columns in the returned cursor are

| Column | Type |
|--------|------|
| 1.RECNO | fldINT32 |
| 2.CATALOG_NAME | fldZSTRING |
| 3.SCHEMA_NAME | fldZSTRING |
| 4.TABLE_NAME | fldZSTRING |
| 5.COLUMN_NAME | fldZSTRING |
| 6.COLUMN_POSITION | fldINT16 |
| 7.COLUMN_TYPE | fldINT32 |
| 8.COLUMN_DATATYPE | fldINT16 |
| 9.COLUMN_TYPENAME | fldZSTRING |
| 10.COLUMN_SUBTYPE | fldINT16 |
| 11.COLUMN_PRECISION | fldINT32 |
| 12.COLUMN_SCALE | fldINT16 |
| 13.COLUMN_LENGTH | fldINT32 |
| 14.COLUMN_NULLABLE | fldINT16 |

Cursor columns are ordered by the procedure name (COLUMN_NAME).

**getProcedureParams()**
```
getProcedureParams (
  pCHAR pszProcName,
  pCHAR pszParamName,
  ppSQLCursor ppCur)
```

Given a procedure name, this method returns a SQLCursor with a list of parameters needed to call the procedure. A search pattern to filter certain parameter names can also be specified in the second parameter.

Columns in the returned cursor are

| Column | Type |
|--------|------|
| 1.RECNO | fldINT32 |
| 2.CATALOG_NAME | fldZSTRING |
| 3.SCHEMA_NAME | fldZSTRING |
| 4.PROC_NAME | fldZSTRING |
| 5.PARAM_NAME | fldZSTRING |
| 6.PARAM_TYPE | fldINT16 |

| Column | Type |
|--------|------|
| 7. PARAM_DATATYPE | fldINT16 |
| 8. PARAM_SUBTYPE | fldINT16 |
| 9. PARAM_TYPENAME | fldZSTRING |
| 10. PARAM_PRECISION | fldINT32 |
| 11. PARAM_SCALE | fldINT16 |
| 12. PARAM_LENGTH | fldINT32 |
| 13. PARAM_NULLABLE | fldINT16 |

Cursor columns are ordered by the procedure name (PARAM_NAME).

**getIndices()**

```
getIndices (
  pCHAR pszTableName,
  UINT32 uIndexType,
  ppSQLCursor ppCur)
```

Given a table name, this method returns a SQLCursor with a list of index columns in the table. One or more eSQLIndexType can be ORed and passed in uIndexType to get metadata about more than one specific index types like Unique.

Columns in the returned cursor are

| Column | Type |
|--------|------|
| 1. RECNO | fldINT32 |
| 2. CATALOG_NAME | fldZSTRING |
| 3. SCHEMA_NAME | fldZSTRING |
| 4. TABLE_NAME | fldZSTRING |
| 5. INDEX_NAME | fldZSTRING |
| 6. PKEY_NAME | fldZSTRING |
| 7. COLUMN_NAME | fldZSTRING |
| 8. COLUMN_POSITION | fldINT16 |
| 9. INDEX_TYPE | fldINT16 |
| 10. SORT_ORDER | fldZSTRING |
| 11. FILTER | fldZSTRING |

Cursor columns are ordered by the procedure name (INDEX_NAME).

New methods can be added to SQLMetaData to return metadata about table and column privileges, available SQL functions and SQL keywords, referential integrity constraints, and so on.

## Data Type Mapping

Data sources represent data in various formats and a common interface like dbExpress should provide a set of generic data types to get individual field values. dbExpress defines a set of logical data types that will surface most of the SQL data types supported by various databases. These logical data types match the ones in BDE for compatibility and also for existing applications to adapt them easily.

However, the mapping from SQL to logical data type may not be the same as in BDE. For example, a new `fldDATETIME` is introduced to represent timestamp data without any data loss. Similarly, numeric data that can't fit in a double are directly mapped into BCD eliminating the need for enabling or disabling BCD. Even though there is a translation between SQL to logical types and vice versa, the performance impact is negligible.

Internally, dbExpress maps database-specific SQL types into database specific physical data types and one or more physical data type maps into a logical data type. Unlike the BDE, dbExpress will not expose the physical data types to the clients; however, with the current frame work database driver developers can choose to return physical data types as well.

On top of the core interface, application developers can create a layer for caching and thereby provide forward and backward scrolling on the result set. Database connections are sometimes very expensive, so a layer for connection pooling can be built. Interfaces for schema creation, import and export data across data sources and all other data-access needs can also be built easily. However, it is very important to have the core runtime data-access layer thin and simpler to provide a high performance database connectivity and for easily adapting to new data sources.

## dbExpress Driver Development

This information is based on a document provided by Ramesh Theivendran, dbExpress Architect.

Database connectivity plays a vital role in almost every business application. Some applications access database extensively (for example; a report writing application) and some sparingly. If you look at the connectivity needs of these applications, they all execute SQL to get data and metadata. Dynamic SQL processing is what database applications need the most. Dynamic SQL allows your application to process any valid SQL statement at runtime. Most database vendor client libraries provide interfaces for dynamic SQL processing like OCI or PRO *C (Dynamic Method 4) for Oracle, CLI for DB2 and other ODBC data sources, CTLIB for Sybase, and E/SQL for Informix.

The various features currently provided by existing database connectivity standards like BDE, ODBC, and JDBC can be broadly classified into three main categories: data access (which includes browsing, bookmarks, and so on), metadata retrieval, and schema creation. Of this the most basic feature a database connectivity standard should provide is an interface to process dynamic SQL. After the basic dynamic SQL processing layer is built, metadata retrieval and schema creation can be easily built on top.

dbExpress is a cross-platform, database-independent and an extensible interface for dynamic SQL processing. dbExpress core interfaces include SQLDriver, SQLConnection, SQLCommand and SQLCursor.

## Understanding the Database Vendor Client

A good understanding of the RDBMS vendor client library is important to provide an efficient connectivity to the underlying database. Database vendors provide precompilers or low-level calls for client to server interaction. Precompilers generate data structures and low level calls to replace the embedded SQL statements in your application. The precompiled sources can then be compiled with any standard compiler.

Depending upon the functionality the precompiler or the low-level calls provide, you could choose one of them to write your own dbExpress driver. While making this decision, make sure you will be able to process dynamic SQL, support all data types including blobs, and also make use of the database-specific features. Some precompilers even allow you to have both embedded SQL statements and low-level calls in your application (for example; Oracle PRO*C and OCI). Now let's look into the basic steps for dynamic SQL processing. Because some readers may be familiar with X/OPEN CAE specification, and for simplicity, I have used the DB2 CLI calls in the code snippets.

## Initializing the Environment

Most database vendor clients have to initialize certain handles before the client can connect to the database server. Usually these initializations involve allocating client resources such as the SQLCA (SQL communications area) and other descriptors for end-to-end communication with the server. DB2 CLI requires an environment handle and a connection handle to be initialized before establishing a database connection. The following code shows how this can be accomplished:

```
SQLHANDLE henv, hdbc;
SQLRETCODE rc;
/* allocate an environment handle */
rc = SQLAllocHandle( SQL_HANDLE_ENV, SQL_NULL_HANDLE, &henv );
/* allocate a connection handle */
if ( SQLAllocHandle( SQL_HANDLE_DBC, henv, hdbc ) != SQL_SUCCESS )
```

```
{
  printf( "ERROR while allocating a connection handle-----n" ) ;
  return SQL_ERROR;
}
```

## Connecting to the Database Server

After the required handles are allocated, a connection can be established by specifying a server, username, and password. You can also set and get certain pre-connect and post-connect properties with the connection handle like autocommit on/off, connection time out (pre-connect set property), and database version info (post-connect get property):

```
/* Set AUTOCOMMIT OFF */
rc = SQLSetConnectAttr( hdbc, SQL_ATTR_AUTOCOMMIT,
  (void *) SQL_AUTOCOMMIT_OFF, SQL_NTS);
if ( SQLConnect( hdbc, Server, SQL_NTS, UserName, SQL_NTS, Password, SQL_NTS)
  != SQL_SUCCESS )
  {
    printf( "ERROR while connecting to %s ------n",Server ) ;
    return SQL_ERROR;
  }
```

## Initializing Statement Handles

A statement handle for a connection must be allocated before any SQL statement can be processed. Most databases allow you to have more than one active statement per connection. On servers that don't, you may have to establish a separate connection to process multiple SQL statements simultaneously. You can also set and get statement level properties with a statement handle:

```
#define ROWSET_SIZE 20
SQLHANDLE hstmt;
rc =SQLAllocHandle( SQL_HANDLE_STMT, hdbc, &hstmt ) ;
/* Set BLOCK FETCH SIZE */
rc = SQLSetStmtAttr( hstmt, SQL_ATTR_ROW_ARRAY_SIZE, (SQLPOINTER) ROWSET_SIZE,
➥0);
```

## Preparing a SQL Statement

Prepare on most servers validates a SQL statement and creates an execution plan. On subsequent execution, the server makes use of the same execution plan. This improves performance and it's recommended to prepare once and execute multiple times if you are processing the same SQL with different runtime parameters. After a SQL statement is successfully prepared, certain database vendor clients will provide information on whether it's an INSERT, DELETE, UPDATE, or SELECT statement, information about the columns in the result set, the number of

parameter markers, and so on prior to executing the SQL statement. Here's a call to
`SQLPrepare` that implements error handling:

```
if ( SQLPrepare(hstmt, szSQL, SQL_NTS) != SQL_SUCCESS )
{
  printf( "ERROR while preparing a SQL statement ------n" ) ;
  return SQL_ERROR;
}
```

## Passing Runtime Parameters

Runtime parameters can be bound by specifying placeholders or parameter markers in the SQL
statement. Depending upon the database you are talking with, there could be one or more ways
to specify parameter markers, like binding by name or binding by number. After a parameterized SQL statement is successfully prepared, you must bind parameter buffers and provide data
or set NULL indicators to all the parameter markers before executing. The following code
shows how to do this:

```
SQLCHAR insert_data[21] ;
SQLINTEGER insert_data_ind ;
for ( iPos = 1; iPos <= noOfParams; iPos ++)
{
  ...
  switch ( dataType )
  {
    case SQL_CHAR:
    /* Bind data to parameter marker */
    rc = SQLBindParameter( hstmt, iPos, SQL_PARAM_INPUT, SQL_C_CHAR,
      SQL_CHAR,20, 0, insert_data, 21, &insert_data_ind );

    break;
    ...
  }
}
```

## Executing a SQL Statement

SQL statements do not always need to be prepared before executing. There are interfaces that
will allow direct execution of a SQL statement. While executing SQL directly, all the client
and server resources are freed immediately after execution and fetching all the result set cursors. So, if an application needs to process the same SQL repeatedly, it is better to prepare the
SQL once and execute it many times. The following code implements error handling for
`SQLExecute` calls:

```
if ( SQLExecute( hstmt ) != SQL_SUCCESS )
{
  printf( "ERROR while executing a SQL statement ------n" ) ;
  return SQL_ERROR;
}
rc = SQLExecDirect( hstmt, szSQL, SQL_NTS ) ;
```

# Binding a Record Buffer

After successfully executing a SQL statement, if it's a SELECT query you can retrieve metadata about the resultset columns. For a INSERT, DELETE, or UPDATE SQL you can get the number of rows affected on the server. When you have determined there is a resultset, you need to allocate a record buffer, which will be used to fetch records. The record buffer size can be computed by summing up all the resultset column lengths plus a four-byte null indicator for each column. For example, if you have two CHAR(20) columns in the resultset, the record buffer size will be $(20 + 1 + 4) * 2 = 50$ bytes. So, depending upon the data type you may need to provide additional buffer for a NULL terminator, size prefixed data, blob handles, and so on. For a clear understanding on the bind buffer requirements for a particular data type, consult the database vendor client library documents. The following code performs buffer bindings for the columns in a result set.

```
SQLSMALLINT noResultCols;
SQLINTEGER noofRowsAffected;
SQLNumResultCols ( hstmt , &noResultCols);
if ( noResultCols )
{
  /* Resultset is available */
  SQLCHAR colname[32] ;
  SQLSMALLINT coltype ;
  SQLSMALLINT colnamelen ;
  SQLSMALLINT nullable ;
  SQLUINTEGER collen;
  SQLSMALLINT scale ;
  SQLINTEGER displaysize ;
  for ( iCol = 1; iCol<= noResultCols; iCol++ )
  {
    /* Describe each column in the resultset */
    rc = SQLDescribeCol( hstmt, ( SQLSMALLINT ) iCol, colname, sizeof(colname),

      colnamelen, &coltype, &collen, &scale, &nullable ) ;
    /* get display length for column */
    rc = SQLColAttribute( hstmt, ( SQLSMALLINT ) iCol, SQL_DESC_DISPLAY_SIZE,
NULL,
      0, NULL, &displaysize ) ;
  }
```

```
}
else
  /* No resultset, should be a INSERT, UPDATE, DELETE or a DDL statement */
  rc = SQLRowCount ( hstmt , &noofRowsAffected );
```

## Fetching Records

After you have prepared a record buffer you can bind the buffer for fetching data and null indicators by iterating through all the resultset columns. Most database vendors provide one or
more ways to bind buffers, like bind by position or bind by name. After providing a buffer for
all the columns, you can fetch a record into the record buffer by calling appropriate fetch calls.
After a record is fetched, all the column null indicators should be examined to see if there is
any valid data. If there is valid data, make a copy of the data from the record buffer to a buffer
provided by the application. Subsequent fetches will fetch records one by one until the EOF
(End Of File) is reached. The following code construct sets up data fetching:

```
for ( iCol = 1; iCol <= noOfColumns; iCol ++)
{
  ...
  switch ( dataType )
  {
  case SQL_CHAR:
    /* Bind buffer for resultset column */
    rc = SQLBindCol(hstmt, iCol, SQL_C_CHAR, (SQLPOINTER) data, 15, ind1);
    break;
    ...
  }
}
while ((rc = SQLFetch(hstmt)) == SQL_SUCCESS)
{
  /* copy record to the client buffer */
  ...
}
if (rc == SQL_NO_DATA_FOUND)
{
  /* copy the last record to the client buffer */
  ...
  rc = SQL_SUCCESS;
}
```

## Free Handles and Disconnect

There could be more than one cursor returned as a result of executing a stored procedure on
certain servers. So, after fetching the first cursor till EOF you can continue to fetch the next
cursor and so on. After all the cursors are fetched, if the statement handles are no longer

needed for repeated execution, you can free the statement handle, disconnect from the database, and free connection and other handles. The following code shows how to free handles and disconnect:

```
rc = SQLFreeHandle( SQL_HANDLE_STMT, hstmt ) ;
rc = SQLEndTran( SQL_HANDLE_DBC, hdbc, SQL_COMMIT ) ;
/* Disconnect for the database */
rc = SQLDisconnect( hdbc ) ;
rc = SQLFreeHandle( SQL_HANDLE_DBC, hdbc ) ;
rc = SQLFreeHandle( SQL_HANDLE_DBC, henv ) ;
```

Now that you have a basic understanding of dynamic SQL processing let's look into the implementation of your own dbExpress driver.

# dbExpress Core Implementation

As explained earlier in this chapter, the four core abstract classes in dbExpress are SQLDriver, SQLConnection, SQLCommand, and SQLCursor. The SQLMetaData metadata access interface is built using the core implementation. To write your own dbExpress driver all these abstract classes should be extended and all the methods should be implemented. For Kylix to instantiate C++ objects they need to have the following as the first three methods: QueryInterface(), AddRef(), Release(). This is the only reason why all the dbExpress classes have these methods. The implementation of AddRef() simply increments a reference count associated with an object. Release() decrements the reference count, and if the reference count is 0, then frees the object.

All the classes have methods to set and get properties that clients can use to pass runtime properties to take advantage of database specific features or to fine tune data access.

## SQLDriver

As explained earlier, SQLDriver is used to configure the connection to a database driver client.

Instead of having an additional layer that determines which dbExpress driver should be loaded and initialized, dbExpress has a unique entry point, getSQLDriverXXX(), for each dbExpress driver. This will be the only call that needs to be exported from your dbExpress driver. Calling getSQLDriverXXX() should return a valid SQLDriver object after loading the vendor client, validating all the entry points and performing database-specific initialization.

SQLDriver has three methods, of which two are for setting and retrieving runtime properties. The third, getSQLConnection(), returns a new instance of a SQLConnection object. If any SQLDriver options are set and if they need to be propagated to the SQLConnection object, make sure these properties are initialized in the SQLConnection object also. This way, you can set properties on the SQLDriver once and they will be automatically propagated to all the SQLConnection objects you get from this SQLDriver.

While implementing the dbExpress interface, do not maintain a lot of state information; this helps to keep the implementation simpler and cleaner. For example, in SQLDriver do not maintain a list of SQLConnection objects when you intend to have a pool of connections. Instead, build the connection pooling as a separate layer.

Refer to Listing 16.1 for a sample SQLDriver implementation.

## SQLConnection

Let's look at some specific implementation details for SQLConnection.

### Connect/Disconnect

The SQLConnection methods connect() and disconnect() wrap the low-level calls that establish and detach a client to database server connection. Connect() takes the servername, username, and password as arguments. If there are additional properties that you might need for establishing a connection (like hostname, protocol, or portno) then you may set those properties using the setOption() method. Similarly, after establishing a connection you could set post-connect options like autocommit. Disconnect() detaches from the database server and frees the connection and other handles associated with it.

### Transaction Support

SQLConnection has the following methods to support transactions: beginTransaction(), commit(), and rollback(). All these methods take a transaction ID to support multiple transactions provided the underlying RDBMS supports the same.

The implementation to support a single transaction is simply to set the autocommit to false, which in turn will start an implicit transaction on the database server when a SQL request is made. Commit() or rollback() can then be called to finish the implicit transaction. After a successful commit or rollback, make sure you set autocommit back to True. On servers that do not support the autocommit behavior you may have to start an internal transaction for each query and commit the same after successfully executing.

Only a few RDBMS like InterBase and Oracle support multiple transactions on a single session. The SQLConnection implementation for these RDBMS maintains a list of transactions started. In dbExpress, transactions are identified by transaction descriptors:

```
typedef struct
{
    UINT32      uTransID;               // Transaction ID
    UINT32      uGID;                   // Global ID
```

```
    eXILType      eTransIsoLevel;        // Transaction isolation level
    UINT32        uCustomIsolation;      // DB specific isolation level

} TransactionDesc;
```

uTransID uniquely identifies a transaction from the list of transactions.

uGID is the global transaction identifier (gtrid) that will be passed to any XA compliant global transaction.

eTransIsoLevel can be set to support one of the standard isolation levels like readcommitted, repeatable read, or dirty read that are supported by most databases. To implement other database-specific isolation levels you could use the uCustomIsolation.

## Command

You need a SQLCommand object to execute any SQL on the database server. SQLConnection method getSQLCommand() allocates statement handles and other associated handles and returns a valid SQLCommand object. SQLConnection properties that might apply to SQLCommand can also be initialized.

Some servers can't have more than one active statement per connection. For those servers, let the client explicitly get a new SQLConnection and a SQLCommand object to execute SQL simultaneously. Because database connections are expensive resources do not silently allocate new connections internally in your implementation. Let the users understand the underlying RDBMS restrictions and this will help them to better design their application. Also cloning new connections can be implemented as a separate layer.

## Error Handling

SQLConnection has two methods, getErrorMessageLen() and getErrorMessage(), to retrieve the SQL error associated with a connection handle. The implementation of getErroMessageLen() calls the vendor error handling calls and gets the error message length and getErrorMessage() simply copies the error message into the client buffer.

Some databases allow retrieving multiple SQL errors. In that case the implementation can repeatedly call the vendor calls until the end of file (EOF) and return the concatenated error message.

Refer to Listing 16.2 for a sample SQLConnection implementation.

## SQLCommand

The SQLCommand implementation is where most of the SQL processing takes place. Each SQLCommand has a statement handle and other associated handles that are needed for executing a SQL on the server.

## Prepare and Execute

SQLCommand has the following methods prepare(), execute(), and executeImmediate() to
process a SQL and return a uni-directional cursor if available. Prepare() takes a SQL statement or a stored procedure name and calls the vendor low-level calls to prepare a SQL on the
server. Before preparing a SQL make sure you replace the dbExpress parameter markers (?)
with the RDBMS supported parameter markers.

In the case of stored procedures, you may have to generate the SQL for calling the stored procedure. (For example, "BEGIN PROC1(); END;" is the SQL for calling PROC1 with no parameters in Oracle). Because the data type and parameter types of stored procedure parameters are
not known until all the parameters are bound, you may have to defer the stored procedure
preparation until execute(). Similarly, on servers that don't support parameter binding (like
MySQL), you may need to replace the parameter markers with the actual data and generate a
valid SQL.

After preparing, if your SQL has parameters to be bound, you need to allocate a parameter list
to hold the IN/OUT parameters:

```
typedef struct Parameter
{
    UINT16          uParamNumber;           //Parameter number
    pCHAR           szName[MAX_NAMELEN];    //Parameter name
    STMTParamType   eParamType;             //Parameter type
    UINT16          uLogType;               //dbExpress logical type
    UINT16          uPhyType;               //Mapped physical type
    UINT16          uSubType;               //Mapped subtype
    INT32           lMaxPrecision;          //Max Precision
    INT32           lMaxScale;              //Max Scale
    pBYTE           pData;                  //IN/OUT data buffer
    UINT32          ulLength;               //Data length
    INT16           iInd;                   //Null indicator
    BOOL            bBound;                 //is a parameter bound
} Parameter;
typedef Parameter* pParameter;
```

execute() and executeImmediate() simply wrap up the vendor calls for executing a SQL. If
there are any parameters involved, check to see if all the parameters are bound. On servers that
don't support direct execution you may need to call prepare internally.

When using stored procedures, make sure the SQL for calling the stored procedure is generated and prepared once.

After successful execution, if there is any result set column, instantiate a new SQLCursor
object. You need to allocate a column list to hold metadata specific to this cursor. Metadata for

each column can be obtained through SQL "describe" calls with the statement handle and specifying the column position in the resultset:

```
typedef struct Column
{
    UINT16   uColNum;              //Column position
    pCHAR    pszColName;           //Column name
    pCHAR    pszTblName;           //Table name

    UINT16   uLogType;             //Mapped logical type
    UINT16   uLogSubType;          //Mapped logical subtype
    INT16    iLogPrecision;        //Mapped logical precision
    INT16    iLogScale;            //Mapped logical scale
    UINT32   uLogLength;           //Mapped logical length

    UINT16   uPhyType;             //Physical type
    INT16    iPrecision;           //Precision
    INT16    iScale;               //Scale
    UINT32   uOffset;              //Column offset in the record buffer
    UINT32   uLength;              //Column length
    UINT32   uNullOffset;          //Column null offset in rec. buffer
    UINT32   uAttribute;           //Column attribute

}Column;

typedef Column* pColumn;
```

After the column SQL types are known, they need to be mapped to appropriate dbExpress logical types. One or more SQL types might get mapped to the same logical type and accessing these SQL types might need special handling. So, as part of the column metadata, always keep a copy of the SQL types, precision, and scale as well.

Based on the column length and data type, the record buffer size can be computed. While computing the record buffer, register the offset for each column data and offset for the column NULL indicators. Blob data should not be part of the record buffer as they could be as huge as two to four gigabytes. Instead, allocate enough room in the record buffer to hold blob locators or handles and null indicators for blob columns. If the RDBMS allows block fetches, then you can allocate an array of record buffers instead of a single one when clients want to perform block fetches. Block fetches significantly improve performance by reducing the network traffic.

Next, iterate through the column list and bind the column buffers and their associated NULL indicators by calling the vendor-specific bind calls (see Figure 16.2).

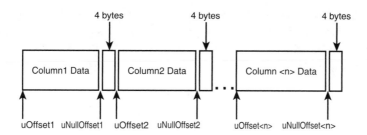

**FIGURE 16.2**
*Offsets for column data and NULL indicators.*

The getRowsAffected() implementation should return the number of rows affected on the server following an UPDATE, INSERT, or DELETE, and this information will be available after a successful SQL execution.

## Parameter Binding

SQLCommand methods setParameter(), getParameter(), and close() take care of all the runtime parameter binding needs. For each parameter marker in the SQL dbExpress clients call setParameter() to bind IN/OUT parameters and getParameter() to get OUT parameter data. In setParameter(), map the logical types to SQL data types and make a copy of the parameter data and store it internally in a SQL format that's needed to bind to the client library. NULL indicators can be set to bind and return NULL.

Also, setParameter() has arguments that will let you specify the OUT parameter buffer requirements; this way you could support returning OUT parameters whose buffer requirements are bigger than the IN parameter. For example, when you have CHAR and VARCHAR types as IN/OUT parameters uLength specifies the size of the IN data, uMaxPrecision can be set to a value higher to uLength to specify the maximum size of the OUT data. So, in case of an OUT or IN/OUT parameter, the larger of uMaxPrecision or uLength is used to allocate the bind buffer. In case of non-character types, uMaxPrecision and uMaxScale should specify the NUMERIC precision and scale for that parameter.

After successful execution, getParameter() returns the output for an OUT or IN/OUT parameter by copying the output data from the parameter buffer and after performing any necessary physical to logical data conversion. After all the OUT or IN/OUT parameters are retrieved and all the result set cursors are fetched, close() frees all the parameter buffers, record buffer, and any other allocated resources for executing the SQL statement.

## Stored Procedure Cursors

On stored procedures that can return more than one cursor getNextCursor() will return the next available cursor, if any. After reaching the end of the current cursor, the implementation for `getNextCursor()` should check if any additional cursors are available by calling the appropriate vendor library calls. If there are, a new `SQLCursor` object should be instantiated and the same steps on `execute()` should be followed. Only a few RDBMS (like Oracle or DB2) support returning multiple cursors.

Refer to Listing 16.3 for a sample `SQLCommand` implementation.

## SQLCursor

`SQLCursor` holds data and metadata with respect to the executed query or stored procedure and has methods to get individual field values. `SQLCursor` implementation uses the `SQLCommand` object associated with it to access the column metadata and the record buffer. Metadata for the cursor columns will be readily available after executing the SQL. However, to access the data `next()` should be called; it wraps the fetch or extended fetch vendor calls to retrieve a record or records into the dbExpress record buffer.

`SQLCursor` data access methods like `getString()` and `getBytes()` check for the column NULL indicator in the null offset and, if the data is not null, uses the column data offset and converts SQL data to dbExpress logical data representation.

Refer to Listing 16.4 for a sample `SQLCursor` implementation.

## SQLMetaData

The `SQLMetaData` interface defines the various database metadata that can be obtained on an opened database connection. The `getSQLMetaData()` method from a `SQLConnection` object will return a `SQLMetaData` object. `SQLMetaData` provides only the metadata needed by DataSnap, Kylix, Delphi, and C++ Builder data-access components. Numerous other database metadata properties are skipped to make the implementation simpler. However, most of these can be surfaced using get and set options on the `SQLMetaData` object and without changing the interface.

New methods can be added to `SQLMetaData` to return metadata about table and column privileges, available SQL functions and SQL keywords, referential integrity constraints, and so on.

# Summary

This chapter provides you with the architectural overview of data access in Kylix, explains why the data access for Kylix is implemented the way it is, and describes how to create your own dbExpress drivers. You should check the FreeCLX Web site (`http://freeclx.sourceforge.net`) and the Borland community Web site (`http://community.borland.com`) for information on the open source dbExpress drivers Borland may have released by the time you read this book.

# Creating a Real-World Application

*By John Kaster*

## IN THIS CHAPTER

In this chapter, you'll create a complete database application, including designing the database and the GUI application to manipulate the data.

## Application Background

Before you can start writing a chapter like this, you have to come up with the "real-world" application to use as an example. We talked about writing an application to provide a searchable GUI interface to all of the examples provided in the book, but we didn't have time to create the application the way we wanted it to be.

Fortunately, my apparently full-time job for David Intersimone, VP of Developer Relations at Borland, (informally titled "special projects director for Borland Developer Relations") provided a solution. For the 2001 Borland Conference (BorCon 2001) in Long Beach, California, we put together a showcase application that demonstrates all of Borland's development products working together. Because we wanted to come up with something reasonably interesting and entertaining, the fictitious company Movi-E-Tailer was created, and an application specification was born.

Several people were involved in producing this showcase application, from Borland's various product groups, and are listed here in no particular order:

- Mike Rozlog, Architect and Technology Evangelist, for the application server Enterprise Java Beans (EJBs)
- Sung Nguyen, Sales Engineer, for the C++ CORBA currency converter
- Blake Stone, JBuilder Architect, for Java Server pages, shopping cart, and mobile phone) client
- Sriram Balsumbramanian, InterBase R&D, for database design and implementation
- John Ray Thomas, Kylix and C++ Builder Product Manager, for Kylix applications
- Thomas Theobald, Delphi Product Manager, for the Web service notifier
- David Intersimone, Vice President of Developer Relations, for defining the needs (the client)
- Pat Kerpan, Vice President of the DSP Group, for TeamSource DSP usage in the collaborative development
- John Kaster, Sr. Manager of Developer Relations, project coordinator and general nag

# Application Description

Movi-E-Tailer sells movies and movie memorabilia. The two requirements fulfilled by Kylix (actually, CLX) were for a GUI application that provides a quick interface for entering information into the database, and a Web-based database navigation system that provides information on the data in the application. Because there were some other things going on at the time (for example, Web services integration using Delphi 6) I actually developed by the CLX GUI application and the base Web server application on Windows with Delphi 6. Then, John Ray Thomas (JT) moved these applications over to Kylix and enhanced the Web server piece to start communicating with a JBuilder-built Java Server Page (JSP).

Because his work on the Web server diverged into supporting another product, we'll stick with the one I originally delivered to him, with a few enhancements I made after the fact.

The pieces of this "real-world" application we will discuss in this chapter are as follows:

- CLX GUI application for database management
- NetCLX Web server for navigating through product offerings

# Database Definition

Because the information in the database dictates a lot of what the application can do, Blake, JT, Sriram, Mike and I talked about what should go into the database definition after Sri and I presented the initial metadata draft. I also called Jeff Overcash (of TeamB and InterBase Express fame) to get some opinions from him for our implementation.

## Tables

After some minor tweaks when I was developing the CLX GUI application, we ended up with the following table definitions, implemented with InterBase 6.

This is a table describing all of the countries, their currency format as a specialized formatting string, and exchange rate compared to the U.S. dollar:

```
CREATE TABLE COUNTRIES
(
  COUNTRY_CODE    CHAR(2) NOT NULL,
  NAME    VARCHAR(60) NOT NULL,
  CURRENCY_FORMAT    VARCHAR(20) NOT NULL,
  EXCHANGE_RATE    DOUBLE PRECISION NOT NULL,
CONSTRAINT PK_COUNTRIES PRIMARY KEY (COUNTRY_CODE)
);
```

Because there is already a standard list of two character abbreviations for all countries on the Internet, the COUNTRY_CODE field is the primary key for this table.

This is the customer table, naturally:

```
CREATE TABLE CUSTOMERS
(
  CUSTOMER_KEY     INTEGER NOT NULL,
  NAME      VARCHAR(25),
  ADDRESS1     VARCHAR(50) NOT NULL,
  ADDRESS2     VARCHAR(50),
  POSTAL_CODE     VARCHAR(10) NOT NULL,
  PHONE      VARCHAR(15),
  REGION_KEY     INTEGER,
  EMAIL      VARCHAR(40),
  EMAIL_PASSWORD     VARCHAR(20),
CONSTRAINT PK_CUSTOMERS PRIMARY KEY (CUSTOMER_KEY)
);
```

This table is a lookup list of movie genres:

```
CREATE TABLE GENRES
(
  GENRE_KEY     INTEGER NOT NULL,
  NAME      VARCHAR(40),
CONSTRAINT PK_GENRES PRIMARY KEY (GENRE_KEY)
);
```

This is the inventory table for specific items:

```
CREATE TABLE INVENTORY
(
  INVENTORY_KEY     INTEGER NOT NULL,
  PART_KEY     INTEGER,
  SUPPLIER_KEY     INTEGER,
  AVAILABLE_QUANTITY     INTEGER,
  SUPPLIER_COST     DOUBLE PRECISION,
  REORDER_QTY     INTEGER,
CONSTRAINT PK_INVENTORY PRIMARY KEY (INVENTORY_KEY)
);
```

This is the main movie table, to which all parts are attached:

```
CREATE TABLE MOVIES
(
  MOVIE_KEY     INTEGER NOT NULL,
  TITLE      VARCHAR(54),
  DESCRIPTION     BLOB SUB_TYPE TEXT SEGMENT SIZE 80,
  IMAGE     BLOB SUB_TYPE -7 SEGMENT SIZE 2048,
  GENRE_KEY     INTEGER NOT NULL,
  IMAGE_FILE     VARCHAR(64),
```

```
TRAILER_URL     VARCHAR(200),
TRAILER_DESC    VARCHAR(60),
ENTRY_DATE      TIMESTAMP,
FEATURED     CHAR(1),
CONSTRAINT PK_MOVIES PRIMARY KEY (MOVIE_KEY)
);
```

This table contains the specific items for an order:

```
CREATE TABLE ORDERLINEITEMS
(
  LINEITEM_KEY     INTEGER NOT NULL,
  ORDER_KEY     INTEGER NOT NULL,
  PART_KEY     INTEGER NOT NULL,
  SUPPLIER_KEY     INTEGER NOT NULL,
  QUANTITY     INTEGER NOT NULL,
  EXTENDED_PRICE     DOUBLE PRECISION,
CONSTRAINT PK_ORDERLINEITEMS PRIMARY KEY (LINEITEM_KEY)
);
```

This is the table of customer orders:

```
CREATE TABLE ORDERS
(
  ORDER_KEY     INTEGER NOT NULL,
  CUSTOMER_KEY     INTEGER NOT NULL,
  ORDER_STATUS     CHAR(1),
  TOTAL_PRICE     DOUBLE PRECISION,
  ORDER_DATE     TIMESTAMP,
  SHIP_DATE     TIMESTAMP,
  CREDIT_CARD     VARCHAR(16) NOT NULL,
  CREDIT_EXP_DATE     CHAR(5) NOT NULL,
CONSTRAINT PK_ORDERS PRIMARY KEY (ORDER_KEY)
);
```

The parts in this table are for a specific movie:

```
CREATE TABLE PARTS
(
  PART_KEY     INTEGER NOT NULL,
  MOVIE_KEY     INTEGER NOT NULL,
  NAME     VARCHAR(54),
  MANUFACTURER     VARCHAR(15),
  PART_TYPE     VARCHAR(11),
  RETAIL_PRICE     DOUBLE PRECISION,
  COMMENT     BLOB SUB_TYPE TEXT SEGMENT SIZE 80,
  IMAGE     BLOB SUB_TYPE -7 SEGMENT SIZE 2048,
  ORDER_COUNT     INTEGER,
```

17

```
    IMAGE_FILE      VARCHAR(64),
    ENTRY_DATE      TIMESTAMP,
CONSTRAINT PK_PARTS PRIMARY KEY (PART_KEY)
);
```

This is a lookup table indicating the various kinds of items that are sold:

```
CREATE TABLE PARTS_TYPE
(
  PART_TYPE     VARCHAR(11) NOT NULL,
  IMAGE_FILE    VARCHAR(48) NOT NULL,
CONSTRAINT PK_PARTS_TYPE PRIMARY KEY (PART_TYPE)
);
```

This table contains a list of all regions for which sales tax or shipping locations are entered:

```
CREATE TABLE REGIONS
(
  REGION_KEY       INTEGER NOT NULL,
  COUNTRY_CODE     CHAR(2),
  STATE_PROVINCE   VARCHAR(20),
  TAX_RATE       DOUBLE PRECISION NOT NULL,
CONSTRAINT PK_REGIONS PRIMARY KEY (REGION_KEY)
);
```

This table contains orders that go out to a supplier:

```
CREATE TABLE REORDERS
(
  REORDER_KEY      INTEGER NOT NULL,
  CUSTOMER_KEY     INTEGER NOT NULL,
  REORDER_STATUS   CHAR(1),
  TOTAL_PRICE      DOUBLE PRECISION,
  REORDER_DATE     TIMESTAMP,
  PART_KEY     INTEGER,
  SUPPLIER_KEY     INTEGER,
  QUANTITY     INTEGER,
CONSTRAINT PK_REORDERS PRIMARY KEY (REORDER_KEY)
);
```

This table is another lookup table used for indicating the status of orders:

```
CREATE TABLE STATUS_CODES
(
  CODE    CHAR(1) NOT NULL,
  DESCRIPTION     VARCHAR(20) NOT NULL,
  IMAGE_FILE      VARCHAR(48),
CONSTRAINT PK_STATUS_CODES PRIMARY KEY (CODE)
);
```

And, finally, this table contains the list of suppliers who provide the parts that can be ordered from the inventory table:

```
CREATE TABLE SUPPLIERS
(
  SUPPLIER_KEY    INTEGER NOT NULL,
  REGION_KEY    INTEGER NOT NULL,
  NAME    VARCHAR(25),
  ADDRESS1    VARCHAR(50) NOT NULL,
  ADDRESS2    VARCHAR(50),
  POSTAL_CODE    VARCHAR(10),
  PHONE    VARCHAR(15),
CONSTRAINT PK_SUPPLIERS PRIMARY KEY (SUPPLIER_KEY)
);
```

## Indices

The following indices provide the quick data retrieval functionality for this database.

This index makes it easy to search for a customer's e-mail address:

```
CREATE UNIQUE INDEX CUST_EMAIL ON CUSTOMERS(EMAIL);
```

This index speeds searching by customer name:

```
CREATE INDEX CUST_NAME_ORDER ON CUSTOMERS(NAME);
```

This index speeds listing the movies in most recent entry order first:

```
CREATE DESCENDING INDEX MOVIES_ENTRY_DATE ON MOVIES(ENTRY_DATE);
```

This index is used to find movies matching a specific genre:

```
CREATE INDEX MOVIES_GENRE_KEY ON MOVIES(GENRE_KEY);
```

This index is used to locate a part by name:

```
CREATE INDEX PARTS_NAME_ORDER ON PARTS(NAME);
```

## Data Constraints

The following constraints help ensure database integrity.

This constraint ensures that the customer location is a valid one contained in the region table:

```
ALTER TABLE CUSTOMERS ADD CONSTRAINT FK_CUSTOMERSREGIONS
  FOREIGN KEY (REGION_KEY) REFERENCES REGIONS (REGION_KEY);
```

17

CREATING A
REAL-WORLD
APPLICATION

This constraint verifies that the customer exists for a specific order:

```
ALTER TABLE ORDERS ADD CONSTRAINT FK_CUSTOMERSORDERS
  FOREIGN KEY (CUSTOMER_KEY) REFERENCES CUSTOMERS (CUSTOMER_KEY);
```

This constraint ensures that the country code entered for a region is valid:

```
ALTER TABLE REGIONS ADD CONSTRAINT FK_REGIONSCOUNTRIES
  FOREIGN KEY (COUNTRY_CODE) REFERENCES COUNTRIES (COUNTRY_CODE);
```

This constraint verifies the region key for a supplier:

```
ALTER TABLE SUPPLIERS ADD CONSTRAINT FK_SUPPLIERREGIONS
  FOREIGN KEY (REGION_KEY) REFERENCES REGIONS (REGION_KEY);
```

## Generators

These generators are used for producing unique keys for the various tables using an integer value as a primary key. The names are self-explanatory:

```
CREATE GENERATOR CUSTOMER_KEY;
CREATE GENERATOR GENRE_KEY;
CREATE GENERATOR INVENTORY_KEY;
CREATE GENERATOR LINEITEM_KEY;
CREATE GENERATOR MOVIE_KEY;
CREATE GENERATOR ORDER_KEY;
CREATE GENERATOR PART_KEY;
CREATE GENERATOR REGION_KEY;
CREATE GENERATOR SUPPLIER_KEY;
```

## Stored Procedures

Stored procedures are great for speeding up the performance of your SQL database application. We'll discuss this in more detail in Chapter 18, "Database Optimizations." (For more information on writing stored procedures with InterBase, refer to your InterBase SQL language reference.)

This stored procedure returns the list of genres that actually have movies assigned to them. There are currently genres in the database that do not have movies assigned to them:

```
CREATE PROCEDURE ACTIVE_GENRES
RETURNS
(
  GENRE_KEY INTEGER,
  NAME VARCHAR(40)
)
AS
BEGIN
```

```
FOR
  SELECT DISTINCT G.GENRE_KEY, G.NAME
  FROM GENRES G
  JOIN MOVIES M ON G.GENRE_KEY = M.GENRE_KEY
  ORDER BY G.NAME
  INTO :GENRE_KEY, :NAME
DO
  SUSPEND;
END
```

As with ACTIVE_GENRES, this stored procedure lists those parts types that have parts associated with them:

```
CREATE PROCEDURE ACTIVE_PARTS_TYPES
RETURNS
(
  PART_TYPE VARCHAR(11),
  IMAGE_FILE VARCHAR(48)
)
AS
BEGIN
  FOR
    SELECT DISTINCT T.PART_TYPE, T.IMAGE_FILE
    FROM PARTS_TYPE T
    JOIN PARTS P ON T.PART_TYPE = P.PART_TYPE
    ORDER BY T.PART_TYPE
    INTO :PART_TYPE, :IMAGE_FILE
  DO
    SUSPEND;
END
```

This stored procedure returns the most popular parts in the database. The number of records to return is passed as the parameter MAX_COUNT:

```
CREATE PROCEDURE MOST_POPULAR_PARTS
(
  MAX_COUNT INTEGER
)
RETURNS
(
  PART_KEY INTEGER,
  MOVIE_KEY INTEGER,
  NAME VARCHAR(54),
  PART_TYPE VARCHAR(11),
  ORDER_COUNT INTEGER
)
AS
```

```
  DECLARE VARIABLE CUR_COUNT INTEGER;
BEGIN
  CUR_COUNT = 0;
  FOR
    SELECT PART_KEY, MOVIE_KEY, NAME, PART_TYPE, ORDER_COUNT
    FROM PARTS ORDER BY ORDER_COUNT DESCENDING
    INTO :PART_KEY, :MOVIE_KEY, :NAME, :PART_TYPE, :ORDER_COUNT
  DO
  BEGIN
    CUR_COUNT = CUR_COUNT + 1;
    IF (CUR_COUNT > MAX_COUNT) THEN
      EXIT;
    ELSE
      SUSPEND;
  END
END
```

This stored procedure returns the top selling movies by counting both the DVD and VHS (videotape) category for all parts in the database. The number of records to return is passed as the parameter MAX_COUNT:

```
CREATE PROCEDURE TOP_SELLERS
(
  MAX_COUNT INTEGER
)
RETURNS
(
  MOVIE_KEY INTEGER,
  TITLE VARCHAR(54),
  IMAGE_FILE VARCHAR(64),
  ENTRY_DATE TIMESTAMP,
  TRAILER_URL VARCHAR(200),
  TRAILER_DESC VARCHAR(60),
  TOTAL_ORDERS INTEGER
)
AS
  DECLARE VARIABLE CUR_COUNT INTEGER;
BEGIN
  CUR_COUNT = 0;
  FOR
    select movie_key, sum(order_count) total_orders
    from parts
    where (part_type = 'DVD') or (part_type = 'VHS')
    group by movie_key
    order by 2 descending
    into :movie_key, :total_orders
```

```
    DO
    BEGIN
      CUR_COUNT = CUR_COUNT + 1;
      IF (CUR_COUNT > MAX_COUNT) THEN
        EXIT;
      ELSE
      BEGIN
        SELECT title, image_file, entry_date, trailer_url, trailer_desc
        FROM movies where movie_key = :movie_key
        into :title, :image_file, :entry_date, :trailer_url, :trailer_desc;
        SUSPEND;
      END
    END
END
```

## Triggers

Database triggers are caused by changes to the data in a table. These triggers are a specialized form of database programming logic, where specific kinds of data events may occur. For InterBase, triggers exist for updating, deleting, and inserting records in a data set.

This trigger occurs before an inserted customer record gets written to the database:

```
CREATE TRIGGER TR_INSERT_CUSTOMER FOR CUSTOMERS
ACTIVE BEFORE INSERT POSITION 0
AS
BEGIN
  IF (NEW.CUSTOMER_KEY is NULL) THEN
    NEW.CUSTOMER_KEY = GEN_ID(CUSTOMER_KEY,1);
END
```

If the customer key is null (meaning it has not been assigned), this trigger will automatically create the customer key. Depending on the way you write your client code to insert records into a database, you may or may not have generated the primary key for a record in the database. This trigger allows for both methods of writing client code: assigning the key yourself, or letting the database do it for you.

This trigger will generate a key for an inserted genres record, if the key has not yet been assigned:

```
CREATE TRIGGER TR_INSERT_GENRES FOR GENRES
ACTIVE BEFORE INSERT POSITION 0
AS
BEGIN
  IF (NEW.GENRE_KEY is NULL) THEN
    NEW.GENRE_KEY = GEN_ID(GENRE_KEY,1);
END
```

This trigger generates a key for an inserted inventory record if required:

```
CREATE TRIGGER TR_INSERT_INVENTORY FOR INVENTORY
ACTIVE BEFORE INSERT POSITION 0
AS
BEGIN
  IF (NEW.INVENTORY_KEY is NULL) then
    NEW.INVENTORY_KEY = GEN_ID(INVENTORY_KEY, 1);
END
```

This trigger generates a movie key, and sets the entry date of the movie to the database server machine's current date and time if it is not set:

```
CREATE TRIGGER TR_INSERT_MOVIES FOR MOVIES
ACTIVE BEFORE INSERT POSITION 0
AS
BEGIN
  IF (NEW.MOVIE_KEY is NULL) THEN
    NEW.MOVIE_KEY = GEN_ID(MOVIE_KEY,1);
  IF (NEW.ENTRY_DATE is NULL) THEN
    NEW.ENTRY_DATE = 'Now';
END
```

This trigger generates a key if necessary, initializes the order count value to zero, and stamps the entry date for the part, all only if needed:

```
CREATE TRIGGER TR_INSERT_PARTS FOR PARTS
ACTIVE BEFORE INSERT POSITION 0
AS
BEGIN
  IF (NEW.PART_KEY is NULL) THEN
    NEW.PART_KEY = GEN_ID(PART_KEY,1);
  IF (NEW.ORDER_COUNT is NULL) THEN
    NEW.ORDER_COUNT = 0;
  IF (NEW.ENTRY_DATE is NULL) THEN
    NEW.ENTRY_DATE = 'Now';
END
```

This trigger generates the region key if needed:

```
CREATE TRIGGER TR_INSERT_REGIONS FOR REGIONS
ACTIVE BEFORE INSERT POSITION 0
AS
BEGIN
  IF (NEW.REGION_KEY is NULL) THEN
    NEW.REGION_KEY = GEN_ID(REGION_KEY,1);
END
```

This trigger generates a new supplier key if the client code has not done so already:

```
CREATE TRIGGER TR_INSERT_SUPPLIERS FOR SUPPLIERS
ACTIVE BEFORE INSERT POSITION 0
AS
BEGIN
  IF (NEW.SUPPLIER_KEY is NULL) THEN
    NEW.SUPPLIER_KEY = GEN_ID(SUPPLIER_KEY,1);
END
```

# Basic Design

At the time of this writing, the remote connectivity DataSnap™ offers isn't available, so we'll do a traditional two-tier database application for the graphical and browser clients. Because it's much easier to produce a Web server interface when there's actually some data in the database, we'll build the graphical client application first to help us put in the data we'll publish for the browser client.

## Data Module

Kylix has a special kind of component container called a Data Module, which is a somewhat misleading term. Many early users of Delphi assumed that only database-centric components could be used on a data module. This is not the case. A data module is simply a container for any component that is not a visual control, and it provides a convenient reference mechanism for the properties in the Object Inspector for these non-visual components from other components in other units.

### Connecting to the Database

As in Chapter 14, "DataCLX Basics," and Chapter 15, "Working with Data-Aware Components," you'll use a `TSQLConnection` component and various `TSQLClientDataSet` components for the tables you want to access. Your data needs for this application are actually simpler than those created for examples in previous chapters, so you don't actually need separate `TDataSetProvider` components to build master detail information. However, we will be requiring access to several different tables and populating some events for them. Rather than go through an exhaustive step-by-step tutorial on setting these components up again as I've done previously, I've summarized the results in Table 17.1. All dataset components refer to the same `TSQLConnection`.

**TABLE 17.1**  Database Components

| Component | Type | Purpose |
|-----------|------|---------|
| dbShowCase | TSQLConnection | Connects to the Movi-E-Tailer database. LoginPrompt is false. |
| cdsMovies | TSQLClientDataSet | Access to the movies table. |
| cdsStatusCodes | TSQLClientDataSet | Access to the status codes lookup table. |
| cdsPartsTypes | TSQLClientDataSet | Access to the parts types lookup table. |
| cdsRegions | TSQLClientDataSet | Access to the region table. |
| cdsCountries | TSQLClientDataSet | Access to the countries table. |
| cdsParts | TSQLClientDataSet | Access to the parts table that points to specific movies. |
| cdsGenres | TSQLClientDataSet | Access to the genres table that is used to categorize movies. |
| dsMovies | TDataSource | Used for the main data entry form visual data-aware controls. |

## Adding Data Constraints and Defaults

There are a variety of ways to improve data integrity in your applications. You can leverage the capabilities of the SQL server you're using by putting foreign key constraints on the data, triggers for validating data, and so on. You can also create custom BeforePost events for your datasets, and put any kind of logic for handling invalid data in there you may want. For a better user experience, a BeforePost event can usually provide a friendlier dialog box to the user than the exception the SQL server will throw.

There's a third way (and there are others I won't be getting into here) to prevent invalid data from being entered in your application, and that's by using lookup fields to provide the user with only the correct choices to assign. For example, for cdsMovies, there is a lookup field on GENRE_KEY that points to cdsGenres. The user will never enter the key value for the genre field. Rather, the user is provided with a combo box that lists the available genres to choose from, thus preventing a data entry error before it ever happens.

Most of the other tables listed are lookup tables, so they don't have a modified list of fields. However, some additional datasets do have lookup fields. cdsParts has lookup fields into the Movies table and the Parts Types table. cdsRegions has a lookup field into the Countries table.

The data defaults for this application case are mainly handled by triggers on the SQL server, but this system also makes use of the `AfterInsert` event to initialize variables with Object Pascal code. For example, the following code is defined in the data module:

```
const
  SMovieKey = 'MOVIE_KEY';
  SRegionKey = 'REGION_KEY';
  SGenreKey = 'GENRE_KEY';
  SPartKey = 'PART_KEY';
var
  TempKey : int64 = 0;
```

The constants are used to refer to the various primary key fields by name in the respective datasets. `TempKey` is a variable that is used to generate a "temporary" key on the client side for any record that has sequence-generated keys on the server

This is the routine that "generates" the temporary key:

```
function TdmShowCase.GetTempKey: int64;
begin
  Dec(TempKey);
  Result := TempKey;
end;
```

These are the `AfterInsert` events that initialize the primary key value on the client side to use a "unique" temporary key:

```
procedure TdmShowCase.cdsMoviesAfterInsert(DataSet: TDataSet);
begin
  DataSet.FieldByName(SMovieKey).AsInteger := GetTempKey;
end;
procedure TdmShowCase.cdsRegionsAfterInsert(DataSet: TDataSet);
begin
  DataSet.FieldByName(SRegionKey).asInteger := GetTempKey;
end;
procedure TdmShowCase.cdsGenresAfterInsert(DataSet: TDataSet);
begin
  DataSet.FieldByName(SGenreKey).asInteger := GetTempKey;
end;
procedure TdmShowCase.cdsPartsAfterInsert(DataSet: TDataSet);
begin
  DataSet.FieldByName(SPartKey).asInteger := GetTempKey;
end;
```

This key will be unique for each client. The only case in which you might run into a problem with this is when you're using briefcase files and have inserted records that have not been applied to the server yet, so you already have some keys with negative integer values. If that's

**17**

CREATING A
REAL-WORLD
APPLICATION

the case, you could simply initialize the TempKey variable to the lowest negative value found, and continue calling GetTempKey from there. This would be easy to do if you use the AfterOpen events on the datasets and set TempKey to the Min of TempKey and the lowest key value of the dataset.

## Updating the Data

After the data has been edited on the client side, you will be updating the SQL database with the latest data values. In many cases, you don't need to customize the updating process at all. For this application, you'll need to intercept the updating process because you're creating temporary keys on the client side that will be re-assigned when the data is updated to the server. This implementation is why the triggers we talked about earlier test the data values they assign for NULL before assigning them.

As I said in Chapter 15, you need to set poPropogateChanges to True for the various SQLClientDataSets to ensure that data changes made while writing to the SQL database are reflected back to the client. poPropogateChanges is a property of the DataSetProvider, but SQLClientDataSet surfaces it as a published property because the DataSetProvider is embedded in the SQLClientDataSet.

Let's look quickly at the dataset-independent routine created for generating key values with InterBase:

```
function TdmShowCase.GetNextKey(KeyGen: string;
  Connection: TCustomConnection): int64;
const
  SSelectKey = 'select GEN_ID(%s,1) NEXTID from RDB$DATABASE';
var
  SQLDataSet: TSQLDataSet;
begin
  SQLDataSet := TSQLDataSet.Create(nil);
  try
    SQLDataSet.SQLConnection := Connection as TSQLConnection;
    SQLDataSet.CommandText := Format(SSelectKey, [KeyGen]);
    try
      SQLDataSet.Open;
      Result := SQLDataSet.FieldByName('NEXTID').asInteger;
    except
      Result := 0;
    end;
  finally
    SQLDataSet.Free;
  end;
end;
```

In this code, KeyGen is the name of the generator to use from the database. The string SSelectKey is InterBase-specific, using one of its internal tables, and also calling the InterBase-specific GEN_ID function to return a sequence-generated value incremented by one. If you were going to write something for Oracle, for example, this part of the code might look like

```
const
  SSelectKey =  'SELECT %s.nextval NEXTID FROM dual';
```

Because dual is the internal table you can use for this in Oracle.

The value that gets generated is explicitly named NEXTID so we can query it in our created SQLDataSet. This version of GetNextKey will also attempt to cast your connection as a TSQLConnection, making this routine dbExpress-specific. It is certainly possible for you to support other database engines with a routine similar to this one. The result returned from this function is zero (0) if it fails for any reason, or the next key value for the generator in question if it succeeds.

Once we have this routine available, it becomes extremely simple to replace the temporary key generated by the client with a corrected sequentially generated key, in the respective BeforeUpdateRecord events. Any changes made in either this event or the AfterUpdateRecord event can be automatically reflected back to the client side as long as poPropogateChanges is True and TField.NewValue is used for assigning the data change. By the way, TField.NewValue can only be assigned in these two events:

```
procedure TdmShowCase.cdsMoviesBeforeUpdateRecord(Sender: TObject;
  SourceDS: TDataSet; DeltaDS: TCustomClientDataSet;
  UpdateKind: TUpdateKind; var Applied: Boolean);
begin
  if UpdateKind = ukInsert then
    DeltaDS.FieldByName(SMovieKey).NewValue := GetNextKey(SMovieKey,
dbShowCase);
end;

procedure TdmShowCase.cdsRegionsBeforeUpdateRecord(Sender: TObject;
  SourceDS: TDataSet; DeltaDS: TCustomClientDataSet;
  UpdateKind: TUpdateKind; var Applied: Boolean);
begin
  if UpdateKind = ukInsert then
    DeltaDS.FieldByName(SRegionKey).NewValue :=
GetNextKey(SRegionKey,dbShowcase);
end;

procedure TdmShowCase.cdsGenresBeforeUpdateRecord(Sender: TObject;
  SourceDS: TDataSet; DeltaDS: TCustomClientDataSet;
```

```
  UpdateKind: TUpdateKind; var Applied: Boolean);
begin
  if UpdateKind = ukInsert then
    DeltaDS.FieldByName(SGenreKey).NewValue :=
GetNextKey(SGenreKey,dbShowcase);
end;

procedure TdmShowCase.cdsPartsBeforeUpdateRecord(Sender: TObject;
  SourceDS: TDataSet; DeltaDS: TCustomClientDataSet;
  UpdateKind: TUpdateKind; var Applied: Boolean);
begin
  if UpdateKind = ukInsert then
    DeltaDS.FieldByName(SPartKey).NewValue := GetNextKey(SPartKey,dbShowcase);
end;
```

In these routines, DeltaDS refers to the delta packet passed in. You're testing the UpdateKind value of the record to determine if this is an inserted record. If it is, re-assign the primary key value. All of these routines call the GetNextKey function to invoke sequence generation.

# GUI Interface

I didn't write all of this code in the order I've presented it, primarily because it usually makes sense to provide your data editing interface at the same time as the data updating code, and do it for every dataset as you move along to make sure each one is working. The process I used was more along the lines of setting up the data access, surfacing the editing interface, and then adding the key generation logic. Once I had the first one done (the Movies table) the rest was easy to implement. It would certainly be possible to create a descendant TSQLClientDataSet that could handle the key generation pieces automatically. However, for me, that's a project for another day.

## Presenting the Data

Now that you have your data access components configured in the data module, you can use visual DataCLX components to modify the data. On the main form, there is a TDBNavigator, a TDBGrid, a TDBImage, and a TDBMemo control. They all refer to the dsMovies data source in the data module. These components allow you to manage the list of movies in the database. The image component will display the movie icon, and the memo control allows you to edit the description of the movie as free-form text.

## Editing the Data

I have also created a general-purpose version of this form that can be used for editing the other datasets that are listed in the data module. Both of these forms could have been designed with a frame that could have been re-used on both as well. I kept them this way because I didn't want to digress into a discussion of frames in this chapter, although frames are very valuable interface design components.

This form has a dataset on it, and a navigator, grid, image, and memo component as well, just as the main form does. The interface for using this form is slightly different, however, because it's designed to support editing any ClientDataSet through the use of a function call. Here's the function:

```
procedure ShowDSEditor(Title: string; DataSet: TCustomClientDataSet;
  GraphicField: string = ''; ImageFile: string = ''; MemoField: string = '');
begin
  if not Assigned(FormDSEditor) then
    FormDSEditor := TFormDSEditor.Create(Application);
  if Assigned(FormDSEditor.ClientDataSet)
    and (FormDSEditor.ClientDataSet <> DataSet)
    and (FormDSEditor.ClientDataSet.ChangeCount > 0) then
  begin
    case MessageDlg('Save changes to ' + FormDSEditor.Caption + '?',
      'Data has been changed.'#10
      + 'Press Yes to save changes,'#10
      + 'No to discard changes,'#10
      + 'or Cancel to abort', mtConfirmation, mbYesNoCancel, 0,
      mbYes) of
    mrYes : FormDSEditor.ClientDataSet.ApplyUpdates(-1);
    mrCancel: Exit;
    end;
  end;

  FormDSEditor.ClientDataSet := nil;
  FormDSEditor.Caption := Title;
  FormDSEditor.DBImage1.DataField := GraphicField;
  FormDSEditor.DBImage1.Visible := GraphicField <> '';
  FormDSEditor.DBMemo1.DataField := MemoField;
  FormDSEditor.DBMemo1.Visible := MemoField <> '';
  FormDSEditor.ImageFileField := ImageFile;
  FormDSEditor.PnlExtraData.Visible := FormDSEditor.DBMemo1.Visible or
    FormDSEditor.DBImage1.Visible;
  FormDSEditor.DataSplitter.Visible := FormDSEditor.DBMemo1.Visible and
    FormDSEditor.DBImage1.Visible;
  FormDSEditor.ClientDataSet := DataSet;
  FormDSEditor.ClientDataSet.Active := True;
  FormDSEditor.Show;
end;
```

You probably noticed a lot of references to `FormDSEditor` in the code. I could have tightened up the code by using `with FormDSEditor do`, but I didn't want the ambiguity a `with` can cause. You will also notice that the `GraphicField`, `ImageFile`, and `MemoField` values all default to a null string. Simply assigning the values of `GraphicField` and `MemoField` to a valid field name of that dataset will cause their respective controls to be visible. `ImageFile` is used to record the filename of the image that may be assigned to `GraphicField`. (More on this a little later.)

Obviously, passing a null string for a field makes its editing control invisible. If both the `GraphicField` and the `MemoField` are null strings, the panel containing both of them and the splitter between them are also made invisible. This is a simple example of using a form to manipulate multiple datasets.

## Extending Functionality

When you look at the data module, you'll notice there is also a `TImageList`, a `TActionList`, and a `TOpenDialog` component present. Before assigning any actions to the `ActionList`, I made sure the `ImageList` was assigned to it, so the default icons for the standard actions I was adding to the `ActionList` were automatically added to the `ImageList`. Then I created the edit menu actions and the file menu actions in the data module, and used the `ActionList` from the main form to build a main menu by assigning the various actions to menu items on the main menu. One of the niceties of actions is the ability to automatically enable or disable actions depending on the state of the application. The following update event will enable or disable the Apply Updates action depending on whether there are actually updates to apply or not:

```
procedure TdmShowCase.actFileApplyUpdate(Sender: TObject);
begin
  actFileApply.Enabled := cdsMovies.ChangeCount > 0;
end;
```

If `ChangeCount` is greater than zero, changes have been made to the dataset. This update event will fire any time the user does something to the application, so the menu option will only be enabled when updates are pending. (Take this as a hint that you want whatever happens in an action update event to run as fast as possible.)

There is also a pop-up menu on the main form that is used to call a file open dialog box to select the image to assign to a movie. This is the action execute event:

```
procedure TdmShowCase.actFileLoadImageExecute(Sender: TObject);
begin
  if OpenDialog1.Execute then
  begin
    OpenDialog1.InitialDir := ExtractFilePath(OpenDialog1.FileName);
    if not (cdsMovies.State in [dsEdit, dsInsert]) then
```

```
      cdsMovies.Edit;
    cdsMoviesIMAGE.LoadFromFile(OpenDialog1.FileName);
    cdsMoviesIMAGE_FILE.AsString := ExtractFilename(OpenDialog1.FileName);
  end;
end;
```

As you can see in this event, it assigns both the filename and the binary image to the data record at the same time. The filename is used for a pre-published image file, which normally makes Web browsing much faster than assigning the mime type for an image request and passing the image as part of an HTTP request. We'll be using the image filename a little later on.

All of the support for editing other datasets in the database is surfaced through "window" selection options. Here are a few of the execute events for the actions editing these files:

```
procedure TdmShowCase.actWinStatusExecute(Sender: TObject);
begin
  ShowDSEditor('Status Codes', cdsStatusCodes);
end;


procedure TdmShowCase.actWinPartsTypesExecute(Sender: TObject);
begin
  ShowDSEditor('Parts Type', cdsPartsType);
end;


procedure TdmShowCase.actWinRegionsExecute(Sender: TObject);
begin
  ShowDSEditor('Regions', cdsRegions);
end;


procedure TdmShowCase.actWinCountriesExecute(Sender: TObject);
begin
  ShowDSEditor('Countries', cdsCountries);
end;


procedure TdmShowCase.actWinPartsExecute(Sender: TObject);
begin
  ShowDSEditor('Parts', cdsParts, 'image', 'image_file', 'comment');
end;


procedure TdmShowCase.actWinGenresExecute(Sender: TObject);
begin
  ShowDSEditor('Genres', cdsGenres);
end;
```

As you can see from this code, the parts table is the only one that has freeform text and image assignment enabled in the generic dataset editor. All of these datasets are edited by the same dataset editor.

If you look at the `fDSEditor`, which is the dataset editor form, you will see that it's a self-contained unit that assumes you'll be passing it a `ClientDataSet` to process. It supports saving and loading briefcase files, assigning images when the dataset has an image field, editing freeform text when applicable, and so on. Because I didn't want to require the showcase data module, it also contains its own `ActionList`, which makes it a self-contained, generic unit you can reuse in multiple applications.

There are many additional enhancements that can be made to this application, simply by employing some of the techniques and components I've discussed Chapters 14 and 15. We'll leave this in its current state (as Guy Kawasaki says, ship it, then fix it!) and move on to the browser client interface.

# Web Interface

There are a variety of details to address when producing a browser client interface. The main paradox is providing an attractive and intuitive interface while also providing pages that are lightweight enough to load quickly on low-bandwidth pages. There are lot of decisions to make about fonts, colors, data grouping, navigation options, and so on. Let's start with formatting issues. We'll use the provided `movies` CGI application for this discussion. It's part of the `CLXApps` project group.

## Formatting

There are at least two different issues when discussing formatting of Web pages. One is the actual cosmetic appearance of the page. The other is representing the data in the database.

### Cosmetics

For the lightest weight HTML pages, it's a good idea to use cascading style sheets. The most important feature of cascading style sheets for me, as a Kylix developer rather than a full-time Web page developer, is that it allows a Web page developer to tweak things and make them look attractive, so I can worry about the functionality of the application and client navigation instead of focusing on tweaking the pages to make them look pretty.

The file `showcase.css` contains the style sheet used at our BorCon presentation. I'll just show an extract of it here:

```
.TitleBar    {
    font-family: Arial, Helvetica;
    font-size: 14pt;
```

```
        line-height: 12pt;
        color: white;
        background-color: #B8ACC2;
        font-weight:bold;
        text-align: center;
}
.MovieTitle  {font-family: Verdana, Arial, Helvetica;
             font-size: 10pt;
             font-weight: bold;
text-align: center;
             text-decoration: none;
             }
```

By using this style sheet and making references to its defined styles, the entire cosmetic appearance of the Web site can be modified without modifying my HTML generation templates or server application.

## Data Representation

NetCLX producers render data to HTML or other markup languages. For more information on these components, see Chapters 19, 20, and 21 on NetCLX, written by Bob Swart. What we'll discuss in this section are components I wrote specifically for this book. They just happened to be very convenient to use for this application.

### Component Scripting through RTTI

These NetCLX extensions support resolution of property references through custom tags. As long as the property referenced is published, these components will resolve it to a string representation.

TPropertyProducer is the root component of these NetCLX extensions, and introduces the capability to resolve property name references for that component itself. Here is the declaration:

```
TPropertyProducer = class(TCustomPageProducer)
private
  FOnGetValue: TGetValueEvent;
  FOnSetValue: TSetValueEvent;
  FParser: TPropertyParser;
  procedure SetOnGetValue(const Value: TGetValueEvent);
  procedure SetOnSetValue(const Value: TSetValueEvent);
  procedure SetSearchOwner(const Value: boolean);
  function GetSearchOwner: boolean;
  function GetErrorHandling: TParserErrorHandling;
  procedure SetErrorHandling(const Value: TParserErrorHandling);
```

```
protected
  function HandleTag(const TagString: string;
    TagParams: TStrings): string; override;
public
  property Parser: TPropertyParser read FParser;
  constructor Create(AOwner: TComponent); override;
  function Lookup(const AExpression: string) : variant; virtual;
  procedure AssignValue(const AExpression, AValue : string); virtual;
published
  property HTMLDoc;
  property HTMLFile;
  property StripParamQuotes;
  property OnHTMLTag;
  {$ifdef MSWINDOWS}
  property ScriptEngine;
  {$endif}
  property ErrorHandling: TParserErrorHandling
    read GetErrorHandling write SetErrorHandling default peException;
  property SearchOwner : boolean read GetSearchOwner write SetSearchOwner;
  property OnSetValue : TSetValueEvent read FOnSetValue write SetOnSetValue;
  property OnGetValue : TGetValueEvent read FOnGetValue write SetOnGetValue;
end;
```

The TPropertyParser is the component that will actually take a property reference and resolve it to a string that can be displayed in HTML. Actually, it does a bit more than that. Consider the following tag:

```
<#property assign="WebAction1.Enabled" value="False"
result="WebAction1.Enabled">
```

When this is evaluated, it will return "False", because WebAction1 was disabled by the assign/value tag parameters. The general syntax for this tag is as follows:

```
<#property [assign=<property reference> [value=<constant or property
reference>]]
  [result=<property reference>]>
```

If you want the tag to embed text into your output, set the result tag parameter. Otherwise, it will simply be used as a primitive scripting mechanism. The result tag is always evaluated last, as the following code shows:

```
resourcestring
  SPropertyTag = 'property';
  SPropertyExpression = 'result';
  SPropertyAssign = 'assign';
  SPropertyValue = 'value';
```

```
...

function TPropertyProducer.HandleTag(const TagString: string;
  TagParams: TStrings): string;
var
  Tag: TTag;
  Assign,
  Value,
  Expression : string;
begin
  Tag := GetTagID(TagString);
  if SameText(TagString, SPropertyTag) then
  begin
    Assign := TagParams.Values[ SPropertyAssign ];
    Value := TagParams.Values[ SPropertyValue ];
    Expression := TagParams.Values[ SPropertyExpression ];
    if (Assign <> '') then // assigning
      AssignValue(Assign, Value);
    if (Expression <> '') then // specific result
      Result := Lookup(Expression)
    else
      Result := '';
  end
  else
    Result := '';
  DoTagEvent(Tag, TagString, TagParams, Result);
end;
```

TComponentPropProducer adds referencing for a specific component you reference as a property, and for searching the owner of the TComponentPropProducer.

```
TComponentPropProducer = class(TPropertyProducer)
private
  procedure SetComponent(const Value: TComponent);
  function GetComponent: TComponent;
protected
  procedure Notification(AComponent: TComponent; Operation: TOperation);
    override;
public
  function Lookup(const AExpression: string) : variant; override;
  procedure AssignValue(const AExpression, AValue : string); override;
published
  property Component : TComponent read GetComponent write SetComponent;
end;
```

With this component, you can access (if you enable it) the published property of any component owned by the same owner as the component property producer.

## Handling Free-form Text

I have a pet peeve about the default NetCLX data producers. When the field in question is a free-form text field, you simply get "(memo)" back as the result because the database content producers use the `TField.DisplayText` method to produce the text representation of the data. I want to actually see the free-form text, with a slight bit of intelligence for handling hard-wrapped lines. So, I created custom versions of two of the DataSet content producers—one for tables, and another one for pages. Here are the methods I implemented for formatting the data, along with a routine they call for gracefully handling hard returns in the text:

```
function HTMLEscape(const sText: string): string;
var
  i, l : integer;
begin
  l := Length( sText );
  Result := '';
  for i := 1 to l do
    case sText[ i ] of
    '<' : Result := Result + '&lt;';
    '>' : Result := Result + '&gt;';
    '&' : Result := Result + '&amp;';
    '"' : Result := Result + '&quot;';
    #13,
    #10 :
      if not (sText[i - 1] in [#13,#10]) then
        Result := Result + '<br>'#13#10;
    #92,
    #160 .. #255 : Result := Result + '&#' + IntToStr( Ord( sText[ i ] ) );
    else
      Result := Result + sText[ i ]
    end; { case }
end;


function TDataSetParamTableProducer.FormatCell(CellRow,
  CellColumn: Integer; CellData: String; const Tag: String;
  const BgColor: THTMLBgColor; Align: THTMLAlign; VAlign: THTMLVAlign;
  const Custom: String): String;
begin
  if SameText(CellData, SBadMemo)
    and (Columns.Items[CellColumn].Field is TBlobField) then
    CellData := HTMLEscape(Columns.Items[CellColumn].Field.AsString);
  Result := inherited FormatCell(CellRow, CellColumn, CellData, Tag, BgColor,
Align,
    VAlign, Custom);
end;
```

From a recent discussion on one of the Borland newsgroups, I've learned there is a much faster HTML encoder than `HTMLEscape` available on CodeCentral. You might want to look for it there. The `FormatCell` routine will format the data for a specific table cell. This version handles free-format fields better.

`SBadMemo` is a `resourcestring` containing the text `"(memo)"` so you can change its value to support multiple languages:

```
procedure TDataSetParamPageProducer.DoTagEvent(Tag: TTag;
  const TagString: String; TagParams: TStrings; var ReplaceText: String);
var
  Field: TField;
begin
  if (TagParams.Count = 0) and Assigned(FDataSet) then
  begin
    Field := FDataSet.FindField(TagString);
    if Assigned(Field) then
    begin
      ReplaceText := Field.DisplayText;
      if SameText(ReplaceText, SBadMemo) then
        ReplaceText := HTMLEscape(Field.AsString);
    end;
  end;
  inherited DoTagEvent(Tag, TagString, TagParams, ReplaceText);
end;
```

This event overrides the default text representation for a DataSet page producer with a nicely formatted version of free-form text.

## Layout

A lot of browser/client problems are addressed with a simple layout that is modular. By doing this, you can change the appearance of a specific data item without breaking the entire generated page content. Let's look at some specific examples. This first HTML template is used to produce the home page:

```
<table border="0" width="100%">
<tr>

<td valign="top" class="genres" width="15%">

<p class="titlebar">Genres</p>
<#property result="dsppActiveGenres.GetContent">
</td>

<td>
```

```
<p class="titlebar">Featured Movies</p>
<table border="0" width="100%">
<tr>
<#property result="dsppFeatured.GetContent">
</tr>
</table>

<p class="titlebar">Best Sellers</p>
<table border=0 width="100%">
<tr>
<#property result="dsppBestSellers.GetContent">
</tr>
</table>

<p class="titlebar">Recent Movies</p>
<table border=0 width="100%">
<tr>
<#property result="dsppRecent.GetContent">
</tr>
</table>

</td>
</tr>
</table>
```

As you can see, it uses the property producer technology I discussed earlier to insert the various sections of the items from the database. The home page producer is a TComponentPropProducer, so it can refer to the other components in the Web module if I set its SearchOwner property to True.

The dsppFeatured.GetContent (as well as the other #property tag results) reference a published property that returns the results of the Content function for the producer. Here's the HTML template for dsppFeatured:

```
<td width="33%">
<p class="movietitle">
<a href="<#server>/movie?movie_key=<#movie_key>"
title="<#title>"><#title></a><br>
<a href="<#server>/movie?movie_key=<#movie_key>" title="<#title>">
<img src="<#path>/images/sm_<#image_file>"></a>
</p>
</td>
```

It simply plugs in a table cell that has a high degree of formatting (at least when you compare it to using an HTML table producer) that has links to movies and more. The table cell width is set to 33 percent because the home page generates three movie references using this. The property RecsToDisplay is set to 3, meaning that three records will be displayed when the Content function is executed, providing three columns for the table. The following code shows how this works:

```
function TDataSetParamPageProducer.Content: String;
var
  Displayed: integer;
  AutoActivate: boolean;
begin
  AssignParameters;
  AutoActivate := not FDataSet.Active;
  if AutoActivate then FDataSet.Open;
  try
    Result := '';
    Displayed := 0;
    repeat
      Result := Result + inherited Content;
      Inc(Displayed);
      if (FRecsToDisplay <> 0) then
        DataSet.Next;
    until (DataSet.Eof) or ((FRecsToDisplay > -1)
      and (Displayed >= FRecsToDisplay));
  finally
    if AutoActivate then FDataSet.Close;
  end;
end;
```

As you can see from this code, if you leave the RecsToDisplay property at 0, the content producer will only merge the current record (behaving exactly like the default TDataSetPageProducer component). Setting it to a value greater than zero will make the component navigate forward through the dataset to the specified number of records. Setting it to -1 will cause it to navigate to the end of the dataset from the current position.

There is also a reference to a special tag for #server that is not a dataset field. This tag substitution is handled by the following code:

```
procedure TwmShowCase.CheckDefaultTag(Sender: TObject; Tag: TTag;
  const TagString: String; TagParams: TStrings; var ReplaceText: String);
begin
  if SameText(TagString, 'server') then
    ReplaceText := Request.InternalScriptName
  else if SameText(TagString, 'path') then
    ReplaceText := 'http://' + Request.Host + WebPath(Request);
end;
```

dsppFeatured has `sqlFeatured` as its `DataSet`. The query for `sqlFeatures` is `select * from movies where featured = 'Y'`. The content producer will limit the record navigation to three records. The other producers work similarly for the data they publish. Some point to the stored procedures described earlier in this chapter rather than having a SQL select statement. Figure 17.1 shows the output of the home page running in Internet Explorer from a Windows box talking to my Linux server box.

**FIGURE 17.1**
*Movi-E-Tailer home page.*

## Navigation

Once data is presented on the Web page, being able to click and move to information specific for an item is an essential feature. When I was working on these custom NetCLX components, I thought it would be extremely convenient to be able to specify the item you were interested in by using it as part of the URL, and setting it up to support parameterized queries easily. This ended up working even better than I expected. That's why these dataset producer component extensions I've been talking about have "Param" in their name—so that you can conveniently assign the values for the parameterized queries they use.

This general-purpose routine takes care of the parameter assignment from the query fields of the URL passed to the Web server in the Web request:

```
procedure DoAssignParameters(Sender: TComponent; DataSet: TDataSet;Request:
TWebRequest);
var
  i: integer;
  Params: TParams;
  CurVal,
  NewVal,
  ParamName: string;
  Changed: boolean;

begin
  if (Request = nil) then
    if not (Sender.Owner is TCustomWebDispatcher) then
      Oops(Sender, SBadOwner)
    else
      Request := TCustomWebDispatcher(Sender.Owner).Request;

  if not Assigned(DataSet) then
    Oops(Sender, SNoDataSet);

  //! This is not working!
  Params := IProviderSupport(DataSet).PSGetParams;

  //! This should go away!
  if not Assigned(Params) then
  begin
    if DataSet is TClientDataSet then
      Params := TClientDataSet(DataSet).Params
    else if DataSet is TSQLDataSet then
      Params := TSQLDataSet(DataSet).Params
    else if DataSet is TSQLClientDataSet then
      Params := TSQLClientDataSet(DataSet).Params;
    if not Assigned(Params) then
      Oops(Sender, SNoParams);
  end;

  Changed := False;

  for i := 0 to Params.Count - 1 do
    if (Params[i].ParamType = ptInput) then
    begin
      ParamName := Params[i].Name;
      if (Request.QueryFields.IndexOfName(ParamName) <> -1) then
```

```
  begin
    CurVal := Params[i].asString;
    NewVal := Request.QueryFields.Values[ParamName];
    if CurVal <> NewVal then
    begin
      Changed := True;
      Params[i].AsString := NewVal;
    end;
  end;
end;

if Changed and (DataSet.Active) then
begin
  DataSet.Close;
  DataSet.Open;
end;

end;
```

The two comments in this code are due to the IProviderSupport implementation not working correctly. It may be fixed by the time you read this. There are two important details to note about this routine: First, that it only assigns parameters whose names match query fields of the request; and second, that the dataset is re-opened only if the value of the parameters change, which is a quick little optimization to prevent unnecessary re-fetches of the data.

The URL http://jfkylix/showcase/movies/genre?genre_key=8 produces the page shown in Figure 17.2.

It generates this page with two producer components. The first one is the component producer for showing the entire genre page. Here is its template:

```
<p class="titlebar"><#property result="wmShowCase.PageTitle"></p>

<table border="0" width="100%">
<#property result="dsppMovieGenre.GetContent">
</table>
```

As you can see, it references the dsppMovieGenre component's content, which points to a SQL component with CommandText set to "select * from MOVIES where genre_key = :genre_key." As you can see, this SQL statement has a parameter for genre_key, which is what automatically makes the selection of the appropriate data from the dataset. Because the RecsToDisplay is set to -1, the entire result set is displayed.

**FIGURE 17.2**

*Science Fiction Genre page.*

The HTML template for this component is simple as well:

```
<tr><td valign="top"><a href="<#server>/movie?movie_key=<#movie_key>"
  title="<#title>">
<img src="<#path>/images/sm_<#image_file>" alt="<#title>" border="0"></a></td>
<td>
<p class="SubTitle">
<a href="<#server>/movie?movie_key=<#movie_key>"
title="<#title>"><#title></a></p>
<p class="description"><#description></p>
<hr>
</td>
</tr>
```

This sets up the link for the movie detail page, which is also a parameterized dataset producer. I'll leave that to you to compile and run so you can see what it looks like.

## Summary

In this chapter, I described a "real-world" application—a GUI client that can be used to build inventory for a Web-based catalogue rapidly, and the Web server application that publishes the information in the database. You found out how to use `ActionLists` and HTML content producers, and how to create custom content producer components.

# Database Optimizations

*by John Kaster*

## IN THIS CHAPTER

In this chapter, you will find tips and techniques for improving the performance of your Kylix database applications. Some of the tips will be specific to the CLX data-aware components. Some of the tips are SQL database server related.

# Introduction

There have been entire books written on the subject of database optimizations, so I'm just going to suggest some of the most common and simple approaches to performance-tuning your Kylix database applications. Some of these techniques involve SQL source code, and others involve either the usage of existing DataCLX components, or simple utility functions that can result in big performance gains when dealing with large datasets.

> **NOTE**
>
> Much of the material for this chapter comes from two TeamB (`http://www.teamb.com`) members I've grown to rely on over the years for deeper technical discussions about database issues: Jeff Overcash and Rob Schieck. In fact, you may find that some of this chapter is extremely similar to material you have seen from them in other venues. This is intentional; if they did a good job presenting the information before, why should I rewrite it and confuse the issue?
>
> You can always find them on the Borland newsgroups, giving newsgroup participants valuable insights into database programming with Kylix, Delphi, C++ Builder, and particularly InterBase. Rob also has excellent database-related resources on his Web site at `http://www.mers.com`.
>
> Most of the information in this chapter is used with InterBase as the database. This is simply because it is the database I have become most familiar with in the past several years. InterBase is my database of choice, and my optimization knowledge is most recent with it. Fortunately, most of the tips in this chapter will apply to any SQL database, although some of the specifics may vary slightly.

# Populate Your Database

Kylix makes it extremely easy to build database applications. This is both a blessing and a curse. It is very easy to develop an application that performs well in tests, and then performs slowly when the system starts becoming loaded with data and users. You should make every attempt to populate your database with data that is either the actual data and amount of data your application will be handling, or some approximation of it.

Most developers don't do this. What most developers do is create their metadata (create their tables and indices), populate each table with a few records (we'll say six), build their application, and then deliver it.

With only six records in each table you won't know during the development process whether you have made an error or not because no matter how you retrieve six records from the database it is always fast. If you had put a hundred thousand records into your customer database, and during the development process you found it took 15 seconds to retrieve a customer, you would know immediately that you have a problem that needs to be fixed.

It's sort of a "pay me now or pay me later" scenario. If you fully populate your database before you start development you'll find your errors and problems during development. Or, you can put six records in your tables and find your errors during production when the heat is really on and you might have to re-factor (which is just the politically savvy term for redesign) some of your application.

## Monitor the SQL Communication

Give a man a fish and feed him for a day, teach him to fish and feed him for life. TSQLMonitor is your fishing pole for doing database development. It allows you to see the conversations that go on between the client and the server.

TSQLMonitor allows you to compare how application changes affect the conversation between your application and the server. It allows you to see exactly how your components are using the database server.

Invest some time in TSQLMonitor (using the generic SQL Monitoring form introduced in Chapter 15, "Working with Data-Aware Components") and it will give you an excellent education on how DataCLX components interact with your SQL server, which will allow you to build highly optimized applications.

If the SQL server you are using supports it, also examine the plans that are used for your data retrieval requests. When you have confused a SQL optimizer, it will often resort to a table scan, which does not use an index. This wastes the performance gains your carefully planned indices could provide. Also, avoid forcing plans if at all possible. Forcing a plan on the database engine can fail if the index becomes unavailable for some reason (disabled during a batch update, for instance).

# Avoid Holding Transactions Open for Long Periods of Time

This is advice you will hear quite often from SQL experts. The problem is, how long exactly is a "long period of time?" The duration of the transaction isn't necessarily as important as what is done with the transaction. If you're going to hold a transaction open for a day and do nothing with it, that is not nearly as severe as holding transactions open all day and running a query every minute and a half. The former will prevent InterBase from doing garbage collection. The latter will also prevent InterBase from doing garbage collection, and in addition will cause InterBase to consume more and more memory to keep track of what is going on in the transaction. The latter can cause significant slowdowns in performance.

For example, one company would open their application in the morning and InterBase would be consuming roughly 180 to 200 megabytes of memory on the server. Because transactions were being held open all day and select queries being run against them, by the end of the day, InterBase was consuming 950 megabytes of memory. The difference in performance was readily visible when the backups were run. With InterBase consuming 950 megabytes of memory, the backup would take an hour to run. If you shut down InterBase and restarted it to free all the memory, the backup would take six minutes.

As you can see, holding transactions open for several minutes isn't a major problem. Holding a transaction open all day and running lots of queries against that transaction can cause major problems.

# Do Not Parameterize Queries that Contain the Verb "Like"

The verb "like" is somewhat tricky to use correctly. Assuming you have an index on the lastname field, the following SQL will cause InterBase to use this index correctly:

```
select * from customer where lastname like 'SCH%';
```

However, the following SQL will be slow and cause excessive load on the InterBase server because it will not use an index:

```
select * from customer where lastname like '%SCH%;
```

The only way InterBase can solve this SQL statement is to do a table scan. This means that InterBase will retrieve every record from disk for the customer table, examine it to see if the lastname field contains a *SCH*. Table scans are slow and should be avoided!

The following queries will cause table scans:

```
select * from customer where lastname like :aparam;
```

This causes a table scan because InterBase doesn't know if you are going to send SCH% or %SCH% as the parameter, so it optimized for the lowest common denominator, which results in a table scan.

It doesn't matter what you submit to the function or what the function is; InterBase cannot tell what the output of the function is ahead of time so it optimizes this query down to a table scan:

```
select * from customer where lastname like upper('something');
```

If you have to perform a lot of queries with case-insensitivity, you may want to create a case-insensitive index either using a custom collation sequence for a column that does case-insensitive collation, or by creating another field in the data record that is the uppercase version of the field you want to index, and setting up a trigger to convert the original value to its uppercase equivalent whenever the data changes.

The only way for InterBase to determine the output of the Upper(lastname) function in this query is to run the lastname field through the function which means a table scan will happen:

```
select * from customer where upper(lastname) like '%SCH';
```

Generally, table scans are slow; indices are fast. Use "like" carefully and your application will fly.

## Avoid Primary Keys and Foreign Keys

Most SQL databases have the capability to declare primary keys and foreign key in your table definitions. Although the declarative aspects of these features make them easy to use, you may want to avoid them.

For primary keys, use a unique index. This allows you to name the index, so when you post a duplicate value to the table you get an exception with an Index name instead of some cryptic engine-creating index name. In addition, unique indices can be deactivated and reactivated to rebuild the indices where primary keys cannot.

Foreign keys are a different story. Let's assume you have a table with a field called Address_State and you want to limit what is accepted in that field to one of the 50 States, so you create a foreign key to a table called States. When you make the foreign key declaration, InterBase will create an index on the Address_State field. The purpose of this index is for when you try to delete a row from the States table. It will allow InterBase to quickly check the Address_State field to ensure the value contained in the States table record that you are trying to delete is not present in the Address_State field.

The performance problem is with the index that is created on the `Address_State` field. If you have 1,000,000 records in your table, and there are 50 states, then there are roughly 20,000 records per state in the `Address_State` field index, making it a very poor index. If the InterBase optimizer chooses this index, there can be problems.

One site that had this problem was running a report that never finished. An examination of the problem revealed that one column had 95,000 rows with the number 3 in it and 5,000 nulls. There was an index on this field created by a foreign key. The InterBase optimizer found this index and the index caused the optimizer to solve the problem backwards. The result was a report/query that could not finish in 10 hours. By dropping the foreign key and its index and replacing it with triggers, the optimizer solved the problem in a couple of minutes, and the reports came out.

## Use Stored Procedures

InterBase allows for selectable stored procedures. This allows you to build a result set on-the-fly, so you can loop through the main table and do individual lookups on the secondary table to get the field(s) that need to be returned. Stored procedures can also be made updatable with the use of triggers in InterBase. The stored procedure in Listing 17.1 executes its secondary `select` statement only for those records matching the first one, but it "flattens" the result set to make it look like only one dataset was queried.

**LISTING 17.1**   The `select_childSchool` Stored Procedure

```
create procedure select_childSchool
returns (name varchar(30), school_name varchar(30))
as
  declare variable school_key integer;
begin
  for select name, school_key from children into :name, :school_key do
  begin
    school_name = null;
    select school_name from schools
      where school_key = :school_key into :school_name ;
    suspend;
  end
end
```

InterBase can create complicated result sets with stored procedures. This allows you to greatly manipulate data to return result sets that cannot be done with normal SQL statements, or much faster than a normal Select statement because all results are gathered on the server without round trips between the client and the server. The following query is used in CodeCentral to count the number of publicly visible entries for each product and category in the database:

```
create procedure snippet_counts
returns
(
  CATEGORY VARCHAR(64),
  CATEGORY_ID INTEGER,
  PRODUCT VARCHAR(64),
  PRODUCT_ID INTEGER,
  SUMMARY INTEGER
)
AS
  declare variable high double precision;
  declare variable low double precision;
begin
  for select category_id, description from category
  where category_id <> 0
  order by description into :category_id, :category do
  begin
    for select product_id, description, low_version, high_version
        from product
        where product_id <> 0 and (not low_version is null )
        order by description
        into :product_id, :product, :low, :high do
    begin
      select count(product_id) from snippet
      where category_id = :category_id and
            product_id = :product_id and
            low_version >= :low and
            high_version <= :high
      into :summary;
      suspend;
    end
  end
end
```

# Be Trigger-Happy

Use triggers, not stored procedures, to enforce relational logic between tables. When you rely on stored procedures, you are hoping that all users, no matter how they will connect to your database, will know to use the stored procedure to insert a record. Insert, Update and Delete logic belongs in a trigger against the table to enforce the required logic for any data change. Note that with Oracle the problem of mutating triggers often pops up. In these cases, stored procedures can be a simpler way to achieve the desired result.

# Be Picky

Let the SQL server do the work for which it was designed. Don't return result sets of 10,000 records for a user to scroll through. We haven't met a human being yet who can work with that much data at once. Force the user to refine the data they want to work with before returning things by designing an application interface that helps them do so.

# Parameterize and Prepare Your Queries for Maximum Performance

Every SQL statement that is sent to InterBase is prepared, either by you or by the tools you use. Preparing a query is a reasonably expensive process, especially over low-speed lines or the Internet. For example, in one project that ran over 28.8Kb dial up lines, the first child took 30 seconds to be returned because of the prepares that had to be done, while subsequent children took 4 seconds each.

In the case of DataCLX, if you don't prepare your statement, it will be prepared for you when you open your `TCustomSQLDataSet` descendant, such as `TSQLDataSet`. DataCLX will leave your query prepared if possible, but several cases will cause it to be unprepared, like changing the `CommandText`. Look at the code in `SqlExpr.pas`, and find the statements for `SetPrepared(False)` or `Prepared := False` to see what will cause your statements to be unprepared. If you know that you have not changed the SQL statement or that it doesn't have parameters, you can pass `True` for the value of the `ExecDirect` parameter when calling the `ExecSQL` method.

# Avoid Fetchalls Like the Plague

A *fetchall* is something you do that causes your application to fetch all the records for a select statement from the database server.

For example, if you have 100,000 people in a database and do a `select * from people where lastname like 'A%'` you will be selecting approximately 10,000 of those records.

Retrieve only what the user needs to start working. Flooding the network is rarely a good thing. All `TCustomClientDataset` descendants have `-1` as the default for the `PacketRecords` property. This tells the dataset component to fetch all the records on opening. On large result sets, this will result in a long delay while everything is being pulled across. Consider setting `PacketRecords` to a low number, like 10, to spread out the network traffic and allow the user to start working faster. Perception is sometimes everything.

If you monitor the SQL communication, you can see the fetches from the server and it is very easy to spot a fetchall happening.

# Rob's Rules of Left Outer Joins

I have never been a fan of left outer joins. They tend to be slow and InterBase will only use an index on the first left outer join in a query. I have several ways of avoiding left outer joins.

For the rest of the discussion, here is some sample data. It is displayed similar to what you will see when talking to InterBase in console mode:

```
SQL> select * from children;
  CHILD_KEY NAME                            SCHOOL_KEY
=========== ============================== ===========

          1 Robert Schieck                           0
          2 Jon Schieck                              1
          3 Diane Schieck                            2
          4 Megan Schieck                            3
          5 Robyn Schieck                            4
          6 Emma Schieck                             5

SQL> select * from schools;

 SCHOOL_KEY SCHOOL_NAME
=========== ================================

          1
          2 Sir Winston Churchill
          3 Oakridges Public School
          4 Lady Churchill Senior Public
```

I have four rules for left outer joins to share with you in the following sections.

## Design Out the Left Outer Join

We have a table (children) with children in it and a field called School_Key that is a foreign key (not declared as such in the table) into the Schools table which has the two fields School_Key and School_Name. Because children under 5 do not go to school, they would have a null value in their School_Key field and you would have to do a left outer join to get all the children with their associated School_Name. In your school table there is a record with the following values:

```
School_key 0
School_Name ''
```

Yes, the `School_Name` field is blank, or an empty string. In the children table, the `School_Key` field is defaulted to 0. Now all the children have a school. Just the ones who are not yet in school or are out of school have a school with no name. When you need to see all the children with their associated schools we can use an inner join instead of an outer join:

```
SQL> select c.name, s.school_name from children c,
  schools s where c.school_key = s.school_key;

NAME                              SCHOOL_NAME
==============================    ================================


Jon Schieck
Diane Schieck                     Sir Winston Churchill
Megan Schieck                     Oakridges Public School
Robyn Schieck                     Lady Churchill Senior Public
```

Please notice that Jon Schieck doesn't go to a school.

## Use a Correlated Subquery

Not all SQL servers can use a correlated subquery, or at least not correctly. You may want to run a test with your SQL server to make sure it will return the correct results. For single column results in an outer join place the outer join as a subentry in the `select` statement. Using the previous example, the query to retrieve all the children and their associate schools would look like this:

```
Select c.Name, (select s.school_name from schools s
  where s.school_key = c.school_key) from children c;
```

The embedded correlated query will run once for every row returned, but if there is an index on the correlated table (usually the primary key) this will still be very fast:

```
SQL> Select c.Name, (select s.school_name from schools s
  where s.school_key = c.school_key) from children c;

NAME
==============================    ================================


Robert Schieck
Jon Schieck
Diane Schieck                     Sir Winston Churchill
Megan Schieck                     Oakridges Public School
Robyn Schieck                     Lady Churchill Senior Public
Emma Schieck
```

The two nulls show up because they have a School_Key but no corresponding entry in the schools table.

## Use a Stored Procedure

Stored procedures that return a result set are very powerful.

Here's a SQL command that uses the stored procedure declared in Listing 17.1:

```
SQL> select * from select_childschool;

NAME                            SCHOOL_NAME
============================= ================================

Robert Schieck
Jon Schieck
Diane Schieck                 Sir Winston Churchill
Megan Schieck                 Oakridges Public School
Robyn Schieck                 Lady Churchill Senior Public
Emma Schieck
```

## Use a Left Outer Join

Sometimes there is no substitute for a left outer join:

```
SQL> select c.name, s.school_name from children c left join schools s
  on C.SCHOOL_KEY = S.SCHOOL_KEY;


NAME                            SCHOOL_NAME
============================= ================================

Robert Schieck
Jon Schieck
Diane Schieck                 Sir Winston Churchill
Megan Schieck                 Oakridges Public School
Robyn Schieck                 Lady Churchill Senior Public
Emma Schieck
```

# For Large Databases or Lots of Users, Cache Your Lookup Tables

As the number of users on your system increases, you need to decrease the load on your server. One way to do that is to start caching your lookup tables. For example, there are 50 states in the United States and the odds of a new one being added on any given day is quite remote, so it is a good candidate to be cached. A `ClientDataSet` is an excellent component for caching the `States` table. With the `States` table in a `ClientDataSet`, you no longer need to join the `States` table in your queries on the InterBase server but can simulate the join using a calculated field on the client side.

To cache it, simply create a `TSQLClientDataSet` component and load it the first time you connect to the database for that instance of the application. The following code assumes that `cdsStates` is the name of the component that points to the `States` table:

```
procedure TForm1.SQLConnection1AfterConnect(Sender: TObject);
begin
  if not cdsStates.Acftive then cdsStates.Active := True;
end;
```

Whenever you connect to the database, which shouldn't be that often, you can verify that your lookup tables are already loaded and populated.

Avoid going to the other extreme of persisting this data between runs of the application. Lookup tables do change, so it is better to take a one-time hit on each startup of the application to get the most current look at these tables than it is to build more intricate logic to determine whether they are dirty. This will reduce the load on the server and allow you to service more users.

## Use Smart Lookups

In some cases, it's not practical to cache your lookup data in a `TClientDataSet`. For example, the CodeCentral Web server validates a variety of lookup tables when the surfer is performing a search of the database. CodeCentral is currently implemented as a CGI application, which means that each connection to the database is closed after the results are passed back to the client. Because some of the tables in CodeCentral have tens of thousands of records, it would be extremely expensive time-wise to load all that into a `ClientDataSet` to use as a cached lookup table. In this case, the following routine gives you a smart lookup, and is generic enough that you can use this same technique in just about any application:

```
function OpenQueryID(const DataSet: TCustomSQLDataSet;
  const FieldName: string; const ID: integer; Param: string = ''): boolean;
var
  Ref : TField;
begin
  Ref := DataSet.FieldByName(FieldName);
  if (not DataSet.Active) or (Ref.asInteger <> ID) then
  begin
    if DataSet.Active then
      DataSet.Close;
```

```
  if Param = '' then
    Param := FieldName;
  DataSet.ParamByName(Param).asInteger := ID;
  DataSet.Open;
  Ref := DataSet.FieldByName(FieldName);
end;
Result := Ref.asInteger = ID;
end;
```

As you can see from the parameter list for this function, it expects the ID field to be an integer. You could make it a variant if you chose, but I find that most key fields are integers anyway. You might want to make it int64 if you're going to be working with really large tables.

The following code snippet assumes USERID is the field name for the key field, and the SQL query is something like select * from users where userid = :user_id, which means the parameter name is different than the field name:

```
if OpenQueryID(SQLDataSet1,'USERID', 1, 'USER_ID') then
  // data processing code here
```

## Turn Off Metadata

When you are done designing your application, set the NoMetaData property to True for your dataset component to avoid fetching the metadata for the table unnecessarily every time you open the dataset. This will tremendously improve the performance of your select statements.

NOTE

This property is not available in the 1.0 version of Kylix, but should be provided in a patch by the time you read this, and also available in Kylix 2.0 and greater. Go to http://www.borland.com/kylix/ to see if the patch is available.

## Need Speed? Turn Off Asynchronous Writes, But Beware of the Risks

By default, InterBase 5.x on NT has forced write or sync writes turned on. This means when InterBase tells NT to write something to disk, NT is not allowed to put it into the OS cache, it must write it to disk immediately.

On Unix platforms, the default is to have force writes off. This means when InterBase tells the Unix operating system to write something to disk, Unix puts it into its cache and writes it out to disk when it is ready.

What is the difference in performance? Inserting 13,000 records via a stored procedure into a table with forced writes on it took 15 minutes; with forced writes off it took 45 seconds.

As with everything, there is a price to be paid and in this case the speed comes with risk. If the InterBase server or the Operating system crashes while InterBase is writing to disk, you stand a good chance of corrupting your database, potentially to the point of making it impossible to repair.

If you choose to turn off "force writes" to improve performance, make sure your computer is on a UPS and do regularly scheduled backups.

# Understand Database Indexing

Developers new to database programming frequently go overboard when indexing the data in their database.

## Understand Selectivity

*Selectivity* means how granular the index is. Selectivity closer to 1 is better; anything over 100 starts to become suspect. A Primary key index, for instance, will be 1 because the index is unique. An index on a field with only two values (such as sex) will have a selectivity of approximately the number of records divided by 2 (~ (# of records)/ 2). Indices take time to maintain, so only build indices on column(s) that will give you good selectivity results.

## Be Careful Using Foreign Keys

As mentioned previously, foreign keys will always create an index on the key fields. Often, if this foreign key is a lookup table, it will have very poor selectivity. Instead use triggers to maintain referential integrity.

## Multi-Column Indices

Multi-column indices always put the most selective items first. InterBase can use a multi-column index and only use partial columns. For instance, if you have a multi-column index on dept_no, proj_no and your select statement selects on dept_no it can use this index because dept_no is first. If you select proj_no, the index can't be used. Most optimizers will be able to select the appropriate index options if you have indices on individual fields.

## Ordering an Index

If you plan on retrieving values in a descending order, create the index in descending order to make sure the optimizer will pick it. For example, order on a date field in descending order to see most recent items first.

## Index Fields Sparingly

Avoid having two indices on a table that start with the same column. This situation can greatly confuse the optimizer. Oracle will always use the index with the least number of columns in it, making multi-column indices worthless (this was a 7.3.4 item; it may be addressed with Oracle 8i or 9).

# InterBase-Specific Tips

The following tips are very InterBase-specific, so I'm reluctant to make claims that they will apply to other SQL database engines. They may or may not, and I recommend trying them with your preferred database to see if they make a difference.

## Do Not Use Large Varchars

InterBase stores chars and varchars internally essentially the same way. Externally, chars are returned to your Delphi application padded with blanks to the length of the field. On the other hand, varchars are presented to your application with no trailing blanks. What most people don't realize is that InterBase passes chars and varchars over the network the same way, fully padded out. To help you visualize this, think of a varchar(32000) with just the letter a in the field. When this field is passed over the network it will be passed as the letter a and 31,999 filler characters.

When you are designing your database, remember that chars and varchars are passed between the client server fully padded out. If you wish to have a long variable length string, consider using a blob.

## Always Build Your Front-End Application Using a Remote Connection

There are two types of connections that you can make, local and remote. A local connection string looks like:

```
\path\to\mydatabase.gdb
```

It uses memory-mapped files to do the communication between your application and the server, and it is deceptively fast. This type of connection is significantly faster than what you can expect when you use a remote server.

A remote connection looks like:

```
localhost:\path\to\mydatabase.gdb
```

or

```
myserver:c:\path\tomydatabase.gdb
```

A remote connection goes through the network to gain access to InterBase, and gives performance that one would expect from a client/server application.

The extra speed of a local connection easily hides serious performance/design problems. These problems will surface when you finally connect to a remote server.

## Use a 2KB or 4KB Page Size for Your Database

The default page size in InterBase 5.x is 1KB, which is too small. Memory is cheap! So is disk space, so you should increase the page size to 2KB or 4KB. I use 4KB by default, and 8KB on systems with large tables. The larger page size results in reduced index depth and the capability to hold larger blobs and records on a single page. All these things increase performance, especially for the indices, if you have long tables.

The only way to change the page size of an existing database is to back it up and restore it with a new page size.

## Understand Index Plans

> **NOTE**
>
> The information in this section for the discussion of index plans is adapted from material written by Bruno Sonnino. For this discussion of plans, it is convenient to use both IBConsole for Linux and InterBaseExpress (IBX), which Jeff Overcash currently keeps up-to-date on his CodeCentral page at http://codecentral.borland.com. You can check there for more recent versions than those included on this book's CD. IBX comes with Delphi 5 and above and C++ Builder 5 and above, but it's not included in the first release of Kylix.

You'll use a test database (called plantest.gdb) provided on the CD that accompanies this book. When a query is submitted to the database server, the server will analyze the involved tables and indexes, generating a plan to optimize the data recovery. You can view the generated plan in the Interactive SQL window of IBConsole on the Plan tab, as shown in Figure 18.1.

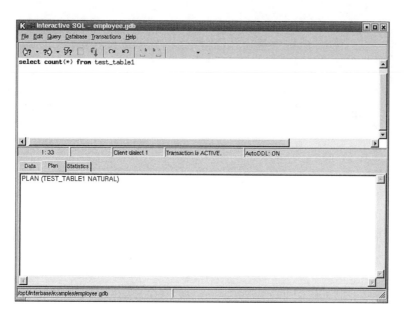

**FIGURE 18.1**

*Viewing the query plan.*

In this figure, you can see that, to recover the record count for TEST_TABLE1, InterBase will use the natural order to scan all rows. For example, if you use the statement

```
SELECT COUNT(*) FROM TEST_TABLE1 WHERE ID BETWEEN 3000 AND 5000
```

the plan is changed to

```
PLAN (TEST_TABLE1 INDEX (RDB$PRIMARY8))
```

indicating the use of the primary index.

The index plan shows how InterBase is recovering the records, and may help you determine which indices to create to optimize the queries. You could use IBConsole to submit your queries and take a look at the plan, but there is a problem: the current version of IBConsole doesn't show the time to execute the query in the Statistics tab, and it is very convenient to know exactly how long it takes to run a query.

Furthermore, dbExpress doesn't have a way to retrieve the plan for the query, so you can't use it to show what happens internally. You could time the queries in a dbExpress application and view the plan in IBConsole, but this is not a practical way. A better way is to use InterBaseExpress (IBX), Borland's components that talk specifically to the InterBase API. Let's create a small program to execute queries, time them, and show their plan.

This application is included on the CD in the folder PlanQry and is shown in Figure 18.2.

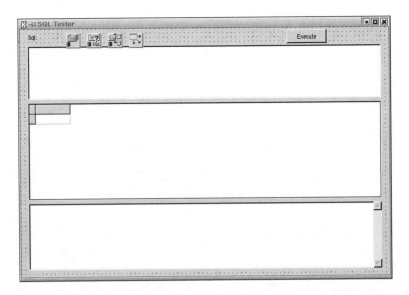

**FIGURE 18.2**

*Application to view the query plan.*

It uses IBX components: a `TIBDatabase`, a `TIBQuery` and a `TIBTransaction` and has three panes. The first pane is a memo for entering your query. When you click the button, the query is executed and its results are shown in the second pane in a `TDBGrid`, which uses the `TDataSource` connected to the `TIBQuery`. The third pane shows the time to execute the query, and the plan used by InterBase for retrieving the query results. The plan is obtained using the `TIBQuery`'s `Plan` property. The `OnClick` event handler for the `Execute` button is:

```
procedure TForm1.Button1Click(Sender: TObject);
var
  ActualTime : TDateTime;
begin
  with IBQuery1 do begin
    if Active then begin
      if IBTransaction1.InTransaction then
        IBTransaction1.Commit;
      Close;
    end;
// assign the memo lines to the SQL property of the TIBQuery
    Sql := Memo1.Lines;
    try
// gets the actual time
      ActualTime := Now;
```

```
// opens the query - if it cannot be opened with Active := True
// (doesn't have a result set)
//    will raise an exception
        if not IBTransaction1.InTransaction then
            IBTransaction1.StartTransaction;
        Active := True;
// shows in the second memo the time to execute the query and its plan
        Memo2.Lines.Add('Time to execute query: '
            +FormatDateTime('hh:nn:ss.zzz',Now-ActualTime));
        Memo2.Lines.Add(Plan);
        Memo2.Lines.Add('------------------------------');
    except
// query doesn't return a result set, execute with ExecSql
        On EDatabaseError do
            if not Active then begin
            // gets the actual time
                ActualTime := Now;
                if not IBTransaction1.InTransaction then
                    IBTransaction1.StartTransaction;
                ExecSql;
                IBTransaction1.Commit;
// shows in the second memo the time to execute the query and its plan
                Memo2.Lines.Add('Time to execute query: '
                    +FormatDateTime('hh:nn:ss.zzz',Now-ActualTime));
                Memo2.Lines.Add(Plan);
                Memo2.Lines.Add('------------------------------');
            end
            else begin
                if IBTransaction1.InTransaction then
                    IBTransaction1.Rollback;
                raise;
            end;
        end;
    end;
end;
```

## Optimizing the Queries

Now you have a way to test your statements. Initially, you will create a statement to retrieve all records from table1 beginning with *B*:

```
SELECT * FROM TEST_TABLE1 WHERE DESCRIPTION BETWEEN 'B' AND 'BZ'
```

The result in the second memo is:

```
Time to execute query: 00:00:00.069
PLAN (TEST_TABLE1 NATURAL)
```

It shows that your query took 69 milliseconds to execute and used the natural order to scan the records. You can try to optimize this query by creating an index on the description:

```
CREATE INDEX TEST_DESC ON TEST_TABLE1 (DESCRIPTION)
```

After re-executing the query, the second memo shows:

```
Time to execute query: 00:00:00.015
PLAN (TEST_TABLE1 INDEX (TEST_DESC))
```

The query took 4.6 times less to execute, and used the index just created. As you can see, it's a good improvement. Now, consider a more complex query, to retrieve the sum of the order values on March/2001:

```
SELECT ORDER_NO, ORDER_DATE,SUM(TOTAL_VALUE) AS TOTVALUE FROM TEST_TABLE2
WHERE ORDER_DATE BETWEEN '3/1/2001' AND '3/31/2001'
GROUP BY ORDER_DATE,ORDER_NO
```

After executing it, the memo shows:

```
Time to execute query: 00:00:12.584
PLAN SORT ((TEST_TABLE2 NATURAL))
```

For this query, the optimizer selected natural order. Let's speed this up with a new index, ordered by ORDER_DATE:

```
CREATE INDEX TEST_ORDER_DATE ON TEST_TABLE2 (ORDER_DATE)
```

Re-executing the query shows this on the memo:

```
Time to execute query: 00:00:06.974
PLAN SORT ((TEST_TABLE2 INDEX (TEST_ORDER_DATE)))
```

This time, the query took half of the time to execute and used the index you created. As you can see, you can have a great speed improvement using the right indexes. You will now use a join between two tables and see the results:

```
SELECT T1.ID,T1.DESCRIPTION,SUM(T2.QUANTITY) FROM
TEST_TABLE1 T1 INNER JOIN TEST_TABLE2 T2 ON T1.ID = T2.PRODUCT_ID
WHERE T1.DESCRIPTION STARTING WITH 'B'
GROUP BY T1.ID,T1.DESCRIPTION
```

This query retrieves the total quantities for records which description starts with B. When you execute it, the result is:

```
Time to execute query: 00:04:35.379
PLAN SORT (JOIN (T2 NATURAL,T1 INDEX (RDB$PRIMARY13,TEST_DESC)))
```

Then, you create a new index, on the PRODUCT_ID field of TEST_TABLE2:

```
CREATE INDEX TEST_PRODUCT_ID ON TEST_TABLE2 (PRODUCT_ID)
```

Executing the query again, you get

```
Time to execute query: 00:01:02.083
PLAN SORT (JOIN (T1 INDEX (TEST_DESC),T2 INDEX (TEST_PRODUCT_ID)))
```

That's a 4-times speed increase. As you can see, the plan has also changed. Before, InterBase scanned all rows in table2 and joined with table1 using the primary key. After creating the new index, InterBase uses the index to select the rows in table1 and then joins with table2.

Sometimes, just reordering the query gives a speed improvement on the execution. This example shows how it is done:

```
SELECT T1.ID,T1.DESCRIPTION,SUM(T2.QUANTITY)
  FROM TEST_TABLE1 T1, TEST_TABLE2 T2
  WHERE T1.ID BETWEEN 2000 AND 3000 and T1.ID = T2.PRODUCT_ID

  GROUP BY T1.ID,T1.DESCRIPTION
```

When you run this query, the memo shows:

```
Time to execute query: 00:01:16.682
PLAN SORT (JOIN (T1 INDEX (RDB$PRIMARY13),T2 INDEX (TEST_PRODUCT_ID)))
```

The query will take more than a minute to execute. You will reorder the WHERE clause, using

```
SELECT T1.ID,T1.DESCRIPTION,SUM(T2.QUANTITY)
  FROM TEST_TABLE1 T1, TEST_TABLE2 T2
  WHERE T1.ID = T2.PRODUCT_ID AND T1.ID BETWEEN 2000 AND 3000

  GROUP BY T1.ID,T1.DESCRIPTION
```

This time, the memo shows

```
Time to execute query: 00:00:06.639
PLAN SORT (JOIN (T2 INDEX (TEST_PRODUCT_ID),T1 INDEX (RDB$PRIMARY13)))
```

This is more than 11 times faster than the first query! When designing your queries you must be very careful with the order you arrange them, as this can be the difference between a slow and a fast application.

## Changing plans

Sometimes, the optimizer doesn't find the optimal plan, and a manual plan is better than the one generated by InterBase. If you elect to override the default plan the optimizer selected, you need to pay special attention to any metadata or index changes you may make to the database because your plan may end up no longer being the best way to perform a query. It is usually

**18**

better to let the optimizer choose the correct plan by keeping your indexes simple and indexing strategically. You should also note that the query optimizer is typically enhanced with every new version of InterBase.

If you decide that you definitely want to specify the plan the query should use, include the PLAN keyword in the SELECT statement.

The following statement illustrates:

```
select order_no,sum(total_value) from test_table2
  where order_date = '3/1/2001' group by order_no
```

When you run the query, you get this result in the memo:

```
Time to execute query: 00:00:06.265
PLAN (TEST_TABLE2 ORDER RDB$PRIMARY11)
```

The optimizer will be using the primary index for table2. This index uses the ORDER_NO field to retrieve the rows. As you want the records for a special date, you can try to use the TEST_ORDER_DATE index, which uses the ORDER_DATE field. This is done with the following query:

```
SELECT ORDER_NO,SUM(TOTAL_VALUE)
  FROM TEST_TABLE2
  WHERE ORDER_DATE = '3/1/2001'
  GROUP BY ORDER_NO
  PLAN (TEST_TABLE2 ORDER TEST_ORDER_DATE)
```

This time, when you run the query, you get this result:

```
Time to execute query: 00:00:00.031
PLAN SORT ((TEST_TABLE2 INDEX (TEST_ORDER_DATE)))
```

That's more than 20 times faster than the previous query. As you can see, just tweaking a little with your queries, changing orders, creating indexes, and modifying the original plan can make your queries fly, which your customers would certainly appreciate. When you are designing your queries, you can use a tool like the one you used here to see what's going on and optimize your queries accordingly.

## Set Your Database Cache Buffers with Gfix

There are lots of ways to set the number of cache buffers on an InterBase server. The best way is to set the number of cache buffers allocated on a per database basis. There is no way to set this value using a GUI interface. You must edit the ibconfig file by hand or use gfix. The command to set the buffers is:

```
Gfix -buffers 10000 -user sysdba -password masterkey \path\to\mydatabase.gdb
```

This will set the cache buffers for `mydatabase.gdb` to 10,000 database pages. This means that the first connection to this database will cause InterBase to add 10,000 database pages of memory to its cache. The second and subsequent users will add zero buffers.

The range for buffers is between 0 and 65,535. The empirical testing Rob has done shows a negligible performance increase going from 10,000 buffers to 20,000, so I typically use 10,000.

## Use Single Processor Machines with InterBase

InterBase (SuperServer Architecture) does not know how to use multiple processors correctly. On NT, if you have multiple processors, the InterBase process will get flipped from processor to processor. It will look like InterBase is using multiple processors but it is not. Empirical evidence points to as much as a 30% decrease in performance due to the flipping of the InterBase process.

If you have a multiprocessor machine and are running InterBase on it, you can run InterBase as an application and set its affinity to one processor to prevent the flipping of InterBase from processor to processor. Multiprocessor support should be available in future releases of InterBase, but it is not available in InterBase 6.0 or lower.

# Summary

In this chapter, you've seen a hodgepodge of database optimization techniques. InterBase was used for most of the SQL server discussions, but much of the information that mentions InterBase specifically will also apply to the database you may choose to use. By using the capabilities of the DataCLX components and your SQL server, you should be able to produce extremely high-performance database applications with Kylix.

# Web

## IN THIS PART

# Apache Web Server Applications

*by Bob Swart (a.k.a. Dr. Bob)*

## IN THIS CHAPTER

Kylix can be used to create Web server applications that run on Linux. However, unlike regular native Linux applications created with Kylix, a Web server application needs a Web server to run. And by Web server I don't mean the hardware (Web server machine), but the software Web server. One of the most common Web servers is Apache, available in most (if not all) Linux distributions that I've seen, but also directly from `http://httpd.apache.org` where you can currently download Apache 1.3.20.

# Web Server Applications

The difference between a regular application and a Web server application is that the latter needs to be deployed in a Web server environment. Web server is the name for both the machine (which I will call "Web server machine") and the hosting application (which I will just call "Web server"). On Linux, the most commonly available Web server is Apache. Web server applications are not run by themselves, but invoked by the Web server. Not spontaneously invoked, but in response to a user (or client) request. Such a request is typically done using the HTTP protocol, in which case the client is using a browser (most often on a different machine) to connect to the Web server (which is configured to respond to incoming HTTP requests on a particular port of the IP-address of the Web server machine). The incoming request contains the name (and location) of the Web server application. For example, the following URL (uniform resource locator) specifies a Kylix application on my Web site:

`http://www.drbob42.co.uk/cgi-bin/hello?login=bob&password=swart`

The first word always specifies the protocol, which is `http` in this example, but can also be `https` for a secure connection. The part immediately after the two slashes (until the next one) denotes the domain name of the particular Web server machine (`www.drbob42.co.uk`). Instead of a domain name you could also specify an IP address, but the domain name `www.drbob42.co.uk` is generally easier to remember than `157.238.47.181` (at least I think so). The location and name of the Web server application can be found between the domain name and the question mark (in this case that's `/cgi-bin/hello`). Right after the question mark you can add pairs of field names and values, where pairs are separated by ampersands: `login=bob&password=swart`. This is just one of the three different ways in which the client can pass information to the Web server application (we'll examine them all in detail in the following two chapters).

## CGI Protocol

Web server applications are started in response to an incoming client request. They typically return output in HTML format (although other formats are possible as well). One of the communication interfaces between the client (Web browser) via the Web server to the Web server application (and back) is called the common gateway interface (or CGI). CGI uses environment variables and the standard input and output files. A simple CGI application is a non-visual application, where the input contains the information (request) sent by the client, and the output (response) is typically the dynamic HTML document that is generated on-the-fly (and sent back to the client with the Web browser). The information that is entered by the client and sent to the CGI application to be used when generating the HTML page is sent using environment variables and the standard input file.

## CGI Forms

But before we can determine what the client wants, let's first take a look at how the client side actually looks. How can a static HTML-page even cause information to be sent over to the Web Server and an CGI application at the server to be executed? For this, you need to use a special HTML extension called Forms. Just like Kylix Forms, a form is a place where controls (such as an edit box, list box, combo box, button or multiline text field) can be used. Unlike Kylix, you have to non-visually design your forms by writing HTML-code.

To verify this, let's make an HTML CGI form using a simple input field named login as follows (save this in a file called `login.htm` so you can use it in a minute):

```
<HTML>
<BODY>
<FORM ACTION="http://www.drbob42.co.uk/cgi-bin/hello" METHOD=GET>
Login: <INPUT TYPE=text NAME=login>
<BR>
Password: <INPUT TYPE=password NAME=password>
<BR>
Level: <SELECT NAME=Level>
  <OPTION VALUE=""> don't care
  <OPTION VALUE="1"> Beginning
  <OPTION VALUE="2"> Intermediate
  <OPTION VALUE="3"> Advanced
</SELECT>
<P>
<INPUT TYPE="RESET" VALUE="Reset Query">
<INPUT TYPE="SUBMIT" VALUE="Get Results">
</FORM>
```

This will result in two edit boxes (one of subtype password, which means that anything you type will be replaced by a * character—safe to input passwords while someone is watching your screen) and a list box or combo box with multiple options that can be selected. There are also two buttons on the form, one of type RESET, to reset the information you've just entered, and one of type SUBMIT, to submit the information you've just entered. So this is the action a client at a Web browsers needs to do to send information to the Web Server: click on the SUBMIT type button (in this case with the text Get Results on it); see Figure 19.1.

**19**

APACHE WEB
SERVER
APPLICATIONS

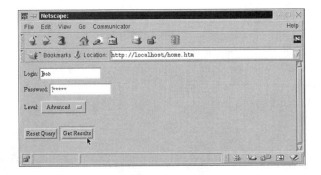

**FIGURE 19.1**

*CGI Form inside Netscape Navigator Web browser.*

But how does the Web Server know which CGI application to start for the data that is sent over? For that you need to take a look at the ACTION parameter of the form itself (the first line of the form code). The ACTION specifies the exact place of the CGI program, in this case http://www.drbob42.co.uk/cgi-bin/hello.

# Apache Web Server

The Apache Web server can be configured to handle Web server applications using the CGI protocol. However, one of the disadvantages of CGI is the fact that after each request, the Web server application will be unloaded again. This takes a lot of unnecessary time, which can be avoided if you could find a way to load the Web server application and have it remain loaded in memory (just like the Web server itself, which is also a process that runs continuously). New client requests would then only have to be routed to the Web server application, resulting in much faster responses.

Of course, I wouldn't mention this if it wasn't possible. With the Apache Web server, you can build so-called dynamic shared objects that can be loaded within the context of the Apache Web server, so they only have to be loaded once (and will not have to be loaded again for subsequent requests).

# Kylix and CGI

You can write CGI applications using any version of Kylix, although the NetCLX support of WebBroker components is only available in Kylix Server Developer and higher (and not Kylix Desktop Developer). However, you can still write Web server applications using Kylix Desktop—without WebBroker—by programming all necessary CGI techniques yourself (looking at environment variables, reading standard input, writing to standard output). A console application will do just fine, but to avoid having to program all CGI details by yourself, I've written a small unit called DrBobCGI that can be used to CGI application development using Kylix (or Delphi for that matter) without the need for WebBroker; the Linux version appears in Listing 19.1. Please use at your own risk (it works fine for me), and refer to my Web site at http://www.drbob42.com/DrBobCGI for more information and the full Windows/Linux version.

**LISTING 19.1**   DrBobCGI

```
unit DrBobCGI;
{===================================================================}
{ DrBobCGI ©   1999-2001 by Bob Swart (aka Dr.Bob - www.drbob42.com }
{ version 1.0 - obtain standard CGI variable values by "value()".   }
{ version 2.0 - obtain CGI values, cookies and IP/UserAgent values. }
{ version 2.1 - obtain Authorisation values (base64-encoded string) }
{ version 3.0 - ported to Kylix 1.0, still works with Delphi 4+ too }
{               Note: DrBobCGI does not work with Delphi 3 or lower }
{ version 3.1 - combining GET and POST fields inside one Data field }
{===================================================================}
interface
type
  TRequestMethod = (Unknown,Get,Post);
var
  RequestMethod: TRequestMethod = Unknown;

var
  ContentLength: Integer = 0;
  RemoteAddress: String[16] = ''; { IP }
  HttpUserAgent: String[128] = ''; { Browser, OS }
  Authorization: String[255] = ''; { Authorization }
  ScriptName: String[128] = ''; { scriptname URL }

  function Value(const Field: ShortString; Convert: Boolean = True):
➥ShortString;
  function CookieValue(const Field: ShortString): ShortString;


implementation
uses
  {$IFDEF LINUX}
    Libc,
  {$ENDIF}
    SysUtils;

  function _Value(const Field: ShortString;
                  const Data: AnsiString; Sep: Char = '&';
```

**LISTING 19.1**   Continued

```
                    Convert: Boolean = True): ShortString;
var
  i: Integer;
  Str: String[3];
  len: Byte absolute Result;
begin
  len := 0; { Result := '' }
  i := Pos(Sep+Field+'=',Data);
  if i = 0 then
  begin
    i := Pos(Field+'=',Data);
    if i > 1 then i := 0
  end
  else Inc(i); { skip '&' }
  if i > 0 then
  begin
    Inc(i,Length(Field)+1);
    while Data[i] <> Sep do
    begin
      Inc(len);
      if (Data[i] = '%') and Convert then
      begin
        Str := '$00';
        Str[2] := Data[i+1];
        Str[3] := Data[i+2];
        Inc(i,2);
        Result[len] := Chr(StrToInt(Str))
      end
      else
        if (Data[i] = ' ') and not Convert then Result[len] := '+'
        else
          Result[len] := Data[i];
      Inc(i)
    end
  end
  else Result := '$'
end {_Value};

var
  Data: AnsiString = '';

  function Value(const Field: ShortString; Convert: Boolean = True):
➥ShortString;
  begin
```

**Listing 19.1** Continued

```pascal
      Result := _Value(Field, Data, '&', Convert)
  end;

var
  Cookie: ShortString;

  function CookieValue(const Field: ShortString): ShortString;
  begin
    Result := _Value(Field, Cookie, ';')
  end;

var
  P: PChar;
  StartData,i: Integer;

initialization
{$IFDEF LINUX}
// Tested on Apache for Linux
  P := getenv('REQUEST_METHOD');
  if P = 'POST' then RequestMethod := Post
  else
    if P = 'GET' then RequestMethod := Get;
  ContentLength := StrToIntDef(getenv('CONTENT_LENGTH'),0);
  Data := getenv('HTTP_QUERY_STRING');
  if Data = '' then
    Data := getenv('QUERY_STRING');
  if Data <> '' then Data := Data + '&';
  Cookie := StrPas(getenv('HTTP_COOKIE'));
  if Cookie = '' then
    Cookie := StrPas(getenv('COOKIE'));
  RemoteAddress := StrPas(getenv('HTTP_REMOTE_ADDR'));
  if RemoteAddress = '' then
    RemoteAddress := StrPas(getenv('REMOTE_ADDR'));
  HttpUserAgent := StrPas(getenv('HTTP_USER_AGENT'));
  if HttpUserAgent = '' then
    HttpUserAgent := StrPas(getenv('USER_AGENT'));
  Authorization := StrPas(getenv('HTTP_AUTHORIZATION'));
  if Authorization = '' then
    Authorization := StrPas(getenv('AUTHORIZATION'));
  ScriptName := StrPas(getenv('SCRIPT_NAME'));
{$ENDIF}

  if RequestMethod = Post then
  begin
```

**19**

**Apache Web Server Applications**

**LISTING 19.1**  Continued

```
    StartData := Length(Data);
    SetLength(Data,StartData+ContentLength+1);
    for i:=1 to ContentLength do read(Data[StartData+i]);
    Data[StartData+ContentLength+1] := '&';
  { if IOResult <> 0 then { skip }
  end;
  i := 0;
  while i < Length(Data) do
  begin
    Inc(i);
    if Data[i] = '+' then Data[i] := ' '
  end;
  if i > 0 then Data[i+1] := '&'
          else Data := '&';

finalization
  Cookie := '';
  Data := ''
end.
```

The unit DrBobCGI has two functions, Value and CookieValue, that can be used by the Web server application to obtain the value of a field name or cookie. Apart from these two functions, I've also put global variables to hold the values for RemoteAddress (the IP address of the client), HttpUserAgent (the name and version of browser), Authorization (base64 encoded), and ScriptName (the name of the Web server application itself).

To complete the example: The following code shows the small console application that can be used to obtain all field values from the HTML CGI form you saw earlier in this chapter:

```
program hello;
{$APPTYPE CONSOLE}
uses
  DrBobCGI;
begin
  writeln('content-type: text/html');
  writeln;
  writeln('<html><body>');
  writeln('<br>Login: ',Value('login'));
  writeln('<br>Password: ',Value('password'));
  writeln('<br>Level: ',Value('Level'));
  writeln('</body></html>');
end.
```

Note the first two lines, which return the content type (a MIME type) followed by an empty line. This is the way to let the Web server tell the client (browser) how to interpret the following data. Apart from HTML texts, you can also return binary images, video streams, or just about anything for which you have a MIME type defined. The next section describes the steps to deploy the console application as a true CGI application on Apache.

## Configuration for CGI

After you compile a Kylix Web server application, you must make sure that it ends up in the cgi-bin directory, which on my machine can be found as the /home/httpd/cgi-bin directory. However, before you can execute it, you first need to tell Apache where to find the libraries that Kylix Web server applications need. For this, you need to manually edit the httpd.conf file (this is the http deamon configuration file—if you can't find it in the /etc/httpd/conf directory on your machine then you can do a "locate httpd.conf" to find it). The changes you have to make can be done as follows:

```
vi /etc/httpd/conf/httpd.conf
```

Add a single line to the end of the file, with the following content (point the LD_LIBRARY_PATH to the bin directory of Kylix):

```
SetEnv LD_LIBRARY_PATH /root/kylix/bin
```

Or point to any other location where Kylix resides (like /usr/local/kylix or /home/kylix or any other place where you have installed Kylix on your machine. Note that in most cases, Kylix may not be available on the final Web server machine, which means that you need to make sure that the required libraries and .so files are deployed on the Web server machine in places where they can be found (like the /lib or /usr/lib directories). For details about which .so files you need, please consult Chapter 13 of the Borland Kylix Developer's Guide manual that comes with your copy of Kylix.

After you've modified the httpd.conf file, you need to explicitly restart the Apache Web server as follows:

```
/etc/rc.d/init.d/httpd restart
```

At this time, you're ready to start a Web browser like Netscape and show the Web server application in action (for example the simple hello.dpr Web server application responding to the CGI HTML form I showed earlier in this chapter); see Figure 19.2.

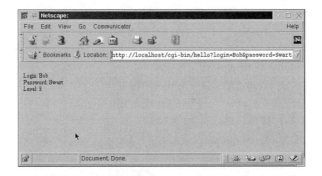

**FIGURE 19.2**
*Result of CGI Web server application in Netscape Navigator.*

## Configuration for DSO

You can use the unit DrBobCGI to produce CGI applications using Kylix Desktop Developer. However, it's much harder to write Apache Dynamic Shared Objects. For this, you should really consider using Kylix Server Developer and NetCLX (the WebBroker components).

The Apache Web server can work with CGI applications as well as DSO shared modules. Unfortunately, the default configuration only supports CGI applications. And it's not a simple switch to turn "on" DSO support, I'm afraid. You actually have to recompile the Apache Web server with DSO support enabled. Version 1.3.20 of the Apache Web server source code can be downloaded from the Apache Web site at http://httpd.apache.org/dist/httpd/apache_1.3.20.tar.gz. (Even if you have a recent distribution of Linux, it never hurts to go to the Apache Web site and look for the latest release with more features, bug fixes, and so on.)

After you've obtained the Apache source code, it's time to turn to pages 22-23 and 22-24 of the Borland Kylix Developer's Guide manual that comes with your copy of Kylix (and get a pen to make a few notes on these pages in a moment).

Basically, you need to perform the following six steps (make sure to login as root because you may need root permissions to uninstall and install Apache):

1. If Apache is already installed, first uninstall the current version of your Apache Web server (this is important, otherwise you may end up with two copies of Apache on your machine). Note that this is not mentioned on page 22-23 of the Kylix manual, but it's something that you should not skip. You can uninstall the Apache Web server as follows:

   ```
   rpm -e apache
   ```

Note that you may want to make a backup of your `httpd.conf` file first (with the configuration settings that you just made for Kylix CGI support in the previous section).

2. Download the latest version of the Apache Web server source code (available from `http://httpd.apache.org`, such as the current latest version 1.3.20 as `http://httpd.apache.org/dist/httpd/apache_1.3.20.tar.gz`).

3. Unpack the `tar.gz` file with the following command:

```
tar xvzf apache_1.3.20.tar.gz
```

4. Go into the root of the source directory, and locate file `config.status`.

5. Add the following lines to `config.status`:

```
#!/bin/sh
##
## Use this shell script to re-run the APACI configure script for
## restoring your configuration. Additional parameters can be supplied.
##
LIBS="/usr/lib/libpthread.so" \
./configure \
"--with-layout=Apache" \
"--enabled-module=so" \
"--enable-rule=SHARED_CORE" \
"$@"
```

Note that the Kylix manual on page 22-24 includes two additional flags, `CFLAGS="-g"` and `CGLAGS_SHLIB="-g"`, that you probably do not want to use, because they cause full debug information to be included in the resulting binary (thanks to Brian Long for pointing that out).

6. Enter the following commands at a terminal in order to compile and install Apache again:

```
chmod 700 config.status
./config.status
make
make install
```

This will result in a new build and installation of Apache on your machine.

In the next two chapters I will show you how to use NetCLX to write Web server applications in Kylix Server Edition with WebBroker—resulting in either a CGI application or a DSO shared object. The good thing about WebBroker is that the resulting target has little influence on the way you program things in your Web module. Apart from the way you start your project (see the next chapter), the major difference between a CGI and DSO module is the place it gets deployed for the Apache Web server. For a CGI application, you must look for the `httpd/cgi-bin` directory (where `httpd/html` is the home directory for the static Web pages). For DSO shared objects, you must look for the `/usr/local/apache/libexec` directory.

**19**

APACHE WEB
SERVER
APPLICATIONS

A final note on using DSO: there appears to be a bug that involves POST variables using DSO only (it works fine using CGI). The next chapter contains a full description as well as a fix that you must apply to unit apachehttp.

## Summary

As I've explained in this chapter, there are two kinds of Web server applications you can make with Kylix: CGI and DSO. And although you can use Kylix Desktop Developer to write CGI Web server applications (for example using the unit DrBobCGI), Chapters 20, "Web Server Development" and 21, "Advanced Web Server Development" will only be using NetCLX—the WebBroker components that are part of Kylix Server Developer.

In this chapter I've tried to explain what a Web server application is, and specifically how you can configure Apache (as Web server) for Web server applications written in Kylix. Chapters 20 and 21 will show in detail how to write actual Web server applications using NetCLX in Kylix Server Developer.

# Web Server Development

*by Bob Swart (a.k.a. Dr.Bob)*

## IN THIS CHAPTER

Web Server Development in Kylix is the area for NetCLX. Apart from the Indy Client and Server components, NetCLX consists of the WebBroker components—proven technology for Web server development that has been available in Delphi on Windows since 1997.

The Kylix WebBroker Technology consists of a New
Web Server Application dialog box; a TWebModule;
and the special TWebDispatcher, TPageProducer, TDataSetPageProducer,
TDataSetTableProducer, and TQueryTableProducer components (not to forget the internal
TWebRequest, TWebResponse, and other supporting classes).

The WebBroker Components are found in Kylix Server Developer only (if you have Kylix Desktop Developer, you need to refer to the previous chapter for creating Web server applications without the WebBroker Technology).

## Web Modules

In this chapter you'll find that the terms *WebBroker* and *Web module* are used to refer to the same thing. Actually, the WebBroker could be seen as a part of the entire Web module (the action dispatcher component, to be precise), but for the purpose of this chapter we can assume both terms refer to the entire collection of the components and support classes.

The WebBroker technology enables you to build standard CGI (Common Gateway Interface) or Apache DSO (Dynamic Shared Object) Web server applications for Linux, without having to worry about too many low-level details. In fact, to the developer, the development of the Web Module application is virtually the same no matter what kind of Web server application is being developed (you can even change from one type to another during development, as you'll see later on). Specifically, the Web Bridge allows developers to use a single API for both Apache CGI and DSO, so you don't have to concern yourself with the differences between these two (or any other Web server application type that may follow in future versions of Kylix). Moreover, Web Server applications are non-visual applications (that is, they run on the Web server, but the "user interface" is represented by the client using a Web browser), and yet the Web Module dialog and components offer us design support, which is still much better compared to writing non-visual ObjectPascal code.

## New Web Server Application

But let's start your first Web server application with Kylix and WebBroker. The New Web Server Application dialog box can be found in the Object Repository, ready to be selected after you choose File, New. (See Figure 20.1.)

If you start the New Web Server Application dialog box (see Figure 20.2), you can specify what kind of Web Server application you would like to create with Kylix. You can either select a CGI standard executable (the default choice) or an Apache Shared Module (DSO).

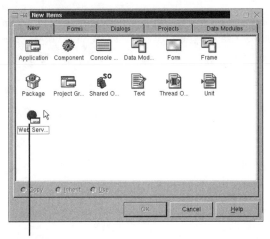

**FIGURE 20.1**

*Object Repository: New Web Server application.*

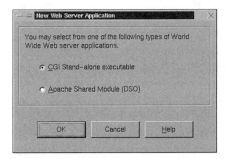

**FIGURE 20.2**

*New Web Server Application dialog box.*

## CGI

A CGI Web Server application is a console application, loaded by the Web Server for each request, and unloaded directly after completing the request. Client input is received on the standard input, and output (usually HTML) is sent back to the standard output. The application object is of type TWebApplication (defined in the unit WebBroker).

The generated source code for a CGI application can be seen in the following code. Note that I have not yet saved the project or Web module, so you still see the default `Project1` and `Unit1` names:

```
program Project1;

{$APPTYPE CONSOLE}

uses
  WebBroker,
  CGIApp,
  Unit1 in 'Unit1.pas' {WebModule1: TWebModule};

{$R *.res}

begin
  Application.Initialize;
  Application.CreateForm(TWebModule1, WebModule1);
  Application.Run;
end.
```

## Apache DSO

An Apache DSO has advantages compared to a CGI application, but can be harder to configure (please refer to Chapter 19, "Apache Web Server Applications," for Apache DSO configuration details). The good news about the WebBroker Technology is that it really doesn't matter what choice you make here. Of course, it does matter for the resulting Web server application (It will be either a CGI standalone executable or an Apache DSO module), but for the remainder of the Web module and the way you can continue creating your Web server application, it really doesn't matter.

The generated source code for a DSO module turns out to be very similar to the generated source code for a CGI application. Compare the previous code (for a CGI standalone executable) with the following (an Apache DSO module), and you'll see the differences for yourself:

```
library Project1;

uses
  WebBroker,
  HTTPD,
  ApacheApp,
  Unit1 in 'Unit1.pas' {WebModule1: TWebModule};

exports
  apache_module name 'Project1_module';
```

```
begin
  Application.Initialize;
  Application.CreateForm(TWebModule1, WebModule1);
  Application.Run;
end.
```

The first difference is that the CGI application is a program (with an additional {$APPTYPE CONSOLE} setting), whereas the DSO module is a library. The second difference is that the CGI application uses the CGIApp unit, whereas the DSO module uses the HTTPD and ApacheApp units. The third and final difference is the fact that the DSO module must export a single entry point called apache_module (and it seems to miss the {$R *.res} resource specifier).

## Apache CGI and DSO

The thing they have in common is, of course, the WebModule1 of type TWebModule1 (in case you didn't change the name or type). And that's something we can use to our benefit: Both projects can use the very same Web module! Once you've accomplished this with both projects also belonging to the same project group, you can switch between a CGI application and a DSO module by selecting the correct project as active project. And you can still use the same single Web module shared by both projects.

The steps needed to reproduce such a project group with two projects (but different targets) and a single shared Web module are as follows:

1. Start Kylix and close default project.
2. Choose File, New and choose Web Server Application.
3. Select CGI and click OK.
4. Save the project and Web module. Specify correct filenames—you won't be able to rename the Web module later because it will be shared by two projects.
5. Start the Project Manager.
6. Right-click on the project group and select Add New Project.
7. Select the Web Server Application icon again.
8. This time, select DSO as option, and click OK.
9. Remove the Web module from the DSO project.
10. Save the DSO project (give it a good name).
11. Right-click on the DSO project in the Project Manager and select Add.
12. Add the unit filename for the Web module to the DSO project.

Now, both the CGI project and the DSO project will be sharing the same Web module. If you save the project group as well, you can quickly switch between these two targets. Otherwise, you'll just have to load the correct project for the specific target.

The benefit of this configuration should be clear: You can prototype and test your Web module using a simple CGI application, but later may want to deploy it (in the real-world) as a DSO shared module because that has a number of additional advantages.

**20**

In this chapter, I will select and work on a CGI application, which requires no further configuration. If you want to select and work on a DSO module instead, you need to make sure that the Apache Web server is configured for DSO modules (see Chapter 19). Apart from that, there are only a few cases where writing a DSO application differs from writing a CGI application, but I will make it clear when this is the case.

# WebBroker Components

After you made a choice (CGI or DSO) in the New Web Server Application dialog box, Kylix generates a new Web module project and an empty Web module. Let's save this new Web server project under the name WebApp42 and the Web module under the name webmod42, as it will be the project to be used for this entire chapter (and the next one).

The Web module is the place to drop the special WebBroker components, such as the PageProducers and TableProducers. The WebBroker components can be found on the Internet tab of the Component Palette (in Kylix Server Developer only); see Figure 20.3.

**FIGURE 20.3**

*Kylix Component Palette—Internet page.*

The Internet tab of the Kylix Component Palette contains the WebBroker components; from left to right: TWebDispatcher, TPageProducer, TDataSetPageProducer, TDataSetTableProducer and TQueryTableProducer. The other three components (TCPClient, TCPServer and UDPSocket) are not part of the WebBroker components, but are also not part of the Indy collection of Internet components, hence their place on the general Internet tab of the Kylix Component Palette.

Apart from those components on the Component Palette, we'll also take a closer look at the TWebModule and the TWebRequest and TWebResponse support classes.

## TWebDispatcher

The TWebDispatcher component is one that you'll seldom need to drop on a Web module. In fact, this component is already built into the Web module itself, and is merely available to transform an existing data module into a Web module (that is: TDataModule + TWebDispatcher = TWeb module).

As a consequence, you can use a data module from a regular Kylix desktop application and turn it into a Web module by adding a TWebDispatcher component to it. Note that the Web Dispatcher will only be used when the application is indeed a Web server application; otherwise it will just be inactive (so there's no harm for the desktop application in turning your data module into a Web module). The end result is a data module (with TWebDispatcher component) that can be re-used by a desktop application as well as a Web server application!

## TWebModule

As I've just explained, a Web module is basically a data module with a TWebDispatcher component to dispatch incoming requests. To what, you may ask? Well, the Web Dispatcher dispatches incoming requests to a specific Action item based on the PathInfo part of the request.

The most important property of the Web module is the Actions property of type TWebActionItems. This is the collection of actions that the Web server application can execute. Each action specifies its own PathInfo as well as actual action that must be taken, as you'll see in a moment. To maintain the TWebActionItems, you need to use the Actions Editor. You can start the Actions Editor in a number of ways. First, you can go to the Object Inspector and click on the ellipsis next to the (TWebActionItems) value of the Action Property. You can also right-click on the Web module and select the Actions Editor to specify the different requests that the Web module will respond to.

Initially, the Actions Editor will be very small, with unreadable columns (see Figure 20.4); you'll have to resize the dialog box and columns to make it readable (unfortunately, the new size is not saved, so the next time you open the Actions Editor it will again be small).

**FIGURE 20.4**
*Web module and* Actions Editor.

Inside the Actions Editor, you can define a number of Web action items of type TWebActionItem (just click Ins to add new items to the list). Each of these items can be distinguished from the others by the PathInfo property. The PathInfo contains extra information added to the request before the Query fields. This means that a single Web server application can respond to different Web action items.

For the examples used in this chapter, you must define five different TWebActionItems, which will be used to illustrate the different usage and capabilities of the Web module components (see Figure 20.5). The next chapter will show some advanced features using a few more action items.

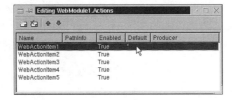

**FIGURE 20.5**
*Web Action Item Editor.*

Note that the first item has no PathInfo specified, and is the (only) default Web action item. This means that it's the TWebActionItem that will be selected when no PathInfo is given, or when no other PathInfo matches the given PathInfo (that is, when the default action is needed). This is the TWebActionItem that will mostly be used to demonstrate a certain effect. The other four PathInfo values must be /hello, /table, /records, and /query, and will be used for the examples throughout the entire chapter.

To write an event handler for a specific TWebActionItem, you need to first select the WebActionItem1 in the Actions Editor (see Figure 20.5). Then go to the Events tab of the Object Inspector and double-click on the OnAction event. This will take you to the code editor where you'll see the following code:

```
procedure TWebModule1.WebModule1WebActionItem1Action(Sender: TObject;
  Request: TWebRequest; Response: TWebResponse; var Handled: Boolean);
begin

end;
```

Before you can write any event-handling code here, you must first learn the details of the parameters. The OnAction event has four arguments: Sender, Request, Response, and Handled. The Sender is the TWebActionItem itself. Handled can be used to specify if processing (this action) has finished yet. However, especially the Request and Response parameters are of crucial importance here, and need some more attention now.

## TWebResponse

Response is an object of type TWebResponse which has a number of properties to specify the generated output. You can specify the ContentType (by default set to text/html), the ContentLength, and other (response) content-related properties. The single most important property, however, is Content itself; a string in which you can put any HTML code that should be returned to the client.

The following code will show the simple line "Hello, Linux world!" inside the browser:

```
procedure TWebModule1.WebModule1WebActionItem1Action(Sender: TObject;
  Request: TWebRequest; Response: TWebResponse; var Handled: Boolean);
begin
  Response.Content := '<h1>Hello, Linux world!</h1>'
end;
```

Of course, you can assign anything to the `Response.Content` property. Usually, it will be of type `text/html`, which is the default value of the `Response.ContentType` property as well. In case you want to return anything else, you need to set the `Response.ContentType` to the correct value. Binary output (such as images) cannot be returned directly using the `Response.Content`, in which case you must use the `Response.ContentStream` property instead. We'll get back to this in the next chapter when you will stream out images.

## TWebRequest

The `Request` parameter of type `TWebRequest` contains a number of useful properties and methods that hold the input query. Based on the used method to send the query (`GET` or `POST`—the value of the `Method` property), the query can be found in the `QueryFields` or the `ContentFields` properties. These two "Fields" are StringGrids, and can be used to select individual items (see Chapter 21, "Advanced Web Server Development," for the steps to retrieve all values for multivalued input items). The `Query` property contains the entire `GET` input string, while the `Content` property contains the entire `POST` input string. In code, you can determine both the request method and input (`Query` or `Content`, depending on the request method) as follows, and return the request back to the requester again:

```
procedure TWebModule1.WebModule1WebActionItem1Action(Sender: TObject;
  Request: TWebRequest; Response: TWebResponse; var Handled: Boolean);
begin
  Response.Content := '<h1>Hello, world!</h1>';
  if Request.Method = 'GET' then
    Response.Content := Response.Content + '<b>GET</b>' +
      '<br>Query: ' + Request.Query
  else
    if Request.Method = 'POST' then
      Response.Content := Response.Content + '<b>POST</b>' +
        '<br>Content: ' + Request.Content
    else
      Response.Content := Response.Content +
        '<b>' + Request.Method + '</b>';
end;
```

Note that you're checking the `Method` property of the `Request` object for the uppercase values `POST` and `GET`. And just in case you ever "fall-through," you include a second `else` clause (in case it's neither `GET` nor `POST`) that will just print the `Request.Method` value.

### GET Versus POST

There are a number of differences between the `GET` and the `POST` protocol that are important to know. When using the `GET` protocol, the query fields are passed on the URL. This is fast, but limits the amount of data that can be sent through. Depending on your client and server machine this is a few kilobytes at most, but that's enough for most cases. A less visible way to pass data is by using the `POST` protocol, where content fields are passed using standard input/output techniques. This is slower, but limited only to the amount of free disk space. Besides, since you cannot see the data being sent on the URL itself, there's also no way of (accidentally) tampering with it and getting incorrect results.

Usually, I prefer to use the `POST` protocol (clean URLs, no limit on the amount of data, but slightly slower), and only use the `GET` protocol when I have a good reason to, as you'll see in the remainder of this chapter.

---

### The POST Bug

There is a bug in the shipping version of Kylix Server Developer when using `POST` in combination with a DSO Web server application. The problem is that the `Request.ContentFields` will remain empty, even if information was posted. The `Request.Content` does have a value; it's just that this value is not broken into individual `ContentFields`.

An unofficial fix, provided by Borland, involves adding one line of code to the file ApacheHTTP.pas (but first you need to make a backup of this file—just in case). In this unit, find the `TApacheResponse.GetStringVariable` function, and add the following case after 15:

```
16: Result := ap_table_get(FRequest_rec^.headers_in,'Content-Length');
```

Now, copy the ApacheHTTP.pas to the `lib` directory (you may also want to add it to your project explicitly)and when you compile it, also compile the fixed ApacheHTTP.pas file and produce new .dcu files that fix this problem.

Note that this is an unofficial fix, and you may need to restore the original version of ApacheHTTP.pas before you can apply any upcoming official fixes or patches from Borland (so always make a backup of your ApacheHTTP.pas and ApacheHTTP.dcu files before you start applying this fix).

# Presenting Content

With what you've written so far, you can run the first version of your WebApp42 Web server application on the Apache Web server on Linux. To actually start the Web server application, you need to write a small local Web page containing an HTML Form that will load the Web module application.

If you moved the CGI application to the cgi-bin directory on your Web server (which is called localhost, but can also be addressed directly by its IP-address), you would need to specify an Action with value http://localhost/cgi-bin/WebApp42, which can be seen in the following HTML Form code:

```
<html>
<head>
<title>Kylix Developer's Guide</title>
</head>
<body bgcolor="ffffcc">
<h1>WebBroker HTML Form</h1>
<hr>
<form action="http://localhost/cgi-bin/WebApp42" method=POST>
Name: <input type=edit name=Name>
<br>
<input type=submit>
</form>
</body>
</html>
```

The WebApp42.htm form needs to be copied to the /home/httpd/html directory on my machine, so we can open it with the http://localhost/WebApp42.htm URL. When you load this Web page in Netscape Navigator, you'll see the WebBroker HTML Form Web page. You are now ready to click on the Submit button to load and start your first Web module application (see Figure 20.6).

If you enter a name in the edit box, like Bob Swart, and then click on the Submit Query button, the WebApp42 Web server application (as specified in the action= clause) will be executed. As it gets executed, it will pass the information you entered using the POST protocol (as specified in the method= clause of the HTML form).

Note that if you've seldom used Netscape Navigator before, or never clicked on the Don't Show This Dialog Again button, you could get the warning dialog box shown in Figure 20.7. This specifies that the information you've just entered will be sent over the network using a normal http connection, which is insecure and could be observed by a third party while in transit. Although this is a useful warning when sending credit card information (which should never be sent over an unsecured connection), in this case you can just click on the Continue Submission button to continue and see the results of WebApp42 in your browser.

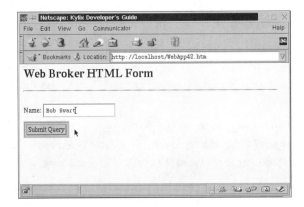

**FIGURE 20.6**

WebApp42.htm *in Netscape Navigator.*

**FIGURE 20.7**

*Netscape Navigator warning.*

The result of the default Web action item can be seen in Figure 20.8.

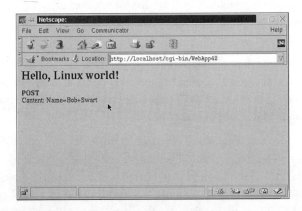

**FIGURE 20.8**

*WebApp42 Results in Netscape Navigator.*

Violà, an HTML Form "tracer." One that will return what (you think) you've specified as input fields. This can be quite helpful when a certain WebActionItem doesn't seem to work, and you need to check if it received the input request in good order. Note that spaces are replaced by plus signs (+), and generally you'll find special characters to be replaced by a percent sign (%) followed by the hexadecimal value of the character itself.

## Simulating GET

Before we continue, I want to share one benefit of using the GET protocol. As I've said before, the GET protocol means that the information is transferred on the URL itself. The request URL and request query (the input fields and values) are separated by a question mark, while the different field-value pairs are separated from each other by an ampersand sign.

If you change the method=POST inside the HTML form to method=GET, you see the full "fat" URL. However, there is another way to see this URL, which can come in very handy when you want to test your Web server application, and that's by manually appending the fields and values on the URL yourself. To test the WebApp42 Web server application responding on the GET protocol (without having to change the HTML form), you can type the following in the address bar of Netscape Navigator:

```
http://localhost/cgi-bin/WebApp42?Name=Bob+Swart&Tool=Kylix
```

You again call the WebApp42 Web server application, passing two fields (Name and Tool) and their values (Name=Bob Swart and Tool=Kylix), this time using the GET protocol, because the fields and values are passed on the URL itself.

You can see the GET result inside Netscape Navigator (see Figure 20.9).

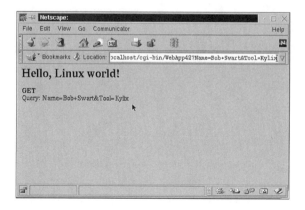

**FIGURE 20.9**

*WebApp42 GET results in Netscape Navigator.*

Whenever you are in a situation where you are not certain that your Web server application is responding correctly to the user input (using the POST protocol), you can always manually enter GET fields and values on the URL and perform a quick test without the need to modify your HTML forms. (Just make sure that your application can use ContentFields as well as QueryFields, as I've shown earlier.)

# PageProducers

Let's continue producing more output. As you probably can imagine, you can put just about anything in the Response.Content string variable, even whole Web pages. Sometimes you might want to return HTML strings based on a template, where only certain fields need to be filled in (with a name and a date, or specific fields from a record in a table, for example). Kylix has two special components that can be used for generating HTML based on a template with certain tags that need to be replaced with dynamic values. The components are TPageProducer and TDataSetPageProducer and are found on the Internet tab of the Kylix Component Palette.

## TPageProducer

Let's start with the generic TPageProducer component. From the Internet tab, drop a TPageProducer on the Web module (see Figure 20.10). It will help you to generate more flexible dynamic HTML.

**FIGURE 20.10**

*Web module and* PageProducer.

A TPageProducer has two properties to specify predefined content. HTMLFile points to an external HTML file. This is useful if you want to be able to change your Web page template without having to recompile your entire application itself. The HTMLDoc property, on the other hand, is of type TStrings and contains the HTML text (this will be hardcoded in the .xfm file).

The predefined content of a TPageProducer component can contain any HTML code as well as special #-tags. These #-tags are "invalid" HTML tags, so they will be ignored by browsers, except for the OnHTMLTag event of the TPageProducer itself. Inside this event, you can change an encountered TagString and replace it with a ReplaceText. For more flexibility, #-tags can also contain parameters, right after the name itself (like a parameter Format=YY/MM/DD to specify the format in which to convert and represent the date).

As an example, let's fill the HTMLDoc property with the following content:

```
<h1>TPageProducer</h1>
<hr>
<#Greeting> <#Name>,
<p>
Today is <#Date> and we're playing with the PageProducers in Kylix...
</p>
```

You can see three #-tags that will fire the OnHTMLTag event of the TPageProducer component. In order to replace each of them with a sensible text, you can write the following code for this OnHTMLTag event:

```
procedure TWebModule1.PageProducer1HTMLTag(Sender: TObject; Tag: TTag;
  const TagString: String; TagParams: TStrings; var ReplaceText: String);
begin
  if TagString = 'Name' then
    ReplaceText := 'Bob' // hardcoded name, for now...
  else
  if TagString = 'Date' then
    ReplaceString := DateTimeToStr(Now)
  else { TagString = 'Greeting' }
    if Time < 0.5 then
      ReplaceText := 'Good Morning'
    else
      if Time > 0.7 then
        ReplaceText := 'Good Evening'
      else
        ReplaceText := 'Good Afternoon'
end;
```

Using a ReplaceText with a fixed value of 'Bob' feels a bit awkward, especially because the HTML form specifically asks the user to enter a name. Can't you just use that value here instead (by using the QueryFields or the ContentFields)? Well, we'd love to, of course, but you're inside the OnHTMLTag event of the TPageProducer component, and not in the OnAction event where you can access the Request object. Fortunately, you *can* access the Request property of the TWebModule itself, which is always assigned to the Request property of the current Action. The same holds for the Response property, by the way.

So, this effectively changes the source code for the OnHTMLTag event as follows:

```
procedure TWebModule1.PageProducer1HTMLTag(Sender: TObject; Tag: TTag;
  const TagString: String; TagParams: TStrings; var ReplaceText: String);
begin
  if TagString = 'Name' then
  begin
    if Request.Method = 'POST' then
      ReplaceText := Request.ContentFields.Values['Name']
    else // GET
      ReplaceText := Request.QueryFields.Values['Name']
  end
  else
  if TagString = 'Time' then
    ReplaceString := DateTimeToStr(Now)
  else { TagString = 'Greeting' }
    if Time < 0.5 then
      ReplaceText := 'Good Morning'
    else
      if Time > 0.7 then
        ReplaceText := 'Good Evening'
      else
        ReplaceText := 'Good Afternoon'
end;
```

By the way, this will be the last time that you check the Request.Method field. From now on we're assuming a POST at all times (but you can still support GET as well as POST using the technique outlined previously).

Before you can finally test this code, you need to write the code for the "/hello" WebActionItem's OnAction event to connect the TPageProducer output to the Response argument:

```
procedure TWebModule1.WebModule1WebActionItem2Action(Sender: TObject;
  Request: TWebRequest; Response: TWebResponse; var Handled: Boolean);
begin
  Response.Content := PageProducer1.Content
end;
```

To activate this specific WebActionItem, you need to be sure to pass the "/hello" PathInfo to the Web module by including the PathInfo string in the ACTION value, or by calling the full URL with the /hello string appended to it.

The easiest way is to use the following HTML Form to start the new WebActionItem:

```
<html>
<head>
```

```
<title>Kylix Developer's Guide</title>
</head>
<body bgcolor="ffffcc">
<h1>WebBroker HTML Form</h1>
<hr>
<form action="http://localhost/cgi-bin/WebApp42/hello" method=POST>
Name: <input type=edit name=Name>
<br>
<input type=submit>
</form>
</body>
</html>
```

If you load this HTML Form in Netscape Navigator and click on the Submit button, you'll get the output shown in Figure 20.11.

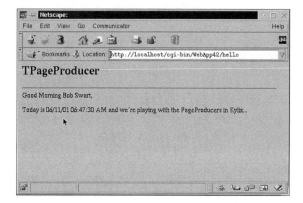

**Figure 20.11**

*Output of* TPageProducer.

Actually, instead of "Good Morning," the example could better have stated "Good Night" in this case (assuming you would never "get up" before 3 AM), by changing the first Time-test as follows:

```
else { TagString = 'Greeting' }
  if Time < 0.125 then
    ReplaceText := 'Good Night'
  else
    if Time < 0.5 then
      ReplaceText := 'Good Morning'
    else
      if Time > 0.7 then
```

```
            ReplaceText := 'Good Evening'
        else
            ReplaceText := 'Good Afternoon'
end;
```

As you can imagine, the TPageProducer component opens up your world to a whole new set of dynamic HTML possibilities. You could even generate a template out of a dataset listing the field names, and then use the PageProducer to provide the values of these field names as well.

## HTMLDoc Versus HTMLFile

So far, you've been using the HTMLDoc Strings property of the PageProducer component to store your HTML template. While this is useful, especially when writing chapters or giving demonstrations, it is not the most powerful way to maintain the HTML template. Apart from the HTMLDoc property, you can also use the HTMLFile property. This doesn't contain the HTML template, but rather points to an external file that contains the HTML template. As such, it can be a bit harder to set up and maintain (if you develop the Web server application on a different machine than the actual Web server where you want to deploy it, you need to remember to copy the HTML template file(s) as well).

One warning: the HTMLDoc and HTMLFile properties cannot be used at the same time! When you enter a value in the HTMLFile property (and move the focus to another property or component to "post" the change in the HTMLFile property), the content of the HTMLDoc property will be cleared. So if you decide to move the content of your HTMLDoc property to an external file specified by HTMLFile, make sure to copy the contents before you enter the filename (been there, done that, got to retype it all over again).

## TDataSetPageProducer

The TDataSetPageProducer component is derived from the TPageProducer you saw in the previous section. Instead of just replacing #-tags with a regular value, the TDataSetPageProducer has a new DataSet property, and will try to match the name of the #-tag with a field name inside the DataSet property, and (if found) will replace the #-tag with the current value of the field. To illustrate the use of this component, drop a TDataSetPageProducer (from the Internet tab) and a TClientDataSet component (from the Data Access tab) on the Web module (see Figure 20.12). In this chapter, you'll work with local MyBase tables and files (in .cds and .xml format); in the next chapter you'll actually use dbExpress to connect to InterBase for a real database Web server application.

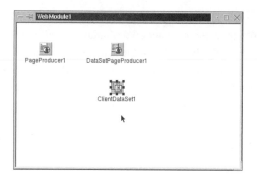

**FIGURE 20.12**
DataSetPageProducer *and* ClientDataSet.

Let's start with the `TClientDataSet` component first, by renaming it from ClientDataSet1 to cdsBiolife. Now, click on the ellipsis next to the `FileName` property to get the dialog box in which you can load a local MyBase .cds or .xml file (see Figure 20.13). The MyBase file can be found in the kylix/demos/db/data directory; select the biolife.xml file.

**FIGURE 20.13**
*MyBase XML files (select biolife.xml).*

Next, set the `Active` property of the cdsBiolife ClientDataSet to `True` (so you don't have to open the dataset by yourself). Next, connect the `DataSet` property of the `TDataSetPageProducer` component to cdsBiolife, and put the following lines in the `HTMLDoc` property (note the four #-tags):

```
<h1>biolife</h1>
<hr>
<br><b>Category:</b> <#Category>
<br><b>Common_Name:</b> <#Common_Name>
<br><b>Species Name:</b> <#Species Name>
<br><b>Notes:</b> <#Notes>
```

These special HTML #-tag codes indicate that you only want to see four specific fields from the `biolife` table. The `TDataSetPageProducer` will automatically replace the #-tags with the actual value of these fields inside the table, so the only code you need to write is for the `TWebActionItem` event handler. Let's use the second `TWebActionItem`, with `/table` as the specific `PathInfo` for this example. Start the `Actions Editor`, click on the third ActionItem, go to the Events tab of the Object Inspector, and double-click on the `OnAction` event to write the following code:

```
procedure TWebModule1.WebModule1WebActionItem3Action(Sender: TObject;
  Request: TWebRequest; Response: TWebResponse; var Handled: Boolean);
begin
  Response.Content := DataSetPageProducer1.Content
end;
```

Recompile the WebApp42 Web server application, and move it to the `httpd/cgi-bin` directory again (otherwise you won't be able to see the new functionality, of course).

Regarding the HTML form, you only need to change the `ACTION=` value to start the third `TWebActionItem` as follows:

```
<form action="http://localhost/cgi-bin/WepApp42/Table" method=post>
```

Note that the `PathInfo` `/Table` is just added to the request URL. If you use any request input (like the `GET` protocol), the question mark is always placed after the `PathInfo`.

The result from running the WebApp42 Web server application with this request is shown in Figure 20.14.

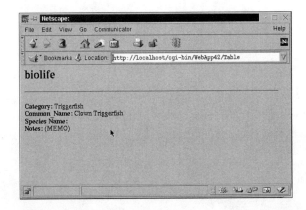

**FIGURE 20.14**

`TDataSetPageProducer` *output.*

Although this looks nice already, there are two things here that you should work on a little bit (to make it even better).

First of all, you don't get the value of the Species Name field, and second, it annoys me a bit to see (MEMO) instead of the actual contents of this Notes field.

The former can be explained by the fact that the Species Name field contains a space, and spaces are used as terminators for the #-tag names, so the TDataSetPageProducer would have been looking for a field named Species here instead of the field Species Name.

We'll take a look at some possible workarounds for this problem. Let's first tackle the (MEMO) problem by making use of the fact that the TDataSetPageProducer is still derived from the TPageProducer, so for every #-tag the OnHTMLTag event is still fired. Inside this event handler, you can simply check the value of the ReplaceText argument to see if it has been set to (MEMO), in which case you should be prepared to change it again to the full contents. This can be done by using the AsString method of the TMemoField, which returns the full contents you want:

```
procedure TWebModule1.DataSetPageProducer1HTMLTag(Sender: TObject; Tag: TTag;
  const TagString: String; TagParams: TStrings; var ReplaceText: String);
begin
  if ReplaceText = '(MEMO)' then
    ReplaceText := cdsBiolife.FieldByName(TagString).AsString
end;
```

Running again gives a more satisfying result already, as shown in Figure 20.15, showing the full contents of the Notes field instead of the text (MEMO).

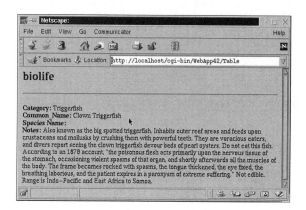

**FIGURE 20.15**

TDataSetPageProducer *output again.*

**20**

There is a slightly easier solution to the (MEMO) problem, which solves it at the DataSet level rather than at the PageProducer level. I just wanted to focus on the WebBroker way first. However, the alternative solution involves going to the cdsBiolife ClientDataSet and right-clicking on this component to start the Fields Editor. Inside the Fields Editor, you need to right-click again and select Add All Fields. This results in a list of all persistent fields inside the cdsBiolife dataset, as can be seen in Figure 20.16.

**Figure 20.16**

*The Fields Editor with the Notes field selected.*

Select the Notes field (as can be seen in Figure 20.16), and go to the Events tab of the Object Inspector. It's the OnGetText event that's the one that you can use to determine what text is returned when the Notes field is interrogated. And instead of returning (MEMO), you want it to return the string representation of the Notes field—the actual readable content. This time, it really takes only one line of code:

```
procedure TWebModule1.cdsBiolifeNotesGetText(Sender: TField;
  var Text: String; DisplayText: Boolean);
begin
  Text := Sender.AsString
end;
```

This time, the result is again the output of Figure 20.15 (you may want to remove the two lines from the DataSetPageProducer OnHTMLTag event handler to verify for yourself that the second solution also works, and in fact works before the DataSetPageProducer can "kick in").

To fix the second problem (no value for "Species Name"), you need to look for a way to use the TDataSetPageProducer to find the values of fields with spaces in their name. This can be done with the same trick that you used before: After the TDataSetPageProducer has a go at replacing the #-tags to the field values, the inherited OnHTMLTag event is called, where you can check to see if a certain ReplaceText is still empty. In this situation, you'll know beforehand that this means that you've received the "Species Name" field name. And personally, I consider it bad database design to use field names with spaces in them in the first place, so I wouldn't mind hard-coding the fix as follows:

```
procedure TWebModule1.DataSetPageProducer1HTMLTag(Sender: TObject; Tag: TTag;
  const TagString: String; TagParams: TStrings; var ReplaceText: String);
begin
  if ReplaceText = '(MEMO)' then
    ReplaceText := cdsBiolife.FieldByName(TagString).AsString
  else
    if (ReplaceText = '') and
       (TagString = 'Species') then
      ReplaceText := cdsBiolife.FieldByName('Species Name').AsString
end;
```

Note that as a security check, when the ReplaceText is empty, you still check to make sure that the original TagString had the value Species. This will produce the correct value for the Species Name field (as can be seen in Figure 20.17).

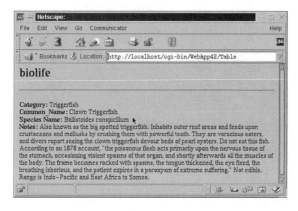

**FIGURE 20.17**

*Correct result of WebApp42 in Netscape Navigator.*

This is a very specific solution that works just fine for the biolife.xml dataset. However, for a more generic solution, you may want to look at a way to encode the field name (inside the HTMLDoc or HTMLFile property) so it can be passed completely inside the TagString, and yet be decoded to the real dataset field name again). Because you must supply the real field name, but cannot use spaces in the #-tag name or its parameters, you must encode the string in a way that you can decode it again to obtain the true field name. And the encoded string can only consist of letters, digits, and the underscore character. The encoding routine is simple: Anything that's not a letter or digit gets encoded by an underscore followed by the hex value of the character that's encoded, like the HTTP % encoding. In fact, when replacing the under-scores with percents, you can use the standard HTTPDecode function (from the HTTPApp.pas unit) to get the real field name back again.

The functions FieldNameEncode and FieldNameDecode are implemented as follows (you must use FieldNameEncode to encode field names that have any characters inside that are not letters of digits, and you must use FieldNameDecode to obtain the real field name again):

```
function FieldNameEncode(const FieldName: String): String;
var
  i: Integer;

  function Hex(B: Byte): String;
  const
    HexChar: PChar = '0123456789ABCDEF';
  begin
    Hex := '_00';
    Hex[2] := HexChar[B SHR $04];
    Hex[3] := HexChar[B AND $0F]
  end;

begin
  Result := '';
  for i:=1 to Length(FieldName) do
    if FieldName[i] in ['A'..'Z','a'..'z','0'..'9'] then
      Result := Result + FieldName[i]
    else
      Result := Result + Hex(Ord(FieldName[i]))
end {FieldNameEncode};

function FieldNameDecode(const FieldName: String): String;
var
  i: Integer;
begin
  Result := FieldName;
  for i:=1 to Length(Result) do
    if Result[i] = '_' then Result[i] := '%';
  Result := HTTPDecode(Result)
end {FieldNameDecode};
```

FieldNameEncoding the field Species Name yields the following HTML code, which you should use in the original HTML file to get the field value. You must change the line with Species Name as follows, to reflect the encoded Species Name fieldname:

```
<h1>biolife</h1>
<hr>
<br><b>Category:</b> <#Category>
<br><b>Common_Name:</b> <#Common_Name>
<br><b>Species Name:</b> <#Species_20Name>
<br><b>Notes:</b> <#Notes>
```

This HTML snippet will fail to find the correct field when used by the TDataSetPageProducer component. However, in your OnHTMLTag event, you can use FieldNameDecode to determine the real field name, and use it as follows:

```
procedure TWebModule1.DataSetPageProducer1HTMLTag(Sender: TObject; Tag: TTag;
  const TagString: String; TagParams: TStrings; var ReplaceText: String);
begin
  if ReplaceText = '(MEMO)' then
    ReplaceText := cdsBiolife.FieldByName(TagString).AsString
  else
    if ReplaceText = '' then
    try
      ReplaceText :=
➥cdsBiolife.FieldByName(FieldNameDecode(TagString)).AsString
    except
      on E: Exception do
        ReplaceText := '(' + E.ClassName + ': ' + E.Message + ')'
    end
end;
```

Note that the try-except clause here makes sure you get to see an error-message instead of an exception being raised on the Web server, terminating the current request. Using these changes in HTML and source code, the result is finally as you'd like it (as well as generic, so it can be reused for other datasets too). The current output is exactly the same as shown in Figure 20.17.

### DataSet and PageProducer

Because the combination of a PageProducer and a DataSet is a very powerful one, I will now spend a little time showing how to use a DataSet and use it to prepare a DataSetPageProducer to list all fields of the DataSet. This includes preparing fields that hold special characters in their name, as you saw in the previous section with the Species Name field.

The result will be a single routine that takes a DataSetPageProducer as an argument, and works on the DataSet property as well as the HTMLDoc property. The DataSet that is connected to the DataSet property is analyzed, and an HTML template that lists the field names inside the DataSet is dynamically producing inside the HTMLDoc property of the DataSetPageProducer. This is a great way to "prepare" the DataSetPageProducer and make it a powerful generic component that can be connected to any dataset and generate HTML that lists the current record of any dataset.

The PrepareDataSetPageProducer procedure is implemented as follows:

```
procedure PrepareDataSetPageProducer(var DSPP: TDataSetPageProducer);
var
  i: Integer;
```

```
begin
  with DSPP do if Assigned(DataSet) then
  begin
    HTMLDoc.Clear;
    HTMLDoc.Add('<h1>'+DataSet.Name+'</h1><hr>');
    if not DataSet.Active then DataSet.Open;
    for i:=0 to Pred(DataSet.FieldCount) do
      HTMLDoc.Add('<br><b>'+DataSet.Fields[i].FieldName+
        '</b>: <#'+
          FieldNameEncode(DataSet.Fields[i].FieldName)+'>');
  end
end;
```

Note that I had to take some precautions. You don't do anything if the `DataSet` property of the `DataSetPageProducer` is not assigned, and you also check to make sure it's opened—it has to be opened in a moment anyway, to resolve the special #-tag field name values that you're generating.

Of course, inside your Web action item, you must make sure that procedure `PrepareDataSetPageProducer` is indeed called at the right moment (before you can call the `DataSetPageProducer.Content` property, which invokes the #-tag for field values replacement process). This is handled inside the `OnAction` event handler for the Web action item as follows:

```
procedure TWebModule1.WebModule1WebActionItem3Action(Sender: TObject;
  Request: TWebRequest; Response: TWebResponse; var Handled: Boolean);
begin
  PrepareDataSetPageProducer(DataSetPageProducer1);
//DataSetPageProducer1.DataSet := nil;
  Response.Content := DataSetPageProducer1.Content
end;
```

The line where I set the `DataSet` property to `nil` can be used as a `debug` statement. The result would be that the generated content of the `HTMLDoc` property would not be processed any further (there is no dataset from which to obtain field values), so the result of calling `DataSetPageProducer1.Content` is just the content of the `HTMLDoc` property—an easy way to check if `PrepareDataSetPageProducer` is working correctly.

Using the `biolife.xml` table from the previous example connected to the `DataSetPageProducer1` component, you could pass `DataSetPageProducer1` to the `PrepareDataSetPageProducer` procedure, to let it overwrite the `HTMLDoc` property with the following, dynamically generated, HTML template:

```
<h1>cdsBiolife</h1><hr>
<br><b>Species No</b>: <#Species_20No>
<br><b>Category</b>: <#Category>
<br><b>Common_Name</b>: <#Common_5FName>
```

```
<br><b>Species Name</b>: <#Species_20Name>
<br><b>Length (cm)</b>: <#Length_20_28cm_29>
<br><b>Length_In</b>: <#Length_5FIn>
<br><b>Notes</b>: <#Notes>
<br><b>Graphic</b>: <#Graphic>
```

As you can see, there are quite a number of field names in `biolife.xml` that had to be encoded (so you can decode them later and retrieve their field values). Specifically, the `Species_20No`, `Common_5FName`, `Species_20Name`, and `Length_20_28cm_29` will need to be decoded before you can obtain their correct field values.

To make the complete example work, you have to write some code in the `OnHTMLTag` event handler for this `DataSetPageProducer`. You need a few lines of code to decode the `TagString` in case the `ReplaceText` is empty (and the `DataSet` property of the `DataSetPageProducer` is assigned; otherwise just leave the `ReplaceText` empty):

```
procedure TWebModule1.DataSetPageProducer1HTMLTag(Sender: TObject;
  Tag: TTag; const TagString: String; TagParams: TStrings;
  var ReplaceText: String);
begin
  if ReplaceText = '' and
    Assigned((Sender AS TDataSetPageProducer).DataSet) then
  try
    ReplaceText := (Sender AS TDataSetPageProducer).
      DataSet.FieldByName(FieldNameDecode(TagString)).AsString;
  except
    ReplaceText := TagString
  end
end;
```

This replaces the hard-coded references to Species Name as well, which is good, because this solution (both `PrepareDataSetPageProducer` and the code inside the `OnHTMLTag` event handler) are now truly reusable for any `DataSet`.

## Customer Test

You can test the re-usefulness of this code by dropping another `TClientDataSet` component on the Web module. Rename it to `cdsCustomer`. You must now load another `MyBase` table file by specifying the location in the `FileName` property of the `cdsCustomer` component. If you click on the ellipsis, you can browse to the `kylix/demos/db/data` directory, where you need the `customer.xml` file (or the `customer.cds` file, if you want to use binary ClientDataSet data instead of MyBase XML data—the content is the same in both cases).

Now, make sure the `DataSetPageProducer` that you already used before is pointing to the `cdsCustomer` ClientDataSet by assigning the `DataSet` property of the `DataSetPageProducer`

**20**

component to cdsCustomer. In the third OnAction handler (the one for the /Table PathInfo) you should already call the PrepareDataSetPageProducer, and the OnHTMLTag event handler of the DataSetPageProducer should also already be implemented with the few lines of code to decode the TagString in case the ReplaceText is empty (see the previous listing). If everything is in place, you can recompile the WebApp42 Web server application, re-deploy it to the cgi-bin directory, and call WebApp42 again with the /Table PathInfo. The result is a dynamic Web page (see Figure 20.18), based on an (also dynamic) HTML template that lists all fields from the cdsCustomer dataset, where the values are presented that are obtained from the first record in the cdsCustomer dataset. (In case you're wondering why you always see only the first record: In the next chapter, I'll show you how to move to other records as well, which requires the maintenance of state information.)

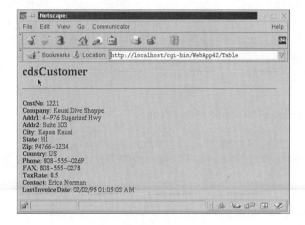

**FIGURE 20.18**

*Dynamic cdsCustomer in Netscape Navigator.*

If you like the output, but do not want to see all fields from the cdsCustomer dataset, you should go back to Kylix and right-click on the cdsCustomer ClientDataSet to start the Fields Editor. Using the Fields Editor you can press Ctrl+F to add all fields (or just right-click for the pop-up menu). Once you have a list of all fields, you can decide which fields to remove so they won't show up in the list of persistent fields, and hence also won't show up in the browser.

## TableProducers

So far, you've seen HTML being prepared and produced for a single record (the first) of a DataSet. But what if you want to view more than one record at a time? For that, you need to move to the last two remaining WebBroker components on the Internet tab of the Kylix

Component Palette: the TDataSetTableProducer (this chapter) and TQueryTableProducer (in the next chapter).

## TDataSetTableProducer

The TDataSetTableProducer also uses a DataSet property, just like the TDataSetPageProducer. This time, however, you get more than one record, and the output is formatted in a grid-like table in HTML. For a first demonstration, drop a third TClientDataSet component on the Web module and call it cdsOrders (to prepare for the Customer-Orders master-detail relationship you're going to build in a little while). Point the filename property to the orders.xml (or orders.cds) MyBase file, which is again stored in the kylix/demos/db/data directory, and open the table by setting Active to True. This is a good time to right-click on cdsOrders and select Add All Fields so you can remove the fields that you don't want (we'll get back to this in a moment).

Now, drop a TDataSetTableProducer on the Web module, and set the DataSet property to the cdsOrders ClientDataSet.

Your Web module should look a bit like Figure 20.19 now (a PageProducer, a DataSetPageProducer, three ClientDataSets—cdsBiolife, cdsCustomer and cdsOrders—and one DataSetTableProducer).

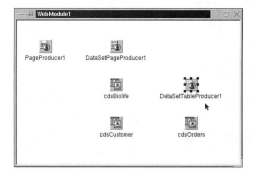

**FIGURE 20.19**
*Web module with* DataSetTableProducer *component.*

The TDataSetTableProducer has a number of properties that are all used to control the HTML code being generated. First of all, the Header and Footer properties hold the lines of text that precede and follow the table output. Then the TableAttributes and RowAttributes properties can be used to define the layout (Alignment, Color, and so on) of the table itself and the rows. A slightly more visual approach to specifying what the table should look like can be experienced using the Columns property and the Columns property editor. From the Object Inspector, start the Columns property editor by clicking on the ellipsis next to the Columns property (THTMLTableColumns) value. This opens the DataSetTableProducer1.Columns editor (which unfortunately, contains somewhat less preview power than the same dialog box that Delphi contains); see Figure 20.20.

Another way to get the same dialog box is by right-clicking on the DataSetTableProducer component and selecting the Response Editor pop-up menu choice.

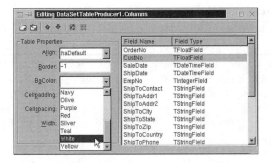

**FIGURE 20.20**

DataSetTableProducer *Columns (Response) Editor.*

Note that the right pane (which now holds the field names and types) is empty if the DataSet is not opened. Because you opened the cdsOrders ClientDataSet already, you immediately see all fields in the Columns editor. Since the cdsOrders contains more than the 13 fields you can see right now, you may want to resize this dialog window. To do this, you have to look for the (almost hidden) splitter just under the list box.

You can now set the output table options, like Border=1 to get a border, a background color by specifying a value for the BgColor property, and so on. Note that individual field (= column) settings have to be done by selecting a field and going to the Object Inspector to set the BgColor, Align (left, center, right) and VAlign (top, middle, bottom, baseline) properties. To change the caption of the fields, you can modify the Title property (again in the Object Inspector). The Title property consists of sub-properties like Align (this time for the title only, not the entire column) and Caption. Hence, to change the title of the ShipToAddr1 field to Shipping Address, you only need to change the Title.Caption property of the ShipToAddr1 field in the Object Inspector (see Figure 20.21).

To get a good feeling of the capabilities of the Response Editor (for the global table options) as well as the Object Inspector (for individual field options), you should now start to play a little while and set some options like background colors, alignments, and so on. When you're finished, just close the Response Editor and continue reading (so I can tell you how you can view the results of what you've just made).

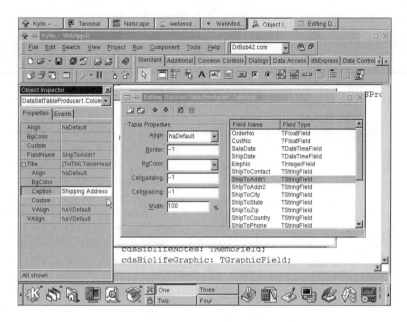

**FIGURE 20.21**

*ShipToAddr1 in Object Inspector.*

For my own enjoyment, I've set the BgColor of the entire table to White. The caption, however, I want to be shown in Yellow, so I need to select all fields in the right pane, move over to the Object Inspector (which will then only show the properties that all fields have in common—including the Title property with the nested Title.BgColor property) and set the Title.BgColor property to Yellow. Alternatively, you may want to select every individual field and set the Title.BgColor by hand, but I prefer to do it all at once (we are using a RAD tool, right?). Apart from this, I also want to indicate that there are two special fields inside the cdsOrders dataset, namely OrderNo (the keyfield of this table) and CustNo (the keyfield with which to link to the cdsCustomer table). I want to give the OrderNo field a yellow BgColor, and the CustNo a red BgColor, so I select these fields and modify their individual BgColor property values.

Most of my changes involve setting BgColor properties. However, I also set the Border property of the global table to 1 (so the result will be a grid-like table), and I changed the Title.Caption of ShipToAddr1 to Shipping Address, as shown in Figure 20.22.

**20**

**NOTE**

It is amazing to see that you not only have all fields, but can already assign property values to these fields. With previous versions of Delphi this was different (yes, I know this book is about Kylix, but please bear with me for a moment). In Delphi, when you start the Response Editor of a TDataSetTableProducer, you cannot immediately assign values to individual field properties. You first have to create persistent fields inside the Response Editor (by clicking on the Add All Fields button—the second one on the right of the toolbar). When you start the Response Editor in Kylix, all fields have been added automatically (it's almost as if you've already clicked on the Add All Fields button). When I first saw this feature, I examined it a little bit further. It appears that Add All Fields is executed whenever there are no persistent fields (which is the case when you first start the Response Editor). You can demonstrate this by removing all fields, which will automatically trigger the Add All Fields action again. Note that this will remove all of your individual field property settings that you made (so it's almost like starting over again), but not the global table property settings, of course.

## Delete Key Bug in the Response Editor

Apart from the support for persistent fields, there is something wrong with the Response Editor as well, I'm afraid. Remember that I wrote that I wanted to set the global table setting Border from –1 to 1? I went to the Border edit box and clicked Delete. Nothing seemed to happen, so I clicked it again twice. I then moved one character to the right and pressed Backspace. That seemed to work, since it now said 1 instead of –1 for the Border property.

So far, so good. I thought. Until I ran the WebApp42 application and noticed that the first three fields of my dataset were not showing in the HTML table. When I went back to the Web module inside Kylix, I noticed that these three fields were no longer part of the list of persistent fields in the list box of the Response Editor (the one that automatically creates a full list when it's made empty—see previous note).

It took me a little while to realize that it was the Delete key that didn't work properly. When you're inside the Border edit box and click Delete, it still deletes a field from the list box, and not a character from the edit box! This is caused by the fact that the Delete key is the shortcut for the delete (field) button. Ouch! This is a nice gotcha, so please watch out for it.

Once you're finished tweaking the HTML table properties, it's time to close the Response Editor and return to the Web module. You are almost done, and only need to make sure that the DataSetTableProducer is used by one of the Web action items. For this, right-click on the Web module and select the fourth Web action item (the one with the /Records PathInfo associated with it, as shown in Figure 20.22).

This will be the last WebActionItem that you'll use in this chapter (the /Query and TQueryTableProducer will be the first one to be covered in the next chapter, when you will connect to a real database using dbExpress instead of local MyBase files).

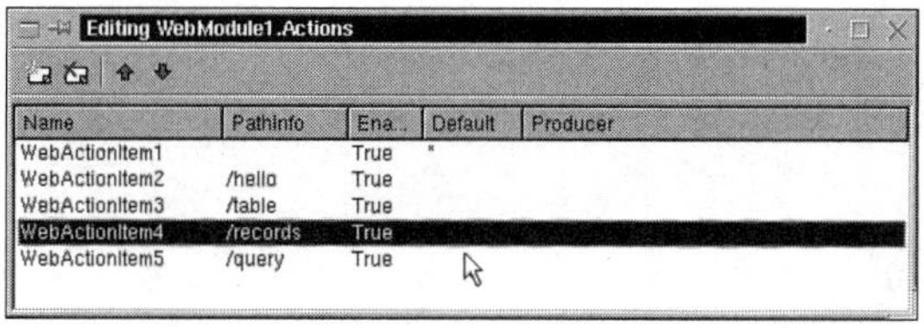

**FIGURE 20.22**
*Web Action Item editor.*

You need to hook the DataSetPageProducer up to this WebActionItem OnAction event handler, and you can just select the WebActionItem4, move to the Object Inspector and double-click on the OnAction event handler to be able to write the following code:

```
procedure TWebModule1.WebModule1WebActionItem1Action(Sender: TObject;
  Request: TWebRequest; Response: TWebResponse; var Handled: Boolean);
begin
  Response.Content := DataSetTableProducer1.Content
end;
```

That's all. You only need to make sure the /Records WebActionItem is fired (by specifying the /Records PathInfo in our request, either by modifying the WebApp42.htm file or by specifying /Records in the URL that you enter in the Location of the Web browser, like you can see in Figure 20.23).

It doesn't look that good, does it? I don't like the empty places in the table that remain gray when no text appears in them. And I've used way too many fields, so I should remove a number of them and make the output a bit more readable.

To start with the latter, let's remove some persistent fields to make the table a bit less wide (and perhaps even fitting on the page). As you may recall, there are two places where you defined persistent fields. One place was inside the Response Editor (where by default all fields were added), and the other place is the original source: the cdsOrders ClientDataSet itself. Before you make your choice and start removing persistent fields from either of these two

places, let's first consider what the difference would be. If you plan to use the fields from the
cdsOrders ClientDataSet in other places as well (for example by a DataSetPageProducer to
produce a detailed overview of a single order), it may not be a good idea to remove persistent
fields here that you need later. In that case, you should move to the Response Editor and
remove the persistent fields that you don't want to see in the browser.

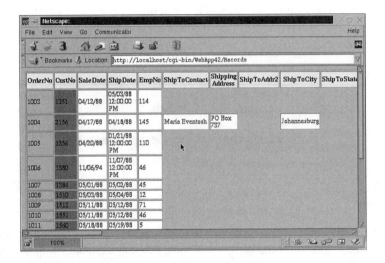

**FIGURE 20.23**

TableProducer *output in Netscape Navigator.*

On the other hand, if the fields from the cdsOrders ClientDataSet are only used by the
DataSetTableProducer to produce the grid-like overview that you see in Figure 20.24
(and the next one), then it's safe to remove the persistent fields from the cdsOrders
ClientDataSet. You also have to remove them from the Response Editor, as you'll see in a
moment, but once you've removed them from the cdsOrders ClientDataSet you are at least
sure that your application isn't making and processing fields that you don't use anyway.

To remove fields from both the cdsOrders ClientDataSet and the Response Editor, first right-
click on the cdsOrders component to start the Fields Editor, and remove the fields that you
don't want. If the list is empty, this means that you get all fields (by default), but in order to be
able to remove fields, you first need to explicitly add them using Add All Fields.

Now, remove all ShipToXXX fields, as well as ShipDate, EmpNo, PO, and Terms; see
Figure 20.24.

**FIGURE 20.24**
*Removing persistent fields using the Fields Editor.*

When you've removed all fields that you don't need from the Fields Editor of the cdsOrders ClientDataSet, move to the DataSetTableProducer and right-click on it to start the Response Editor. Because you removed persistent fields from the cdsOrders ClientDataSet, you now need to make sure the Response Editor isn't listing fields that are no longer present.

The good thing about the Response Editor, as you can see in Figure 20.25 (with the ShipToXXX fields already removed from the Response Editor list box) is that the persistent fields that have been removed in the Fields Editor (and who are no longer present) are shown without Field Type information. This isn't too strange, considering they're gone, so no field type information can be found anyway. Just select these fields and remove them to "synchronize" the Response Editor with the Fields Editor.

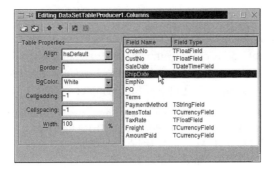

**FIGURE 20.25**
*Removed persistent fields inside the Response Editor.*

Once all fields have been removed that are not wanted, you can recompile and redeploy the WebApp42 Web server application. This time, the result looks much better already; see Figure 20.26.

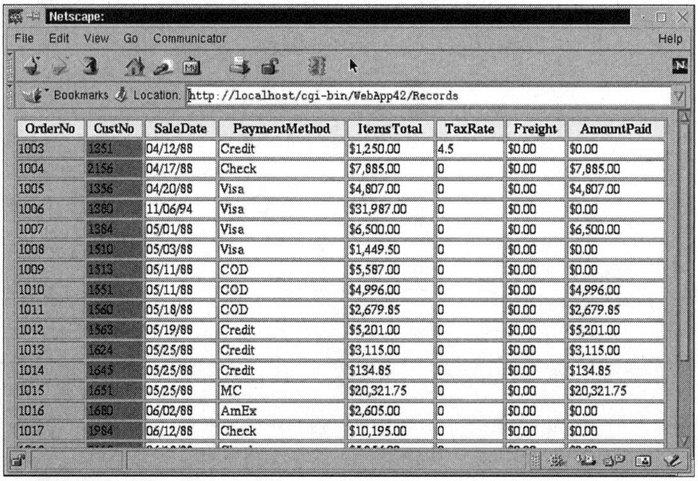


| OrderNo | CustNo | SaleDate | PaymentMethod | ItemsTotal | TaxRate | Freight | AmountPaid |
|---|---|---|---|---|---|---|---|
| 1003 | 1351 | 04/12/88 | Credit | $1,250.00 | 4.5 | $0.00 | $0.00 |
| 1004 | 2156 | 04/17/88 | Check | $7,885.00 | 0 | $0.00 | $7,885.00 |
| 1005 | 1356 | 04/20/88 | Visa | $4,807.00 | 0 | $0.00 | $4,807.00 |
| 1006 | 1380 | 11/06/94 | Visa | $31,987.00 | 0 | $0.00 | $0.00 |
| 1007 | 1384 | 05/01/88 | Visa | $6,500.00 | 0 | $0.00 | $6,500.00 |
| 1008 | 1510 | 05/03/88 | Visa | $1,449.50 | 0 | $0.00 | $0.00 |
| 1009 | 1513 | 05/11/88 | COD | $5,587.00 | 0 | $0.00 | $0.00 |
| 1010 | 1551 | 05/11/88 | COD | $4,996.00 | 0 | $0.00 | $4,996.00 |
| 1011 | 1560 | 05/18/88 | COD | $2,679.85 | 0 | $0.00 | $2,679.85 |
| 1012 | 1563 | 05/19/88 | Credit | $5,201.00 | 0 | $0.00 | $5,201.00 |
| 1013 | 1624 | 05/25/88 | Credit | $3,115.00 | 0 | $0.00 | $3,115.00 |
| 1014 | 1645 | 05/25/88 | Credit | $134.85 | 0 | $0.00 | $134.85 |
| 1015 | 1651 | 05/25/88 | MC | $20,321.75 | 0 | $0.00 | $20,321.75 |
| 1016 | 1680 | 06/02/88 | AmEx | $2,605.00 | 0 | $0.00 | $0.00 |
| 1017 | 1984 | 06/12/88 | Check | $10,195.00 | 0 | $0.00 | $0.00 |

**FIGURE 20.26**

`DataSetTableProducer` *output in Netscape Navigator.*

# Customizations

Apart from removing a number of fields, there are a few more ways you can tweak and customize the output a little further. First of all, you may want to "flag" certain amounts of money with a special color. Like the $0.00 amount in the AmountPaid column, which indicates that nothing has been paid, yet. Or you may flag the COD strings in the PaymentMethod columns with a blue color, since this is also something to pay attention to.

Both of these changes can be done in the `OnFormatCell` event of the `TDataSetTableProducer` component. All you need to do is check if the `CellColumn` equals 7 and `CellData` contains $0.00 and then assign Red to the `BgColor`, or, if the `CellColumn` equals 3 and `CellData` is COD you should change the `BgColor` to Blue, for example:

```
procedure TWebModule1.DataSetTableProducer1FormatCell(Sender: TObject;
  CellRow, CellColumn: Integer; var BgColor: THTMLBgColor;
  var Align: THTMLAlign; var VAlign: THTMLVAlign;
  var CustomAttrs, CellData: String);
begin
  if (CellColumn = 3) and (CellData = 'COD') then
    BgColor := 'Blue'
  else
    if (CellColumn = 7) and (CellData = '$0.00') then
      BgColor := 'Red'
end;
```

Note that CellColumn starts counting from zero. Also note that the Red and Blue values are defined in the THTMLBgColor type (and are the same values that you could use for the BgColor property in the Response Editor and Object Inspector). Executing this new code produces the output in Figure 20.27 (compare that to Figure 20.26 to see the difference of a few new lines of code).

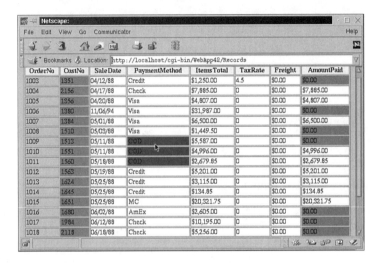

**FIGURE 20.27**
*Revised* TableProducer *output in Netscape Navigator.*

## Master-Detail Relationship

Now, as the last example of this chapter, you'll combine the functionality and output from the DataSetPageProducer (a single Customer record) with the output from the DataSetTableProducer (a set of Orders), so they give a list of orders for that particular customer.

Before you can lay out the resulting HTML, however, you first need to construct the master-detail relationship itself, using the cdsCustomer and cdsOrders ClientDataSets. To do so, you need a TDataSource component (from the Data Access tab of the Component Palette). Connect its DataSet property to the cdsCustomer ClientDataSet (the master). You can then use this DataSource as the value for the MasterSource property of the cdsOrders ClientDataSet (the detail dataset). After you've set that up, you only need to specify the link between the cdsCustomer and cdsOrders datasets, and you can do that by clicking on the ellipsis for the MasterFields property of the cdsOrders detail dataset. This will pop up the Field Link Designer dialog box (see Figure 20.28), in which you can connect the CustNo field from cdsCustomer with the CustNo field from the cdsOrders datasets.

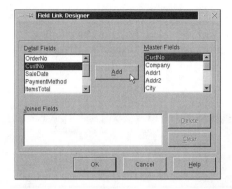

**FIGURE 20.28**
*Field Link Designer for* CustNo *fields.*

Once you click on Add, the CustNo-CustNo link will define the master-detail relationship between cdsCustomer and cdsOrders. You can then close this dialog box by clicking the OK button, and prepare the HTML output.

Ideally, you would like to see one master Customer record with all detail Order records that belong to it. Assuming that the Customer dataset is positioned right, you can start by obtaining the DataSetPageProducer.Content output, followed by the DataSetTableProducer.Content output. In short, you can modify the event handler for the /Records Web action item as follows to do what you want:

```
procedure TWebModule1.WebModule1WebActionItem4Action(Sender: TObject;
  Request: TWebRequest; Response: TWebResponse; var Handled: Boolean);
begin
  PrepareDataSetPageProducer(DataSetPageProducer1);
  Response.Content := DataSetPageProducer1.Content;
  Response.Content := Response.Content + '<hr>' +
    DataSetTableProducer1.Content
end;
```

Note that you first assign the DataSetPageProducer.Content value to Response.Content, and then just add the DataSetTableProducer1.Content to it. Because the Response.Content is just a long string (containing HTML in this case), you can add anything you want to it.

Now, before you compile and redeploy the new WebApp42 Web server application, you may want to remove some extra fields from the cdsCustomer ClientDataSet, so the output will look a bit nicer. In Figure 20.29, I've removed the Addr2, Fax, and TaxRate fields to make the output fit on one page inside the browser.

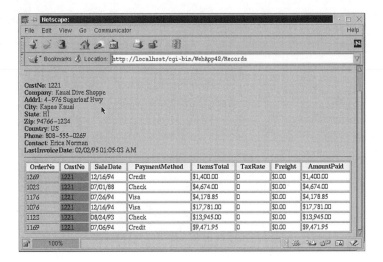

**FIGURE 20.29**

*Final master-detail output in Netscape Navigator*

This wraps up the introduction chapter on Web server development with Kylix and the WebBroker Technology. The good news is that the code is cross-platform, and will also compile with Delphi 6 Professional (in case you care about cross-platform application development).

## Summary

You've seen a lot already—web modules, Web action items, Page Producers, and Table Producers for CGI and DSO modules. You've encountered problems, and solved them or produced workarounds. And you produced some pretty useful and powerful sample programs along the way. I hope to have shown that the Kylix WebBroker technology is a powerful set of tools for Internet server-side application development.

And we've only just begun. Hopefully, by now you're wondering "What about the next customer?" and "What if I want to search for a specific customer or order?" The next chapter covers more advanced topics such as maintaining state (for browsing) and the TQueryTableProducer (which can be used for searching in a real database).

**20**

# Advanced Web Server Development

*by Bob Swart (a.k.a. Dr. Bob)*

## IN THIS CHAPTER

In Chapter 20, "Web Server Development," you saw Web server development support in Kylix with the WebBroker Technology (also called NetCLX). In this chapter, I want to follow-up with a number of advanced features and real-world solutions, starting with a dbExpress database connection, the use of the TSQLQueryTableProducer, maintaining state information, returning images (which is a bit difficult with Kylix) and finally some cross-platform strategies.

# New WebApp42

Because you'll be doing a few different things compared to last chapter, it maybe easier to start with a new Web server application instead of continuing with the previous one (WebApp42 from last chapter). You can start a new Web server application by choosing File, New and selecting the Web Server Application Wizard. Again, select the CGI standalone application as Web server application type, save your new Web module in file WebMod42.pas and your Web server project in WebApp42.dpr (note that these are the same filenames you used in the last chapter, so you should put the projects in different directories—which is always a good idea anyway).

Before you can continue, you need to make a few Web action items (just like you did in the last chapter). Six to be exact: /query, /image, /table, /field, /browse, and a last one with an empty PathInfo property value; see Figure 21.1.

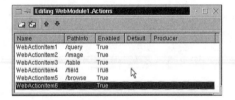

**FIGURE 21.1**

*Web Action Items Editor.*

Make sure to set the Default property of this last WebActionItem to True so it's indeed the default (last) action that will be triggered when the incoming request doesn't match any of the other PathInfo values.

## Producer and ProducerContent

In the previous chapter, you always wrote one or more lines of code in the OnAction event handler of each Web action item. Most of the time, the code consisted of just one line, like:

```
Response.Content := DataSetPageProducer.Content;
```

For situations like the above, where you only want to redirect the output of one of the producer components to the Response.Content property, you can avoid having to write even that

Advanced Web Server Development

CHAPTER 21

871

21

ADVANCED WEB
SERVER
DEVELOPMENT

single line of code by using the `Producer` property of the `WebActionItem`. The `Producer` property can point to any `PageProducer` or `TableProducer` component, and will automatically obtain the `Content` value of the associated (Content) `Producer` component when the Web action item itself is triggered. This is convenient, and also very nice, because you can assign a different `Producer` component to the `Producer` property when needed (resulting in truly customizable Web broker applications—but perhaps a bit harder to manage).

## dbExpress

As I explained in Chapter 20, the Web module can be seen as a data module with a special `WebDispatcher` component inside (to dispatch the incoming requests to the different Web action items). Because it is a data module, albeit a special one, you can easily drop data access components on it. And while you've been using standalone `ClientDataSet` components so far, it's time to use a real DBMS connection using dbExpress, such as InterBase (the main reason why I want to use the InterBase database that ships with Kylix, so everyone can join in with the examples in this chapter).

> **NOTE**
>
> The Kylix CD contains the installation files for InterBase 5.6, but if you would rather use InterBase 6, you can find the installation files for that particular version on the Kylix Companion Tools CD (in the `interbase_6` directory). For the code in this chapter it doesn't matter which version of InterBase you use, but it's nice to know you have a choice.

To be able to work with InterBase, you need to go to the dbExpress tab and start with a `TSQLConnection` component. Set its `ConnectionName` property to `IBLocal`. Apart from setting the `ConnectionName` property, you may have to right-click on the `SQLConnection` component and start the Connection Properties editor to make sure the database is pointing to an existing filename (for me that's the `employee.gdb` file in the `/usr/interbase/examples` directory, but the location may be different on your machine, depending on whether you installed InterBase as root or normal user); see Figure 21.2.

To verify the existence of the database, you should now close the Connections Editor and try to set the `Connected` property of the `SQLConnection` component to `True`. This will result in the Database Login dialog box for username sysdba, which should get the ultra-secret password *masterkey*.

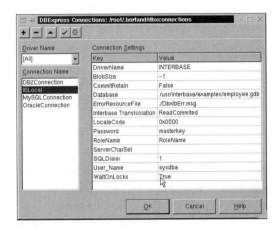

**FIGURE 21.2**

*Connection properties—IBLocal database.*

Once you've verified that you can connect to the IBLocal database, you should make sure that the Database Login Prompt isn't shown at runtime (obviously, that would be a bad idea for a Web server application running on a Web server). To do so, you must set the LoginPrompt property of the SQLConnection component to False.

Now it's time to drop one of the actual dbExpress data accessing components, such as TSQLDataSet, TSQLTable, TSQLQuery, or TSQLStoredProc. You can use any of them (see Part IV, "DataCLX," for more details about these components), but to demonstrate the capabilities of the TSQLQueryTableProducer in the next section, I want to start by using a TSQLQuery component now. You must use the SQLConnection property of the SQLQuery component to connect it to the SQLConnection component. Next, click on the ellipsis for the SQL property, which will open up a string list editor to type in your SQL query. For now, I'll keep it simple, with the following SQL statement:

```
SELECT * FROM CUSTOMER
```

After you've written the SQL query, you can activate it by closing the SQL string list editor and setting the Active property of the SQLQuery component to True (this executes or "opens" the query). Once this component is active, the result is a read-only unidirectional dataset that we can use to feed components like the TDataSetTableProducer and the TSQLQueryTableProducer.

# TDataSetTableProducer

Let's first start where the last chapter ended, with a TDataSetTableProducer. Drop one on the Web module and assign its DataSet property to the SQLQuery component. Your Web module should now look like the one shown Figure 21.3.

**FIGURE 21.3**
*Web module with SQLConnection, SQLQuery, and DataSetTableProducer.*

Right-click on the DataSetTableProducer to start the Response Editor, give the table a nice background color and a border, and remove all fields you don't want to see (see the previous chapter for full details on how to do that). When you're done tweaking, you're left with a yellow table that shows only the CUST_NO, CUSTOMER, CONTACT_FIRST, CONTACT_LAST, PHONE_NO, CITY, and COUNTRY fields. Too bad you can't preview the results in the Response Editor (you can in Delphi for Windows)—you'll actually have to compile, deploy, and start the WebApp42 application to see the results.

Before you can view the results in a browser, you need to actually use the DataSetTableProducer in one of the Web action items you defined. For now, let's use the default Web action item (the empty one). Select this item in the Object Inspector, and set its Producer property to the DataSetTableProducer component. If you watched carefully, you may have noticed that the PathInfo for this Web action item suddenly changed from being empty to being the name of the DataSetTableProducer component that you assigned to it (namely DataSetTableProducer1); see Figure 21.4.

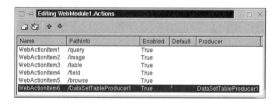

**FIGURE 21.4**
*Default WebActionItem with new PathInfo value.*

This is not a bug, but a little feature (and only happens to Web action items if the `PathInfo` property is still empty). It doesn't really matter at this time because the last Web action item was set to be the default one anyway, so you can still call the `WebApp42` application without any `PathInfo` value specified at all, and still the default Web action item will be triggered.

**NOTE**

Assigning the name of the `ContentProducer` (like a `PageProducer` or `TableProducer`) to the `Producer` property helps the Web dispatcher to make sure that each `Producer` is connected to at most one Web action item (zero or one, but not more). If you happen to connect a `ContentProducer` to the `Producer` property of another Web action item, the `Producer` property of the first Web action item (which was also set the same `ContentProducer`) will be set to `nil` again.

Before you continue, you must first compile `WebApp42` and make sure to place the resulting `WebApp42` executable file in the `cgi-bin` directory again, so you can call it from Netscape Navigator with the result shown in Figure 21.5.

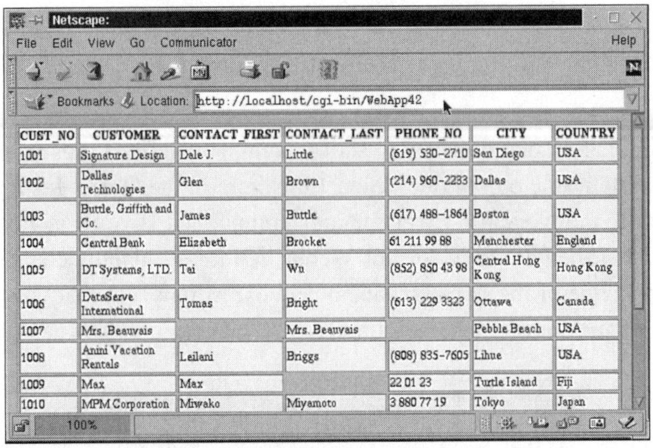


| CUST_NO | CUSTOMER | CONTACT_FIRST | CONTACT_LAST | PHONE_NO | CITY | COUNTRY |
|---|---|---|---|---|---|---|
| 1001 | Signature Design | Dale J. | Little | (619) 530-2710 | San Diego | USA |
| 1002 | Dallas Technologies | Glen | Brown | (214) 960-2233 | Dallas | USA |
| 1003 | Buttle, Griffith and Co. | James | Buttle | (617) 488-1864 | Boston | USA |
| 1004 | Central Bank | Elizabeth | Brocket | 61 211 99 88 | Manchester | England |
| 1005 | DT Systems, LTD. | Tai | Wu | (852) 850 43 98 | Central Hong Kong | Hong Kong |
| 1006 | DataServe International | Tomas | Bright | (613) 229 3323 | Ottawa | Canada |
| 1007 | Mrs. Beauvais | | Mrs. Beauvais | | Pebble Beach | USA |
| 1008 | Anini Vacation Rentals | Leilani | Briggs | (808) 835-7605 | Lihue | USA |
| 1009 | Max | Max | | 22 01 23 | Turtle Island | Fiji |
| 1010 | MPM Corporation | Miwako | Miyamoto | 3 880 77 19 | Tokyo | Japan |

**FIGURE 21.5**

*Output of* `DataSetTableProducer`.

## `TSQLQueryTableProducer`

Now, let's move over to the `TSQLQueryTableProducer` component, also from the Internet tab. The `TSQLQueryTableProducer` produces output that is similar to the `TDataSetTableProducer`. The difference between these two components is not based on the fact that you must connect a

TSQLQuery component to the TSQLQueryTableProducer (after all, you can already connect any TDataSet or TDataSet-derived component, including TSQLQuery to the TDataSetTableProducer), but is based on the fact that the TSQLQueryTableProducer has special support for automatically filling in the parameters of a parameterized TSQLQuery (that is, where the SQL statement contains a parameter that has to be given a value at runtime).

Drop a TSQLQueryTableProducer component on the Web module, and connect its Query property to the TSQLQuery component you've used in the previous example. This, however, will result in the same output as the TDataSetTableProducer. The real strength of the TSQLQueryTableProducer can be shown when you add a parameter to the SQL statement, such as:

```
SELECT * FROM CUSTOMER
 WHERE (COUNTRY = :COUNTRY)
```

This is a SQL query with one parameter. The parameter starts with a colon and has the name of the field you want it to connect to. This is by convention, and will help you later. You now need to specify the type of the parameter in the Parameter Property Editor of the TSQLQuery component. Click on the ellipsis next to the Params property in the Object Inspector. This will open up the Query Parameters Editor. Select the COUNTRY parameter in the list (which only shows one parameter anyway), and go to the Object Inspector to set the value of DataType to ftString, the ParamTyp to ptInput and leave the Value property empty.

Close the Query Parameters Editor again. You can open the TSQLQuery component (set Active to True) to check if you didn't make any typing mistakes. Now, click on the TSQLQueryTableProducer, and assign the Query property to the TSQLQuery component. Note that the TSQLQueryTableProducer contains the same properties to customize its output as the TDataSetTableProducer (see the previous section and previous chapter for more details), so go ahead and have some fun.

The TSQLQueryTableProducer works by looking for the parameter name (COUNTRY in this case) among the ContentFields (or QueryFields, if you're using the GET method), and filling in the value of the Field as the value for the Parameter. In this case, it means you need a sample HTML startup file defined as follows:

```
<html>
<body bgcolor=ffffcc>
<h1>WebBroker HTML Form</h1>
<hr>
<form action="http://localhost/cgi-bin/WebApp42/query" method=post>
Country: <input type=edit name=Country>
<p>
<input type=submit>
</p>
```

```
</form>
</body>
</html>
```

If you view this HTML form in Netscape Navigator it will look like Figure 21.6.

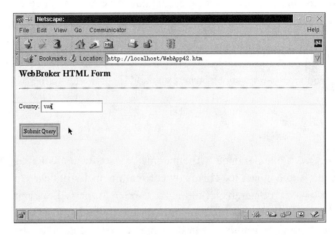

**FIGURE 21.6**

*HTML Form inside* WebApp42.htm.

Note that the name of the input field is Country, which is exactly the name of the Query para-meter (the parameter names are not case-sensitive). If you fill in a value, like **USA** (see Figure 21.6), you should get all customers from this particular country. As long as you set the MaxRows property of the TSQLQueryTableProducer to a real high value (999 will do fine in this case), you're pretty sure you see all detail records. Note that generally setting the MaxRows property to a high value (especially for the TDataSetTableProducer) will result in more records that are shown, but also bigger and certainly slower output. The latter is not only caused by the fact that the output is simply bigger and has to be transferred over the network, but also by the fact that an HTML table doesn't show itself until the closing </table> tag is reached. This means that for a really big table with 999 rows, you may actually see a blank browser window for a while until suddenly the entire table is drawn.

Anyway, to finish this example, you only need to connect the TSQLQueryTableProducer to the Producer property of the first Web action item (the one with the /query PathInfo) or write one single line of code in the OnAction event handler for the aforementioned /query Web action item:

```
procedure TWebModule1.WebModule1WebActionItem1Action(Sender: TObject;
  Request: TWebRequest; Response: TWebResponse; var Handled: Boolean);
```

Advanced Web Server Development

CHAPTER 21

877

21

ADVANCED WEB
SERVER
DEVELOPMENT

```
begin
  Response.Content := SQLQueryTableProducer1.Content
end;
```

With the `WebApp42.htm` file showing in the browser, which will start the `WebActionItem` with the /query `PathInfo`, you can enter **USA** in the Country edit box, and click on the Submit Query button to finally get the result shown in Figure 21.7.

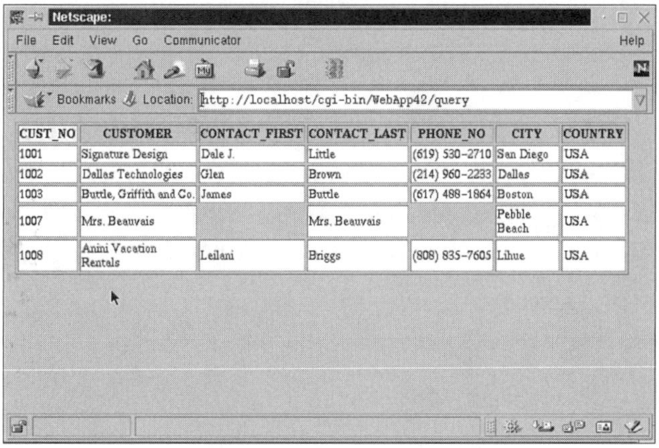

**FIGURE 21.7**
`TSQLQueryTableProducer` *output in Netscape Navigator.*

This works really nice; the only disadvantage is that the visitor (and user) of your Web site will have to know in advance which values can be entered in the Country box—without typos or mistakes. And that's easier said than done because I know there is a customer from The Netherlands. But to find that particular record from the `CUSTOMER` table, you have to enter **Netherlands** (without *The*).

## PrepareSQLQueryTableProducer

Wouldn't it be nicer if you were somehow able to produce a list box from which the visitor could select among all the possible values for this query parameter? Yes, of course it would, so I've built one and called it `PrepareSQLQueryTableProducer` (just like the `PrepareDataSetPageProducer` routine you saw in the previous chapter). The function takes a `DataSet` and fieldname as arguments, and returns an HTML string that produces an HTML listbox control (using the `<select>` ... `</select>` HTML tags, with `<option>` for each individual option):

```
function PrepareSQLQueryTableProducer(const DataSet: TDataSet;
  const FieldName: String): String;
```

```
var
  Values: TStringList;
  i: Integer;
begin
  Result := '<select name="' + FieldName + '">';
  Values := TStringList.Create;
  try
    Values.Sorted := True;
    if not DataSet.Active then DataSet.Open;
    DataSet.First;
    while not DataSet.Eof do
    begin
      Values.Add(DataSet.FieldByName(FieldName).AsString);
      DataSet.Next
    end;
    for i:=0 to Pred(Values.Count) do
      Result := Result + '<option value="' + Values[i] + '">' + Values[i];
  finally
    Values.Free;
    Result := Result + '</select>'
  end
end {PrepareSQLQueryTableProducer};
```

Note that to hold the individual values for the fieldname, I'm using a `StringList` component with the `Sorted` property set to `True`, which will not only sort the list of possible field values, but will also eliminate all duplicate values for me. Quite helpful in this case!

The output is a single HTML string that can be embedded in the HTML form you wrote earlier, to produce the following new content for `WebApp42.htm`:

```
<html>
<body bgcolor=ffffcc>
<h1>WebBroker HTML Form</h1>
<hr>
<form action=http://localhost/cgi-bin/WebApp42/query method=post>
Country:
<select name="Country">
  <option value="Belgium">Belgium
  <option value="Canada">Canada
  <option value="England">England
  <option value="Fiji">Fiji
  <option value="France">France
  <option value="Hong Kong">Hong Kong
  <option value="Italy">Italy
  <option value="Japan">Japan
  <option value="Netherlands">Netherlands
```

Advanced Web Server Development

**CHAPTER 21**

879

**21**

ADVANCED WEB
SERVER
DEVELOPMENT

```
  <option value="Switzerland">Switzerland
  <option value="USA">USA
</select>
<p>
<input type=submit>
</p>
</form>
</body>
</html>
```

Note that unlike the `PrepareDataSetPageProducer`, you cannot really use the
`PrepareSQLQueryTableProducer` function to directly work on the `SQLQueryTableProducer`.
This time, it's just a helpful function to support you in producing a good HTML form with all
available options (and no way to make input mistakes), as you can see in Figure 21.8, which
shows the generated HTML string embedded in your previous HTML form.

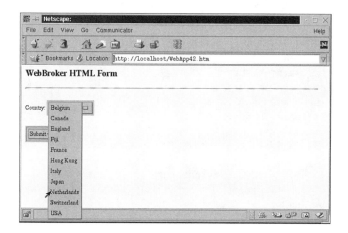

**FIGURE 21.8**

*Generated list box with entries for* `SQLQueryTableProducer`.

After you select a country from the list and click on the Submit Query button, the output is still
the same as before—it's only the selection mechanism (and hence the usability level of your
Web server application), which has improved significantly!

Now, let's focus on another important aspect when doing real-world Web server application
development: maintaining state information to browse and navigate through a dataset.

# Maintaining State Information

To illustrate the benefits of the ability to maintain state, let's first drop a TDataSetPageProducer component on the Web module, and use it to show the content (of only one record) of the CUSTOMER table as well. In the end of this section you want to walk through the entire set of CUSTOMERs, so let's also drop a new dbExpress data access component: a TSQLTable to connect directly to the entire table (instead of using a TSQLQuery component).

Point the SQLConnection property of the TSQLTable component to the SQLConnection component. Next, select the CUSTOMER table inside the TableName property and set the Active property of the SQLTable component to True. Now, point the DataSet property of the DataSetPageProducer component to the SQLTable component and add the following content to the HTMLDoc property, which was generated semi-automatically with a little help and some minor modifications from the PrepareDataSetPageProducer method (see previous chapter) listing all fields from the CUSTOMER table:

```
<#Navigator>
<hr>
<b>CustNo</b>: <#Cust_No><br>
<b>Customer</b>: <#Customer><br>
<b>Contact First</b>: <#Contact_First><br>
<b>Contact Last</b>: <#Contact_Last><br>
<b>Phone No</b>: <#Phone_No><br>
<b>Address #1</b>: <#Address_Line1><br>
<b>Address #2</b>: <#Address_Line2><br>
<b>City</b>: <#City><br>
<b>State/Province</b>: <#State_Province><br>
<b>Country</b>: <#Country><br>
<b>Postal Code</b>: <#Postcal_Code><br>
<b>On Hold</b>: <#On_Hold><br>
<hr>
<#Navigator>
```

Note that apart from the 12 fields from the CUSTOMER table, I've also included a #Navigator tag (twice), which can be used in a moment to produce a navigator-like set of buttons that you can use to, indeed, navigate (for which you need state information about the current record).

To see the houtput from the DataSetPageProducer component, you need to connect it to a Web action item, and in this case you can use the default Web action item again (the one currently connected to the DataSetTableProducer). After you recompile the WebApp42 application (and make sure it's placed inside the cgi-bin directory again) you can view the output inside Netscape Navigator, which should look like Figure 21.9 (note that the #Navigator tags have just been replaced by empty strings for now, we'll get back to those in a minute).

Advanced Web Server Development

CHAPTER 21

881

21

ADVANCED WEB
SERVER
DEVELOPMENT

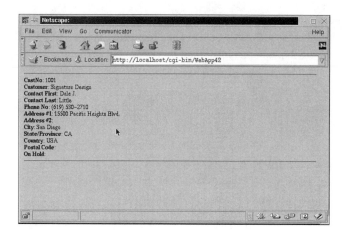

**FIGURE 21.9**

*Output of* DataSetPageProducer *in Netscape Navigator.*

Using hthe TDataSetPageProducer component you can see all fields from one specific record in a dataset. Seeing a single record from a table in a Web browser is real fine, but of course you'd like to see the next record as well, and the next, and the last, and back to the first again. In short, you need the capability to browse through the records in the table. And you need this using the TDataSetPageProducer and code you've written so far, but you will have to extend it just a little bit to produce a navigator that supports browsing.

The main hproblem you have to solve when it comes to moving from one record to another in a Web browser is maintaining state information; which record (number) are you currently looking at? HTTP (HyperText Transfer Protocol—the protocol that is used by the browser and Web server to communicate with each other) is a stateless protocol, so you must find a way to store the information.

Saving state information can be done in three different ways: using fat URLs, cookies, or hidden fields. In the following sections I will use the DataSetPageProducer connected to the CUSTOMER table, and will show how each of the three possible solutions can help you to maintain state and provide navigation support.

## Fat URLs

A common way to retain state information is by adding form variables with their value to the URL itself. Adding a RecNr value (that specifies the Record Number of the table), this could lead to the following ACTION URL:

```
<form action="http://localhost/cgi-bin/WebApp42?RecNr=1" method=post>
```

Note that the general METHOD to send form variables is still POST, although the state (RecNr) variable is passed using the GET protocol. This means you'll see the RecNr and its value appear on the URL: something that can be experienced with some search engines on the Web as well.

Apart from a form action method, you can also directly construct a fat URL that contains a jump to the first record, by creating a simple link, as follows:

```
<a href="http://localhost/cgi-bin/WebApp42?RecNr=1">First</a>
```

The RecNr=1 part (right after the question mark) indicates the jump to the first record. A jump to the last record can be enforced by making sure to jump very far. The easiest way to simulate this is by specifying –1 as RecNr value (so the Web server application should and will be able to conclude that it must walk until the end of the table):

```
<a href="/cgi-bin/WebApp42?RecNr=-1">Last</a>
```

Now, assuming that you know the current RecNr (this is the state you have to maintain), you can also specify the previous and next steps, as follows:

```
<a href="http://localhost/cgi-bin/WebApp42?RecNr=',RecNr-1,'">Prev</a>
<a href="http://localhost/cgi-bin/WebApp42?RecNr=',RecNr+1,'">Next</a>
```

The four lines with the First, Last, Prev, and Next links are just what you need to generate inside the OnHTMLTag event handler for the DataSetPageProducer for the #Navigator tag. The only question is: how do you know the correct value of RecNr? Well, because you're passing RecNr in the fat URL, you can use the QueryFields to get its value. And if it's not available, yet, then obviously you've just started and RecNr should be set to 1. In code, this can be done as follows:

```
var
  RecNr: Integer;
begin
  RecNr := StrToIntDef(Request.QueryFields.Values['RecNr'],1);
```

The StrToIntDef makes sure that the default value of RecNr will be set to 1 (whenever the QueryFields.Values of 'RecNr' doesn't return a valid value that can be turned into an integer.

## Navigation

This part is the same whether you're using fat URLs, cookies or hidden fields (however, I will say it only once). Right after you've obtained the value for RecNr, you should not forget to position the SQLTable that contains the CUSTOMER records (otherwise you may think you're at RecNr=2, but still see the first record). This can be done with the follow code snippet:

```
if not SQLTable1.Active then SQLTable1.Open; // Open when needed
SQLTable1.First;
```

```
if RecNr = -1 then
begin
  RecNr := 1;
  while not SQLTable1.Eof do
  begin
    Inc(RecNr);
    SQLTable1.Next
  end
end
else
  for i:=1 to Pred(RecNr) do SQLTable1.Next;
if SQLTable1.Eof then // went past Eof, need to backtrack!
begin
  Dec(RecNr); // one before Eof
  SQLTable1.First;
  for i:=1 to Pred(RecNr) do SQLTable1.Next
end;
```

Right after you've correctly positioned the table, you can use the DataSetPageProducer to actually produce the correct output. The fieldnames for the correct record will be replaced automatically, leaving only the #Navigator to be replaced inside the OnHTMLTag event handler. The only problem you still need to solve is the question "how do you know the value of RecNr inside the OnHTMLTag event handler"? Well, there can be two answers. The first one is simple: you can again retrieve the value of RecNr from the QueryFields.Values['RecNr'] statement. However, suppose that at some moment in time, you want to change the way you maintain state (from using fat URLs to using cookies or hidden fields). At that moment, you need to make two changes in the way RecNr is retrieved (and chances are that you'll forget about the second one inside the OnHTMLTag event handler), which leads to less maintainable code. The second, and in my view better, solution is to add a class field to the Web module, which holds the value of RecNr for us. Is this safe? Yes, because each incoming request gets its own instance of a Web module (even if you have an Apache DSO shared module). The only potential danger when using a shared object that is kept in memory is that the RecNr field may still hold a value from a previous request. Just make sure to initialize it with the StrToIntDef before you access the content of the DataSetPageProducer and you should be set.

This changes the declaration of the Web module inside unit WebMod42 as follows:

```
type
  TWebModule1 = class(TWebModule)
    SQLConnection1: TSQLConnection;
    SQLQuery1: TSQLQuery;
    DataSetTableProducer1: TDataSetTableProducer;
    SQLQueryTableProducer1: TSQLQueryTableProducer;
    SQLTable1: TSQLTable;
```

```
    DataSetPageProducer1: TDataSetPageProducer;
    procedure WebModule1WebActionItem6Action(Sender: TObject;
      Request: TWebRequest; Response: TWebResponse; var Handled: Boolean);
  private
    { Private declarations }
    RecNr: Integer;
  public
    { Public declarations }
  end;
```

With the code for the (default) OnAction event handler being as follows:

```
procedure TWebModule1.WebModule1WebActionItem6Action(Sender: TObject;
  Request: TWebRequest; Response: TWebResponse; var Handled: Boolean);
var
  i: Integer;
begin
  RecNr := StrToIntDef(Request.QueryFields.Values['RecNr'],1);
  if not SQLTable1.Active then SQLTable1.Open; // Open when needed
  SQLTable1.First;
  if RecNr = -1 then
  begin
    RecNr := 1;
    while not SQLTable1.Eof do
    begin
      Inc(RecNr);
      SQLTable1.Next
    end
  end
  else
    for i:=1 to Pred(RecNr) do SQLTable1.Next;
  if SQLTable1.Eof then // went past Eof, need to backtrack!
  begin
    Dec(RecNr); // one before Eof
    SQLTable1.First;
    for i:=1 to Pred(RecNr) do SQLTable1.Next
  end;

  Response.Content := DataSetPageProducer1.Content
end;
```

Note that because you have to position the SQLTable before you can process the
DataSetPageProducer.Content, you can no longer use the Producer property of the default
Web action item (using the Producer property will trigger the DataSetPageProducer.Content
property function before the OnAction event handler is fired, therefore using an incorrectly
positioned table). In other words: you should make sure that the Producer property is cleared

again (which, incidentally, will not clear the value of the corresponding `PathInfo` name (which was set to `DataSetTableProducer1` in the beginning of this chapter), but that still doesn't matter because it's still the default Web action item anyway).

Finally, you need the following support code inside the `OnHTMLTag` event handler:

```
procedure TWebModule1.DataSetPageProducer1HTMLTag(Sender: TObject;
  Tag: TTag; const TagString: String; TagParams: TStrings;
  var ReplaceText: String);
const
  WebApp42 = '/cgi-bin/WebApp42';
begin
  if TagString = 'Navigator' then
    ReplaceText :=
    '<a href="' + WebApp42 + '?RecNr=1">First</a>  ' +
    '<a href="' + WebApp42 + '?RecNr=' +
    IntToStr(RecNr-1) + '">Previous</a>  ' +
    '<a href="' + WebApp42 + '?RecNr=' +
    IntToStr(RecNr+1) + '">Next</a>  ' +
    '<a href="' + WebApp42 + '?RecNr=-1">Last</a>  ' +
    '(<b>' + IntToStr(RecNr) + '</b>)<br>'
end;
```

Note that you use a string constant to refer to the location of WebApp42, and that you haven't specified the domain, but rather started with /cgi-bin, which indicates the cgi-bin directory in the root of the domain that is currently used. As a consequence, you can compile and deploy this application on more than one machine, and anyone connected to a specific Web server (domain) will always be directed back to that domain because follow-up requests will all be routed to the /cgi-bin/WebApp42 of the same domain. In fact, I have used this to deploy the WebApp42 Web server application on my native Linux box (a desktop), my laptop (running Windows 2000, with VMWare running Linux inside) and the Web server of TDMWeb, my ISP of the http://www.drbob42.co.uk Web site. I did not have to recompile or change a single statement to make it work on all three machines, just by using the previous reference to /cgi-bin/WebApp42.

In the final executable, the constant definition for WebApp42 is moved to the top of the implementation section, so all routines share just one definition. (You only have to update it in one location if it needs to change, for example if you want to change the name of the executable.)

## Fat URLs in Action

When you recompile and redeploy the WebApp42 Web server application and start the default Web action item again, you see the result shown in Figure 21.10.

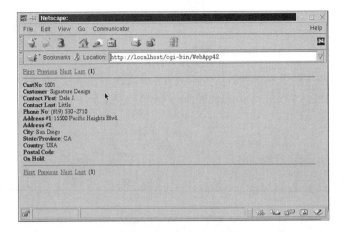

**FIGURE 21.10**

WebApp42 *output with Navigator.*

Note that you're at the first record (RecNr=1) and you can click a few times on the Next link to get to the next records, which can be seen in Figure 21.11.

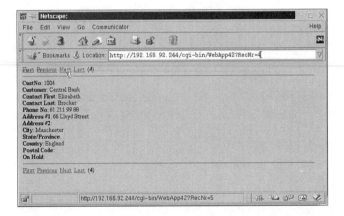

**FIGURE 21.11**

WebApp42 *output with Navigator at* RecNr=4.

As you can see, the value of RecNr is shown on the URL. If you place a lot of fields and values on the URL, this gets very big, or fat. Hence the nickname "fat URLs."

# Cookies

Cookies are sent by the server to the browser. When using cookies, the initiative is with the Web server, but the client has the capability to deny or disable a cookie. Sometimes, servers even send cookies when you don't ask for them, which can be a reason why some people don't always like cookies (like me, for example).

Cookies can be set as part of the `Response`, using the `SetCookieField` method. Like CGI values, a cookie is of the form *name=value*, so you can put a `RecNr=`*value* in there without much trouble:

```
var
  Cookies: TStringList;
begin
  Cookies := TStringList.Create;
  try
    Cookies.Add('RecNr='+IntToStr(RecNr));
    Response.SetCookieField(Cookies,'','',Now+1,False);
  finally
    Cookies.Free
  end;
```

Note that you are using a `TStringList` to set up a list of cookie values. Each list of cookies can have a `Domain` and `Path` associated with it to indicate which URL the cookie should be sent to. You can leave these blank, of course. The fourth parameter specifies the expiration date of the cookie, which is set to `Now` plus 1 day, so the next time the user is back the cookie will have expired. The final argument specifies whether the cookie is sent over a secured connection (which I just set to `False`).

Now, assuming the user accepts the cookie, then having set the cookie is still only half the work. In a follow-up `WebActionItem` `OnAction` event you need to read (eat?) the value of the cookie, to determine how far to step with the `SQLTable` to be able to show the next records. In this case, cookies are part of the `Request` class, just like the `QueryFields`, and they can be queried directly using the `CookieFields` property:

```
begin
  RecNr := StrToIntDef(Request.CookieFields.Values['RecNr'],1);
```

Other than that, cookies work just like any CGI content field. Just remember that while a content field is part of your request, so should always be up to date, a cookie may have been rejected, resulting in a possible older value (which was still on your disk a few sessions ago).

## Hidden Fields

Hidden fields is the third, and in my opinion most flexible (less error-prone, less bothersome), way to maintain state information. The HTML syntax for a hidden field called RecNr with a value of 1 is as follows:

```
<input type=hidden name=RecNr Value=1>
```

Hidden fields are invisible to the end-user, but the names and values are sent back (using the protocol specified by the method attribute of the HTML form) to the Web server and Web module application as soon as the user hits any of the submit buttons.

To implement hidden fields for your situation, you need to write a new HTML form, specifying the default WebActionItem, the hidden field RecNr, and use four different submit buttons (each with a different caption and hence a slightly different effect):

```
<form action="/cgi-bin/WebApp42" method=post>
<input type=hidden name=RecNr value=1>
<input type=submit name=Submit value=First>
<input type=submit name=Submit value=Previous>
<input type=submit name=Submit value=Next>
<input type=submit name=Submit value=Last>
</form>
```

Now, instead of looking at the value of RecNr (which is the current value), you also need to look at the value of the submit button (i.e. the value for SUBMIT), and perform an action on the value of RecNr accordingly. In pseudo code, this action should be as follows:

```
case SUBMIT of
  First: RecNr := 1
  Previous: Dec(RecNr);
  Next: Inc(RecNr)
  Last: RecNr := -1
end;
```

As an alternative, you could also create four different HTML forms, each with their own correct value of (the hidden field) RecNr, and each with their own submit button. However, it's easier and looks nicer to have just one form with four different buttons, as you can see in Figure 21.12.

Advanced Web Server Development

CHAPTER 21

889

21

ADVANCED WEB
SERVER
DEVELOPMENT

## FIGURE 21.12

WebApp42 *output with Navigator using hidden fields.*

The OnAction event handler is modified only in the section that needs to obtain the value of
RecNr (which now not only needs to obtain the hidden value of RecNr, but also the value for
SUBMIT to process RecNr into the actual value of RecNr):

```
procedure TWebModule1.WebModule1WebActionItem6Action(Sender: TObject;
  Request: TWebRequest; Response: TWebResponse; var Handled: Boolean);
var
  i: Integer;
  Submit: String;
begin
  RecNr := StrToIntDef(Request.ContentFields.Values['RecNr'],1);
  Submit := Request.ContentFields.Values['Submit'];
  if Submit = 'First' then RecNr := 1
  else
    if Submit = 'Last' then RecNr := -1
    else
      if Submit = 'Previous' then Dec(RecNr)
      else
        if Submit = 'Next' then Inc(RecNr);
  if not SQLTable1.Active then SQLTable1.Open; // Open when needed
  SQLTable1.First;
  if RecNr = -1 then
```

```
begin
  RecNr := 1;
  while not SQLTable1.Eof do
  begin
    Inc(RecNr);
    SQLTable1.Next
  end
end
else
  for i:=1 to Pred(RecNr) do SQLTable1.Next;

if SQLTable1.Eof then // went past Eof, need to backtrack!
begin
  Dec(RecNr); // one before Eof
  SQLTable1.First;
  for i:=1 to Pred(RecNr) do SQLTable1.Next
end;

Response.Content := DataSetPageProducer1.Content
end;
```

And of course the OnHTMLTag event handler had to be modified to produce the dynamic HTML form with the hidden RecNr field as well as four submit buttons:

```
procedure TWebModule1.DataSetPageProducer1HTMLTag(Sender: TObject;
  Tag: TTag; const TagString: String; TagParams: TStrings;
  var ReplaceText: String);
const
  WebApp42 = '/cgi-bin/WebApp42';
begin
  if TagString = 'Navigator' then
    ReplaceText :=
    '<form action="' + WebApp42 + '" method=post>' +
    '<input type=hidden name=RecNr value=' + IntToStr(RecNr) +'>' +
    '<input type=submit name=Submit value=First>  ' +
    '<input type=submit name=Submit value=Previous>  ' +
    '<input type=submit name=Submit value=Next>  ' +
    '<input type=submit name=Submit value=Last>  ' +
    '(<b>' + IntToStr(RecNr) + '</b>)' +
    '</form>'
end;
```

The source code on this book's CD contains both the fat URL and the hidden fields solution, using IFDEFs to allow you to select which maintaining state solution you wish to use (at compile time).

Advanced Web Server Development

**CHAPTER 21**

891

21

ADVANCED WEB
SERVER
DEVELOPMENT

The techniques used here to keep state information and use it to browse through a table can be used in other places as well, of course. Note that while you used the RecNr to retain the current record number, you could also pass the current (unique) key values, and use them to search for the current record instead. This can turn out to be more precise, especially when browsing a dynamic table where lots of users are adding new records while you're browsing it.

# Advanced Page Producing

You saw what the individual PageProducers and TableProducers can do. However, it gets really interesting once you combine these components and connect the "output" of one to the "input" of another. Especially if you combine this with the ability to dynamically create the ContentProducing components themselves as well (so you can in fact start with an empty Web module and use three Web actions items, namely /table, /field, and /browse).

The example you're going to build at this time is a dbExpress table viewer, but with the capability to dynamically specify the table name and field names. This is the purpose of the WebActionItems with the /table, /field, and /browse PathInfo. First, select the WebActionItem with the PathInfo /table, which will be executed to show a dynamic list of table names from which you can select a table to inspect. You will write an OnAction event handler now for the Web action item.

To get a list of available TableNames for the IBLocal SQLConnection, you can simply call the GetTableNames method of the SQLConnection component, passing a StringList as an argument:

```
procedure TWebModule1.WebModule1WebActionItem3Action(Sender: TObject;
  Request: TWebRequest; Response: TWebResponse; var Handled: Boolean);
const
  WebApp42 = '/cgi-bin/WebApp42';
var
  TableNames: TStringList;
  i: Integer;
begin
  Response.Content := '<h1>Table Selection</h1><hr><p>';
  TableNames := TStringList.Create;
  TableNames.Sorted := True;
  try
    with SQLConnection1 do
    begin
      Connected := True; // just in case
      GetTableNames(TableNames)
    end;
    Response.Content := Response.Content +
      'Please select a database table.' +
```

```
        '<form action="' + WebApp42 '/field" method=post>' +
        '<table>';
     Response.Content := Response.Content +
        '<tr><td align=right>Master: </td><td><select name="master">';
     for i:=0 to Pred(TableNames.Count) do
        Response.Content := Response.Content +
          '<option value="' + TableNames[i] + '">'+TableNames[i];
     Response.Content := Response.Content +
        '</select></td></tr>';
     Response.Content := Response.Content +
        '</table><p>' +
        '<input type=reset> <input type=submit>' +
        '</form>';
   finally
     TableNames.Free
   end
end;
```

The resulting selection list can be seen in Figure 21.13 inside Netscape Navigator.

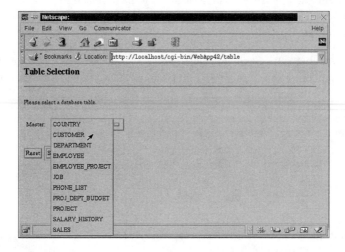

**FIGURE 21.13**

*Table selection.*

After you select a TableName and click on the Submit button, the /field WebItemAction is executed, which is implemented as follows:

```
procedure TWebModule1.WebModule1WebActionItem4Action(Sender: TObject;
  Request: TWebRequest; Response: TWebResponse; var Handled: Boolean);
const
```

Advanced Web Server Development

CHAPTER 21

893

21

ADVANCED WEB
SERVER
DEVELOPMENT

```
  WebApp42 = '/cgi-bin/WebApp42';
var
  i: Integer;
begin
  Response.Content := '<h1>Table Fields</h1><hr><p>' +
    '<form action="' + WebApp42 + '/browse" method=post>' +
    '<input type=hidden name="master" value="' +
      Request.ContentFields.Values['master'] + '">';
  with TSQLTable.Create(nil) do
  try
    SQLConnection := SQLConnection1;
    TableName := Request.ContentFields.Values['master'];
    FieldDefs.Update; // no need to actually Open the Table
    Response.Content := Response.Content +
      '<table><tr><td width=200 bgcolor=FFFF00> <b>Table: </b>' +
        TableName + ' </td>' +
      '<tr><td bgcolor=cccccc valign=top>';
    for i:=0 to Pred(FieldDefs.Count) do
      Response.Content := Response.Content +
        '<input type=checkbox checked name="M' +
          FieldDefs[i].DisplayName + '" value="on"> ' +
          FieldDefs[i].DisplayName + '<br>';
  finally
    Free
  end;
  Response.Content := Response.Content +
    '</td></tr></table><p>' +
    '<input type=reset> <input type=submit>' +
    '</form>'
end;
```

Note that you now need to pass the Table field with the previously selected values to the next
Web page (so you can use it to combine with the selected FieldNames). This is done by pass-
ing a hidden field called Master (yes it's called Master, because you'll be extending it with a
Detail as well in a moment).

Executing this OnAction event finally results in a form with the /browse PathInfo, where you
can select the fields from the table you've selected in the previous step. Note that the selected
field names may optionally be encoded and decoded using your previously written
FieldEncode and FieldDecode methods (refer to Chapter 20) to be sure they can be handled
by the TDataSetPageProducer. This is left as an exercise for the reader, but only involves a
few additional lines of code.

The output of the /field action can be seen in Netscape Navigator in Figure 21.14.

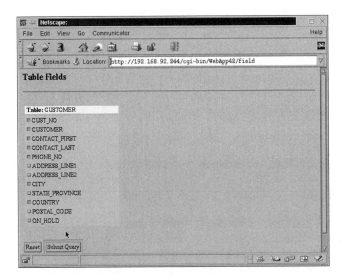

**FIGURE 21.14**

*Specifying table fields.*

After you select a number of fields, such as CUST_NO, CUSTOMER, CONTACT_FIRST,
CONTACT_LAST, PHONE_NO, CITY, and COUNTRY, and click on the Submit button, the final
/browse TWebItemAction is executed, which is implemented as follows:

```
procedure TWebModule1.WebModule1WebActionItem5Action(Sender: TObject;
  Request: TWebRequest; Response: TWebResponse; var Handled: Boolean);
const
  WebApp42 = '/cgi-bin/WebApp42';
var
  Master: TSQLTable;
  Str,Submit: String;
  i: Integer;
begin
  Str := '<h1>Table Contents</h1><hr><p>' +
    '<form action="' + WebApp42 + '/browse" method=post>' +
    '<input type=hidden name="master" value="' +
      Request.ContentFields.Values['master'] + '">' +
    '<input type=submit name=Submit value="First"> ' +
    '<input type=submit name=Submit value="Previous"> ' +
    '<input type=submit name=Submit value="Next"> ' +
    '<input type=submit name=Submit value="Last">';
  Master := TSQLTable.Create(nil);
  with Master do
  try
    SQLConnection := SQLConnection1;
```

Advanced Web Server Development

**CHAPTER 21**

895

21

ADVANCED WEB
SERVER
DEVELOPMENT

```
TableName := Request.ContentFields.Values['master'];
Open;
for i:=0 to Pred(Fields.Count) do
  if Request.ContentFields.Values['M'+Fields[i].FieldName] = 'on' then
    Str := Str +
      '<input type=hidden name="M' + Fields[i].FieldName + '" value="on">';
// locate correct record
RecNr := StrToIntDef(Request.ContentFields.Values['RecNr'],1);
Submit := Request.ContentFields.Values['Submit'];
if Submit = 'First' then RecNr := 1
else
  if Submit = 'Last' then RecNr := -1
  else
    if Submit = 'Previous' then Dec(RecNr)
    else
      if Submit = 'Next' then Inc(RecNr);
if not Active then Open; // Open when needed
First;
if RecNr = -1 then
begin
  RecNr := 1;
  while not Eof do
  begin
    Inc(RecNr);
    Next
  end
end
else
  for i:=1 to Pred(RecNr) do Next;
if Eof then // went past Eof, need to backtrack!
begin
  Dec(RecNr); // one before Eof
  First;
  for i:=1 to Pred(RecNr) do Next
end;

Str := Str +
  '<input type=hidden name=RecNr value=' + IntToStr(RecNr) + '>';

// display fields
Str := Str + '<table cellspacing=4>';
for i:=0 to Pred(Fields.Count) do
  if Request.ContentFields.Values['M'+Fields[i].FieldName] = 'on' then
    Str := Str + '<tr><td valign=top align=right><b>' +
           Fields[i].FieldName + ':</b> </td><td>' +
      '<#' + Fields[i].FieldName + '></td></tr>'
```

```
    else
      Str := Str + '-';
  Str := Str + '</table>';
  with TDataSetPageProducer.Create(nil) do
  try
    HTMLDoc.Clear;
    HTMLDoc.Add(Str);
    DataSet := Master;
    Str := Content;
  finally
    Free
  end;
finally
  Close;
  Response.Content := Str + '</form>';
end
end;
```

Note that because you want to browse through the result, you need to keep the value of the Table as well as all selected FieldNames. These are all passed as hidden fields (even though the Action specifies the same /browse PathInfo, you still need to supply them in every step).

The final output, in which you can browse through the table, showing all the fields you've selected, can be seen in Netscape Navigator in Figure 21.15.

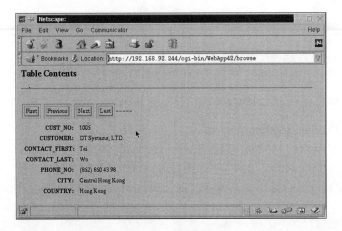

**FIGURE 21.15**

TDataSetPageProducer *browsing* CUSTOMER.

Now, if you think you're done, you're wrong. Apart from selecting one table, what's going to stop you from selecting two tables and producing a "live" master-detail relationship and

Advanced Web Server Development

**CHAPTER 21**

897

21

ADVANCED WEB
SERVER
DEVELOPMENT

overview between them (using a dynamically created `DataSetPageProducer` component for the master fields and a dynamically created `DataSetTableProducer` component for the detail grid)?

# Images

For the final part of this chapter, you need to open up the `WebApp42` project from the previous chapter. A final extension to the `OnHTMLTag` event can be made to resolve image fields that normally produce the string `'(GRAPHIC)'` only, such as the graphics field of the `biolife.xml` or `biolife.cds` table. The idea is simple: Replace the `'(GRAPHIC)'` string with an image, where the source is another call to the Web Module application (but this time to the special `/image` `WebActionItem` that only exists to produce a binary image as output). I've started a new Web server application called `cgi42` for this purpose, so the calls to itself should also reflect the new name `cgi42`. In other words, the generated HTML source for the image should look as follows:

```
<img src="/cgi-bin/cgi42/image?RecNr=42>
```

Where `RecNr` is the current record number for which you need to produce the binary image (preferably in a format that all browsers support, such as JPG, GIF or PNG).

The extended implementation of the `OnHTMLTag` event (see Chapter 20 for the original implementation that connects to `cdsBiolife`)—to produce this HTML code—is as follows:

```
procedure TWebModule1.DataSetPageProducer1HTMLTag(Sender: TObject; Tag: TTag;
  const TagString: String; TagParams: TStrings; var ReplaceText: String);
const
  cgi42 = '/cgi-bin/cgi42';
var
  DataSet: TDataSet; // little trick so we don't have to hardcode cdsBiolife
begin
  if Sender IS TDataSetPageProducer then
    DataSet :=  (Sender AS TDataSetPageProducer).DataSet
  else DataSet := nil;
  if ReplaceText = '(MEMO)' then
  begin
    if Assigned(DataSet) then
      ReplaceText := DataSet.FieldByName(
        FieldNameDecode(TagString)).AsString
  end
  else
  if ReplaceText = '(GRAPHIC)' then
  begin
    if Assigned(DataSet) then
      ReplaceText :=
```

```
      '<IMG SRC="' + cgi42 + '/image?RecNr=' +
       IntToStr(RecNr) + '&FieldName=' +
       FieldNameDecode(TagString) +
       '" border=1 alt="Bitmap (' +
       IntToStr(RecNr) +
       ') visible with Internet Explorer'  + '">'
  end
  else
    if ReplaceText = '' then
    try
      if Assigned(DataSet) then
        ReplaceText := DataSet.FieldByName(FieldNameDecode(TagString)).AsString
    except
      on E: Exception do
        ReplaceText := '(' + E.ClassName + ': ' + E.Message + ')'
    end
end;
```

The /image WebActionItem needs to assign the TGraphicField from the biolife.xml table to
the Response. Note that this is the example where you cannot use the Response.Content property directly, but you should use the Response.ContentStream property (to send the binary
image) instead. By the way, this also means you need to set the value of the
Response.ContentType property (to image/bmp):

```
procedure TWebModule1.WebModule1WebActionItem6Action(Sender: TObject;
  Request: TWebRequest; Response: TWebResponse; var Handled: Boolean);
var
  RecNr: Integer;
  TheFieldName: String;
begin
  RecNr := StrToInt(Request.QueryFields.Values['RecNr']);
  TheFieldName := Request.QueryFields.Values['FieldName'];
  Table.MoveBy(RecNr - Table.RecNo); // go to right record
  ImageStream := TMemoryStream.Create;
  (Table.FieldByName('Graphic') AS TGraphicField).SaveToStream(ImageStream);
  if ImageStream.Size > SizeOf(TGraphicHeader) then
  begin
    // set ImageStream to skip Paradox header
    ImageStream.Position := SizeOf(TGraphicHeader);
    Response.ContentType := 'image/bmp';
    Response.ContentStream := ImageStream;
    Response.SendResponse
  end
end;
```

Of course, this solution can also be extended with the browsing capabilities that you developed
earlier in this chapter (using the GET links or the POST buttons), which results in the complete

Advanced Web Server Development

**CHAPTER 21**

899

**21**

ADVANCED WEB
SERVER
DEVELOPMENT

(but rather long) Listing 21.1 of the dynamic biolife image project. Note that this project is cross-platform, and compiles with Kylix as well as Delphi 6, which will be discussed in the next section of this chapter, hence the reason why I wanted to include the full listing at this time.

**LISTING 21.1**   The Dynamic Biolife Image Project

```
unit webmod;
interface
uses
  SysUtils, Classes, HTTPApp, DB, DBClient, HTTPProd, DSProd;

type
  TWebModule1 = class(TWebModule)
    ClientDataSet1: TClientDataSet;
    ClientDataSet1SpeciesNo: TFloatField;
    ClientDataSet1Category: TStringField;
    ClientDataSet1Common_Name: TStringField;
    ClientDataSet1SpeciesName: TStringField;
    ClientDataSet1Lengthcm: TFloatField;
    ClientDataSet1Length_In: TFloatField;
    ClientDataSet1Notes: TMemoField;
    ClientDataSet1Graphic: TGraphicField;
    DataSetPageProducer1: TDataSetPageProducer;
    procedure WebModule1WebActionItem2Action(Sender: TObject;
      Request: TWebRequest; Response: TWebResponse; var Handled: Boolean);
    procedure DataSetPageProducer1HTMLTag(Sender: TObject; Tag: TTag;
      const TagString: String; TagParams: TStrings;
      var ReplaceText: String);
    procedure WebModule1WebActionItem1Action(Sender: TObject;
      Request: TWebRequest; Response: TWebResponse; var Handled: Boolean);
  private
    { Private declarations }
    RecNr: Integer;
  public
    { Public declarations }
  end;

var
  WebModule1: TWebModule1;

implementation
{$R *.xfm}
```

**LISTING 21.1**  Continued

```
type
{ Paradox graphic BLOB header }

  TGraphicHeader = record
    Count: Word;                { Fixed at 1 }
    HType: Word;                { Fixed at $0100 }
    Size: Longint;              { Size not including header }
  end;

{$IFDEF LINUX}
const
  cgi42 = '/cgi-bin/cgi42';
{$ENDIF}
{$IFDEF MSWINDOWS}
const
  cgi42 = '/cgi-bin/cgi42.exe';
{$ENDIF}


function FieldNameEncode(const FieldName: String): String;
var
  i: Integer;

  function Hex(B: Byte): String;
  const
    HexChar: PChar = '0123456789ABCDEF';
  begin
    Hex := '_00';
    Hex[2] := HexChar[B SHR $04];
    Hex[3] := HexChar[B AND $0F]
  end {Hex};

begin
  Result := '';
  for i:=1 to Length(FieldName) do
    if FieldName[i] in ['A'..'Z','a'..'z','0'..'9'] then
      Result := Result + FieldName[i]
    else
      Result := Result + Hex(Ord(FieldName[i]))
end {FieldNameEncode};

function FieldNameDecode(const FieldName: String): String;
var
  i: Integer;
```

**LISTING 21.1**   Continued

```pascal
begin
  Result := FieldName;
  for i:=1 to Length(Result) do
    if Result[i] = '_' then Result[i] := '%';
  Result := HTTPDecode(Result)
end {FieldNameDecode};


procedure PrepareDataSetPageProducer(var DSPP: TDataSetPageProducer);
var
  i: Integer;
begin
  with DSPP do if Assigned(DataSet) then
  begin
    HTMLDoc.Clear;
//  HTMLDoc.Add('<h1>'+DataSet.Name+'</h1><hr>');
    HTMLDoc.Add('<#Navigator><hr>');
    if not DataSet.Active then DataSet.Open;
    for i:=0 to Pred(DataSet.FieldCount) do
      HTMLDoc.Add('<br><b>'+DataSet.Fields[i].FieldName+
        '</b>: <#'+
          FieldNameEncode(DataSet.Fields[i].FieldName)+'>');
    HTMLDoc.Add('<hr><#Navigator>');
  end
end;


procedure TWebModule1.WebModule1WebActionItem2Action(Sender: TObject;
  Request: TWebRequest; Response: TWebResponse; var Handled: Boolean);
{ this is the default WebActionItem with an empty PathInfo value }
var
  i: Integer;
{$IFDEF POST}
  Submit: String;
{$ENDIF}
begin
{$IFDEF POST}
  RecNr := StrToIntDef(Request.ContentFields.Values['RecNr'],1);
  Submit := Request.ContentFields.Values['Submit'];
  if Submit = 'First' then RecNr := 1
  else
    if Submit = 'Last' then RecNr := -1
    else
      if Submit = 'Previous' then Dec(RecNr)
```

**LISTING 21.1** Continued

```
      else
        if Submit = 'Next' then Inc(RecNr);
{$ELSE}
  RecNr := StrToIntDef(Request.QueryFields.Values['RecNr'],1);
{$ENDIF}
  if not ClientDataSet1.Active then ClientDataSet1.Open; // Open when needed
  ClientDataSet1.First;
  if RecNr = -1 then
  begin
    RecNr := 1;
    while not ClientDataSet1.Eof do
    begin
      Inc(RecNr);
      ClientDataSet1.Next
    end
  end
  else
    for i:=1 to Pred(RecNr) do ClientDataSet1.Next;

  if ClientDataSet1.Eof then // went past Eof, need to backtrack!
  begin
    Dec(RecNr); // one before Eof
    ClientDataSet1.First;
    for i:=1 to Pred(RecNr) do ClientDataSet1.Next
  end;

  PrepareDataSetPageProducer(DataSetPageProducer1);
  Response.Content := DataSetPageProducer1.Content
end;


procedure TWebModule1.DataSetPageProducer1HTMLTag(Sender: TObject;
  Tag: TTag; const TagString: String; TagParams: TStrings;
  var ReplaceText: String);
var
  DataSet: TDataSet; // little trick so we don't have to hardcode cdsBiolife
begin
  if Sender IS TDataSetPageProducer then
    DataSet := (Sender AS TDataSetPageProducer).DataSet
  else DataSet := nil;
  if ReplaceText = '(MEMO)' then
  begin
    if Assigned(DataSet) then
      ReplaceText := DataSet.FieldByName(
```

**LISTING 21.1** Continued

```
          FieldNameDecode(TagString)).AsString
end
else
if ReplaceText = '(GRAPHIC)' then
begin
  if Assigned(DataSet) then
    ReplaceText :=
      '<IMG SRC="' + cgi42 + '/image?RecNr=' +
        IntToStr(RecNr) + '&FieldName=' +
        FieldNameDecode(TagString) +
          '" border=1 alt="Bitmap (' +
          IntToStr(RecNr) +
          ') visible with Internet Explorer'  + '">'
end
else
begin
  if ReplaceText = '' then
  begin
    b TagString = 'Navigator' then
    begin
      ReplaceText :=
    {$IFDEF POST}
      '<form action="' + cgi42 + '" method=post>' +
      '<input type=hidden name=RecNr value=' + IntToStr(RecNr) +'>' +
      '<input type=submit name=Submit value=First>  ' +
      '<input type=submit name=Submit value=Previous>  ' +
      '<input type=submit name=Submit value=Next>  ' +
      '<input type=submit name=Submit value=Last>  ' +
      '(<b>' + IntToStr(RecNr) + '</b>)' +
      '</form>'
    {$ELSE}
      '<a href="' + cgi42 + '?RecNr=1">First</a>  ' +
      '<a href="' + cgi42 + '?RecNr=' +
      IntToStr(RecNr-1) + '">Previous</a>  ' +
      '<a href="' + cgi42 + '?RecNr=' +
      IntToStr(RecNr+1) + '">Next</a>  ' +
      '<a href="' + cgi42 + '?RecNr=-1">Last</a>  ' +
      '(<b>' + IntToStr(RecNr) + '</b>)<br>'
    {$ENDIF}
    end
    else
    try
      if Assigned(DataSet) then
        ReplaceText :=
```

**LISTING 21.1**   Continued

```
            DataSet.FieldByName(FieldNameDecode(TagString)).AsString
      except
        on E: Exception do
          ReplaceText := '(' + E.ClassName + ': ' + E.Message + ')'
      end
    end
  end
end;


procedure TWebModule1.WebModule1WebActionItem1Action(Sender: TObject;
  Request: TWebRequest; Response: TWebResponse; var Handled: Boolean);
{ this is the WebActionItem with the /image PathInfo }
var
  RecNr: Integer;
  TheFieldName: String;
  ImageStream: TmemoryStream;
{$IFDEF POST}
  Submit: String;
{$ENDIF}
begin
{$IFDEF POST}
  RecNr := StrToIntDef(Request.ContentFields.Values['RecNr'],1);
  Submit := Request.ContentFields.Values['Submit'];
  if Submit = 'First' then RecNr := 1
  else
    if Submit = 'Last' then RecNr := -1
    else
      if Submit = 'Previous' then Dec(RecNr)
      else
        if Submit = 'Next' then Inc(RecNr);
{$ELSE}
  RecNr := StrToIntDef(Request.QueryFields.Values['RecNr'],1);
{$ENDIF}
  ClientDataSet1.Open;
  try
    TheFieldName := Request.QueryFields.Values['FieldName'];
    ClientDataSet1.MoveBy(RecNr - ClientDataSet1.RecNo); // go to right record
    ImageStream := TMemoryStream.Create;
    (ClientDataSet1.FieldByName('Graphic') AS
      TGraphicField).SaveToStream(ImageStream);
    if ImageStream.Size > SizeOf(TGraphicHeader) then
    begin
      // set ImageStream to skip Paradox header
```

**LISTING 21.1**  Continued

```
      ImageStream.Position := SizeOf(TGraphicHeader);
      Response.ContentType := 'image/bmp';
      Response.ContentStream := ImageStream;
      Response.SendResponse
    end
    else
      Response.Content :=
        'RecNr = ' + IntToStr(RecNr) + '<br>' +
        'FieldName = ' + TheFieldName + '<br>' +
        'Size = ' + IntToStr(ImageStream.Size);
  except
    on E: Exception do
      Response.Content :=
        'Error: ' + E.Message + '<hr>' +
        'RecNr = ' + IntToStr(RecNr) + '<br>' +
        'FieldName = ' + TheFieldName + '<br>' +
        'Size = ' + IntToStr(ImageStream.Size);
  end
end;

end.
```

The output of this application can be seen in Internet Explorer or Windows 2000 (I'll explain the reason for Internet Explorer in a moment), and looks just about perfect (see Figure 21.16).

As you may have realized by now, I'm showing the output in Internet Explorer (because the image won't appear inside Netscape Navigator). And that's because the only problem about the presented solution is the fact that the `biolife.xml` (and `biolife.cds`) files contain a graphic field that is stored in the BMP format (the native windows bitmap type). And BMP files can only be shown by the Microsoft Internet Explorer browser—Netscape Navigator is not able to show BMP files. For Netscape Navigator, you could try to convert the BMP file into a JPG or PNG image instead. However, in that case you need to use the `QGraphics` unit. And it turns out that the `QGraphics` unit cannot be used in a console (non X) application because you'll get the error message `cannot connect to X server`. In other words, Web server applications written in Kylix cannot use the `QGraphics` unit (and continue to work). So, you have to make sure the bitmaps are stored in the JPG or PNG format in the first place (either by modifying the `biolife.xml` and `biolife.cds` files, or by referring to external bitmaps in the JPG or PNG format).

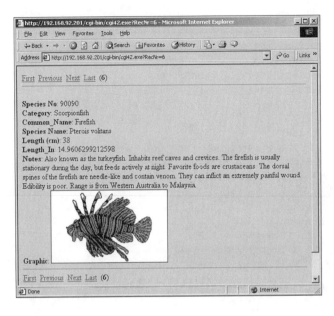

**FIGURE 21.16**
*Output of* cgi42 *inside Internet Explorer (on Windows 2000).*

As a general recommendation, I would suggest storing images in databases in JPG format (when size matters) or in PNG format (when quality matters), but not in the BMP file format (not if you want to produce Web server applications using Kylix, and want to be able to view the image in a browser other than Internet Explorer). So the techniques described here will work in real-world situations (but just not 100 percent perfect with the biolife tables that are provided as sample data files with Kylix itself).

# Cross-Platform Strategies

The WebBroker technology is now part of NetCLX. Or is actually called NetCLX, as some people say. Regardless of the details, being part of NetCLX means that the WebBroker technology is cross-platform, so you should be allowed to write a Web module application using Kylix and move it over to Delphi 6 without many problems. Actually, so far the two WebApp42 applications and especially the cgi42 application (for the dynamic images) will compile with Kylix as well as Delphi 6 as long as you've continued to work on a CGI executable. If you've worked on an Apache DSO module, you need to change the project wrapper (to CGI or any of the native Windows Web server project types) if you want to recompile it with Delphi.

There are a number of minor changes that are required when you want to recompile the WebApp42 applications in a Windows environment. The most obvious is that under Windows,

Advanced Web Server Development
**CHAPTER 21**

907

21

ADVANCED WEB
SERVER
DEVELOPMENT

the CGI executable requires the .exe extension (and the dynamic HTML forms that you generate should also include this .exe, hence the reason for working with a global constant string WebApp42 that can be modified using IFDEFs as follows:

```
{$IFDEF MSWINDOWS}
  const
    WebApp42 = '/cgi-bin/WebApp42.exe';
{$ENDIF}

{$IFDEF LINUX}
  const
    WebApp42 = '/cgi-bin/WebApp42';
{$ENDIF}
```

Apart from that change, you will have problems keeping the dbExpress driver references cross-platform (although dbExpress itself is cross-platform, the drivers that implement the functionality run on either Windows or Linux). Especially the SQLConnection component that has a LibraryName and a VendorLib property that both point to .so files on Linux and DLLs on Windows. And the location of the database as specified inside the Params property of the SQLConnection component will also be using / on Linux and \ on Windows as path delimiters (apart from the fact that the database file itself will often be located in different places as well). But these problems can be solved by dynamically assigning the properties to the SQLConnection component, again using IFDEFs as follows:

```
procedure TWebModule1.WebModuleBeforeDispatch(Sender: TObject;
  Request: TWebRequest; Response: TWebResponse; var Handled: Boolean);
begin
  SQLConnection1.Connected := True
end;


procedure TWebModule1.SQLConnection1BeforeConnect(Sender: TObject);
begin
  with Sender AS TSQLConnection do
  begin
  {$IFDEF MSWINDOWS}
    LibraryName := 'dbexpint.dll';
    VendorLib := 'GDS32.DLL';
    Params.Values['Database'] := 'd:\delphi6\data\employee.gdb'
  {$ENDIF}
  {$IFDEF LINUX}
    LibraryName := 'libsqlib.so.1';
    VendorLib := 'libgds.so.0';
    Params.Values['Database'] := '/usr/interbase/examples/employee.gdb'
  {$ENDIF}
  end
end;
```

This code uses the `OnBeforeDispatch` event handler of the Web module to activate the `SQLConnection` component (which is not connected at design-time). And in the `OnBeforeConnect` event handler of the `SQLConnection` component you can use `IFDEFs` to set the platform-specific properties `LibraryName` and `VendorLib` as well as the `Database` (which can be found in the `Params` property of the `SQLConnection` component).

The only disadvantage is that the Web module won't be cross-platform and active at design-time in both the Kylix (Linux) and Delphi 6 (Windows) environments, but I guess it's best to select one environment to develop the Web module application, and another one to use as simple compiler (producing an executable for "the other" platform).

## Summary

You've seen it all. Web modules, Web action items, page producers and table producers, for CGI and DSO. You've encountered problems, and solved them or produced workarounds. And you produced some pretty useful and powerful sample programs along the way.

All in all, I hope to have shown that the Kylix WebBroker technology is a powerful set of tools for Internet server side application development. I will keep pushing Web Modules to the limit in my daily work and on my Web site at `http://www.drbob42.com`.

# INDEX

## SYMBOLS

& (ampersand) character (C/C++), 63

@ (at) character
in Object Pascal code, 63
in variable addresses, 87

^ (caret) character
accessing variable information using, 631
addressing pointer memory using, 142

$ (dollar sign) character, as hexadecimal symbol, 87

= (equal) character, as equality operator, 86

/ (front slash) character, as division operator, 84-85

< (less than) character, as inequality operator, 86

% (percentage) character, in class searches, 739

+ (plus) character, string concatenation using, 85,

; (semicolon) character, in data field lists, 693

_(underscore) character, in class searches, 739

## A

abstract classes
building components from, 490
creating descendants, 491
TComponent, 491
TControl, 493
TCustomControl, 490, 493
TGraphicControl, 491, 492
TWidgetControl, 490

# Delphi™ 6 Developer's Guide

*Steve Teixeira and Xavier Pacheco*

0-672-32115-7
$64.99 US/$97.45 CAN

Steve Teixiera and Xavier Pacheco offer the best techniques and tricks for Delphi 6. Learn to apply real-world applications, solutions, and projects to your own programs to become a more efficient and better Delphi developer. Included in this edition is the latest information on CLX™, DataSnap™, Web Services/BizSnap™, wireless application development, and more.

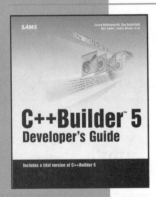

# C++Builder™ 5 Developer's Guide

*Jarrod Hollingworth, Dan Butterfield, Bob Swart, Jamie Allsop*

0-672-31972-1
$59.99 US/$89.95 CAN

*C++Builder™ 5 Developer's Guide* is your key to unlocking the full potential C ++Builder. The text provides comprehensive coverage of all major C++Builder5 features, including InternetExpress™, ADOExpress, InterBase®, TeamSource™, CodeGuard™, and more. In addition, you'll discover how to take advantage of enhanced support for MIDAS™, CORBA®, and COM+.

# Pure Corba®

*Fintan Bolton*

0-672-31812-1
$49.99 US/$74.95 CAN

*Pure CORBA®* is a practical guide to writing CORBA-compliant applications in C++ and Java™. This book focuses on the CORBA standard itself rather than on any particular ORB. Equal priority for C++ and Java is ensured by presenting code fragments and examples in both languages throughout. The book is self-contained and requires no previous knowledge of distributed systems or of CORBA application development. Pure CORBA is for experienced C++ and Java programmers.

# What's On the CD-ROM?

On the CD-ROM you will find all of the examples developed in the book, Kylix 2 Open Edition, and Kylix 2 Trial Edition.

# Installation Instructions

## Linux/UNIX

These installation instructions assume that you have a passing familiarity with UNIX commands and the basic setup of your machine. As UNIX has many flavors, only generic commands are used. If you have any problems with the commands, please consult the appropriate manual page or your system administrator.

Insert the disc into your CD-ROM drive.

If you have a volume manager, mounting of the CD-ROM will be automatic. If you don't have a volume manager, you can mount the CD-ROM by typing

`mount -tiso9660 /dev/cdrom /mnt/cdrom.`

> **NOTE**
>
> `/mnt/cdrom` is just a mount point, but it must exist when you issue the mount command. You may also use any empty directory for a mount point if you don't want to use `/mnt/cdrom`.

Open the `readme.htm` or `readme.txt` file for descriptions and installation instructions.

### NOTE

This CD-ROM uses long and mixed-case filenames requiring the use of a protected-mode CD-ROM Driver.